PENGUIN BOOKS

HENRY JAMES
A LIFE IN LETTERS

Henry James was born in 1843 in New York City, of Scottish and Irish ancestry. His father was a prominent theologian and philosopher, and his elder brother, William, is also famous as a philosopher. He attended schools in New York and later in London, Paris and Geneva, entering the Law School at Harvard in 1862. In 1865 he began to contribute reviews and short stories to American journals. In 1875, after two prior visits to Europe, he settled for a year in Paris, where he met Flaubert, Turgenev and other literary figures. However, the next year he moved to London, where he became so popular in society that in the winter of 1878–9 he confessed to accepting 107 invitations. In 1898 he left London and went to live at Lamb House, Rye, Sussex. Henry James became a British citizen in 1915, was awarded the Order of Merit, and died in 1916.

Henry James wrote some twenty novels, the first published being *Roderick Hudson* (1875). Other titles include *The Europeans*, *Washington Square*, *The Portrait of a Lady*, *The Bostonians*, *The Princess Casamassima*, *The Tragic Muse*, *The Spoils of Poynton*, *The Awkward Age*, *The Ambassadors* and *The Golden Bowl*.

Philip Horne was educated at Cambridge University and is currently a Reader in English Literature at University College, London. He has published *Henry James and Revision: The New York Edition* (1990), edited James's *A London Life*, *The Reverberator* and the Penguin edition of *The Tragic Muse*.

Henry James:
A Life in Letters

Edited by PHILIP HORNE

PENGUIN BOOKS

PENGUIN BOOKS

Published by the Penguin Group
Penguin Books Ltd, 27 Wrights Lane, London w8 5tz, England
Penguin Putnam Inc., 375 Hudson Street, New York, New York 10014, USA
Penguin Books Australia Ltd, Ringwood, Victoria, Australia
Penguin Books Canada Ltd, 10 Alcorn Avenue, Toronto, Ontario, Canada m4v 3b2
Penguin Books India (P) Ltd, 11 Community Centre,
Panchsheel Park, New Delhi – 110 017, India
Penguin Books (NZ) Ltd, Cnr Rosedale and Airborne Roads, Albany, Auckland, New Zealand
Penguin Books (South Africa) (Pty) Ltd, 5 Watkins Street,
Denver Ext 4, Johannesburg 2094, South Africa

Penguin Books Ltd, Registered Offices: Harmondsworth, Middlesex, England

First published by Allen Lane The Penguin Press 1999
Published in Penguin Books 2000
1 3 5 7 9 10 8 6 4 2

Printed in England by Clays Ltd, St Ives plc

For Judith and Olivia

Contents

Acknowledgements

This book would not have been possible without the hospitality, generosity, support and assistance of a great number of people, which it is a pleasure to record. I am grateful first of all to the late Alexander R. James for his gracious encouragement, and to his daughter Bay for her sympathy and her kind permission to publish materials on which she holds copyright. I am very grateful also to the British Academy for the Small Research Grant in 1989 which allowed me to gather the first mass of material for this book, and for subsequent grants which have helped with its completion. I am doubly grateful to Michael Worton, Dean of Arts at University College London, both for repeated and crucial support from the Dean's Travel Fund and for his expert advice on some of my French translations. Also to the English Department of University College London, especially for the term of leave which allowed me to finish this book; and to the Chambers Fund of the department for much assistance.

I must particularly thank Cathy Henderson of the Harry Ransom Center in Austin, who took the trouble in 1991 to bring me into contact with Steven Jobe, to whom I owe a deep debt for his heroic work compiling the *Calendar* of James's letters, which has saved me several years and made this a better book. It has been a pleasure and a rare piece of luck to coincide with him. I would also like to thank his associate Susan E. Gunter, whose *Biographical Register of Henry James's Correspondents* (still in progress) is already an extraordinary resource. I also wish to acknowledge a general debt to previous editors of James's letters. While many published books have been invaluable, I am especially grateful to those who have let me see work in progress: Michael Anesko, Rayburn Moore and Rosella Mamoli Zorzi.

For their special kindness and trouble I am indebted to my parents; as well as to Susie Boyt; David Bromwich and Georgann Witte; Jane Dietrich; Pat and T. Lux Feininger; Giles Foden; Tamara Follini; Siobhan Kilfeather; Mark and Charlotte McCann; Ernest Mehew; Karl Miller; Adrian Poole; Neil Rennie; Christopher Ricks; Adam Strevens; Peter Swaab; Sir John and Lady Vinelott; Hugh and Carolinne White. Henry Woudhuysen went to heroic pains in inspecting my transcriptions, and has saved me from many errors. I have been lucky in having to do with Penguin, and especially with Tim Bates, Paul Keegan, Anna South, Robert Mighall, Peter Ford and Richard Duguid; I have appreciated their trust and generosity.

I thank my colleagues at UCL for their encouragement and assistance, especially Valerie Adams, Rosemary Ashton, Ardis Butterfield, Danny Karlin, Charlotte Mitchell, John Sutherland, David Trotter and Keith Walker. Also the patient staff of the college computer helpdesk; and Helen Hayward.

I am grateful to: Jackson C. Boswell; J. A. De Bruyne; the late Leon Edel; Louise Fradenburg; Rick Gekoski; Lyndall Gordon; Glenn Horowitz; Roslyn Jolly and Simon Petch; Jim McCue; Sarah Pattle and Colin at Associated Response; Yopie Prins; George Ramsden; Marian Rooney and Thom Calderon; the Society of Authors; Andrew Taylor; Adeline Tintner and Henry Janowitz; Peter A. Walker; Kim Scott Walwyn; Fred Wegener; A. N. Wilson; Greg Zacharias.

I would also like to express my gratitude for the kindnesses of the staff in all the libraries which I have visited or with which I have corresponded, above all to Lesley Morris, Denison Beach, Thomas Ford, Susan Halpert, Jennifer Lopez, Jennie Rathbun, Virginia Smyers, William Stoneman, Emily Walhout, Melanie Wisner and Jozef Zajac at the Houghton Library, who have been consistently helpful over a long period. I am indebted also to: Jean Ashton (Rare Book and Manuscript Library, Columbia University); Jean Beckner (Special Collections Librarian, Honnold/Mudd Library, Claremont, California); Alan Bell (London Library); Michael Bott (Reading); Iain G. Brown (National Library of Scotland); Nan J. Card (Curator of Manuscripts, Hayes Library); Jacqueline Cox (King's College Library, Cambridge); Rodney Dennis (Houghton Library); Bill Fagelson and Patrice Fox (Texas); Annette Fern and Fredric Woodbridge Wilson (Harvard Theatre Collection); Wayne Furman (Berg Collection); Bonnie Hardwick (Bancroft Library); Colin Harris, Nicky Pound and T. D. Rogers (Bodleian, Modern Reading Room); Sarah Hodson (Huntington Library); Mary-Jo Kline (John Hay Library, Brown University); Michael Meredith (Eton College); Christine Nelson, Robert Parks and Charles E. Pierce, Jr (Pierpont Morgan Library); Michael Plunkett and Christina M. Deane (University of Virginia Library); Jean F. Preston and Margaret M. Sherry (Princeton Library); Christopher Sheppard (The Brotherton Collection, Leeds University Library); Virginia H. Smith (Massachusetts Historical Institute); John D. Stinson (Rare Books and Manuscripts, New York Public Library); David Wigdor (Library of Congress); Patricia C. Willis (Beinecke Rare Book and Manuscript Library, Yale).

I am grateful to the following for their hospitality, helpfulness or permission to reproduce material held by them, and mostly for all these kindnesses:

ACKNOWLEDGEMENTS

The Abernethy Library, Middlebury College, Vermont; the Baker Library, Dartmouth College, Hanover, New Hampshire; the Bancroft Library, Berkeley, California; the Berg Collection, New York Public Library; the Bibliothèque Nationale de France, Paris; the British Library, London; the Bodleian Library, University of Oxford; the trustees of the Boston Public Library; John Hay Library, Brown University, Providence, Rhode Island; Cheshire County Council for material in the Cheshire Record Office, Chester; Joseph Regenstein Library, University of Chicago; the Mrs Humphry Ward Collection, Special Collections Department, Honnold Library, Claremont, California; Special Collections, Miller Library, Colby College, Waterville, Maine; Rare Book and Manuscript Library, Butler Library, Columbia University, New York; Library of Congress, Washington, DC; Department of Rare Books, Olin Library, Cornell University, Ithaca; Cambridge University Library; Dorset Natural Historical and Archival Society, Dorset County Museum, Dorchester; the Provost and Fellows, Eton College; the Fitzwilliam Museum, Cambridge; the Folger Shakespeare Library, Washington DC; Hillhead Library, Glasgow University; Rutherford B. Hayes Presidential Center, Fremont, Ohio; the Houghton Library, Harvard University; Hove Reference Library, East Sussex; Department of Manuscripts, Henry E. Huntington Library, San Marino, California; King's College Library, Cambridge; the Frederick R. Koch Collection, Beinecke Rare Book and Manuscript Library, Yale University; the Brotherton Collection, Leeds University Library; John Rylands University Library, University of Manchester; Massachusetts Historical Institute, Boston; Pierpont Morgan Library, New York; Manuscripts and Archives Room, New York Public Library; Pattee Library, Pennsylvania State University; Harvard Theatre Collection, the Houghton Library; the Library, University of Reading; Manuscripts Division, National Library of Scotland, Edinburgh; College Archives, Smith College, Northampton, Massachusetts; Tate Gallery, Millbank, London; Manuscripts Division, Department of Rare Books and Special Collections, Princeton University Library; Harry Ransom Humanities Research Center, University of Texas at Austin; Manuscripts and Rare Books Room, University College London; Doheny Library, University of Southern California, Los Angeles; C. Waller Barrett Collection, Alderman Library, University of Virginia; the Master and Fellows of Trinity College, Cambridge; the Yale Collection of American Literature, Beinecke Rare Book and Manuscript Library, Yale University.

Only one of these letters is in a private collection; I thank myself for permission to publish it.

Above all I would like to thank Judith Hawley, to whom the book is dedicated, for everything.

Introduction

'He was so admirable a letter-writer that *they* will constitute his real and best biography.' This was said not of Henry James, but by him, of his brother William (in Letter 275). Applied to the correspondence of Henry himself, another admirable letter-writer, such a statement carries much conviction. If biography is literally life-writing, then whose writing better than the one's who lived the life in question? If that person is one of our greatest writers, the case is proportionately strengthened.

There is competition around James for biographical primacy. One can hardly ignore the late Leon Edel's massive five-volume *Life of Henry James*, which the late A. L. Rowse described as 'the single greatest work of biography produced in our century'. But in James's own words? From James himself we have two autobiographical books and part of a third, in which he takes himself up to the 1870s and his early years in England (*A Small Boy and Others* (1913), *Notes of a Son and Brother* (1914) and *The Middle Years* (1917)). In their chronology these great books, whose subject, like that of Wordsworth's *Prelude*, is the growth of a writer's mind, leave out most of James's career. This book sets out to render an account of James's whole span from 1864, when he attained his (legal) maturity and began to publish, to his death in 1916.

The best reason for reading literary biography is an interest in a writer's works, and in how they came into being. *Henry James: A Life in Letters* takes the form it does in the belief that James's letters are *among* his works; that many of them are in themselves major works or contain major writing; and that a thoughtfully presented selection can constitute an involving narrative – a narrative of passionate creation. James, himself often dubious about the public exposure of the private, was alive to the richness of the field; he told his old friend Charles Eliot Norton in 1899 that if a correspondence had 'the real charm', he 'would give it all the glory of the greatest literature' (*Henry James Letters* IV, 123; hereafter HJL).

Letters observe different conventions from those of, say, novels, where the author customarily takes on the responsibility of introducing the characters and settings to the paying public. Private correspondents of a past time, who already share a frame of reference with their audience of (usually) one, and who are exercising what James called 'the unremunerated pen', can leave the unaided modern reader, whom they often neglect to bring into the picture, at something of a loss. The ideal is to have one's explications from the horse's mouth. On New Year's Day 1908 James's typist, Theodora Bosanquet, recorded in her diary (now in the Houghton Library, Harvard) that 'Mr James wrote letters . . . and, dear man, explained all about the people he was writing to – I *do* enjoy his letter-writing mornings.' Explaining where possible in James's own vivid words from elsewhere, or those of some close witness, I have tried to produce a similar enjoyment. When James himself first presented in print a set of letters, putting together his (reluctantly written) memoir of a pretentious American sculptor-poet in Rome, *William Wetmore Story and His Friends* (1903), the practice he evolved was a remarkably imaginative way of reading them, attempting the fullest possible recovery of the time and place and relation within which they had their original sense. After quoting one letter he remarks, 'Ghosts enough, verily, with a little encouragement, would peep out of the foregoing' (1, 257) – then spends several pages teasing the phantoms out into a dense fabric of reminiscences and anecdotes. The system here of introductory headnotes and accompanying footnotes aims to help readers feel and understand by how full and sometimes tangled a web James himself was connected with his world.

I have been influenced also by James's forceful words to Edmund Gosse in 1912, on the editing of the letters of their dead friend George Meredith:

What lacerates me perhaps most of all in the Meredith volumes is the meanness and poorness of editing – the absence of any attempt to project the Image (of character, temper, quantity and quality of mind, general size and sort of personality,) that such a subject cries aloud for; to the shame of our purblind criticism. [*Selected Letters of Henry James to Edmund Gosse, 1882–1915*, 273; hereafter SLHJEG]

I have tried in this book to make James project his own 'Image', by taking quotations from the whole body of his writings (including much unpublished correspondence); but I have sought also to give an image of his place and time by weaving in quotations and information derived from other sources. James's is not here the only voice; others, often critical of James, make themselves heard, including Theodore Roosevelt, Edith Wharton, George Bernard Shaw and H. G. Wells. The James in this book is unavoidably the centre of interest, but is a 'centre' partly in the Jamesian sense (used, e.g., in Letter 170) of a character whose temper, quantity and quality of mind cannot be separated from the world he or she witnesses and lives through.

This James, then, does not entirely conform to the antithesis he himself drew and was drawn by, between the essentially solitary artist and the urbane socialite. He wittily conjures this division shortly after his settlement in London in 1877, writing to his sister Alice of his surprise and disappointment in meeting at a dinner a poet he greatly admires, Robert Browning. James deplores Browning's unpoetic behaviour, his 'shrill interruptingness', but then reconciles himself to the apparent contradiction with the conceit that 'evidently there are 2 Brownings – an esoteric & an exoteric. The former never peeps out in society, & the latter hasn't a ray of suggestion of *Men & Women*.' (Letter 38.) This notion, later made the basis of a short story, 'The Private Life' (1892), is a joke more than a full truth, an exaggeration designed to entertain Alice back in Cambridge, Massachusetts, or the reader of the story, and to make a point: that the alienation of the artist, in modern society at least, makes necessary the adoption of a protective covering, a social persona. But to say that the poet Browning was not 'really' at the dinner is only a conceit; it must be just as true that the poet in Browning *was* really there, thinking, feeling, performing and reacting in a way not finally separable from his creative activity.

James was a social novelist, writing about the workings of society as well as the minds of his characters, and he can be seen as 'socially engaged' in a sense beyond the famous social engagements with which his life was crowded, the country-house-parties and the London dinners. In *The Awkward Age* (1899) and his great late travel-meditation *The American Scene* (1907), for instance, he shows a profound concern with the understanding, development and future fate of the civilization he inhabited. And even in what he liked to think of as the monk-like cell of a writer's retirement he was addressing an audience, and needing to please the magazine editors, publishers and critics at least enough to be constantly published and to earn a comfortable living (his income from the family estates being in itself insufficient).

This book therefore tries, within reason, to explain 'all about' the people James is writing to – to evoke as required the circumstances mentioned, his literary activities of the time, his travels, some of the links and disjunctions between his circles of acquaintance, and his attitudes where they can be known. This has led me to steer between two current generic models. Most modern literary biographies, often compellingly, offer strong readings of the documentary material (usually, above all, correspondence), quoting parts but mostly just summarizing, paraphrasing and interpreting; while nearly all scholarly editions of letters now obey austere conventions which make even a minimal narrative linkage difficult. I have wanted to present the letters, the primary texts, in their integrity as far as possible, but to make it possible to follow through them a clear story of what James did and wrote. I have therefore evolved a form which allows his letters to be read as a continuous, condensed narrative, keeping 'interpretative' interference to a minimum (though, where external evidence seems to contradict James's claims, the fact is indicated). The letters should thus be available for the reader's own interpretations, and have not been put through the secondary processing which in bad cases can leave the reader of biography doubting the biographer's account but unable to get back to the primary material.

To put it another way, I have found myself refashioning the Victorian 'Life and Letters', which Christopher Ricks has called 'a genre within biography that is now thoughtlessly underrated and misrepresented' (*Essays in Appreciation* (1996), 201). The form, which works best through a rich selection of material, can offer the reader constant suggestive openings for interest in unobtrusive patterns of juxtaposition, recurrence and contrast, out of which fresh and unpredictable understandings may emerge. Above all, perhaps, it is to be valued as giving first place to the writer's own words, which with James are likely to be of livelier interest than the biographer's own. *Henry James: A Life in Letters* attempts to make the case for James's letters as his 'real and best biography'.

II

Half of the letters in this book have not previously been published. I have drawn for whole texts on thirty-three archives in the United States, Britain and France – for quotations and information on perhaps as many more – because James's vast correspondence is extraordinarily scattered, in a way which reflects his own wide experience. Estimates of the total number of letters surviving vary considerably, but 12,000 to 15,000 seems a likely range. James himself was capable of being aghast at his overcommitment; he told his friend Lizzie Boott in 1886 that 'My correspondence is the struggle of my life!' (HJL III, 135.) He was however at the same time addicted to the epistolary pen or typewriter as a substitute for the conversation which physical separation made impossible. A characteristic passage from a fiercely candid, eloquently critical letter in 1899, lecturing Mrs Humphry Ward on the technique of fiction, shows him pausing for a halt, attempting to stop, but then pulled forward again by what he *has* to say:

But there is too much to say about these things – & I am writing too much – & yet haven't said ½ I want to – *and*, above all, there *being* so much, it is doubtless better not to attempt to say pen in hand what one can say but so partially. And yet I *must* still add one or two things more. [Letter 170]

It is quite possible that James wrote many more letters than the estimated 15,000. On 7 August 1905 he pulls himself up in a letter to the Chicago novelist Robert Herrick as he starts to justify his revisions for the New York Edition with the statement that 'it is 1 o'clk a.m., & I've written 7 letters' (Letter 220). The register of James's correspondence heroically assembled by Steven Jobe, the *Calendar of the Correspondence of Henry James*, which lists all known letters, notes only one other letter for this date. Should two out of seven be the overall survival rate for James's correspondence, it would suggest he may have written something over 40,000 letters in his lifetime.

There has never been a complete edition of James's letters, surprising as that might seem for one of America's greatest writers. The general collection I have already quoted, *Henry James Letters* (1974–84), by Leon Edel, the great pioneer in James scholarship, comes in four big volumes, which contain altogether 2,345 pages and 1,100 letters: a generous sampling, but scarcely a substitute for a full record. Before that *The Letters of Henry James* (1920) was the work of Percy Lubbock, a young friend of James and the James family's choice of editor, and the 936 pages of its two large volumes contain 403 letters. The selections are strikingly divergent: Edel's, despite its greater capacity, reprints only 173 of those in Lubbock's, leaving out 230, well over half, of the letters in Lubbock's out-of-print edition. The picture gets even more complicated: *Henry James Letters* also omits 28 of the 120 letters Leon Edel himself had put into a single volume in 1955 (*Selected Letters of Henry James*); while his single-volume *Henry James: Selected Letters* (of 1987) includes about two dozen previously unpublished letters.

These general editions by Lubbock and Edel have been the best concentrations of James letters, but many other letters have been published one at a time or in groups, or in editions of individual correspondences. Until Steven Jobe published his first *Calendar* of them in the *Henry James Review* in 1990, it was difficult to get a clear sense even of James's published letters; an updated version of the *Calendar* from October 1994 lists 125 printed sources, some of them extremely out of the way. In recent years some of the editions of James's individual correspondences have been invaluable, notably Michael Anesko's W. D. Howells, George Monteiro's John Hay and Henry Adams, Rayburn Moore's Edmund Gosse and Macmillan, Lyall Powers's Edith Wharton, and the Skrupskelis–Berkeley edition of William James.

Such partial publications are extremely welcome in themselves, and I have drawn gratefully on them here. Many James scholars have been advocating for years the production of a complete edition of the letters – a huge undertaking, but one without which the general understanding of James is inhibited. Early in the 1990s the possibility was mooted of a facsimile multi-volume edition of the manuscript originals of all the letters – only for the project to fall through as financially unfeasible. It was therefore a surprise when, following some polemics on the subject at the New York University conference for James's Sesquicentennial in 1993, the University of Nebraska Press announced early in 1997 a thirty-volume *Complete Letters of Henry James* under the general editorship of Peter Walker and Greg Zacharias, to begin publication early in the twenty-first century and to take about fifteen years. The *Complete Letters* will be founded on the awe-inspiring labours of Steven Jobe. Even those who will not leap to devour this massive edition should welcome it for the sake of the mass of fascinating material, and the quantity of good writing, it will make available, significantly changing our understanding of James, and of his place in the American and British literary cultures of the late nineteenth and early twentieth centuries.

Among the more complex of the problems to be faced by the Nebraska project is that of the surviving James letters *not* in archives. Many of James's letters are still not *in* libraries: they are in the hands of private collectors, or in the hands of the descendants or heirs of the recipients. In the following letters, James mentions as friends or familiars a number of people he seems very likely to have corresponded with, people he knew well, or had business relations with, like his relations the Tweedys, J. M. Barrie, Charles Milnes Gaskell, Alice Bartlett (later Warren), Auguste Laugel, J. Comyns Carr and Charles Frohmann. Yet no letters to any of these have yet been traced, while in the letters that survive there are numerous references to further (still untraced) letters that James has written or means to write. It may be that some recipients acted on the instruction to 'Burn this' (or some comic variation on that formula) that James attached to frankly gossiping letters – letters that are often of particular interest to later readers. Having delivered himself on the subject of the play *Votes for Women* (1907) by Elizabeth Robins, James commands his correspondent Lucy Clifford, 'Only repeat me, quote me, betray me not – and burn my letter with fire or candle (if you have *either*! Otherwise wade out into the sea with it and soak the ink out of it).' (HJL IV, 436.) In 1910, moreover, after his health had begun to decline, James, who was deeply concerned with privacy, had a large bonfire in which he burned a great number of personal documents and manuscripts, doubtless including letters *from* him which he had retrieved from the effects of correspondents who had died (notably his sister Alice and his close friend Constance Fenimore Woolson). Yet burnings and soakings, and even losings, seem likely to account for only some of those missing, and it is in any case known that a great number are in private hands.

It is easy to believe in the modern world that everything written by a great writer is in the public domain. But many of James's works in the epistolary form are quite invisible, while others can be traced only in auction catalogues, where the asking price for a single letter can be $4,000–6,000, or £3,200, prices beyond the scope of most underfunded libraries. Questions to the auctioneers after the event will often take one only a certain distance. The free market, and the law of supply and demand, mean that to publish a letter reduces its rarity and thus its value on the market. Auction catalogues, announcing a sale of James letters, thus like to say '*Not in Edel*'. While this situation can increase our gratitude for the generosity of collectors who give permission for their letters to be reproduced, it is understandable that some collectors wish to keep the very existence of their letters secret. There is a legend that James read *Du Côté de chez Swann* in 1914 and wrote to Proust; no such letter has been traced, but any reader of *The Aspern Papers* can imagine a collector rubbing his hands over the treasure in the strong-room of some château. In 1996 I found that a letter to the magazine editor Robert Underwood Johnson, which I had seen in 1989 on deposit in the Morgan Library in New York, had turned up for sale in a London book-dealer's, and bought it – exactly in order to give myself permission to include it here (it is Letter 133).

III

As said above, of the 296 letters to 115 correspondents included in this book, half have not previously been published. They have been selected from the widest possible coverage – over nearly a decade – of the archival material from Bloomsbury to Berkeley, from the oak-panelled rare book room of the Baker Library at Dartmouth College in New Hampshire to the formica-topped tables of the Central Library in Hove, where James's letters to Lord and Lady Wolseley have incongruously ended up. Just over a third of the letters come from the single largest archive, the Houghton Library in Harvard, where the James family papers are held, and there are numbers in double figures from the Beinecke in Yale, the Alderman Library in Charlottesville, the Bodleian in Oxford, the Harry Ransom Humanities Research Center in Austin, Texas, and the Firestone in Princeton. But I have seen material in and from quite a few more, working closely since 1992 with Steven Jobe, as well as combing the printed sources, in order to be able to make a fresh selection properly representing the extraordinary quantity of fascinating material in the multitude of extant letters that have been seen by few (and, given James's difficult hand-writing, read by fewer).

The past selections of James's correspondence understandably reflect lines of critical and biographical curiosity highly respectable in themselves but necessarily not congruent with those of the turn of another century. There have been so many interests to bear in mind in choosing the items for *Henry James: A Life in Letters* – above all intrinsic quality, but also narrative relevance, novelty, comedy, critical acuity, force of expression, biographical significance, emotional suggestiveness, relation to recipient, date, place, source – that formulation of all the powerful criteria in operation would scarcely be possible. Even so, I have tried to keep in mind, and satisfy, angles of interest on James that have opened up more recently – taking into account the perspectives of feminism, gender studies, publishing history and literary theory.

There is much here of James's thinking about women and women writers; many of those with whom he is concerned have recently come back into focus after long neglect (e.g. Elizabeth Robins and Mrs Humphry Ward). James's ambivalent reactions to feminism can be traced in his direct dealings both with suffragists and with the anti-suffragist Mrs Ward. There is plenty of concern with sex, both heterosexual and homosexual, to intrigue further those who are puzzled about the mystery of James's relation to what in 'Browning in Westminster Abbey' he called 'the great relation between man and woman'. I have not particularly set out to answer the question of James's sexuality, and had better put on record that none of the correspondence I have read in the archives strikes me as resolving it, though some of the new letters here may help to reframe it. Wilde and his rival André Raffalovich, and James's non-heterosexual friends Howard Sturgis and Hugh Walpole, prompt James to interestingly mixed responses.

In September 1912 Hugh Walpole recorded James saying to him, 'I've had one great passion in my life – the intellectual passion. What that has been for me I cannot say.' What dominated James's life was literature, and I have kept that the controlling concern in a variety of ways. Writing to other writers about their work, James can be an overwhelming, spontaneous critic, meaning to pay polite compliments but bursting out into robust expressions of dissatis-faction and statements of artistic principle. Writing about his own work, he makes disconcerting concessions about structure or conception, or strongly defends it, or jokingly makes the highest claims in the style of hyperbolic advertisements (thus an 1870 story 'is one of the greatest works of "this or any age"' (Letter 19)). I have tried to characterize in passing those with whom James had professional dealings – publishers, magazine editors, literary agents, theatrical managers and others – sufficiently to bring out the spectrum of possibilities for him. The resulting narrative should make vivid the contingent difficulties of his life as a well-established but always insecure author during a period of really extraordinary changes in the conditions of the literary market as well as in the literary tradition.

James had many projects which the reader of his completed and published works would barely suspect, projects either never started or never brought to final form. A travel essay on Sicily, a review essay on Jane Austen, a descriptive book on *London Town*, a sequel to *The American Scene* describing his travels to California (to have been called *The Sense of the West*), plays for disappointing actors and companies, novels interrupted by illness or war – all of these remained unwritten or unfinished, unpublished or unproduced. I have included some of these dead ends to evoke the uncertainties and frustrations of a writer's career as it is lived. In letters to publishers and editors James is often writing to the moment, the last moment, pleading for more space or time. In letters to theatre people, whose collaborative enterprise both drew and repelled him, we have a rare opportunity to see him discussing practical questions of art with his artistic collaborators.

Certain shapes emerge in reading these letters in sequence, suggesting ways of thinking, sometimes speculative, about sets of circumstances and how they may have borne on aspects of James's career. I hope readers will be stirred to form their own ideas about the configurations of his extraordinarily complex life. In the 1860s and 1870s, for example, James's older friend from Cambridge, Massachusetts, the culturally well-connected Charles Eliot Norton, can be sensed as a formative influence on him, though one against which the young writer struggles. A secular preacher of the value of European civilization to America with strong links in England, a friend of Carlyle and Ruskin and Clough and Mrs Gaskell, Norton first publishes the young critic in the *North American Review*, and then when James comes to Europe is in London to give him valuable introductions, which can be seen as the basis of his later social success in London when he settles in 1877. Norton's lessons in culture are serious and valuable, but only part of James responds to his high-minded solicitations.

Sequences of incidents, also, in a succession of letters, can coalesce into some degree of topical coherence; stretches of years come into new perspectives. After the successes of the late 1870s, James suffers a whole series of setbacks in the 1880s, affecting his relation to his homeland. The death of a parent each time casts a shadow over his two successive return visits to the U.S. after his settlement in Europe. The nationalist fuss over 'Daisy Miller' (1878) and the violent American reaction against his *Hawthorne* (1879) combine to raise James's profile uncomfortably. Then his friend, editor and supporter William Dean

Howells writes an essay in his defence that only provokes a storm of further controversy – unhappily coinciding with the death of Henry James Senior. The ill-feeling of which James becomes the inadvertent focus may have set James's image and his ideological meaning in America for the rest of his career; at any rate it appears to lie behind the extraordinary assault on James as an expatriate and a 'bolter' by the young Theodore Roosevelt in a speech to the Brooklyn Young Republicans (mentioned in Letter 78). The arrangement with his new publisher Osgood, made in the wake of his father's death, for *The Bostonians*, James's last completed novel set in America, and various other works, ends badly: James is attacked for his alleged caricature of a real Boston personage, Miss Peabody, and then the book is not critically welcomed; Osgood goes bankrupt and after a period of financial anxiety James salvages only some of the money he has worked for. By the end of the 1880s his commercial situation is so reduced that Frederick Macmillan is cutting the advance he offers for *The Tragic Muse*. A measure of desperation, then, may make especially attractive the overture from the actor-manager Edward Compton, inviting James to write a dramatization of his 1877 novel *The American* and putting him on the path which leads to the disastrous première of *Guy Domville*.

Other patterns to be discerned in sequences of these letters might include the way the expense of the outright purchase of Lamb House in 1899 engenders more financial anxiety in James, a pressure that leads him to take on the succession of contractual commitments which produces, in rapid order, *The Ambassadors*, *The Wings of the Dove* and *The Golden Bowl* – among the most demandingly complex and serious of modern novels, masterpieces that could not be called by any stretch of the imagination pot-boilers, yet that seem to arise out of the productive rage set off by James's threatened domestic economy. One of the rewards of reading James's correspondence is the emergence of such narratives from the juxtapositions of evidence; and yet there is also a reward in the way the creative processes elude reductive explanation. As James wrote to Graham Balfour in 1901, biography cannot truly penetrate the mysteries of the imagination: 'I speak as from the literary vision, the vision for which the rarest works pop out of the dusk of the inscrutable, the untracked.' (HJL IV, 213.)

IV

I have felt it crucial to produce as accurate as possible a text, and where original manuscripts are known to survive I have carefully transcribed them (or worked from xerox or microfilm copies). Where letters have been published before,

I have attempted to be at least as accurate as previous editors. My precursors have sometimes nodded, quite understandably when one sees some of the pages James turned out at what must have been high speed. Thus Lubbock, and, following him, Edel, have read in Letter 223, where James is praising Wells's *Kipps*, 'the book has, throughout, such extraordinary life; everyone in it, without exception, and every piece and part of it, is so vivid and sharp and *raw*'. This last word was always particularly striking, apt enough perhaps for the acute social embarrassment that informs Wells's novel, but unexpected coming from the James who tends to prefer the cooked to the raw and one of whose images for the imagination is a stewpot. And indeed, when one pores over the marks on James's page, the word comes out '*done*'. In Letter 9, to Thomas Sergeant Perry in 1867, where James in unusually prophetic mode is trying to define the nature of the cultural opportunity for young Americans, he writes:

We must of course have something of our own – something distinctive & homogeneous – & I take it that we shall find it in our "moral consciousness," our unprecedented spiritual lightness and vigour.

James's inverted commas round '"moral consciousness"' appear here for the first time in print, although the letter has been published at least four times; and they make sense as a trace of irony about the term, coming appropriately enough from the son of the eccentric theological thinker Henry James Senior, who amused his offspring by deploring priggishly virtuous behaviour as 'flagrant morality'. Small as both these examples are, they make a considerable difference to each passage's sense and to the interpretations we might place on it; and the pursuit of accuracy has produced many such new and closer readings in the pages that follow.

Although I have preserved James's spelling and punctuation (provided his sense can be followed), most readers will be grateful that I have not attempted to reproduce variants on the page. The Textual Notes at the back give among other details an account of the appearance of the manuscript in most cases, including James's insertions and, where I have been able to decipher them, his cancellations – for he often rewrites as he goes, and one can follow the dramatic process of his construction of a sentence: James writing the bland word and then inserting the expressive; or writing the word that is too rudely true and replacing it with one somewhat politer. I have tried to present these in a form where they can be browsed through; it is often of interest that the clinching phrase in a sentence is a subsequent insertion.

I have provided translations on the page where there are longer passages in a foreign language, but, in order not to clutter the text, James's many phrases and words of French, Italian, Latin and German are listed in alphabetical order (by first foreign word) in a Glossary of Foreign Words and Phrases at the back of the book. James has a fine ear for idiom, even in a foreign language, and usually resorts to such terms where no phrase in English would convey quite the right shading.

The index is complete in its listing of persons' names and the titles of books or plays, so that cross-referencing in the main text can be kept to a minimum. The reader will be able to find every mention of a particular person by consulting the index. There are also a number of thematic entries.

V

The dramatic intensity of thought which produces his often-blotted pages informs James's choice of words and building of sentences in most of what follows, putting the freshness and seriousness of life in his letters. From the flirtatious playfulness of his charming note of 1865 to Lilla Cabot (Letter 3) to the startling self-parody of his 1907 dialogue-letter to Fanny Prothero (Letter 239), his self-conscious language, never without a glint of humorous possibility, strives to entertain – perhaps to entertain James himself as much as his addressee. Such entertainment can in less jocular moods be a serious activity, a stoical ironic acceptance of whatever happens. James can be trusted to find 'interest', as he tells the gloomy Henry Adams in Letter 280, though it is something that must be constantly cultivated in the face of blankness or disaster. In his great letter to Wells in 1915, bruised by the parodic scorn of him in the younger writer's *Boon*, he restates the idea as an even more active creed for the creative writer:

I hold that interest may be, *must* be, exquisitely made & created, and that if we don't make it, we who undertake to, nobody & nothing will make it for us. [Letter 289]

This interest is *made* by the artist not only for himself but for others; he lives to communicate interest, to make it for his society out of the relations which constitute that society.

Near the end of his life, in the stress of wartime and the pain of what would be his final illness, one of the final literary acts of this admirable letter writer, whose ceaseless making of interest occupied a lifetime, was to select for an anthology a passage from the works of William James, his late elder brother. He chose the end of the essay 'Is Life Worth Living?' Its view of life is in a broad sense religious, and also poetic, for it argues that the individual consciousness has to *make* its own significance:

If this life be not a real fight, in which something is eternally gained for the universe by success, it is no better than a game of private theatricals from which one may withdraw at will. But it *feels* like a real fight – as if there were something really wild in the universe which we, with all our idealities and faithfulnesses, are needed to redeem . . . These then are my last words to you: Be not afraid of life. Believe that life *is* worth living, and your belief will help create the fact. [Letter 294]

Through all his hardships and setbacks, the philosopher's younger brother continually testified to the value of artistic effort – not just in 'Art', the specialized activity of a few, but also in the innumerable small acts of everyday life, the rituals and exchanges of the social world and their endless creation of significance. His correspondence, a considerable part of this creative effort, was, he sometimes complained, 'the struggle of my life'; but then life, he would finally agree with William, was a 'real fight', an engagement in which something was 'gained for the universe'.

Note on the Text

James's handwriting is notoriously difficult to read, but decades of practice make it easier. I present the following letters as accurately as possible, following James's spellings and abbreviations and punctuation throughout, and working in most cases both from original manuscripts and from xerox or microfilm copies of manuscripts, but nearly always from an original or a reproduction of it. The description at the head of each letter gives addressee, date, source and a note of previous publication (if any). Further details will be found in the appendix of 'Textual Notes' at the back of the book. The category 'Published' should be self-explanatory; a few letters described as 'Unpublished' may have been previously quoted from in print, but have not been presented in letter form (with address, date, superscriptions and subscriptions, etc.). 'Partly published' means a text was presented *as* a letter (usually in an edition of letters) but with marked or unmarked elisions.

The introductory headnote to a letter is intended both to evoke the situation the letter directly or indirectly addresses, and to sketch a narrative of James's activities. The footnotes offer further information at the point where I hope it is most helpful in the reading of a letter. Where it can be done economically, I have indicated the sources of my citations, using many abbreviations in order to break up the text as little as possible. James, whose fiction often finds interest in blazing documents, destroyed most of the letters he received in periodic bonfires. A number have survived, and where possible I quote or describe the letters from others mentioned by James.

To produce a clear reading text, addresses, dates and subscriptions have been ranged right and relineated, for clarity and economy, and on the ground that it would be impossible in print exactly to reproduce the varieties of layout in James's letters, written and typed on all sorts of paper over a fifty-one-year period. In James's handwritten letters paragraph breaks are mostly marked only by a long dash without a new line; in such cases I have omitted the dash and started a new paragraph in order to present a more readable text. Where James has a single underlining for titles or emphasis, I use italic; where he has a double underlining, I use italic with a single underlining. Information about James's cancellations and insertions, and about other textual details (library call-numbers, notes on dating, etc.), is reserved for the 'Textual Notes'. In a few places I have used editorial square brackets to supply punctuation or missing words or, where manuscripts are unknown and I am working from a previous transcription, to correct obvious errors affecting James's sense.

I have primarily though not exclusively aimed in my annotation to assist the reader who proceeds chronologically through the letters, and to explain and describe as matters come up. I have wanted to trace and make clear as many references as possible, in order to render the complex world in which James moves. Longer passages in foreign languages are translated on the page where they occur or in footnotes; words and phrases are translated in the glossary at the back, arranged alphabetically by first foreign word in each instance. The very full index is intended for readers who wish to refer back or forward; but also to make the book accessible for those dipping in or for use as a work of reference.

Lists of Abbreviations

In order to clutter the text as little as possible, while providing sources for the many quotations, I have made use of the following abbreviations:

MC	manuscript copy
MS	manuscript
TC	typed copy
TS	typescript
AHJ	Alice Howe James (1849–1922; wife of WJ)
AJ	Alice James (1850–92)
HJ	Henry James (1843–1916)
WJ	William James (1842–1910)

ARCHIVE REFERENCES

Abernethy	Abernethy Library, Middlebury College, Vermont
Baker	Baker Library, Dartmouth College, Hanover, New Hampshire
Bancroft	Bancroft Library, Berkeley
Berg	Berg Collection, New York Public Library
Bib. Nat.	Bibliothèque Nationale de France, Paris
BL	British Library, London
Bodleian	Bodleian Library, University of Oxford
BPL	Boston Public Library
Brown	John Hay Library, Brown University
Cheshire	Cheshire Libraries, Arts and Archives, Chester
Chicago	Joseph Regenstein Library, University of Chicago
Colby	Miller Library, Colby College, Waterville, Maine
Columbia	Butler Library, Columbia University, New York
Congress	Library of Congress, Washington DC

Cornell	Department of Rare Books, Olin Library, Cornell University
CUL	Cambridge University Library
Dorset	Dorset Natural Historical and Archival Society, Dorset County Museum, Dorchester
Eton	Eton College
Fitzwilliam	Fitzwilliam Museum, Cambridge
Folger	Folger Shakespeare Library, Washington DC
Glasgow	Hillhead Library, Glasgow University
Hayes	Rutherford B. Hayes Library, Fremont, Ohio
Horne	Author's Collection
Houghton	Houghton Library, Harvard University
Hove	Central Library, Hove, East Sussex
Huntington	Department of Manuscripts, Henry E. Huntington Library, San Marino, California
King's	King's College Library, Cambridge
Leeds	Brotherton Collection, Leeds University Library
Manchester	Rylands Library, University of Manchester
Mass. Hist. Inst.	Massachusetts Historical Institute, Boston
Morgan	Pierpont Morgan Library, New York
NYPL	Manuscripts and Archives Room, New York Public Library
Penn	Pattee Library, Pennsylvania State University
Princeton	Department of Rare Books and Special Collections, Princeton University Library
Pusey	Pusey Theater Library, Harvard University
Reading	Library, University of Reading
Scotland	Manuscripts Division, National Library of Scotland, Edinburgh
Smith	College Archives, Smith College, Northampton, Massachusetts
Tate	Tate Gallery, Millbank, London
Texas	Harry Ransom Humanities Research Center, University of Texas at Austin
UCL	Manuscripts and Rare Books Room, University College London
UCSC	Doheny Library, University of Southern California, Los Angeles
Virginia	C. Waller Barrett Collection, Alderman Library, University of Virginia
Wren	Trinity College Library, Cambridge
Yale	Beinecke Library, Yale University

GENERAL COLLECTIONS OF HENRY JAMES LETTERS

HJL	*Henry James Letters*, edited by Leon Edel, 4 vols., Harvard University Press, Cambridge, Massachusetts, and London, 1974–84.
LHJ	*The Letters of Henry James*, edited by Percy Lubbock, 2 vols., Macmillan and Scribner's, London and New York, 1920.
SL1	*Selected Letters of Henry James*, edited by Leon Edel, Farrar, Straus & Cudahy, New York, 1955; Rupert Hart-Davis, London, 1956.
SL2	*Henry James: Selected Letters*, edited by Leon Edel, Harvard University Press, Cambridge, Massachusetts, and London, 1987.

OTHER COLLECTIONS OF OR INCLUDING HENRY JAMES LETTERS

AMRP	George Monteiro, '*The Atlantic Monthly*'s Rejection of "The Pupil": An Exchange of Letters between Henry James and Horace Scudder', *American Literary Realism, 1870–1910*, 23 (1990), 75–83.
CC	Clare Barbara Kozol, *Creator and Collector: The Unpublished Letters of Henry James to Isabella Stewart Gardner*, University Microfilms, Ann Arbor, 1973 (Columbia University PhD, 1973).
CF	E. V. Lucas, *The Colvins and their Friends*, Scribner's, New York, 1928.
CHJHA	*The Correspondence of Henry James and Henry Adams, 1877–1914*, edited by George Monteiro, Louisiana State University Press, Baton Rouge and London, 1992.
CHJHM	*The Correspondence of Henry James and the House of Macmillan, 1877–1914: 'All the Links in the Chain'*, edited by Rayburn S. Moore, Louisiana State University Press, Baton Rouge, 1993.
CP	*The Complete Plays of Henry James*, edited by Leon Edel, Rupert Hart-Davis, London, 1949.
CWJ	*The Correspondence of William James: William and Henry*,

edited by Ignas K. Skrupselis and Elizabeth M. Berkeley, 3 vols., University Press of Virginia, Charlottesville, Virginia, and London, 1992–4.

FLHJWM 'Four Letters from Henry James to William Meredith', *Desiderata*, 1 (2 April 1948), 1–4.

FMFSCHJ Brita Lindberg-Seyersted, *Ford Madox Ford and His Relationship to Stephen Crane and Henry James*, Humanities Press International, Atlantic Highlands, New Jersey, 1987.

HBB Henry Brewster, 'Fourteen Letters', *Botteghe Oscure*, 19 (1957), 182–94.

HJAD Leon Edel, *Henry James: les années dramatiques*, Jouve & Cie., Paris, 1931.

HJAH H. Montgomery Hyde, *Henry James at Home*, Methuen, London, 1969.

HJBL Leon Edel and Lyall H. Powers, 'Henry James and the *Bazar* Letters', *Bulletin of the New York Public Library*, 62 (February 1958), 75–103; as reprinted as a brochure in *Howells and James: A Double Billing*, New York Public Library, 1958.

HJEWL *Henry James and Edith Wharton: Letters, 1900–1915*, edited by Lyall H. Powers, Weidenfeld & Nicolson, London, 1990.

HJHGW *Henry James & H. G. Wells: A Record of their Friendship, their Debate on the Art of Fiction, and their Quarrel*, edited by Leon Edel and Gordon N. Ray, Rupert Hart-Davis, London, 1958.

HJJH George Monteiro, *Henry James and John Hay: The Record of a Friendship*, Brown University Press, Providence, 1965.

HJJH2 David W. Pancost, 'Henry James and Julian Hawthorne', *American Literature*, 50 (1978–9), 461–5.

HJLACBAM *Henry James: Letters to A. C. Benson and Auguste Monod*, edited by E. F. Benson, Elkin Mathews & Marrot, London, 1930.

HJRLS *Henry James and Robert Louis Stevenson: A Record of Friendship and Criticism*, edited by Janet Adam Smith, Rupert Hart-Davis, London, 1948.

HJVH Robert Secor, 'Henry James and Violet Hunt, the "Improper Person of Babylon"', *Journal of Modern Literature*, 13/1 (March 1986), 3–36.

Lettere *Lettere a Miss Allen (Letters to Miss Allen)*, edited by Rosella Mamoli Zorzi, Rosellina Archinto, Milan, 1993.

LFL   Michael Anesko, *Letters, Fictions, Lives: Henry James and William Dean Howells*, Oxford University Press, New York, 1997.

LPC   S. P. Rosenbaum, 'Letters to the Pell-Clarkes from their "Old Cousin and Friend" Henry James', *American Literature*, 31 (1959–60), 533–7.

MLL   George Soames Layard, *Mrs Lynn Linton: Her Life, Letters and Opinions*, London, 1901.

MLT   Compton Mackenzie, *My Life and Times*, 10 vols., Chatto & Windus, London, 1963–71.

OD   Victoria Welby-Gregory, *Other Dimensions: A Selection from the Later Correspondence of Victoria, Lady Gregory*, Jonathan Cape, London, 1931.

PPLGB   Adeline Tintner, 'Pater in *The Portrait of a Lady* and *The Golden Bowl*, Including Some Unpublished Henry James Letters', *Henry James Review*, 3 (winter 1982), 80–95.

RRR   Jerome McGann, 'Revision, Rewriting, Rereading; or, "An Error [Not] in *The Ambassadors*", in *Henry James's New York Edition: The Construction of Authorship*, edited by David McWhirter, Stanford University Press, Stanford, California, 1995, 109–22.

SLHJEG   *Selected Letters of Henry James to Edmund Gosse: A Literary Friendship*, edited by Rayburn S. Moore, Louisiana State University Press, Baton Rouge and London, 1988.

TF   *Theatre and Friendship: Some Henry James Letters with a Commentary by Elizabeth Robins*, G. P. Putnam's Sons, New York, 1932.

TLHJJC   *Three Letters from Henry James to Joseph Conrad*, edited by G. Jean-Aubry, Curwen Press, London, 1926.

TSPB   Virginia Harlow, *Thomas Sergeant Perry: A Biography*, Duke University Press, Durham, North Carolina, 1950.

TULM   'Three Unpublished Letters and a Monologue by Henry James', *London Mercury*, 6 (1922), 492–501.

OTHER MATERIAL CITED

A   Henry James, *Autobiography: A Small Boy and Others; Notes of a Son and Brother; The Middle Years*, edited by Frederick W. Dupee, Criterion Books, New York, 1956.

AACCI   Michael Anesko, 'Ambiguous Allegiances: Conflicts of Culture and Ideology in the Making of the New York Edition', in *Henry James's New York Edition: The Construction of Authorship*, edited by David McWhirter, Stanford University Press, Stanford, California, 1995, 77–89.

AEP   James Hepburn, *The Author's Empty Purse and the Rise of the Literary Agent*, Oxford University Press, 1968.

AJB   Jean Strouse, *Alice James: A Biography*, Houghton Mifflin, Boston, 1980.

BHJ   Leon Edel and Dan H. Laurence, *A Bibliography of Henry James* (The Soho Bibliographies, VIII), third edition, revised with the assistance of James Rambeau, Clarendon Press, Oxford, 1982.

CLJC   *Complete Letters of Joseph Conrad*, edited by Frederick Karl and Laurence Davies, projected 8 vols., Cambridge University Press, Cambridge and New York, 1983– .

CTW:C   Henry James, *Collected Travel Writings: The Continent*, edited by Richard Howard, Library of America, New York, 1993.

CTW:GBA   Henry James, *Collected Travel Writings: Great Britain and America*, edited by Richard Howard, The Library of America, New York, 1993.

DAJ   *The Diary of Alice James*, edited by Leon Edel, Rupert Hart-Davis, London, 1965.

DLAJ   *The Death and Letters of Alice James*, edited by Ruth Bernard Yeazell, University of California Press, Berkeley, Los Angeles, and London, 1981.

EGLL   Ann Thwaite, *Edmund Gosse: A Literary Landscape*, Secker & Warburg, London, 1984.

Friction   Michael Anesko, *'Friction with the Market': Henry James and the Profession of Authorship*, Oxford University Press, New York and Oxford, 1986.

HJAL   Leon Edel, *Henry James: A Life*, Harper & Row, New York, 1985.

HJR   Philip Horne, *Henry James and Revision: The New York Edition*, Clarendon Press, Oxford, 1990.

HWB   Rupert Hart-Davis, *Hugh Walpole: A Biography*, Harcourt, Brace & World, 1952.

Jameses   R. W. B. Lewis, *The Jameses: A Family Narrative*, André Deutsch, London, 1991.

LC I	Henry James, *Literary Criticism: Essays on Literature, American Writers, English Writers*, edited by Leon Edel and Mark Wilson, The Library of America, New York, 1984.
LC II	Henry James, *Literary Criticism: French Writers, Other European Writers, The Prefaces to the New York Edition*, edited by Leon Edel and Mark Wilson, The Library of America, New York, 1984.
LCVF	John Sutherland, *The Longman Companion to Victorian Fiction*, Longman, Harlow, 1988.
LEW	*The Letters of Edith Wharton*, edited by R. W. B. Lewis and Nancy Lewis, Simon & Schuster, New York and London, 1988.
LHA	*The Letters of Henry Adams*, edited by J. C. Levenson, Ernest Samuels, Charles Vandersee and Viola Hopkins Winner, 6 vols., Harvard University Press, Cambridge, Massachusetts, 1982–8.
LLAJ	*Her Life in Letters: Alice James*, edited by Linda Anderson, Thoemmes Press, Bristol, 1996.
LLWDH	*Life in Letters of William Dean Howells*, edited by Mildred Howells, 2 vols., Doubleday, Doran & Co., Garden City, New York, 1928.
LOW	*The Letters of Oscar Wilde*, edited by Rupert Hart-Davis, Harcourt, Brace & World, Inc., New York, 1962.
LR&E	*Literary Reviews and Essays by Henry James on American, English and French Literature*, edited by Albert Mordell, Twayne, New York, 1957.
LRLS	*The Letters of Robert Louis Stevenson*, edited by Bradford A. Booth and Ernest Mehew, 8 vols., Yale University Press, New Haven and London, 1994–5.
LWJ	*The Letters of William James*, edited by his son Henry James, 2 vols., The Atlantic Monthly Press, Boston, 1920.
MHW	John Sutherland, *Mrs Humphry Ward: Eminent Victorian, Pre-eminent Edwardian*, Clarendon Press, Oxford, 1990.
N	*The Complete Notebooks of Henry James*, edited with introductions and notes by Leon Edel and Lyall H. Powers, Oxford University Press, New York and Oxford, 1987.
NHJ	*The Notebooks of Henry James*, edited by F. O. Matthiessen and Kenneth B. Murdock, Oxford University Press, New York and Oxford, 1955.
OED	*Oxford English Dictionary*.

PE	*The Painter's Eye: Notes and Essays on the Pictorial Arts by Henry James*, edited by John L. Sweeney, Rupert Hart-Davis, London, 1956.
SA	Henry James, *The Scenic Art: Notes on Acting and the Drama, 1872–1901*, edited by Allan Wade, Rupert Hart-Davis, London, 1949.
SLWDH	W. D. Howells, *Selected Letters*, edited by George Arms, Richard H. Ballinger, Christoph K. Lohmann and John K. Reeves, 6 vols., Twayne Publishers, Boston, 1979–83.
TCWJ	Ralph Barton Perry, *The Thought and Character of William James*, 2 vols., Little, Brown, Boston and Toronto, 1935.
WDHAC	*W. D. Howells as Critic*, edited by Edwin H. Cady, Routledge & Kegan Paul, London and Boston, 1973.

Henry James (hereafter HJ) was born on 15 April 1843 at 21 Washington Place in New York City. He was a grandson of the strict Presbyterian William James of Albany (d. 1832), an Irish immigrant who amassed a large fortune ($1,300,000 and much land), but also a son of Henry James 'Senior' (1811–82), fifth of a generation of eleven children which abstained from business in what HJ called a 'rupture with my grandfather's tradition and attitude'. Henry James Senior had rebelled against his father's moralistic prescriptions and been forced to contest a punitive last will and testament to obtain his share of the estate, money he then used to follow his calling as a peripatetic Swedenborgian philosopher and social controversialist, a friend of Ralph Waldo Emerson and Thomas Carlyle among other notable figures of the time.

HJ was the second of Henry James Senior's five children by his wife Mary (née Walsh, 1810–82). His elder brother was the future psychologist and philosopher William James (hereafter WJ), 1842–1910; his younger siblings were, in order, Garth Wilkinson James ('Wilky'), 1845–83; Robertson James ('Bob'), 1846–1910; and the remarkable Alice James (hereafter AJ), 1848–92. The young Jameses seldom remained long in one place; their restless father, moving between Manhattan and Albany, between America and Europe, took them through a succession of eccentric family homes – New York, Paris, London, Geneva, Boulogne, Bonn, Newport (Rhode Island), Cambridge (Massachusetts).

In the letters that follow we pick up HJ as a young author, shortly before his twenty-first birthday. About 11 July 1863 HJ had been drafted in Newport for army service in the Civil War, but then exempted on 29 August by reason of physical disability (probably a back strain). It was in 1864 that 'Henry James Junior' (as HJ was known till 1883) began his career in print, after a false start at Harvard Law School in 1862–3. He can already describe himself as 'a literary man'.

1. To Thomas Sergeant Perry
25 March 1864

Colby MS   Published HJL I, 49—51

The James family had returned in summer 1858 from one of their educational sessions in Europe and spent a year in Newport, Rhode Island, which became their main home for some years (from October 1859 to September 1860 they were again in Europe). HJ made friends at the Rev. W. C. Leverett's school there with Thomas Sergeant Perry (1845—1928). WJ and (to a small extent) HJ studied painting in Newport with the French-trained William Morris Hunt (1824—79). Another student in Hunt's studio, as HJ recalled in 1914, was the friendly, Francophile artist and 'man of the world' John La Farge (1835—1910), reader of Browning and Balzac, who became 'at once . . . quite the most interesting person we knew', and who in 1860 married Perry's elder sister Margaret (1840—1925). The extraordinarily well-read Perry was 'from the first an exemplary . . . and a discouraging friend'. Literary ambition and youthful high spirits inform the HJ–Perry correspondence.

From 1860, according to Perry's reminiscences, HJ 'was continually writing stories, mainly of a romantic kind. The heroes were for the most part villains, but they were white lambs by the side of the sophisticated heroines, who seemed to have read all Balzac in the cradle and to be positively dripping with lurid crimes.' (LHJ I, 8.) In the autumn of 1862 HJ joined the Harvard Law School – in the event only for part of a year. A 1909 fragment, 'The Turning Point of my Life', marks this as his beginning in literary production: 'I brought away with me certain rolls of manuscript that were quite shamelessly not so many bundles of notes on the perusal of so many calfskin volumes.' HJ had already published one (anonymous) story by the time of this letter, 'A Tragedy of Error' in The Continental Monthly, *a short-lived magazine edited by Mrs Martha Elizabeth Duncan Walker Cook, in February 1864 (the magazine expired in this same year). Leon Edel suggests that the 'modern novel' mentioned in this letter may be HJ's second published story, 'The Story of a Year', published in the* Atlantic Monthly *in March 1865 – and that the* Atlantic *made difficulties before printing it.*

Newport, Friday, March 25*th* 1864.

Dear Sarge – Your second letter quite put me to the blush. (If you examine my paper with Willie's microscope you will see that it reflects a faint ruby tinge.)[1] I had been meaning to give some sort of civil answer to your first,

---

1. WJ had earlier in the year enrolled in Harvard Medical School.

from day to day; but my pen, ink and paper – yea, even my small stock of wits – were engaged in advance. The printer's devil was knocking at the door. You know a literary man can't call his time his own. I wonder that you have enough for letter writing. What I mean is that I had made up my mind to finish a certain task or die in the attempt. The task is unfinished: and I have embraced the alternative. This [is] a spiritual, supernatural message. I write with a pen snatched from my angel-wing. It is very pleasant up here but rather lonely, the only other inhabitants being Shakespeare, Goethe and Charles Lamb. There are no women. Thackeray was up for a few days but was turned out for calling me a snob because I walked arm-in-arm with Shakespeare. I am rather sorry, for I am dying to hear the end of *Denis Duval*: that is an earthly expression.[2] Now I am immortal. Heigh-ho. I am lucky in having Goethe all to myself, for I am the only one who speaks German. I translate a good many of Elia's puns.[3] I don't think G. quite relishes them. Elia is delicious. He always flies about with a pen in his ear – a relic of his clerkship days. He looks a good deal like the picture of the harpies in Doré's Dante. He and W. S. have great times together. Elia is forever spouting out quotations from the Plays, which Shake never recognises. –

Nay, to speak seriously, or at least, soberly, the task I mentioned was to rewrite that modern novel I spoke of to you and get it off my hands within a certain number of days. To do this I had to husband my (physical) writing powers. I failed; still, it is almost finished and will go in a day or two. I have given it my best pains: bothered over it too much. On the whole, it is a failure, I think; tho' nobody will know this, perhaps, but myself. Do not expect anything: it is a simple story, simply told. As yet it hath no name and I am hopeless of one. Why use that vile word novelette. It reminds me of chemisette. Why not say *historiette* outright? Or why not call it a bob-tale? I shall take the liberty of asking the *Atlantic* people to send their letter of reject. or accept. to you. I cannot again stand the pressure of avowed authorship (for the present;) and their answer could not come here unobserved. Do not speak to Willie of this. I will not begin again the old song about being lonely; although just now I am quite so; Wilkie is gone to New York. As for John La Farge, he comes to Newport so seldom that his company goes for little. I think I shall run up

2. William Makepeace Thackeray (1811–63) had died before finishing *Denis Duval*, which, however, continued to be serialized in the *Cornhill Magazine* till June 1864. Thirty-four years later HJ moved into Lamb House, Rye, Sussex – next to Winchelsea, where the novel opens; and he published a meditative essay, 'Winchelsea, Rye and "Denis Duval"', in *Scribner's Magazine* (January 1901), recalling 'the poetry of its original appearance'.

3. Charles Lamb (1775–1834) was best known for the quasi-autobiographical *Essays of Elia*, which appeared in 1820–23.

to Boston some day to see him. _Do_ come down some Saturday, as you say. Now that the Spring is waking up to some sense of her duty it is good to be out of doors. I walk a little every day, and by sitting and standing and staring and lingering and sniffing the air, contrive to get a certain amount of exercise. The great event since you went off has been a grand Sanitary concert: here the Rhodian Sappho loved – or at least flirted, – and sung.[4] Here your humble servant performed the duties of one: attired like an English footman, he showed folks to their seats.

I am impatient for your Wasson-killer.[5] My friend, read the 4_th_ Act of the Mercht. of Venice and be merciful.[6] What a fearful state for a man! I wonder if he is aware of your presence in the world; if he sniffs you from afar. I suppose he is attacked with epileptic fits and unaccountable tremblings. He may die before your article comes out: in which case it could serve for an epitaph. _A propos_ of Wasson, Father has been having quite a correspondence with your old love Miss Gail Hamilton, or Mary Abby Dodge.[7] I believe I told you while you were here that he had written her an anonymous letter, suggested by one of her articles. A short time ago, he received a letter from her saying that she had just been reading the "Substance and Shadow,"[8] and that she was convinced that the letter and the book were by the same hand; and thanking him warmly for both. Then he answered her; and yesterday heard from her again: a very good, healthy letter, with a promise of her next book.

Monday. So much I wrote yesterday. To-day I saw John and got your 3_d_ letter!!! Oh beloved Friend! Oh joyous tidings! Oh magnanimous youth! Halleluia! Oh laggard time! Come! Come! Come to your _H.J._

---

4. In _Notes of a Son and Brother_ (1914), HJ recalls 'performances, dramatic and musical . . . in aid of the great Sanitary Commission'. The 'Rhodian Sappho' may be Julia Ward Howe (1819–1910), poet of 'The Battle Hymn of the Republic' (1862), hostess and reformer, who lived at this time in Lawton's Valley, Newport.

5. In March 1864 Perry had published in _Harvard Magazine_ a (parodic) short story; in April he published there an essay on the Transcendentalist author David A. Wasson (1823–87).

6. _The Merchant of Venice_, IV. i. 181–3: 'The quality of mercy is not strained. / It droppeth as the gentle rain from heaven / Upon the place beneath.'

7. Mary Abigail Dodge (pseud. Gail Hamilton; 1833–96), essayist and poet, author of _Country Living and Country Thinking_ (1862), soon to be editor of _Our Young Folks_ (1865–7).

8. _Substance and Shadow: or, Morality and Religion in their Relation to Life: an Essay on the Physics of Creation_ (1863), by Henry James Senior.

2. *To Charles Eliot Norton*
11 November [1864]

Houghton MS or MC   Unpublished

In May 1864 the whole James family moved to 13 Ashburton Place, Boston. HJ made his critical as well as fictional début in print in this year, when the world of American magazines was about to become freshly active following the end of the Civil War in April 1865. He also made influential friends. In Notes of a Son and Brother *he recalled his thrill at 'the offered cup of editorial sweetness': 'I had addressed in trembling hope my first fond attempt at literary criticism to Charles Eliot Norton, who had lately . . . come to the rescue of the North American Review, submerged in a stale tradition and gasping for life, and he had not only published it in his very next number – the interval for me of breathless brevity – but had expressed the liveliest further hospitality, the gage of which was thus at once his welcome to me at home.' In October 1864 the* North American Review, *published like the* Atlantic *by Ticknor & Fields and which Norton edited with James Russell Lowell (1819–91) from 1864 to 1868, printed HJ's review of Nassau W. Senior's* Essays on Fiction. *Norton (1827–1908) devoted his life to what HJ called in a 1908 memorial essay 'the civilising mission' – a friend and editor of Ruskin, he wrote on medieval art and culture and translated Dante. His relations with HJ's father were prickly. He was soon to be a co-founder (with Edwin Lawrence Godkin (1831–1902)) of the* Nation *(New York) in 1865; the HJ of 1915 recalled, 'I contributed, in my young innocence, an "important" article to the first number of the enterprise' (LC II, 178). HJ subsequently became a regular contributor.*

HJ was in Northampton, Massachusetts (where he later set the opening of Roderick Hudson*) as 'a patient in a "Water Cure"' for the constipation that plagued him, together with back problems, in his early years.*

Northampton, November 11*th*

My dear Mr. Norton.

I herewith transmit, in accordance with your request, the long-awaited notice of *Azarian*.[1] Like many long awaited things it is not such a success as might be desired. It was written at a disadvantage. You will, however, judge of it for yourself. I have in my mind a much better notice wh. may one of these days

1. HJ's review of *Azarian* by Harriet Elizabeth Prescott Spofford (1835–1921) appeared in the *North American Review* of January 1865 (C, 268–77). 'Of human nature there is not an unadulterated page in the book . . . We would earnestly exhort Miss Prescott to be *real*, to be true to something.'

get uttered *à propos* of something else. I will send the two remaining notices, viz: those of "Emily Chester" and the "Gypsies of the Danes' Dyke" before the end of the month.[2] I hope you will not regret it if on these likewise, conscience should compel me to be 'severe.'

Most truly your's
Henry James jr.

3. To Lilla Cabot (later Perry)
[May 1865?]

Colby MS   Unpublished

HJ's second published story – signed this time – was 'The Story of a Year' in the Atlantic Monthly *of March 1865.*

Lilla Cabot (1848–1933), daughter of the Boston surgeon Dr Samuel Cabot, was a poet and talented painter. Her mother was a cousin of the eminent poet, Harvard professor and diplomat James Russell Lowell (1819–91). Her brother Arthur Tracy Cabot (d. 1912), who graduated from Harvard in 1872, was to become a doctor and a Fellow of the American Academy. In the spring of 1874 she married HJ's close friend Thomas Sergeant Perry. She kept the following letter for many years, and wrote on the envelope: 'My first letter from H. James when I was a schoolgirl. I was staying with Aunt Anna Lowell and was going to Harvard Square to post some letters after supper in late May. I heard steps running after me and H.J. asked if he might go with me. After posting the letters I said goodnight as I had to go to my cousin's for a locket I had left there the night before. He proposed that I sh'ld. let him go with me and go for a walk afterwards. I got my locket and dropped it when he picked it up and gave it to me. I was a shy girl and feeling embarrassed by his man of the world manner and by knowing he was "an author" I accidentally dropped it again and this time he picked it up and put it in his pocket and said it was the will of Providence he sh'ld always keep it. I had the dignity of shy youth and said nothing meaning to ask for it again when he took me home from our walk but we went to the top of a hill to see a view he knew of and he talked so interestingly that we did not get home till 10.30 and I hurried into the house and

2. HJ's review of *Emily Chester* by Mrs Anne Moncure Crane Seemüller (1838–72), 'emphatically a dull book' with 'a questionable moral tendency', was in the January 1865 *North American Review*. There was no review in the magazine of *The Gypsies of the Danes' Dyke: A Story of Hedge-side Life in England, in the Year 1855* by George S. Phillips (January Searle) (Ticknor & Fields, Boston, 1864): HJ acknowledged to Norton on 1 December that 'the Gypsy book does not deserve so elaborate a handling as I have given it' (HJL I, 57).

forgot the locket till the next morning when I wrote him a stiff little note asking him to give my locket to the bearer and finding it very stiff and prudish I added in a P.S. "Did you see Miss Poke's poem in the Cambridge Chronicle this morning called the "Rape of a locket". This is his reply and I kept it because I knew he was an Author! My brother who was my messenger (he was in college & had come to call on me) said "Well Lilla I never knew a man take so long to write a short note". But never was a note read with such pride! H. James seemed so grown up to me! Seldom has any note been kept so long but the author's celebrity has quite justified my youthful sense of its value.'

My dear Miss Cabot —

    I had of course wildly dreamed of keeping, wearing & cherishing your locket — but I must part from it just as I'm getting used to it. — In sterner truth I had quite forgotten having taken it — it was sojourning sweetly in my waistcoat pocket, just over my heart, when your note was handed me. I'm sorry you should have had the trouble of sending for it — though I can't altogether regret an accident which has opened a correspondence between us. Who can tell where it may end? I don't say *when*: I hope never — never till I cease to be your most faithful —

H. James jr.

I will look up Miss Poke's poem. It was very kind of her not to have written a *Dunciad*, *à mon adresse*.[1]

4. To Charles Eliot Norton
31 July [1865]

Houghton MS   Published HJL I, 61

In July 1865 HJ had three (unsigned) pieces — on Matthew Arnold, Louisa M. Alcott and Goethe — in the North American Review, *edited by Norton and James Russell Lowell, as well as two in issues of the weekly* Nation, *which Norton and Godkin started in that month.*

1. A search in the 1865 *Cambridge Chronicle* revealed of course no such poem as Miss Poke's 'Rape of a Locket'.

Boston.
13 Ashburton Pl.
July 31*st*

My dear Mr. Norton.

Would the *N.A.R.* like a notice of *Thoreau's Letters* fr. an outside, *i.e.* an extra-Concord point of view? Unless some such view is taken, I fear the lesson of the book will be lost. I will be glad to take it, if you so desire, according to my lights.[1] I should also be well pleased to have you suggest any other book for criticism. As I start tomorrow for the Wh. Mts., will you be so good as to address me, at your leisure, *North-Conway, N.H.*?

With kind regards to Mrs. Norton, believe me

very faithfully your's
H James jr

I importune you thus early, lest some Thoreau-ite should be before me. Only remember my offer & answer at yr. perfect convenience.

5. To Thomas Sergeant Perry
Friday morn [1865]

Colby MS   Published TSPB, 276–7

When he got to North Conway, New Hampshire, in the White Mountains, HJ spent part of what he would remember in Notes of a Son and Brother *as a 'splendid American summer' with (among others) Oliver Wendell Holmes (1841–1935), a future chief justice of the U.S. Supreme Court, John Chipman Gray (1839–1915), a Harvard law professor to be, and HJ's brilliant, troubled, exciting cousin Minny Temple (1845–70) (with an escorting aunt, and three sisters). They made up a 'fraternising, endlessly conversing group . . . under the rustling pines'. It is not clear which 'romance' HJ is writing of here; his next fiction to be published was 'A*

---

1. The *North American Review* review of *Letters to Various Persons* by Henry David Thoreau (1817–62) *was* done by someone else. On 11 September HJ wrote to Norton that 'I shall send *Thoreau* to the *Nation* as you suggested. He is not yet begun upon' (HJL I, 62); but this came to nothing. HJ never wrote at length about Thoreau, but discussed him in *Hawthorne* (1879): 'Whatever question there may be of his talent, there can be none, I think, of his genius . . . He was imperfect, unfinished, inartistic; he was worse than provincial – he was parochial; it is only at his best that he is readable. But at his best he has an extreme natural charm . . . He was Emerson's independent moral man made flesh – living for the ages, and not for Saturday and Sunday; for the Universe, and not for Concord' (ch. IV).

Landscape Painter' in the Atlantic Monthly *of February 1866. I have provisionally dated this as after HJ's time in North Conway.*

> Ashburton Place.
> Friday morn.

A myriad thanks, dear Boy, for your heaven-inspired letter. Of course it is more delightful than I can say to hear your good opinion of the romance; which I value infinitely more than a chorus of promiscuous praise. But what I am especially grateful for is the fact that you should have written to me at the dictate of a mood of feeling so kindly & expansive. "Keep a doin' of it." I have had nothing in a very long time please me so much as yr. expression – so full and so spontaneous – of confidence & sympathy.

Yr. letter touches upon great questions.

The Book of Job! I know it but little. W. Holmes has often spoken of its charms to me.[1]

I appreciate yr. sense of mystery – I delight in seeing you *ferment*. One day a rich wine will come of it. I should like to see you before you go to Newport – but put not yrself out. Give my love to your visitors.

> Yours ever
> *H.J. jr.*

6. To Charles Eliot Norton
28 February [1866]

Houghton MS   Published HJL I, 63–4

HJ had written to Norton in October, the day after his review of Schérer's Nouvelles Études sur la littérature contemporaine *had appeared in the* Nation, *proposing 'an article on "Recent French Criticism"', 'a review say of Sainte-Beuve, Taine, Renan (as an Essayist) and Schérer' (HJL I, 62). HJ was in the future to write on all these figures: Charles Augustin Sainte-Beuve (1804–69), Hippolyte Adolphe Taine (1828–93), Ernest Renan (1823–92) and Edmond Schérer (1815–89).*

1. Holmes had in 1864 returned, 'so handsome' and 'marked with military distinction', as HJ recalled, from the Civil War – and begun to study law at Harvard, where WJ had met him. In the summer of 1865 Holmes was reading 'no end of poetry' in reaction against the ugliness of the war. He soon became a friend of HJ, and they travelled together up to North Conway on 1 August 1865. Holmes had an imaginary 'Society of Jobbists' devoted to getting the job done.

Boston, February 28*th*

My dear Mr. Norton:

I undertake a begging-letter. I beg in the first place that you will out of the abundance of your kindness, allow me to retract my proposal to deal critically with Mrs. Stowe, in the N.A.R. I have been re-reading two or three of her books & altho' I see them to be full of pleasant qualities, they lack those solid merits wh. an indistinct recollection of them had caused me to attribute to them; & it is only such merits as these that in my present state of intellectual exhaustion consequent upon having pumped up faint praise for a succession of vapid novels in the *Nation*, will restore vigour & enthusiasm to my pen.[1] The fact of the proposal having been (as I believe) mine, makes me regret my indisposition both the more & the less: the less because it reminds me that you had probably not set your heart upon the article. If its omission will cause an aching void in the Review (or anywhere else) I will of course apply myself to the task. Otherwise I beseech you to avert your gaze & allow me to back out gracefully. I will promise for the future, not to undertake reviews without a better knowledge of the facts of the case.

And this remark applies somewhat to the second clause of my petition.

To come at it, at once: I am loth, *moi chétif*, to engage with the French critics next June or at all, for the present.

I honestly feel incompetent to the enterprise. That is, I could of course put together a certain number of inoffensive commonplaces & uncontested facts about them, & the article would stand written. But I had rather not touch them till I feel that I can do it easily & without stretching: for except under these circumstances, what I should write would be stiff and laboured. I have written the Taine part of the review & it fails signally to satisfy me & would fail equally to satisfy you. I therefore would feel very grateful to you for sinking the scheme just now.

Do not think me either very lazy or very fastidious, but believe me simply tolerably shrewd where the interests of the Review are concerned. Do not trouble yourself, if my representations satisfy you, to answer. I will take your silence for a merciful assent, & not for that of contempt for the instability of my character, or as a token of your having cut my acquaintance.

Ever most truly your's
H. James jr.

1. There was no review at all of Harriet Beecher Stowe (1811–96), author of *Uncle Tom's Cabin: or, Life Among the Lowly* (1851) in the *North American Review* of 1866. In 1875 HJ did review one novel by her in the *Nation* – dismissively: 'none of Mrs. Stowe's ladies and gentlemen open their mouths without uttering some amazing vulgarism'.

7. *To William Conant Church*
21 May 1866

NYPL MS   Unpublished

In 1866 the James family had – while they searched for a permanent home – what
HJ would recall as 'a long summer, from May to November, spent at the then rural
retreat of Swampscott, forty minutes by train northward from Boston'. Thirty-nine
years later, at Coronado Beach, California, HJ would recall 'that (probably August)
day when I went up to Boston from Swampscott and called in Charles St. for news
of O.W.H., then on his 1st flushed and charming visit in England, and saw his
mother in the cool dim matted drawingroom of that house (passed, never, since,
without the sense), and got the news, of all his London, his general English, success
and felicity, and vibrated so with the wonder and romance and curiosity and dim
weak tender (oh, tender!) envy of it, that my walk up the hill, afterwards, up
Mount Vernon St. and probably to Athenaeum was all coloured and gilded, and
humming with it, and the emotion, exquisite of its kind, so remained with me that
I always think of that occasion, that hour, as a sovereign contribution to the germ
of that inward romantic principle which was to determine, so much later on (ten
years!), my own vision-haunted migration.' (N, 239.) ('O.W.H.' was Oliver
Wendell Holmes.)

Church (1836–1917) and his brother, Francis Pharcellus Church (1839–1906),
were founder-editors of The Galaxy, *a New York magazine which first appeared*
on 1 May 1866, and where the story in question here, 'A Day of Days', appeared
on 15 June 1866.

Swampscott, Mass.

Dear Sir: – I have at your request added 5 M.S. pages (as few as I could) to
my story. I agree with you on reflection, that it will be the better for them &
I enclose them herewith.

Truly your's
Henry James jr.

W. C. Church esq.

May 21st, '66

P.S. Suppose (if it is not too late to make a change) you call the story: – *Tom*
Ludlow's Letters, instead of the actual title. Isn't it a better name?

H.J. jr.

8. To William Dean Howells
10 May [1867]

Houghton MS   Published LFL, 59

The Ohioan William Dean Howells (1837–1920), like HJ the literary son of a Swedenborgian father, had returned in 1865 from a consular post in Venice (the reward for a campaign biography of Lincoln) and had found a position at the new Nation *in New York under E. L. Godkin. Then from 1 March 1866, he moved to Boston to become assistant editor of the* Atlantic Monthly *under James T. Fields. Charles Eliot Norton helped him find a house in Cambridge, Massachusetts. HJ and he met in the summer of 1866, around the time of Howells's great success with* Venetian Life, *and forged an alliance. In November 1866 the James family moved again, to the house they had found at 20 Quincy Street, Cambridge. By December Howells was telling E. C. Stedman of a talk with HJ 'two or three hours long, in which we settled the true principles of literary art' (SLWDH I, 271). In 1867 came* Italian Journeys, *the 'papers' referred to in this, the earliest letter from HJ to Howells known to survive.*

Cambridge – May 10*th*

Dear Howells –

Thanks again for your papers – They are utterly charming, & a 100 times the most graceful, witty and poetical things yet written in this land. I especially liked the chapter on Ferrara. – *Que n'y suis-je-pas!* But they are all delightful and I await the rest. Your manner seems to me quite your own & yet it reminds one vaguely of all kinds of pleasant & poignant associations. Thou hast the gift – "go always!" I like the real levity of your lightness & the real feeling of your soberness; and I admire the delicacy of your touch always & everywhere.

The worst of it is that it is almost *too* sympathetic. You intimate, you suggest so many of the refinements of the reality, that the reader's soul is racked by this superfluous enjoyment. But as I say, I think I can stand another batch.

– Your's always
H.J. jr.

9. *To Thomas Sergeant Perry*
20 September [1867]

Colby MS   Published HJL I, 74–9; SL2, 13–17; SL1, 48–53; TSPB, 282–6

In August 1866 Perry had gone to Europe after graduating from Harvard – to England, Paris, Germany, Spain, Switzerland. In Dresden he spent a week in June 1867 with WJ, who was three years his senior; from October the two would lodge together in Berlin, where Perry learned German.

Cambridge – Sept 20*th*

Mon cher vieux Thomas: –

J'ai là sous les yeux depuis hier ta gentille lettre du 4 7*bre*. Je fus bien aise de te savoir de retour à Paris, que tu n'as sans doute pas quitté. Je crois que tu ne regretteras jamais d'y avoir passé une grosse partie de ton temps; car enfin, quoiqu'on en dise, c'est une des merveilles de l'univers. On y apprend à connaître les hommes et les choses, et pour peu qu'on soit parvenu à y attrapper le sentiment de *chez soi*, quelque genre de vie que l'on mène plus tard, on ne sera jamais un ignorant, un ermite – enfin un provincial. – Tu as dépensé toute une page de ta lettre à me parler de l'Exposition.[1] – Que le diable l'emporte, cette maudite baraque! Nous en avons bien assez, même ici à Cambridge. J'aurais bien mieux aimé que tu m'eusses parlé de toi, que tu m'eusses donné de tes nouvelles intimes. (En voilà, des imparfaits du subjonctif! Après cela dira qui voudra que je ne sais pas le Français!) Je me suis donné hier le plaisir d'aller chez tes camarades, Storey et Stratton, recueillir de tes nouvelles.[2] Ces messieurs ont été bien bien aimables, ils m'ont fait part des lettres qu'ils ont reçues de toi pendant l'été. J'en ai beaucoup ri, de ces lettres folles et charmantes. On ne peut avoir plus d'esprit, ni une gaillardise de meilleur ton. Ah mon cher, que je t'en porte envie, de tes courses et de tes aventures, et de ton humeur Rabelaisiaque! – Décidément, je plante là mon français: ou plutôt c'est lui qui me plante. [TRANSLATION: 'My dear old Thomas: – I have before my eyes, since yesterday, your kind letter of the 4

1. The first Great Exhibition at Paris was held in 1855 in the Champs-Élysées.
2. Moorfield Storey (1845–1929) was a classmate of Perry's, a lawyer and author. In the fall of 1867 he went to Washington D.C. as secretary to the statesman Charles Sumner. Later he returned to the Boston area. Charles Stratton was another classmate, a sharer of Perry's irreverent wit, who like Storey became a lawyer.

September. I was happy to know you had come back to Paris, which you have probably not yet left. I think you will never regret having spent a large part of your time there; for in the end, whatever may be said about it, it's one of the marvels of the universe. There one learns to know men and things, and if only one gets to the point of feeling *at home* there, whatever kind of life one leads later, one will never be an ignorant person, a hermit – that is, a provincial. You spent a whole page of your letter telling me about the Exhibition. – The devil take it, that cursed fairbooth! We have quite enough of them, even here in Cambridge. I'd much have preferred that you should have talked about yourself, that you should have given some personal news about yourself. (There are imperfect subjunctives for you! After that I defy anyone to say that I don't know French!) I yesterday gave myself the pleasure of going to see your friends Storey and Stratton, to gain news of you. These gentlemen were very amiable, and shared with me the letters they had received from you over the summer. I laughed a good deal over those mad and charming letters. One could not be wittier, nor be amusing in a better tone. Ah my dear friend, how envious I am of you, of your movements and your adventures, and of your Rabelaisian humour! – Definitely, I'm abandoning my French at this point: or rather it is my French which abandons me.'] – As I say, Storey & Stratton read me and lent me a large portion of your recent letters, beginning with a long one from Venice to the former. Many of your gibes of course I didn't understand, the context being absent. But I understood enough to enjoy the letters very much and to be able to congratulate you on your charming humour. (How detestable this *you* seems after using the Gallic *toi*!) Let me repeat in intelligible terms that I'm very glad to think of you as being as much as possible in Paris – city of my dreams! I feel as if it would count to my advantage in our future talks (& perhaps walks.) When a man has seen Paris somewhat attentively, he has seen (I suppose) the biggest achievement of civilization in a certain direction & he will always carry with him a certain little *reflet* of its splendour. – I had just been reading, when your letter came, Taine's *Graindorge*, of wh. you speak.[3] It seems to me a truly remarkable book in the way of *writing* & description, but to lack very much the deeper sort of observation. As a writer – a man with a language, a vocabulary & a style, I enjoy Taine more almost than I do any one; but his philosophy of things strikes me as essentially superficial & as if subsisting in the most undignified subservience to his passion

3. In the *Nation* of 6 May 1875, HJ reviewed an English translation of Taine's work, *Notes on Paris: The Life and Opinions of M. Frédéric-Thomas Graindorge*, and recalled that 'eight years ago', on its first appearance, it 'was voted by all good critics a rather melancholy mistake', Taine 'being too serious to succeed in a *jeu d'esprit*'.

for description. – I have also read the last new Mondays of Ste. B., & always with increasing pleasure. Read in the *7th* (I think) if you haven't already, an account of A. de Vigny. – Truly, exquisite criticism can't further go. – Have you read *M. de Camors*, by Octave Feuillet? – a sweet little story! Read by all means, if you haven't, (I assume that you have the time,) *Prosper Randoce*, by V. Cherbuliez.[4] It's a work of extraordinary skill & power & I think takes the rag off all the French Romancers, save the illustrious G. Sand, *facile princeps*. I read recently, by the way, this lady's *Memoirs* a compact little work in ten volumes. It's all charming (if you are not too particular about the exact truth) but especially the two *1st* vols., containing a series of letters from her father, written during Napoleon's campaigns. I think they are the best letters I ever read. But you doubtless know the book.[5] – In English I have read nothing new, except M. Arnold's *New Poems*, wh. of course you will see or have seen. – For real & exquisite pleasure read Morris's *Life & Death of Jason*. It's long but fascinating, & replete with genuine beauty.[6] – There is nothing new of course in the universe of American letters – except the projected resuscitation of *Putnam's* Magazine.[7] Great news, you see! We live over here in a thrilling atmosphere. – Well, I suppose there *are* thrills here; but they dont come from

4. HJ had first read Sainte-Beuve's *Causeries du lundi* (1851–62) while at Harvard Law School in fall 1863; *Les Nouveaux Lundis* appeared between 1863 and 1870. Alfred Victor de Vigny (1797–1863) was a sombre Romantic philosopher-poet of spiritual anguish and disillusion, though also of lofty idealism. In the *Nation* of 30 July 1868, HJ reviewed an American translation of *M. de Camors* by the popular Octave Feuillet (1821–90). The novelist endeavours through a narrative of intrigues and depravity 'to show us his hero in all the nakedness of his moral penury', HJ declares, but 'To stir the reader's moral nature and to write with truth and eloquence the moral history of superior men and women, demand more freedom and generosity of mind than M. Feuillet seems to us to possess.' In October 1873 in the *North American Review*, HJ praised *Prosper Randoce* by Victor Cherbuliez (1829–99), Swiss-born French novelist, as 'admirably ironical' in its portrayal of 'a Parisian scribbler, with a genius three parts tinsel to a fourth part silver, and a *morale* containing very little pure metal indeed'.

5. George Sand was the pseudonym of Amandine-Aurore-Lucille Dupin (1804–76), Baronne Dudevant, for HJ 'the greatest of all women of letters' (LC II, 775). HJ refers to *Histoire de ma vie* (1854–5).

6. Matthew Arnold (1822–88), great English critic and poet, brought out *New Poems* in 1867, including 'Thyrsis', his pastoral elegy on the loss of his Oxford friend Arthur Hugh Clough. The influential William Morris (1834–96), also English, painter, poet, designer and later Socialist, published in 1867 *The Life and Death of Jason*, a poem in rhymed couplets. HJ reviewed it in the *North American Review* of October 1867, praising Morris's 'comprehensive sense of form, of proportion, and of real completeness' in the handling of the narrative.

7. From 1868 to 1870 *Putnam's Magazine* appeared under the editorship of E. C. Stedman as a revival of *Putnam's Monthly Magazine* (1853–7); in 1870 it merged with the new *Scribner's Monthly*.

the booksellers – not even from Ticknor & Fields, publishers of *Every Saturday*.[8] I applaud your high resolves with regard to work, when you get home. You will always have my sympathy & co-operation. – Have you in view a *particular office* here at Harvard, for wh. you are particularly fitting yourself, or meaning so to do? – Upon this point, on wh. I have long felt a natural curiosity I have as yet failed to obtain satisfaction.[9] Tell me all about it & unfold your mind to your devoted H.J. – I should think that by the time you get home you will have become tolerably well saturated with the French language & spirit; & if you contrive to do as much by the German, you will be a pretty wise man. There will remain the Classical & the English. On the 1st I say nothing. *That* you will take care of; and I suppose you will study Latin & Greek by the aid of German & *vice-versa*. But the English literature & spirit is a thing which we tacitly assume that we know much more of than we actually do. Don't you think so? Our vast literature & literary history is to most of us an unexplored field – especially when we compare it to what the French is to the French. – Deep in the timorous recesses of my being is a vague desire to do for our dear old English letters and writers *something* of what Ste. Beuve & the best French critics have done for theirs. For one of my calibre it is an arrogant hope. *Aussi* I don't talk about it. – To enter upon any such career I should hold it invaluable to spend two or three years on English soil – face to face with the English landscape, English monuments and English men and women. – At the thought of a study of this kind, on a serious scale, and of possibly having the health and time to pursue it, my eyes fill with heavenly tears and my heart throbs with a divine courage. – But men don't accomplish valuable results *alone*, dear Sarge, and there will be nothing so useful to me as the thought of having companions and co laborers with whom I may exchange feelings and ideas. It is by this constant exchange & comparison, by the wear and tear of living & talking & observing that works of art shape themselves into completeness; and as artists and workers, we owe most to those who bring to us most of human life. – When I say that I should like to do as Ste. Beuve has done, I don't mean that I should like to imitate him, or reproduce him in English: but only that I should like to acquire something of his intelligence & his patience and vigour. One feels – I feel at least, that he is a man of the past, of a dead generation; and that we young Americans are (without cant) men of the future.

8. Ticknor & Fields, the major Boston publishing house, published not only the *Atlantic Monthly* and the *North American Review* but also *Our Young Folks* and *Every Saturday*, which Thomas Bailey Aldrich ran from 1865 to 1872, and which was to compete with *Harper's* in the English reprint market.

9. Before he returned to Harvard, Perry arranged a tutorship in French and German.

I feel that my only chance for success as a critic is to let all the breezes of the west blow through me at their will. We are Americans born – *il faut en prendre son parti*. I look upon it as a great blessing; and I think that to be an American is an excellent preparation for culture. We have exquisite qualities as a race, and it seems to me that we are ahead of the European races in the fact that more than either of them we can deal freely with forms of civilisation not our own, can pick and choose and assimilate and in short (aesthetically &c) claim our property wherever we find it. To have no national stamp has hitherto been a defect & a drawback; but I think it not unlikely that American writers may yet indicate that a vast intellectual fusion and synthesis of the various National tendencies of the world is the condition of more important achievements than any we have seen. We must of course have something of our own – something distinctive & homogeneous – & I take it that we shall find it in our "moral consciousness," our unprecedented spiritual lightness and vigour. In this sense at least we shall have a national *cachet*. – I expect nothing great during your lifetime or mine perhaps: but my instincts quite agree with yours in looking to see something original and beautiful disengage itself from our ceaseless fermentation and turmoil. You see I am willing to leave it a matter of instinct. God speed the day. – But enough of "abstract speculation", marked as it is by a very concrete stupidity. I haven't a spark of your wit & humor, my boy, and I can't write amusing letters. Let me say, now while I think of it, that I was quite unaware until I heard it the other evening from Ben Peirce, of how serious your accident had been on Mt. Vesuvius.[10] In writing to you after 1st hearing of it, I believe I didn't even speak of it. A 1000 pardons for my neglect. My poor dear fellow: accept all my retrospective commiseration. It must have been the very devil of an exasperation. And you carry a classic wound – a Vesuvian scar! – Ah why was I not there (i.e. at the hotel) to sponge your gory face, and to change your poultices? – Well, thank the Lord it was no worse. I always said so, when we used to walk on the hanging rock at Newport. – I have used up all my letter with nonentities, and have no space nor strength for sweet familiar talk. No news. The summer (like a civil young man in the horse car) is giving its seat to the mellow Autumn – the glorious, the grave, the divine. We are having October weather in September: *pourvu que ça dure*. This is *American* weather – worth all the asphaltic breezes of Paris. – I have been all summer in Cambridge – *sans découcher une seule nuit*. Tiens! mon français qui me retrouve! – It has been quite cool & comfortable, but "stiller

10. Ben Peirce (1844–70), a mining engineer, and his elder brother James Mills Peirce (1834–1906), a future Harvard mathematics professor, were in Paris at the same time as Perry in 1867, and seemingly also in Naples (near Vesuvius).

than chiselled marble" – Vide Tennyson.[11] I have a pleasant room with a big soft bed and good chairs, and with books and shirt-sleeves I found the time pass rapidly enough. – I'm sorry to hear you say that your plans may not agree with Willie's for the winter. I hope you may adjust them. You'll of course find it pleasant enough to be together; but I hope neither of you will sacrifice any thing to your serious interests. I should suppose of course that *you* will prefer Berlin. We are expecting daily to hear from W. He wrote 8 weeks ago that he was feeling much better: news wh. gladded my heart. – I haven't seen John all summer; but I heard from him yesterday. – Your sister is again a mother: a little girl, & doing well.[12] But this you will have heard. I draw to a close. My letter is long but not brilliant. I can't make 'em brilliant until some one or something makes me brilliant. A 100 thanks for the photos. About has a capital, dear face; & Sardou a highly refined & Parisian one.[13] – By all means send your own & others. Write punctually. – Farewell, *mon vieux*. Tout à toi

H.J.

10. To Francis Pharcellus Church
23 October [1867]

NYPL MS   Published HJL I, 73–4

In the years up to 1870 HJ contributed five stories (and one short play) to the Churches' Galaxy, and nine to the Atlantic. As Leon Edel says, 'The allusion here appears to be to "The Story of a Masterpiece"' (it appeared – in two instalments, not 'all at once' – in the Galaxy, V (January–February 1868)).

Cambridge – Oct 23*d*

My dear Sir: –

I recd. your note and the enclosed cheque – for which many thanks.

11. In Tennyson's 'A Dream of Fair Women' (1832), the first legendary beauty the narrator sees is Helen of Troy: 'At length I saw a lady within call, / Stiller than chiselled marble, standing there; / A daughter of the gods, divinely tall, / And most divinely fair.' (*The Poems of Tennyson*, edited by Christopher Ricks (1987), 1, 484–5 (ll. 85–8)).
12. The little girl was Margaret La Farge, who with her family would visit HJ at Lamb House in 1903.
13. Edmond About (1828–85), brilliant French journalist and moralizing novelist and editor of *Le XIXe Siècle*, met HJ in London in 1879. HJ in 1875 called Victorien Sardou (1831–1908), a successful French playwright, 'this supremely skillful contriver and arranger'.

I am sorry the story is not a little shorter but I am very glad that you are to print all at once. As for adding a paragraph I should strongly object to it. It doesn't seem to me necessary. Silence on the subject will prove to the reader, I think, that the marriage *did* come off. I have little fear that the reader will miss a positive statement to that effect & the story closes in a more dramatic manner, to my apprehension, just as I have left it.[1]

Yours most truly –
H. James jr.

F. P. Church esq.
(over)

P.S. – Let me reiterate my request that I may see a proof. This I should particularly like to do.

HJ jr.

11. To Thomas Sergeant Perry
13 May [1868]

Colby MS   Unpublished

Perry remained in Berlin for the academic year, even after WJ left in January 1868, returning to the U.S. in August 1868. He seems to have taken offence at HJ's words in a letter of 27 March 1868: 'Vrai, are you not another T. S. Perry than the "boy Sargy" of bygone days – a languid, florid cosmopolite, clad in black velvet, knowing in French wines, actors, actresses and sich.' In that letter HJ paints Cambridge life in drab colours: 'I see none indeed but the Nortons and Howells' (HJL I, 82–3).

Cambridge, May 13*th*, a.m.
Dear Sarge – I recd. this morning at first with joy & then with horror & anguish your letter of April 13th. – Dear sensitive child, what under heaven

1. There *is* an additional paragraph at the end of 'The Story of a Masterpiece', a tale which consciously reworks Browning's poem 'My Last Duchess'. The hero, Lennox, has commissioned a portrait of his beautiful fiancée from a talented painter who turns out to be a disillusioned old lover of hers; and the portrait unintentionally conveys to him the truth of her character, 'a certain vague moral dinginess'. Anguished, he hacks the painting with a dagger. The extra

had I done to make you feel so sore! I quite forget the colors of the little
fancy-picture drawn in my letter — but you may be sure that any attempt at a
portrait was consciously a mere fancy-picture. — My words — harmless jocosities
— were used in the utter vacancy & laxity of mere good nature & fantasy —
and as for their being dictated by anything said or written by Ware or by
Willy, 'tis a certain truth that neither of those persons have yet spoken of you
but in the barest generalities & the most perfect kindness.[1] It has been a matter
of regret with me all winter that, in default of letters from yourself Willy didn't
drop more allusions to your pursuits & your manners. For what I said, then,
I alone am responsible, & for the evil suspicions & accusations therein contained,
which seem overmuch to have wounded your feelings, your own brilliant
imagination, dear Sarge, must be held accountable. Allons, in future I will risk
no jokes, *j'ai la main lourde*. Believe me then for this once, that the sketch in
my letter was the irresponsible, irrational off-spring of a sportive fancy, taking
no acct. whatever of probability, & having no reference to anything seen,
heard, suspected or even seriously fancied or conjectured. I quite deny that
the "subject" therefore, as you call it, should cast a shade over our correspondence, & for my own part I certainly don't mean to allow it to do so. Your
picture of me on my pilgrim rack is truer & harsher than any I ever mentally
formed of you; but it gives me a loathsome feeling of pharisaism to think that
you suspected me of wanting to show my teeth at you & revile you for
venturing to take your ease in Europe. I certainly should have reviled you if
you hadn't. If you were stained with all the vices of Gomorrah I should still
bow to you in Beacon St.; & as it is, indeed as you are (say) only with those
of Berlin, I will still extend you my hand. — But a truce to these mutual
recriminations. I was loath to remain any longer under your impeachment of
harboring injurious thoughts & talking of that whereof I know nothing. You
took au grand sérieux what was at best a very thin jest & by me forgotten [as]
soon as uttered. I ought to have written in a ( ) what Artemus Ward was
wont to do.[2] I am sorry to have caused you a moment's discomfort of feeling
& can assure you that your vices were never imaged with such vividness as
to cause me a tenth part of such suffering. — Why ah why, dear child, instead
of writing these futile words of self defence, didn't you tell me something that

---

paragraph, which presumably reflects HJ's feeling about the Churches' insistence, begins: 'I
need hardly add that on the following day Lennox was married.'

1. William Ware, an architect, had shared quarters with Perry in Paris.

2. HJ puts here a pair of empty brackets. Artemus Ward (pseud. of the recently dead Charles
Farrar Browne (1834–67), American humourist) published *Artemus Ward: His Book* (1862) and
Artemus Ward: His Travels (1865). Typical parentheses in Artemus Ward read '(N.B. This is
rote Sarcastical . . .)' or '[N.B. – This is Sarkassum.]' or '[A jew desprit]'.

I didn't know & would have been glad to hear? Remove from your mind this baleful shadow of misconception & *write me a fair & joyous note.*

I came yesterday from Newport where I had been staying at the Tweedies with a select party – Minnie T., Mr. & Miss Boott (whom I believe you know or have met) John Gray, &c, &c. I saw your sister, who seemed beautiful – yet was lonely – John being, perforce, constantly in N.Y.[3] He said you were coming home *at once* & I was surprised to see no mention of such intent in your letter. I am glad you're [getting well?] into German, tho' I deprecate the lewd & immoral Herder.[4] I shall be absent fr. C., all summer – where? – I know not; except that the mts. will receive me.[5] But in the autumn I shall be here & await you. –

Don't forbear to write or I shall become more abusive still; & now that you have let me in the inquisitorial Dock, who knows what I may not discover? – Farewell –

> Tout à toi – as of old –
> *H.J. jr*

12. To George Abbott James
20 March [1869]

Houghton MS   Unpublished

In 1868 HJ mostly remained in Cambridge, writing. In March that year he told Perry, 'I write little and only tales, which I think it likely I shall continue to manufacture in a hackish manner, for that which is bread.' (HJL I, 84.) (He published six stories in 1868.) In November he wrote to Grace Norton in England, evoking his Cambridge life: 'I am leading the quiet life which I so long ago formed the habit of – the only very audible sound in its quietness being still the scratching

3. Minny Temple was a friend of the Bootts – Francis (1813–1904), a widower and American composer, who lived mainly in Italy, and his only child, Elizabeth (Lizzie) Boott (1846–88). Lizzie would study painting in Paris with Thomas Couture (1815–79), the teacher of Manet and of William Hunt (Hunt taught WJ and La Farge). The others here are John Chipman Gray, Margaret Perry La Farge, who must have been at least five months pregnant, and John La Farge.

4. (The paper here is creased and the words only half visible.) Johann Gottfried Herder (1744–1803) was an associate of Goethe and a crucial figure in the *Sturm und Drang* movement in German Romantic literature. He claimed that folk poetry (including Ossian and Shakespeare) was the highest achievement of the creative imagination. Perry was reading Herder and Goethe.

5. HJ spent some time around the start of August 1868 in Jefferson, New Hampshire, where, as he wrote to Oliver Wendell Holmes, 'there are woods; there are women' (SL I, 54).

of this decidedly indifferent pen.' (Unpublished Houghton MS, bMS Am 1094 (871).)

HJ got his turn in Europe only after WJ and his friends Perry, Holmes and others. The family financed his travels, both for the sake of his health (his back and his digestion both caused him discomfort) and for that of his cultural development. He landed at Liverpool on 27 February 1869, 'a somewhat disabled young man who was about to complete his twenty-sixth year', as he put it in his unfinished recollections in The Middle Years (1917); and immediately wrote to his parents that he had acquired an English accent (Unpublished Houghton MS, bMS Am 1094 (1752)).

George Abbott James (b. 1838), probably not related to the Jameses, Ohio-born and wealthy, became a Boston lawyer. In 1864 he married Elizabeth Cabot Lodge, whose brother Henry became Senior Senator for Massachusetts. His sister married the artist John Chandler Bancroft, whom HJ knew from Newport and Miss Upham's boarding-house in Cambridge. HJ had met George James at Harvard Law School, and was as Notes of a Son and Brother says struck by 'his splendid aspect' and 'flush of life and presence'.

London 7 Half-Moon St. Piccadilly
March 20*th*

My dear George –

I have just rec'd a letter from home in wh. mention is made of an invitation which, in ignorance of my departure, you were so good as to send me. I need no more than this little pretext to drop you at this late hour a line of farewell & a word of apology for not having made an appearance in Beacon St. before going off. My departure was so unexpected & sudden that I was compelled to make all my adieus by proxy & to concentrate all my exertions upon getting my shirts into my valise & myself into the New York train. Farewell then, most regretfully, to your excellent self & to Mrs James & Mrs Lodge, as well as to your sister, if she is still with you.

I feel quite as if I were scribbling this note as I have done others, from Quincy St. Cambridge & as if it were going to be carried to you on a blessed horsecar & not on an – anything but blessed – Atlantic steamer. I have been now some three weeks in this mighty metropolis & have fairly purchased the right I think, to speak of it as the darkest & dingiest of cities – especially when seen, as I see it now, from the basement of an ancient lodging house in a narrow, albeit highly respectable street, with the brightness of heaven obscured at once by a steady deluge of rain & a vast wire screen, destined to repress the curiosity of the populace. Nevertheless, like everything else, the old place has its points – which you know quite as well as I – & I shall have spent a very pleasant month here. I have seen a moderate number of people & things & made the most of my small opportunities.[1] After three years of Cambridge, you know, a very little, even, of London will go a great way! I hanker after the Continent, but I mean, by hook or by crook, to stick it out in England (somewhere or other[)] a few weeks longer. The trouble with an American in England is that, as an outsider, he can find comparatively little to enjoy. The beauty of England is all private property, & unless he is duly initiated he will see very little of it by strolling over the land. One of these days I may get a chance at it all as an *insider*, but I must forego it for the present. Moreover as I say I find abundant use for my superficial faculties in merely looking at what turns up from day to day.

I already feel as if Boston were the baseless fabric of a vision & shall have to depend upon letters to keep me convinced of its reality.[2] One from you, I needn't say, would go far towards it. You can think of me – when you've so little else to do that your thoughts take such a turn – as shut up within these four seas for the next six weeks, then as lolling away the summer on some Swiss Mountain side – then as treading with rapture the elastic asphalte of the Boulevards. This I assure you, shines from afar to the lonely resident on Piccadilly.

I shall know well enough how to think of you – as to the general outline – but shall always be glad to hear of any new lights & shades – using the last word of course in a purely relative sense. Àpropos of outlines, &c, do give *mes hommages* to the Sybil[3] – & believe me, as regards yourself, more familiarly,

Most faithfully yours

Henry James jr

1. HJ's opportunities were less scant than this suggests, partly because the well-connected Charles Eliot Norton was in London with his wife Susan Ridley Sedgwick Norton (1838–72), and his sisters Jane (1824–77) and Grace (1834–1926). By this time HJ had met, among others: the intellectual Leslie Stephen (1832–1904), future father of Virginia Woolf, the positivist philosophers John Henry Bridges (1832–1906) and Frederic Harrison (1831–1923) (the latter at the Nortons'), and the sanitary reformer Sir John Simon (1816–1904), a friend of Ruskin's; the Swedenborgians William White and J. J. Garth Wilkinson (1812–99); Dickens's daughter Kate, the poet Aubrey De Vere (1814–1902), and, most notably perhaps, William Morris and John Ruskin himself. The day after this letter HJ would lunch with Charles Darwin.
2. *The Tempest*, IV. i. 150. Not for the last time HJ applies Prospero's famous speech to America: 'Our revels now are ended. These our actors, / As I foretold you, were all spirits, and / Are melted into air, into thin air; / And like the baseless fabric of this vision, / The cloud-capped towers, the gorgeous palaces, / The solemn temples, the great globe itself, / Yea, all which it inherit, shall dissolve; / And, like this insubstantial pageant faded, / Leave not a rack behind.'
3. The 'Sybil' was not identified.

13. To Henry James Senior
17 September [1869]

Houghton MS   Unpublished

HJ's constipation took him from London and the company of the Nortons to Malvern, near the Welsh border, and Dr Raynor's expensive water-cure on 31 March 1869. He stayed three weeks. On leaving Malvern, HJ spent three weeks more touring England – Worcester, Tintern Abbey, Raglan Castle, Newport, Chepstow, Gloucester, Warwick Castle, Kenilworth, Stratford-on-Avon, Oxford, Blenheim Palace, Tewkesbury, Salisbury, Ely, Winchester and Oxford – before returning to London and the company of the well-connected Nortons. On 10 May he wrote to his father of George Eliot, whom he had visited: 'in this vast ugliness resides a most powerful beauty which, in a very few minutes, steals forth and charms the mind, so that you end as I ended, in falling in love with her' (HJL I, 116). On 14 May he left London, calling at Boulogne and Paris, for Geneva and a summer of energetic walking in Switzerland, where at Vevey (again near the Nortons) he read John Stuart Mill's new book, The Subjection of Women. *He descended into Italy on foot late in August, and taking Norton's advice on itinerary, made his way to Venice via Lake Maggiore and Lake Como, Milan, Pavia, Brescia, Verona and Vicenza.*

Venice, Hotel Barbesi
Sept. 17*th*

Dear father –

I have as yet hardly more than time to let you know by this hasty scrawl that I have at last arrived among these blessed isles – in fact that I have been here two days. My 1*st* act, the morning after my arrival was to take a gondola to the bankers & ask for my letters. They were not as numerous as I had hoped – but there were enough of them to create a little heaven – within this larger heaven about me: one from you of Aug. 27*th*, from Cambridge, one from mother from Pomfret & one from Willy, do., which seemed to have suffered great delay & mischances having been soaked to death with salt water; – not however that I couldn't easily read it.[1] Its date was the last of July & in case of his having wondered at my not having got it before, tell him I couldn't possibly have read it with greater rapture than just as I did. I bade my gondolier turn into the Grand Canal, & there stretched in voluptuous ease beneath my awning, as we lapsed & swerved & gurgled along this glorious liquid path, I

1. HJ's parents and brother and sister were at Pomfret, Connecticut for the summer.

devoured the paternal, maternal, fraternal words. Ah, je vous aime bien, allez! Your letters were full of good things & good news. The Lord be praised for your blissful Summer at Pomfret! Willy's statement of his mild improvement caused me to howl again! May it proceed with inexorable consistency. The only bad bit in your letter was what you say about poor Wilky's crop & the worm. I had just been reading in the *Times* an article celebrating the fine crop of the year & was fancying him happy in a comfortable harvest.[2] Poor dear boy; if this gorgeous wicked old Venice had any consolation for him he should have it.

I wrote you last from Verona, where I spent three excellent days. The place is full of admirable things, such as ought to be quietly studied & enjoyed. The great arena lords it over the whole with stupendous Roman inelegance. But after this come two other great works of which I wish (a wish now likely to become chronic) I might enclose you proper photographs: the tombs of the Scaligers & the Ch. of San Zenone. The former are a little group of monumental sepulchres in a little medieval church-yard in the heart of the old city & exhibit I fancy a denser accumulation of artistic labor & deep aesthetic intent than can anywhere else be found in the same compass. The atmosphere in the little iron-bound circle which encloses them seems absolutely thick & heavy with research & beauty. The whole thing is tremendously serious. San Zenone is about the most worshipful & religious edifice I have yet beheld: – a beauty so vast & tranquil, so chaste & formal that it wrings tears from the eyes. On my way from Verona I spent 24 hours at Vicenza. It is easily described by saying that Vicenza is Palladio – the place having been his home & the great scene of his operations. What one looks at is the outsides of about a hundred palaces – the town swarms with 'em. I enjoyed them vastly, but since coming here & getting hold of a vol. of Ruskin's *Stones of V.*, I find he pronounces Palladio infamous & I must blot out that shameful day.[3] Of Venice generally I shall attempt to say nothing, as yet – unless how astonishingly well one knows the place without having been here. Atmospherically it is a good deal like Newport. I have already contrived to see a good many pictures – having been to the 3

2. On 9 September 1869 *The Times* noted the report of the Agricultural Department in Washington: 'All the important cotton-growing States of the country are said to report improvements in the general condition and promise of the cotton crop . . . The general cotton crop of the country . . . has as yet been comparatively little injured by worms.'

3. Andrea Palladio (1508–80) built many palaces in Vicenza but also a number of churches in Venice, including S. Giorgio Maggiore. In HJ's story 'Travelling Companions' (*Atlantic*, November–December 1870) the narrator visits Vicenza, 'looking at Palladio's palaces and enjoying them in defiance of reason and Ruskin' – whose *The Stones of Venice* (1851–3) is a passionate defence of Gothic architecture, and aspects of the feudal attitudes it expresses, against modern secularism and commercialism.

strongholds – the ducal palace, the Academy & the Scuola of San Rocco. It's all a perfect bedazzlement of genius. I hope soon to write Willy a good letter about the various "artists." He may be interested to know *en attendant* that the grand Titian already trembles, nay, actually sinks, in the scale. There is a greater than he in the terrible Tintoretto – & a greater than either possibly in the sublime John Bellini. Titian's famous things here, the *Assumption*, the *Presentation* of the little Virgin are disappointing.[4] But of all this anon.

Gondolas are celestial. I have one by the day: the gondolier is my slave & creature. It's most imperial. I have been two afternoons to the Lido at sunset: I say no more.

If you see Howells tell him I have a letter on the stocks. I'm glad to hear your news of your book.[5] You will of course mail or in some way despatch a copy to me. Address it & address all future letters (jusquà nouvel ordre) *Cura MM. Em. Fenzi & Cie Banquiers Florence*. (I rewrite: *Em. Fenzi & Cie*.) I shall stay here at least a couple of weeks. I thought of taking a lodging, but looked at some & found them dearer than the hotel & besides very lonely. I had heard neither of Kitty Emmet's baby nor of Elly's husband. May they both turn out satisfactory. I hope Kitty is better & prospering. But I don't a bit like Elly marrying that Methusaleh. Is Minny coming abroad? Has J.L.F. sailed? I get no news of A.K. I fancy they are now in Milan, on their way to Florence.[6]

4. The Palace of the Doges, founded in 800, contains many major works of art, as does the Accademia delle Belli Arti on the other side of the Grand Canal. The Scuola di San Rocco contains works by Jacopo Tintoretto (1518–94). Titian (Tiziano Vecelli) (*c.*1487/90–1576) was usually thought the greatest of Venetian painters, with his *Assumption* (1516–18) at the Church of the Frari the basis of his fame. HJ said in 1882: 'At Venice, strange to say, Titian is altogether a disappointment.' (CTW:C, 302–3.) HJ told WJ eight days after this that 'the greatest of them all – Tintoretto – . . . ends by becoming an immense perpetual moral presence, brooding over the scene' (CWJ I, 93). Giovanni Bellini (*c.*1430–1516), the son of one painter and younger brother of another, was the greatest of Venetian Madonna painters.
5. Henry James Senior gave W. D. Howells a copy of his *The Secret of Swedenborg* by 5 September, and Howells reviewed it in the December *Atlantic Monthly*, of which he was by now practically in charge, though he did not become official editor till 1 July 1871.
6. Katherine Temple Emmet (1843–95), elder sister of Minny Temple, married Richard Stockton Emmet (1821–1902) in September 1868, and had a small boy in July 1869. Ellen James Temple (1850–1920), Minny Temple's younger sister, married her cousin Christopher Temple Emmet (1822–84) and moved to California (she remarried in 1891). Minny Temple, who was seriously ill with tuberculosis, had written optimistically to HJ on 6 June 1869, 'If you were not my cousin I would write & ask you to marry me & take me with you – but as it is, it wouldn't do' (HJAL, 105). John La Farge was not in good health and did not go to Europe at this period. Aunt Kate was Catharine Walsh (1812–89), HJ's mother's sister, whose two-year-long, unsuccessful marriage to Captain Charles H. Marshall in 1853–5 interrupted her long residence with the James family. She was travelling in Europe with Henry Wyckoff, Helen Ripley and Mrs Helen Wyckoff Perkins and her husband. HJ finally coincided with her in Rome.

The mosquitoes are infernal here just now & they will probably take Venice on their exit. Thank mother & W. for their letters, & Alice for that wh. she of course has written & is now *en route*. Thank you, dear dad, for everything. I get no more Nations: where is the hitch? Yours till I write again

H.J. jr.

14. To Grace Norton
11 November [1869]

Houghton MS   Unpublished

After leaving Venice, HJ spent October in Florence, feeling his problems with back and bowels 'so intolerable that I have well nigh made up my mind to leave Italy & fly to England' (CWJ I, 115). But when the Nortons arrived on about the 22nd for two years in Italy, HJ visited Pisa with them, and then, leaving them to return to Florence and the Villa d'Elci where they were staying, finally went on to Rome. Arriving on the morning of 30 October, he 'went reeling & moaning thro' the streets, in a fever of enjoyment', as he wrote to WJ (CWJ I, 116).

Charles's younger sister Grace, who never married, was a lifelong confidante of HJ's. She was active in literature and later in life published Studies in Montaigne *(1904) and other works on the same subject.*

Rome, Hotel de Rome, Nov. 11*th*.[1]

Dear Grace —

Rome is sublime, but you are sublimer! Base tho' I am, I am not insensible to the delicate insight with which you divined that, *in spite* of my baseness & my apparent oblivion of all human decencies, I was not only worthy but even anxious to hear from you. Your letter came to me yesterday at the end of a heavy Roman day & lightened most palpably the weight of the twenty four hours past & to come. It doesn't do to stand too much alone among all these swarming ghosts of the past & there can be no better antidote to their funereal contagion than a charming modern living feminine letter.

My dear Grace, I was not only anxious to hear from you: I will say more: I will actually assert that I was *worthy*! I have been holding my peace neither because I was false nor fickle nor faithless but simply — if it's not too lame &

1. In Murray's 1867 *Handbook of Rome and its Environs*, the Hotel de Rome is described as 'on a large scale', with 250 beds.

impotent a conclusion – because I've been too perpetually tired to take up a pen.

After roaming thro' the city all day I have generally in the evening collapsed into languor & stupefaction. Having come to Rome with very vague previsions as to my stay I have gone roundly to work sight-seeing, so that in case of a proximate departure I should have drunk as deeply as possible of the enchanted draught. I have tacitly rejected the thought of putting you off even provisionally with half a dozen lines & I have most illogically waited until some super-natural intervention should have compelled me to spend a morning in my room – or brought me home in the evening fresh & elastic & the least bit good company. I don't say that this is the case this evening: but we must effect a compromise.

Your letter was all delightful, save your mention of Charles's being unwell. What is the use of having such a sunny haven of rest – of being master of the villa d'Elci – if you are going to overwork yourself like a *bourgeois*? Do let me hear when you next write that he is better – better even than before & being rapidly made over anew by the magic of your home. Meanwhile give him my love & God-speed for a Florentine winter.

It's poor work writing from Rome, if you pretend in the least to write up to the level of your impressions! Expect a most common-place scrawl.

I find Rome – *interesting*: I can't say more. In this quality it exceeds everything I have yet seen & falls not a whit below my pre-conceptions. Other places are pleasing, picturesque, pretty, charming; but Rome is thoroughly serious. Heaven knows it's picturesque enough: but it has in this respect a depth of tone which makes it differ not only in degree but even in kind, from Florence & Venice. I have been out of doors so constantly from the moment of my arrival & have had such a crowding multitude of impressions that my brain contains as yet but a confused mass of brilliant images which I devoutly trust will be reduced with time to some degree of harmony & logic: but as yet they are barely available for epistolary purposes.

My mind swarms with *effects* of all kinds – to be introduced into realistic novels yet unwritten.

But I must get rid without delay of my confession. I came hither, as I foresaw I should have to, by the night express & saw no more of the road than was visible between sunrise & 10 o'clock. Don't lament, however. I shall see it all in detail on my way back. After going to my hotel & a hasty "wash" & breakfast I let myself loose on the city. It was decide[d]ly one of the days of my life. I roamed about in every direction from noon till dusk & when I came home to dinner had pretty well taken the cream off of Rome. My senses being a good deal quickened by excitement I think that if I had been compelled to depart that evening I should have felt myself to have got a good solid impression of the subject – & would have ventured to discuss it at an evening-party. I *do* find Rome "*rubbishy*" – magnificently, sublimely so.[2] Amid many of the heaps of rubbish I have lingered & gloated with the fondest fascination. I spent a long sunny morning (besides various secondary visits) lounging & maundering & murmuring in the Coliseum; & an afternoon very much in the same fashion at the Baths of Caracalla.[3] I enjoyed a magnificent sunset there, on the summit, quite by [my]self; & I think I never had quite so intimate a *tête à tête* with the genius of the past. We were literally face to face – & eye-to-eye. Another long sunny cloudy breezy morning at the Palace of the Caesars which (since you were here probably) has been under the auspices of Napoleon III excavated & revealed in the most wondrous manner.[4] Much too have I loafed & lingered in the Forum. Two good long stares have I had at those unutterably *manly* sculptures which adorn the arch of Constantine. Few things tell so well the Roman tale.[5] Decidedly I veto Female Suffrage. Again & again have I taken the measure of that noblest & simplest & sweetest of statues – the kind old Marcus Aurelius at the Capitol. It makes even Roman bronze mild & humane & pathetic.[6] At the Pantheon I have said at least a dozen good round Pagan prayers. It seems to me *exquisitely* sublime & I don't believe I shall ever get from architecture a purer cleaner sensation.[7] As for St. Peter's I decidedly go in for it: – tho' indeed as you suggest I'm extremely glad "it aint no bigger." But it *is* big without a doubt & furnishes the mind

2. In the opening verse-letter of the narrative poem *Amours de Voyage* (pub. 1858) by Charles Eliot Norton's late friend Arthur Hugh Clough, the hero Claude writes to his friend Eustace that 'Rome disappoints me much; I hardly as yet understand, but / *Rubbishy* seems the word that most exactly would suit it.'

3. The vast ruins of the Baths of Caracalla, covering 140,000 square yards, were described by HJ to AJ on 7 November 1869 as 'a collection of perfectly mountainous masses of brickwork' (HJL I, 163).

4. The Palace of the Caesars on the Palatine Hill was first built by Augustus, then variously remodelled and extended by Tiberius, Caligula, Nero, Vespasian and Titus. In 1861 the site had been purchased by Napoleon III, whose French garrison protected Pius IX's Vatican against Italian nationalism, for excavation and the laying-open of the remains.

5. The Arch of Constantine, covered in reliefs, was built over the Via Triumphalis to commemorate Constantine's victory over Maxentius.

6. This was the only ancient equestrian statue which had been preserved entire, moved to the site where HJ saw it by its admirer Michelangelo. HJ had written of Marcus Aurelius, in an 1866 *Nation* review of *The Works of Epictetus*, 'He was simply a moralist; he had a genius for virtue. He was intensely a man among men, an untiring observer, and a good deal of a satirist.'

7. Murray's *Handbook* cites the commentator Forsyth calling its portico 'positively the most sublime result that was ever produced by so little architecture'. Erected in 27 BC as a pagan temple, it was later consecrated as a church.

with a perfectly satisfactory standard & example of vastness. It's internal physiognomy strikes me as uncommonly magnificent & I should never dream of wishing it other. The glorious whole swallows up the inglorious parts & you get one rich transcendent effect.[8]

To the Vatican I have paid of course many visits & almost feel as if I have seen a fair portion of it. Its richness & interest are even greater than I supposed; the great things are more numerous & greater. That there *are* such things is certainly a great comfort to the feeble conscientious mind. I had finally got into a wretched muddle in the Florentine galleries with regard to pictures & painters & my likes & dislikes: but now that pitiful fever is quenched – & these cool immortals quite make me forget the tawdry colorists. Within the last couple of days however I confess I have been reminded of them at a couple of the private Galleries. I saw to day at the Doria palace your old man of Titian with a rose & a jewel.[9] He is well enough; but I fancy your maturer judgement would think him the least bit of a humbug. I fear it would enlighten you in a similar manner as to the merits of the *Empress Helena* of Paul Veronese, of which you speak. I am sorry my dear Grace to blight your young illusions; but in compensation I commend to you the fine P.V. at the *Pitti*, over a door – a Baptism of our Lord.[10] I *have* seen to day one really great picture – one of those works which draw heavily on your respect, & make you feel the richer for the loss: the portrait of Innocent X, by Velasquez at the Doria Palace.[11] Also a Corregio – a mere sketch, but most divinely touched – & a glorious Claude which leaves Turner nowhere; *car enfin* it's in good taste.[12] This is not

8. St Peter's, whose famous dome was the design of Michelangelo, was begun in 1450. Murray's comments seem to find an echo in HJ's: 'The Interior, in spite of all the criticisms of architects, is worthy of the most majestic temple of the Christian world. Whatever may be the defects in particular details, . . . we believe that the minds of most persons who enter it for the first time are too much absorbed by the unrivalled unity of its proportions to be influenced by such professional pedantry.'

9. Not identified. Murray mentions '*Titian*. A fine Male Portrait' in the Palazzo Doria-Pamphili without further details.

10. The painting of St Helena, the mother of the emperor Constantine, by Paolo Veronese (c.1528–88), was in the Vatican picture-gallery. Veronese's 'Baptism of Christ', painted c.1578–80, is in the Palatine Gallery of the Pitti Palace in Florence.

11. Pope Innocent X had been the founder of the Pamphili family. Velázquez (Don Rodriguez de Silva, 1599–1660) worked chiefly in Spain, but painted the Pope during a visit to Rome in 1651. HJ's character Daisy Miller would later be seen beside this portrait in compromising company.

12. Murray notes, spelling the name differently, '*Coreggio*. A cartoon of Glory crowning Virtue.' Antonio Correggio (so spelt now; 1494/1489–1534) worked mostly in Parma. Claude Lorraine (1600–82), born in France, worked in Italy from an early age, specializing in atmospheric classical landscapes. In 'Roman Rides' (1873) HJ says the Doria Palace has 'two famous specimens' of Claude's 'splendid scheme of romance'. Joseph Mallord William Turner (1775–1851) was the

everything but it's much. If it were everything, by the way, I think I should like the *Transfiguration* a little better. It's well enough once in a while I suppose, to have a disappointment.[13] I paid Rafael the high compliment of choosing his immortal work as the occasion of mine: in that way I shall be sure to remember it. M. Angelo's *Moses*, on the other hand leaves much less to be desired than I fancied.[14] It seems to me a work of really heroic merit.

You ask about your old friend *San Clemente*. I paid him a visit the other afternoon & found him full of sweet antiquity & solitude. It's since you were here I suppose, that he has been found to have an elder brother buried beneath the soil, on whose prostrate form he has settled himself so placidly. I was too late to explore: but shall not fail to return.[15]

Too late; my dear Grace those words remind me of the actual flight of time. You must let this hasty scribble serve as a note of my deep enjoyment. I do wish I could put into my poor pale words some faint reflection of the color & beauty of this glorious old world. But you have it all in memory; & then – *que dis-je?* – you have in fact something very nearly as good. I know some of the secrets of the Florentine hills: I know your garden, your terrace, your prospect: you certainly have Italy quite as well as I.

I am most happy to learn of your felicity & contentment. May it know no interruption. I trust that Charles has exhausted all possible pretexts for getting tired – & that in common with you all, he will devote himself to inventing pretexts for taking his perfect ease – troubled by no more painful effort than once in a while to remember that I think of you as you my dear Grace have done so divinely & that in token of the same I have hereby sent you my love: – Farewell. I sometimes wish that instead of having come to this terrible serious Rome I were wintering peacefully in calm aesthetic Florence. But in some fashion or other I shall put Rome thro'; & then I hope shall take another look at the banks of the Arno. Many thanks for your account of my vacant room.

---

controversial English Romantic landscapist championed by Ruskin: in 1873 HJ wrote that, 'Magic is the only word for his rendering of space, light, and atmosphere.'

13. Raphael (1483–1520) left this work still to be completed at his death. On 7 November 1869 HJ described himself to his sister as 'staring stupidly at the *Transfiguration* and actually *surprised* at its thinness' (HJL I, 166).

14. Michelangelo Buonarotti (1475–1564) sculpted his 'Moses' as part of a commission from Pope Julius II. In a letter to WJ on 27 December 1869, HJ recorded that 'I went this morning to bid farewell to M. Angelo's *Moses* at St. Pietro in Vincoli & was so tremendously impressed with its sublimity that on the spot my intellect gushed forth a torrent of wisdom & eloquence' (CWJ I, 133).

15. Murray: 'This church, long considered as one of the most ancient and unaltered of the early Christian edifices of Rome, has lost a good deal of its interest from the recent discovery of a still more ancient one beneath.'

I'm afraid it has a more liberal vacancy than I shall avail to fill: but I shall do what I can, be sure. But at this rate you'll certainly not accuse me of lacking the power of expansion. So with Roman brevity – Goodbye.

Most faithfully your's
H. James jr.

P.S. I have been feeling since coming to Rome, in spite of inevitable fatigue, very much better than in Florence. – I address to Fenzi as I don't know your proper superscription.

15. To Charles Eliot Norton
25 March 1870

Houghton MS   Unpublished

Despite his reassurance to Grace Norton, HJ's health remained precarious, particularly his digestion, and he was regular in briefing WJ on 'what you term so happily my moving intestinal drama' (CWJ I, 138). In December he visited Naples, then on 28 December left Rome for Assisi, Perugia and Florence, where he saw the Nortons, who were remaining there for the winter. His constipation drove him from Italy: calling at Genoa, Mentone, Nice, Marseilles and Avignon, he made a ten-day stop at Paris, admiring the cookery, the Louvre and the Théâtre Français; then came to London on 4 February, and two days later completed 'the gradual fatal relentless progression from Florence to Malvern' (CWJ I, 143).

Malvern, March 25*th* 1870.

My dear Charles – I received this morning with very great satisfaction your letter of the 21*st* – & altho' I feel as if to reply properly to certain portions of it, I ought to allow myself a little longer space for reflection – yet its general effect upon my spirits is to move me to pour forth without delay, a torrent of thanks longings & regrets! I find it a great relief to get from yourself rather than – optimistically – from Jane & Grace, some report of your health, even tho' it be so poor a one. I had been cheerfully nourishing the illusion that you are really better & that your physical troubles had quite fallen into the background. But this seems a vain hope to indulge, so long as our physics haven't fallen into the background altogether. I most earnestly hope that the coming spring will do for you what you speak of as possible, whether with a view to sending you to London or elsewhere. But that you express an objection to going northward I should venture to say something about the Italian lakes – to say even that if you were to go there we possibly might meet. But I discreetly reflect that Como is a long journey from Florence – & a still longer one from London. But wherever you spend the summer it can hardly help being in Italy, & I suppose I shan't fall short of the truth in thinking of you as backed by a delicious *mise en scène*, anywhere. Not a day passes that I dont think of your well-remembered *mise en scene* at Florence. Three or four days since came to me Jane's kind letter with Grace's well-imagined enclosure – which seemed as I opened it to send forth a perfume of Tuscan spring. All that the spring must be at Florence I feel as if I might almost claim that I can vividly fancy. I had indeed, as I'm most happy to remember, a glimpse of the divine city in early October before the Summer was altogether dead. It was in those days that I saw the Certosa – of which my memory tallies most lovingly with your description. Yes, I saw it to perfection – in all its mellow mediaevalism – uplifting three mild monastic turrets out of the green into the blue.[1] It gave me a very poignant pang to read what you say of the Italy of your former visits & to reflect that I have sate *en tête à tête* with a man who has really lived in the world of the *Chartreuse de Parme*. À propos of the C. de P. I have just been reading it – with real admiration. It seems to me stronger and more truthful than the author's books of profound observation, theory &c. It is certainly a great novel – great in the facility & freedom with which it handles characters & passions.[2] On the whole I incline to agree with you that I ought to rejoice in not being haunted by these memories of old Italy. I confess that during my last month in the country I was continually struck with the enormous bulk of the still lingering ineradicable past – so that at times I could think with positive cheerfulness of that projected visit of mine, twenty years hence. Not for twenty years, at least, shall I be willing to go back to Naples, & rejoice

1. The Certosa in Val d'Ema in Florence. Norton's letter of 21 March 1870 from the Villa d'Elci described this old Carthusian monastery as 'so untouched by the 19*th* century. There was a monk there making candles for the pious, for church ceremonies, who looked as if he had never heard the word Revolution, & who certainly was ignorant of Voltaire & Franklin, & Renan & Emerson & the Atlantic Monthly.' (Unpublished Houghton MS, bMS Am 1094 (374.)) HJ described it in the 1873 'Florentine Notes'.

2. *La Chartreuse de Parme* (1839) by Stendhal (Marie Henri Beyle, 1783–1842), which follows its hero Fabrice del Dongo through intrigues at a minor Italian court. HJ wrote in 1874 of the exclusiveness of Stendhal's doctrine of self-justifying '*passion*, the power to surrender one's self sincerely and consistently to the feeling of the hour': 'In the "Chartreuse de Parme," where every one is grossly immoral, and the heroine is a kind of monster, there is so little attempt to offer any other [doctrine], that through the magnificently sustained pauses of the narrative we feel at last the influence of the writer's cynicism, regard it as amiable, and enjoy serenely his clear vision of the mechanism of character, unclouded by the mists of prejudice' (LC II, 817).

most heartily over Sara's good fortune in going to Spain.[3] I wish I were only with you to have the benefit of her letters. What a thankless grasping spirit a year of travelling begets in the unregenerate mind – what a discontentment with favors conferred – what a perpetual demand for more! I say this apropos of the fierce envy I feel of poor Sara. In reality it is only when one of your Florentine letters breaks with a momentary splash the placid surface of my – more than resignation (if the least bit less than rapture) that I cease to feel that in my own proper person I am a very fair object of envy. England is certainly not Italy – but most incontestably it *is* England. I feel this with less of excitement perhaps than when I was here before but with more of conviction. Deep aesthetic delights are constantly possible – delights to be religiously prized by one who has a fair amount of Cambridge, Mass. in prospect & retrospect. My chief amusement here is my walks which I am able to make very long & frequent, & many of them are full to overflowing with admirably picturesque incident & matter delightful to eye & fancy. Yesterday morning if I had thought of Florence it would have been almost in charity. I walked away across the country to the ancient town of Ledbury, an hour of the way over the deer-cropped slopes & thro' the dappled avenues of Eastnor Park (Earl Somers's –) a vast & glorious domain & as immensely idle & charming & uncared for as anything in Italy.[4] And at Ledbury I saw a noble old church (with detatched *campanile*) & a churchyard so full of ancient sweetness, so happy in situation & characteristic detail, that it seemed to me (for the time) – as so many things do – one of the memorable sights of my European experience. On the whole I try to make the most in the way of culture, of all my present opportunities. I think it less of a privilege to see England than to see Italy but it is a privilege nevertheless, & one which I shall not in future years forgive myself for having underestimated. It behooves me as a luckless American diabolically tempted of the shallow & the superficial, really to catch the flavor of an old civilization (it hardly matters which) & to strive to poise myself for one brief moment at least, in the attitude of observation. Think of me then as regretting Italy, but making the best of England.

While I speak of regrets let me say what I feel as to the manner in which a singularly unsympathetic fate deals between me & Grace. Jane's letter left me no doubt as to what I had so strangely suspected – Grace's non-receipt of a letter I sent her almost immediately on my arrival here – soon enough to pass

3. Sara Sedgwick (1839–1902), a friend of AJ, was the sister of Theodora Sedgwick, of Norton's wife Susan Ridley Sedgwick Norton (1838–72) and of Arthur Sedgwick (1844–1915), lawyer and editor. In 1877 Sara married William Erasmus Darwin, the eldest son of Charles Darwin.
4. Ledbury is about five miles south-west of Great Malvern, and Eastnor Park, the estate of Earl Somers, is just outside the town.

muster as an answer to one she had sent me to Paris.[5] What has become of it I know not but I *do* know (I think) that my standing in any quarter of Grace's affections nearer to her heart than her charity could ill afford to dispense with the humble testimony of that misguided missive. Pray let her know at any rate that it went: I hope soon to furnish her with any needful consolation (beyond this knowledge) for its not having arrived. You ask about my plans – concerning which I believe I recently hinted somewhat in writing to Jane.[6] I hope to be a couple of mos. longer in England – a couple of weeks longer in this place. I am less the better for my 8 weeks here than I hoped to be: still I am the better. My subsequent projects are a jumble of Switzerland – two or three German springs – Paris &c. I shall probably return home in October. I get no home news worth repeating – unless I were to enclose you bodily a very good letter from Howells.[7]

Susan you say is 'delightfully well' – delightfully for me, assure her with my love. Seriously, dear Charles, for your own continued indisposition, je n'en reviens pas. I can only hope that you overestimate the inactivity wh. results from it. At any rate I rejoice most warmly in your uninterrupted enjoyment of the good things about you. With Italy in the present & your children in the future you have *de quoi vivre*. You give no especial news of your mother, which I interpret as the best. Farewell. Love to all. Most affectionately yours –

H. James jr.

16. To Mary Walsh James (mother)
26 March [1870]

Houghton MS   Published HJL I, 218–23; SL1, 60–64

On 17 November 1869, Minny Temple in Pelham, thinking of joining her recently married sister in California, had written to HJ, 'Think of me, over the continent. "When shall we meet again, / Dearest & best, / Thou going Easterly, / I, to the West?" as the song saith.' (Unpublished Houghton MS, bMS Am 1094 (437).)
But she died on 8 March 1870, at New Rochelle, of tuberculosis.

5. Probably HJ's letter of 18 February 1870, saying how he missed Florence and had enjoyed Paris (Unpublished Houghton MS, bMS Am 1094 (879)).
6. No letters to Jane Norton are known to survive from this period.
7. A long letter of 2 January and 6 March 1870 (LFL, 69–74).

Malvern March 26*th*

Dearest mother –

I rec'd. this morning your letter with father's note, telling me of Minny's death – news more strange & painful than I can find words to express. Your last mention of her condition had been very far from preparing me for this. The event suggests such a host of thoughts that it seems vain to attempt to utter them. You can imagine all I feel. Minny seemed such a breathing immortal reality that the mere statement of her death conveys little meaning; really to comprehend it I must wait – we must all wait – till time brings with it the poignant sense of loss & irremediable absence. I have been spending the morning letting the awakened swarm of old recollections & associations flow into my mind – almost *enjoying* the exquisite pain they provoke. Wherever I turn in all the recent years of my life I find Minny somehow present, directly or indirectly – & with all that wonderful ethereal brightness of presence which was so peculiarly her own. And now to sit down to the idea of her *death*! As much as a human creature may, I fancy, she will survive in the unspeakably tender memory of her friends. No attitude of the heart seems tender & generous enough not to do her some unwilling hurt – now that she has melted away into such a dimmer image of sweetness & weakness! Oh dearest mother! oh poor struggling suffering *dying* creature! But who complains that she's gone or would have her back to die more painfully? She certainly never seemed to have come into this world for her own happiness – or that of others – or as anything but as a sort of divine reminder & quickener – a transcendent protest against our acquiescence in its grossness. To have known her is certainly an immense gain: but who would have wished her to live longer on such a footing – unless he had felt within him (what I felt little enough!) some irresistible mission to reconcile her to a world to which she was essentially hostile. There is absolute balm in the thought of poor Minnie & *rest* – rest & immortal absence! But viewed in a simple human light, by the eager spirit that insists upon its own – her death is full to overflowing of sadness. It comes home to me with irresistible power, the sense of how much I knew her & how much I loved her. As I look back upon the past, from the time I was old enough to feel & perceive, her friendship seems literally to fill it – with proportions magnified doubtless by the mist of tears. I am very glad to have seen so little of her suffering & decline – but nevertheless every word in which you allude to the pleasantness of that last visit has a kind of heart-breaking force.[1] "Dear

---

1. Minny Temple visited the Jameses in Cambridge for a week from 19 November 1869. WJ wrote to HJ on 5 December that 'She was delightful in all respects, and although very thin, very cheerful.' (CWJ I, 129.)

bright little Minny!" as you most happily say: what an impulse one feels to sum up her rich little life in some simple compound of tenderness & awe. Time for you at home, will have begun to melt away the hardness of the thought of her being in future a simple memory of the mind – a mere pulsation of the heart: to me as yet it seems perfectly inadmissible. I wish I were at home to hear & talk about her: I feel immensely curious for all the small facts & details of her last week. Write me any gossip that comes into your head. By the time it reaches me it will be very cheerful reading. Try & remember anything she may have said & done. I have been raking up all my recent memories of her & her rare personality seems to shine out with absolutely defiant reality. Immortal peace to her memory! I think of her gladly as unchained from suffering & embalmed forever in all our souls & lives. Twenty years hence what a pure eloquent vision she will be.

But I revert in spite of myself to the hard truth that she is *dead* – silent – absent forever – she the very heroine of our common scene. If you remember any talk of hers about me – any kind of reference or message pray let me know of it. I wish very much father were able to write me a little more in detail concerning the funeral & anything he heard there. I feel absolutely *vulgarly* eager for any fact whatever. Dear bright little Minny – God bless you dear mother, for the words. What a pregnant reference in future years – what a secret from those who never knew her! In her last letter to me she spoke of having had a very good photograph taken, which she would send. It has never come. Can you get one – or if you have only the house copy, can you have it repeated or copied? I should very much like to have it – for the day when to think of her will be nothing but pure blessedness. Pray, as far as possible, attend to this. Farewell. I am melted down to such an ocean of love that you may be sure you all come in for your share.

Evening. I have had a long walk this afternoon & feel already strangely familiar with the idea of Minny's death. But I can't help wishing that I had been in closer relations with her during her last hours – & find a solid comfort at all events in thinking of that long never-to-be-answered letter I wrote to her from Florence.[2] If ever my good genius prompted me, it was then. It is no surprise to me to find that I felt for her an affection as deep as the foundations of my being, for I always knew it: but I now become sensible how her image softened & sweetened by suffering & sitting patient & yet expectant, so far away from the great world with which so many of her old dreams & impulses were associated, has operated in my mind as a gentle incentive to action & enterprise. There have been so many things I have thought of telling her – so

2. HJ's letter is not known to survive.

many stories by which I had a fancy to make up her losses to her – as if she were going to linger on as a graceful invalid to listen to my stories! It was only the other day however that I dreamed of meeting her somewhere this summer with Mrs. Post.[3] Poor Minny! how much she was not to see! It's hard to believe that she is not seeing greater things now. On the dramatic fitness – as one may call it – of her early death it seems almost idle to dwell. No one who ever knew her can have failed to look at her future as a sadly insoluble problem – & we almost all had imagination enough to say, to ourselves at least, that life – poor narrow life – contained no place for her. How all her conduct & character seem to have pointed to this conclusion – how profoundly inconsequential, in her history, continued life would have been! Every happy pleasant hour in all the long course of our friendship seems to return to me, vivid & eloquent with the light of the present. I think of Newport as with its air vocal with her accents, alive with her movements. But I have written quite enough – more than I expected. I couldn't help thinking this afternoon how strange it is for me to be pondering her death in the midst of this vast indifferent England which she fancied she would have liked. Perhaps! There was no mourning in the cold bright landscape for the loss of her liking. Let me think that her eyes are resting on greener pastures than even England's. But how much – how long – we have got to live without her! It's no more than a just penalty to pay, though, for the privilege of having been young with her. It will count in old age, when we live, more than now, in reflection, to have had such a figure in our youth. But I must say farewell. Let me beg you once more to send me any possible talk or reminiscences – no matter how commonplace. I only want to make up for not having seen her.

I resent their having buried her at N. Rochelle. She ought to be among her own people.[4] Good night. My letter doesn't read over-wise; but I have written off my unreason. You promise me soon a letter from Alice: the sooner the better. Willy I trust will also be writing. Good night, dearest mother –

Your loving son
H. James.

Write me who was at the funeral &c. – I shall write next from here – then probably from London.

3. On 13 February 1870 HJ had written to WJ that Aunt Kate 'mentions that Mrs. Post has asked Minny to go abroad with her' (CWJ I, 146). Mary Minturn Post was Minny Temple's cousin.

4. Leon Edel tells us that later she was removed from New Rochelle and buried near her parents in Albany Rural Cemetery.

17. To James Thomas Fields
15 July [1870?]

Houghton TC   Unpublished

Still unwell, HJ reluctantly sailed for America on 30 April 1870 on the Scotia. *He told Grace Norton, before he left, 'It's a good deal like dying'; and, once back in the U.S., 'how characteristic every thing strikes me as being – everything from the vast white distant sky – to the stiff sparse individual blades of grass' (HJL I, 233, 240).*

Fields (1817–81) was editor of the Atlantic Monthly, *and Boston's foremost publisher, shining for the young HJ, as he remembered in 1915, 'with the reflected light of Longfellow and Lowell, of Emerson and Hawthorne and Whittier'. With his attractive young wife Annie Adams Fields (1834–1915), equally 'addicted to the cultivation of talk and wit', Fields ran a virtual* salon *on Charles Street. Fields was indulgent to HJ's early fiction even though feeling, HJ later recalled, 'that such a strain of pessimism in the would-be picture of life had an odd, had even a ridiculous, air on the part of an author with his mother's milk scarce yet dry on his lips' (LC I, 163–5, 170). If the dating of this letter is correct, HJ probably refers to the story 'Travelling Companions', published in the* Atlantic's *November and December issues, or possibly to 'A Passionate Pilgrim' (March–April 1871).*

Cambridge
July 15th.

My dear Mr. Fields –

I leave you the manuscript of a story. I have tried to keep it within the compass of a single no., but it may have exceeded it. Probably it has. If this appears, I have marked a place for division; page 85. – Let me add that I should be grateful for a more or less immediate cheque.

Yours very truly
H. James Jr.

18. To James Thomas Fields
25 July [1870]

Houghton TC   Unpublished

The summer of 1870 saw HJ visiting the fashionable resort Saratoga Springs for a month, Lake George for a week, Pomfret, Connecticut, for a fortnight en famille *and Newport for a further fortnight. He wrote travel pieces for the* Nation *based on these travels. HJ would confide to Grace Norton in September that 'I am doing no work of consequence', but also that 'I shall see all I can of America and* rub it in, *with unfaltering zeal' (HJL I, 245, 246). His 'Saratoga' (11 August) called it the place in America 'where the greatest amount of dressing may be seen by the greatest number of people' (CTW:GBA, 753).*

Saratoga Springs
July 25th.

My dear Mr. Fields.

I have just received from home your note with the enclosed cheque. I am sorry you had to puzzle out my story yourself – and feel that, under the circumstances, you have treated me very well. Many thanks!

Yours very truly
H. James Jr.

P.S. My devotions, please, to Mrs. Fields.

19. To James Thomas Fields
15 November [1870]

Houghton TC   Published HJL I, 248

Fields was not personally to publish HJ's first novel, Watch and Ward, *the story mentioned here, in the* Atlantic; *Howells took over as full editor on 1 July 1871, and it appeared in five parts from August to December 1871.*

Cambridge
Nov. 15th.

[My dear Mr. Fields.]

I told Howells this morning, on his mention of your proposal to defer for a couple of months the publication of my story, that my own preference was for immediate publication – and this he said he would communicate to you. I find, however, on reflection that if it suits you better to delay it, I shall be well pleased to have it lie over. My wish to have it appear in the January number was prompted by the desire to 'realize' upon it without delay. If, as it is, you can enable me to do so, I shall not regret your keeping back the work – to do so, of course I mean, on the three parts already in your hands. The two others then will have been joined with them before publication begins – which probably will turn out to be a relief to my own mind. There is only one drawback: if you wish to take cognition of the tale, you lose the comfort of doing so in the proof: the m.s. I can recommend to no man's tolerance. Perhaps you will content yourself with my assurance that the story is one of the greatest works of "this or any age."

Yours very truly
H. James Jr.

P.S. I should like Mrs. Fields to know that I last night heard our friend Nillson.[1] What a pity she is not the heroine of a tale, and I didn't make her!

20. To Grace Norton
27 November 187[1]

Houghton MS   Published HJL I, 263–6

Watch and Ward *was coming to the end of its run in the* Atlantic. *HJ had written about it to Charles Eliot Norton in August that 'The subject is something slight; but I have tried to make a work of art, and if you are good enough to read it I trust you will detect my intention. A certain form will be its chief merit.' (HJL I, 262.) Howells's* A Wedding-Journey *ran in the same magazine, July–December 1871. The Nortons were still in Europe, by now in Dresden, sending back to HJ photographs of Venice and works of art – staying away from their home in Shady Hill, Cambridge.*

Cambridge Nov. 27th '70.
My dear Grace.

Your excellent photograph has come – accompanied by your still more excellent note. Blessings innumerable upon your head for your ingenious kindness in sending the picture. Yes, my well-remembered Frati are all there & my little *compagnon de voyage* – & *almost* the Prior.[1] It's a leaf out of my own unwritten journal.

1. Christine Nillson, a Swedish opera singer here visiting Boston, appears in the opening chapter of Edith Wharton's novel of 1870s New York, *The Age of Innocence* (1920).
1. The reference has not been traced.

I won't interpolate here any vain apologies for my long delayed notice of your magnificent letter of August last from Innsprück – deep in the tangled web of my existence some palpable excuse might be discovered; but I thank you now as freshly and heartily as if the letter had come yesterday. I have just been reading it over. It is charmingly graphic about poor old Innsprück & charmingly amiable about poor old me, – poor Roger, Nora, the Signora *e tutti quanti*.[2] It is hardly worth while, now, attempting to enlighten you upon any point of the master-piece in which the former creations figure; by the time you get this you will have perused it to the bitter end – & you will have been confirmed or confuted as fate & occasion decree. But if it has beguiled a few of your something dolorous Germanic half-hours & given you a theme for a moment's thought or talk – "the author will not have labored in vain." Really, I'm not writing a preface; I merely wish to thank you before hand for any sort of final sentiment you may entertain on the subject. Have you or Charles or any of you, by the way, been reading in the recent *Revues des 2. M.* V. Cherbuliez's new novel?[3] If not, do it at your earliest convenience. It is tremendously fine – with all sorts of fineness & is quite the author's *magnum opus* as yet. But this en parenthèse. In looking over your letter, there is everything to re-read; but nothing definitely to answer – save indeed, those confidential remarks about Howells and his wedding-journeyers. But touching them, too, you will by this time have been confirmed or confuted. I suppose I'm not far wrong in guessing the former. Poor Howells is certainly difficult to defend, if one takes a stand-point the least bit exalted; make any serious demands & it's all up with him. He presents, I confess, to my mind, a somewhat melancholy spectacle – in that his charming style & refined intentions are so poorly & meagrely served by our American atmosphere. There is no more inspiration in an American journey than *that*! Thro' thick & thin I continue however to enjoy him – or rather thro' thin & thinner. There is a little divine spark of fancy which never quite goes out. He has passed into the stage which I suppose is the eventual fate of all secondary & tertiary talents – worked off his less slender primitive capital, found a place and a routine & an income, and now is destined to fade slowly & softly away in self-repetition and reconcilement to the Common-place. But he will always be a *writer* – small but genuine. There are not so many after all now going in English – to say nothing of American.

These are Cambridge topics – what have I to add to them? Really nothing

2. Roger, Nora and the Signora are characters in *Watch and Ward*.
3. The latest novel by Victor Cherbuliez was *La Revanche de Joseph Noirel* (1871), which originally appeared in the *Revue des Deux Mondes*, 15 July–1 October 1871. HJ's plot outline of it resembles his own later *The Princess Casamassima*.

— save that I count off the days like a good Catholic a rosary, praying for your return.

Nov. 30*th* I was interrupted the other day & now that I begin afresh, it's a terrifically cold windy dusty Thanksgiving. I'm glad I didn't finish my letter, for scribbling thus to you is a service very appropriate to the day. Alice & Sara S. have gone down to spend it at Newport & you may believe that your health will be drunk in the two places in this hemisphere which know you best.[4] I believe I was on the point, just above, of attempting a sketch of the *vie intime* of Cambridge, at the present moment; but it's well I came to a stop; it would have been a sketch without a model. Shady Hill still exists, I believe — I take it on trust — I shan't fairly know it till you are back again. There are no new social features. Mrs. Dr. Freund *née* Washburn, & husband have come to dwell here — the latter a graceful winning *distingué* German — a German Jew, yet apparently a Christian Gentleman![5] Mrs. W*m* Washburn, *née* Sedgwick-Valerio, is also expected, I believe, on a visit. This will interest Susan.[6] Also Mr. J. T. Fields lectured here on *Cheerfulness* lately (as who should say: I know I'm a humbug & a fountain of depression, but grin and bear it) & Mr. Longfellow feasted him afterwards at supper. A propos of wh: Mr. Longfellow is just issuing a new poem *The Divine Tragedy*, on the Passion & Crucifixion.[7] I don't suppose it will be quite as strong a picture as the San Cassano Tintoretto; but it will have its points.[8] Lowell seems to write nothing. I believe he is given

4. AJ's best friend of the time was Sara Sedgwick. In an 1887 letter to WJ, AJ referred to Grace Norton, whom apparently she disliked for 'her mouthing ineptitudes, her 3 century old anecdotes and her snobbish pretentiousness', as 'the ancient houri of Kirkland St' (AJB, 137).
5. In January 1872 HJ reports to Elizabeth Boott: 'We are just now witnessing the forlorn and homesick state of poor Dr. Freund — husband of Miss Washburn that was, who is striving vainly and pitifully to acclimatize and domesticate himself.' (HJL I, 269.) In 1873 WJ mentions a German doctor, Wilhelm Alexander Freund (1833–1918), returning to Breslau 'with wife & brats' (CWJ I, 192); in 1874 AJ recorded being told Freund had '*lost* three children' (LLAJ, 53).
6. Presumably William Washburn is the 'Billy Washburn' WJ describes in 1869 having a story called 'Fair Harvard' anonymously published: 'Characters & action absolutely *nil*. All his old jokes embalmed there without exception. Much coarseness of allusion &c.' (CWJ I, 131). His wife is presumably a relation of Susan Norton (née Sedgwick).
7. Henry Wadsworth Longfellow (1807–82), editor, professor, author, poet (*Hiawatha*), published *The Divine Tragedy* in 1871.
8. When HJ first saw Tintoretto's small painting of the *Crucifixion* in the little church of San Cassano in Venice in September 1869, he told WJ it was 'the greatest picture it seemed to me as I looked at it I ever saw' (CWJ I, 96). In 1872 he would write of it: 'It was the whole scene that Tintoret seemed to have beheld in a flash of inspiration intense enough to stamp it ineffaceably on his perception; and it was the whole scene, complete, peculiar, individual, unprecedented, that he committed to canvas with all the vehemence of his talent.' (CTW:C, 343.)

over to the study of Low French – I use the term in a historic & not a moral sense. I am told further more that he is going abroad in the Spring; but this of course you know.

You lead quiet lives; but you can match this base gossip, I imagine.

Your tremendous sally on the beauties of the German Tongue did me good. I have an apprehension that I shall never know it decently & I am ravished to believe it's not worth my while. But don't come & tell me now that you like it better for knowing it better; for I count upon you for backing me in my scorn.

I try & figure Dresden & your walks and haunts (if the word is not too flattering) as I have always tried to do, with your successive *emménagements*; & with tolerable success, perhaps this time, as I have my brother W*m* to prompt and suggest. But he, poor creature, speaks kindly of Dresden, knowing it only in Summer, & especially – miserable mortal! – never having been to Italy.

You allude, with a kind of mitigated enthusiasm, of the Gallery. Has Deutschland rubbed off on Titian & P. Veronese? – do they – have they learned to – speak Italian with a German accent?

I think I can say as something more than a figure of speech that I envy you your musical opportunities; for I find as I grow older that I listen a little less stupidly than of yore, & as I zealously cultivate my opportunities, I don't despair of being able someday to recognize an air at the five hundredth repetition. Tell Sally, with an embrace, that I hope in a couple of years, to be wise enough to know how well she fiddles.

I should like vastly to get a hint of Charles's impressions & opinions of Germany. I hope they are not all as unfriendly as I am sorry to hear Germany threatens to be to him. I wish he would write a couple of letters or so to the *Nation*, which doesn't seem to grow rich as it grows old. But really I am very generous, wishing him to write to the *Nation*; if he has any spare inclinations in that line, do tell him with my love, that I wish he would direct his letter to me. (I suppose, by the way – I believe I never mentioned it – that he got safely a letter of mine of some three months since.)

I must leave myself space to assure you of the interest I take in your various recent mysterious hints about the "nearness" of your return. I don't know whether I care exactly to have this "nearness" translated into literal months – whether I don't prefer to leave it vague & shadowy & shrouded in the hundred potentialities born of my mingled wish to see you & my desire that you continue to see what you may in Europe. I wish you at once to stay as long as you can & to come as soon as you can. Does that mean next autumn – & does *that* mean next summer in England? I think the ideal thing for a long stay in Europe is to spend the first & the last few months in England. But these are doubtless very premature & importunate inquiries & reflections. I have only one distinct request – do come, for heaven's sake, so that we can have a great stretch together before I realize that fantastic dream of mine of another visitation of England and Italy. I want to talk things threadbare with you before I see them. But you'll think I've made a pretty good beginning now! I begin to sniff the sacred turkey, & to hear the rattling evolutions of the parlor-maid. You have I suppose a little corner of patriotic piety in your mind – sufficient to feel the pleasant pang I would fain evoke at this image of the classic Yankee feast. Farewell. Commend me most affectionately to one & all – especially to your Mother – Yours always, dear Grace –

H. James jr

21. To Charles Eliot Norton
4 February 1872

Houghton MS   Published HJL I, 271–4; SL2, 90–93

Norton's wife Susan died in Dresden in February 1872, just after the birth of their son Richard.

Cambridge Feb. *4th* '72.

My dear Charles –

I hear of you from time to time, but I have an unsatisfied desire to hear from you – or at any rate, to talk *of* you directly, myself. Alice received a couple of days since a charming note from Susan, which was an approach to immediate news of you & has done much to put my pen into my hand. Let me use it first to thank Susan most tenderly for her altogether amiable mention of myself – both as man & author![1]

I am in constant expectation of a letter from Jane or from Grace & I come down to breakfast every morning & stride to my plate with a spiritual hunger for this possible letter hugely in excess of that which coffee & rolls can satisfy. But as yet I have to content myself grimly with the coffee & rolls. Jane & Grace may be affected by the knowledge that this state of things is not conducive

---

1. This might refer to HJ's recent appearances in the *Atlantic* (*Watch and Ward*, August–December 1871; 'A Change of Heart' (short play), January 1872); or in the *Galaxy* ('At Isella', August 1871; 'Master Eustace', November 1871).

to that breakfast-table cheerfulness & smilingness which I presume figures in their programme for a Christian life.

It is not that I have any thing very new & strange to relate. In fact, when one sits down to sum up Cambridge life *plume en main*, the strange thing seems its aridity. A big bustling drifting snow-storm is the latest episode – & we try to believe that, owing to the remarkably "open weather" that has preceded it, it has a certain charm. I have been spending a quiet stay-at-home winter, reading a good deal and writing a little. Of people or things in which, or whom, you are interested especially I have seen little. But who and what are the particular objects of your interest? You must write and tell me – for I hardly know what tastes and sympathies you may be forming in these many months of silence and absence. To the formation of what tastes does a winter in Dresden conduce? A few *dis*tastes, possibly, come into shape. Tell me of them too, for I want to be assured that in the interest of "general culture" a winter in Germany is not *de rigueur*.

I have vague impressions of your being disappointed in the gallery. But happy man, to have a gallery even to be disappointed in!

But it will be made up to you in New York, when you come back, by the rare collection of old masters who are to form the germ of what it seems so odd to have the Revue des 2. Mondes calling the *Musée* de N.Y.[2] You will of course adjourn thither from ship-board!

But I'll not talk of your coming back yet awhile, but try rather to forward you some native odds & ends.

The public mind seems to be rather vacant just now, save as to a vague contemplation of the close of the English Treaty.[3] I fancy there is something irrational and premature in the present English irritation on the subject. I doubt whether our direct demands, in so far as the country supports them, are not such as can be fairly satisfied. The English seem exasperated by the very copious setting forth of our injuries; I suppose we have stated our case strongly, to gain moderately. At all events the matter is not, thank heaven, in the hands, of the two big foolish nations, but, I trust, in that of men of the last discretion, who feel that the vexing ghost *must* be laid.

Among those who ask about you when we meet is Gurney – though we meet but rarely. I don't know whether it's fancy, but he has to me the air of a man

2. HJ wrote in the June *Atlantic*, with moderated enthusiasm, about 'The Dutch and Flemish Pictures in New York', referring to them as 'the germ of what it is so agreeable to have the *Revue des Deux Mondes* talking of currently as the *Musée de New York*' (SA, 52) – that is, the Metropolitan Museum of Art.

3. The 'English Treaty' referred to here was signed in Washington, and settled a dispute in international law between the two nations about the responsibilities of neutral powers.

almost oppressed and silenced and saddened by perfect comfort and happiness.[4]

Lowell, to my regret, I never see. With Longfellow I lately spent a pleasant evening & found him bland and mildly anecdotical. Have you seen his new book – the *Divine Tragedy*? I believe it's voted but a partial success. He is not quite a Tintoretto of verse. Howells is making a very careful and business-like editor of the *Atlantic*. As a proof of his energy – he has induced me to write a monthly report of the Fine Arts in Boston!! It's pitiful work and I shall of course soon collapse for want of material.[5]

You, like all the world here I suppose, have been reading Forster's *Dickens*. It interested, but disappointed me – through having too many opinions & "remarks" & not enough facts & documents. You have always, I think, rated Dickens higher than I; so far as the book *is* documentary, it does not, to my sense, add to his intellectual stature.[6] But of this we shall discourse in coming days over the succeeding volumes.

Have I come to the end of our common acquaintance? You know, I suppose, the Charles Perkinses – with whom I lately spent an evening. Mrs. P. is spicy & Mr. P. – sugary, shall I say? – no, full of sweetness and light – especially sweetness. He is repeating before the Lowell Inst. a course of lectures on Ancient Art, which he gave last winter to the University. Careful and sound, but without the divine afflatus.[7]

There is more or less good lecturing going on. John Fiske is giving a long course in town on Positivism – quite a large performance, in bulk & mass, at any rate; & Wendell Holmes is about to discourse out here on Jurisprudence.[8]

4. Ephraim Whitman Gurney (1829–86), Harvard Professor of History, who was dean of the faculty from 1870 to 1875, and editor of the *North American Review*. In 1868 he married Ellen Sturgis Hooper, sister of Marian ('Clover') Hooper Adams, wife of Henry Adams (1838–1918) (in 1870 he handed the review's editorship on to Adams).

5. HJ contributed art pieces in January, February, March and June.

6. John Forster (1812–76) published his life of his friend Charles Dickens in three volumes (1872–4). Norton had told HJ on 11 April 1869 of his conversation with Dickens at a banquet in Liverpool: 'It is a delightful experience to be with Dickens, – his simplicity, his sincerity, his sweetness are so great, and his large sympathy & genial acceptance of the world as it comes good & bad together are a capital corrective of one's own fastidiousness & reserve.' He had reported Dickens saying of 'the character & tone of society in London' that 'These things are the portent of a break up. Society is no longer a community. It has lost its cohesive force.' (Unpublished Houghton MS, bMS Am 1094 (369).) HJ had reviewed *Our Mutual Friend* unforgivingly for the *Nation* on 21 December 1865.

7. Charles Callahan Perkins (1823–86) was a Boston etcher and art critic who had lived in Rome and Paris and had a summer home at Newport. He was one of the founders of the Boston Museum of Fine Arts in 1870. He was also for a time the conductor of the Handel and Haydn Society.

8. The extraordinarily learned John Fiske (1842–1901), U.S. historian and philosopher of evolution, published *Outlines of Cosmic Philosophy* in 1874, expounding the evolutionary theories

The latter, some day, I think, will *percer*, as the French say, & become eminent – in a specialty, but to a high degree. He, my brother, & various other long-headed youths have combined to form a metaphysical club where they wrangle grimly & stick to the question. It gives me a headache merely to know of it.[9]

I belong to no club myself and have no great choice of company either to wrangle or to agree with. If it didn't sound weak-mindedly plaintive & fastidious, I would say I lacked society. I know no "nice men" – that is, passing few, to converse withal. The only one we often see is Arthur S. – who by the way, has gone to N.Y. to comfort & assist Godkin in his sudden illness.[10]

I suppose of course you always see the *Nation*. I don't know whether it strikes you as it does us; but I fancy its tone has been a good deal vitiated – & in a miserable, fatal sort of way. Godkin seems to me to come less rather than more into sympathy with our "institutions." Journalism has brutalized him a good deal, & he has too little tact, pliancy and "perception."

I confess that my best company now-a-days is that of various vague moonshiny dreams of getting to your side of the world with what speed I may.

I carry the desire (this confession is mainly for Jane) to a morbid pitch, & I exaggerate the merits of Europe. It's the same world there after all & Italy isn't the absolute any more than Massachusetts. It's a complex fate, being an American, & one of the responsibilities it entails is fighting against a superstitious valuation of Europe.

It will be rather a sell, getting over there and finding the problems of the universe rather multiplied than diminished. Still. I incline to risk the discomfiture!

Feb. 5th a.m. I was obliged to interrupt myself yesterday & must now bring my letter to a close – if not to a point! The 24 hours have brought forth nothing

---

of Herbert Spencer. He had a bushy beard and smoked a meerschaum. At Harvard he was considered an atheist, and never became a professor, but remained an assistant librarian.

9. The originator of philosophical 'Pragmatism', Charles Sanders Peirce (1839–1914), recalled in 1906: 'It was in the earliest seventies that a knot of us young men in Old Cambridge, calling ourselves, half-ironically, half-defiantly, "The Metaphysical Club," – for agnosticism was then riding its high horse, and was frowning superbly upon all metaphysics, – used to meet, sometimes in my study, sometimes in that of William James.' Other members included O. W. Holmes Jr, John Fiske and another advocate of Darwinism, Chauncey Wright (1830–75). Peirce also said, 'It was there that the name and doctrine of pragmatism saw the light.' (TCWJ I, 534, 535.)

10. Arthur George Sedgwick (1844–1915), brother of Theodora and Sara Sedgwick Darwin and Susan Sedgwick Norton, was a lawyer, and author, an editorial associate of Godkin's first on the *Nation* (1872–84) and then on the New York *Evening Post* (1881–5). After founding the *Nation* in 1865, the Irish-born Godkin edited it till 1881; then edited the New York *Evening Post* (1883–1900). His books include *The Danger of an Office-holding Aristocracy* (1883) and *Unforeseen Tendencies of Democracy* (1898).

momentous – save a little party last night at Mrs. Dorr's (*arida nutrix leonum!* as some one called her) where I communed with a certain Miss Bessie Minturn of N.Y., whom Mrs D. tenders you as "*probably* the most learned woman now living!" Imagine the grimace with which you accept her! But if she's blue – it's a heavenly blue. She's a lovely girl.[11]

I was going on to say above that no small part of this scandalous spiritual absenteeism of mine consists of fantastic encounters with you and yours in various choice spots of the shining Orient – so that I shall listen with infinite zeal to any hint of your future movements & tendencies.

It seems to me I have now been about as egotistical as the most friendly heart can desire. Be thus assured of the value I set on the practice! Tell me how you are & where you are, – morally & intellectually. I suppose you can bring yourself once in a while to read something not German. If so, I recommend: Taine's Notes sur l'Angleterre & Renan's Réforme Morale: the latter curiously fallacious in many ways, but a most interesting picture of a deeply conservative soul.[12] And in the way of a novel, Cherbuliez's last. I don't see how *talent* can go further. I have heard of Grace, Theodora & Eliot's journey to Berlin. If I might have the story from Grace! Your mother, I trust, continues well. Give her my filial regards – & commend me fraternally to Susan, Jane & the rest. Your children, I suppose, are turning into so many burly little heroes & heroines for Otto Pletsch.[13] Farewell, dear Charles. Respond only at your perfect convenience & believe me ever yours

H. James jr.

22. To Charles Eliot Norton
19 November [1872]

Houghton MS   Published HJL I, 309–10

On 11 May 1872, HJ embarked for Europe on the s.s. Algeria, *landing at Liverpool ten days later. This time, he was cicerone to AJ, who was recovering from a nervous*

---

11. Mrs Dorr may be the wife of Charles H. Dorr, whom HJ saw in Paris in November 1872 when he 'called on me & chirped away as usual' (HJL I, 313), and probably in Florence in 1874 (HJL I, 440). A Miss E. T. Minturn contributed to the *Nation* after 1876.

12. HJ reviewed the Taine in the *Nation* of 25 January 1872. Ernest Renan's *La Réforme intellectuelle et morale* (1871) was an attempt to come to terms with democracy, in the aftermath of defeat in the Franco-Prussian War of 1870.

13. The German Otto Pletsch was an internationally known illustrator of children's books such as *Chimes and Rhymes for Youthful Times!* (1871) and *Aunt Bessie's Picture Book* (1872).

collapse in 1868, and their Aunt Kate (Catherine Walsh). They went on to London, then to Paris, and then spent the summer in Switzerland, northern Italy and Germany. In October HJ saw AJ and Aunt Kate off at Liverpool, and returned to Paris, where he 'struck up a furious intimacy with James Lowell' (HJL I, 308). The widowed Norton was in London.

44 Rue Neuve St. Augustin
Tuesday evening. Nov. 19.

Dear Charles:

I thought your first note excellent when it came, but I think it is even better now, since it has brought your second. Of your criticism or your repentance I don't know which I prefer, & thank you heartily for the affectionate terms of both. You say the inventor of a work of art is always right. In a certain sense; but the critic is always right too: that is the impression of an intelligent observer has always an element of truth & value. I should be sorry ever to write anything which mightn't suggest a question of its being right or wrong, at points. But ah, *probability*! bugbear of the fictionist! Who will ever hit the happy medium between the too little & the too much – the prosaic matter of course?[1]

All is well with me, as you kindly hope, & I am glad to hear it is with you in spite of rain & mud & early darkness. I am fighting the same enemies, backed up by the cold, & vowing every day that the Paris climate is too detestable for another day's endurance. But I like my life here & shall probably endure it for some weeks more – unless indeed M. Thiers & the assembly between them treat us to another revolution & make an exodus prudent.[2] We are *en pleine crise* & I suppose you will have got the news of yesterday's session. Is this unhappy people booked for eternal chaos – or eternal puerility? I don't know what the day has brought forth & am curious for tomorrow's news; the republic may even now be decapitated.

I dwelt in a serener air for a couple of hours this morning, in walking thro' the Louvre with Emerson. I found him at Lowell's hotel, with his daughter

1. This discussion probably concerns 'Guest's Confession', HJ's only fiction published in 1872 (*Atlantic*, October–November).
2. Louis-Adolphe Thiers (1797–1877), suppressor of the Paris Commune, had been since the summer of 1871 president of the French Republic, a position he held till May 1873. Twelve days after this letter HJ wrote to WJ: 'There has been a prolonged battle between Thiers & the majority (monarchical) in the chamber, ending or tending to end in the discomfiture, well-deserved, of the latter. Thiers is really a sublime little creature, in his way, & . . . I can believe anything of monarchical blindness & folly.' (CWJ I, 181–2.)

when I went over there to dine on Sunday, according to my wont, & he then benevolently suggested our seeing the pictures together. Even when he says nothing especial, his presence has a sovereign amenity, & he was peculiarly himself this morning. His perception of art is not, I think, naturally keen; & Concord can't have done much to quicken it. But he seemed to appreciate freely the splendor of the Louvre, & that of Paris generally.[3] But he's not one of your golden Venetians, whose society I decidedly envy you. Golden indeed they must seem in murky London. Love to every one – *especially to Grace* for her delightful answer to my letter of ten days since. N.B. This last message to be conveyed *literatim*. I believe she hath a conscience.

Good night. Yours always, dear Charles

H. James jr

23. To Charles Eliot Norton
31 March [1873]

Houghton MS   Published HJL I, 361–3

The Nortons were in London, seeing much of Thomas Carlyle and planning to return to the U.S. on 15 May. Norton had written to HJ, who had been in Rome since before Christmas, on 13 March, and then again on 23 March reporting a talk with Ruskin: 'I read to him what you say of Tintoret, which had greatly pleased me when I first read it yesterday, in the Nation of March 6th. – It would have been pleasant to you to see the cordial admiration he felt for your work, and to hear his warm expression of the good it did him, to find such sympathies & such appreciations, and to know that you were to be added to the little list of those who really, & intelligently & earnestly care for the same things that have touched him most deeply, & influenced his life most powerfully. – You may be pleased from your heart to have given not merely pleasure, but stimulus, to a man of genius very solitary, & with very few friends who care for what he cares for.' (Unpublished Houghton MS, bMS Am 1094 (378).) Ruskin had wished that HJ instead of Sidney Colvin could have been chosen as Professor of the Fine Arts at Cambridge.

3. The sixty-nine-year-old Emerson was on his way to Egypt, recovering from the shock of a fire in his Concord house. He had seen Norton in London, and in Paris stayed in the Hôtel de Lorraine with his friend J. R. Lowell. He and his daughter left Paris on 21 November.

Roma 101 Corso *4° po.*
March 31*st*

Dear Charles –

Nothing could have given me more substantial pleasure than your note about Ruskin – the invidious comparison as to Mr. Colvin included. If there is any stimulus in the case it is certainly I who have felt it. I can well understand that it should be a gratification to Ruskin to encounter late in life a cordial assent to a cherished opinion never very popular and to which years have not, I suppose, brought many adherents. Tintoret I have never seen (save by Ruskin) spoken of with the large allowance that he demands.

Your letter has been the great news with me – I don't know that I have any other. I am growing daily fonder of Rome, & Rome at this season is growing daily more loveable. My only complaint is of the climate, which takes a good deal more strength from you than it gives. But Rome with a *Snap* in the air would not be Rome, & the languor that one continually feels has something harmonious & (intellectually) profitable in it. 'Society' continues, in spite of the departure of two or three of its ornaments. Last night at the Storys I met Matthew Arnold & had a few words with him. He is not as handsome as his photographs – or as his poetry. But no one looks handsome in Rome – beside the Romans.[1]

So you're acquainted with Story's Muse – that brazen hussy – to put it plainly. I have rarely seen such a case of *prosperous* pretension as Story. His cleverness is great, but the world's good nature to him is greater.[2]

I am very sorry your harsh weather continues, for an English spring is too good a thing to be spoiled. I wish I could take you out on my balcony & let you look at the Roman house-tops & loggias & sky & feel the mild bright air. But this is questionably kind.

1. William Wetmore Story (1819–95), expatriate American sculptor, essayist and poet, whose salon in Rome at the Palazzo Barberini included the Brownings, Hawthorne, Thackeray, Elizabeth Gaskell and Walter Savage Landor. Under pressure from the Story family, HJ half-reluctantly wrote a memoir, *William Wetmore Story and his Friends*, in 1903, in which he recalled this first meeting with Matthew Arnold (1822–88), 'in prose and verse, the idol of my previous years' (HJL II, 208), whom he had spotted in a café the day before.

2. HJ's 13 March letter to Norton had told of his being subjected to three hours of Story's reading part of his 'five-act tragedy on the history of *Nero*!', a performance HJ attributed to vanity (HJL I, 353). Norton replied (23 March): 'I have known Story – and all the potential tragedies of Nero – for years. It is a comic spectacle, not without its sadness.' HJ reviewed *Nero* anonymously in the *Nation* on 25 November 1875: 'The subject, especially as Mr. Story presents it, is too complete a monotony of horror . . . the whole work would have gained by compression and by occasional cancellings.' (LR&E, 237, 239.) Even in his memoir of Story, HJ was unrelenting towards *Nero*: 'I find its most attaching page, I confess, its dedication' (to Fanny Kemble) (HJL II, 254).

Your note of ten days since came safely & was most welcome. There were several things in it to reply to which your story of Ruskin has chased out of my head.

I *do*, for instance, believe in criticism, more than that hyperbolical speech of mine would seem to suggest.[3] What I meant to express was my sense of its being, latterly, vastly overdone. There is such a flood of precepts & so few examples – so much preaching, advising, rebuking & reviling, & so little *doing*: so many gentlemen sitting down to dispose in half an hour of what a few have spent months & years in producing. A single positive attempt, even with great faults, is worth, generally most of the comments & amendments on it. You'll agree to that.

Again, I wished to repudiate the charge of my patriotism being "serene."[4] It has come to that pass, you see, that I'm half ashamed of it. I wish it *were* serene. I don't pretend in the least to understand our national destinies – or those of any portion of the world. My philosophy is no match for them, & I regard the march of history very much as a man placed astride of a locomotive, without knowledge or help, would regard the progress of that vehicle. To stick on, somehow, & even to enjoy the scenery as we pass, is the sum of my aspirations.

As to Christianity in its old applications being exhausted, civilization, good & bad alike, seems to be certainly leaving it pretty well out of account.[5] But the religious passion has always struck me as the strongest of man's heart, & when one thinks of the scanty fare, judged by our usual standards, on which it has always fed, & of the nevertheless powerful current continually setting towards all religious hypotheses, it is hard not to believe that *some* application of the supernatural idea, should not be an essential part of our life.

I don't know how common the feeling is, but I am conscious of making a

3. Norton's letter from London on 13 March had concluded: 'And let me say as my last word that I think you perverse in your feelings in regard to Criticism. I can account for them only by the fact that you have read only the critical notices of the Atlantic Monthly of late. I quite agree with you that the world would gain if they were silenced.' (Unpublished Houghton MS, bMS Am 1094 (377).)

4. Norton (13 March): 'I look forward to life at home without any misgivings, though your serene patriotism is beyond my attainment. I do not accept even American institutions, social or political, as finalities. I believe in a distant future not in the present as I used to do, & in this faith America is as good a home as another, perhaps a better than any other in some minor respects.'

5. Norton (13 March): 'Christianity as a creed, & the ascetic morality based on the popular conception of the Christian doctrine have nearly run their course: their influence has become a thing of tradition, rather than an actual force exercising control over the conduct & character of man. And it must take a long time to establish the new morality which is to be the organizing power & animating spirit of the new society.' He mentions a striking article by Leslie Stephen in the March *Fortnightly Review*, called 'Are We Christians?'

great allowance to the questions agitated by religion in feeling that conclusions & decisions about them are tolerably idle.

But I meant to write you no letter – only to thank you: & this is more than a note & less than what it should be otherwise. Farewell dear Charles. Love to each & all – I sent you a _criticism_ of _Middlemarch_ in the _Galaxy_ lately. Did it come? – If you positively don't at all like _M_. you will probably say that such criticism as that ought to be silenced.[6] Yours always

H. James jr

24. To Henry James Senior and Mary Walsh James (parents)
14 August [1873]

Houghton MS   Unpublished

HJ left Rome in May, and spent the early summer in Switzerland before arriving in July at Homburg, where gambling had been newly abolished. 'Homburg Reformed' appeared in the Nation _of 28 August._

Homburg v. d. Hohe
Kisseleff-Strasse
Aug. 14_th_

Dearest parents.

Less than a week ago came to me your combined letter of July 20 – & 22_d_, written apparently just before your intended departure for the North.[1] It seemed to indicate a comfortable & agreeable state of things & was fondly read & re-read. The time is coming round again for me to begin to look for a letter from some point or other of your journey. I hope this has been uninterruptedly prosperous & that I shall hear of everything that befalls you. I thank you kindly for all the expressions of yearning affection in your letters & respond to them with all the enthusiasm of my nature – both in their sentimental & material aspects. I should like to sit between you on the sofa, holding a hand of you apiece – & I should like also to sit between you at dinner, putting your generosity to the test by my inroads into salmon & peas, corn & tomatoes,

6. HJ's review of _Middlemarch_ was in the _Galaxy_ of March 1873 ('"Middlemarch" is a treasure-house of details, but it is an indifferent whole' (LC I, 958)). Norton to HJ (13 March): 'I wish I could think as well of her book as you do. It is impossible.'
1. AJ and Aunt Kate went on a Canadian tour in 1873; they were met by HJ's parents at St John's, Newfoundland.

melons & ice-cream – luxuries unknown to this ponderous land of sodden veal & odorous cabbage.

I wrote to you about a week ago – something more & to W*m* a few days later, & I suppose my letters are safely arriving. Aunt Mary T. who is lodged below me here, told me yesterday that she was writing to mother.[2] I don't know what news she gave of me, but she related at any rate that I had become their fellow-lodger. I quitted my hotel yesterday (where a change in the weather – toward cold – had made my room uncomfortable) & took up my quarters in this house – where I luckily discovered a most agreeable little chamber at a most agreeable little price. I go still to the hotel for my meals, as I don't like, like the Jacksons, to eat alone & economise the society of the Tweedies for more desperate hours.[3] They are very well & happy – more so than I had yet seen them in Europe – & more and more delighted with Homburg. But A.M. will have told you everything in her letter. I too remain on excellent terms with H., which has been surpassing itself these last days in the way of delightful & salubrious air. The weather which had been intensely hot for some time lately changed to cold, with a good deal of wet; but the cold & the damp themselves are of a most delightful quality – & so free from sharpness that they cushion you about like great soft, supporting bolsters. I took a long walk through the charming spreading Hardtwald the other day with Mr. Tweedy, to the little old French village of Friederichsdorf – founded 200 years since by a colony of Huguenot refugees & French as ever to this day. The woods and the air seemed full of the breath & brilliancy of an American autumn; & I would have been homesick if I hadn't reflected that I ought to be contented with enjoying American sensations among old world privileges. The woods here are an immense blessing & stretch away and away for miles, in their green interior stillness all traversed by wandering paths and half-cleared grassy vistas. For people with whom a little of the everlasting Kursaal goes a great way, they are quite the making of Homburg.

This is all very well, but what I have chiefly at heart to descant upon is the fact that the last week has ushered in a marked improvement in my health & that I have distinct previsions of being better and better as more weeks and months and years elapse. Now at last, physically, I think I understand myself. It has taken me long to learn, blind & erring mortal that I am, but I shall

2. Uncle Edmund and Aunt Mary Temple Tweedy, well-off Newporters and intimates of the Jameses, had for years been the foster parents of HJ's Temple cousins, whose parents, Catherine James (HJ Sr's sister) and Captain Robert Temple (Mary Tweedy's brother) had died young. They were in Paris with HJ, AJ and Aunt Kate in September 1872, and HJ had also seen them in Rome at Christmas 1872.
3. The Jacksons were not identified.

preserve the knowledge in the most sacred recesses of my soul. If I were at home I would close mother round her delicate waist and lift her to ethereal heights in celebration of this latest. As it is I can only bid you be happy with me in your still parental hearts and count upon the now (I trust) less and less obstructed development of a graceful activity!

Your principal home-news was that of Wilky's intended marriage.[4] I can imagine he shouldn't enjoy waiting & yet I hope he isn't doing any thing irredeemably imprudent. As mother says, a single year's probation is less than very many couples submit to. But it is perhaps not for me, disengaged, to cast the stone.

I mentioned, I think, in my last my letter from W*m* whose enjoyment of his holiday can hardly have been greater than mine of his account of it.

Now, I suppose, you have "connected" with A.K. & Alice & are perhaps looking over the Atlantic from some breezy northern shore and exhaling soft sighs toward Homburg. Perhaps these Arctic susurrations were the cause of our late *refroidissement*. I hope you found Alice & A.K. at any rate, perfectly blowsy with health, & with appetite for whale's blubber, rein-deer steaks & all other local delicacies.

I rec.'d of the 2 Atlantics you must have sent only the one containing the Roman Holiday.[5] It's strange what becomes of them. But you needn't bother about the other, as I've sent for it to London.

With improved health, I look forward to more work. I yesterday despatched a tale in III. parts to the *Galaxy* – with regret, as it is the best written thing I've done. But it was the only thing I could do. I must approach English organs on some other basis than American subjects – unless they are very "racy" & of the Bret Harte & Joaquin Miller type.[6]

I expect to stay on here at least three weeks more, after which my plans are unformed. I did think of making straight back to Italy; but I have had unpleasant developments with my *teeth*, now unvisited for more than a year, which make the assistance of a 1*st* rate dentist urgent. I am thinking of finding it wise to go straight (*via* Cologne) to Paris & having it out with Burrage.[7] It won't hurt

4. HJ's younger brother Garth Wilkinson James (1845–83) married Caroline Eames Cary in 1873. The James family did not warm to her.
5. 'A Roman Holiday' was in the *Atlantic* of July 1873; 'Roman Rides' in that of August.
6. *Madame de Mauves* was published in two longish parts, February–March 1874, in the *Galaxy*. Bret Harte (1839–1902) (real name Francis Brett), was an immensely popular Western short-story writer and poet, author of e.g. *The Luck of Roaring Camp, and Other Sketches* (1870). Joaquin Miller (1839–1913) (real name Cincinnatus Hiner), was a successful poet and playwright of the West (in e.g. *Songs of the Sierras* (1871)).
7. Burrage is not among the names of Paris dentists listed in the 1878 Baedeker *Paris and its Environs*. HJ uses the name in *The Bostonians* (1886).

me, I suppose, to keep out of Italy till time has assured me that I'm as much better as I believe. But I give you no new address till I next write. My blessings on all yourselves, dearest parents —

H.J. jr

25. To William Dean Howells
3 May [1874]

Houghton MS   Published HJL I, 443–5; LFL, 95–6

In October 1873 HJ returned to Italy, where he was joined by WJ in November. They went together to Rome on 28 November, returning to Florence after a month. WJ left HJ in February and arrived back in the U.S. about the middle of March.

Dr Josiah Holland (1819–81), editor of Scribner's Monthly, *wrote early in 1874 to HJ's father, who was handling his literary business in the U.S., asking for a novel to be serialized in the magazine. But HJ wrote home that 'I feel myself under a tacit pledge to offer first to the* Atlantic *any serial novel I should now write – and should consider myself unfriendly to Howells if I made a bargain with* Scribner *without speaking first to him' (HJL I, 435). Howells accepted HJ's demand of $1,200, equalling the* Scribner's Monthly *offer.*

Roderick Hudson, *the first novel HJ would acknowledge, was begun in Florence in the spring of 1874, and was to run in the* Atlantic *for all twelve months of 1875. To finance the large undertaking, HJ would publish in the course of 1874 five short stories, seventeen travel pieces and eighteen assorted reviews. The Preface to* Roderick Hudson *in 1907 recalls the early composition of the novel in 'the high, charming, shabby old room which . . . looked out, through the slits of cooling shutters, at the rather dusty but ever-romantic glare of Piazza Santa Maria Novella'.*

Florence, Piazza Sta. Maria Novella
May 3*d*.

Dear Howells —

I rec'd. some days ago from my father the little note you had sent him, signifying your acceptance of my story for next year's *Atlantic*, & have had it at heart ever since to drop you a line in consequence.

I'm extremely glad that my thing is destined to see the light in the Atlantic rather than in tother place & am very well satisfied with the terms. My story is to be on a theme I have had in my head a long time & once attempted to write something about. The theme is interesting, & if I do as I intend & hope,

I think the tale must please. It shall, at any rate have all my pains. The opening chapters take place in America & the people are of our glorious race; but they are soon transplanted to Rome, where things are to go on famously. Ecco. Particulars, including name, (which however I incline to have simply that of the hero), on a future occasion. Suffice it that I promise you some tall writing. My only fear is that it may turn out taller than broad. That is, I thank you especially for the clause in the contract as to the numbers being less than twelve. As I desire above all things to write close, & avoid padding and prolixity, it may be that I shall have told my tale by the 8*th* or 9*th* number. But there is time enough to take its measure scientifically. I don't see how, in parts of the length of Aldrich's *Prudence Palfrey* (my protagonist is *not* named Publicius Parsons,) it can help stretching out a good piece.[1]

Of Aldrich's tale, I'm sorry to say I've lost the thread, through missing a number of the magazine, & shall have, like Dennett, to wait till it's finished.[2]

Why do you continue to treat me as if I didn't care to hear from you? I have a vague sense of unnumbered notes, despatched to you as an editor, but in which your human side was sufficiently recognized to have won from you some faint response. If you knew how dismally & solitudinously I sit here just now before my window, ignorant of a friendly voice, & waiting for the rain-swept piazza to look at last as if it would allow me to go forth to my lonely pranzo at a mercenary trattoria – you would repent of your coldness. I suppose I ought to write you a letter flamboyant with local color; but the local color just now, as I say, is the blackest shade of the pluvious, & my soul reflects its hue. My brother will have talked to you about Florence and about me, sufficiently too, I suppose, for the present. Florence has become by this time to me an old story – though like all real masterpieces one reads and re-reads it with pleasure. I am here now but for a few weeks longer, & then I shall leave Italy – for a many a year, I imagine. With ineffable regret for many reasons; contentedly enough for others. But we shall have a chance before long to talk of all this. I return home at the end of the summer (& hope to bring my tale with me substantially completed). To many of the things of home I shall return with pleasure – especially to the less isolated, more freely working-& talking-life.

Don't wait for this, however, to let me hear from you; but write me meanwhile, if it's only to tell me you're glad I'm coming. I have had no

1. Thomas Bailey Aldrich (1836–1907), a poet and storywriter, would succeed Howells as editor of the *Atlantic Monthly* (1881–90). His *Prudence Palfrey* appeared in the *Atlantic*, January–June 1874.
2. John R. Dennett (1837–74), the notoriously severe literary critic of the *Nation*, had recently moved to Cambridge, Massachusetts. He was a friend of T. S. Perry and Arthur Sedgwick.

personal news of you in an age, but I trust you are nestling in prosperity. It's a hundred years since I heard of your wife's health: but I trust it is good, even at the advanced age which this makes her. What are you doing, planning, hoping? I suppose your Venetian tale is almost off your hands – I long to have it on mine.[3] (I'm delighted by the way to hear you like "Eugene Pickering:" *do*, oh do, if possible put him through in a single number.)[4] Lowell has just passed through on his way to Paris. I got great pleasure from his poem, which he read me in bits. I'm impatient to see it all together.[5] Farewell, dear Howells; the rivulets on the piazza run thin, and I must trudge across & quaff the straw-covered fiaschetto: I shall do it, be sure, to your health, your gentilissima sposa's & your children's. Yours always

H.J. jr

26. To William Dean Howells
[19 or 26 March 1875]

Hayes MS   Published HJL I, 475; LFL, 114

As HJ's 1907 Preface recalled, '"Roderick Hudson" was further, was earnestly pursued during a summer partly spent in the Black Forest and (as I had returned to America early in September) during three months passed near Boston.' Indeed, 'the book was not finished when it had to begin appearing in monthly fragments' (in January 1875), and HJ completed it in New York, where he spent the winter.

His first book, A Passionate Pilgrim, and Other Tales, *was published by James R. Osgood & Company on 31 January 1875 – followed on 29 April by a collection of his travel writings,* Transatlantic Sketches, *from the same publisher. Howells, whose* A Foregone Conclusion *HJ had just praised anonymously both in the* Nation *and the* North American Review, *reviewed the storybook, glowingly and anonymously, in April's* Atlantic: *'Like it or not, you must own that here is something positive, original, individual, the result of long and studious effort in a well-considered line, and mounting in its own way to great achievement.'*

3. Howells finished his first full novel, *A Foregone Conclusion*, in July, the month in which its first instalment appeared in the *Atlantic*. HJ would write two unsigned reviews of Howells's book, one in the *North American Review* (January 1875), the other in the *Nation* (7 January 1875).
4. HJ's story was published in the *Atlantic* in two numbers, October–November 1874.
5. J. R. Lowell's 'Agassiz' was printed in the *Atlantic* of May 1874. The zoologist Louis Agassiz, whom WJ had accompanied on his 1865 expedition to Brazil, had died in December 1873.

111 east 25*th* st.
Friday evening.

Dear Howells —

I read this morning your notice of A P.P. & — well, I survive to tell the tale! If kindness could kill I should be safely out of the way of ever challenging your ingenuity again. Never was friendship so ingenious — never was ingenuity of so ample a flow! I am so new to criticism (as a subject,) that this rare sensation has suggested many thoughts, & I discern a virtue even in being overpraised. I lift up my hanging head little by little & try to earn the laurel for the future, even if it be so much too umbrageous now. Meanwhile I thank you most heartily. May your fancy never slumber when you again read anything of mine!

I hope to be in Cambridge for two or three days about April 10*th*, if by that time there is any symptom whatever of sprouting grass or swelling buds. We will take a walk together & you will help my town-wearied eyes to discover them. I will bring with me the "balance" as they say here, of my novel or at least the greater part of it. I hear rumors that you are coming this way (i.e. to New Jersey:) I hope it won't be at just that time.[1] Of course you won't be here, with whatever brevity, without looking me up. The wheel of life revolves, here, but it doesn't turn up any great prizes. I lead a very quiet life & dwell rather in memories & hopes than in present emotions. With love to your house,

Yours ever — more than ever —
H. James jr.

27. *To Francis Pharcellus Church*
1 December [1875]

NYPL MS   Published HJL II, 8–9

Roderick Hudson *appeared (slightly revised) in book form in November 1875, HJ's third book of a momentous year. He stayed at 111 East 25th Street from January to July 1875, writing copiously for the New York* Nation, *to which that year he contributed fifty-eight pieces; after which he went back to the parental home for three months. Then he returned to Europe, this time quasi-permanently — financed by an arrangement made through his friend the poet, journalist, novelist and*

---

1. The Howellses did in fact visit the Pennsylvania Moravian settlement late in March, returning to Cambridge only on 13 April. It is not clear when or if HJ paid his Cambridge visit.

statesman John Hay (1838–1905), as Paris correspondent for the New York Tribune *– arriving in the French capital on 11 November.*

HJ's lodgings in the heart of Paris, which he kept till mid November 1876, were, as he told his father, 'a snug little troisième *with the eastern sun, two bedrooms, a parlor, an antechamber and a kitchen. Furniture clean and pretty, house irreproachable, and a gem of a* portier, *who waits upon me.' (HJL II, 6.) HJ was quick off the mark: his first* Tribune *letter was dated 22 November. F.P. Church (1839–1906) was one of the proprietors of the New York* Galaxy, *where a number of HJ's short stories had been published.*

Paris.
Rue de Luxembourg 29.
Dec 1st

My dear Mr. Church –
[Text of first page missing in manuscript.]
[. . .] this before I left N.Y.

I propose to take for granted, as soon as I can, that you will be ready to publish, on receipt of them, the opening chapters of a novel. I have got at work upon one sooner than I expected, & particularly desire it to come out without delay. The title of the thing is the "The American." I hope you will not consider that it will interfere with such other serials as you may have under way, nor deem it a drawback if it runs over into next year. I will send you as promptly as possible the first of the *MS*.. Yours very truly –

H. James jr[1]

28. To Mary Walsh James (mother)
11 January [1876]

Houghton MS   Unpublished

HJ was writing The American, *but also his letters to the daily* New York Tribune, *appearing between 11 December 1875 and 26 August 1876. In addition, he wrote a good deal for the* Nation, *of which Auguste Laugel (1830–1914) was Paris correspondent.*

HJ was starting to make the acquaintance of the circle of French writers grouped

1. On 3 December HJ told WJ, 'I shall speedily begin, in the *Galaxy*, another novel: it is the best I can do' (CWJ I, 245).

around Flaubert and Turgenev – notably Edmond de Goncourt, Alphonse Daudet and Émile Zola.

Rue de Luxembourg 29.
Jan 11<u>th</u>.

Dearest mother –

I have been waiting to write again, until I rec.'d something from home. This morning arrived your letter of Xmas. day, & I immediately seized the pen. I had received about two weeks before a letter from W*m.* of *Dec. 11th* which I do not think I had acknowledged. Write as often as you can, but don't wonder if I don't write oftener. I have so much & such constant writing to do that it is about all I am up to. Besides I have had, these two months, a great many letters to write.

Your letter, dearest mammy, was of course most welcome; I had only heard from you once since I had been away! – the letter you wrote after your return from Milwaukee. So Wilky has a daughter – strange as it may seem.[1] I wish him joy. I'm glad for variety's sake it is a girl. I am sorry to hear of his rheumatism, & hope he will get off easily. The next points were your projected *salon* (which I cannot too warmly applaud, & in which, in my mind's eye, I behold you & Alice, ravishingly attired: *i.e.* you in your old black, & she in her old (or new) brown, officiating with triumphant grace.)[2] It is too terrible to think of Dido's exile, & sent to Bob, as you said.[3] She occupies the tenderest corner of my heart, & remains enshrined in my imagination as the ideal of female loveliness. I am glad to hear such good things of her successor, & I hope he will keep all his promises. I am pining for a dog, but – even if as I am living now it were convenient to keep it – I can't afford to buy a nice one.

I have very little news. Xmas & New Year have come & gone, but I had – alas! – no Xmas & no New Year. I passed the festive season in solitary *recueillement*. Nothing happens to me worth relating; & I see no one of consequence. I do a good deal of work, which is the principal thing; but outside of this my days are a blank. I am not engulfed in society, & tho' I have done my best to become so, the result does not seem to impend. The half dozen charming houses to which it would be pleasant to go of an evening do not

1. HJ's brother Wilky and his wife Carrie had a daughter, Alice, on 24 December 1875, after a son, Joseph, in 1874. Wilky was working in Milwaukee. His Civil War wounds were troubling him, and he was starting to suffer from a 'rheumatic heart' (*Jameses*, 313).
2. Mrs James had been inspired by the example of an acquaintance to hold some 'receptions', and was 'to be at home on Thursday evenings in January' (DLAJ, 71).
3. Dido was a family dog. She was replaced by a Scotch terrier pup called Bunch.

open their doors to me. No one in fact, appears to receive of an evening; the only time people are visible is in the afternoon. I have seen nothing more of Turgeneff since I last mentioned him, though I have called upon him, & mean to return to the charge shortly.[4] He doesn't appear (nor do any of the literary class) to practise the sacred rites of hospitality – at least as we understand them. I think I mentioned in my last my acquaintance with Gustave Flaubert.[5] I called upon him again a while since, one afternoon, & sat with him a couple of hours, chattering famously, & greatly liking him. He is an excellent old fellow, simple, naïf, & *convaincu*, in his own line, & extremely kind & friendly, not to say affectionate. He has almost eclipsed Turgeneff in my affections. I am going again, next Sunday, to see him, & shall find him surrounded by his disciples. I see little of the Laugels. I have called, devotedly, several times, on the ladies, who are slow, but L. is never visible. They apparently don't entertain, & to know them leads to nothing very interesting. Mrs. Kemble gave me a letter to M*me* Mohl, a famous saloon-keeper; but her husband has lately died, her saloon is extinct, & she is inconsolable & invisible.[6] Was Mrs. Perkins's offer of letters a joke?[7] If not, pray make her do what she can, & before this winter is over.

The only man I see here familiarly is C. Peirce with whom I generally dine a couple of times a week.[8] He is a very good fellow – when he is not in

4. Ivan Sergeevich Turgenev (1818–83), the Russian novelist and playwright, was one of HJ's major contemporary influences. In a letter the previous day, HJ had told Lizzie Boott that, 'He is extremely simple, candid – almost infantine – *in somma* he is a true, ideal genius.' (Unpublished Houghton MS bMS Am 1094 (516).) HJ had published a long essay on him in April 1874.
5. HJ was ambivalent about most of the works of Gustave Flaubert (1821–80), but liked the man and greatly admired *Madame Bovary* (1857). Flaubert's *cénacle* or literary coterie included such writers as Émile Zola, Alphonse Daudet, the brothers Goncourt and Guy de Maupassant.
6. Fanny Kemble (1809–93) was the mother of HJ's friend from his days in Rome, Sarah Butler Wister, and thus grandmother of Owen Wister (1860–1938), author of *The Virginian*. Mme Mohl (1790–1883) was the former Mary Clarke, daughter of an expatriate Scottish naval widow, who in her youth had charmed Chateaubriand and thus Mme Récamier, and later had her own Paris *salon*. Her husband died on 3 January 1876, and 'Her one interest in life henceforth was her husband's memory and work' (Kathleen O'Meara, *Mme Mohl, Her Salon & Her Friends* (1885)). HJ described her to WJ as 'a little old woman of ninety with her grey hair in her eyes, precisely like a Skye terrier, a grotesque cap & a shabby black dress' (CWJ I, 256–7).
7. This is probably the 'spicy' wife of the Charles Perkins, cosmopolitan Boston etcher and art critic, whose lectures HJ had attended in 1872. It might be the former Jane Sedgwick Watson, who had married the Boston lawyer Edward Perkins, five years her junior, a decade before (DLAJ, 74).
8. Charles Sanders Peirce, whom WJ recommended HJ in December 1875 to treat 'more or less chaffingly' to get through his prickly exterior: 'the way to treat him is after the fabled "nettle" receipt: grasp firmly, contradict, push hard, make fun of him, and he is as pleasant as any one'. Moreover, 'he is a man of genius and there's always something in that to compel

ill-humour; then he is intolerable. But, as W*m* says, he is a man of genius, &
in such, in the long run, one always finds one's account. He is leading here a
life of insupportable loneliness & sterility – but of much material luxury, as
he seems to have plenty of money. He sees, literally, not a soul but myself &
his secretary. I suppose you have seen me again (mutilated & spoiled) in the
Revue.[9] My translator (with whom I have had some correspondence) is a M.
Lucien Biart, the author of weak novels published by Hetzel, & rather a
second-rate individual, I fear.[10] But I have sent him *R.H.*, as he intimates that
he has not yet done with me. I have written ½ a doz. letters to the Tribune –
where those that have been published sicken me with their flaunting headings.
Subjects are woefully scarce; nevertheless I shall stomach it out for this winter.
When they are slow to appear you may know it is the Tribune's fault – not
mine. I have sent a lot of things to the *Nation*, since my arrival, which I suppose
you recognise.[11] The slip from Appleton's journal was very good criticism.[12]
Tell me if you hear any thing about the *sale* of R.H. I think of sending it to
an English publisher (Chatto & Windus or Sampson & Low,) to propose

one's sympathy' (CWJ I, 246). Peirce never found an academic position in the U.S. and spent
his last years in poverty.

9. A translation of HJ's story 'Eugene Pickering' – as 'Le Premier Amour d'Eugène Pickering
– Une Femme Philosophe' – appeared in the *Revue des Deux Mondes* on 1 January 1876; 'The
Last of the Valerii' had appeared in the same journal on 15 November 1875 as 'Le Dernier des
Valerius'.

10. Some of the works of Lucien Biart, which often dealt with Mexico and the U.S. (such as
Aventures d'un jeune naturaliste (1869) and *À travers l'Amérique* (1876)), were translated into
English. He would also translate 'The Madonna of the Future' and 'A Passionate Pilgrim'. He
never did translate *Roderick Hudson*.

11. Since the start of November 1875, HJ had published in the *Nation* notices of Andrew
Wilson's Eastern travels, Henry Irving's *Macbeth*, W.W. Story's *Nero*, Alvan S. Southworth's
African travels, a collection of Thackerayana, London sights, Charles de Mazade on French
literature, Ernest Renan at Ischia, George Barnett Smith's literary studies, the Misses Hill and
their Australian travels, and A. P. Russell's miscellaneous extracts.

12. The short notice of *Roderick Hudson* in the New York *Appleton's Journal of Literature, Science
and Art* judges that the book might be accepted as 'the long-expected "great American novel" '
but for HJ's 'deficiency of dramatic faculty'. It begins: 'As a specimen of ingenious and
sustained psychological analysis, Mr. Henry James, Jr.'s, "Roderick Hudson" . . . is a wonderful
production; but as a novel it fails to stand the crucial test. It is surprising, indeed, that a book
which is so good in many ways – so subtle in its insight, so full of the finest fruits of culture,
and so eloquent withal – should fail so utterly in the essential point of impressing us with the
objective reality of the people to whom it introduces us . . . The motives of any given course
of action, the influence of antecedents and circumstances upon character, and the complex effects
which in human life flow from an apparently simple cause, he can trace with marvellous skill;
but he does not seem able to construct in thought the process by which a person reveals his
personality, and becomes human in the apprehension of others.' (18 December 1875, 793.)

republication.[13] I expect to begin a novel in the April *Galaxy*; to run thro' nine numbers – to December. *Say nothing whatever of this*: especially to Howells, to whom I had offered it, to appear later, & to whom I must write & explain that I can't afford to wait. But I must close my letter: wh. I am afraid has a lugubrious sound. But this is nonsense. I am very happy & very well, &, for the present, very well content with Paris. My health has been steadily better & better ever since my arrival in Paris, & suffices to all my needs. For a week now we have had *real* winter – detestable. Before it was only play. But it will be short-lived. Love to all – & to Wilk & Bob. Success to your parties. Je t'embrasse, beloved mammy, à la folie.

Your
H.J. jr.

29. *To William Dean Howells*
3 February [1876]

Houghton MS   Published HJL II, 22–3; SL2, 122–4; LFL, 115–16

Paris, Rue de Luxembourg, 29.
Feb. 3*d*

Dear Howells –

Ambiguous tho' it sounds, I was sorry to get your letter of the 16*th* ult. Shortly after coming to Paris, finding it a matter of prime necessity to get a novel on the stocks immediately, I wrote to F. P. Church, offering him one for the *Galaxy*, to begin in March, & I was just sending off my first instalment of MS. when your letter arrived. (The thing has been delayed to April.) It did not even occur to me to write to you about it, as I took for granted that the Atlantic could begin nothing till June or *July*, & it was the money question solely that had to determine me. If I had received your letter some weeks before I think my extreme preference to have the thing appear in the Atlantic might have induced me to wait till the time you mention. But even of this I am not sure, as by beginning in April my story, making nine long numbers, may terminate & appear in a volume by next Xmas. This, with the prompter

13. *Roderick Hudson*, first published in November 1875 in the U.S. by Osgood, was not published in England till June 1879, when it came out in what a note calls 'minutely revised' form from Macmillan in three volumes.

monthly income (I have demanded $150 a number,) is a momentous consideration. The story is "The American" – the one I spoke to you about (but which, by the way, runs a little differently from your memory of it.) It was the only subject mature enough in my mind to use immediately. It has in fact perhaps been used somewhat prematurely; & I hope you find enough faults in it to console you for not having it in the *Atlantic*. There are two things to add. One is that the insufferable *nonchalance*, neglect & ill-manners of the Churches have left me very much in the dark as to whether my conditions are acceptable to them: & I have written to them that if they are not satisfied they are immediately to forward my parcel to you. The other is that I would, at any rate, rather give a novel to the Atlantic next year, (beginning, that is, in January) than this. So far as one party can make a bargain, I hereby covenant to do so. I expect to have the last half of the summer & the autumn to work on such a tale; for I shall have obviously to settle down and produce my yearly romance. I am sorry, on many accounts that the thing for the present stands as it does, but I couldn't wait. I hope you will find something that will serve your turn.[1]

Why didn't you tell me the name of the author of the very charming notice of *R.H.* in the last *Atlantic*, which I saw today at Galignani's? I don't recognize you, & I don't suspect Mrs. Wister. Was it Lathrop?[2] If so please assure him of my gratitude. I am doing as I would be done by & not reading your story in pieces. Will you mail me the volume when it appears? I should like to notice it.[3]

Yes, I see a good deal of Tourguéneff & am excellent friends with him. He has been very kind to me & has inspired me with an extreme regard. He is everything that one could desire – robust, sympathetic, modest, simple, profound, intelligent, naïf – in fine angelic. He has also made me acquainted with G. Flaubert, to whom I have likewise taken a great fancy, & at whose house I have seen the little *coterie* of the young realists in fiction. They are all charming

---

1. In the event HJ switched magazines: *The American* began in the *Atlantic Monthly* in June 1876 and ran till May 1877.
2. Galignani's, No. 224 rue de Rivoli, was a well-stocked English-language reading-room. HJ's friend Sarah Butler Wister did review *Roderick Hudson*, but in the April 1876 *North American Review*. It was George Parsons Lathrop (1851–98), assistant editor of the *Atlantic* 1875–7, Hawthorne's son-in-law and author of *A Study of Hawthorne* (1876), who reviewed *Roderick Hudson* in the February 1876 issue. Though deploring 'its manifest and at times even offensive want of compression', he gave 'unqualified praise to the boldly broken ending of the story, which so completely lends it the air of a detached piece of life, without injuring its individual completeness'.
3. Howells's serial *Private Theatricals* appeared in the *Atlantic* from November 1875 to May 1876. Perhaps because of threatened legal action from satirized New England hoteliers, there was no book publication till 1921, when it came out as *Mrs Farrell*.

talkers – though as editor of the austere *Atlantic* it would startle you to hear some of their projected subjects. The other day Edmond de Goncourt (the best of them) said he had been lately working very well – on his novel – he had got upon an episode that greatly interested him, and into which he was going very far. *Flaubert*: "What is it?" *E. de G.* "A whore-house *de province*."[4]

I oughtn't to give you any news – you yourself were so brief. Indeed I have no news to give: I lead a quiet life, & find Paris more like Cambridge than you probably enviously suppose. I like it – (Paris) – much, & find it an excellent place to work.

I am glad my *Tribune* letters amuse you. – They are most impudently light-weighted, but that was part of the bargain. I find as I grow older, that the only serious work I can do is in story-spinning.

Farewell. With a friendly memory of your wife & children

Yours very truly
H. James jr

30. To Grace Norton
31 March [1876]

Houghton MS   Unpublished

Grace Norton was in the Norton family home at Shady Hill in Cambridge, Massachusetts. This letter identifies her as the author of the review of Roderick Hudson *in the* Nation, *9 March 1876, which was evidently shortened by the magazine. The review contrasts* Roderick Hudson's *'thoughtful and elaborate observation' with 'the greater simplicity of his earlier work'. It also touches on the expatriation of the characters: 'each one – it would almost appear, as if unconsciously to the author – is in his or her individual way a constant reminder that Americans lose much of their rightful charm and interest when transplanted from their own habitat and exhibited among the more cultivated growths of foreign life'. She sees in the fluctuations of the relation between Rowland Mallet and Roderick Hudson 'so strange a flaw in the story as to damage it throughout'; the character of Rowland is 'over-elaborated'. But the review contains some praise, as where 'The simplicity*

4. Goncourt's heroine in his grim *La Fille Élisa* (1877: 'Elisa the Prostitute') is the daughter of a Paris midwife sometimes reduced by penury to carrying out abortions. After a childhood full of 'érotiques détails, des matérialités de la procréation' ('erotic details, the physical realities of procreation'), she runs away at sixteen to the miserable provincial whorehouse HJ mentions, where she becomes a prostitute. She ends up in prison, where she eventually dies. Reviewing the novel in the *Nation*, HJ called Goncourt 'intolerably unclean' (LC II, 404).

and directness and quietness of the plot make the interest of its gradual development a matter of very considerable artistic skill, since it relies wholly on the phases and transformations of the characters involved.'

Paris Rue de Luxembourg 29.
March 31st

My dear Grace –

Any thing which is the cause of my getting a letter from you is a very good thing – but your lively emotion on the subject of the article on *R.H.* in the *Nation* has only that justification. I have just got your letter & have been sitting wreathed in the broadest smiles while I read it.[1] My dear Grace, there is something exquisitely superfluous in your agitation – something indeed worse than superfluous – pernicious & fatal. I had read the review in question, & had thought the article was extremely kindly, graceful, neatly turned, felicitous – everything that a review should be. Your letter is not a reassurance, but almost a discomfiture, & it has set me puzzling my head over the article most unmercifully to try and find something displeasing in it. With the best will in the world, I haven't succeeded. But I am willing, like the "Marchioness" in the "Curiosity Shop" (with her orange peel & water) to 'make believe a good deal' and pretend that there is, so that I may seem to have a right to all the kindly, friendly, affectionate & lovely things that you say to me in your letter.[2] It would be worth while to be damaged a little, once a year or so, to have one's wounds bound up with such magical fingers. Your article was charming, your letter was charminger still, and you, dear Grace, are the best of women & the cleverest of scribes. I am extremely sorry you had so much bother & ennui with your composition; it was very generous of you to undertake to notice the book at all. Behold me then healed of wounds I have never felt, wiping away tears I have never shed, all because in this world it is well to take all one can get & if reparation isn't à propos now it is very well to lay in a stock of it in view of future contingencies. Some of these days I shall feel some wrong less because of the balm you have poured on my tender places.

1. In Milton's *L'Allegro*, the poet calls on the goddess Euphrosyne to bring 'Nods and Becks, and Wreathed Smiles / Such as hang on *Hebe*'s cheek' (ll. 26–9).
2. In ch. LXIV of Dickens's *The Old Curiosity Shop* (1841), 'the Marchioness' (in fact a 'small servant') is kept 'very short' by her employers. After they go to bed, she comes out 'for bits of biscuit, or sangwitches that you'd left in the office, or even pieces of orange peel to put into cold water and make believe it was wine'. She tells Dick Swiveller about this drink that 'If you make believe very much, it's quite nice, . . . but if you don't, you know, it seems as if it would bear a little more seasoning, certainly.'

You are quite right about my *woulds*: several of them are erroneous. But this, I think is not a defective sense, but mere carelessness & culpably hasty reading of proof. (Here, indeed, I am very glad the *Nation* witheld your animadversions upon my folly from the publicity & eternity of print.) I think my *shoulds* are right: i.e. wherever they occur. There is only not enough of them.[3] The "ought to" I used as a colloquialism (some people are talking,) because of the (, as I am conscious, deserved) reproach often cast upon me of making my characters express themselves too neatly & bookishly. But it is certainly ugly, & I will in future compass realism by some other device. Many thanks for your allusion to this. As to the "suppositions which have taken shape & serve as a solvent," I don't think they are quite unpardonable.[4] It is the suppositions, & not the shape, which are the solvent – though I confess they would have had more of that fluidity which is becoming in a solvent if they had not taken shape. I should say by analogy, a solvent *did* solve. The adjective is neuter but the noun is active. (I suppose that what you contest, however, is the meaning of the word. I really think that – tho' of course I don't remember – I chose it precisely for the idea of *melting down*, in the more literal sense, & not of offering a solution in the borrowed one.) Lastly, the metaphor about muffling shame in a splendor that asks no questions is indeed a trifle mixed; but it is essentially a loose metaphor – it isn't a simile – it doesn't pretend to sail close to the wind.[5] Still, it is certainly very happy that that splendor *does* ask no questions: the fewer the better.

I thank you most sincerely for noting those weak spots: it is invaluable, indispensable, to a style to feel itself watched, vigilantly. I wish I had more of it than the public of the American magazines furnishes.

I say nothing about other matters, because it is 1½ o'clock *a.m.* Paris is always Paris & I am always I, and your very faithful friend. I am busy, contented, with plenty to observe, think about & enjoy. Paris has great qualities

3. Cambridge Mass. was watching HJ's p's and q's. WJ wrote to him on 1 January 1876 to report that Professor F. J. Child liked *Roderick Hudson* but felt that 'you misuse your shalls & wills &c, and use the word sympathetic too often' (CWJ I, 250).
4. In the first American edition of *Roderick Hudson*, Rowland Mallet says: 'I desire to harm no one; but certain suppositions have taken place in my mind which serve as a solvent to several ambiguities' (ch. XI). In the revised 1879 three-volume Macmillan British edition, 'certain suppositions have taken shape in my mind which serve as the answers to two or three riddles'.
5. On the next page, Rowland comments on Christina Light's motive – her humiliation by the revelation of her illegitimacy – for her grand marriage to Prince Casamassima. She is 'the proudest girl in the world, deeply wounded in her pride, and not stopping to calculate probabilities, but muffling her shame, with an almost sensuous relief, in a splendor that stood within her grasp and asked no questions'. In 1879 it is 'a splendour that stood within her grasp and would cover everything'.

as a residence, & I shouldn't wonder if I were to live here forever. But I shall make visits to Shady Hill. Mrs. Childe is a charming woman – an exact fit to the term.[6] Farewell, dear Grace; injure me, indemnify me, but continue to love me & do everything but forget me. Yours, more than ever,

H. James jr.

31. To Thomas Sergeant Perry
[2 May 1876]

Colby MS   Published HJL II, 44

Dear Thomas –

I have just recd. your postal card, & will with pleasure look up the photos. I have little doubt I can find them. I got from you a note some fortnight since which I have had at heart to answer, but a glut of writing – especially a terrible *encombrement* of letters – must be my excuse for delay.

So Miss Bessie Lee marries? What a lovely thought for F. Shattuck![1] I remember her with a quite intense & peculiar admiration & should like to make bold to tell her so. (Excuse me: I have just discovered that the rear of my sheet is bescribbled.) –

Yes, I have seen Daudet several times. He is a little fellow (very little) with a refined & picturesque head, of a Jewish type. Former private secretary of the Duc de Morny.[2] A brilliant talker & *raconteur*. A Bohemian. An extreme imitator of Dickens – but *à froid*, without D.'s real exuberance. *Jack* has had immense success here – ça se vend comme du pain. M*me* Sand en raffole. The stepfather is a portrait – Pierre Véron, editor of the

6. The wife of General Robert E. Lee's nephew Edward Lee Childe (1836–1911), a friend of the Nortons, this 'very graceful, elegant and clever Frenchwoman', as HJ called her on 8 February 1876, was the former Blanche de Triqueti (HJL II, 27).

1. Elizabeth Perkins Lee, a cousin of the Jameses' friend Fanny Morse, married in June 1877 Dr Frederick Cheever Shattuck (1847–1929), who was later to become a professor of clinical medicine at Harvard. In April 1873 WJ had found her 'very "nice"' (CWJ I, 230).

2. The Duc de Morny (1810–65) was President of the Legislative Body, an elegant, urbane, man of the world, and himself a writer. In 1860, he took on the young Daudet as an *attaché du cabinet* but died unexpectedly in 1865, due, said some, to the attentions of the dubious Dr Olliffe, a fashionable Irish physician whose daughter Florence, as Mrs Hugh Bell, would be a good friend of HJ. Daudet caricatured Olliffe in *Le Nabab* (1877).

Charivari.[3] The book to me was dreary & disagreeable, & in spite of cleverness intrinsically weak. I prefer an inch of Gustave Droz to a mile of Daudet.[4] Why the Flaubert circle don't like him is their own affair – I don't care. I heard M. Zola characterize his manner sometime since as *merde à la vanille*. I send you by post Zola's own last. – *merde au naturel*. Simply hideous.[5] Yours ever in extreme haste

H. James jr

32. To Mrs Ellen Louise Chandler Moulton
20 October [1876]

Congress MS   Published HJL II, 69

HJ remained in Paris till July 1876, 'turning into an old, and very contented, Parisian' (HJL II, 51), writing The American, *his* Tribune *letters back to New York, and other criticism. The* American *began in the June* Atlantic, *and his late Preface recalls how 'much was still unwritten' and the great 'variety of scenes of labour' in which he struggled to complete it. He went till September into the French provinces – Étretat in Normandy, the Childes' Chateau de Varennes, and Biarritz. By late July he was writing to WJ that 'my last layer of resistance to a long-encroaching weariness and satiety with the French mind & its utterance has fallen from me like a garment. I have done with 'em, forever, & am turning English all over' (CWJ I, 271).*

At the end of August HJ also broke off his journalistic arrangement with Whitelaw Reid and the Tribune: *'If my letters have been "too good" I am honestly afraid that they are the poorest I can do, especially for the money! I had better, therefore, suspend them altogether' (HJL II, 64). When he returned to Paris, he could not get back into his apartment, which he had given up for the summer; and he had to wait to get into a new apartment at the same address.*

Ellen Louise Chandler Moulton (1835–1908), a cousin of the poet E. C. Stedman

3. HJ's appreciative 1890 essay on Daudet calls the character of the hero's stepfather the 'success of the book' – the 'author of *Le Fils de Faust*, an uncirculated dramatic poem in the manner of Goethe, and centre of a little group of *ratés* – a collection of dead-beats, as we say to-day, as pretentious, as impotent, as envious and as bilious as himself'. 'The subject of *Jack* is the persecution of the boy by this monstrous charlatan' (LC II, 241). Pierre Véron was a friend of Daudet's in his early period in literary Paris. *Le Charivari*, founded in 1832, was a satirical illustrated magazine, the prototype of *Punch*.

4. In 1871 HJ had praised the talents of Gustave Droz (1832–95) as an *amuseur* and social commentator in novels like *Le Cahier bleu de Mlle Cibot* (1868) and *Autour d'une source* (1869), predicting his career 'cannot fail to be brilliant' (LC II, 274).

5. The latest novel by Zola was *Son Excellence Eugène Rougon* (1876).

and herself an author, collected poets and had a Friday salon in Boston attended by Longfellow, Holmes, Whittier and Lowell, among others. From 1870 she was the Boston literary correspondent of the New York Tribune, *and spent her summers in Europe.*

29 Rue du Luxembourg.
Oct 20*th*

My dear Mrs. Moulton —

I am glad you have found a dwelling that suits you & hope it will prove agreeable & comfortable. I will soon give myself the pleasure of calling upon you. The names of the two best volumes of tales by Mérimée are *Colomba*, & *Carmen*.[1] The former is the best, but both are good; though they may not please you especially. They are not in the least sentimental. There are a great many good short stories, or *nouvelles*, in French, though not so many I think, as is supposed. Those of Alfred de Musset are very charming, & consist of 2 volumes entitled respectively simply *Contes* & *Nouvelles*.[2] The latter are the best, & are admirable. They, on the contrary, are very sentimental. Extremely good also are the tales of Henry Mürger — tales & short novels. Of these there are several volumes (published by Michel Lévy & costing but 1. franc. 25.) The "Scènes de la Vie de Bohême," The "Buveurs d'Eau," the "Pays Latin" & two or three others, are all charming.[3] Some of the short tales of Balzac are also excellent — though always disagreeable.[4] Tourgénieff's short stories — *Nouvelles Moscovites, Etranges Histoires* &c., I suppose you know.[5]

1. Prosper Mérimée (1803–70) wrote plays and (especially short) fiction, including: 'La Vénus d'Ille' (1837), which John La Farge had once persuaded HJ to translate (a New York periodical refused the translation, now lost); 'Colomba' (1840); and 'Carmen' (1845), the basis of Bizet's opera.
2. Alfred Charles de Musset (1810–57), poet and playwright, famous for his liaison with George Sand in 1833–5, but also for the elegance, irony and melancholy of his writing. His short stories are not usually much attended to. HJ in June 1877, acknowledging that 'they are the most mannered of his productions', referred to 'Emmeline', 'Les Deux Maîtresses' and 'Frédéric et Bernerette' as 'masterpieces' (LC II, 617).
3. The main productions of Henry Mürger (1822–61), a French novelist of German extraction, are: *Scènes de la vie de Bohême* (1847–9), on which Puccini based his opera *La Bohème*; *Le Pays latin* (1851); and *Les Buveurs d'eau* (1855).
4. Honoré de Balzac (1799–1850), French novelist of the massive *Comédie Humaine*, was a lifelong inspiration and irritant to HJ. In a long essay in December 1875 HJ singles out for praise certain of Balzac's tales: 'Le Colonel Chabert', 'L'Interdiction', 'La Femme abandonnée', 'La Grenadière', 'Le Message', 'Le Curé de Tours' and 'Un Debut dans la vie' among them.
5. In his large essay on Turgenev of April 1874, HJ declares that 'some of his best performances are tales of thirty pages' (LC II, 974).

I am almost forgetting two charming collections of Nouvelles & Contes by Théophile Gautier.[6] These are wonderfully picturesque. I have all these books in America, but haven't them here, I am sorry to say, as they would be quite at your service. Yours very truly

Henry James jr.

33. *To William Dean Howells*
24 October [1876]

Houghton MS   Published HJL II, 70–72; SL2, 136–7; LFL, 122–3

29 Rue de Luxembourg.
Oct. 24*th*

Dear Howells –

Many thanks for your letter & the promise of *Hayes*, which I shall expect.[1] Thanks also for your good opinion of the notice of *D.D.*, which charmed & reassured me. I was rather afraid that you would think its form beneath the majesty of the theme.[2] Many thanks, furthermore, for your continuing to like the *American*, of which I shall send you by the next mail another instalment. (I sent you one by the last, & I shall very soon send you the closing pages.) Your appeal on the subject of the *dénoûement* fairly set me trembling, & I have to take my courage in both hands to answer you. In a word M*me* de C. doesn't marry Newman, & I couldn't possibly, possibly, have made her do it. The whole pivot of the dénoûement was, in the conception of the tale, in his losing her; I am pretty sure this will make itself clear to you when you read the last quarter of the book. My subject was: an American letting the insolent foreigner go, out of his good nature, after the insolent foreigner had wronged him & *he* had held him in his power. To show the good nature I must show the wrong

6. Théophile Gautier (1811–72), French poet, novelist and travel writer, influentially expresses in his poem 'L'Art' a view of art as the supreme value. HJ admired him as 'the apostle of visual observation – the poet of the look of things'; but remarked of his fiction that 'he cared for nothing and knew nothing in men and women but the epidermis' (LC II, 353, 366).

1. Howells had published the month before a campaign biography of the Republican presidential candidate Rutherford B. Hayes (1822–93), his wife's cousin, who would win by a small margin in November.

2. HJ's essay in dialogue form on George Eliot's new work, 'Daniel Deronda: A Conversation', was published in the *Atlantic* in December 1876.

& the wrong of course is that the American is cheated out of Mme de Cintré. That he should only have been scared, & made to fear, for a while, he was going to lose her, would have been insufficient – non è vero? The subject is sad certainly, but it all holds together. But in my next novel I promise you there shall be much marrying. Apropos of this I have it on my conscience to mention that I am in correspondence with Scribner about a serial to begin in their magazine in June next. Nothing is yet settled, but I suppose something will be. The vision of a serial in Scribner does not, I may frankly say, aesth[et]ically delight me; but it is the best thing I can do, so long as having a perpetual serial running has defined itself as a financial necessity for me.[3] When my novels (if they ever do) bring me enough money to carry me over the intervals I shall be very glad to stick to the *Atlantic*. Or I would undertake to do this if I could simply have money down for my MS., leaving the Magazine to publish at its leisure. My novel is to be an *Americana* – the adventures in Europe of a female Newman, who of course equally triumphs over the insolent foreigner.[4]

Yes, I couldn't help translating those croquet-verses of Turgenieff, tho' I don't share the Russian eagerness for War. T. himself is full of it, & I suspect it is coming. The air is full of it & all the world here expects it.[5]

I think I shall thrive more effectually than here in London, to which city I propose before long to emigrate – if I don't go to Italy. But I shan't, at any rate, winter here. You manage to tell me very little about yourself. What are you writing? Yours very truly, with love at your fireside,

H. James jr.

3. By 18 December 1876, when HJ wrote again to Howells, the Scribner plan had been abandoned, as Scribner's could not start publication of another novel till November 1877, and could not guarantee even that. Scribner's published HJ's story 'Four Meetings' in their *Monthly* in November 1877, and his novel *Confidence* in 1879–80.
4. An early mention, apparently, of the theme of *The Portrait of a Lady* (1881).
5. For the *Nation* of 5 October 1876, HJ translated (from French) a poem by Turgenev in which Queen Victoria plays croquet with the severed heads of Christians massacred by the Turks in Bulgaria. After the Franco-Prussian War, an alliance was devised by Bismarck in 1873 between Germany, Austria-Hungary and Russia, but broke up with the Eastern Crisis of 1875–8. Russia backed Bulgarian nationalist agitations against oppression in 1875–6 by Bulgaria's Turkish occupiers, and formally went to war with Turkey in 1877–8.

34. To Thomas Sergeant Perry
12 January [1877]

Houghton TC   Published TSPB, 294–5

HJ crossed the English Channel on 10 December 1876, and was quickly settled in Mayfair. He wrote to AJ, 'I have an excellent lodging in this excellent quarter – a lodging whose dusky charms – including a housemaid with a fuliginous complexion, but a divine expression and the voice of a duchess – are too numerous to repeat' (HJL II, 82).

On 25 November 1881, reviewing the past years in his notebooks, HJ would remark that 'if you learn to know your London you learn a great many things. I felt all this in that autumn of 1876, when I first took up my abode in Bolton St. I had very few friends, the season was of the darkest and wettest; but I was in a state of deep delight. I had complete liberty, and the prospect of profitable work; I used to take long walks in the rain. I took possession of London; I felt it to be the right place.' (N, 218.)

3 Bolton St. Piccadilly
Jan. 12*th*

Dear Thomas –

I got both your letters, that of Xmas day (forwarded from Paris) & that of just after. I bless your baby, & wish it all the merits & attractions of its Parents & of its lovely Godmother, to which I doubt not it will add a peculiar grace of its own. – I am glad you are disposed to translate John Tourgueneff's novel, & trust, indeed, that some publisher will smile.[1] I count the days till I read it. Yes, I am *intimissimo* with John himself & esteem it a comfort. If you knew him personally, you would almost hate his books, comparatively!

Your acct. of the N.A.R. makes my heart bleed, but I hope that if it is to be done to death by the proprietor & the parson, it will yield you some profit *en attendant*.[2] What are you writing about? I would have sent you Gobineau, if I had not supposed that dear Miss Möller plied you with foreign literature

1. Perry's translation of *Virgin Soil* was published in the 'Leisure Hour' series in Boston in 1877. He had translated Turgenev's *Dimitri Roudine (Rudin)* in 1873, as well as three of his short stories.

2. HJ had written for the *North American Review* when it was edited by his friends Lowell and Norton (1864–8), then by E. W. Gurney (1868–70), and by Henry Adams (1870–76). In 1876 Charles Allen Thorndike Rice (1851–89) bought the quarterly magazine and moved it to New York, where he edited it as a monthly till his death.

gratis, & speedily enough.[3] (Besides Wm. writes me that book-post now pays a duty.) Àpropos of Miss Möller, do some day give her a message from me – my friendly remembrances & assurance of interest in the shop &c. Do it handsomely – in German.

Yes, London seems like a powerful big & busy place – much more interesting & inspiring, though much less agreeable, & for a lonely celibate, less convenient, than Paris. I subscribe to Mudie's & have 6 books at a time (now 2 uncut) – a 60*th* of which I read![4] I don't mean to try to "collaborate" on the London Magazines, tho' surely a novelist, among them is greatly wanted. Someday, if I pile up my fame, I may be less easy; but meanwhile I make shift with our own vulgar organs. But they *are* vulgar; & you may fancy what they seem here. My instinct is to *hide* them as soon as the postman has delivered them. But though overpowered by the quantity of British literature, I can't say I am [word illegible] by the quality. If they want a novelist they want also a critic: witness the flimsy article on G. Sand in the current *Blackwood*. – I have seen very few people; but I am to dine next week with Andrew Lang of the *Academy*. I met him 'tother day, & he is charming, tho' Scotch.[5] I will write of him. The Editor of the Acad. (Appleton) I haven't seen.[6] I kiss the hands of your wife, & the bald head of your baby, & wish you, dear Tom, the best prosperity possible.

Ever yours
H.J. jr.

I am told it is the deuce to get money out of the London Mags. Half the work is done by rich dilettanti gratis.

3. Comte Joseph-Arthur de Gobineau wrote *Nouvelles asiatiques*, which HJ reviewed in the *Nation* (7 December 1876), and Perry in the *Atlantic* (June 1877). Schoenhof & Moeller, 'Importers of Foreign Literature', at 40 Winter Street, Boston, ran, as HJ told Perry in 1878, 'a *vastly* better shop than any of the kind in London' (TSPB, 301).
4. Started in 1842 by Charles Edward Mudie, Mudie's Circulating Library (which lasted till 1937), based on the institution of the three-volume novel, allowed customers to subscribe by the year for as many volumes as they would pay for.
5. Andrew Lang (1844–1912) came from Oxford in 1875 to settle in London as a prolific man of letters, in the spheres of poetry, anthropology, Homeric scholarship, melodramatic fiction, fairy-tales and *belles-lettres*. HJ's next letter to Perry, in late February, commented that 'tho' amiable, he is too busy for social life', and called his output 'all pretty thin' (TSPB, 295). As a critic Lang disliked HJ's fiction, and HJ was to deplore to Edmund Gosse in 1912 his '*cultivation*, absolutely, of the puerile imagination and the fourth-rate opinion' (HJL IV, 638).
6. Charles Edward Cutts Birch Appleton (1841–79), an Oxford man, founded the *Academy* in 1869, and edited it till his early death.

35. To William Dean Howells
2 February [1877]

Houghton MS   Published HJL II, 96–7; LFL, 125–6

What HJ would recall as his 'prospect of profitable work' in London included in the longer term his most serious undertaking so far, The Portrait of a Lady, *for which, however, he needed 'full elbow room'.* The American *was still running in Howells's* Atlantic *till May 1877, and HJ floated the idea for a shorter novel.*

3 Bolton St Piccadilly W.
Feb. 2d

Dear Howells. –

I sent you a few lines three days since with my last bundle of copy; but now comes your letter of Jan. 20*th* which prompts me to send a few more.

I quite understand that you should not be able to begin another serial by H.J. jr until after the lapse of a year at least. Your readers & your contributors would alike remonstrate. I shall be glad, however, if you could begin to print a *six-months' tale* sooner than a longer one, to do something of those dimensions.[1] But I should not make use of the subject I had in mind when I last alluded to this matter – that is essentially not compressible into so small a compass. It is the portrait of the character & recital of the adventures of a woman – a great swell, psychologically; a *grande nature* – accompanied with many "developments." I would rather wait and do it when I can have full elbow room. But I will excogitate something for the shorter story, & shall endeavour to make it something of an "objective," dramatic & picturesque sort. Only let me know well in advance when you should commence publication. In January '78?

I agree with you in thinking that a year seems a long time for a novel to drag thro' a magazine – especially a short novel that only fills one volume when republished. But I think that the real trouble is not that any novel that the Atlantic would publish in a year is too long, but that it is chopped up in too fine pieces. Properly such a thing as the *American* should have been put thro' in 5 or 6 months, in numbers of 30 or 35 pages. To wait a month for a 20 minutes' nibble at it, would, it seems to me, if I were a reader, put me into a fatally bad humor with it. I have just been making this reflection apropos of your little "Comedy" – which is extremely pretty & entertaining. But one

1. This became *The Europeans*, which appeared in the *Atlantic* in four numbers from July to October 1878.

wants to go through with it. Your young-lady talk is marvellous – it's as if the devil himself were sitting in your inkstand. *He* only could have made you know that one girl would say that another's walking from the station was *ghastly*!![2] Yours ever

H.J. jr.

36. To William James
29 March [1877]

Houghton MS   Published CWJ I, 282–5; partly published LHJ I, 52–4; SL2, 147–9

HJ was quickly initiated into London society, in widening circles that seem to have opened up from letters of introduction from Charles Eliot Norton, Henry Adams and J. R. Lowell. He also wrote about English art, plays, books and life for American magazines.

THE ATHENAEUM CLUB. PALL MALL.
March 29*th*

Dear W*m* –

I will write you a few lines before I leave this place this evening. I thanked you for your last letter thro' mother a few days since – a letter of wh. I forget the exact date; (you described your brain-lecture &c.)[1] I have been dining here, & then sitting awhile to read the last no. of the 19*th* Centy! (I won't send it you as I send it to Mrs. Lockwood, who can't afford to buy it & would never see it otherwise.)[2] Vide in the same Prof. Clifford's thing at the end.[3]

2. Howells's play *Out of the Question* (*Atlantic*, February–April 1877), which contains a debate about social equality, starts with Miss Leslie Bellingham saying, 'No, Maggie. The stage didn't bring me here. I walked' and Miss Maggie Wallace replying, 'Why, Leslie! How perfectly ghastly!'
1. Not identified. In 1878 WJ gave a set of lectures at Johns Hopkins on 'The Brain and the Mind'.
2. HJ had met the New York writer and religious thinker Florence Bayard Lockwood (1842–98), wife of Major Benoni Lockwood, through Sarah Butler Wister. He saw her in Paris in 1876.
3. William Kingdon Clifford (1845–79), British mathematician and metaphysician, professor of applied mathematics at University College London from 1871, like T. H. Huxley took the British empirical tradition towards naturalism and positivism. 'The Influence upon Morality of a Decline in Religious Belief' appeared in the *Nineteenth Century* 26 (April 1877). In 'The Will to Believe' (1896), WJ calls Clifford 'that delicious *enfant terrible*'. Clifford's widow, Sophia Lucy Clifford (*née* Lane) (1846–1929), who became a professional novelist when his death from consumption left her with two small children, was a good friend of George Eliot and of HJ.

London life jogs along with me, pausing every now & then at some more or less succulent patch of herbage. I was almost ashamed to tell you thro' mother that I, unworthy, was seeing a bit of Huxley.[4] I went to his house again last Sunday evening – a pleasant easy, no-dress-coat sort of house (in our old Marlboro' Place, by the way.)[5] Huxley is a very genial, comfortable being – yet with none of the noisy & windy geniality of some folks here, whom you find with their backs turned when you are responding to the remarks that they have very effusively made you. But of course my talk with him is mere amiable generalities. These, however, he likes to cultivate, for recreation's sake, of a Sunday evening. (The slumbering Spencer I have not lately seen here; I am told he is terribly "nervous".)[6] Some mornings since, I breakfasted with Lord Houghton again – he invites me most dotingly.[7] Present: John Morley, Goldwin Smith (pleasanter than my prejudice agt. him) Henry Cowper, Frederick Wedmore & a monstrous cleverly-agreeably-talking M.P., Mr. Otway.[8] John

4. Thomas Henry Huxley (1825–95) was an immensely influential comparative anatomist, a scientific and educational thinker, a popular promoter of evolutionary theory in the wake of Charles Darwin's 1859 *Origin of Species*.

5. Just before Christmas 1855, the James family had rented 10 Marlborough Place in St John's Wood.

6. The nervous system of Herbert Spencer (1820–1903), enormously influential evolutionary philosopher, individualist thinker, psychologist and sociologist, had given way under the strain of writing *Principles of Psychology* (1870–72). WJ used the book in his Harvard teaching. HJ had written on 28 February that 'I often take an afternoon nap beside H.S. at the Athenaeum' (CWJ I, 281).

7. Richard Monckton Milnes (1809–85), first Baron Houghton, was a Cambridge friend of Alfred, first Baron Tennyson (1809–92), poet laureate from 1850, as well as of Arthur Hallam and Thackeray, and later of Browning, Swinburne and many others. A Conservative M.P., then a Liberal, one of the earliest serious English collectors of the Marquis de Sade, he wrote poetry and a *Life and Letters of Keats* (1848). He first had HJ to one of his breakfasts on 14 February 1877; by 5 May HJ was writing to Henry Adams, who knew him, that 'He has been really most kind & paternal, & I have seen, under his wing, a great variety of interesting & remarkable people' (CHJHA, 35).

8. John Morley (1838–1923), later Viscount Morley of Blackburn, was a Liberal statesman and literary man, lifelong friend of Leslie Stephen. He edited the *Fortnightly Review* (1867–82), and from 1880 the daily *Pall Mall Gazette*. From 1883 he was an M.P. He was a reader for Macmillan and editor from 1877 of the 'English Men of Letters' series, for which HJ wrote his *Hawthorne*. He is thought to have written the negative Macmillan's report on HJ's *French Poets and Novelists*, which calls it 'honest scribble work and no more'. Morley was close to positivist thinkers like T. H. Huxley and Frederic Harrison. Goldwin Smith (1823–1910), historian and controversialist, educated at Eton and Oxford, became a professor at the newly founded Cornell in 1868 and then moved to Toronto where he settled, frequently returning to England and actively publishing on history, literature, religion and politics. Henry Cowper (1836–87) was an M.P. Frederick Wedmore (1844–1921) was a painter-etcher, art-critic and novelist; three months later HJ called him 'an amiable weakling of the aesthetic school, who writes in the Academy' (CWJ I, 289).

Morley has a most agreeable face, but he hardly opened his mouth. (He is, like so many of the men who have done much here, very young looking.) Yesterday I dined with Lord Houghton – with Gladstone, Tennyson, Dr. Schliemann (the excavator of old Mycenae &c) & half a dozen other men of "high culture."[9] I sat next but one to the Bard, & heard most of his talk which was all about port-wine & tobacco: he seems to know much about them, & can drink a whole bottle of port at a sitting with no incommodity. He is very swarthy & scraggy & strikes one at first as much less handsome than his photos.: but gradually you see that it's a face of genius. He had I know not what simplicity, speaks with a strange rustic accent & seemed altogether like a creature of some primordial English stock, a 1000 miles away from American manufacture.

Behold me after dinner conversing affably with Mr. Gladstone – not by my own seeking, but by the almost importunate affection of Lord H. But I was glad of a chance to feel the "personality" of a great political leader – or as G. is now thought here even, I think, by his partisans, ex-leader. That of Gladstone is very fascinating – his urbanity extreme – his eye that of a man of genius – & his apparent self surrender to what he is talking of, without a flaw. He made a great impression on me – greater than any one I have seen here: though 'tis perhaps owing to my naïveté, & unfamiliarity with statesmen. Dr. Schliemann told me 2 or 3 curious things. 1º he is an American citizen having lived some years in America in business. 2º though he is now a great Hellenist he knew no word of Greek till he was 34 years old, when he learned it in 6 weeks (!!) at St. Petersburg. *Ce que c'est d'être Allemand!* The other men at Houghton's dinner were all special notabilities. Next me sat a very amiable Lord Zouche – noted as the unhappy young peer who a short time since married a young wife who three or four months after her marriage eloped *bel et bien* with a Guardsman.[10]

Sir Arthur John Otway (1822–1912) was a Liberal M.P., and Deputy Speaker of the House of Commons, 1883–5.

9. William Ewart Gladstone (1809–98), remarkable Liberal statesman and author, four times prime minister (1868–74, 1880–85, 1886 (briefly: his first Irish Home Rule Bill was defeated), 1892–4), was another friend of Tennyson. Heinrich Schliemann (1822–90), German archaeologist, was famous for his questionable discovery of Troy (his *Trojanische Alterhümer* ('Troy and its Remains') appeared in 1874). An English translation of the work HJ refers to here – *Mycenae: A Narrative of Researches and Discoveries at Mycenae and Tiryns* – came out in 1878 with a preface by Gladstone.

10. Robert Nathaniel Cecil George (1851–1914), Lord Zouche of Haryngworth, had in July 1875 married Annie Mary Eleanor Fraser (b. 1857), daughter of the eighteenth Lord Saltoun of Abernethy. She left him after three months.

Did I tell you that I some time since spent an evening with F. T. Palgrave?[11] (Strictly between ourselves – i.e. as regards H. Adams, & every one else, – I dont particularly like him: but he is evidently very respectable. He is a tremendous case of culture, & a "beggar for talk" such as you never faintly dreamed of. But *all* his talk is kicks & thrusts at every one going, & I suspect that, in the last, analysis, "invidious mediocrity" would be the scientific appellation of his temper. His absence of the *simpatico* is only surpassed by that of his wife. (This sounds pretty scornful; & I hasten to add that I imagine he very much improves on acquaintance. I shall take a chance to see.)[12] Did I tell you too that I had been to the Oxford & Cam. boat-race? But I have paragraphed it in the *Nation*, to wh. I refer you. It was for about 2 minutes a supremely beautiful sight; but for those 2 minutes I had to wait a horribly bleak hour & a ½, shivering, in mid-Thames, the sour March-wind.[13] I can't think of any other adventures: save that I dined 2 or 3 days since at Mrs. Godfrey Lushington's (they are very nice, *blushing* people) with a parcel of quiet folk: but next to a divine little Miss Lushington (so pretty English girls can be!) who told me that she lived in the depths of the City, at Guy's Hospital, whereof her father is administrator. Guy's Hospital – of which I have read in all old English novels. So does one move all the while here on identified ground.[14] This is the eve. of Good Friday, a most lugubrious day here – & all the world (save 4000,000 or so) are out of London for the 10 days' Easter holiday. I think of making two or three excursions of a few hours apiece, to

11. Francis Turner Palgrave (1824–97) worked in the education department 1855–84, but is best known as a friend of Tennyson's and for *The Golden Treasury of best songs and Lyrical poems in the English Language* (1861). He was a friend of Henry Adams, who recalled in *The Education of Henry Adams* (1918) that 'His literary taste, condensed into the *Golden Treasury*, helped Adams to more literary education than he ever got from any taste of his own … Literature, painting, sculpture, architecture were open field for his attacks, which were always intelligent if not always kind, and when these failed, he readily descended to meaner levels.'

12. HJ did find Palgrave improve on closer acquaintance. On 21 May 1878 he wrote to AJ: 'He is a good fellow, as one knows him better, & his abuse of all the world a bark that is much worse than his bite. He is, I imagine, the most disappointed man in England. He was the great man of his day at college & was expected to set the world on fire. But here he is at middle age only an inspector of schools, & an editor of little books of verses. He feels it much & it has soured him.' (Unpublished Houghton MS, bMS Am 1094 (1583).)

13. HJ's piece in the *Nation* (12 April 1877) records his standing 'for an hour in the fierce, raw wind that sweeps over Barnes Bridge' (CTW:GBA, 273).

14. Godfrey Lushington (1832–1907) was an Assistant Under-Secretary of State in the Home Department from 1876. His wife was a sister of the widow of the English poet Arthur Hugh Clough (who had been a friend of J. R. Lowell and Charles Norton), and with another sister, Mrs Arthur Coltman, they were very hospitable to HJ. Guy's Hospital is, for instance, where Bob Sawyer in *The Pickwick Papers* was a student, and where Mrs Gamp's husband dies in *Martin Chuzzlewit*.

places near London whence I can come back to sleep: Canterbury, Chichester &c: (but as I shall communicate them for lucre I won't talk of them thus.)[15] Farewell, dear brother, I won't prattle further. Thank father for the 2 cuts from the *Galaxy* – tho I wish he had sent a line with them. I enclose $2.00 I accidentally possess. Add them to that $12.00 & spend them for any cost I may put you to. Have you rec'd. your *Maudsley*?[16] Don't you think very well of Hayes, & are not things in a brightening way?[17] Encourage Alice to write to me. My blessings on yourself from your faithful

H.J. jr.

Ask Alice to keep these London scrawls of mine: I may be glad to refer to them later.

37. *To William Dean Howells*
30 March [1877]

Houghton MS   Published HJL II, 104; SL2, 149–52; LFL, 126–8

Unfortunately Howells's 'long letter' protesting at the ending of The American *does not survive.*

3 Bolton St. W.
March 30*th*

Dear Howells –

I am supposed to be busily scribbling for lucre this morning; but I must write you three lines of acknowledgment of your welcome long letter. It's most interesting portion was naturally your strictures on the close of my tale, which I accept with saintly meekness. These are matters which one feels about as one may, or as one can. I quite understand that as an editor you should go in for "cheerful endings"; but I am sorry that as a private reader you are not struck with the inevitability of the *American* dénoûement. I fancied that most folks would feel that M*me* de Cintré *couldn't*, when the pivot came, marry

15. 'An English Easter' appeared in *Lippincott's Magazine* (of Philadelphia) in July 1877, recording HJ's experiences in London, Canterbury and Rochester.
16. Probably *Body and Mind: An Inquiry into Their Connection and Mutual Influence* (1869) by the British psychologist and physiologist Henry Maudsley (1835–1918).
17. The Republican Rutherford B. Hayes had won the American presidency by a small margin in November 1876.

Mr. N.; and what the few persons who have spoken to me of the tale have expressed to me (e.g. Mrs. Kemble t'other day) was the fear that I should really put the marriage through. *Voyons*; it would have been impossible: they would have been an impossible couple, with an impossible problem before them. For instance – to speak very materially – where could they have lived? It was all very well for Newman to talk of giving her the whole world to choose from: but Asia & Africa being counted out, what would Europe & America have offered? M*me* de C. couldn't have lived in New York; depend upon it; & Newman, after his marriage (or rather *she*, after it) couldn't have dwelt in France. There would have been nothing left but a farm out West. No, the interest of the subject was, for me, (without my being at all a pessimist) its exemplification of one of those insuperable difficulties which present themselves in people's lives & from which the only issue is by forfeiture – by losing something. It was cruelly hard for poor N. to lose, certainly: but *que diable allait-il faire dans cette galère?* We are each the product of circumstances & there are tall stone walls which fatally divide us. I have written my story from Newman's side of the wall, & I understand so well how M*me* de Cintré couldn't really scramble over from *her* side! If I had represented her as doing so I should have made a prettier ending, certainly; but I should have felt as if I were throwing a rather vulgar sop to readers who don't really know the world & who don't measure the merit of a novel by its correspondence to the same. Such readers assuredly have a right to their entertainment, but I don't believe it is in me to give them, in a satisfactory way, what they require.

I don't think that "tragedies" have the presumption against them as much as you appear to; & I see no logical reason why they shouldn't be as *long* as comedies. In the drama they are usually allowed to be longer – non è vero?

But whether the *Atlantic* ought to print unlimited tragedy is another question – which you are doubtless quite right in regarding as you do. Of course you couldn't have, for the present, another evaporated marriage from me! I suspect it is the tragedies in life that arrest my attention more than the other things & say more to my imagination; but, on the other hand, if I fix my eyes on a sun-spot I think I am able to see the prismatic colors in it. You shall have the brightest possible sun-spot for the 4-number tale of 1878.[1] It shall fairly put your readers eyes out. The idea of doing what you propose much pleases me; and I agree to squeeze my buxom muse, as you happily call her, into a 100 of your pages. I will lace her so tight that she shall have the neatest little figure in the world. It shall be a very joyous little romance. I am afraid I can't tell you at this moment what it will be; for my dusky fancy contains nothing joyous

1. *The Europeans* appeared in the *Atlantic* in four numbers, July–October 1878.

enough: but I will invoke the jocund muse & come up to time. I shall probably develop an idea that I have, about a genial, charming youth of a Bohemianish pattern, who comes back from foreign parts into the midst of a mouldering & ascetic old Puritan family of his kindred (scene, imaginary locality in New England 1830,) & by his gayety & sweet audacity smooths out their rugosities, heals their dyspepsia & dissipates their troubles. *All* the women fall in love with him (& he with them – his amatory powers are boundless;) but even for a happy ending he can't marry them all. But he marries the prettiest, & from a romantic quality of Xtian. charity, produces a picturesque imbroglio (for the sake of the picturesque I shall play havoc with the New England background of 1830!) under cover of which the other maidens pair off with the swains who have hitherto been starved out: after which the beneficent cousin departs for Bohemia (*with his bride, oh yes!*) in a vaporous rosy cloud, to scatter new benefactions over man-, & especially, woman-, kind!

(Pray don't mention this stuff to any one. It would be meant, roughly speaking, as a picture of the conversion of a dusky, dreary domestic circle to epicureanism. But I may be able to make nothing of it. The merit would be in the amount of *color* I should be able to infuse into it.) – But I shall give you it, or its equivalent, by Nov. next. It was quite by accident I didn't mention the name of your admiress. Nay there are two of them! The one I spoke of, I think, is Lady Clarke – a handsome charming woman, of a certain age, the wife of a retired & invalid diplomatist, who lives chiefly on her estate in Scotland.[2] She "takes in" the *Atlantic* & seems to affect you much. The other is Mrs. Coltman, a modest, blushing & pleasing woman, who also has the *Atlantic*, & who can best be identified by saying that she is the sister of the widow of A. H. Clough, the poet – Lowell's friend. She is to take me some day soon down to Eton & show me an inside-view of the school, where her rosy little British boys are. Both of these ladies descanted to me on the *Atlantic* & your productions & said nary a word to me of my own masterpieces: whereby I consider my present action magnanimous! Àpropos: the young girl in your comedy is extremely charming; quite adorable, in fact; & extremely real. You make them wonderfully well.[3]

What more shall I say?

Yes, I find London much to my taste – entertaining, interesting, inspiring,

2. Lady Clark (d. 1897) was the former Charlotte Coltman, daughter of Mr Justice (T. J.) Coltman, and had in 1851 married Sir John Forbes Clark (1821–1910), who was a diplomat till he resigned in 1855. They were hospitable to Americans, including Henry Adams, John Hay and Clarence King, and HJ visited them at the Scottish estate, Tillypronie, Aberdeenshire, in September 1878 and September 1881.
3. The heroine of Howells's *Atlantic* comedy, *Out of the Question*, is Leslie Bellingham.

even. But I am not, as you seem to imply, in the least in the thick of it. If I were to tell you whom I see; it would make a tolerably various list: but the people only pass before me panoramically, & I have no relations with them. I dined yesterday in comp'y. with Browning at Smalley's — where were also Huxley & his wife & the editor & editress of the *Daily News*: among the cleverest people I have met here.[4] Smalley has a charming house & wife, & is a very creditable American representative; more so than the minister, who, I am told, has never returned a dinner since he has been here.[5] Browning is a great chatterer but no *Sordello* at all.

We are lost in admiration of Mr. Hayes; may his shadow never grow less! Blessings on your home. Yours always truly

H. James jr.

38. To Alice James
8 April [1877]

Houghton MS   Unpublished

HJ's sister was living quietly at home with the James parents at 20 Quincy Street on the edge of Harvard Yard in Cambridge, Massachusetts. His letters to her are full of gossipy accounts of his adventures in the English world from which he was consciously gathering material and seeking inspiration.

Here, for example, after meeting the poet Browning, HJ sketches the mystery which later became the crux of his fantastic story 'The Private Life' in 1892, a mystery he recalls in the 1909 Preface to that tale: 'I have never ceased to ask myself, in this particular loud, sound, normal, hearty presence . . . what lodgement,

4. After the death of his wife Elizabeth Barrett Browning in 1861, the poet Robert Browning (1812–89) had returned from Italy to London. His *Sordello* (1840) was a watchword for baffling complexity, and *Men and Women* (1855) his most successful collection. George Washburn Smalley (1833–1916), European correspondent for the *New York Tribune* from 1866 to 1895, had called on HJ in Paris. He and his wife lived in London and introduced HJ to many people, getting him temporary membership of the Savile Club. As HJ wrote to WJ the next year, 'Reared in New England Abolitionism & asceticism they never had any "society" in the early part of their career, & in consequence they go in for it now, tooth and nail' (CWJ I, 297). Frank Harrison Hill (1830–1910), from an underprivileged Lincolnshire background, worked as a tutor before in 1861 becoming editor of *The Northern Whig*. In 1862 he married Jane Dalzell Finlay (d. 1904), daughter of the paper's proprietor; she continued to write literary articles and reviews, chiefly in the *Saturday Review*. In 1865 Hill joined the *Daily News* and in 1869 became its editor till 1886.

5. The U.S. Ambassador to Great Britain in 1876–7 was Edwards Pierrepont (1817–92).

*on such premises, the rich proud genius one adored could ever have contrived . . .
The whole aspect and allure of the fresh sane man, illustrious and undistinguished
. . . was mystifying; they made the question of who then had written the immortal
things such a puzzle.' In the story, the narrator figures out that there are two of
him: 'One goes out, the other stays at home. One is the genius, the other's the
bourgeois.'*

3 Bolton St. Piccadilly.
April 8*th*.

My dearest sister: I was "so very pleased" as they say here, to receive your
letter of March 24*th*, which was a much needed proof that you had not "fainted
by the wayside," & that the family had not accidentally omitted to mention it.
Your letter contained many interesting items – especially the history of Nanny
Kotch's friend Miss Smith, which I found as choice a morsel as those I daily
read in the English papers & am sometimes tempted to consider a monopoly
of this happy isle.[1] It would go well with the tale I yesterday perused of an
old man & his wife, who were both deaf & dumb, & who lived on an annual
pension of £5.00, paid them by the Cordwainers' Society – the condition of
the same being that they received no help from the parish. They were unable
to work & utterly destitute, but they were afraid to ask for help lest the pension
should be stopped. *Sur ces entrefaîtes*, they were found dead of starvation in
the attempt to live on £5.00 a year!![2]

But let me turn to more cheerful themes – tho where to find them I hardly
know. This is a rainy Sunday afternoon – a dreadfully dreary sort of thing in

1. Nanny or Nancy Kotch was a friend of AJ, who said of her in 1873, 'I learn from William
that she converses with men just as she does to us, about her *intense existence, yearning* and *her
despairs* etc. – is it not extraordinary truly? . . . she is just a little wearisome to me' (LLAJ,
30). Miss Smith could not be identified.
2. *The Times*, Saturday, 7 April 1877, p. 10: 'INQUESTS. Last evening Mr. Humphreys held an
inquiry, at the Whittington and Cat Tavern, Bethnal-green, into the circumstances attending
the death of Mary-Ann Nash, 71 . . . On Tuesday evening, on witness calling on his mother,
he entered deceased's room, which was almost void of furniture and without a fire. The deceased
and her husband, who were deaf and dumb, were lying apparently in a dying state. He called
his mother's attention to them, but she replied that she had had enough of them. He then fetched
Dr. Lillie, who ordered the husband to be taken at once to the Infirmary. The deceased,
however, was dying, and did die in his presence one hour and a half afterwards. The deceased
and her husband were in receipt of £5 per annum each from the Cordwainers' Company, but
in the event of their receiving parish or other relief the money would have been forfeited. For
that reason they did not apply to the parish . . . Dr. Lillie said the cause of death was exhaustion
from privation and destitution. He never saw a worse case in his life, the deceased having been
completely starved to death.'

London. I usually consecrate Sunday afternoons to visits it being the only time one has a chance of finding ladies at home: but to day I abstain, from an aversion, on the one side, to get wet & muddy in my peregrinations, & a thrifty indisposition, on the other, to encounter an accumulation of cabfares: as I have lately come to a realization of the havoc that these latter have made in my slender fortune. There is however no happiness in London unless one allows a goodly margin for them, & the great part they play is by itself sufficient to make this a dearer place than N.Y. or even Paris. So I will pay an afternoon call on my sister in spite of the fact that she will probably not offer me a cup of 5 o'clock tea in a bit of highly remarkable old china, on a Japanese table about as high as a footstool. The sprightliness of her conversation will however compensate for the absence of this picturesque incident of a Quincy St. afternoon.

I am glad to hear you say that "nothing is too trivial" to relate from my London observations, for I have sometimes feared that I bored you with a string of barren enumerations. But this time I have few even of trivialities to unfold, as the London world has just been passing thro' the dead season of the Easter holidays. This, together with Passion Week, makes a sudden & complete social stoppage; "every one" goes out of town, invitations hang fire & a gloomy hush broods over the place. I suppose there will be a resurrection next week, but meanwhile I have been nowhere & seen no one. Stay I remember that on Good Friday I partook of a very pleasant dinner at the Smalleys', who do everything that is regular & who since, I believe, have departed for Torquay. Present at their dinner were Robt. Browning, Mr. & Mrs. Huxley, Mr. & Mrs. Frank Hill, editor & editress of the *Daily News*, & my humble self. The Hills are quite the cleverest folk I have met here – I have seen more or less of Mrs. H. Hill himself is a really superior talker & says nothing but what is very good – though on this occasion he was shut up by the chattering and self-complacent Robert B., who I am sorry to say, does not make on me a purely agreeable impression. His transparent eagerness to hold the *dé de la conversation* & a sort of shrill interruptingness which distinguishes him have in them a kind of vulgarity.[3] Besides which, strange to say, his talk doesn't strike me as very good. It is altogether gossip & personality & is not very beautifully worded. But evidently there are 2 Brownings – an esoteric & an exoteric.[4] The former never peeps out in society, & the latter hasn't a ray of suggestion of *Men & Women*. I think it was the day after this that I dined with a very pleasant old

3. In French a *dé* (m.) is a die in gaming (or a thimble); hence, 'to monopolize the conversation'.
4. 'esoteric . . . exoteric': a pair of terms going back to Aristotle and Pythagoras. The first means 'designed for, or appropriate to, an inner circle of advanced or privileged disciples'; the second, in contrast, 'communicated to outsiders, intelligible to the public' or 'commonplace, simple' (OED).

gentleman who seems kindly disposed to me – a Mr. Phillips-Jodrell who lives round the corner, in Stratton St, where his dwelling looks into the garden of Devonshire House. He is an old bachelor of fortune & culture, a liberal, charitable, a retired fox hunter, a valetudinarian, & a friend of many Americans of 40 years ago.[5]

He is very fond of giving small dinners, talking of old books &c, & is a very pretty specimen of a certain sort of fresh-colored, blue-eyed simple-minded yet cultivated (two things which go together so much here) old English gentleman. His dinner consisted of young liberal M.P.s &c – my eternal fate! I meet none but statistical people.

I have seen no one else, save that I called yesterday p.m. on Mrs. Duncan Stewart, (the mother of the clever Mrs. Rogerson whom I have mentioned to you) a rather picturesque & agreeable old lady, who has lived always in good London society, wears voluminous *capotes* & capes of old white lace, talks of Lady Morgan & Mrs. Norton &c.[6] The latter has just been married by the way, at 75 years of age, in a Bath-chair, to a great Scotch laird, Sir W*m* Stirling Maxwell, the author of the 'Cloister-Life of Chas V.': a fact that Mrs. Kemble cited to me the other day as a proof that the English were the most romantic of all people & the most capable of great passions; Sir W*m* Stirling having been in love with Mrs. N. for the last 40 years & prevented hitherto from marrying her.[7] Lady Morgan, said Mrs. Duncan Stewart, kept a saloon & was

5. Probably Thomas Jodrell Phillips, born in 1807 in Manchester and educated at Trinity College, Cambridge. Phillips was called to the bar at the Inner Temple in 1835. In 1868 he assumed the surname and arms of the Jodrells by Royal Licence, becoming Thomas Phillips-Jodrell.

6. Sketching his novella 'A London Life' in his notebook in 1887, HJ imagined 'an old lady – like Mrs. Duncan S[tewart] – only of rank – a genial, clever, worldly, old-fashioned, half-comforting, half shocking old lady' (N, 38). She had known Washington Irving and Leigh Hunt, and was widowed in 1869. The previous month HJ described her daughter, the unhappily married Mrs James Rogerson (née Christina Stewart), as 'a clever, liberal woman who invites me to dinner every four or five days' (HJL II, 101). Lady Morgan, born Sydney Owenson in Dublin (1783?–1859), was a poet, novelist and society figure of considerable fame, notably for her novel *The Wild Irish Girl* (1806). The granddaughter of the playwright and politician Richard Brinsley Sheridan (1751–1816), Caroline Elizabeth Sarah Sheridan (1808–77), a great beauty, prolific poet and occasional novelist praised by James Hogg, married the Hon. George Chapple Norton (1800–75) in 1827. 'The marriage was wretched' (LCVF, 469). In 1836 her husband charged the politician Lord Melbourne with alienating her affections; and in 1853, though separated, he attempted to claim as his own her literary copyrights. She keenly supported the 1853 Divorce Bill. In 1875 Norton died.

7. Sir William Stirling Maxwell (1818–78), baronet, Spanish scholar, historian and collector, author of *The Cloister Life of the Emperor Charles the Fifth* (1852), lost his first wife in 1874 and on 1 March 1877 married 'Mrs. N.'. She was by then an invalid, and died on 15 June the same year.

a very good maîtresse de maison. "She always drew people out & made them show their best. To me she always said: 'Come out of your corner there and show your shoulders!'"

I had a plan of making some excursions into the country; but the wretched weather – perpetual rain – has brought it to nought. I went down one afternoon to Rochester, however, (of whose charming old castle I enclose you a photo.) & another day tried Canterbury, but had my pleasure spoiled by tremendous & constant rain. I sent you some photos of the immensely interesting Cathedral. (Pray keep these & glue them in a book with others I will send of such places as I see. If you will thus exercise your peculiar talent for me I shall be very glad to find the things in the future). I had one pleasant afternoon lately – I went down by train with Robert Cunliffe & we took a long walk in Richmond Park.[8] This accessibility of such charming places is a great redemption of much of the dreariness of London. You go after lunch & you are back in time to dress for dinner.

I hope you are having a lovelier spring than me, & that all is going well at home. I had this a.m. a visit from Benoni Lockwood, who is in Europe for a few weeks, & who gave me an optimistic acct. of Hayes & the political situation.[9] *Send me a photo. of Hayes* – don't fail.[10] I hope father prospers & figure to myself that you have begun again to take the air in the phaeton. Do you take Bunch with you & is he [as] charming in his conduct as Dido?[11] I hope you don't drop him under the wheel – that horrid instant which seemed to make me a murderer – lives in my memory. Thank father much for looking at my proof – I hope it doesn't tire him. Do you hear anything particular from Bob. & Wilk? Please tell A.K. (to whom I hope you sometimes send my letters) that I should like extremely to hear from her. She must have had rather a dismal winter, in the midst of N.Y. tribulations. Are the Ripleys living with Cousin H.? What is left of poor Helen R.?[12] I shall be very glad to see Sara

8. Sir Robert Cunliffe and his pretty wife were young English friends of Henry Adams, to whom HJ mentions on 5 May 1877 a recent walk with him in Richmond Park (HJL II, 110).
9. Major Benoni Lockwood was the husband of HJ's friend Mrs Florence Lockwood.
10. On 22 March, HJ had asked his father to send him a photograph of the new president. In 1881 HJ favourably compared the portrait of the following president, James A. Garfield, to that of Hayes.
11. Dido was the previous, and Bunch the current James family dog.
12. HJ's Aunt Kate, Catherine Walsh (1812–89), had in 1869 been in Europe with Henry Wyckoff, Helen Ripley and Mrs Helen Wyckoff Perkins and her husband. On 31 January HJ had told his mother he had not heard before of Joseph Ripley's death, 'and can well conceive of poor Helen's desolation'. Now 'Poor Helen', presumably Helen Ripley, was staying with 'Cousin H.P.' (HJL II, 95).

S.[13] Tell her to notify me immediately she arrives. Love to all, sweet sister & general blessings.

Yours ever
H.J. jr.

I have been reading in a rough edition which I won't send you, besides wanting to keep it for review, Tourgenieff's new novel *Terres Vierges*: the French translation. It has fine things, but I think it is decidedly inferior to his earlier works. I hear from Paris that it has fallen so flat in Russia that it has not even been reprinted from the magazine, & T is much accablé.[14]

39. To Elizabeth Boott
26 May [1877]

Houghton MS   Unpublished

Lizzie Boott now lived at Bellosguardo, above Florence, with her widowed father Frank Boott. The pair were acknowledged by HJ as the basis for the figures of Gilbert and Pansy Osmond in The Portrait of a Lady. *Lizzie studied painting with Thomas Couture and later married the American painter Frank Duveneck.*

3 Bolton St. W.
May 26*th*

Dear Lizzie –

Many thanks for your noble displeasure over the conclusion of my novel, & for Miss Bartlett's as well.[1] Will you enclose her this note, which is addressed

13. Sara Sedgwick, sister of Theodora and Arthur, friend of AJ and the Cambridge Nortons, came to England in 1877, staying in the country with her cousin Mrs Nix. By the autumn she was engaged to William Darwin, banker son of the naturalist Charles. She was, HJ said in 1878, 'very sweet, soft, gentle and without initiative' (HJL II, 150).
14. HJ's unsigned review of *Virgin Soil* in the *Nation* of 26 April 1877 emphasized Turgenev's 'superiority' rather than this novel's inferiority. On 18 April HJ sent on to the Russophile T. S. Perry 'the cheap (and nasty) reprint of *Terres Vierges* which John Turgenieff lately sent me – having kept it only to review it' (HJL II, 108).
1. HJ had in 1873 gone riding in the Roman Campagna with Alice Bartlett, and read Tasso's poetry with her twice a week. He had told Lizzie Boott on 11 November 1876, 'I esteem her rather a good fellow than a lovely woman. I couldn't love her.' (Unpublished Houghton MS, bMS Am 1094 (524).) She is said to have given HJ the germ of 'Daisy Miller' (HJL IV, 262n.). She had been the companion in the Via della Croce of the separated wife – whom HJ found

to both of you? After your approval, *à toutes deux*, nothing could give me greater delight than your censure; & indeed I am not sure that the thought of moving you to wrath – noble, indignant, magnanimous emotion – has not something even more exquisitely grateful than the idea of your simple tame satisfaction. Generous, admirable, sublime you are, both of you, & I kiss the hem of your garments: that, namely, of Miss Bartlett's riding-habit, & of your (Miss Boott's) painting-blouse. Such readers are worth having – readers who really care what one does & who pay one the divine compliment of taking things hard. I will dedicate my next novel to both of you under the emblem of a mahl-stick & a riding-whip intertwined.[2] I feel, indeed, as if I had been rapped about the head with each of these instruments; but, as I say, the pleasure & honor were greater than the pain.

Of course I hold you mortally wrong, & deem my dénoûement the only possible one. What would you have had? Come, now, they couldn't have married, when it came to the point, & I never meant they should, or that the reader shld. expect it. It was very well for Newman to want it, & for M*me* de C. to fancy for a few weeks it was possible: but she was *not* in love with him, &, in fact, she could never have crossed the Rubicon. What then could he have done to recover her? She was irrecoverable. It seemed to me that in putting it into Newmans power to forgive & contemptuously "let off" the haughty Bellegardes, I was doing quite the most dramatic & inspiring thing. I think Miss Bartlett's Welsh Bard would have appreciated it.[3] However I am a realist, & he wasn't; & I am never more of one than in saying that I salute you both to the earth, & adore you completely. We will discuss details some day under Italian olives & figs (or rather *over* them) (that is the figs) & in that situation love & admire each other so that we can't differ. I obsequiate your father & believe that he likes the last pages.

> Yours more than ever
> H. James jr

'charming' – of the eminent Massachusetts Senator Charles Sumner (1811–74), who was waiting for a divorce (after which she resumed her maiden name as Alice Mason) (CWJ I, 198).

2. HJ draws in the middle of his text the emblem he mentions, with the painter's mahl-stick and the riding-whip crossed like swords. I am especially grateful to the staff in the Houghton Library for helping me to decipher 'mahl-stick'.

3. Perhaps the author of the medieval work *The Mabinogion*, translated into modern English by Lady Charlotte Guest between 1838 and 1849.

40. To Mary Walsh James (mother)
15 March [1878]

Houghton MS   Published SL 1, 79–80

HJ remained in Bolton Street, making occasional country visits in, for instance,
Shropshire and Warwickshire, until September 1877, when he went back to Paris
for a month of writing, then on to Florence and Rome, where he spent seven weeks.
He returned to London in December, eager for concentrated work on The Europeans.

March 15*th*

Dearest mammy –

Only a word to thank you for your letter of March 2*d*, acknowledging my
explanation about the Scribner cheque last summer. Now it is all right.[1]

I am much pleased with your other news – about W*m*'s success in Baltimore,
of wh. I was sure in advance; & A.'s visit to N.Y.[2] I am sorry W.'s eyes still
demand care, as I suppose that, in consequence I shall have no details from
him: but I trust A. will write me a keen analysis of her N.Y. observations. I
congratulate her on her female-lunch-cooperative-Society, which strikes me as
a brilliant idea. I would willingly be present in the humble garb of an Irish
waiter – or are the waiters female too? I am surprised father has not yet rec'd.
a copy of my book, which I posted *instantly* with my own hands: I hope it
promptly turned up. A number of people here have spoken to me of it with
much appreciation.[3] The story Howells is to publish is *by no means* the one of
which I wrote you last summer that it would be to the American "as wine
unto water." *That* is still on my hands; but I hope to do something with it this
summer. I have offered it again to Lippincott.[4] (*Silence* on this point.) "The

1. On 17 February HJ had had painstakingly to explain to his mother that the previous summer
he had got *Scribner's Monthly* to send his father a draft for $300 (for 'Four Meetings' (November
1877) and 'Longstaff's Marriage' (August 1878)) to meet a draft he had made on their account,
expecting to go abroad sooner than he did.
2. WJ had given a set of lectures at Johns Hopkins, where he was being thought of for a
position, on 'The Brain and the Mind'. AJ had returned from New York with a cold, and before
long she had a breakdown, attributed by biographers to the disturbance of WJ's marrying.
3. *French Poets and Novelists* was published by Macmillan on 19 February 1878.
4. HJ was still biding his time for the effort of *The Portrait of a Lady*, which on 23 July 1878
he told WJ 'is only begun; I am doing other things just now' (CWJ I, 306). In 1877 HJ had
contributed three travel sketches and a review to the Philadelphian *Lippincott's Magazine*, edited
by John Foster Kirk (1824–1904), and in 1878 they published the story 'Théodolinde' (May)
and an essay on 'The British Soldier' (August). But the magazine never took a novel by HJ;

Europeans" is a much slighter & shorter affair – which I have pledged myself to get into a 100 pages of the *Atlantic*, & which will be much squeezed & minimized by this circumstance. Still, I think you will find it pretty & good. The donnée is interesting – & the art will be superior. Howells has quite enough of it in his hands to begin immediately; but I am afraid he won't. (Please say *nothing* about the other story, which is the one that will cover you with fame.) If I could only afford to wait, *that* might come out here also in the *Cornhill* or *Macmillan*; but for this I must wait for what I do next afterward. I have dined out a good deal lately: but with moderate interest, & will reserve the record till I next write to A. Blessings to all from your faithful

H.

41. To Frederick Macmillan
[1 August 1878]

BL MS   Published CHJHM, 16

HJ remained in London, with a couple of country excursions, until September 1878. In 1877, after hearing from Smalley that Frederick Macmillan (1851–1936) had thought of asking to publish The American *in England, he had approached him to propose his publishing* French Poets and Novelists *(and Macmillan did, in February 1878, despite a gloomy reader's report probably from John Morley). On 31 July Frederick Macmillan had agreed to HJ's latest, on a 'half-profits' contract: 'We shall be glad to publish "The Europeans" on the terms I mentioned yesterday, that is, we will assume the entire risk of the undertaking, and share with you any profits that may arise. I hope the British public may take to the book in such a way as to make these same profits enormous.' (CHJHM, 15.) The novel ran in the* Atlantic *from July to October.*

Dear Macmillan –

I meant to have written you yesterday that I am very glad you undertake the book. As regards the profits I am afraid there is not much danger of their being "enormous," exactly; but even if they are only moderate, it will be a beginning of my appearance before the British public as a novelist – as *the*

1878 was the year in which Kirk returned 'Daisy Miller' to its author, as HJ's Preface later recalled, 'with an absence of comment that struck me at the time as rather grim', explicable only by the idea that it must 'have passed with the Philadelphian critic for "an outrage on American girlhood".'

novelist of the future, destined to extract from the B.P. eventually (both for himself & his publishers) a colossal fortune! You shall have the rest of the copy the moment it arrives & proofsheets shall receive the promptest attention. Kind regards in St. John's Wood, & *bon voyage* for Etretat.[1]

Yours very truly
Henry James

42. To William Ernest Henley
[6 October 1878]

Morgan MS   Unpublished

HJ finally published in a British magazine in June – the controversial 'Daisy Miller', for which Leslie Stephen's Cornhill *paid him £95.* French Poets and Novelists *had established him critically in London, and a 'graceful & complimentary' review brought him into correspondence with W. E. Henley about 'dear old Balzac' (Unpublished Morgan MS (MA 1617. 1) 9 March [1878]). Henley (1849–1903), poet and man of letters, had lost a foot in boyhood, and had battled to keep the other. He was a friend of HJ's acquaintance Leslie Stephen, who had introduced him in 1875 to another invalid with a swagger, Robert Louis Stevenson (1850–94), whose collaborator he would become until they fell out. He came up to London in 1877 to work on, and soon edit, a new weekly,* London, *and later edited the* Magazine of Art *(1881–6),* The Scots Observer *which became* The National Observer *(1888–94), and the* New Review *(1895–8), where he serialized* What Maisie Knew. *On 28 August HJ had written to Henley encouraging him to write on Turgenev, for whom they shared an enthusiasm. (I have not found the second, 'longer article' mentioned below.)*

The Europeans *was published by Macmillan, stretched over two volumes, on 18 September 1878; and Henley praised it in print, calling HJ 'an exponent of the refined, eclectic realism of Turgénieff' and* The Europeans *'perhaps the purest piece of realism ever done'.*

Dear Mr. Henley –

Here are the little Americo-"Europeans," with the author's kind regards, which I am afraid of writing inside, lest the post should protest.

1. Frederick Macmillan had married Georgiana Elizabeth Warrin (d. 1943) of Newtown, Long Island, in 1874 while he was working at the company branch in New York, and they had a home at 2 Elm Tree Road, St John's Wood. Étretat was the fashionable Normandy resort, about which HJ had written for the New York *Tribune* in August 1876.

I read your paper on Tgff., many weeks since, with a great deal of pleasure, & I hope you are likely to get to work at the longer article you proposed. The other was full of well-said things. He will bear a great deal of talking about, & of his manner of writing there has never been enough in England. I wish George Eliot were a little more like him.

I have it in my conscience to say that I don't particularly know George Meredith.[1]

I haven't read "Richard Feverel," but have made a note of it.

A good play is a good thing, & I wish all prosperity to yours.[2] Attend well to those French devils, who know everything that can be known about the Dramatic Art (I mean the art of the drama,) for modern conditions: Dumas fils, Emile Augier, even Sardou. I am a great admirer of Dumas fils, & think the "Demi-Monde" & the "Fils Naturel" the 1st modern comedies. Have you read Sardou's *Haine*? If you haven't Emile Augier I will gladly lend him to you.[3] Have you found the missing Tgffs.?

1. This might prick HJ's conscience: in his letter of 28 August he enthusiastically picks up Henley's unfavourable comparison of the poet and novelist Meredith (1828–1909) with Turgenev: 'Rather! George Meredith strikes me as a capital example of the sort of writer that Turgénieff is most absolutely opposite to – the *un*realists – the *literary* story-tellers. T. doesn't care a straw for an epigram or a phrase – his inspiration is not a whit literary, but purely and simply, human, moral. G.M. cares, I should say, enormously for epigrams and phrases. He's a mannerist, a *coquette*, in a word: like that pitiful prostitute, Victor Cherbuliez. Turgénieff hasn't a grain of coquetry!' (HJL II, 183). Henley mentions Meredith's controversial *The Ordeal of Richard Feverel* (1859) in his review in the *Academy* (9 August 1879) of the revised English issue of *Roderick Hudson* – to HJ's advantage. But Henley and Stevenson dedicated their play *Beau Austin* to Meredith 'with Admiration and Respect' in 1884.
2. In the autumn and winter of 1878 Henley and Stevenson evolved the melodrama of a master carpenter and deacon of the wrights who leads a double life; *Deacon Brodie* was privately printed in 1880 in an early draft, and first staged at Bradford on 21 December 1882.
3. On 1 May HJ had written to WJ of his 'most earnest & definite intention 'to commence at playwrighting as soon as I can', claiming that 'I have thoroughly mastered Dumas, Augier & Sardou' (CWJ I, 301). Alexandre Dumas (*fils*) (1824–95) was natural son of the author of *The Three Musketeers*; *Le Demi-Monde* (1855) and *Le Fils naturel* (1858) were among his early successes. Émile Augier (1820–89) was famous for *L'Aventurière* (1848), the first play HJ saw at the Théâtre Français, and *Les Lionnes pauvres* (1858), a study of adultery. Victorien Sardou (1831–1908), whose photograph Perry had sent HJ in 1867, was a highly successful theatrical craftsman; HJ lent Henley his *La Haine* (1875). In a further letter, dated only 'Friday', HJ responds to Henley's responses: 'I'm sorry you dislike Dumas fils so much – or rather so exclusively. In one way – as a "moralist" – he is detestable & a childish charlatan: but as a dramatist, I think he understands the business like none of the others. Sardou is very clever, certainly; but he seems to me only a more modern Scribe – dealing mainly in *ficelles* & machinery, &, in sentiment, very arid & vulgar. But he is phenomenally skilful & this *Haine* is very powerful.' (Unpublished Morgan MS (MA 1617. 2.)) Henley wrote on Dumas *fils* in the *Saturday Review*, comparing him with Scribe and mentioning *Les Lionnes pauvres* and *La Haine*.

I hope you are finding work to your need, & contentment, & have no particularly actual grievance against fate.

Faithfully yours
H. James jr

3 Bolton St.
Sunday.

43. To Elizabeth Boott
30 October [1878]

Houghton MS   Published HJL II, 189—91

HJ was staying with a friend of Lord Houghton's and Fanny Kemble's, the eccentric widow Mrs Richard Greville (Sabine Matilda Thellusson), an adorer of Tennyson, whom she took him to see at Aldworth. In his unfinished memoir The Middle Years, *where he reverses the order of the Tennyson and George Eliot visits, he writes of the 'innocent fatuity' of 'this large, elegant, extremely near-sighted and extremely demonstrative lady, whose genius was all for friendship, admiration, declamation and expenditure' (A, 579).*

Telegrams and Parcels: Milford Station, Surrey.
THE COTTAGE, MILFORD, GODALMING
Oct 30*th*

Dear Lizzie —

I haven't your last letter here, & I must answer it from memory — which will be easy to do however, because I remember its pleasant purport very vividly. Also that of your father's, which came with it, & for which I beg you to thank him very tenderly. I must entreat you both again to consider this as a kind of double effusion, addressed to you equally, & to try and stretch it out into something bigger & better than it is. I have just now so much writing on hand that if I can hit two birds with one stone I feel a kind of economical glee.

You are a marvellous critic, dear Lizzie, & in your observations on the *Europeans* you showed the highest discrimination. 1/ Yes, Mr. Wentworth *was* a reminiscence of Mr. Frank Loring, whose frosty personality I had always in my mind in dealing with this figure.[1] 2*d* The off-hand marrying in the end was

1. *Not*, which has been often said, the Boston publisher (Aaron K. Loring), who in 1880 pirated *A Bundle of Letters*, which HJ had published in his friend Theodore Child's *Parisian*. Dr Francis Boott Loring was the son of Judge Edward G. Loring, and attended to Marian (Clover) Hooper Adams.

commandé – likewise the length of the tale. I *do* incline to melancholy endings – but it had been a part of the bargain with Howells that *this* termination should be cheerful and that there should be distinct matrimony. So I did it off mechanically in the closing paragraphs. I was not at all weary of the tale at the end, but I had agreed to write it in *100 Atlantic* pages, & its abrupt ending came from outward pressure – not from internal failing. 3*d* You are quite right to hate Gertrude, whom I also personally dislike!

Your sympathetic mind, & your father's, will be gratified to learn that the book is succeeding here quite brilliantly & in a manner to be very propitious to whatever I may do hereafter.

I am paying a short visit to an amiable friend in Surrey – a lovely little place, an hour & ¼ from London. She is a clever widow, (don't tell the Realist!) – Mrs. Greville by name, whom you may have heard me mention.[2] She is not young, & she is ugly; but she has a touch of genius – a charming house – and a delightful mother, who lives with her. Also a very nice married sister, who is here on a visit. I am the only man in this trio of *devoted* gentlewomen; so you see I do well to stop in England! To day my hostess drove me 7 miles through a lovely country to lunch with Tennyson who is an intimate friend of hers (to the point of her *kissing* him somewhere – quite *en famille* – every ¼ of an hour) & who has in this part of the country an adorable estate where he spends 3 or 4 months of the year, alternating with his house in the Isle of Wight. He read out "Locksley Hall" to me, in a kind of solemn, sonorous chant, & I thought the performance, & the occasion sufficently impressive.[3] Tomorrow I go to lunch with George Eliot, who also lives near.[4] So you see I am in good company.

I suppose this will find you in Rome, where I hope your installation will be comfortable & your winter brilliant. I won't harrow you up by saying that

2. 'The Realist', who becomes a figure of frequent reference between HJ and Lizzie Boott, is unidentified, but Lyndall Gordon has suggested she may be Mrs Philip Livingstone Van Rensselaer, an eager American expatriate whom HJ had known in Rome and would see in London.

3. In *The Middle Years* HJ recalled himself as listening 'dissentingly' to the reading, sighing in secret, 'Oh dear, oh dear,' and judging Tennyson 'wasn't Tennysonian'. At luncheon Tennyson had startled HJ by discussing the Marquis de Sade, but because 'neither knowing nor communicating knowledge', he shocked no one at the table.

4. The visit to George Eliot and George Henry Lewes at their Witley villa was notoriously ill-omened and awkward. Mrs Greville importunately pressed on their hosts a 'pair of blue-bound volumes' (*The Europeans*), only for Lewes to thrust them back at the departing HJ, unaware that he was their author: 'Ah those books – take them away, please, away, away!' In his recollection of the visit HJ does not seem to realize that Lewes, who died on 30 November, was seriously ill at the time (Lewes's diary: 'Can't read for more than an hour' (Rosemary Ashton, *G. H. Lewes: A Life* (1991), 276)).

you will miss Miss B.; nor will you need that I should.[5] But I earnestly hope you will find a little civilized society, or some single Christian comrade. I have been seeing Mrs. Mason lately in London, where she still is, in very good spirits about her daughter's marriage. Young Balfour has been much with them & seems a decent, reasonable youth. But Mrs. M. is to me now less interesting than she has ever been, since she has become a sort of appendage to a rather ordinary English family & a devotee of a commonplace son in law! She is charmed with the Balfour people, who belong altogether to the class of "swells," & is going back to Scotland to stay many more weeks with them. She hopes this winter to get to Rome, before they go home in the spring for the marriage. Then the young people are to come out here again, & live in Liverpool, where Balfour (who is a younger son) is in business. Mrs. M. expects to live "near" them; but I don't know how she will manage it.[6] International marriages have certainly their uncomfortable side! I have news from home both bad & good. Bad in that my father has lost a great deal of money: good in that Alice, thank heaven, is just lately a great deal better. This good more than balances the evil. But I am afraid that her health will remain for a long time delicate & precarious, & that they have a pretty sad, sober winter before them.

Thank your father for all his good literary advice – it falls in quite with a programme of my own, which will, I suppose, be more or less executed. I sent him (to 44) Swinburne's last volume, which I hope has reached him safely & which I beg him to receive as a small token of my sentiments.[7] (It contains by the way, with a great deal of unpleasant rubbish, a large number of magnificent passages & stanzas.[)] I hope the verses your father mentioned will, as a whole, prove suitable for his musical purpose. I also sent him an *Atlantic* & a Harper.

I trust dear Lizzie that you will find in your Roman situation, this year, the elements of happiness. You have them always, in your virtues & talents – your sweetness & light. Remember that one of the first elements in my happiness is hearing from you. My blessing to your father to whom I before long will write. Ever yours

H.J. jr

---

5. Alice Bartlett married a Texan called Warren. In February 1905 HJ nearly visited her in Aiken, South Carolina, on his way to Florida.
6. Alice Mason's daughter Isabella Weyman Hooper (from her first marriage to Marian Adams's cousin, William Sturgis Hooper (1833–63)), married Edward Balfour of Balbirnie in October 1879.
7. The second series of *Poems and Ballads* (1878) by Algernon Charles Swinburne (1837–1909) was more subdued than the first series in 1866, which HJ seems to have found disagreeable and which reflected Swinburne's repudiation of Christianity and interest in the Marquis de Sade.

44. To Julian Hawthorne
15 January 1879

Bancroft TC   Published HJJH2, 461–5

John Morley of Macmillan, mastermind of the 'English Men of Letters' series, who had met HJ at Lord Houghton's, wrote to him on 9 October 1878 proposing 'a short book on Washington Irving, or on Hawthorne' (Unpublished Houghton MS, bMS Am 1094 (362)).

Julian Hawthorne (1846–1934), son of Nathaniel and schoolmate of Wilky and Bob James, was himself a minor novelist. He spent many years in England, where he reviewed for the Spectator, *and saw HJ at the houses of Lord Houghton, the Smalleys, and others. On 13–14 January 1878 HJ had told his mother of hearing that 'poor Julian Hawthorne is . . . in great destitution & distress' and wondered greatly 'that he doesn't go home' (Unpublished Houghton MS, bMS Am 1094 (1860)). Julian Hawthorne's later life was unhappy: in 1913 he was sent to Atlanta Penitentiary for his involvement in a Canadian mining-stock fraud.*

> 3 Bolton Street, Piccadilly.
> Jan. 15th, 1879

My dear Mr Hawthorne:

I must thank you without delay for your very liberal response to my appeal, and your kind allusions to hospitality. In expressing a disposition to go to Hastings, I was far from wishing to give you any trouble or responsibility, and I beg you to banish all such ideas. I should betake myself to the inn, and we shall engage in a conversational walk. As regards this, however, there is no hurry. I am not obliged to get at work upon the little book for a month or two – and I had vastly better wait to see you, until that event, which you mention as impending, in your own family, has been accomplished. I beg leave to present Mrs Hawthorne my best wishes.[1] If you will drop me a line, at your convenience, after this, I will specify a day for presenting myself.

I am well aware that it will not be an easy matter to give an account of your father's life and genius save on a very modest scale. I have undertaken the task reluctantly, and chiefly for three reasons: – I. The Editor desired greatly it should be done, and was evidently determined that it should be by some one.

1. On 22 January HJ wrote to Julian Hawthorne that 'I am very glad to hear of your little girl having come happily into the world' (Unpublished Virginia MS, 6251-a #558). It was not till 26–8 February that HJ managed to spend his thirty-six hours in Hastings.

II. – It seemed to me that, this being the case, it should, if possible, be done by an American. III. – I could think (in all modesty) of no American who didn't seem likely to do it worse than I. – For, with 1000 thanks for your compliment to my own critical powers, I must say that I don't think we *are* a race of accomplished critics.[2] – I feel as if, also, I ought to notify you that I don't find the circumambient people a "detestable" one. On the contrary! I could never bring myself to live, regularly, among a people I should distinctly dislike, – it would be too gross a wrong both to myself and to them. But we will talk of that too. With all good wishes, very truly yours

H. James, Jr.

I shall send you herewith a copy of the American edition of "The Europeans": it being a pity you should remain longer in ignorance of so sublime a work.[3]

45. To William Ernest Henley
5 February [1879]

Morgan MS   Unpublished

3, BOLTON STREET, PICCADILLY. W.

My dear Mr. Henley –

I am very glad to get news of you again. I had been wondering what turn yr. affairs were taking. You will say, I suppose, that the "turn" is wanting – they are too damnably rectilinear. I hope your play will indeed make a deflection.

I will send you my book with pleasure; but I am afraid you will be disappointed at finding that the "other stories" are simply the "Internat. Episode," & one even shorter one. But such as it is you are very welcome to it.[1]

2. In the event Julian Hawthorne approved of HJ's *Hawthorne*: 'It is an honest and painful piece of work, and will endure' (*Memoirs of Julian Hawthorne*, 127). John Morley wrote to HJ on 13 October 1879: 'I am delighted with your work. It will certainly be one of the most attractive of the whole Series. In truth, it interests me more than most of the illustrious subject's own work.' (Unpublished Houghton MS, bMS Am 1094 (363).)
3. Julian Hawthorne received *The Europeans* on 17 January and three days later called it 'entertaining'.
1. On 15 February 1879, Macmillan brought out in two volumes *Daisy Miller: A Study; An International Episode; Four Meetings*. On 9 April HJ acknowledged Henley's praise: 'I am glad you liked my little story that is no story (it is more impudent, even, in this respect than my wont)' (Unpublished Morgan MS (MA 1617.4)).

Yes, I saw Edinburgh in September last – saw it & fell in love with it. What a picturesqueness – it is quite operatic.[2] Zola's play is said to have been tidied up into insipidity. Have you read his volume of *Théâtre?* It is very bad, with the most fatuous prefaces; but if you haven't & will say so, I will send it you.[3]

I never read a word of Sacher-Masoch. I read very little fiction & I had been warned off from him. I never read a story unless it comes very highly recommended; but if you recommend S.-M., I will try him.[4] Yes the review in the N.A.R. was stupid.[5] The human mind, generally speaking, is dull.

Yours very truly

H. James jr

Feb. 5th

46. To Jane Dalzell Finlay (Mrs Frank Harrison) Hill
21 March [1879]

Princeton MS   Published HJL II, 219–23; SL2, 159–62; SL1, 103–8

In January 1877, shortly after settling in London, HJ wrote to his brother William of a dinner at which 'I took in a very nice, ugly woman, Mrs. Hill, wife of the Daily News' *(HJL II, 89). Mrs Hill reviewed the* Daisy Miller *volumes in her husband's pages, and took exception to 'An International Episode', in which a Boston girl, Bessie Alden, finally refuses the English Lord Lambeth, after his relatives have rudely tried to discourage her. Mrs Hill declared: 'We feel bound to protest against the manners of Lord Lambeth and Mr. Percy Beaumont, in "An International Episode," being received as typical of the manners of English*

2. Henley had spent much time in hospital in Edinburgh. HJ's 'In Scotland' was in the *Nation* (10 and 24 October 1878).

3. An adaptation of Zola's novel *L'Assommoir* by Busnach and Gastineau opened at the Ambigu in Paris on 18 January 1879. Zola himself wrote to Flaubert, 'Entre nous, la pièce ne vaut pas grand'chose . . . Le roman a été massacré' ('Between ourselves, the play is almost worthless . . . The novel has been done to death'). *The Era* on 26 January reported that the adaptation 'toned down very considerably the crude language of the novel, and the situations have also undergone considerable change'. HJ lent Henley the volume of *Théâtre* (which had come out in September 1878, including *Le Bouton de Rose* and *Thérèse Raquin*) and did not want it back.

4. Leopold von Sacher-Masoch (1836–95), German author of *Venus im Pelz* (*Venus in Furs*), etc. On 9 April HJ told Henley, whose anti-puritanical views led him into sexually controversial areas, 'No, I haven't touched Sacher-Masoch.'

5. Probably that of *The Europeans* and *Daisy Miller* by Richard Grant White (1821–85), founder-editor of *Yankee Doodle* in 1846, in the *North American Review*, which charges HJ with failing fully to imagine his characters – 'this lack of individuality and vital force in their personages is the great defect of all Mr. James's novels' (January 1879).

gentlemen.' When on 18 January 1879 the story had just first appeared in Leslie
Stephen's Cornhill Magazine *(December–January), HJ wrote to his mother of*
easily bruised British sensitivities: 'I shall keep off dangerous ground in future. It
is an entirely new sensation for them (the people here) to be (at all delicately)
ironized or satirized, from the American point of view, and they don't at all relish
it' (HJL II, 213).

March 21st
3, BOLTON STREET, PICCADILLY. W.

My dear Mrs. Hill –

I must thank you without delay for the little notice of *Daisy Miller* & the
"3 Meetings," in this morning's *D.N.*, in which you say so many kind things
so gracefully.[1] You possess in great perfection that amiable art. But, shall I
confess it? (you will perhaps guess it,) my eagerness to thank you for your
civilities to two of my tales, is slightly increased by my impatience to deprecate
your strictures with regard to the third. I am distressed by the evident disfavour
with which you view the "Internat. Episode;" & meditating on the matter as
humbly as I can, I really think you have been unjust to it. No, my dear Mrs.
Hill, *bien non*, my 2 young Englishmen are not represented as "Arries"; it was
perhaps the fond weakness of a creator, but I even took to myself some credit
for the portrait of Ld. Lambeth, who was intended to be the image of a loveable,
sympathetic, excellent-natured young personage, full of good feelings & of all
possible delicacies of conduct.[2] That he says "I say" rather too many times is
very probable (I thought so, quite, myself, in reading over the thing as a book:)
but that strikes me as a rather venial flaw. I differ from you in thinking that
he would, in fact, have been likely to say it with considerable frequency. I
used the words because I remembered that when I was fresh to England &
first began to "go out," I was struck with the way in which they flourished
among the younger generation, especially when the younger generation was

1. As Leon Edel points out, 'Three Meetings' is the title of a Turgenev story, HJ's being 'Four
Meetings'.
2. HJ is retorting to this passage in the review: 'There are undoubtedly, in England, and out
of it, plenty of 'Arries, 'Arries in all grades of society, 'Arries even going about with the dread
title "lord." Had Mr. James chosen to draw for our amusement an 'Arry, he would have done
it with his wonted humour and truth, and greatly amused we should have been. But Lord
Lambeth and Percy Beaumont are not 'Arries. They are very worthy, stupid, honest gentlemen,
and acquit themselves consistently as such in all they do. Why then should they be represented
as habitually talking like arrant 'Arries? Men who have been to a public school and college do
not preface all their remarks with "Oh, I say!" That is not the slang of the stable or the club.
That is the slang of the street . . .'

of the idle & opulent & pleasure-loving type. Depend upon it, it is not only "Arry" who says "I say." There are gentlemen & gentlemen – those who are constantly particular about what they say, & those who go in greatly for amusement & who say anything, almost, that comes into their heads. It has always seemed to me that in this latter racketing, pleasure-loving "Golden Youth" section of English society, the very atmosphere was impregnated with slang. A year ago I went for six months to the St. James's Club, where (to my small contentment, personally,) the golden youth of every description, used largely to congregate, & during this period, being the rapacious & shameless observer that you know, I really made studies in London colloquialisms. I certainly heard more "I says," than I heard ever done before; & I suppose that 19 out of 20 of the young men in the place had been to a public school. However, this detail is not of much importance; what I meant to indicate is the (I think) incontestable fact that certain people in English society talk in a very off-hand, informal, irregular manner, & use a great many roughnesses & crudities. It didn't seem to me that one was bound to handle their idiosyncrasies of speech so very tenderly as to weigh one idiom very long against another. In a word the Lord Lambeths of the English world are, I think, distinctly liable, in the turn of their phrases, just as they are in the gratification of their tastes – or of some of them – to strike quiet conservative people like your humble servant as vulgar. I meant to do no more than just rapidly indicate this liability – I meant it to be by no means the last impression that he would leave. It doesn't in the least seem to have been so, with most people, & if it didn't sound fatuous I should say that I had been congratulated by several people whom I supposed to be of an observing turn upon the verisimilitude of his conversation.

If it didn't seem fatuous, too, or unmannerly, to inflict upon you so very bulky a bundle of exposition as this letter has grown into, I should go on to say that I don't think you have been liberal to the poor little women-folk of my narrative.[3] (That liberal, by the way, is but a conciliatory substitute for some more rigid epithet – say *fair*, or *just*.) I want at any rate to remonstrate with you for your apparent assumption that in the two English ladies, I meant to make a resumé of my view of English manners. My dear Mrs. Hill – the idea is fantastic! The two ladies are a picture of a special case, & they are certainly not an over-charged one. They were very determined their manners should not be nice; it would have quite defeated the point they wished to make,

---

3. Mrs Hill continues, provocatively: 'nor are the manners of his English fine ladies pretty. Perhaps he does not consider that English manners are pretty, and we have no doubt he has had ample means of judging.'

which was that it didn't at all suit them that a little unknown American girl should marry their coveted young kinsman. Such a consummation certainly does not suit English duchesses & countesses in general – it would be quite legitimate to draw from the story an induction as to my conviction on that point. The story was among other things an attempt at a sketch of this state of mind, &, given what I wished to represent, I thought the touches by which the attitude of the duchess & her daughter is set forth, were rather light and discreet than otherwise. A man in my position, and writing the sort of things I do, feels the need of protesting against the extension of his idea in which, in many cases, many readers are certain to indulge. One may make figures & figures without intending generalizations – generalizations of which I have a horror. I make a couple of English ladies doing a disagreeable thing – *cela s'est vu*; excuse me! – & forthwith I find myself responsible for a representation of English manners! Nothing is my *last word* about anything – I am interminably supersubtle & analytic – & with the blessing of heaven, I shall live to make all sorts of representations of all sorts of things. It will take a much cleverer person than myself to discover my last impression – among all these things – of anything. And then, in such a matter, the bother of being an American! Trollope, Thackeray, Dickens, even with their big authoritative talents, were free to draw all sorts of unflattering English pictures, by the thousand. But if I make a single one, I am forthwith in danger of being confronted with a criminal conclusion – & sinister rumours reach me as to what I think of English society. I think more things than I can undertake to tell in 40 pages of the Cornhill. Perhaps some day I shall take more pages, & attempt to tell some of these things; in that case, I hope, there will be a little, of every sort, for every one! Meanwhile I shall draw plenty of pictures of disagreeable Americans, as I have done already, & the friendly Briton will see no harm in that! – it will seem to him a part of the natural fitness!

Since I am in for it – with this hideously egotistic document – I do just want to add that I am sorry you didn't find a little word of appreciation for the 2 other women's figures in the *I.E.*, which I really think a success. (You will smile at the artless crudity of my vanity!) The thing was the study – a very sincere, careful, intendedly minute one – of the state of mind of a couple of American women pressed upon by English circumstances – & I had a faith that the picture would seem life-like & comprehensible. In the case of the heroine I had a fancy it would even seem charming. In that of the elder sister, no, I hadn't such a faith; she is too garrulous, &, on the whole, too silly; – it is for a silly woman that she is offered. But I shld. have said it was obvious that her portrait is purely objective – she is not in the least intended to throw light upon the objects she criticises (English life & manners &c;) she is intended to throw light on the American mind alone, & its way of taking things. When I attempt to deal with English manners I shall approach them through a very different portal than that of Mrs. Westgate's intelligence! I was at particular pains to mark the limitations of this organ – by some of the speeches I have put into her mouth – such as the grotesque story about the Duke who cuts the Butterworths. In a word she is, throughout, an ironical creation!

Forgive this inordinate & abominable scrawl – I certainly didn't mean to reward you for your friendly zeal in reading so many of my volumes by despatching you another in the innocent guise of a note. But your own frankness has made me expansive – & there goes with this only a grain of protest to a hundredweight of gratitude. Believe me, dear Mrs. Hill, very faithfully yours

H. James jr

47. To William James
15 June [1879]

Houghton MS   Published CWJ I, 312–17

HJ was finishing his novel Confidence, *of which he had by mid May sent half to Scribner's Magazine.*

June 15*th*
3, BOLTON STREET, PICCADILLY. W.

Dear William –

I have been balancing for some moments between addressing this letter to our common (or rather, uncommon) mother, or to you; I have decided for you on the general ground of having long intended & desired to write to you, – as well as the special one of having received a letter from you (accompanying one from your Alice) some fortnight ago. But please give mother very tenderly to understand that I adore her none the less, & that I have before me now two good letters from her – one received some ten days since, & the other last night; the latter enclosing a most charming letter from Bob, & also an extract from the Springfield Republican which in its crude & brutal vulgarity strikes me as anything but charming.[1] The American newspaper tone strikes one over here, where certain reticences & ménagements, a certain varnish of good

1. This may refer to the review of *Daisy Miller; An International Episode; Four Meetings* in the issue of 31 December 1878.

manners & respectful way of saying things, still hold their own, as of too glaring, too scorching, an indecency. But never mind that.

I wrote to Alice just a week ago – much more briefly than I could have desired, but I hope my letter will have reached her safely, as it contained a little document which constituted its only value.[2] I gather from father's *p.s.* to mother's letter of last night that your wife is so well on the way to her normal condition again that you have no longer any cause for anxiety.[3] I delight in the image, indistinctly as I yet perceive it, of your infantine Henry & cordially hope he will be a fount of comfort & entertainment to you. He will be for many a day the flower of Quincy St. & I hope he will bloom with dazzling brilliancy. I can fancy the interest you will take (as a psychologist) in watching his growth, & can trust you to give him a superior education.

Let me say before I go any further that I have *not* yet heard definitely from Knowles about your MS.[4] – He told me the other day that he was *greatly* crowded with philosophic & psychologic papers (I don't know whose) but that he shld. (though he thought on this ground the presumption was against yours) be sorry to decide not to take it till he had looked at it more closely. He is keeping it for this purpose, but I hope soon to hear from him. If he doesn't take it I have hopes of being able to get it printed somewhere – I will try everything I can.

Mother has lately given me a good deal of information about you – e.g. with regard to your plan of building a house upon father's "grounds." It seems a bright particular idea, & I deeply regret that delays & difficulties interpose themselves. It is an odious thought that you should have so small an income, & I am very sorry to hear that the inconsiderate Bowen shows the reverse of a tendency to resign.[5] But patience will see any game out, & yours I trust will brighten materially before your supply of this commodity is exhausted. A curse indeed must your deficient eye-sight be! – I wonder greatly at the work you manage to do.

Bob's letter, enclosed by mother, was very delightful, & has helped to dispel the impression of the rather dark account of him & of his possible future contained in your letter. It is strange that with his intelligence & ability – as one seems to perceive it in his letters – he shouldn't arrive at more successful

2. This letter is not known to survive.
3. WJ and Alice Howe (Gibbens) James (hereafter AHJ) had a first child, a further Henry James, on 18 May 1879.
4. Sir James Thomas Knowles (1831–1908), architect, in 1877 founder and editor of the *Nineteenth Century*, friend of Gladstone and Tennyson. CWJ suggests the 'MS' is WJ's 'Rationality, Activity, and Faith', published in the *Princeton Review* in July 1882.
5. Francis Bowen (1811–90), a Harvard philosopher critical of WJ.

occupations. I am very sorry for him, & I wish I were nearer to him & able to see him sometimes & perhaps help him along a little. His account of Wilkie's manière d'être is quite to the life & is on the whole favorable as regards the amenity of existence for poor W. But into what a queer social *milieu* he must have planted himself. Some months ago he sent me a friend of his from Milwaukee, with a letter of introduction, describing him as his most beloved intimate & requesting me to make him *mine*! The friend was a French-teacher – an old Frenchman who appeared to have been in Milwaukee for many years & to have quite unlearned his native tongue, which he pronounced & spoke in the most barbaric & incomprehensible fashion. He seemed very stupid & common & had nothing at all to say (even about Wilkie) but that he desired I should try to find him *pupils* for the few weeks that he was to remain in London – or failing this, that I should do the same in Edinburgh, whither, I believe, he afterwards betook himself. He was in every way a most curious apparition – (he appeared to speak no English, & his French was atrocious –) & not an encouraging specimen of the social resources of Milwaukee. Wilkie wrote – "Show him London, & above all show him yourself!" I was as tender as possible with him, but I was not sorry when he vanished. (N.B. Never repeat this to Wilky – who had evidently been very kind & humane to the poor old man.)

I feel at moments as if I could write you 50 pages of general & particular reflections upon my own manner of life, occupations, observations, impressions &c – but when it comes to the point, in giving any account of London days & London doings, one hardly knows where to begin. I suppose this is a proof that such days are full, such doings numerous, & that if one could, by a strong effort detach one's self from them & look at them as objectively, as a person living quite out of it & far away from it, (like yourself) would do – there would be many more things worth dwelling upon than one falls here into the way of seeing. To dwell on *nothing*, indeed, comes to be here one's desire as well as one's habit – & half the facts of London life are tolerable only because they exist to you just for the moment of your personal contact with them. Heaven have mercy on you if you were obliged to drag them about in memory or in esteem! I am sinking also rapidly into that condition of accepted & accepting Londonism when impressions lose their sharpness & the idiosyncrasies of the place cease to be salient. To see them, to feel them, I have to lash my flanks & assume a point of view. The confession is doubtless a low one, but I have certainly become a hopeless, helpless, shameless (and you will add, a *bloated*,) cockney. No, I am not bloated – morally; I am philosophic to lean-ness – to stringiness. Physically, it's another affair, & I am bloated *tant que vous voudrez*. I am as broad as I am long, as fat as a butter-tub & as red as a British materfamilias. On the other hand, as a compensation, I am excellently well! I am working along very quietly & steadily, & consider no reasonable share of fame & no decent literary competence out of my reach. Apropos of such matters, mother expresses in her last night's letter the hope that I have derived much gold from the large sale (upwards of 20 000 copies) of my two little Harper stories. I am sorry to say I have done nothing of the sort. Having in advance no prevision of their success I made a very poor bargain. The *Episode* I sold outright (copyright & all!) for a very moderate sum of ready money – so I have had no percentage at all on its sale! For Daisy Miller I have rec'd. simply the usual 10% – which, as it sells for twenty cents, brings me but 2 cents a copy. This has a beggarly sound, but the Harpers sent me the other day a cheque for 200 $. This represents but meanly so great a vogue – but you may be sure that I shall clinch the Harpers in future; as having now taught them my value I shall be able to do. A man's 1st successes are those, always, by which he makes least. I am not a grasping business-man – on the contrary, and I sometimes – or rather, often – strike myself as gaining wofully less money than fame. My reputation in England seems (considering what it is based on) ludicrously larger than any cash payments that I have yet received for it. The Macmillans are everything that's friendly – caressing – old Macmillan physically *hugs* me; but the delicious ring of the sovereign is conspicuous in our intercourse by its absence. However, I am sure of the future – that is the great thing – & it is something to behave like a gentleman even when other people don't. I shall have made by the end of this year very much more money than I have ever made before; & next year I shall make as much as that again. As for the years after that, – nous verrons bien. The other night, at a "literary gathering," the excellent Cotter Morison came at the "urgent request" of *celui-ci* to introduce me to Edmond About, who is here in a sort of 2d rate "International Literary Congress" which appears to have made a foolish *fiasco*.[6] About seized me by both hands & told me that what he wished of me (beyond the pleasure of making my acquaintance) was that I should promise to give him a translation of my next novel for the feuilleton of his paper, the XIX*e* Siècle. "Voyons, cher Monsieur James, je tiens à cela très-sérieusement – je tiens à ce [que] vous me donniez la parole. Mettez la main sur un traducteur qui vous satisfasse – envoyez-moi le manuscrit – je vous donne ma parole qu'il

6. James Cotter Morison (1832–88) was the positivist author of *Life and Times of St Bernard, Abbot of Clairvaux* (1863), biographies of Gibbon and Macaulay, and *The Service of Man: An Essay towards the Religion of the Future* (1887). Edmond François Valentin About (1828–85), Parisian novelist and editor of *Le XIXᵉ Siècle*, whose photograph Perry had sent to HJ in 1867, presided at the second session of the Congrès Littéraire International in London from 9 June 1879.

n'attendra pas. Je sais que vous êtes très-puissant, très-original, que vous êtes en train de vous poser ici comme personne; etc., etc." [TRANSLATION: 'You see, my dear Mr James, I hold to this very seriously – I hold to your giving me your word on it. Lay your hand on a translator you like – send me the manuscript – I give you my word it will not be kept waiting. I know you are highly vigorous and original, that you are in the process of establishing yourself here like nobody else; etc., etc.'] I gave him my promise, & I shall probably send him "Confidence;"[7] but what strikes me in everything of this kind is the absurd, the grotesque, facility of success. What have I done, juste ciel? It humiliates me to the earth, & I can only right myself by thinking of all the excellent things I mean to do in the future.

The other night John Fiske rose, moonlike, above my horizon – apparently very well & happy, & I immediately invited him to dine with me to meet Turgenieff next week – the latter coming over by invitation to receive the D.C.L. degree at Oxford – a very pretty attention to pay him – (to which I imagine James Bryce chiefly put them up.)[8] He has promised solemnly (by letter from Paris) to dine with me on the 20*th*; & it is quite on the cards that he shld. play me false; but I trust he wont. I wish you were here to share & adorn the feast – Fiske on his return will tell you about it.

Henry Adams & his wife arrived a few days since & are staying at the Milnes Gaskells.[9] I have seen them but once or twice & find them rather compressed & depressed by being kept from getting into quarters of their own. Gaskell has taken a great house in London on purpose to entertain them, & this seems to weigh upon their spirits. Henry A. can never be in the nature of things a very gracious or sympathetic companion, & Mrs. A. strikes me as toned down & bedimmed from her ancient brilliancy; but they are both very pleasant, & doubtless when they get into lodgings will be more animated. I have had as yet very little talk with them.

I have scrawled you a great many pages – but it seems to me I have told you none [of] the things I meant to in sitting down. But I must pause – I have already written two letters before this. I hope you will get all possible good of your vacation – that your eyes will heal – and that your bride & babe will flourish in emulation.

7. Nothing by HJ ever appeared in the magazine.
8. John Fiske (1842–1901), Harvard historian and philosopher of evolution, lived three doors from the Jameses on Quincy Street. Turgenev received his honorary degree on 18 June. James Bryce (1838–1922), British statesman and author, was ambassador to the U.S. from 1907 to 1913.
9. HJ had visited Charles Milnes Gaskell (1842–1919) and his new wife Lady Catherine (1856–1935), by whom HJ was very struck, at their country home, Wenlock Abbey, the previous July.

Every now & then (irrelevantly) I meet Mallock & have a little talk with him.[10] He has promised to come & see me; but he never does – to my regret. I think he wants to, but is defeated by a mixture of English shamefacedness & London accidents. I regret it much for I have a strong impression I should like him & we should get on. But I shall probably see more of him some time – his face expresses his intelligence. Farewell. My blessings on mother, father, sister, & – if she is there, God bless her!, as they say here, – upon the aunt. Many greetings to your Alice – I suppose you will get into the country with her and the infant. I take much interest in the latter, & if ever you shld. get tired of him, shall be very glad to adopt him. Fraternally yrs.

H. James jr

I enclose to Alice (single) a very pleasant letter from Lowell, which I beg her to keep for me.

48. To William Dean Howells
17 June [1879]

Houghton MS   Published HJL II, 243–4; LFL, 134–5

The 'aching fragment' to which HJ refers is The Portrait of a Lady.

June 17th.
3, Bolton Street, Piccadilly. W.

Dear Howells.

Many thanks for the flattering note of the fair Washingtonian. These responsive throbs & thrills are very gratifying – as you of course have known for a long time.[1]

I had been meaning to write a word of answer to your letter of the other day, which was extremely pleasant, in all ways.

10. William Hurrell Mallock (1849–1923), a High Anglican Tory from Balliol, Oxford, had made himself known in 1877 with *The New Republic: or culture, faith and philosophy in an English country house*, which satirizes Ruskin, Arnold, Pater, T. H. Huxley and others.
1. This note – presumably a response to 'Daisy Miller' or 'An International Episode' – is not known to survive. Neither is Howells's 'letter of the other day' – which may have prefigured his letter to J. R. Lowell of 22 June remarking how 'The thing went so far that society almost divided itself in Daisy Millerites and anti-Daisy Millerites', and generalizing that 'we are in a fair way to have a pretty school of really native American fiction' (SLWDH II, 230–31).

I am delighted to hear of the flourishing condition of my fame in the U.S. & feel as if it were a gt. shame that I shouldn't be there to reap a little the harvest of my glory. My fame indeed seems to do very well everywhere – the proportions it has acquired here are a constant surprise to me; it is only my fortune that leaves to be desired.

I hope very much to send you sometime in the autumn a *short* story (size of the *Pension B*;) I don't see my way just now to promising anything larger, & for such a purpose I have a very good subject – a real subject – not a mere pretext like the P.B. – *en tête*.[2] I am pledged to write a long novel as soon as possible, & am obliged to delay it only because I can't literally afford it. Working slowly & painfully as I do I need for such a purpose a longish stretch of time during which I am free to do nothing else, & such liberal periods don't present themselves – I have always to keep the pot-a-boiling. The aforesaid fame, expanding through two hemispheres, is represented by a pecuniary equivalent almost grotesquely small. Your account of the vogue of *D.M.* & the *I.E.*, for instance, embittered my spirit when I reflected that it had awakened no echo (to speak of) in my pocket. I have made 200 $ by the whole American career of D.M. & nothing at all by the Episode (beyond what was paid – a very moderate sum – for the use of it in Harper's Magazine.) The truth is I am a very bad bargainer & I was born to be victimized by the pitiless race of publishers. Excuse this sordid plaint; & don't indeed take it too hard, for after all I shall have made this year much more than I have ever made before, & shall little by little do better still.

Don't regret having declined the *Episode*: I never offered it to you. You mistake in thinking it to be the same as a certain novel about a Europeanizing heroine touching which I wrote you. That is quite another affair & is a very long story. It is the same as the novel I just now spoke of which I am waiting to write, & which, begun some time, since has remained an aching fragment.

Why don't you take measures to issue your own things here as well as at home? It would be, I shld. think, well worth your while. The other day at a brilliant dinner party a lady sitting next me began eagerly – "You who are an American, *do* you know anything about Mr. Howells? – You know him personally? Oh, tell me *everything* about him. His books have enchanted me!

2. This hope may have turned into *Washington Square*. On 3 January 1880, in a letter to Howells, HJ says, 'I blush to record that my short story has perforce stretched itself into a long one – three nos. – & I have (virtually) sold it to the persuasive *Scribner*, who, however, will probably not publish it for a year. I tried to squeeze it down for you, but it was no use. It seemed to me absurd to offer you anything in more than one instalment – when I am to give you so many instalments later in the year.' (LFL, 142.) In the event *Washington Square* went to the *Cornhill* (June–November 1880) and *Harper's New Monthly Magazine* (July–December 1880).

&c". I painted you in the tenderest tints, & I imagine there are many – or would be, if you would give them a chance – who would have the same bright yearning as my neighbor, who was not young or pretty, but who was a clever old woman of the world. What has struck me here, is the almost absurd facility of success. Here are 15 years that I have been addressing the American public, & at the end of a few months I appear to have gone as far with this one as I ever got at home.

I am very happy to hear of your teeming projects for work – the blessing of nature & the smile of circumstance rest upon them all.[3] I remember very well your children's "deserted city," with its bushy vistas & grassy cross-roads. I used very often to play there – alone! Won't you dine with me on the 20*th*, to meet Turgenieff? I wish you might, indeed.[4] He is in England for a few days, & I have asked John Fiske to meet him, who will tell you of him. A happy summer & a bushel of compliments to your house. Ever yours

H. James jr

49. To William Dean Howells
[14 or 15 July 1879]

Houghton MS   Published HJL II, 251–2; LFL, 136

HJ was building to an even higher pitch of conspicuous productivity. Confidence *appeared in* Scribner's Monthly *from August 1879 to January 1880. The next year,* Washington Square *would run simultaneously in Leslie Stephen's* Cornhill Magazine *(June–November) and* Harper's New Monthly Magazine *(July–December) – simultaneity being desirable both because of the larger income and the absence of an Anglo-American copyright agreement. And here HJ starts to solidify the arrangements for the publication of* The Portrait of a Lady, *which in fact began its long run (fourteen instalments) in* Macmillan's *in October and the* Atlantic *in November 1880.*

3. Howells was finishing his next novel, *The Undiscovered Country*, serialized in the *Atlantic* (January–July 1880) – but also made starts on several other works.
4. Howells was in the U.S. all year, but he called Turgenev 'one of the profoundest literary passions of my life' after being introduced to his works by the pioneering T. S. Perry, probably in the early 1870s. Those who actually attended HJ's dinner were Bryce, Hugh Arnold-Forster (1855–1909), author and politician, Turgenev's translator W. R. S. Ralston (1828–89), who worked in the British Museum, Cotter Morison, the banker John Cross (b. 1840, soon to marry George Eliot) and Mowbray Morris (1847–1911), editor of *Macmillan's Magazine* from 1885.

REFORM CLUB, PALL MALL. S.W.

My dear Howells. –

Your letter of June 29*th*, asking me for a novel for next year came to me three days since, & I have been thinking over your proposal. I am under certain pledges to the *Cornhill* & *Macmillan*; but having sifted them out & boiled them down, I have come to the conclusion that I may properly undertake to furnish you a glowing romance about the time you propose. That is if my conditions suit you. These bear on two or three points. For instance I have a desire that the next *long* story I write be *really* a long one – i.e. as long as the *American* at least – though very preferably told in a smaller number of longer instalments. As you speak of having *4* novels in one year I am afraid that this *won't* suit you. I think that what I should like would be 6 or 7 numbers of 25 pages apiece. I should also like to begin about the middle of the year – June or July – hardly before, & not later.

I shall also feel inspired, probably, to ask more for my tale than I have done for any of its predecessors. If I publish in *Macmillan* or the *Cornhill* I can double my profits by appearing also in *Harper*, & I shall have, to a certain extent, to remember this in arranging to appear in one periodical exclusively.[1] But I shall not, in this respect, be at all unreasonable. You had better let me know how these things suit you before you announce me: especially the matter of length. I don't feel as if it would be worth my while to pledge myself so long in advance to furnish a *short* novel – a thing like the *Europeans* or like *Confidence*, now appearing in *Scribner*. I must try and seek a larger success than I have yet obtained in doing something on a larger scale than I have yet done. I am greatly in need of it – of the larger success. Yours ever

H. James jr

1. As HJ told Macmillan on 22 July, 'the *Atlantic* has always objected to "simultaneity" with the English magazines'. However, HJ had incited Howells the novelist on 17 June to 'take measures to issue your own things here as well as at home', and Howells had written back to HJ 'to propose simultaneity with *Macmillan* or the *Cornhill* for his own forthcoming novel' (i.e. *The Undiscovered Country*). The effect for Howells the *Atlantic* editor, HJ calculates to Macmillan, is that 'I suppose he wouldn't raise his prohibition as to mine', in which case 'you would of course be welcome to begin my story at the same time he does' (CHJHM, 38). On 23 August HJ welcomed Howells's willingness to 'entertain the idea of simultaneity' (LFL, 139).

50. *To William James*
16 December [1879]

Houghton MS   Published CWJ I, 321–2

HJ crossed to Paris for three months, with Confidence *written, at the end of August, rejoining the Adamses who had since June been in London, 'very pleasant, friendly, conversational, critical, ironical' (HJL II, 246). They dined together most nights and went to the theatre three times a week. HJ finished there in September his study of Hawthorne.* Washington Square *seems to have been written mostly in Paris and finished in London by February 1880.*

WJ probably read the comparatively unsuccessful experimental novel Confidence *either in* Scribner's Monthly, *where it ran from August 1879 to January 1880, or in an advance copy of the two-volume English Chatto & Windus edition (HJ made an effort to find a more remunerative publisher than Macmillan), which was published on 10 December 1879. The next year's novel was 'big':* The Portrait of a Lady.

Dec. 16th
3, BOLTON STREET, PICCADILLY. W.

My dear William –

Only a line to acknowledge your note of Nov. 27*th* acknowledging my return of your MS., & containing strictures on *Confidence* &c.[1] The latter were I think just (as regards the lightness of the tale;) but I also think that, read as a whole, the thing will appear more grave. I have got (heaven knows!) plenty of gravity within me, & I don't know why I can't put it more into the things I write. It comes from modesty & delicacy (to drop those qualities for the moment;) or at least from the high state of development of my artistic conscience, which is so greatly attached to *form* that it shrinks from believing that it can supply it properly for *big* subjects, & yet is constantly studying the way to do so; so that at last, I am sure, it will arrive. I am determined that the novel I write this next year shall be "big."

I am sorry you "outgrow" so, & hardly know what remedy to suggest – as I can't like Joshua, bid Science to stand still.[2] But keep up your heart, & sometime you will have your year or so of leisure in Europe – which I will

1. WJ's MS was that rejected earlier in the year by Knowles of the *Nineteenth Century*, and more recently by the *Contemporary*. WJ's 'note of Nov. 27*th*' is not known to survive.
2. WJ was anxious to make contact with the pioneers in Germany of the new fusion of physiology and psychology. cf. Joshua 10: 12: 'Then spake Joshua to the Lord in the day when the Lord delivered up the Amorites before the children of Israel, and he said in the sight of

endeavour, in the future, to further. I trust your eyes continue to improve. I have just written to father – & refer you to the Quincy St. letter. I am returned as you see, from Paris, & am settled down again in this dusksome but satisfactory town. I gave up Italy, *rapport au* cold. I am full of work, projects, &c; & save for an occasional big head-ache (tea or no tea) am in very good health. I brought a dozen pr. gloves from Paris for Alice, to post here, as more safe; but shall have to send them pair by pair, till the dozen is told. Bid her receive them with my love, (I address them to you) but not acknowledge them till they have all arrived. A comfortable Xmas! Your picture of the "squab-like" babe went to mon *coeur d'oncle*!

> ever yr.
> H.J. jr

51. To John S. Barron
21 December [1879]

Virginia MS   Unpublished

To WJ on 10 November 1879 HJ had complained that 'The vulgarly-edited North American has had for the last seven months [two papers] . . . concerning which it will give me no satisfaction whatever, not even that of returning them' (CWJ I, 320). Charles Allen Thorndike Rice had 'in a mercenary manner' cashed in on the vogue of 'Daisy Miller' by printing as a signed article in April 1879 a book-notice that should have been published anonymously (HJL II, 229). Barron was one of Rice's employees.

> Dec. 21st
> 3, BOLTON STREET, PICCADILLY. W.
> J. S. Barron Esq.

Dear Sir.

I never received your note of acceptance of my article on Ste. Beuve. I sent my two articles at Mr. Rice's urgent invitation twice repeated, and the only notice of them that was taken, during a period of six months that followed, was an expression of doubt from Mr. Rice, sent in reply to an urgent inquiry of my own, that any use could be found for them. I immediately replied to

---

Israel, Sun, stand thou still upon Gibeon; and thou, Moon, in the valley of Ajalon.' The sun and moon do as commanded, and the Israelites avenge themselves on the Amorites.

this that if by the time my letter should arrive the same doubt still should exist, I would wish them sent without delay to an address which I gave. Of this no notice whatever was taken, & you now write me that you "hope to be able" to publish the Sainte-Beuve during the next few months. I greatly regret that under the circumstances you should have seen fit still to detain it, and I must repeat most emphatically my request that you send it back to me on receipt of this. I wish to withdraw it altogether from the *North American Review*, to which I must refuse myself the honour of attempting to contribute.[1] I am truly yours

H. *James jr*

52. To John S. Barron
19 January 1880

Virginia MS   Unpublished

REFORM CLUB, PALL MALL. S.W.

Dear Sir –

I rec'd. this morning your letter of Jan 5*th*. I am sorry to say I have at present no prospect of being able to contribute anything more to the N.A.R. I am engaged in work which leaves me no time for writing "articles", my day for which has, I think, pretty well passed away.[1] If I should be able to do anything, however, I will let you hear of it.

I am afraid a comparison between English & American manners would, in any case, be rather too invidious and ticklish a theme – especially while I continue to reside in England. Yours very truly

H. *James jr*

John S. Barron esq
Jan. 19*th* 1880

1. HJ's 'Sainte-Beuve' was published in the *North American Review* in January 1880. The other article in question, on the *Lettres d'Eugène Delacroix*, was withdrawn by HJ and placed in the *International Review* of April 1880.

1. With the composition in quick succession of *Confidence*, *Washington Square* and *The Portrait of a Lady*, HJ seems henceforth to have written only one or two ' "articles" ' before mid 1882. HJ did not publish in the *North American Review* again till 1899.

53. To William Dean Howells
31 January [1880]

Houghton MS   Published HJL II, 266–8; LFL, 146–8

HJ's Hawthorne *was published in England by Macmillan on 12 December 1879, and in the U.S. by Harper & Brothers on 15 January 1880. By 22 February HJ would be writing to Lizzie Boott, 'The American press, with 2 or 3 exceptions, seems furious over my poor little Hawthorne. It is a melancholy revelation of angry vanity, vulgarity & ignorance. I thought they would protest a good deal at my calling New England life unfurnished, but I didn't expect they would lose their heads and their manners at such a rate. We are surely the most-thin-skinned idiots in the world, & I blush for my compatriots.' (Unpublished Houghton MS, bMS Am 1094 (557).)*

Jan. 31st

3, Bolton Street, Piccadilly. W.

My dear Howells –

Your letter of Jan. 19th, & its inclosure (your review of my *Hawthorne*) came to me last night, & I must thank you without delay for each of them.[1]

I am very happy to hear the effects of the fire were so minimized by the moment at which it took place; & evidently, both in your letter & in your article, you had been writing in a smokeless air.[2] Your review of my book is very handsome & friendly & commands my liveliest gratitude. Of course your graceful strictures seem to yourself more valid than they do to me. The little book was a tolerably deliberate & meditated performance, & I should be prepared to do battle for most of the convictions expressed. It is quite true I use the word provincial too many times – I hated myself for't, even while I did it (just as I overdo the epithet "dusky".) But I don't at all agree with you in thinking that "if it is not provincial for an Englishman to be English, a Frenchman French &c, so it is not provincial for an American to be American."[3]

1. Howells's review was in the *Atlantic* of February 1880.
2. On 28 December 1879, the offices of Houghton, Osgood & Company in Boston, publishers of the *Atlantic*, were destroyed by fire. Neither the magazine nor any of Howells's or HJ's works were adversely affected.
3. Howells had written, 'If it is not provincial for an Englishman to be English, or a Frenchman French, then it is not so for an American to be American; and if Hawthorne was "exquisitely provincial," one had better take one's chance of universality with him than with almost any Londoner or Parisian of his time.'

So it is not provincial for a Russian, an Australian, a Portugese, a Dane, a Laplander, to savour of their respective countries: that would be where this argument would land you. I think it is extremely provincial for a Russian to be very Russian, a Portugese very Portugese &c; for the simple reason that certain national types are essentially & intrinsically provincial. I sympathize even less with your protest against the idea that it takes an old civilization to set a novelist in motion – a proposition that seems to me so true as to be a truism.[4] It is on manners, customs, usages, habits, forms, upon all these things matured & established, that a novelist lives – they are the very stuff his work is made of; & in saying that in the absence of those "dreary & worn-out paraphernalia" which I enumerate as being wanting in American society, "we have simply the whole of human life left," you beg (to my sense) the question. I should say we had just so much less of it as these same "paraphernalia" represent, & I think they represent an enormous quantity of it. I shall feel refuted only when we have produced (setting the present high company – yourself & me – for obvious reasons, apart) a gentleman who strikes me as a novelist – as belonging to the family of Balzac & Thackeray. Of course, in the absence of this godsend, it is but a harmless amusement that we should reason about it, & maintain that if right were right he should already be here. I will freely admit that such a genius will get on *only* by agreeing with your view of the case – to do something great he must feel as you feel about it. But then I doubt whether such a genius – a man of the faculty of Balzac & Thackeray – *could* agree with you! When he does I will lie flat on my stomach & do him homage – in the very centre of the contributors' club, or on the threshold of the Magazine, or in any public place you may appoint![5]

But I didn't mean to wrangle with you – I meant only to thank you & to express my sense of how happily you turn those things.

I am greatly amused at your picture of the contributing blood-hounds whom

4. Howells takes issue with HJ's 'theory, boldly propounded, that it needs a long history and "a complex social machinery to set a writer in motion" . . . After leaving out all those novelistic "properties," as sovereigns, courts, aristocracy, gentry, castles, cottages, cathedrals, [&c.] . . . by the absence of which Mr. James suggests our poverty to the English conception, we have the whole of human life remaining, and a social structure presenting the only fresh and novel opportunities left to fiction . . . No man would have known less what to do with that dreary and worn-out paraphernalia than Hawthorne.'

5. Howells himself had invented and inaugurated 'The Contributors' Club' in the *Atlantic*, with contributions remaining anonymous, beginning in January 1877. Soliciting material, he urged the existing writers: 'You can attack, defend, praise, or blame any body you like in the C.C. All we require is that you shall be lively' (SLWDH II, 141n.). HJ remarked to Perry in August 1880, 'The principles on which he edits the *Atlantic* indicate a low standard, certainly, & the vulgarity of that magazine often calls a patriotic blush to my cheek' (TSPB, 308).

you are holding in check. I wish, immensely, that you would let them fly at me – though there is no reason, certainly, that the decent public should be bespattered, periodically, with my gore.

However my tender (or rather my very tough) flesh is prescient already of the Higginsonian fangs.[6] Happy man, to be going, like that, to see your plays acted.[7] It is a sensation I am dying, (though as yet not trying,) to cultivate. What a tremendous quantity of work you must get through in these years! I am impatient for the next *Atlantic*. What is your *Cornhill* novel about?[8] I am to precede it with a poorish story in three numbers – a tale purely American, the writing of which made me feel acutely the want of the "paraphernalia."[9] I *must* add, however, (to return for a moment to this) that I applaud & esteem you highly for not feeling it; i.e. the want. You are entirely right – magnificently & heroically right – to do so, & on the day you make your readers – I mean the readers who know & appreciate the paraphernalia – do the same, you will be the American Balzac. That's a great mission – go in for it! Wherever you go, receive, & distribute among your wife & children, the blessing of yours ever –

H. James jr

54. To William Dean Howells
18 April [1880]

Houghton MS   Published HJL II, 284–6; LFL, 148–9

HJ left England in mid March in order to work on The Portrait of a Lady, *spending three or four days in Paris en route for Florence, where he arrived on 28 March. He began, as he told his father, by 'taking a holiday pure and simple' (HJL II, 277), then returned to Florence to work, seeing much of the Bootts.*

6. Thomas Wentworth Higginson (1823–1911), the Unitarian clergyman, poet and critic who was an early sponsor of Emily Dickinson's poetry, may have written the hostile review of *Hawthorne* in *Scribner's Monthly* (April 1880).
7. Howells had translated a Spanish tragedy by 'Estébanez', pseudonym of Manuel Tamayo y Baus, and it was produced by the actor-manager Lawrence Barrett as *Yorick's Love*, opening on 20 January in Boston.
8. In the *Atlantic* (January–July), Howells's *The Undiscovered Country* had just begun (without simultaneous publication in Britain). Leslie Stephen of the *Cornhill* had written to Howells in December 1879 proposing simultaneity for his next novel, *Dr Breen's Practice*, but later in 1880 he withdrew the offer because the novel would not be ready as soon as he expected.
9. *Washington Square* was in fact in six numbers.

Florence, April 18*th*

Carino Amico —

The most caressing epithets of a caressing language are not out of place in regard to the particular motive of my writing to you. My imagination seeks eagerly for anything that will ease me off a little & rob my letter of its sting. This sting resides, brutally speaking, in my earnest wish that you may find it not fatally inconvenient to begin my promised serial in *October* instead of *August*! A postponement of two whole months! – the thing will probably have to you an impudent sound. But I throw myself on your mercy & urge upon your attention that the story shall be a 100 per cent better by each day that you have to wait. My motives for this petition are twofold. In the first place I withdrew a month ago from London & its uproar, its distractions & interruptions, in order to concentrate myself upon my work. But if London is uproarious, Italy is insidious, perfidious, fertile in pretexts for one's haunting its lovely sights & scenes rather than one's writing-table; so that, in respect to my novel, it has been a month lost rather than gained. In the second place I think I wrote you before that I lately finished a serial tale for the *Cornhill*. This has proved by the editor's measurement longer than by my own, so that instead of running through *4* numbers, it will extend to *six*. As it begins in *June* this will make it terminate in *November*; & it will be agreeable to *Macmillan* that the novel for them, & you, shall not begin till the thing in the *Cornhill* is virtually leaving the scene. Behold, dear Howells, my reasons; I trust they will seem to you worthy of a compatriot & a Christian, & that the delay won't cause you any material discomfort. It will leave me a chance to get forward a good deal further than I should otherwise do, before beginning to publish. I shall assume that I have touched you by this appeal, & shall proceed in consequence; but a line in answer (to 3 Bolton St. Piccadilly,) will nevertheless be very welcome.

Come back to Italy as soon as you can; but don't come with a master-piece suspended in the air by the tenderest portions of its texture; or else forbid yourself the pleasure of paying your proper respects to this land of loveliness.

I have just come back from a ten days' run to Rome & Naples, and shall be in this place for the longer or shorter time that I remain absent from England.[1] Florence is delightful, as usual, but I am lacerated with the effort of

1. HJ had left Florence almost immediately after his arrival, spending two or three days in Rome, then gone on to Posilippo near Naples to stay with his friend from Paris in 1875, the Russian painter Paul Joukowsky (1845–1912), a new intimate of the Richard Wagners near by and future set-designer for *Parsifal*. HJ declined to meet the composer, 'as I speak no intelligible German and he speaks nothing else' (HJL II, 283). He returned to Florence via Rome, where he saw the Storys.

turning myself away from Rome, where I feared I shouldn't do much work, but which is, to Florence, as sunlight unto moonlight.

I hope that, putting aside the untoward incident embodied in this letter, everything is well with you. I read your current novel with pleasure, but I don't think the subject fruitful, & I suspect that much of the public will agree with me.[2] I make bold to say this because, as the thing will be finished by this time, it won't matter that my rude words discourage you. Also, I am in a fine position to talk about the public's agreeing with me!

But if you do, sometimes, I don't care about the others! Greet me your wife & children, & believe me your devotissimo —

H. James jr

55. To Eliza Lynn Linton
6 October [1880]

Abernethy MS   Published HJL II, 303–4; SL1, 171–2; MLL, 233–6

HJ returned in late May, earlier than he had hoped, to London, where in early June WJ spent a month with him before going on to the Continent. HJ remained in England, paying some country visits, and pushing on with The Portrait of a Lady. *For various reasons, the novel was delayed to start in* Macmillan's *in October and in the* Atlantic *of November. Also for various reasons, chief of which was the* Portrait's *being 'but half completed' (HJL II, 295), in July HJ postponed his planned return visit to the U.S. till the following year.*

The vigorous Eliza Lynn Linton (1822–98) started her career as a novelist in 1846, but is best known for offending many of her contemporaries by essays in the Saturday Review *attacking feminism and the New Woman. These were collected in England as* The Girl of the Period *(1869); HJ had reviewed the American edition/version,* Modern Women, and What Is Said of Them, *in 1868 in the* Nation *(22 October), showing sympathy for the predicament of the Girl under attack: 'The whole indictment represented by this volume seems to us perfectly irrational' (LC I, 24). Her letter to HJ apparently does not survive, but she seems to have quarrelled with a friend over the character of Daisy Miller.*

2. *The Undiscovered Country* deals seriously with spiritualism, Shakerism and scientific doubt in New England, and was indeed found puzzling though impressive by Howells's readers. In July HJ read it in book form, and commented 'that it is the least *entertaining* of your books'; though 'On the other hand the subject is a larger & heavier one than you have yet tried, & you have carried it off with great ease & the flexibility which shows how well you have learned your art' (LFL, 151, 152).

REFORM CLUB
Oct. 6th

My dear Mrs. Lynton,

I will answer you as concisely as possible – & with great pleasure – premising that I feel very guilty at having excited such ire in celestial minds & painfully responsible at the present moment.

Poor little D.M. was (as I understand her) above all things *innocent*. It was not to make a scandal – or because she took pleasure in a scandal – that she "went on" with Giovanelli. She never took the measure, really, of the Scandal she produced, & had no means of doing so: she was too ignorant, too irreflective, too little versed in the proportions of things. She intended infinitely less with G. than she appeared to intend – & he himself was quite at sea as to how far she was going. She was a flirt – a perfectly superficial and unmalicious one; and she was very fond, as she announced at the outset, of "gentlemen's society." In Giovanelli she got a gentleman who to her uncultivated perception was a very brilliant one – all to herself; and she enjoyed his society in the largest possible measure. When she found that this measure was thought too large by other people – especially by Winterbourne – she was wounded; she became conscious that she was accused of something of which her very comprehension was vague. This consciousness she endeavoured to throw off; she tried not to think of what people meant & easily succeeded in doing so; but to my perception, she never really tried to take her revenge upon public opinion – to outrage it & irritate it. In this sense I fear I must declare that she was not *defiant*, in the sense you mean. If I recollect rightly, the word "defiant" is used in the tale – but it is not intended in that large sense; it is descriptive of the state of her poor little heart which felt that a fuss was being made about her and didn't wish to hear anything more about it. She only wished to be left alone – being, herself, quite unaggressive. The keynote of her *character* is her innocence – that of her *conduct* is of course that she had a little sentiment about Winterbourne that she believed to be quite unreciprocated – conscious as she was only of his protesting attitude. But even here I didn't mean to suggest that she was playing off Giovanelli against Winterbourne – for she was too innocent even for that. She didn't try to provoke & stimulate W. by flirting overtly with G. – she never believed that Winterbourne was provokable. She would have liked him to think well of her – but had an idea from the first that he cared only for higher game; so she smothered this feeling to the best of her ability (though at the end a glimpse of it is given) & tried to help herself to do so by a good deal of lively movement with Giovanelli. The whole idea of the story is the little tragedy of a light, thin, natural, unsuspecting creature being sacrificed, as it were, to a social rumpus that went on quite over her head & to which she stood in no measurable relation. To deepen the effect I have made it go on over her mother's head as well. She never had a thought of scandalizing any body – the most she ever had was a regret for Winterbourne.

This is the only witchcraft I have used – & I must leave you to extract what satisfaction you can from it.[1]

Again, I must say, I feel "real badly," as D.M. would have said, at having supplied the occasion for a breach of cordiality. May the breach be healed herewith! –

You are detestably enviable to be at Cadenabbia. I hope you are either coming back soon or staying in Italy for the whole winter – as I expect to go thither for a long stay after the New Year. Wherever you are, believe in the very good will of yours faithfully

H. James jr.

56. To Charles Eliot Norton
13 November 1880

Houghton MS   Partly published LHJ I, 74–5

Nov. 13th 1880
3, BOLTON STREET, PICCADILLY. W.

My dear Charles.

I have waited to thank you for your beautiful volume (the handsomest yet issued, I think, from the American press,) so that I might have the satisfaction of reading it first.[1] This pleasure I have now had, & can therefore express a more deliberate gratitude. This pleasure has been great; I have enjoyed every line of the interesting story you have told so well. The labour[,] knowledge, care, that you have been able to put into it, I can of course but vaguely measure (though I have been struck by the copiousness & exactness of detail & the way all your details are verified;) but the charm of the narrative is easily appreciated, & the success with which you have given the history of each church a really dramatic interest. I am delighted that such a valuable piece of work should have been done by an American – even by such a terribly

---

1. HJ is often drawn to Othello's insistence that he won Desdemona not by magic but by his narrative art: 'This only is the witchcraft I have used' (1. iii. 168).

1. *Church-Building in the Middle Ages: Venice, Siena, Florence* (Harper & Bros., New York, 1880).

adulterated one as yourself! It makes up for the New York Herald & the "Contributors" Club in the *Atlantic*. There is some hope for us yet, & you at least can never consistently despair.

I envy you more than I can say your Italian studies & your large & intimate knowledge of the great Italian period. I try always to add a little to my own – for me it is the most valuable knowledge I can acquire; but in London there are too many distractions & abstractions (mainly of the so-called social kind) & I shall never know anything worthwhile until I succeed in making an uninterrupted stay of some length in Italy. But I don't know when that will be; for the next *long* absence I make from England must be for a very different purpose – to revisit the Western World. If your book made me homesick for Italy, what must it have made you? I believe however that there must have been many hours when in your quiet study at Shady Hill you felt yourself in Florence – & lived again there – & not in the Florence of to-day (where the illusion would perhaps after all have been less perfect) but in that of the 15*th* century. I hope you are going on – that you will relate some other chapters of the wonderful story. Be sure that when you do, I shall always be one of the most receptive of your readers.

I was extremely sorry to hear from Grace not long since (I wrote to her by the way a week ago,) that you were somewhat weak in health.[2] I hoped this had ceased to be the case (&, by hoping, had ended by believing it to be so.) I wish you could take a good holiday & spend it in these countries. I have got to feel like such an old European that I could almost pretend to help to do you the honours. I am at least now a thoroughly naturalized Londoner – a cockney "convaincu." I am attached to London in spite of the long list of reasons why I should not be; I think it on the whole the best point of view in the world. There are times when the fog, the smoke, the universal uncleanness, the combined unwieldiness & flatness of much of the social life – these & many other matters – overwhelm the spirit & fill it with a yearning for other climes; but nevertheless one reverts, one sticks, one abides, one even cherishes! Considering that I lose all patience with the English about fifteen times a day & vow that I renounce them for ever, I get on with them beautifully & love them well. Our dear Vasari, I fear, couldn't have made much of them, & they would have been improved by a slight infusion of the Florentine spirit; but for all that they are, for me, the great race – even at this hour of their possible decline.[3] Taking them altogether, they are more complete than other folk,

2. HJ wrote to Grace Norton on 7 November (the letter is in HJL II, 313–15).
3. Giorgio Vasari (1511–74), though himself a painter and architect, is best known for perhaps the most significant book in the whole history of art, *The Lives of the Most Excellent Italian Architects, Painters and Sculptors* (1550, enlarged 1568).

more largely nourished, deeper, denser, stronger. I think it takes more to make an Englishman, on the whole, than to make any one else – & I say this with a full consciousness of all that often seems to me to have been left out of their composition. But the question is interminable, & idle into the bargain.

I am passing a quiet autumn – London has not yet waked up from the stagnation that belongs to this period. The only incident of consequence that has lately occurred to me was my dining a few days since at the Guildhall, at the big scrambling banquet which the Lord Mayor gives on the 9th November to the Cabinet, foreign Ministers, &c. It was uncomfortable but amusing – you probably have done it yourself. I met Lowell there – whom I see, besides, with tolerable frequency.[4] He is just back from a visit to Scotland which he appears to have enjoyed, including a speechmaking at Edinburgh. He gets on here, I think, very smoothly & happily; for though he is critical in the gross, he is not in the detail, & takes things with a sort of boyish simplicity. He is universally liked & appreciated, his talk enjoyed &c (as well it may be after some of their own!) & his poor long-suffering wife is doing very well: I therefore hope he will be left undisturbed by Garfield, to enjoy the fruition of the long period of discomfort he has passed through.[5] It will be in the highest degree indecent to remove him – though I wish he had a pair of secretaries that ministered a little more to the idea of American brilliancy. Lowell has to do *that* quite by himself. Even if he remains here for a good while (which I trust he will – I think he is *really* quite willing) Mrs. Lowell is not destined apparently to emerge from the seclusion which after all but becomes her. But I must close, dear Charles. Do write me some time when your other labours are light.

I am to spend a day or two at Basset before long, when I shall see Lily, who I hope is happy there.[6] My love to all her brothers & sisters – especially to the sister Margaret. Believe me always faithfully yours

H. James jr

4. In the autumn of 1880 J. R. Lowell was transferred from his diplomatic posting in Madrid to become American Minister in London, his secretaries being William Jones Hoppin (b. 1820) and Ehrman Syme Nadal (1843–1922). Lowell's (second) wife Frances Dunlop Lowell, whose health was poor and who suffered intermittently from painful bouts of insanity, died early in 1885.
5. The Republican James Abram Garfield (1831–81) was elected as twentieth president of the U.S. in the election of 1880. HJ requested his portrait from home, and displayed it on his mantelshelf. Garfield's term ended with his assassination.
6. 'Lily' was Elizabeth Gaskell Norton (1866–1958), daughter of Charles Eliot Norton. At Basset she was staying, accompanied by a French governess, with Sara Sedgwick Darwin and William Darwin.

57. To William Dean Howells
5 December [1880]

Houghton MS   Published HJL II, 320—22; LFL, 156—8

The Portrait of a Lady *started its fourteen-instalment run in the* Atlantic *in*
November 1880. Howells wrote, commenting on the characters of HJ's heroine,
Isabel Archer, her friend Henrietta Stackpole, an American journalist, and the
politically advanced Lord Warburton, who proposes to Isabel early in the story.

Dec. 5th.
3, Bolton Street, Piccadilly. W.

Dear Howells.

I didn't mean to put the screw on you to the extent of *two* volumes of native
fiction, & am much obliged to you for your generosity. I shall not attempt to
read the books just now, but keep them for the larger leisure of a journey
abroad, later in the winter. Dizzy's "Endymion," which is the actuality of the
hour here, has almost fatally disgusted me with the literary form to which it
pretends to belong.[1] Can the novel be a thing of virtue, when such a contemptibly
bad novel as that is capable of being written – and read? Perhaps, however,
Aldrich and the Grandissimo will reconcile me to this branch of art.[2] I asked
you about the latter because I had observed one or two notices of him which
seemed to indicate (in superlative terms) that the G.A.N. had at last arrived;
but from the moment that public opinion had not forced him on your own
perusal, I was willing to give the G.A.N. another chance.

Your strictures on my own story seem to me well-founded (don't say that
I don't take criticism like an angel.) The girl is over-analysed, & her journalistic
friend *seems* (whether she is or not) overdrawn. But in defense of the former
fault I will say that I intended to make a young woman about whom there

1. *Endymion* was the last novel of Benjamin Disraeli (1804–81), first Earl of Beaconsfield,
statesman and man of letters, Conservative prime minister in 1868, and from 1874 to 1880.
In August 1870, reviewing his *Lothair* for the *Atlantic*, HJ had spoken of his 'deplorable
levity'.
2. Thomas Bailey Aldrich (1836–1907) published his novel *The Stillwater Tragedy* in the *Atlantic*
(April–September 1880), and Howells reviewed it in the November issue. *The Grandissimes* by
the Southern writer George Washington Cable (1844–1925) had also been much praised, and
hailed as the 'Great American Novel' ('G.A.N.'), a phrase coined in an essay of that name by
the novelist John De Forest (1826–1906) in the *Nation* (9 January 1868). HJ had mentioned
these works on 11 November when he asked Howells to 'send me once in a while some good
American book', but he never commented in print on either (LFL, 155).

should be a great deal to tell & as to whom such telling should be interesting; & also that I think she is analysed once for all in the early part of the book & doesn't turn herself inside out quite so much afterwards. (So at least it seems to me – perhaps you will not agree with me). Miss Stackpole is not I think really exaggerated – but 99 readers out of a 100 will think her so: which amounts to the same thing. She is the result of an impression made upon me by a variety of encounters & acquaintances made during the last few years; an impression which I had often said to myself could not be exaggerated. But one must have received the impression, & the home-staying American doubtless does not do so as strongly as the expatriated; it is over here that it offers itself in its utmost relief.

That you think well of Lord W. makes me regret more than I already do that he is after all but a secondary figure. I have made rather too much of his radicalism in the beginning – there is no particular use for it later.

I must have been strangely vague as to *all* the conditions of my story when I first corresponded with you about it, & I am glad to have wrung from you the confession that you expected it to be in six numbers, for this will teach me to be more explicit in future. I certainly supposed I had been so in this case – the great feature of my projected tale being that it was to be long – longer than its predecessors. Six months, for a regular novel, is a very small allowance – I mean for dealing with a long period of time & introducing a number of figures. You make your own stories fit into it, but it is only by contracting the duration of the action to a few weeks. Has not this been the case in all of them? Write one that covers a longer stretch of months or years, and I think you will see that it will immediately take more of the magazine. I believed that in this case you positively desired something voluminous & I believed equally that I had announced my voluminosity well in advance. I am afraid that it will be a characteristic of my future productions (in, I hope, a reasonable measure;) but I will be careful to put the points on my i's.

I complain of you that you will never write to me save of the weather – as if you had just been introduced to me at an evening party! That is very well: especially as you describe it beautifully – but I would rather you told me what you are doing, writing, enjoying, suffering, hearing, seeing. About all these things you are very mysterious. Your description of the impudent Cambridge winter, however, is vivid – with the earth like a stone & the sky like a feather. Here the earth is like a Persian rug – a hearth-rug, well besprinkled with soot.

I hear every now and then that you are soon coming abroad; but I sincerely hope you won't have the perversity to take just the time when I am coming home, as I hope (this time seriously,) to do next year. Your wife, I am sure, would not do this. Tell her I believe it, & remain faithfully yours

H. James jr

I think you may be sure Mrs. Orr got your book: but I will make a point of ascertaining.[3]

58. To Thomas Bailey Aldrich
14 July [1881]

Houghton MS   Unpublished

Both HJ's mother and Grace Norton seem to have written to him late in 1880 about marriage: he told the latter, 'I shall not marry, all the same . . . I am too good a bachelor to spoil' (HJL II, 323). He left London about 9 February 1881 for Italy. As he recalled in November, 'I wished to get away from the London crowd, the London hubbub, all the entanglements and interruptions of London life; and to quietly bring my novel to a close' (N, 220). Till his return on 12 July he was in Venice, with which he reported he had 'fallen deeply and desperately in love' (HJL II, 355).

On 1 March 1881, Aldrich took over the Atlantic *from Howells, who was tired of editing and had made a lucrative deal for a novel a year with the publisher J. R. Osgood, who had set up on his own. Aldrich thus inherited* The Portrait of a Lady, *which had been running serially in the magazine since November 1880 and was meant to finish in the November issue.*

3 Bolton St. Piccadilly
July 14*th*

Dear Aldrich.

I send you by this post another of those parcels which you so promptly & gracefully acknowledge. This is your *October* copy.

And I send with it a confession, a petition, an entreaty: (touching which I have just written also to H., M. & Co.)[1] I have had to ask Macmillan *for one more month* – a short instalment this time. *Macmillan* has nobly consented, &

---

3. Alexandra Sutherland Orr (1828–1903), sister of the eminent painter Sir Frederick (later Lord) Leighton (1830–96), was an intimate, and the first biographer, of Robert Browning, as well as a praiser of Howells (in an 1880 essay).

1. Houghton, Mifflin & Co., who published the book in the U.S. on 16 November 1881.

I hope you will not be less magnanimous. I have been working over the conclusion of my tale & it perforce spills over into 15 pages (or so) of the *November* Macmillan, (which makes your December.) Meanwhile, the three last numbers will *all be shorter* than their predecessors, & you will therefore grudge me less perhaps my exorbitant demands of space. I hope this won't inconvenience you quite too utterly, as they say here. The instalment I send you today is, to begin with, of but *20* pages, & the two last will be somewhat shorter. Have courage, then, & remember that you will at last get (for the present,) altogether rid of me. I have just come back from Venice, fortunately for me; as from that relaxing clime I could never have written to you so offensively.[2] Forgive me & believe me ever in haste yours

H. James jr

59. To Alice Howe Gibbens James
6 August [1881]

Houghton MS   Unpublished

HJ, who was staying with his publishers, had not yet met AHJ, his sister-in-law.

Holme Lodge, Walton-on Thames
2, ELM TREE ROAD, ST. JOHN'S WOOD.[1]
Aug. 6th.

Dear Alice.

I received about a fortnight ago a co-operative note from William & you. He had supplied the sentiments, & you the penmanship; so it seems to me that to you this effort of my own pen should be addressed. I should have answered you before, but since my return from the continent I have had an accumulation of duties of every kind which has made me postpone familiar letters. I have been occupied for instance a good deal in seeing Alice, who has been in the

2. In his 1907 Preface to *Portrait of a Lady* HJ recalled: 'I had rooms on Riva Schiavoni, at the top of a house near the passage leading off to San Zaccaria; the waterside life, the wondrous lagoon spread before me, and the ceaseless human chatter of Venice came in at my windows, to which I seem to myself to have been constantly driven, in the fruitless fidget of composition, as if to see whether . . . the ship of some right suggestion . . . mightn't come into sight' (LC II, 1070).

1. HJ has written the Walton address above the printed London address of the Macmillans.

country near London, & with whom I have, naturally had much conversation.[2] She is doing very well in spite of one or two drawbacks, & seems to be both enjoying her life here and gaining strength from it. It is of course very quiet, but she and Miss Loring do whatever they like & see a good deal of the picturesque. I am sorry she doesn't see more people; but that, for the present, seems impossible. She will at any rate, I think, go home much refreshed & encouraged. I am glad to find myself in England again, after a four months' absence, especially as we are having a remarkably beautiful summer. It is what we call in America a "real" summer – so real that the poor Britons don't know what to make of it & suffer anguish from the visibility of the sun. The heat, indeed, during much of July was intense; but now the heavens only smile, without scorching. I am spending a couple of days about 15 miles from London, in a little cottage occupied for the summer by Fred. Macmillan & his pretty little American wife, whom William encountered here. It is very rustic and bowery, very quiet and very "restful" – close to the river, near Hampton Court & c. Tell William I thank him kindly for his remarks on my novel – especially on the character of the depraved Osmond. I am afraid it won't be in my power, however, to change him much at this late day. As however he was more intended than W*m* appears to have perceived, to be disagreeable & disappointing, it may be that the later numbers of the story have already justified my first portrait of him. I think on the whole he will be pronounced good – i.e. horrid.

I hear from mother that you are enjoying life and leisure in the Adirondack, & that the infant Harry is in danger from the Cows.[3] Remember that I haven't seen him yet, & rescue him at any price: I will make it up to you. I hope your rustication is doing you all good, & that when I come home I shall find you fat and brown & lusty. I am beginning to feel the nearness of that event, & to anticipate both social & vegetable delights. The breeze from the lawn is fluttering my paper, & the big lawn-tennis net (which occupies half the small garden) is shaking amain. I have promised myself to write two other letters before lunch, so I send you all my blessing & remain ever affectionately yours

H. *James jr*

2. HJ's sister AJ (the problem of the Alices' names was never settled) had arrived in England with her friend Katharine Loring in June 1881, before HJ, who had not been notified of her coming, returned from Venice. After some travelling they left for the U.S. again on 20 September. 3. This was a cabin (called the 'Putnam Shanty') near the village of Keene Valley in New York State, where WJ and his wife AHJ had spent their honeymoon. AJ (sister) had been there in 1878, and commented 'the shanty lacks nothing in the way of discomfort' (DLAJ, 81).

60. To Thomas Bailey Aldrich
31 August [1881]

Houghton MS   Unpublished

3 Bolton St. Piccadilly.
Aug. 31*st*

My dear Aldrich.

You will be glad to get the last of me, in the final pages of my too, too solid serial, which I send you by this post. It is a *little* longer – that is this last instalment is – than I promised. But it is by several pages shorter than its predecessors. How extremely entertaining are the 2 nos. already published of Howells's new story.[1] The interview between the he-&-she-doctors admirable! Ever yours

H. James jr

61. To Houghton, Mifflin & Co.
23 November [1881]

Houghton MS   Unpublished

With The Portrait of a Lady *completed, HJ embarked for his postponed visit to America – his first for six years – on 20 October 1881. He stayed first with his parents and sister AJ in Quincy Street, Cambridge, then moved to the Brunswick Hotel in Boston, where on 25 November he opened a notebook and, reviewing the last years of ambition and fulfilment, took stock of his position. 'My choice is the old world,' he wrote, 'my choice, my need, my life.'*

In 1880 Houghton, Mifflin & Co. had formed when J. R. Osgood (1836–92) dissolved his partnership with Henry Oscar Houghton (1823–95). In the division, Houghton, Mifflin retained all Osgood's earlier titles, including eight of HJ's, among them Roderick Hudson. *The book form of HJ's grand new novel appeared from Houghton, Mifflin on 16 November, and a week later he wrote to them, in the tone of American business, as the first reviews were appearing.*

1. Howells's new novel, *Dr Breen's Practice*, was being serialized in the *Atlantic* from August.

Cambridge Nov. 23*d*.
Messrs. Houghton, Mifflin & Co.

Dear Sirs.

I had some talk yesterday with one of your gentlemen (in Park St.,) which appeared to be all that is necessary to be said just now in relation to *Roderick Hudson*. I desire that the American edition of the book should remain for the present out of print. The English edition is virtually a new book, & a very superior one; & it is only in that form that I wish it presented again to the American public.[1] As however the American public appears to be in no hurry for it (although the novel in question has had more success in England than any of my other productions,) it seems to me it had better be left to wait for it. I do not, accordingly, suggest a new issue of *Roderick Hudson* now. Let it become scarce!

There is another point of which I wish to speak.

Ten percent. royalty on the retail price of my volumes seems to me a very beggarly profit. Let me request then that it be raised then to *twenty*. My next half-yearly account in that case will present a less meagre appearance than the last that you sent me. Please let me receive your assent to this.[2] Yours very truly

H. James jr

62. To Frederick Macmillan
27 December [1881]

BL MS   Published CHJHM, 66–7

At the end of November HJ went to New York and stayed till 23 December at 115 East 25ᵗʰ Street with his old friend Edwin L. Godkin, editor of the Nation, *and his son Lawrence, before returning to Cambridge for Christmas.*

Cambridge, Mass.,
Dec. 27*th*

My dear Macmillan.

Will you kindly inquire what mistake there was regarding the sending out one of my *Portraits* according to my list? I was notified a few days since that

1. HJ had brought out *Roderick Hudson* with Macmillan – its first English appearance – in June 1879, in three volumes, with a note specifying that, 'It has now been minutely revised, and has received a large number of verbal alterations. Several passages have been rewritten.'
2. Houghton, Mifflin & Co. declined HJ's demand; and Osgood, learning of HJ's dissatisfaction with his former partners, stepped back in and became HJ's publisher again.

the copy to be addressed – "Countess of Rosebery, Mentmore, Leighton Buzzard," had not, up to Dec. 1*st*, reached the *destinataire*. But hold: I may have given another address; i.e. *Dalmeny, Edinburgh*![1] Will you at any rate please ask whether to one or other of these addresses a copy of my novel was sent? I fondly hope that the others went out in order.

I wrote to you (from here) a few days after my arrival in these climes, & though there was nothing particular in my letter to answer have had ever since a sort of yearning to hear from you. Like the German woman of letters mentioned by Heine, who always wrote with one eye fixed on her MS. & the other on some man – I too pass my life in a sort of divergent squint.[2] One of my orbs of vision rests (complacently enough) on the scenes that surround me here; the other constantly wanders away to the shores of Old England; & takes the train for Euston as soon as it arrives.

I wrote to you from Cambridge, but I have not been here ever since then. I have spent a month, most agreeably, in New York (staying, the whole time, with E. L. Godkin, a most genial host,) & came on here to pass Xmas in the bosom of my family. I have done so, very pleasantly, and tomorrow I return to N.Y. & to further adventures. My winter, thus far, has gone on very happily, though I cannot say it has been devoted to literary composition. No, I have only been seeing American life; from about 9 o'clock a.m., daily, to considerably past midnight. I have done a great deal & been charmingly treated; but I begin to long, powerfully, for a studious seclusion which I am afraid is still distant. If I can't, before long, obtain it otherwise I shall return to Europe for it. New York is a big place, & is rapidly becoming an interesting one. I am struck, throughout, with the rapid & general increase of the *agreeable* in American life, & the development of material civilization. As we are having moreover a winter at once extraordinarily mild & charmingly bright, my impressions are

1. In 1881 HJ had visited both Mentmore and Dalmeny, country homes of Archibald Philip Primrose (1847–1929), fifth Earl of Rosebery, a Liberal statesman, promoter of an idealistic view of Empire, and historian. He was prime minister in 1894–5. His wife Hannah (1851–90), was the daughter of Sir Meyer de Rothschild. (In fact *The Portrait of a Lady* was sent to Dalmeny.)

2. Heinrich Heine (1797–1856), the great German Jewish poet who moved to Paris in 1831, generalizes in his *Geständnisse* (*Confessions*) of 1854 about women – only excepting the Countess Ida von Hahn-Hahn (1805–80), a poet and novelist: 'Wenn sie schreiben, haben sie ein Auge auf das Papier und das andere auf einen Mann gerichtet, und dieses gilt von allen Schriftstellerinnen, mit Ausnahme der Gräfin Hahn-Hahn, die nur ein Auge hat.' (*Sämtliche Schriften*, ed. Klaus Briegleb, Munich, 1968–76, VI, i, 453.) I am grateful to Rosemary Ashton for finding this passage, and for her translation: 'When they write, they have one eye on the paper and the other on a man, and this is true of all authoresses, with the exception of the Countess Hahn-Hahn, who has only one eye.'

decidedly genial. Also my book is selling – largely, for one of mine.[3] I hope it is doing something of the kind *chez vous*. I have seen a good many English notices, & appear to myself to have got off on the whole very well. Look, if you can put your hand on it, at a Review in the *Tribune* for Dec. 25*th* – very glowing, & well-written.[4] Write me – something, anything, provided it speak to me of London! I hear you are having a "fine" winter, & I am sorry; for I love, as they say here, to think of the dear old dingy air. Keep some pleasant evening in May clear for me to dine with you. I send *mille tendresses* to Mrs. Macmillan & remain with all good wishes very faithfully yours

H. James jr

63. To Edwin Laurence Godkin
22 January [1882]

Houghton MS   Unpublished

In the first week of 1882 HJ went via New York to the nation's capital, where his friends the Adamses were now based – at first, as he told Turgenev's English translator W. R. S. Ralston on 7 January, with the intention of 'settling myself here for two or three months' (Unpublished Berg MS, 64B4494).

Washington.
723 15*th* St. Jan. 22*d*

My dear Godkin.

Though Washington is very pleasant, I like to keep communication with New York well established. I must therefore thank you for your friendly note & assure you that I hold you in the most grateful memory. I take careful note of what you say about the downy couch on which I slept so softly – if not so

3. In the first six weeks *The Portrait of a Lady* sold 2,937 copies in America, and 5,530 by the end of 1882. This was success for HJ, but compare Twain's *The Adventures of Huckleberry Finn* (1885), of which 30,000 copies were printed and sold.

4. Few English reviewers were enthusiastic, and on 11 December the New York *Tribune* had printed excerpts from *Athenaeum* ('a dull book') *Spectator*, and *Academy* ('A novelist has to tell a story'). The unsigned review on 25 December 1881, by HJ's friend John Hay, was thus a retort: 'There is positively no incident in the book – there is not one word of writing for writing's sake; there is not a line of meretricious ornament. It is a sober, consistent study of a single human character, with all its conditions and environments, in situations not in the least strained or exceptional. There is nothing exceptional about the book but the genius of the author, which is now, more than ever before, beyond question.'

late! – for three weeks being again at my service in February: & I venture to remark at present that my stay in this place will probably not exceed the *tenth* of that month. About that date – (I shall notify you of course more exactly) – I shall be delighted to come back to you. That is, if you will take me back after hearing of the company I have been keeping. The Adamses consider it very bad – though I notice that they are eagerly anxious to hear what I have seen & heard at places which they decline to frequent. After I had been to Mrs. Robeson's they mobbed me for revelations, & after I had dined with Blaine, to meet the President, they fairly hung upon my lips.[1] I shall try & get you & Lawrence into that attitude when I return. Not however that I shall have anything very wonderful to relate, for the inside life here is neither adapted to my opportunity nor to my desires; & the outside, though pleasant enough, doesn't bristle with startling events. My ordinary pastimes are going to see Mrs. Adams at 5 o'clock; my extraordinary ones are occasionally dining out. So long as that resource lasts a little, I shall remain here; when it fails me, I shall flee. Washington is too much of a village – though the absence of trade & stockbroking is delightful. It is too niggerish, & that has rubbed off on some of the whites.[2] I had some talk with the President the other evening & took a shine to him. He seemed to me a good fellow – but then I don't know his record, & don't want to know it. Oscar Wilde is here – an unclean beast.[3] The British Minister is dull, though apparently appreciative; but he has a ravishing young daughter.[4] Give my love to Lawrence & believe me ever yours –

H. James jr

1. Mrs Mary I. Ogston Robeson, wife of New Jersey Congressman George Maxwell Robeson (1829–97), controversially sponsored Oscar Wilde (1856–1900) during his visit to Washington. HJ described her to Isabella Stewart Gardner as 'fifty years old & fundamentally coarse. Very charming, however, with a *désinvolture* rather rare chez nous' (HJL II, 373). The Republican president from 1881 to 1885, Chester A. Arthur (1830–86), who was distantly related to HJ by marriage, assumed him 'to be the son of Uncle William, and wouldn't be disillusioned . . . I felt that if I had any smartness in me, I ought, striking while the iron was hot, to apply for a foreign mission' (HJL II, 371). The other guests of James G. Blaine, later Republican presidential candidate, included the British minister, the Governor of California, Generals Sherman and Hancock, Andrew Carnegie and Allen Thorndike Rice of the *North American Review*.
2. Compare HJ in 1897, advising the actress Elizabeth Robins: 'Somehow I like even Nell Gwynne mouthing Dryden rather to *quote* "niggers" than to say it too much off her own bat or too trippingly off her own tongue' (TF, 195).
3. On the night of 22 January, as HJ wrote to Isabella Stewart Gardner the next day, he went to Harriet Loring's, 'and found there the repulsive & fatuous Oscar Wilde, whom, I am happy to say, no one was looking at' (HJL II, 372).
4. Sir Lionel Sackville-West (1827–1908) served as British minister in Washington from November 1881 till his recall in 1888. Victoria was, as HJ wrote to Sir John Clark on 8 January,

64. To George Abbott James
[2 February 1882]

Houghton MS   Unpublished

HJ planned to stay in Washington till mid February, spend a fortnight in New York, make a tour in the South, and spend April in the Boston area. But on 27 January a note arrived from his brother Robertson saying his mother was ill. On 29 January she died after an attack of bronchial asthma. HJ arrived in Cambridge on Tuesday, 31 January, the day before the funeral.

20 Quincy St.
Cambridge. Thursday

My dear George.

I thank you heartily for your affectionate note – it touches me to be remembered. I have lost the sweetest, tenderest, wisest, most beneficent of mothers – & I simply *bleed* accordingly. But nothing can hurt *her* more.

I should like to see you; I mean also about a matter of practical advice. My mother's death has caused me to modify all my plans for the coming months – I wish to remain near my father. I do not wish however to be in Cambridge – but to have a habitation of my own, & to this end to take some furnished rooms in Boston. I know nothing about the ways & means of discovering such places – whether there [are] any agents, &c – but it occurs to me that you, who know Boston so well, may have an idea. I really know it so little. I mention it to you thus immediately, because it is a thing I wish to arrange *at once*. I wish more than ever now to return to my work (laid aside for many months,) & I cannot do so until I find myself in quarters of my own. Perhaps you know of the existence of one or two places such as I am looking for – what they call in England "chambers" – ? – a good sitting-room bed-room & bath-room, in a decent house & situation. If you do, or you have an idea of how one even *begins* to look for such things, do drop me a line. I shall have to go into town immediately & constantly & would come & see you. Excuse this eminently practical appeal; it is not to give you any trouble. All my three brothers are here – the first time we have been together in 15 years. Kind thanks to your wife. Ever faithfully yours

H. James jr

---

his 'most attractive little ingénue of a daughter, the *bâtarde* of a Spanish ballerina, brought up in a Paris convent, and presented to the world for the first time here' (HJL II, 367). She became the mother of the writer 'Vita' Sackville-West (1892–1962).

65. To Edmund Clarence Stedman
20 April [1882]

Berg MS   Unpublished

HJ moved into rooms at 102 Mount Vernon Street, Boston, on 9 February 1882.
It was here he wrote his (unproduced) dramatization of 'Daisy Miller'.

Stedman (1833–1908), a wealthy New York poet and anthologist also successful
on Wall Street, was a friend of Howells and an Atlantic contributor. He knew HJ
from New York in 1875.

102 Mt. Vernon St.
Boston. April 20*th*

Dear Mr. Stedman.

Howells has just read me a portion of a letter from you in which you make
inquiry about foreign lodgings, & as he (who hasn't been in foreign lands for
a good many years) seemed rather at a loss how to advise you, I ventured to
say to him that perhaps I might be able to give you a few suggestions. If they
prove to be at all useful, I shall be very happy.

In *Venice* there are lots of furnished rooms, which are let by the day, week
or month, & where the tenants usually dine & breakfast at the restaurants &
cafés. I spent the months of March, April, May & June last at *No. 4161, Riva*
dei Schiavoni, where I had a little fourth floor (4 rooms) which were meagrely
& hideously furnished, but where the rent was so low, the view so divine (four
windows on the lagoon,) & the situation so convenient, that it was a very
tolerable situation.[1] I wrote there the larger part of my last novel. (I had to
feed out, entirely, – in the Piazza: the best place is the Café Quaddri. The
house I speak of, you would perhaps deem too modest: try then the Casa
Barbieri – there are three different branches of the establishment, all on the
Grand Canal. Or try the Casa Chitarin (where there are Baths.) Or the Casa
Foscolo (beautiful.)[2] Any gondolier knows these places; knows also lots of
other addresses of lodgings (wherever you see a white paper on the blind.)
You will be rather late for Rome, but thanks to that fact (the thinning out of

1. HJ's notebook in 1881 remembers it as 'una bellezza; the far-shining lagoon, the pink walls
of San Giorgio, the downward curve of the Riva, the distant islands, the movement of the quay,
the gondolas in profile'. Baedeker's *Northern Italy* (1879): '*Private Apartments* are easily obtained.
The rents of those on the *Grand Canal* and the *Riva degli Schiavoni* are the highest.'
2. The Café Quadri (correct spelling) is in the Piazza San Marco. Chitarin's hotel had a salt-water
bath. I did not find the Casa Barbieri and the Casa Foscolo in Baedeker.

the strangers,) will have your pick of rooms. Those on the *Corso* are the best (with sun.) Walk up and down, & go in & ask wherever you see a card hung out with *Camere Mobigliate*. There are dozens of such. There too you will dine abroad. I don't think you spoke of Florence, but there are many little apartments there. Try the house on the corner of the Piazza Sta. Maria Novella & Via della Scala, I forget the number (I think 10 or 12) where I once had excellent quarters for several months – though the buxom landlady won't (any more than the one in Venice) remember my name.[3] They never do! I used to know Switzerland very well – but I don't know Germany much. In the former country, it is an embarrassment (of riches) to recommend you the rural retreat you desire. Don't bury yourself too much or you will be bored. I am not particularly fond of Switzerland myself; would give it all for one hour of Italy. But the places are legion, & of every kind. Do you want a mountain or a valley, a lake or an altitude, a town or a lonely dell? (The towns are rural enough.) The upper part of the Lake of Geneva (from Lausanne to Villeneuve) is a chain of little resorts; & the lake of Lucerne the same. In the former case the scenery is tame, though lovely; in the latter, superb. Doubtless, however, you know all that. Try the Axenstein, & Seelisberg, on the L. of Lucerne; though I am bound to say they are not *quiet*. Or try the glorious Grindelwald – though *that* is not quiet, either.[4] The truth is none of the *good* places in Switzerland *are* quiet in July in August. If a place is wrapped in repose, there are probably objections to it.

A few years ago I spent two summers in Germany: one at Homburg (near Frankfurt;) the other at Baden Baden.[5] The latter place (now that the gaming is dead & gone) is an enchanting spot & if I wished to settle down for a few weeks (in Germany) & do a little work I should choose it again. (I wrote a large part of *Roderick Hudson* there.) It has every comfort, lots of quiet, & the loveliest scenery I know; I am much addicted to walking & in this respect Baden is delightful. I worked all the morning, & spent the afternoons strolling through the Black Forest. In the evenings I listened to the music at the Kursaal: it was a charming summer. Excuse this dry & inadequate enumeration. Perhaps it may assist you a little. I go abroad on May 10*th* – & hope we may meet. Yours very truly –

H. James jr

3. The number was 10; HJ wrote the beginning of *Roderick Hudson* there in April–June 1874.
4. The Kurhaus Axenstein was a spa hotel near Brunnen on the Lake of Lucerne, and Seelisberg was, according to Baedeker, 'a favourite health-resort' across the lake from it. Grindelwald, properly the village of Gydisdorf, is 'a favourite summer resort' (Baedeker's *Switzerland* (1883)) near the Jungfrau mountain. HJ was in Lucerne from July to August 1869; and at Villeneuve and in Grindelwald in July 1872.
5. HJ was in Homburg from July to September 1873, and in Baden-Baden from June to August 1874.

66. To Edwin Lawrence Godkin
5 June [1882]

Houghton MS   Unpublished

The Times of 2 June 1882 carried a dispatch from Dublin recording death threats, police reinforcements and the shooting of a young man called Trimble in County Cavan, where HJ's grandfather William James of Albany had been born. Godkin was an Anglo-Irishman. HJ was back in Bolton Street by 22 May.

3 Bolton St. Piccadilly
June 5*th*.

My dear Godkin.

It was my plan to write to you from Ireland, if Ireland should prove inspiring: but I am sorry to say she did not. I disembarked at Cork, on the 9*th* day of a beautiful voyage, & spent three or four days in that city & in Dublin – but I soon perceived that to get even a glimpse of the Irish Revolution I shld. have to take several days & wander about the country – a course for which I was not prepared, having neither the time nor acquaintances, nor letters of introduction[.] Cork & Dublin offered nothing abnormal save a good many constables & soldiers & the latter place a better than the usual British Hotel. There was no inducement to resolve my impressions into eloquent prose; so I have waited till to-day to send you my greeting. It is only the more cordial – as separation has become more serious. I have had time to resume my vicious little habits – writing my letters here, for instance, & to begin & look at New York through the golden mists of memory. They show it to great advantage – make it poetical & "tender." London seems big & black & actual – it is a brutal sort of place compared with New York. But I revert to it with a kind of filial fondness – which is a proof, I suppose, that I have become brutalized. It seems complicated & complete, & very "smart" or very foul, according to the way you look at it. What strikes me most is the fine physique & handsome appearance of the people – alas, they beat us there. I have seen Lowell, who is in good spirits, in spite of transatlantic rumblings, & has invited me to dinner to-night – to meet (inter alios) the Countess of Jersey![1]

Knowles has asked me to write in the 19*th* Century a rejoinder to Matt.

---

1. Margaret Elizabeth Child-Villiers (1849–1945), Countess of Jersey, daughter of the second Baron Leigh, married in 1872 the seventh Earl of Jersey, and entertained on a grand scale at Osterley Park, Isleworth, on the edge of London (HJ stayed there in June 1886).

Arnold's article about America; but after thinking a bit of it I have declined, in compliance with a vow I long since took not to descend into the arena of controversy & never to embark on a *defense* of my native land, which seems to me rather worse than an attack upon it.[2] Let the English discuss America among themselves; meanwhile it does well enough; & I limit my ambition to producing from time to time a soigné work of art! Hold on to your plan of coming over & let Lawrence do the same. It will give you lots to think about. Meanwhile I have relapsed – but I am none the less of both of you the very faithful & grateful

H. James jr

67. To Sir John Clark
13 November [1882]

Virginia MS   Unpublished

HJ stayed in London for the summer of 1882, seeing the Howells family who came for seven weeks from the end of July before going on to the Continent. HJ himself left London on 12 September for Paris and, after a few days, Touraine and other provinces, on the six-week excursion that became A Little Tour in France. *In 1900 HJ recalled that work as 'sketches on "drawing-paper" and nothing more', as seeking 'the benefits of the perception of surface' rather than 'the perception of very complex underlying matters'. He was back in Paris about 1 November, staying in the large and expensive Grand Hotel in the Boulevard des Capucines, next to the recently built Opera House.*

Paris Grand Hotel.
Nov. 13*th*

My dear Laird.

I won't pretend to tell you why, having desired to write to you for many weeks, I only today bring my desire to a point; for I am not good at these explanations – they never really justify one – they are wanting in the famous quality of lucidity. Suffice it that I have often thought of you & have sent you all sorts of disembodied epistles. The rain is descending in customary torrents & the gorgeous fabric of the Opéra, which I see from my windows, looms

---

2. Arnold's 'A Word about America', which appeared in the *Nineteenth Century* (May 1882), was his response to attacks on him which claimed he regarded America as vulgar.

vaguely through a curtain of water. My thoughts wander away to your Scotch mountains & moors, & I ask myself what *your* situation can be just now, if this is the best that a dazzling capital can do for one of the most faithful of its votaries.[1]

Perhaps I shall hear from you that the sun of Tillypronie has never ceased to shine, & that you sit on your terrace & watch the smoke of your cigar (excuse my forgetting whether you smoke or not,) rise into the blue – or the blues! I have been talking about you with the John Hays & with the genial King, who is lodged below me here & who convokes us sometimes (Hay & me – with others) to the most gorgeous feasts – when he is not buying old silk tapestries, or the petticoats of M*me* de Pompadour, to cover New York chairs, or selling silver mines to the Banque de Paris, or philandering with Ferdinand Rothschild, who appears unable to live without him.[2] These allusions to Tillypronie are the touch of nature which makes us all Kin & which makes it also impossible I should forbear any longer to send you a greeting. Receive it, my dear Laird, as tenderly as it's sent. I think that what has most *attendri* myself is hearing from Mrs. Hay (who kindly read me some extracts from a letter of Lady Clark's) that you are coming to Folkestone for the winter. This is a most lovely fact. I gather that you don't care at all for that classic refuge of the seasick; but this fact is perfectly indifferent to me. It is enough that Folkestone is but two or three hours from London & that I shall be able – *si vous le voulez bien* – to go & see you there. You will see that I shall avail myself of this facility. Kindly write me & tell me when you migrate, & whether (as I think Mrs. H. told me) you don't stop awhile in London on your way. I have [been] wandering about the provinces ever since the middle of September – that is, till 15 days ago, & learning more about France than I ever learned before. What I have learned I will tell you, some time, at Folkestone; it is for the most part to the credit of this interesting country. Touraine, Anjou, Poitou, Gascony, Provence, Burgundy – I have examined them all (more or less,) & seen many picturesque & curious things. Paris is the same old Paris – on the whole I am very fond of it, though I dislike this particular quarter. I have a

1. The Clarks' 'supremely comfortable house' at Tillypronie in Aberdeenshire was said by HJ in 1878 to enjoy 'the conveniences of Mayfair dove-tailed into the last romanticism of nature' (HJL II, 184, 186).
2. The remarkable, many-talented Clarence King (1842–1901) was a geologist, head of the U.S. Geological Survey, and a friend of Hay and Adams (he is important in *The Education of Henry Adams*). He wrote *Mountaineering in the Sierra Nevada* (1872). The French-born Ferdinand de Rothschild (1839–98), who lived in England from 1860, was a collector and patron of the arts. In July 1885 HJ spent five days at Rothschild's newly completed French château – Waddesdon Manor, Buckinghamshire – and wrote of 'the gilded bondage of that gorgeous place' (HJL III, 98).

good many old friends here – & when I am only *de passage* (a passage of three weeks, as now) my life is too much of a scamper & a scramble. I maintain however that Paris is a good place to work, if you succeed in beginning. The theatres are dull, the restaurants are ruinous, the streets are (for Paris,) dirty. People pretend to feel very insecure & to hear the *grondement* of subterraneous revolutions. The government is shaky & lives but from day-to-day & the air has a certain little odour of dynamite. The rain also falls with a persistency worthy of a better cause. With these drawbacks however, Paris is delightful! I haven't seen the Westons, though I have tried twice; *elles étaient dans leurs malles*, watching each other's sick-beds, &c.[3] I am to be here but a week longer, & after that am to bask in the sun of Bolton St. Kindly address me there. Permit me to send my love to Lady Clark & to assure you of the undying friendship of yours very faithfully

Henry James jr

68. To Theodore Child
5 December [1882]

Virginia MS   Unpublished

HJ returned to London on 20 November.

He had met Theodore Child (d. 1892), then a London journalist writing for the Pall Mall Gazette, *at Étretat in 1876. He saw him again soon after arriving in London to settle, and they became good friends. Child became Paris correspondent of the* Daily Telegraph, *and HJ wrote to his Parisian friend William Henry Huntington (1820–85) on 23 April 1879, 'He is an Oxford man & a young journalist (Pall-Mall Gazette &c) & though a bit of a Bohemian & furthermore (on the testimony of his nose) a Jew, I don't feel as if I were outraging the sanctity of your private life. Child is not a phenix, but he is modest, honest, ingenuous & excellent, & the worst he can do to you will be not to thrill you with violent emotion of any kind.' (Unpublished Virginia MS, 6251–c420, Box 5.) Child edited* The Parisian, *to which HJ contributed; and he would die, as HJ recorded in the Preface to vol. XIV of the New York Edition, 'prematurely and lamentedly, during a gallant professional tour of exploration in Persia' (LC II, 1221).*

---

3. The two Miss Westons were aunts of Elizabeth Bates Chapman Laugel, wife of the *Nation*'s Paris correspondent Auguste Laugel. They had helped HJ socially in Paris in 1875–6.

3 Bolton St. Piccadilly
Dec 5*th*

My dear Child.

Your friendly letter increases my regret at not having seen you in Paris. If I had managed to catch Huntington,[1] I certainly should have seen you as well, but I failed in that good-fortune through the limitations of my time, as I had many – too many – irons on the fire. Do you absolutely never come to London? I am afraid you have forgotten that this Philistine city has after all du bon. So much so that I at any rate am very glad, at the beginning of the winter, to find myself back at a British fireside. I spent six weeks in France, in the provinces, before coming to Paris & visited 20 villes du Midi – some of which, like London, had du bon. I looked at M. Rabusson in the Revue, & found him dirty sans le moindre talent.[2] What the devil is coming over you Frenchmen? – ces messieurs seem to me to have lost the perception of anything in nature but the genital organs. The French imagination ne sort pas de là. You will probably think these strictures of the most prudish hypocrisy.[3] Thank you all the same for your account of Daudet's new novel, which sounds very curious & interesting, and which I await with interest.[4] Tell him that an American, not without talent, adores him, & spent a day at Tarascon not long ago solely for the love of him & of his Tartarin.[5] I have read three or four of Renan's papers, & am anxious for the book.[6] The said Renan is a queer mixture. He has an enchanting mind, but it needs ventilation, awfully. I should like to see

1. Huntington was European correspondent for the *New York Tribune*. HJ described him to WJ in 1876, while in Paris writing his own letters for the *Tribune*, as 'the most amiable, loosely-knit optimist on the planet; a very good creature, but an extreme Bohemian' (CWJ I, 259).

2. Henry Rabusson's *Dans le Monde* appeared in three parts in the *Revue des Deux Mondes* from 15 October to 15 November. The first instalment follows a young cavalry officer, the marquis de Trémont, and the plotting which gets a young woman into his apartment: 'cinq jours durant, ce fut une orgie d'amour' ('it was a five-day-long orgy of love').

3. Edmond de Goncourt, *Journal: Mémoire de la vie littéraire (1879–1890)*, III, ed. Robert Ricatte: Wednesday, 31 August 1881: 'A libertine Englishman claimed that the best place to pick up women, in Paris, was the omnibus offices, and the observation came from one who knew his Paris. It was Theodore Child who told me that . . .' (my translation).

4. Daudet's next novel was *L'Evangéliste* (1883), serialized in *Le Figaro* from December 1882 to January 1883, which gave HJ the idea of *The Bostonians* (N, 21).

5. The twenty-ninth chapter of *A Little Tour in France* recounts three hours spent in the Southern town of Tarascon 'chiefly for the love of Alphonse Daudet, who has written nothing more genial than "Les Aventures Prodigieuses de Tartarin" ', one of three novels about this hero, 'a hunter of lions and charmer of women', a cowardly braggart repeatedly forced to live up to his boasts. HJ, 'bribed with gold', translated the third, *Port Tarascon*, in 1890 (CHJHM, 158).

6. Ernest Renan's *Souvenirs d'enfance et de jeunesse* were appearing in the *Revue des Deux Mondes*, the fifth and sixth instalments on 1 and 15 November.

your books, & envy you that good company. I don't collect – I fear possessions – which seem also to fear me. I envy you your new pieces, & other Parisian things, & am never absolutely unlikely to go & see a few. Love to H.W.H. Tout à vous

H. James jr

69. To James Ripley Osgood
8 April 1883

Congress MS   Unpublished

Receiving word of his father's last illness, HJ sailed for the U.S. on 12 December 1882, reaching New York on 21 December, the day of the funeral in Cambridge, Massachusetts. Consoled by learning his widowed father had 'longed so to die' (HJL II, 403), HJ stayed on in the small house on Mount Vernon Street to which his father and sister had moved. As his father's executor, and with WJ away in Europe, he travelled to Milwaukee in temperatures of 20° below zero to see his younger brothers, and then to Syracuse to see the family properties (the estate was valued at $95,000).

In Boston, HJ kept busy, writing: 'En Provence' for the Atlantic *(July–November 1883, then February, April–May 1884) – which became* A Little Tour in France. *He also arranged with Macmillan for a collected edition of his fiction so far, to appear in November 1883.*

After his expression of frustration with Houghton, Mifflin & Co., HJ, like Howells and Twain, had come to an agreement with the former partner Osgood, now independent. He assembled for Osgood a volume of three tales, The Siege of London *('The Pension Beaurepas', 'The Point of View' and the title story), which was swiftly brought out on 24 February 1883, and the travel collection* Portraits of Places. *Here he outlines his next big novel,* The Bostonians, *in a letter that he the same day copied with slight differences into his notebooks.*

131 Mount Vernon St.
April 8th 1883.

Dear Mr. Osgood.

I take a few moments before going out of town to say a few words about the novel I spoke of to you to-day. (Proposal I.)

The scene of the story is laid in Boston & its neighbourhood; it relates an episode connected with the so-called "women's movement." The characters

144

who figure in it are for the most part persons of the radical & reforming class, who are especially interested in the emancipation of woman, giving her the suffrage, releasing her from bondage, co-educating her with men &c. They regard this as the great question of the day – the most urgent & sacred reform. The heroine is a very clever & gifted young woman, associated by birth & circumstances with a circle immersed in these ideas & in every sort of new agitation – daughter of old abolitionists, transcendentalists, spiritualists, &c. She herself takes an interest in the cause; but she is an object of still greater interest to her family & friends, who have discovered in her a remarkable natural talent for public speaking, by which they believe her capable of moving large audiences & rendering great aid in the liberation of her sex. They cherish her as a kind of apostle & redeemer. She is very pleasing to look upon, & her gift for speaking is a kind of inspiration. She has a dear & intimate friend, another young woman who, issuing from a totally different social circle (a rich, conservative, exclusive family) has thrown herself into these questions with intense ardour, & has conceived a passionate admiration for our young girl, over whom, by the force of a completely different character, she has acquired a great influence. She has money of her own, but no talent for appearing in public; & she has a dream that her friend & she together (one by the use of her money the other by her eloquence) may, working side by side, really revolutionize the condition of women. She regards this as a noble & inspiring task, a mission to which everything else should be sacrificed, & she counts implicitly on her friend. The latter however makes the acquaintance of a young man who falls in love with her & in whom she also becomes much interested, but who, being of a hard-headed & conservative disposition, is resolutely opposed to female-suffrage & all similar innovations. The more he sees of the heroine the more he loves her & the more determined he is to get her out of the clutches of her reforming friends, whom he utterly abominates. He asks her to marry him, & does not conceal from her that if she does so she must entirely give up her "mission." She feels that she loves him; but that the sacrifice of the said mission would be terrible, & that the disappointment inflicted on her friends, & especially on the rich young woman, would be worse. Her lover is a distant relative of the rich young woman, who in an evil hour, by accident, & before she was acquainted with his opinions (he has been spending ten years in the West) has introduced him. She appeals to her friend to stand firm – appeals in the name of their intimate friendship & of all the hopes that are centered on the young girl's head. The tale relates the struggle that takes place in the mind of the latter. The struggle ends (after various vicissitudes,) with her letting everything go, breaking forever with her friend, in a terrible final interview, & giving herself up to her lover. There are to be several other characters, whom I have not mentioned – reforming & radical types – & as many little pictures as I can introduce of the woman's rights' agitation. I propose that the story shall be of the length of 150 pages of the *Atlantic*; & I desire to receive $4500 for it. (This means that I shall definitely make it of the length of what I called six "parts." I first spoke of five – that is, 125 pages of the *Atlantic*.)[1]

As regards the period at which I should be able to give it (or the greater part of it) to the printers, I am afraid that November first is the earliest date.[2] The reason of this is partly that I wish to write something else first; & this other production I shall also make the subject of a proposal to you which I here subjoin.

Proposal No II.

I wish to write *before* beginning the novel above-described another "international episode"; i.e. a story of the same length & character as "Daisy Miller", the "Internat. Episode" & the "Siege of London." (The length to be that of two instalments of the *Cornhill* – the form in which those three tales appeared.) The name to be "Lady Barberina." I have treated (more or less) in these other things the subject of the American girl who marries (or concerning whom it is a question whether she *will* marry) a British aristocrat. This one reverses the situation & presents a young *male* American who conceives the design of marrying a daughter of the aristocracy. He is a New Yorker, a good deal of an Anglomaniac & a "dude;" & as he has a good deal of money she accepts him & they are united. The 1st half of the tale takes place in England. In the 2d the parties are transported to New York, whither he has brought his bride, & it relates their adventures there, the impressions made & received by the lady, & the catastrophe. I don't know exactly the relation of the *Atlantic* page to that of the *Cornhill*; but I call it roughly (about) 50 pages of the *Atlantic*. I will give you this to do what you choose with (reprint &c.) for $1000. And that you may conveniently reprint it I will undertake to furnish you, later, with two short stories, of the length of the *Pension Beaurepas* & the *Point of View*, which could make up a volume with it. I should propose to include in this volume the little story (reprinted some time ago in England) entitled "Four

1. In the event HJ settled for $4,000 for all rights (including foreign) for five years, on delivery of manuscript, in an unconventional contract. He had himself, without success, offered the novel to the *Century* magazine, which had started in 1881 as a replacement for *Scribner's Monthly* under the poet Richard Watson Gilder (1844–1909); but Osgood got them to pay *him* for it. Six parts of the *Atlantic* would make a novel just under half the length of *The Portrait of a Lady*.
2. *The Bostonians* did not begin its year-long run in the *Century* till February 1885.

Meetings," which I spoke of to you the other day (when I said that it *might* have appeared with the *Siege of London*.[3] And this brings me to –

Proposal No III

This is simply that I write & give up to you the "Lady Barberina" *and*, as well, the two short tales which I have just mentioned as calculated to appear in book-form with it, *before* I go forward with the novel described in Proposal No I. That is, write the substance of a book, in three stories (respectively of the lengths I have mentioned,) & in which the "Four Meetings" will make a fourth; & then having in the interval let Proposal No I remain exactly where it is (except as regards date of beginning to publish) take it up & go on with it, so that your magazine may have the story therein treated (or enough of it to begin to print) by *about* the New Year. This will give me more time for that story – which, as I think over it, I should a good deal prefer to have. In a word I would rather do the short things now and the longer ones later, remaining equally willing to let you have them all. For the *three* short things taken together – "Lady Barberina" & her two companions – $2500 seems to me a fair price.[4] (I got $500 from the Century for the *Point of View*, which appeared in one instalment. For the *Siege of London* I got from the Cornhill $750.) A smaller sum than this would not represent the *volume*, in addition to the appearance of the tale in periodicals. I do not speak definitely of the time I shall be able to give you these tales; but will only say that you shall have them one by one – the "Lady Barberina" first – at as early a date as possible. The other day Gilder (of the *Century*) said in writing to me – "Haven't you got any more short stories in you: short as *Four Meetings*, & as good?" I mention this to show you that there is a demand for these productions. He had asked me this two or three times before.

---

3. 'Lady Barberina' appeared in the *Century* (May–July 1884), and was collected in October 1884 in *Tales of Three Cities* for Osgood, together with 'The Impressions of a Cousin' (*Century*, November–December 1883) and 'A New England Winter' (*Century*, August–September 1884). HJ wrote on 10 March 1884 to Osgood's partner Benjamin Ticknor, saying he would 'much rather not call it "Impressions" &c; and I think that "*Tales of Three Cities*" will do very well – the three cities being New York, London, & Boston, & there being considerable reference to the places in the stories. This will probably be judged fairly "attractive," though I shall be accused of cribbing it from Dickens.' (Unpublished Yale MS, Za James 20.) In fact 'Four Meetings', which had been published in England in 1879, was put in the volume of stories called *The Author of Beltraffio*, published by Osgood in February 1885.
4. HJ received $2,000 for 'Lady Barberina' and the two other stories in *Tales of Three Cities*, as well as 'Four Meetings'.

This is a long letter; but I hope you will understand the relation that my "proposals," clumsily joined one to the other, bear to each other. The important ones are the *1st* & *3d*: the *2d* is, as it were, superfluous, being included in the *3d*. I repeat that I should prefer to do you the short things first & the novel afterward, within limits of time to be hereafter settled between us. I shall also have to hear from you how my property in the *copyright* of the productions in question is affected by the arrangement we are discussing. I don't suppose I make it over to you *forever*? That is an idea from which I shrink.

My address in New York will be till the *17th* – *115 east 25th St*. After that, till the *24th*, *Wormeleys Hotel, Washington*.

Yours ever
Henry James

70. *To Thomas Sergeant Perry*
[June 1883?]

Colby MS   Unpublished

In November 1882 there had appeared in the Century *magazine Howells's civil but provocative 'Henry James, Jr.', declaring the 'art of fiction', exemplified by HJ's 'impartiality', 'a finer art in our day than it was with Dickens and Thackeray'. The resulting controversy, picking up from those about* Daisy Miller *and* Hawthorne, *damagingly affected attitudes to HJ in both Britain and America for at least a decade. In an article in the Tory* St James's Gazette *(London) of 5 July 1883, called 'An American on American Humour' and dated 'Boston, June 1883', Howells's friend Perry takes up the topic of the literature produced by a democracy. His article, which may have been revised after HJ's comments, takes Mark Twain as chief representative of the powerfully influential American style of humour, the 'vulgarizing, denigrating spirit' which attacks 'zeal as well as affectation'. Perry identifies 'one great animating spirit which . . . is obviously the core of democracy: the importance, namely, of the people, of the present, by the side of which all traces of aristocracy, of the past, are valueless'. Whitman is 'the constructive side of this spirit': Perry cites his demand in* Specimen Days *for 'a new-founded literature not merely to copy and reflect existing surfaces, or to ponder what is called taste – not only to amuse, pass away time, celebrate the beautiful, the refined, the past, or exhibit technical, rhythmic, or grammatical dexterity – but a literature underlying life, religious, consistent with science, handling the elements and forces with competent power, teaching and training men'. Perry remarks, 'This is a statement that is open to criticism, but it expresses definite dissatisfaction with recognizable literary methods.'*

131 Mt. V. St.
Monday a.m.

Dear Thomas.

I return your little article. The young Cockerel is much obliged to you – but I am not sure that H.J. jr catches your meaning.[1] Who are "the people?" I think it odious for any class to arrogate that title more than another, & I think the passage you quote from Walt Whitman mere drivel. But we will talk of this.[2] I pretend to be one "of the people", moi. And I can imagine no coterie-literature more coterie than a class of novel devoted to the portrayal of the professional democrat. Tout à vous

H. James

71. To Grace Norton
11 December [1883]

Houghton MS   Unpublished

In July the Atlantic *started to run 'En Provence' (*A Little Tour in France*) – the book HJ would still be writing when he returned to London at the end of August. HJ thought of taking a house in Elm Tree Road, St John's Wood (the Macmillans' street); but then, as he told Grace Norton on 14 November, was kept in Bolton Street by 'distance, dampness &c – & vis inertiae – much work, & a sudden sense of being very well off where I am'. HJ's brother Wilky died in Milwaukee – HJ called it to WJ a 'blessed liberation' – after years of ill health, on 15 November (CWJ I, 372).*

In the same letter to Grace Norton HJ referred to the controversial, but immensely influential, American lecture tour (seventy speaking engagements) of his favourite English critic. On 7 and 17 November, and then 1 December, Matthew Arnold – who actually stayed with the Nortons – had lectured in Boston. 'I take much interest in poor Matt. Arnold's career, & fear that it won't be brilliant. Have you seen, heard, heeded, scorned, evaded – & invited – him? – I am very fond of him, & if he is more or less ridiculous over there shall love him the more. I am in the act of

1. Marcellus Cockerel is a stridently and humorously patriotic American in HJ's comic tale of national differences, 'The Point of View'.

2. On 'Tuesday p.m.', evidently the next day, HJ responded to Perry's (lost) reply: 'Dear Thomas / I will dine with you tomorrow at 6.30 with gt. pleasure, & explain to you that I didn't suspect you of battering *me* personally with W.W. – as well as listen to your own explanation of anything – or everything – in the world that you will. Yours ever *H. James jr.*' (Unpublished Colby MS.)

writing a short notice about him (to accompany a portrait) in Macmillan's new magazine.' He also reassured her at the end of his difficult year: 'Don't think of me as troubled, depressed or worried. I am steadily learning not to be at all, & I recommend you my sagesse, *which I will do up for you in a formula as soon as I have condensed it a little more.' (Unpublished Houghton MS, bMS Am 1094 (953).) She cannot have received this before sending the letter (not extant) to which HJ replies here.*

3 Bolton St. Mayfair.

Dec. 11*th*

Dear Grace.

Here is a little letter – a very little one – in lieu of that bigger one which I don't see my way just now to write. Yours of the 19*th* ult. calls it forth; & I must begin by thanking you tenderly for that. I thank you tenderly all the time & try & imagine you in all sorts of comfortable & entertaining – entertained – & generally *mitigated* – positions.

You were not mitigated at all, however, apparently, when you went to hear my poor dear Matt. Arnold. Aren't you a little hard on him, & don't you scold *him* a little when you represent him as "scolding"? I am very fond of him, & indeed delight in him – & for my sentiments in regard to him (a little arranged & embellished) I refer you to an article in the January *Illustrated Macmillan*, in which I freely admit that I am simply fulsome. But I think you are unfair to grudge him his relieving his mind on the subject of the horrors of the horsecars.[1] Surely, (for the impression they make on the arrived European especially) they can scarcely be exaggerated. To me, all the while I was in the U.S., they were unspeakable – & that is why I didn't speak of them.[2] But surely one ought to be able to do so without becoming unpopular – they are

1. Arnold wrote to his sister on 15 November in horror of 'What it is in the towns, to have practically no cabs and to be obliged to use trams' (*Letters of Matthew Arnold* (1895), ed. George W. E. Russell, 2 vols, II, 230).

2. HJ did write of them, at the start of *The Europeans* (1878), where Eugenia watches 'a strange vehicle . . . : a huge, low omnibus, painted in brilliant colours, and decorated apparently with jingling bells, attached to a species of groove in the pavement, through which it was dragged, with a great deal of rumbling, bouncing, and scratching, by a couple of remarkably small horses. When it reached a certain point the people . . . projected themselves upon it in a compact body – a movement suggesting the scramble for places in a life-boat at sea – and were engulfed in its large interior.' E. L. Godkin said of Henry James Senior that 'When in his grotesque moods he maintained that to a right-minded man, a crowded Cambridge horse-car "was the nearest-approach to Heaven upon earth"' (LWJ I, 115). HJ's father wrote an unpublished piece called 'The Omnibus, and Its Morality'.

so great an abuse and so much the ugliest thing in a country where so much is ugly. But I must check my pen, or I shall make you think that I too am scolding.

I am just back from a little Saturday-to-Monday visit to Sara Darwin. It had been long due, as the last one I had paid her was between three & four years ago, & it proved very pleasant. Sara was lively (for her) & seems wanting in no element of happiness but health, vigour & vitality!! Darwin is better than ever – a jewel of a husband & a modest flower of human beings. Margaret flourishes like a young palm-tree, appears very well & happy, is majestic & elegant; & wears the *m*ost beautiful *bleu-ciel* dresses, with everything "to match." There was no one there but Miss Darwin, who struck me as dullish & queer, but probably harmless; & William & I took a ten-mile walk on the lovely frosty Sunday, through a country delightfully rural & old-English, & then came back & lunched on cold pheasant & hock. Mrs. Kemble is in town for the winter – very fairly well for her, but preoccupied by the advent of Mrs. Leigh (her daughter whose husband has now a church) in London (Bryanstone Square.)[3] In that family advents always preoccupy – the presumption is always that they are hostile, & Mrs. L. is an *enfant terrible* – of fifty! This is all my little letter to-day, dear Grace. You shall have another very soon. You will have heard of the death of Lady Rose – in her chair, as her maid was putting on her cap. Poor Mrs. Tweedy![4] Ever your very faithful

Henry James

72. To William Dean Howells
21 February 1884

Houghton MS   Published HJL III, 27–9; LFL, 241–4

On 29 January 1884 HJ wrote to Osgood asking not to be strictly held to the clause in his contract for The Bostonians, *etc., stating that 'the said works shall take precedence of any other works of fiction to be written by said James'; he wanted to write for Dana of the New York* Sunday Sun *a couple of tales for lucrative*

3. In 1877, after a visit to Mrs James (Frances Butler) Leigh and her clergyman husband in Stratford-upon-Avon, HJ wrote that 'the Leighs themselves are not interesting' and that Mrs Leigh 'is inferior both to her mother and sister' (HJL II, 148).
4. The former Charlotte Temple, aunt to HJ's Temple cousins and sister of Mrs Edmund Tweedy, married Sir John Rose (1820–88), a Scot active in Canadian government until his resignation and settlement in England about 1868. HJ liked her 'good manners, good sense and good humor' (HJL II, 7).

syndication – 'Georgina's Reasons' and 'Pandora'. He pleaded that 'I have not enough ready money to carry me through the time it will take me to complete my novel' ('Friction', 86).

HJ crossed to Paris – which with Turgenev dead he found the poorer – on 2 February 1884. While in Paris, he first met the young American painter John Singer Sargent (1856–1925) through Henrietta Reubell, a friend of Whistler and Wilde. In March, back in London, he introduced him to many of his English friends. In July, Sargent in turn introduced HJ to the French writer Paul Bourget (1852– 1935).

Paris. Feb. 21st 1884.

My dear Howells.

Your letter of the 2d last gives me great pleasure. A frozen Atlantic seemed to stretch between us, & I had had no news of you to speak of save an allusion, in a late letter of T.B.A., to your having infant-disease in your house.[1] You give me a good account of this, & I hope your tax is paid for the year at least. These are not things to make a hardened bachelor mend his ways.

Hardened as I am, however I am not proof against being delighted to hear that my Barberina tale entertained you.[2] I am not prepared even to resent the malignity of your remark that the last 3d is not the best. It isn't; the Ameri. part is squeezed together & écourté. It is always the fault of my things that the head and trunk are too big & the legs too short. I spread myself always, at first, from a nervous fear that I shall not have enough of my peculiar tap to "go round." But I always (or generally) have and therefore, at the end, have to fill one of the cups to overflowing. My tendency to this disproportion remains incorrigible. I begin short tales as if they were to be long novels. Àpropos of which, ask Osgood to show you also the sheets of another thing I lately sent him – "A New England Winter." It is not very good – on the contrary; but it will perhaps seem to you to put into form a certain impression of Boston.

What you tell me of the success of Crawford's last novel sickens & almost paralyses me.[3] It seems to me (the book) so contemptibly bad & ignoble that the idea of people reading it in such numbers makes one return upon one's self & ask what is the use of trying to write anything decent or serious for a

1. Aldrich mentioned that Howells's son John had had scarlet fever.
2. 'Lady Barberina' was not published till May–July 1884 in the *Century*; Osgood, Howells's publisher as well as HJ's, may have shown him proof-sheets.
3. Francis Marion Crawford (1854–1909), a prolific American writer born in Italy, whose mother and stepfather, the Luther Terrys, HJ knew in Rome in the 1870s, had a great success with *To Leeward* (1883), which sold 9,787 copies in its first year.

public so absolutely idiotic. It must be totally wasted. I would rather have produced the basest experiment in the "naturalistic" that is being practised here than such a piece of sixpenny humbug. Work so shamelessly bad seems to me to dishonour the novelist's art to a degree that is absolutely not to be forgiven; just as its success dishonours the people for whom one supposes one's self to write. Excuse my ferocity, which (more discreetly & philosophically) I think you must share; & don't mention it, please, to any one, as it will be set down to green-eyed jealousy.

I came to this place three weeks since – on the principle that anything is quieter than London; but I return to the British scramble in a few days. Paris speaks to me, always, for about such a time as this, with many voices; but at the end of a month I have heard all it has to say. I have been seeing something of Daudet, Goncourt, & Zola; & there is nothing more interesting to me now than the effort & experiment of this little group, with its truly infernal intelligence of art, form, manner – its intense artistic life. They do the only kind of work, to-day, that I respect; & in spite of their ferocious pessimism & their handling of unclean things, they are at least serious and honest. The floods of tepid soap and water which under the name of novels are being vomited forth in England, seem to me, by contrast, to do little honour to our race. I say this to you, because I regard you as the great American naturalist. I don't think you go far enough, and you are haunted with romantic phantoms & a tendency to factitious glosses; but you are in the right path, & I wish you repeated triumphs there – beginning with your Americo-Venetian – though I slightly fear, from what you tell me, that he will have a certain "gloss."[4] It isn't for me to reproach you with that, however, the said gloss being a constant defect of *my* characters; they have too much of it – too damnably much. But I am a failure! – comparatively. Read Zola's last thing: *La Joie de Vivre*. The title of course has a desperate irony; but the work is admirably solid & serious.[5]

I haven't much London news for you. I see the genial Gosse occasionally, & the square-headed Tadema, whose *d*'s & *t*'s are so mixed; & they frequently ask about you.[6] Miss Fenimore Woolson is spending the winter here; I see her

4. Howells never wrote this projected historical novel, in which a young New England ship's captain was to sail to Venice and become romantically involved with a Venetian noblewoman.
5. Edmond de Goncourt felt that in *The Joy of Living* (1884) Zola was indecent in 'making copy out of his mother's death', and in 1903 HJ wrote of it as one of Zola's 'explorations of stagnant pools . . . which make us wonder what pearl of philosophy, of suggestion or just of homely recognition, the general picture, as of rats dying in a hole, has to offer' (LC II, 889).
6. HJ had met Edmund William Gosse (1849–1928), later one of Britain's most successful men of letters, in 1879; it was only after HJ's return from America that their friendship grew. Sir Lawrence Alma-Tadema (1836–1912) was an Anglicized Dutch painter, often of classical subjects, of whom HJ wrote in 1882, the year he met him: 'Such painting as Mr. Tadema's

at discreet intervals, & we talk of you and Mrs. *you*.[7] She is a very intelligent woman, & understands when she is spoken to; a peculiarity I prize, as I find it more & more rare.

I am very happy as to what you tell me of Perry's having a large piece of work to do; & I pray it may yield him some profit & comfort. Sad indeed has been hitherto the history of his career, & the cynical indifference of the public to so good a production (in spite of weaknesses of form) as his *18th Century* makes me blush for it.[8] As you see, I am blushing a good deal for the public now. Give Perry my love, please, when you see him next, & tell him I am acutely conscious of owing him, & indeed his wife, a letter; they shall really have it soon. Addio – stia bene. I wish you could send me anything *you* have in the way of advance-sheets. It is rather hard that as you are the only English novelist I read (except Miss Woolson), I shouldn't have more comfort with you. Give my love to Winny: I am sure she will dance herself well.[9] Why doesn't Mrs. Howells try it too? Tout à vous,

Henry James

73. To Theodore Child
8 March [1884]

Virginia MS   Published HJL III, 36–7

Alphonse Daudet had appreciated HJ's essay on him in the August 1883 Century, and HJ's translation for the November 1883 Century of Daudet's reminiscence of Turgenev. Compliments had been exchanged, and on 12 February, accompanied by Theodore Child, HJ had spent an evening at Daudet's in Paris and been struck by his 'remarkable personal charm' (CWJ I, 375). Child gave an (anonymous) account

---

makes the painting of many of his fellows in England look like schoolboy work' (PE, 210). Alma-Tadema's wife was Gosse's sister-in-law.

7. Constance Fenimore Woolson (1840–94), grandniece of Fenimore Cooper, New Hampshire-born novelist of Southern life, became close friends with HJ after a letter of introduction from Henrietta (Temple) Pell-Clarke (1853–1934). They had met in Florence in 1880.

8. HJ wrote to Perry on 6 March 1884 of his news from Howells that Perry had 'a whole encyclopaedia to write': *From Opitz to Lessing* was published by Osgood in October 1884, dedicated to Howells. Perry had published *English Literature in the Eighteenth Century* in 1883.

9. Winifred, Howells's eldest daughter, was about to make her social début in Boston, but in the event was prevented by worsening health. She had had a breakdown in the fall of 1880. After many other efforts she was treated by Silas Weir Mitchell (1829–1914), a poet and novelist as well as a physician, for what seemed a psychologically rooted disorder, but died unexpectedly in 1889 from 'a sudden failure of the heart' (SLWDH III, 147).

in the Atlantic *'Contributors' Club' in May 1884 of this occasion, which was attended by Goncourt, Zola, Coppée and Loti. They remembered HJ from Flaubert's, and he heard their discussion of the torments of style. Child remarked that 'The young Frenchman leads a free-and-easy café life, into which it is best not curiously to inquire', and that these French writers, 'mostly men of humble origin', found it difficult to represent 'society ladies'. HJ was back from Paris on 29 February, but kept in touch through Child.*

3 Bolton St. W.
March 8*th*

Dear Child.

I thank you cordially for your letter & the various *primeurs* you enclose. Goncourt's preface I immediately return, no other human eye having beheld it.[1] It is interesting, & I agree with much of it. But there is something indefinably disagreeable to me in what that man writes[,] something hard – irritated, not sympathetic. Why also shld. the note of egotism, of vanity, of the claims he makes for himself, be condemned to sound in every Frenchman's utterance, sooner or later? However, I am for the roman d'analyse, sans intrigue & sans ficelle, tant qu'il voudra, & also, Dieu sait!, for writing exquisitely & resisting reportage. And why the devil will he make us wait twenty years for those wonderful Memoirs! – & 20 years after his death too.[2] In your place, with your opportunities, I should secretly poison him tomorrow, so that the 20 years may commence to run. *Mlle. Tantale* must be a sweet thing, & I confess there are moments when such emanations seem to me to sound the *glas* of a literature.[3] Nevertheless, I am sorry that the divine Daudet is going to Virtuefy his souillon.[4] Puisque souillon il y a, I shld. say let her be a real one. The said Daudet, however, cannot put three words together that I don't more or less

1. Edmond de Goncourt (1822–96), French novelist and man of letters, outlived his brother Jules (1830–70), with whom he had collaborated, by many years. They were known for the *roman documentaire*, the novel of painstaking research. The preface here is probably that to *Chérie*, Goncourt's new novel, serialized in *Gil Blas* from 11 March. Its preface was published in *Le Figaro* on 17 April, the day of the book's publication.
2. In July 1883 Edmond de Goncourt told the Daudets of the journal he had been keeping, and, encouraged by them, published extracts from 1886 onwards. HJ would write in October 1888 on the sexual and personal frankness of the journal: 'If instead of publishing his Journal M. de Goncourt had burned it up we should have been deprived of a very curious and entertaining book; but even with that consciousness we should have remembered that it would have been impertinent to expect him to do anything else.' (LC II, 406.)
3. I have not been able to identify '*Mlle. Tantale*'.
4. Fanny, the central character of Daudet's *Sapho* (1884) as published, is a model, no longer young.

adore them. I enter into your divided feelings about Paris – though fortunately, for myself, I have worked into quiet waters; I find life *possible* in London (on condition of swearing at it) & the ideally arranged existence (by the year) for me would be 5 mos. of London, 5 of Italy (mainly Rome), a month for – Paris & a month for the imprévu. I have settled down again into this Indian village, & the matutinal tea & toast, the British coal-scuttle, the dark back-bedroom, the dim front sitting-room, the *Times*, the hansom cab, the London dinner, the extension of the franchise, partagent my existence. This place *is* hideously political, & there don't seem to me to be three people in it who care for questions of art, or form, or taste. I am lonely & speechless. Everything around me is woolly, stuffy, literal, unspeakably Philistine. I went, however, to see Salvini last night, & he is the greatest of the great.[5] Stick to your bright little Parisian 5ième, to the light & easy civilization of the Gauls. Don't rashly make an exchange which is like refusing a riz de veau à la jardinière for a dish of tripe & onions! Yours ever, cynically,

Henry James

74. To Edmund Gosse
9 June [1884]

Leeds MS   Published SLHJEG, 31–2

On 26 March HJ noted that 'Edmund Gosse mentioned to me the other day a fact which struck me as a possible donnée. *He was speaking of J.A.S., the writer (from whom, in Paris, the other day I got a letter), of his extreme and somewhat hysterical aestheticism, etc.: the sad conditions of his life, exiled to Davos by the state of his lungs, the illness of his daughter, etc. Then he said that, to crown his unhappiness, poor S.'s wife was in no sort of sympathy with what he wrote; disapproving of its tone, thinking his books immoral, pagan, hyper-aesthetic, etc.' HJ's story, 'The Author of "Beltraffio"', a tragic portrait of a writer's marriage, appeared in the* English Illustrated Magazine *(June–July 1884).*

HJ had met John Addington Symonds (1840–93), author of The Renaissance in Italy *(1875–6), in February 1877, lunching with Andrew Lang, and found him 'a mild, cultured man, with the Oxford perfume' (CWJ I, 280). He had sent Symonds his essay on Venice of November 1882, and* Portraits of Places, *probably late in 1883.*

5. Tommaso Salvini (1829–1915), born in Milan, was for many years the leading Italian actor; HJ had praised for the *Atlantic* his performances in Boston in January 1883 shortly after his father's death. In March–April 1884 Salvini was playing at Covent Garden, and HJ again wrote about him, this time for the *Pall Mall Gazette* (27 March).

It is now well known that Symonds was secretly homosexual, the author of Memoirs *documenting his inner struggles and of the privately printed* A Problem of Modern Ethics *(1891), of which Gosse would lend HJ a copy. But at this time Gosse may have had another perspective on the unhappy Symonds marriage, through the analysis the consumptive Robert Louis Stevenson gave to their common friend Sidney Colvin in early April 1882, from Davos in Switzerland, where Symonds lived for his health: 'A stupid woman, married above her, moving daily with people whose talk she doesn't understand . . . No two people were ever less formed to make each other comfortable; happy, they could never hope to make each other — the root of that, comprehension, being absent . . . You see that Symonds is to be pitied in his marriage, and you see that it is not her fault but her misfortune . . .' (LRLS III, 312–13.) In 1890, the married Gosse wrote to Symonds, 'I know all you speak of — the solitude, the rebellion, the despair. Years ago I wanted to write to you about all this, and withdrew through cowardice. I have had a very fortunate life, but there has been this obstinate twist in it!' (Anne Thwaite*, Edmund Gosse: A Literary Landscape *(1984), 194–5.)*

3 Bolton St. W.
June 9th

My dear Gosse.

Thanks — many — for your note about *Beltraffio*. I am delighted you see some life in it & have an appetite for the rest. Of course it is tragic — almost (I fear) repulsively so. But the 2*d* part is better written than the 1*st*, & I agree with you in thinking the thing is more solid than many of my things. I feel it to be more *packed* — more complete. But I shall do much better yet! Meanwhile you obey a very humane inspiration whenever you murmur *bravo*! in the ear of the much-attempting & slowly-composing, easily-discouraged & constantly dissatisfied fictionist. Your ever grateful

Henry James

P.S. Perhaps I *have* divined the innermost cause of J.A.S.'s discomfort — but I don't think I seize, on p. 571, exactly the allusion you refer to. I am therefore devoured with curiosity as to this further revelation. Even a post-card (in covert words) would relieve the suspense of the perhaps-already-too-indiscreet — H.J.[1]

1. Page 571 of the *English Illustrated Magazine* finds the narrator in a quiet late-evening talk in Mark Ambient's study, recognizing 'that in his books he had only said half of his thought, and what he had kept back — from motives that I deplored when I learnt them later — was the richer part'. On the same page Ambient learns that his wife blames him for the illness of their child, and comments, '"Beatrice must be very happy — she has an opportunity to triumph!"'

75. To Alphonse Daudet
19 June [1884]

Houghton MS   Published HJL III, 44–6

Daudet sent HJ a copy of his novel Sapho, *which had been serialized in* L'Echo
de Paris *(16 April to 28 May 1884). In it a young man from Provence, Jean
Gaussin, comes to Paris to pursue a diplomatic career and meets Fanny Legrand
at a masked ball. He is increasingly drawn to her; they start to live together; then
he learns of her many sexual entanglements in the past. He is disgusted and torn
by jealousy, and cannot rid himself of his dependence on her.*

3 Bolton St. Piccadilly W.
London. 19 Juin.

Mon cher Alphonse Daudet.

J'aurais dû déjà vous remercier de tout le plaisir que vous m'avez fait en
m'envoyant *Sapho*. Je vous suis très-reconnaissant de cette bonne et amicale
pensée, qui s'ajoutera désormais, pour moi, au souvenir du livre. Je n'avais
pas attendu l'arrivée de votre volume pour le lire – mais cela m'a donné
l'occasion de m'y remettre encore et de tirer un peu au clair les diverses
impressions que tant d'admirables pages m'ont laissées. Je n'essaierai pas de
vous rapporter ces impressions dans leur plénitude – dans la crainte de ne
réussir qu'à deformer ma pensée – tout autant que la vôtre. Un nouveau livre
de vous me fait passer par l'esprit une foule de belles idées, que je vous
confierais de vive voix – et de grand coeur – si j'avais le bonheur de vous voir
plus souvent. Pour le moment je vous dirai seulement que tout ce qui vient de
vous compte, pour moi, comme un grand évènement, une jouissance rare et
fructueuse. Je vous aime mieux dans certaines pages que dans d'autres, mais
vous me charmez, vous m'enlevez toujours, et votre manière me pénètre plus
qu'aucune autre. Je trouve dans *Sapho* énormément de vérité et de vie. Ce
n'est pas du roman, c'est de l'histoire, et de la plus complète et de la mieux
éclairée. Lorsqu'on a fait un livre aussi solide et aussi sérieux que celui-là, on
n'a besoin d'être rassuré par personne; ce n'est donc que pour m'encourager
moi-même que je constate dans *Sapho* encore une preuve – à ajouter à celles
que vous avez déjà données – de tout ce que le roman peut accomplir comme
révélation de la vie et du drôle de mélange que nous sommes. La fille est
étudiée avec une patience merveilleuse: c'est un de ces portraits qui épuisent
un type. Je vous avouerai que je trouve le jeune homme un peu sacrifié –
comme étude et comme recherche – sa figure me paraissant moins éclairé – en

comparaison de celle de la femme – qu'il ne le faudrait pour l'intérêt moral –
la valeur tragique. J'aurais voulu que vous nous eussiez fait voir davantage
par où il a passé – en matière d'expérience plus personnelle et plus intime
encore que les coucheries avec Fanny – en matière de rammollissement de
volonté et de relâchement d'âme. En un mot, le drame ne se passe peut-être
pas assez dans l'âme et dans la conscience de Jean Gaussin. C'est à mesure que
nous touchons à son caractère même que la situation devient intéressante – et
ce caractère, vous me faites l'effet de l'avoir un peu négligé. Vous me direz
que voilà un jugement bien anglais, et que nous inventons des *abstractions*,
comme nous disons, afin de nous dispenser de toucher aux grosses réalités.
J'estime pourtant qu'il n'y a rien de plus réel, de plus positif, de plus à peindre,
qu'un caractère; c'est là qu'on trouve bien la couleur et la forme. Vous l'avez
bien prouvé, du reste, dans chacun de vos livres, & en vous disant que vous
avez laissé l'amant de Sapho un peu trop en blanc, ce n'est qu'avec vous même
que je vous compare. Mais je ne voulais que vous remercier et répondre à
votre envoi. Je vous souhaite tout le repos qu'il vous faudra pour recommencer
encore! Je garde de cette soirée que j'ai passée chez vous au mois de Février une
impression toute colorée. Je vous prie de me rappeler au souvenir bienveillant de
Madame Daudet, je vous livre la main et suis votre bien dévoué confrère

Henry James.

[TRANSLATION: "My dear Alphonse Daudet, / I should have already thanked
you for all the pleasure you''ve given by sending me *Sapho*. I am very grateful
to you for this kind and friendly thought, which will henceforth be associated
for me with the memory of the book. I had not waited for the arrival of your
volume to read it – but its coming prompted me to set about it again and to
clarify a little the different impressions so many admirable pages have left on
me. I won't try to report these impressions to you in their fullness, lest I
succeed only in twisting my meaning – as well as yours. A new book by you
sends a host of beautiful thoughts crowding through my mind, which I would
confide to you face to face – and most willingly – if I was lucky enough to
see you more often. For the moment I will simply say to you that everything
that comes from you counts for me as a great event, a rare experience of intense
and fruitful pleasure. I like you better on some pages than on others, but you
always charm me and carry me away, and your style touches me more than
any other. I find in *Sapho* an enormous amount of truth and life. It is not
fiction, it is history, and of the most complete and insightful kind. When one
has done a book as solid and as serious as that, one needs reassurance from no
one; it is therefore only to encourage myself in my own efforts that I note in
Sapho another proof – to add to those you've already given – of all that the

novel can accomplish as a revelation of life and of the odd mixture we all are. The woman is studied in detail and with marvellous patience; it's one of those portraits which say everything about a type as a subject. I will confess to you that I find the young man somewhat neglected – as a study and as an object of inquiry – his figure seeming to me less lit up – in comparison with the woman's – than it would need to be for the moral interest, the tragic value. I would have liked you to make us see more what he went through – with regard to still more personal and intimate experience than his sexual adventures with Fanny – with regard to the softening of his resolution and the slackening of his spirit. In a word, the drama does not perhaps sufficiently take place in the soul and the consciousness of Jean Gaussin. It is as we progressively come into contact with his actual personality that the situation becomes interesting – and this personality you strike me as having a little neglected. You will tell me this is a very English judgement, and that we invent *abstractions*, as we say, in order to enable ourselves to avoid dealing with harsh realities. I believe however that there is nothing more real, more positive, more worth painting, than a personality; it is there that one really finds colour and form. You have thoroughly proved it, moreover, in each of your books, and when I tell you that you have left Sapho's lover a little too blank, it is only with yourself that I compare you. But I simply wanted to thank you and to respond to your gift. I wish you all the repose that will be necessary for you to start writing yet again! I treasure a brightly coloured memory of that evening in February which I spent at your house. I ask you to commend me to Mme Daudet, I offer you my hand and am your very devoted colleague / Henry James']

76. To Edgar Fawcett
31 July [1884]

Princeton MS   Unpublished

Edgar Fawcett (1847–1904) was a friend of Julian Hawthorne and T. B. Aldrich, a regular contributor to the Atlantic Monthly, *and an extraordinarily fluent author of novels, verse and plays. His fiercely agnostic, quasi-Naturalist novels often attacked the clergy or New York's high society. Howells and others noted HJ's influence on his writing as early as 1881. His essay 'Henry James's Novels', one of the first major general essays on HJ, appeared in the* Princeton Review, *XIV (July 1884), 68–86. He ranked HJ high: 'there is little doubt that he deserves today to be called the first of English-writing novelists'.*

3 Bolton St. Mayfair
July 31st

My dear Edgar Fawcett.

Your generosity is inexhaustible. I come back from a visit in the country to find your volume of poems (with its charming title) on my table. I lose no time in thanking you for it, for the two novels which have preceded it, & for the copy of the *Princeton Review*, with its munificent notice of my productions.[1] This last especially moves me to grateful acknowledgment. You treat me far too well, & your praise is, like all your writing, very rich. I feel, on laying down your article, as if I had swallowed a jug-full of lucent syrup tinct with cinnamon.[2] But strange to say, the liquid sweetness agrees with me, & I can only thank the friendly dispenser. If I were in N.Y. or (better) you were in London, I would talk [to] you about your novels, which have had for me much suggestion. You are right to stick to American life: I wish I knew it as well as you. *Don't* stick to verse (unless you want to very much;) I don't mean because your verse is not good; but because I am jealous of poetry – of its taking a young talent when English prose (as a real form, an art,) is so sadly neglected. Whatever you do, however, you will continue to have the cordial good wishes of yours very faithfully

Henry James

77. To Benjamin Holt Ticknor
28 September 28 [1884]

Yale MS   Unpublished

On 6 August 1884, HJ's notebook pictures him as 'Infinitely oppressed and depressed by the sense of being behindhand with the novel – that is, with the start *of it, that I have engaged, through Osgood, to write for the* Century.' *He went to Marine Parade, Dover, for seven or eight weeks till late September 1884 in order to write. He told WJ on 5 October, 'It is a better subject than I have ever had before, & I think will be much the best thing I have done yet. It is called "The Bostonians." I shall be much abused for the title but it exactly & literally fits the story, & is much the best, simplest & most dignified I could have chosen.' (CWJ I, 383.)*

1. The volume of poems is presumably *Song and Story, Later Poems* (1884); Fawcett's 1884 novels were *Tinkling Cymbals, Rutherford, An Ambitious Woman* and *The Adventures of a Widow*.
2. Keats, 'The Eve of St Agnes', XXX: 'A heap / Of candied apple, quince, and plum, and gourd; / With jellies soother than the creamy curd, / And lucent syrops tinct with cinnamon.'

Benjamin Ticknor was Osgood's partner in Osgood & Co., publishers of A Little Tour in France *on 5 September 1884.*

3 Bolton St. Piccadilly

Sept 28<i>th</i>

Dear Mr. Ticknor.

I find the 6 copies of the *Little Tour* on my return from a long absence in the country; for which many thanks. I should like you to send me ½ a dozen more, & to direct a few author's copies to be sent to the addresses I enclose.[1] I ought to have given you these names before; but better late than never. The opening chapters of "The Bostonians," the novel for the *Century*, have gone to New York, the next are following, & I earnestly hope they will begin publication with as little delay as possible. Please keep the list of names for the *Little Tour* & use it again for the forthcoming "Tales," when that volume appears.[2] I lately published an article (The Art of Fiction) in *Longman*, without appending a warning as to the U.S. copyright. But I did this on purpose, as the paper was not a story. I don't like to flaunt that American claim here for anything but stories, & consider that the reproduction (partial or entire) of that article in the U.S. will have done me more good than harm – as it will have advertised my fictions.[3] When you write me again will you kindly enclose Howells's new address?[4] Ever yours

Henry James

1. The sheets containing these names are now with another letter to Ticknor of 26 June [1885] in the Library of Congress: 'Mr. Richardson, the architect, whose initials I don't know'; William James Esq.; Miss Grace Norton; Mrs. Lodge; T. B. Aldrich Esq.; Mrs. Owen Wister; Miss Emma Lazarus; Mrs. Walsh (Aunt Kate).
2. *Tales of Three Cities* ('The Impressions of a Cousin', 'Lady Barberina', 'A New England Winter') was published by Osgood on 17 October 1884.
3. 'The Art of Fiction' was indeed pirated in Boston, by Cupples, Upham & Company, in November 1884, bound together with Walter Besant's essay of the same title (which the same publisher had pirated in August). HJ himself collected it in *Partial Portraits* (1888).
4. Howells had recently bought a house at 302 Beacon Street, Boston.

78. To Grace Norton
14 November [1884]

Houghton MS   Unpublished

Reviews of A Little Tour in France *were appearing as one of the most scurrilous presidential contests in American electoral history was being played out, and despite his absence – or because of it – HJ became involved. In October 1884 Theodore Roosevelt spoke to the Brooklyn Young Republican Club, justifying his sudden support for the aggressive imperialist James G. Blaine, who had been implicated in a financial scandal, as (unsuccessful) presidential candidate against the Democrat Grover Cleveland, who had been revealed as having had an adulterous affair and an illegitimate child. (Roosevelt had opposed Blaine at the convention, and some of Blaine's more fastidious opponents – 'Mugwumps' or 'bolters' – had left the party.) The Democratic* New York Times *reported: 'Mr. Roosevelt said that his hearers had read to their sorrow the works of Henry James. He bore the same relation to other literary men that a poodle did to other dogs. The poodle had his hair combed and was somewhat ornamental, but never useful. He was invariably ashamed to imitate the British lion. In Mr. Roosevelt's opinion there were many traits in the "Poodle Henry James" that the independents of the Henry James order of intellect had in common. These men formed quite a number of the bolters this year. They were possessed of refinement and culture to see what was wrong, but possessed none of the robuster virtues that would enable them to come out and do the right.' (Sunday, 19 October 1884.)*

AJ and her friend Katharine Loring arrived at Liverpool on 11 November.

Adelphi Hotel. Liverpool
Nov. 14th

My dear Grace.

Your two documents – or rather three – the rejected vindication, Garrison's note, & your own – came to me just before I came to this place – four days ago – to meet Alice, which I have done, with the expected sequel of remaining here some days with her, she being quite knocked up with the voyage.[1] We go, however, to London tomorrow, & then, for the next weeks, to Bournemouth.[2]

---

1. Neither 'note' is known to survive. Wendell Phillips Garrison (1840–1907), son of the abolitionist William Lloyd Garrison, was from 1865 to 1906 literary editor of the *Nation*, for which HJ wrote many reviews in the 1870s.

2. Once AJ got to London, HJ installed her at 40 Clarges Street, near Bolton Street. She was such an invalid that she did not go out for nine weeks (Katharine Loring being in Bournemouth

Let me thank you both gratefully & amusedly for your adventure with the cudgels on my behalf. It was delightfully feminine of you to think that the Nation would have printed that article – in itself duly feminine, to begin with. But it is all the more agreeable to me & I read it with the sense of being a public more *choisi* than it would have found in the other case. Garrison's note is very reasonable – but I could understand the situation better if I had seen the article you speak of in the *Nation*, which I have not yet done. I gather it is rather nasty, & if it is I don't think it friendly of the *Nation* to have published it.[3] I should be the last to expect or desire it to puff me because I am an old contributor (& a friend of the Editors!) but there is an alternative – i.e. saying nothing, rather than holding one up to scorn. My "Little Tour" is a book that could easily be passed in silence. But I am writing – heaven knows why! – as if I cared about reviews! I don't, honestly, & rarely read them – finding them rarely worth it. Yours only, published or unpublished, are of interest to me. What was Roosevelt's allusion to, or attack upon, me, in his speech? I have heard nothing, & know nothing, of it. I never look at the American papers – I find them (with the exception of the *Nation*, which, however, I don't see at all regularly,) intolerable. At the end of four days in this dreary place I feel completely out of the world & am already homesick for London. Write a review of me with "digs", dear Grace, & it will have more success.

I wrote you a longish letter a couple of weeks ago, & you will be getting it by this time.[4] I thank you for your generous wrath, zeal & eloquence – none of it is lost, any more than your other virtues on yours ever

Henry James

---

with her sister Louisa, also an invalid, most of that time); she had an attack in late December. At the end of January AJ went to Bournemouth; in April HJ went down to be near her.

3. The *Nation*'s anonymous review of *A Little Tour in France* is indeed hostile. HJ's approach is criticized as excessively 'personal': 'The point of view throughout is the sentimental, the dilettante. The superficial aspect treated is the purely picturesque. Now, in France this is a great mistake' (No. 1008, 23 October 1884, 358–9).

4. HJ had on 3 November written to her about her 'rare faculty of taking the world tragically' and about AJ's impending arrival and his recent essay 'The Art of Fiction'. He also told her, 'I shall never marry . . . I am both happy enough and miserable enough, as it is, and don't wish to add to either side of the account.' (HJL III, 52, 54.)

79. To Theodore Child
29 November [1884]

Virginia MS   Unpublished

3 Bolton St. W.
Nov 29<u>th</u>.

My dear Child.

Your letter was a stimulating – though I may add a depressing – excuse my Irish sequences – whiff of Paris; & your essay on the studio-poverty of the English tongue very amusing.[1] I am much grieved at your account of our poor dear old Huntington; & I wish you would very kindly forward him the enclosed.[2] It is only a weak, vain word of friendly sympathy; but such as it is I should like him to get it.

I think you make too much of the before-mentioned absence of artistic slang in our philistine tongue: though I admit there is a certain void. There are certain things the anglo-saxon mind never attempts to say, n'en éprouvant pas le besoin. If the fancy shld. take it, it would be much bothered for want of a vehicle, doubtless; but the French, I think, have run too much to clichés of that sort. They don't seem to have made them (the French) any tidier – witness the general literary foulness on which you animadvert. I [don't] think it a fault in a language, in a word, to have kept technical terms out [of] the literary current – that is, to have kept them out more than the French have done. Poor Sir J. Reynolds' small vocabulary didn't make him paint the worse.[3] Your account of Goncourt's "court" is appalling: I didn't suppose that Challot[?] showed himself dans le monde.[4] A pox on M*me* Daudet; elle est bien susceptible. What do you say of M*me* Hugues?[5] The demoralization of your country seems to me complete. Escape before the doom of Gomorrah descends on it – escape to this virtuous clime where I see that the Very Rev. the Dean of Hereford

1. I have not located Child's 'essay'; HJ may be referring to a passage in Child's letter.
2. HJ had heard from Child by 10 October 1883 of their friend Huntington's illness (HJL III, 6).
3. Sir Joshua Reynolds (1723–92), one of the greatest English painters of the eighteenth century, was also the author of the highly influential *Discourses* on art (1769–90), delivered to the students of the Royal Academy, of which he was the first president.
4. I have found no trace of a 'Challot' in Goncourt's Journal or Mme Daudet's memoirs.
5. Perhaps Madame Hugues Le Roux, wife of the French journalist (1860–1925) who was a friend of Paul Bourget.

was yesterday arrested for indecent behaviour – with a young man! – in Hyde Park.[6] Ce que c'est de nous! Yours ever

H. James

Do write again. I shld. be glad of more news of Huntington.

80. To Robert Louis Stevenson
5 December [1884]

Yale MS   Published HJL III, 57–8; HJRLS, 101–2

HJ and Stevenson had first met at lunch with Andrew Lang in 1879. HJ's sense of Stevenson then (for T. S. Perry) had been: 'a shirt-collarless Bohemian and a great deal (in an inoffensive way) of a poseur' *(HJL II, 255). Stevenson's of HJ in 1881 (to their friend Henley, disagreeing about* Washington Square, *'an unpleasant book'): 'a mere club fizzle (fizzle perhaps too strong, on representations from the weaker vessel) and no out-of-doors, stand-up man whatever' (LRLS III, 159).*

HJ's response under the same title to Walter Besant's 'The Art of Fiction' in turn provoked Stevenson to 'A Humble Remonstrance', which took issue with HJ's insistence that 'The only reason for the existence of a novel is that it does compete *with life.'*

3 Bolton St. Piccadilly
Dec. 5th

My dear Robert Louis Stevenson
    I read only last night your paper in the December *Longmans*, in genial rejoinder to my article in the same periodical on Besant's lecture, & the result of that charming half-hour is a friendly desire to send you three words. Not words of discussion, dissent, retort or remonstrance, but of hearty sympathy, charged with the assurance of my enjoyment of everything you write. It's a

6. The *Pall Mall Gazette* for 16 December 1884, under the heading 'The Charge against the Dean of Hereford', records that, 'At the Central Criminal Court yesterday the grand jury had before them the bill of indictment against the Dean of Hereford for alleged immoral conduct with a young man in Hyde Park last month. After a long investigation the grand jury came into court and announced that they ignored the bill. The announcement was received with some applause by the court.' The Dean was the Hon. and Very Reverend George Herbert, and the young man Charles Telfer or Trefer.

luxury, in this immoral age, to encounter some one who *does* write – who is really acquainted with that lovely art. It wouldn't be fair to contend with you here; besides, we agree, I think, much more than we disagree, & though there are points as to which a more irrepressible spirit than mine would like to try a fall – that is not what I want to say – but on the contrary, to thank you for so much that is suggestive & felicitous in your remarks – justly felt & brilliantly said. They are full of these things, & the current of your admirable style floats pearls & diamonds. Excellent are your closing words, & no one can assent more than I to your proposition that all art is a simplification.[1] It is a pleasure to see that truth so neatly uttered. My pages, in Longman, were simply a plea for liberty: they were only half of what I had to say, & some day I shall try & express the remainder.[2] Then I shall tickle you a little, affectionately, as I pass. You will say that my liberty is an obese divinity, requiring extra-measures; but after one more go I shall hold my tongue. The native *gaiety* of all that you write is delightful to me, & when I reflect that it proceeds from a man whom life has laid much of the time on his back, (as I understand it) I find you a genius indeed. There must be pleasure in it for you too. I ask Colvin about you whenever I see him, & I shall have to send him this to forward to you.[3] I hope the present Season is using you tenderly, & I am with innumerable good wishes yours very faithfully

Henry James.[4]

1. Stevenson's essay closes by advising the young writer to bear in mind that 'although, in great men, working upon great motives, what we observe and admire is often their complexity, yet underneath appearances the truth remains unchanged: that simplification was their method, and that simplicity is their excellence'.
2. HJ had said as much to Grace Norton in early November: 'I mean . . . to publish another article on the subject – for the [one] in *Longman* was only about half even of the essence of what I have to say' (HJL III, 53).
3. Sidney Colvin (1845–1927), a close friend of Stevenson as well as Gosse, was Slade Professor of Fine Art at Cambridge from 1873 to 1885, and keeper of prints and drawings at the British Museum from 1883 to 1912. He also wrote biographies of Landor and Keats. He was to be Stevenson's literary executor and edit the posthumous Edinburgh edition (1894–7) and letters (1899 and 1911), etc.
4. Stevenson replied to this letter on 8 December, saying he was pleased at the prospect of a sequel to 'The Art of Fiction', in order to educate the public about the art of literature; that he was glad HJ liked his works; and that he wished HJ could write 'as it were an episode from one of the old (so-called) novels of adventure'. He invited HJ to Bournemouth, where, coincidentally, AJ was soon to join Katharine Loring.

81. To Thomas Bailey Aldrich
3 January 1885

Houghton MS   Unpublished

On 12 December 1884, HJ told Perry, 'I have been all the morning at Millbank Prison (horrible place) collecting notes for a fiction scene. You see I am quite the Naturalist.' (HJL III, 61.) HJ later described The Princess Casamassima *as inspired by settling in London, by 'the habit and the interest of walking the streets' (LC II, 1086). But he was forced to write to Aldrich on 30 December 1884 to postpone its start in the* Atlantic *from July to September 1885: 'I work better, I think, as I grow older, but I also work more slowly, & the novel I have been writing for the* Century *("The Bostonians") has outstretched & elongated its issue to a degree to force me to postpone, a few weeks, ulterior proceedings. Two months more will give me plenty of margin, & when the "Princess Casamassima" does begin it will be so magnificent that you will be delighted (so to speak) to have waited for it.' (Unpublished Houghton MS, bMS Am 1429 (2580).)*

HJ's article on George Eliot's Life as Related in Her Letters and Journals *(1885) by her widower, John Walter Cross, appeared in the* Atlantic *of May 1885. Lord Brabourne's 1884 edition of* Letters of Jane Austen *was not reviewed in the* Atlantic *in 1885.*

3 Bolton St. W.
Jan 3d '85

Dear Aldrich.

I quite omitted to say to you in my last that as a kind of compensation for any wrong I may do by the postponement of my novel for 2 months I shall be very glad to write you a couple of shortish articles: on George Eliot's Life & Letters, which are coming out here in two or three weeks; & 1 on those of Jane Austen, (her Letters) which appeared a short time since.[1] As the latter book is possibly to be treated of in your pages, actually, I will do the other

---

1. HJ never directly addressed Jane Austen's work in his criticism. His letter of 23 June 1883, to the brilliant but hapless poet and critic George Pellew (1860–92), who had won a prize for a dissertation on her, comments that he would have made more than Pellew of Jane Austen's 'genius – of the extraordinary vividness with which she saw what she did see, and of her narrow unconscious perfection of form'. Pellew has acutely noted 'the want of moral illumination on the part of her heroines, who had undoubtedly small and second-rate minds and were perfect little she-Philistines'. But that contributes to their interest – 'a sort of simple undistracted concentrated feeling which we scarcely find any more' (SL2, 189).

1st. I will obtain George Eliot as soon as she appears, & let you have the article quickly. You will then, if necessary, have time to warn me off Jane Austen. In haste ever yours

Henry James

82. To William James
14 February [1885]

Houghton MS   Published HJL III, 68–70; CWJ II, 7–9; SL2, 201–4

On 6 March 1884 HJ had written jocularly to T. S. Perry of The Bostonians *as 'a remorseless exploitation of Boston', saying 'Look out, in Marlborough St.; I am especially hard on the far end' (TSPB, 316). The novel began in the* Century *in February 1885, and at once offended Bostonian sensitivities. It must have been about this time that HJ insisted to Osgood, who had sold the novel to the* Century *and was to publish the book, that 'the charge in regard to this serial's containing "personalities" is idiotic & baseless: there is not the smallest, faintest portrait in the book' (Unpublished MS fragment, Congress (#1955).)*

3 Bolton St. W.
Feb. 14*th*

Dear William

I am quite appalled by your note of the 2*d,* in which you assault me on the subject of my having painted a "portrait from life" of Miss Peabody![1] I was in some measure prepared for it by Lowell's (as I found the other day) taking for granted that she had been my model, & an allusion to the same effect in a note from Aunt Kate. Still, I didn't expect the charge to come from you. I hold that I have done nothing to deserve it, & think your tone on the subject singularly harsh & unfair. I care not a straw what people in general may say about Miss Birdseye – they can say nothing more idiotic & insulting than they have already said about all my books in which there has been any attempt to represent things or persons in America; but I should be very sorry – in fact deadly sick, or fatally ill – if I thought Miss Peabody *herself* supposed I intended to represent her. I absolutely had no shadow of such an intention. I have not

---

1. WJ's 'note of the 2*d*' is not known to survive. Elizabeth Palmer Peabody (1804–94), pupil of Emerson, acquaintance of Henry James Senior and Transcendentalist reformer, founded the first American kindergarten in Boston in 1860.

seen Miss Peabody for 20 years, I never had but the most casual observation of her, I didn't know whether she was alive or dead, & she was not in the smallest degree my starting point or example. Miss Birdseye was evolved entirely from my moral consciousness, like every person I have ever drawn, & originated in my desire to make a figure who should embody in a sympathetic, pathetic, picturesque & at the same time grotesque way, the humanitary & *ci-devant* transcendental tendencies which I thought it highly probable I should be accused of treating in a contemptuous manner in so far as they were otherwise represented in the tale. I wished to make this figure a woman, because so it would be more touching, & an old, weary battered & simple-minded woman because that deepened the same effect. I elaborated her in my mind's eye – & after I had got going reminded myself that my creation would perhaps be identified with Miss Peabody – *that* I freely admit. So I bore in mind the need of being careful, at the same time that I didn't see what I could do but go my way, according to my own fancy, and make my image as living as I saw it. The one definite thing about which I had a scruple was some touch about Miss Birdseye's spectacles – I remembered that Miss P.'s were always in the wrong place; but I didn't see, really, why I should deprive myself of an effect (as regards this point,) which is common to a thousand old people. So I thought no more about Miss Peabody *at all*, but simply strove to realize my vision. If I have made my old woman *live* it is my misfortune, & the thing is doubtless a rendering – a vivid rendering, of my idea. If it is at the same time a rendering of Miss Peabody I am absolutely irresponsible – & extremely sorry for the accident. If there is any chance of its being represented to *her* that I have undertaken to reproduce her in a novel I will immediately write to her, in the most respectful manner, to say that I have done nothing of the kind, that an old survivor of the New England Reform period was an indispensable personage in my story, that my paucity of data & not my repletion is the faulty side of the whole picture, that, as I went, I had no sight or thought of her, but only of an imaginary figure which was much nearer to me, and that in short I have the vanity to claim that Miss Birdseye is a creation. You may think I protest too much; but I am alarmed by the sentence in your letter "– It is really a pretty bad business," & haunted by the idea that this may apply to some rumour you have heard of Miss Peabody's feeling *atteinte*. I can imagine no other reason why you should call the picture of Miss Birdseye a "bad business" or indeed any business at all. I would write to Miss P. on the chance – only I don't like to *assume* that she feels touched, when it is possible that she may not, & know nothing about the matter. If you can ascertain whether or no she does & will let me know, I will, should there be need or fitness, immediately write to her. Miss Birdseye is a subordinate figure in the *Bostonians*, & after appearing in the *1st* & *2d* numbers, vanishes till toward the end, when she re-enters, briefly, & pathetically & honourably dies. But though subordinate, she is I think, the best figure in the book, she is treated with respect throughout, & every virtue of heroism & disinterestedness is attributed to her. She is represented as the embodiment of pure the purest philanthropy. The story is, I think, the best fiction I have written, & I expected you, if you said anything about it, would intimate that you thought as much – so that I find this charge on the subject of Miss P. a very cold douche indeed.

I shall be very willing to let little Howard James have $25, to be taken by you out [of] the money you say you owe me – by which I think you mean the money you had *prélevé* (or borrowed) from my share of the Syracuse rents to pay for Father's book (that is, for your half of the costs.)[2] In writing to B. Temple to tell him I withheld the $100, I enclosed him a tendollar greenback.[3]

About Alice I have written to AK. two or three times quite lately, & there ought to be an agreement between you that she always forwards you my notes. I sent her a word this a.m. with a very short note of Alice's, & one of K. Loring's, both just received by me from Bournemouth enclosed. Alice is evidently now rather stationary, but not *bad*.[4] She has been a month at Bournemouth but has not yet left her room. Her *legs* seem always a serious question. K. Loring & Louisa will probably remain at B. till the end of April, & then go elsewhere. I shall then go to Alice, who, however, may subsequently rejoin the Lorings in the place they go to. They spend the summer in Europe. I don't think the climate has anything at all to do with Alice's state. She isn't in the least in touch with it, always in doors, with the same profuse fires, never reached by the outer air. I am sorry – very – for your botherations about your house. Ever yours

H. James.

2. Howard James (1866–1920) was a cousin, son of Henry James Senior's youngest brother, who tried acting at this time, before later becoming a doctor. WJ was looking after the family real estate in Syracuse. 'Father's book' was *The Literary Remains of the Late Henry James*, edited and with a long introduction by WJ, and published by Osgood in 1884.
3. Their cousin Robert Temple (b. 1840), brother of Minny Temple and Henrietta Pell-Clarke, was in prison in Montana for forgery, and writing to family members asking for the $250 to get him out.
4. AJ had had a serious attack in December.

83. To William James
15 February [1885]

Houghton MS   Published HJL III, 71–2; CWJ II, 10–11

3 Bolton St. W.
Feb. 15*th*

Dear William.

Let me say as a p.s. to my letter of yesterday that I was wrong in telling you to take the $25 for Howard James from the Syracuse money you owe me, as I have assigned this as you know altogether to Alice, to whom of course you continue to pay it, & I want it to go to her intact. She appears scarcely to touch it, & her idea is to "save it up" for me, but I wish her to have it, all the same. The subtraction of the money to pay for my ½ of Father's book was an exceptional case, arranged between us. Therefore I will send you one of these very next days a postal order or a £5 note, for the $25. Today is a Sunday, & I can do nothing.

I have been thinking over the rest of my novel, in relation to Miss Birdseye, & it seems to me that even if Miss Peabody *should* think I meant to portray her (which, however, heaven forfend!) she cannot on the whole feel that what I had in mind is not something very fine & is not tenderly & sympathetically expressed. The later apparition & death of Miss B. is the prettiest thing in the book, & even should it be resentfully insisted that the picture is a portrait (I am told, on all sides, here, that my *Author of Beltraffio* is a living & scandalous portrait of J. A. Symonds & his wife, whom I have never seen) I believe the story will remain longer than poor Miss P.'s name or fame, & I don't hold that it will be an obloquy or ground of complaint for her, to be handed down as having suggested anything so touching & striking. In a word, after you have read the book I don't think it will seem to you any more wounding for her to be known as Miss Birdseye than to be known as Miss P. But probably, later, if the episode *does* strike people as I think it will, they will deny then that I *did* have Miss P. in my mind, or that they ever said so; they will never give me the credit of having wished to represent her gracefully!

As I told you yesterday I never wished or attempted to represent her *at all*, or dreamed of it, & to be accused of doing so is a poor reward for having laboriously bodied forth out of the vague of imagination, & with absolute independence of any model that my own wits did not afford me, a creature who is (as I think) interesting & picturesque. If you think it so bad a business now, perhaps you will think that the sequel does *not* better it – but I can do nothing more than I have done, at this last hour – except, as I say, write a letter of absolute protest to Miss Peabody.

You don't tell me whether you had any rejoinder from Godkin to the letter you wrote about the review of your book.[1] When I had read the article it was absolutely impossible for me not to write to him on my own account, & as I told him that the notice was "contemptible, &, under the circumstances, barbarous," he may see fit to terminate our acquaintance. Melancholy, after 20 years! Ever yours

H. James

84. To Theodore Child
16 February [1885]

Virginia MS   Unpublished

3 Bolton St. W.
Feb. 16*th*

Dear Child.

Your interesting letter of the 10*th* has been lying on my table for several days, tempting me to a response for which, till this moment, the licence has been wanting. I expect, every time I hear from you, to learn that everything is over with Huntington but perhaps the hope – the hope that he may have ceased to suffer, which I confess I earnestly entertain – is father – too much – to the thought. I heard yesterday that Smalley had gone to Paris & I hope that seeing him (for they are very old friends,) may ease him off or pass the time for him a little. I sympathise in your longing for quelque chose de bien méridional, & think (though a black rain is falling here & the sun, for the moment, disowns us,) that I should feel it still more if I were chained to the

1. The *Nation* on 15 January 1885 contained an anonymous review of *The Literary Remains of Henry James*, declaring that on the whole 'the volume has no literary interest'. WJ wrote to Godkin, complaining of an excess of 'impartiality': 'Poor Harry's books seem always given out to critics with antipathy to his literary temperament; and now for this only and last review of my father – a writer exclusively religious – a personage seems to have been selected for whom the religious life is complete *terra incognita*.' (LWJ I, 240.) HJ wrote too, but his letter seems not to survive. Godkin wrote back in distress to both brothers, explaining that the critic in question had been chosen by another of the editors, Garrison.

pavé de Paris. The moral climate of that city strikes me as so unpleasant par le temps qui court that the cruder civilization & less organised Priapism of some southern land present themselves as, by contrast, almost Arcadian. I am deeply pained at your revelation in regard to the "little thing".[1] Poor dear fascinating, beautiful, but I fear rather crapulous little thing! He ought to know that any American publisher was foredoomed to lâcher "Sappho" as soon as he had looked at it, & required no journalist to explain to him that it couldn't possibly pass, in English. Your history of Goncourt, his *grenier* & his dirty little companions, is very sad: it completes the impression of something perverse & disagreeable that in the midst of so much that was interesting, I got from that visit to him I paid with you last February (I see by a notebook it was the *6th*.)[2] And for him to be working at this point of his career upon Paris actresses of the last century – i.e. resuscitating defunct whores – completes the picture.[3] There is in all this a strange smell of décadance! Here we are much more proper. The only engrossing topic is Sudan tragedy – only yet in its *1st* act – on which I won't entertain you; though every thing there, & here, conspires to make this such an interesting, exciting moment to be in England that you ought to envy me.[4] People do also talk a little about George Eliot's Life, which has just been published in 3 fat volumes by her *2d* husband (& which to me is very interesting) & they talk so Britannically![5] It is full of a deep decency, earnestness, constant, strenuous labour, & a comfortable English prosperity – yet what is most alluded to – there are long discussions as to whether she was "right" – is the scandalous Bohemian fact that she lived 25 years, conjugally, with G. H. Lewes without having married him. It makes me feel how far one is from the pavé de Paris. I have still my little dream of going to Paris for 10 days, before long, but nothing is definite as yet.[6] What prevents me is unfinished work – serial-novels – which presses me, so that I can't leave them.[7] Always remember how much your little chronicles interest me, & send me one

1. *Le Petit Chose* is the title of a Daudet novel.
2. This notebook does not seem to survive. Goncourt inaugurated his celebrated *Grenier* ('Attic') on 1 February 1885, with a Sunday gathering of fifteen or sixteen male intellectuals for discussion, including Zola, Daudet, Maupassant, the novelist Huysmans and the poet Hérédia.
3. I have not found a Goncourt book answering this description, but the Goncourt brothers together had published in the 1860s a small book called *Les Actrices*, and had collaborated on a study of eighteenth-century painters.
4. HJ's military friend Lord Wolseley was involved as leader of the Gordon Relief Expedition of 1884–5.
5. The book was reviewed by HJ in the *Atlantic* of May 1885.
6. HJ did not get to Paris until September 1885.
7. *The Bostonians* and *The Princess Casamassima*.

on any pretext. Give my love, please, to Huntington: I shall get news of him
from S.

Tout à vous
H. James

85. *To John Hay*
13 May [1885]

Brown MS   Published HJJH, 97–8

By mid April HJ, who was about to join AJ in Bournemouth, had completed The
Bostonians, *but not yet had it all 'type-copied' for transmission to the U.S. The pre-*
vious year he had read Hay's own anonymously published novel The Breadwinners,
and on 3 May 1884 had written to his sister he was sure it was Hay's and that it had
'a great deal of crude force & is ce qu'on a (lately) fait de mieux in the American novel,
after Howells & me' (Unpublished Houghton MS, bMS Am 1094 (1605)).

St Alban's Cliff, Bournemouth
May 13*th*

My dear Hay.

I am immensely touched & gratified by your friendly note anent the *Bostonians*
& the noble Lamar.[1] It was a kind thought in you that led you to repeat to
me his appreciative judgment of my rather reckless attempt to represent a
youthful Southron. It makes me believe for a moment that that attempt is less
futile than it has seemed to me on seeing the story in print; & I am delighted,
at any rate, that the benevolent Senator should have recognized in it some
intelligence of intention, some happy divination. He himself, for that matter is
in it a little, for I met him once or twice in Washington & he is one of the few
very Mississippians with whom I have had the pleasure of conversing. Basil
Ransom is made up of wandering airs & chance impressions, & I fear that as
the story goes on he doesn't become as solid as he ought to be. He remains a
rather vague & artificial creation, & so far as he looks at all real, is only fait
de chic, as the French say. But if you ever get a chance, without betraying to

1. Lucius Quintus Cincinnatus Lamar (1825–93) was a member of the Confederate government
during the Civil War, but subsequently a popular senator from Mississippi who was in 1885
made Secretary of the Interior. He was a friend of the Henry Adamses. In a speech of 1860 in
the House of Representatives he had argued that slavery was constitutional, calling abolitionism
'this fanatical revolution'.

Lamar that you betrayed him, do whisper to him that it gave me very great pleasure to know that in the figure of B.R. he did recognize something human & Mississippian. His word is a reward. So is your own, my dear Hay. It *do* please me if some one says that I write tidily, & if that some one happens to be some one who knows what he is talking about I celebrate the day. I am down in this mild spot (mild in every sense but being very cold) to look after my sister, who is here in a state of wretched invalidism, & to escape the rush and crush of tout ce que vous savez in London from this time on.[2] I shall probably be out of town for most of the season, & hope to have something to show for it. Nevertheless I feel as great a pang to hear that King isn't to arrive by the next train for Liverpool, as if I were at my door in Bolton St. to see him pass to his own. Mexico, lackaday![3] That has an evil sound. What a mixture of a life! But I believe he is coming back as firmly as I believe that I am never going away. Give my tender love to him when you have a chance, & tell him the British barmaid mourns his absence in plaintive *h*elegies!

The laird & lady of Tillypronie were in town for a couple of months in a lame & languid condition, I am very sorry to say. She is very feeble, & poor dear Sir John is not much better. I feel more than ever the curse & blight of their solitary home being in that remote mountain fastness: a ridiculous perch for two infirm & impecunious *vieillards*. They ought to have a decent flat, in South Kensington, but instead of that they have a protuberance in Caledonia stern and wild. Luckily they have let their London house, to Lord Napier of Magdala.[4] I mourn Lowell already & hate his successor in advance.[5] It is a wanton stroke of fate: without a redeeming feature. The air is thick with politics of course, but the shock of battle is for the moment averted. I ween, however, it's a truce only, & a growling one. I send a most gallant message to Mrs. Hay, & my blessing on the smaller wisps. I hope you are in tolerable form & am ever very faithfully & gratefully yours

Henry James.

2. George Monteiro cites Sir John Clark, the 'laird of Tillypronie', writing to Hay about HJ on 20 October 1885: 'I am afraid the poor fellow is much hampered by that most impracticable of Crosses – I was going to say crises – an hysterical & of course exacting Sister.'
3. Clarence King was made president of his mining company in the spring of 1885, after his two-year holiday in Europe, and returned to his mines in Mexico. In May 1884 the joke of those like HJ in the King–Hay–Adams circle was that King had abandoned his millionaire friends like Ferdinand Rothschild and preferred dining with 'publicans, barmaids, and other sinners' (HJ to AJ, 3 May 1884, HJJH, 172).
4. Robert Cornelis Napier (1810–90), first Baron Napier of Magdala, was an eminent military man.
5. With Cleveland's election to the U.S. presidency, Lowell was replaced in 1885 as Minister to England by Edward J. Phelps.

86. To Benjamin Holt Ticknor
26 June [1885]

Congress MS   Unpublished

*On 21 August 1885 HJ was to write to WJ that 'this year has been disastrous'
(CWJ II, 25). The Bostonians had already gone vastly over schedule and over
length, on a contract with his American publisher, J. R. Osgood & Co., which was
to give him a flat $4,000 for serial and book rights for five years in the U.S.
(permanently in foreign markets). On 2 May, in Bournemouth, he saw in* The
Times *that Osgood had gone into receivership. HJ had for some time been fretting
about the non-payment of various moneys due him under his contract, and WJ had
to advance him $1,000 on 22 May for current expenses.*

*On 2 June it was announced that Ticknor & Co., under Osgood's partner Ticknor,
son of William Davis Ticknor (1810–64), would take over the business of Osgood
& Co. Since HJ had been advised by Frederick Macmillan not to send off the last
section of the novel, and Osgood had not observed his contractual obligations, HJ
retained the copyright and was in a position to negotiate.*

3 Bolton St. W.
June 26*th*

Dear Mr. Ticknor.

I have your letter of the 10*th*.

I have written to Mr. Warner that I shall be glad to leave you the Bostonians
for $4000 down *on a new contract*.[1]

This contract to modify in 2 particulars the old.

1*st*. To apply only to the United States, & leave me the English market: i.e.
leave me free to make my own arrangement to publish the book here.

2*d*: To restore me at the end of *five years* all the American rights, without
conditions.

My original contract with your former firm was so insanely unprofitable for
me, that I must claim this relief now that that firm is broken up. If it had lasted
I should have swallowed my mistake in silence, though greatly repenting of
it: but I must rectify it in some small degree, in these altered conditions. The
changes I ask for still leave you the book on tremendously low terms. The
Atlantic gives me $4,200 for the *simple serial use* of the novel I begin there in
September; & for the $4000 now in suspension between us you will have had

1. Joseph Bangs Warner was the James family attorney.

the serial use of the *Bostonians* & the American sales, which I am sure will be larger than those of any other book of mine, for the long period I mention (5 years) into the bargain.[2] I trust you will see the justice of the alteration I desire; in which case I shall, as I say, be very glad to leave you the book.

As regards future books of mine I must put off correspondence on that point for the present. I should wish first to know whether your new firm assumes the liabilities of your old, or whether what you propose to me is to remit my unpaid royalties (on 5 books) & "start fresh".[3] Truly yours

H. James

87. To Robert de Montesquiou
21 August [1885]

Bib. Nat. MS   Published HJL III, 96

It was August before Ticknor finally turned down HJ's $4,000 demand (about £800 for book and *serial), delaying the £500 advance (on a 15 per cent royalty) HJ eventually received in a new deal with Macmillan, who published the book in Britain (16 February 1886) and America (19 March 1886). (The* Century *had months previously paid Osgood in full for the serial publication; that money was forfeit.)*

On 2 June 1885, HJ had dispatched the first instalment of The Princess Casamassima *to Aldrich and the* Atlantic, *promising 'The 2d instalment will follow in a week or two – don't be nervous!' (Unpublished Houghton MS, bMS Am 1429 (2584).) On 10 August, still in Bournemouth, he recorded in his notebook that he needed to clarify its 'future evolution'. He was launched on the writing and had begun to send off manuscript, but many details of the novel remained vague to him – 'owing to the fact that I have been so terribly preoccupied – up to so lately – with the unhappy* Bostonians, *born under an evil star'.*

On 2 and 3 July 1885 HJ had found himself caught in town. Through his recent friend Sargent, he became London guide and introducer (to Whistler, for instance) of three grand visiting French aesthetes, originals of characters in Marcel Proust's À la recherche du temps perdu: *Count Robert de Montesquiou-Fézensac (1855– 1921), homosexual man of letters, the cultured doctor Jean-Samuel Pozzi (1846– 1918), and the composer Prince Edmond de Polignac (1834–1901). After another stay in Bournemouth, HJ returned to town, till on 1 August shifting to Dover for*

2. *The Princess Casamassima* ran in the *Atlantic* from September 1885 to October 1886. HJ had sent off the first chapters by June.

3. The five books were: *Daisy Miller: A Comedy* (the play); *The Siege of London*; *Portraits of Places*; *A Little Tour in France*; *Tales of Three Cities*.

what he called on 28 August 'a very secluded & meditative month' (to Lady Wolseley, Unpublished Hove MS).

15 Esplanade,
Douvres:
ce 21 août.

Cher Monsieur de Montesquiou

Je suis bien aise de savoir que vous avez gardé un aussi bon souvenir de votre trop court passage à Londres, & vous envoie ce mot pour vous engager à y retourner sans crainte de voir se gâter vos belles impressions. Je crois que l'interêt que vous avez trouvé à beaucoup de choses ne ferait que s'accroître avec une plus intime connaissance – & que pour vous, comme pour tous ceux qui ont fini par s'attacher à la vie anglaise, le premier aspect & la surface un peu terne (de bien des éléments) se trouvera n'avoir été qu'une mesure trompeuse des jouissances qui vous attendent! Soyez certain, dans tous les cas, que chaque fois que vous reparaîtrez vous ferez bien du plaisir à yours very faithfully

Henry James

[TRANSLATION: 'I am happy to learn that you have preserved so good a memory of your too-short time in London, and I send you this note to urge you to return with no fear of spoiling your favourable impressions. I believe the interest you found in so many things could only grow with more intimate acquaintance – and that for you, as for all who have ultimately become attached to English life, the first appearance and the rather dull surface (of many of the elements) will turn out to have given a misleading indication of just how many great delights await you! Be sure, in any case, that each time you come back here you will give much pleasure to yours very faithfully / Henry James']

88. To Benjamin Holt Ticknor
27 August [1885]

Virginia MS   Unpublished

Dover
August 27*th*

Dear Mr. Ticknor.

I have signed the cancellation-papers sent me by Mr. Warner, & returned one of them to him. I did this rather because I wished to wind up the whole matter than because I was struck with the fitness of the clause of which you had requested the insertion, to the effect that I should relieve you of your stereotype plates.[1] Please debit me with the amount of the cost of them & *see that they are destroyed*, as I have no use for them. Mr. Warner also transmitted me your offer to take the *Bostonians* on sale, giving me 20 percent. I am much obliged to you; it is already arranged that Messrs. Macmillan dispose of the book in the U.S.

Truly yours
Henry James

89. To William James
9 October 1885

Houghton MS Published HJL III, 101–2; CWJ II, 29–31

On 11 September, hard-pressed, HJ crossed to Paris, where he took his old apartment in the renamed rue de Luxembourg till the end of October. On 18 September he wrote to Fanny Stevenson: 'Ah, to whom do you say it – that the devil of the serial at one's back mortifies the man & murders the artist? – If some one would make me des rentes I would write 20 lines a day.' (Unpublished Yale MS, MS Vault Stevenson 4959.)

In May WJ had lent HJ $1,000 'for current expenses', which he was now paying back in instalments. Their brother Robertson, an alcoholic, had decided to make WJ and Warner, the family lawyer, trustees of his share of the estate in order to prevent himself from selling it and squandering the proceeds. The Princess Casamassima had begun what would turn out to be a fourteen-month run in the Atlantic *in September. WJ had made further comments on* The Bostonians.

29 Rue Cambon.
Oct. *9th* 1885

Dear William.

This must be a very short effusion, mainly to enclose you another draft of $250, & to thank you for 2 letters, both received during the month that I have been spending in Paris. The 1st was from Cambridge & was about Bob's having made you his trustee &c.; the 2d from Keene Valley, acknowledging

1. As Michael Anesko explains, this was by now an old-fashioned clause which put the expenses on authors.

my former draft, the power of attorney &c, & containing several pages of advice & warning *àpropos* of the "Bostonians."[1] For these last I thank you heartily & think it very nice of you to have taken the trouble to write them. I concur absolutely in all you say, & am more conscious than any reader can be of the redundancy of the book in the way of descriptive psychology &c. There is far too much of the sort of thing you animadvert upon – though there is in the public mind at the same time a truly ignoble levity & puerility & aversion to any attempt on the part of a novelist to establish his people solidly. All the same I have overdone it – for reasons I won't take time to explain. It would have been much less the case if I had ever seen a proof of the *Bostonians*; but not a page have I had before me till the magazine was out. It is the same with the *Princess Casamassima*; though that story will be found probably less tedious, owing to my having made to myself all the reflections your letter contains, several months ago, & never ceased to make them since. The *Princess* will, I trust, appear more "popular." I fear the *Bostonians* will be, as a finished book, a fiasco, as not a word, echo or comment on the serial (save your remarks,) have come to me (since the row about the 1st 2 numbers) from any quarter whatever. This deathly silence seems to indicate that it has fallen flat. I hoped much of it, & shall be disappointed – having got no money for it I hoped for a little glory. (What do you mean, by the way by saying – "now that I am to lose nothing by Osgood!" I lose every penny – not a stiver shall I have had for the serial, for which he received a large sum from the *Century*.) But how can one murmur at one's success not being what one would like when one thinks of the pathetic, tragic ineffectualness of poor Father's lifelong effort, & the silence & oblivion that seems to have swallowed it up? Not a person to whom I sent a copy of your book, in London, has given me a sign or sound in consequence, & not a periodical appears to have taken the smallest notice of it.[2] It is terribly touching & – when I think of the evolution of his productions & ideas, fills me with tears. Edmund Gurney spoke to me with extreme enthusiasm of your preface, but said he considered it dispensed him from reading the rest.[3]

I have been all this month (from Sept. 10*th*,) in a perfectly empty, & very

1. Keene Valley, New York, was the summer place where WJ and his family went in the Adirondacks, the 'Putnam Shanty'. The pages about *The Bostonians* are missing from the Houghton manuscript of WJ's letter.
2. WJ had reported that only six copies of *The Literary Remains of Henry James* had been sold in six months.
3. Edmund Gurney (1847–88), a fellow of Trinity College, Cambridge, and a main founder of the Society for Psychical Research in 1882, was one of a group of philosophers to whom WJ had given a paper in London in February 1883.

dull & provincial Paris, which however I have enjoyed very much. I have had my time to myself, worked, gone to the theatre &c. I shall stay another 2 or 3 weeks, as some of my friends are coming back – including Bourget, who, to my great regret, has been wholly absent. The Bootts come next week. I can't give you any impressions of Paris – partly because they aren't much worth it, & partly because I must catch the train to go & dine at Versailles with poor Charlotte King.[4] Alice is settled at 7 Bolton Row, & Katherine will *probably* be with her another month. I won't write about her now – I shall be sure to do it so much, later. Thank your wife for a sweet note, acknowledging my photographs. I am delighted that Keene Valley poured so much satisfaction into you. May it remain. I tremble to ask about Bob. Ever, in haste, your affectionate

Henry

90. To Thomas Bailey Aldrich
29 April [1886]

Houghton MS   Published SL1, 113–14

Over the autumn and winter of 1885–6, HJ worked on The Princess Casamassima, *which was spreading beyond the agreed bounds. Returning from Paris on 1 November, he took 'a "residential flat" in Kensington, on a long lease . . . very good, with air, light, space, a lift (to the fourth floor, where it is "located")' (HJL III, 106). With decorating and furnishing, he only got in 'definitively' on 6 March.*

April 29th
13, DE VERE MANSIONS WEST, W.

My dear Aldrich.

I am obliged to throw myself on your mercy – your magnanimity – with regard to the remainder of my *July* Princess, which goes to you to-day, & the still remainder (of August &c) which is to follow. That is, I *must* ask you to give me another month (the 13*th* – September,) to finish the everlasting tale.

4. Charlotte Matthews King was a Europeanized maternal cousin who spent her last years in Versailles. Earlier in 1885 she had upset HJ with a 'crazy effusion about *my* being her executor' (CWJ II, 5). In ch. xx of *A Small Boy and Others* (1913), HJ recalled the 'singularly sharp and rounded image of our cousin Charlotte', whom he last saw in 'an old-world rez-de-chaussée at Versailles'.

Of course for that extra instalment I ask for no payment, as I contracted with the publishers to do the thing up in 12 numbers. I can't – I am too damnably voluminous. I must make a Book Fourth (instead of having only Three, as I intended;) to consist of the August & this added September parts. These will end the story in glory; & I hope they won't bother or oppress you too much. I must *begin* Book Four with Part Eleven – so that, to divide properly, I have made this July number of a good deal less than the usual length. I hope you won't mind this – & don't see why you should – as I am throwing you in a number gratis, in which all deficiencies of copy will be made up. There have been several numbers that have fallen a little short of 25 pages.[1] It relieves me immensely to have decided to ask you this favour – for I have been feeling terribly squeezed, & I pray you take it not too editorially, but humanly, imaginatively & with allowances for him whose calculations previsions & adjustments, are woefully apt to be erratic, but who is nevertheless yours with some little pride as well as much contrition

Henry James

91. To William James
13 June 1886

Houghton MS   Published CWJ II, 41–3; HJL III, 121–3

On 9 May 1886 WJ wrote to HJ retracting his 'growling letter' of the previous autumn about The Bostonians; *reading it now, 'my enjoyment has been complete' (CWJ II, 38–9). HJ was to use Osterley as the basis of Summersoft, the great house at the opening of his 1888 story, 'The Lesson of the Master'.*

June 13th 1886
Osterley Park, Southall, W.

Dear William.

As I have just written to Aunt Kate & asked her to forward you the letter it is bad economy, no doubt, to give you at the same moment, a letter for yourself. But on the other hand I have a moment of leisure & the sharp consciousness of having since I last gave you of my direct news heard copiously & liberally from you. So I will just seize this fleeting occasion to thank you

1. The average length overall (of the fourteen instalments HJ wrote) was 22½ *Atlantic* pages, the shortest being 17 and the longest 33. (HJ was paid for 300 pages, and provided 319.)

for your letter received I think nearly a month ago, on the subject of the *Bostonians*. Everything you said in it gratified me extremely – & very superfluous was your retractation of what you wrote before (last autumn, while the thing was going on in the magazine & before you had more than dipped into it.) I myself subscribe just as much to those strictures now as I did then – & find'em very just. All the middle part is too diffuse & insistent – far too describing & explaining & expatiating. The whole thing is too long & dawdling. This came from the fact (partly) that I had the sense of knowing terribly little about the kind of life I had attempted to describe – & felt a constant pressure to make the picture substantial by thinking it out – pencilling & "shading." I was afraid of the reproach (having *seen* so little of the whole business treated of,) of being superficial & cheap – & in short I should have been much more rapid, & had a lighter hand, with a subject concerned with people & things of a nature more near to my experience. Let me also say that if I have displeased people, as I hear, by calling the book the Bostonians – this was done wholly without invidious intention. I hadn't a dream of generalizing – but thought the title simple & handy, & meant only to designate Olive & Verena by it, as they appeared to the mind of Ransom, the southerner & outsider, looking at them from New York. I didnt even *mean* it to cover Miss Birdseye & the others; though it might very well. I shall write another: "The Other Bostonians." However, this only by the way; for after one of my productions is finished & cast upon the waters it has, for me, quite sunk beneath the surface – I cease to care for it & transfer my interest to the one I am next trying to float. If Aunt Kate sends you the letter I have just written to her you will receive it almost as soon as you do this one. It will tell you that Katherine L. came over about three weeks ago (she has left Louisa at Ems, with W*m* Loring & his wife;) & a few days later conveyed Alice to Leamington.[1] Alice appears to have been greatly – too greatly, & somewhat disappointingly fatigued by the journey; but she is now emerging from this bad sequel – & at any rate has suffered *less* than from any similar effort she has made since she came to England. K.L. will stay with her 3 weeks longer, & very possibly come back to her later in the Summer. I have no doubt that during the next three months Alice will form *habits* of going out (in her chair) & that will be the beginning of a much better order of things. Katherine, who had not seen her for 7 months, finds her, in spite of the knock-up of the journey, wonderfully better.

I am spending this Whitsunday down at this fine old place, (close to London)

---

1. Louisa was Katharine Loring's consumptive younger sister; William Caleb Loring was her younger brother, a lawyer married to Susan Mason Lawrence Loring.

of which Lord Jersey is the happy proprietor.[2] Lowell is in the house, & a few others, of no particular importance. Lowell, who has returned to England on a visit, as a private individual, is no less happy than when he was here as Minister; rather, indeed, I think, more so, as he has no cares nor responsibilities – & his "social position" is (bating precedence, as to which they let him off easily,) quite as good.[3] They are making, in London, an extraordinary lion of Dr. Holmes, who strikes me as rather superannuated & extinct (though he flickers up at moments) & is moreover dazed & bewildered by the row.[4] He is handicapped, unfortunately by having with him his singularly, inexplicably common daughter Amelia – who throws a kind of lurid light of consanguinity on some of *Wendell's* less felicitous idiosyncrasies.

Of course you are hearing all about Gladstone's defeat a week ago; which I don't deplore, for though it seems to me that Home Rule must come, his whole conduct in forcing it upon a house of Commons not in the least elected to pronounce for it – so that it might be done by *him* & him only – has been a piece of high political egotism.[5] I don't know how the G.O.M. looks at the distance of across the seas, but seen on this spot he appears to me to have become rather baleful & demagogic. His talk about the "people's heart" the "classes" &c, is unworthy of a man having his responsibilities; & his influence, or rather his boundless authority, is demoralizing – his name is a kind of fetich with so many millions & the renunciation of personal judgment, before him, so complete. But the whole drama is very interesting. There are to be new elections next month exclusively on the Home Rule issue, & it will be momentous to see what they bring forth. All the England one doesn't see may be for it – certainly the England one does is not. It seems highly probable that whatever happens here, there will be civil war in Ireland – they will stew, in a lively enough manner, in their own juice.

Edward Hooper, who is out here, lunched with me the other day & I pumped him vigorously for information about Cambridge & Boston. He would scarcely

2. Victor Albert George Child Villiers (1845–1915), seventh Earl of Jersey, was a British colonial administrator; his wife was Margaret Elizabeth (Leigh), Countess of Jersey. HJ, who had met them through Lowell, called Osterley 'a fine old Georgian house'.

3. Lowell had been American Minister in England from 1880 to 1885, and had returned to the U.S. early in the summer of 1885, after Cleveland's election to the presidency in November 1884 and the consequent change of administration.

4. Oliver Wendell Holmes (1809–94), father of Wendell, one of HJ's earliest friends, was the famous Boston doctor and author known as 'the autocrat of the breakfast table'. Wendell's compromising sister was Amelia Jackson Holmes Sargent (1843–89).

5. Gladstone, the 'Grand Old Man', Liberal prime minister once again, had introduced the Irish Home Rule Bill, which was defeated on 7 June 1886 – a defeat which led to the fall of his government.

talk, however, of anything but poor Richardson – whose departure I much deplore.[6] I hope the approach of the long vacation lifts you up. I am about to be called to lunch & can only squeeze in my love to Alice & many fraternal & avuncular assurances from yours ever affectionately

Henry James

P.S. You had better send this to A.K. in exchange for hers

92. *To Robert Louis Stevenson*
30 July [1886]

Yale MS   Unpublished

Only on 7 July 1886 did HJ send the last (October) copy of The Princess Casamassima *to Aldrich: 'It concludes the interminable work.' (Unpublished Houghton MS, bMS Am 1429 (2602).) On 20 July he went down to Bournemouth to see Stevenson, and on 23 July he proposed to Robert Underwood Johnson (1853–1937) of the* Century *an essay on Stevenson, one on the French actor Coquelin (published January 1887), and a third on London, like his 'Venice': 'I shld. make it awfully good.' (Unpublished Houghton MS, bMS Am 1094.2 (3).)*

On 29 July Stevenson wrote to HJ about the twelfth instalment of The Princess Casamassima *in the August* Atlantic – *the one HJ mentions in his 29 April letter to Aldrich – that 'This number brightens up again like anything; and Hyacinth and the Prince are Ex-qui-site, Sir, exquisite' (LRLS V, 296). Stevenson, unlike HJ, had great successes in 1886 – with* Kidnapped, *the work mentioned here, and* The Strange Case of Dr Jekyll and Mr Hyde.

July 30*th*
13, DE VERE MANSIONS WEST, W.

My good Louis.

You obeyed an enlightened, as well as a humane, impulse in sending a word of encouragement about the *Princess*. That the last part should cause you to palpitate was more than I had hoped – I feared that virtue had gone out of it.

6. Edward William Hooper (1839–1901), lawyer, brother of Marian ('Clover') Hooper Adams, Henry Adams's wife. Henry Hobson Richardson (b. 1838), Harvard classmate of Henry Adams and Paris-trained architect, died on 27 April 1886. He had worked for WJ in 1880 and 1885, as well as for John Hay, and for Adams and Ephraim Gurney, both of whom were married to Edward Hooper's sisters.

This gives me a certain trust that the remainder may be, if not better, at least not essentially worse, than these August pages – & that I may seem to get into port without shipwreck – or at any rate without loss of life.

I have seen various reviews of your book, & sent you one or two. They are all admiratory in a high degree – but they are but poorly discriminatory or gustatory. Such, however, is the contemporary critic. I trust there has come further good news of Sam – but *I* see no yacht on the horizon.[1] Many greetings to your good lady.

Ever your
H. James

What I *hear* about *Kidnapped* is universal ecstasy.

93. To Julian Russell Sturgis
20 September [1886]

Houghton TC   Unpublished

Julian Sturgis (1848–1904), a cousin of Marian ('Clover') Hooper Adams, was the eldest brother of Howard Overing Sturgis (1855–1920) and son of the wealthy American expatriate banker Russell Sturgis. He was brought to England at seven months and attended Eton and Oxford, becoming a British subject in 1877. He trained as a barrister, was a friend of the poet and novelist George Meredith and in 1883 took an Irish wife. In 1878 he began a career as a comic novelist. In 1880 HJ had written to Perry about 'the gentle Julian', 'He is a dear sweet fellow, and with a considerable literary talent of a light order; but I question whether his tissues have not been fatally relaxed by the uncrumpled rose-leaf character of his origin & breeding' (TSPB, 307–8).

HJ had forwarded Sturgis's verse-play Count Julian *to the American actor-manager Lawrence Barrett (1838–91), who in 1885 had mounted Browning's play* A Blot in the 'Scutcheon *in Philadelphia, and who in 1884 had proposed to HJ dramatizing* The Portrait of a Lady. *On 14 September HJ wrote to Sturgis enclosing Barrett's verdict: 'I am not surprised that he finds it "won't do" – I didn't expect he would. I hasten to add that this is because I myself found your drama very well-written indeed . . .' HJ explained Barrett's 'immense fear of a play being literary, or, as*

1. Samuel Lloyd Osbourne (1868–1947), Stevenson's stepson, born in San Francisco, with whom Stevenson was to collaborate on several works. He had been in poor health, but by mid July was 'decidedly better' after 'a day on Mrs. Jenkin's yacht' (LRLS V, 283), and at the end of July was on a trip to the Scilly Isles with relatives. In 1887 he decided to be known as 'Lloyd'.

you will see by his letter, poetic' (Unpublished Houghton TC, Lubbock: bMS Am 1237.16). Count Julian: A Spanish Tragedy *was published in 1893.*

34 De Vere Gardens, W.
Sept. 20th [1886].

My dear Julian,

Your letter touches and interests me much and I am grateful to you for the offering of the beautiful repudiated drama, which in the theatre of my imagination acts itself so well. Hold up your head, your heart, and your pen – and keep striking – that is the only thing. The world, stupid and vulgar as it is, and a large part of which has about as much literary sense as the chair on which I sit (or, rather, much less – for the chair is *mine* and has known the contact of my superior person) – the world which has so much fathomless insensibility and ignorance, will yet, in one of its softer and more sensitive spots, end by feeling and hearing. You have much talent and the rare accomplishment of knowing how to write. You are also young, vigorous, and ambitious. I am not yet prepared to admit, few illusions as I have about the taste of the time, and the *train dont vont les choses* in the world of letters, that these advantages – especially the knowing how to write – can avail nothing. Many people – I know – hate one for that; but many others like and indeed love one – and it is in these one must believe – for these one must work. I sympathise with you much in these particular disappointments of attempting to work for the stage – though I have suffered, practically, but little – save in the whole general disillusionment that has come over me with regard to trying at all. When I was younger that was really a very dear dream with me – but it has faded away with the mere increase of observation – observation, I mean, of the deadly vulgarity and illiteracy of the world one enters, practically, in knocking at a manager's door.[1] Besides I think, I confess, less highly of the drama, as a form, a vehicle, than I did – compared with the novel, which can do and say so much more. "Count Julian" shows me that you can still write a play that a manager will welcome – if you will do it *in prose*. They are mortally afraid of verse – "et pour cause". What can the poor wretches do with it? I think one must accept that. In the case of Barrett's refusing Count Julian I think too one must make the part of this: that he didn't regard C.J. as enough of a part – I mean in quantity – for himself. It is not enough "worked up" – he hasn't enough to do – is not enough on the stage &c. No actor, in Barrett's situation,

---

1. HJ had been disappointed in 1882 with the failure of the Mallory brothers at their Madison Square Theatre in New York to produce his *Daisy Miller: A Comedy in Three Acts*.

wants a *play* – what he wants is a *part*. And then I suppose you know that he is really very bad. Come and see me when you return. I am to be all the autumn in London. Believe me ever yours

Henry James.

94. To Thomas Bailey Aldrich
12 June 1887

Houghton MS   Published HJL III, 185–6

The Princess Casamassima *came out in book form on 22 October 1886 in Britain and on 2 November in the U.S. HJ confessed to WJ in September 1886 that he had been resting from work, the production of* The Bostonians *and* The Princess Casamassima, *'one on top of the other & both so exceedingly long, . . . having quite exhausted me' (CWJ II, 49). At the beginning of December he left London, encouraged by his sister AJ, and on 8 December – via Milan and Pisa – he arrived at Bellosguardo in Florence, where for a month he sublet the Villa Brichieri from Constance Fenimore Woolson, then moved into the Hôtel du Sud. Towards the end of his Florentine stay, HJ wrote to WJ that 'I have been driving the pen very steadily, and have produced a number of short things (I am going on to produce a good many more)' (CWJ II, 58). On 21 February he left for six weeks in Venice as the guest of the wealthy American Katherine De Kay Bronson (1834–1901), at the Palazzino Alvisi, her guest apartment, often used by Browning. He returned to Florence and the Villa Brichieri in early April, taking the downstairs apartment while Constance Fenimore Woolson was upstairs. Late in May HJ returned to Venice, this time to stay with the Bostonians Daniel Sargent Curtis (1825–1908) and Ariana Randolph Wormeley Curtis (1833–1922) at the Palazzo Barbaro, which they had bought in 1885.*

On 12 January one of HJ's Florentine circle, Eugene Lee-Hamilton (1845– 1907), the half-paralysed poet stepbrother of Violet Paget (Vernon Lee, 1856– 1935), had told HJ of Captain Edward Silsbee, 'the Boston art-critic and Shelley-worshipper', and his richly frustrating encounter with the ancient Claire Clairmont, 'Byron's ci-devant mistress', whose papers he coveted. This became 'The Aspern Papers', which appeared in the Atlantic *in three shortish parts (March–May 1888).*

Venice June 12*th* '87.
Dear Aldrich.
    I send you herewith (in another parcel,) the first half of the type-copy of a story – without having sounded you first on the subject. You may see in this

a subtle device to entrap you – to make you print it the more submissively from your having it on your hands. If you don't dislike it – & I don't see why you should, as it is brilliant, & of a thrilling interest – I shall be very glad that you should print it early. If you do I will give you another of the same – or of a somewhat smaller length. This thing ("The Aspern Papers") makes 2 parts of the maximum size – that of the longest instalment of the *Princess*. I think it would suffer a grave injury from being cut otherwise. As you liked long instalments of the *Princess* I hope you won't object to them in this case. I should add that the tale is eminently proper. For the rest, voyez plutôt. The second half is in London, being type-copied, & I am expecting it within *a week*. The moment it comes it will follow its mate. It will thus reach you in about eight days after the latter.[1] Will you please say to Messrs. Houghton and Mifflin that I shall be much obliged to them for sending me a cheque on your telling them that you print the story; (and I hope you won't tell them that you don't.) I blush to own it, but I am in want of money – & it would be a convenience to have it without waiting for publication. I leave them to fix the amount.

I have been spending this whole winter in Italy – & have pulled up here – in this effulgent steambath – to say good-bye. I return to London in July – & my address is of course always *34 De Vere Gardens W*. When do *you* return?

A portion of the 2*d* part of my story has just come in from the copyist – & I send that too, in an envelope by itself. It makes about a third of the said second part, which is a little longer than the 1*st*. So you will receive (with this) 2 oblong packets. I shall be very glad to hear they have reached you safely – & am ever, faithfully yours,

Henry James

95. To Robert Louis Stevenson
2 August [1887]

Yale MS   Published HJL III, 128

HJ arrived back from Italy on 20 July. On 23 July he wrote to Grace Norton of his new large project: 'I am just beginning a novel about half as long (thank God!) as the Princess *– and which will probably appear, at no very distant day, as a volume, without preliminary publication in a magazine. It will be called (probably)* The Tragic Muse; *but don't tell of it' (HJL III, 198). He went down to Bournemouth*

---

1. HJ dispatched the second part on 21 June.

on 30 July to see Stevenson, who had been more gravely ill even than usual, and saw him in London before he sailed from Tilbury (with a gift of a case of champagne) on 21 August. The Stevensons went to Saranac Lake in the Adirondacks, whence in 1888 they departed for the South Seas.

Sir Henry Rider Haggard (1856–1925), author of King Solomon's Mines *(1885), published* She *in the* Graphic *from October 1886 to January 1887, and the book came out in 1887.*

34 De Vere Gardens. W.
Aug. 2d

My dear Louis.

I left you on Sunday p.m. without a farewell. – but I thought it better to spare you that palaver; as there seems a probability of my seeing you so soon in town. I should have been very glad to stop over yesterday – but my time has been terribly ploughed into of late – & the hours became too sordidly precious to me here. In short I *had* to come back. This is to tell you *that*, in sorrow; & to relieve myself a little further on the subject of the unspeakable Haggard. Since I saw you I have finished Solomon & read half of "She". Ah, par exemple, c'est trop fort – & the "40*th* thousand" on the title-page of my *She* moves me to a holy indignation. It isn't nice that anything so vulgarly brutal should be the thing that succeeds most with the English of to-day. More even than with the contemptible inexpensiveness of the whole thing I am struck with the beastly *bloodiness* of it – or it comes back to the same thing – the cheapness of the hectatombs with which the genial narrative is bestrewn.[1] Such perpetual killing & such perpetual ugliness! It is worthwhile to write a tale of fantastic adventure, with a funny man &c, & pitched all in the slangiest key, to kill *20 000* men, as in Solomon, in order to help your heroes on! In *She* the narrator himself shoots through the back (I think) his faithful servant Mahommed, to prevent his being boiled alive, & describes how he "leaped into the air" like a buck, on receiving the shot. He himself is addressed constantly by one of the personages of the tale as "my Baboon"![2] Quel genre! They seem to me works in which our race & our age make a very vile figure

1. HJ writes 'hectatombs', combining the classical 'hecatomb' (OED: 'a great number of persons, animals, or things, presented as an offering, or devoted to destruction') with the recent invention the 'hectograph' ('An apparatus for multiplying copies of writing', for which the first OED entry is 1880).
2. In ch. VIII of *She*, the cannibal hot-pot scene, the narrator, Ludwig Horace Holly, shoots 'the diabolical woman who had been caressing Mahomed'. 'The bullet struck her in the back and killed her . . . [T]o my terror and dismay, Mahomed, by a superhuman effort, burst from

– & they have unexpectedly depressed, so that he looks to *you* for consolation, yours ever faithfully

Henry James

P.S. I mean consolation *printed* – don't think of answering this. I hope my visit didn't have a bad morrow.

96. To Robert Louis Stevenson
5 December [1887]

Yale MS   Published HJL III, 205–7; HJRLS, 167–9; LHJ I, 132–3

On 1 October HJ sketched for WJ a broad vista of his ambitions: 'I now simply want elbow-room for the exercise, as it were, of my art. I hope during the next ten years to do some things of a certain importance.' (CWJ II, 72.)

At Saranac Lake, Stevenson was taking a cure under a Dr Trudeau, staying in what he called 'our wind-beleaguered hilltop hatbox of a house', where in the December thermometer 'the mercury . . . curls up into the bulb like a hibernating bear' (LRLS VI, 77). Writing a note of introduction on 18 December for Owen Wister, future author of The Virginian, *HJ sketched the family: 'You will find him a queer, unique, dishevelled, undressed, nondescript, fascinating, loveable fellow. There is a youthful fresh, complacent Scotch mother, a poor sightless (or almost so) American stepson, & a strange California wife, 15 yrs. older than Louis himself, but almost as interesting.' (Unpublished Congress MS.) They had been reading* Roderick Hudson en famille, *and Stevenson declared it 'one of the best works I ever heard' (LRLS VI, 61; c. 20 November).*

My dear Louis.

I could almost hate poor Roderick H. (in whom, at best, as in all my past & shuffled off emanations & efforts, my interest is of the slenderest,) for making you write so much more about him than about a still more fascinating hero.

---

his tormentors, and, springing high into the air, fell dying upon her corpse. The heavy bullet from my pistol had driven through the bodies of both, . . . saving her victim from a death a hundred times more horrible. It was an awful and yet a most merciful accident.' HJ is thus not quite accurate about Holly's intentions. It is the wise old chieftain Billali who calls the ugly Holly 'my Baboon'.

If you had only given me a small instalment of that romantic serial, The Mundane Situation of R.L.S.? My dear fellow, you skip whole numbers at a time. Your correspondent wouldn't. I am really delighted you can find something at this late day in that work in which my diminutive muse first tried to elongate her little legs. It is a book of considerable good faith, but I think of limited skill. Besides, directly my productions are finished, or at least thrust out to earn their living, they seem to *me* dead. They dwindle when *weaned* – removed from the parental breast, & only to flourish, a little, while imbibing the milk of my plastic care. None the less am I touched by your excellent & friendly words. Perhaps I am touched even more by those you dedicate to the less favoured *Portrait*.[1] My dear Louis, I don't think I follow you here. Why does that work move you to such scorn – since you can put up with Roderick, or with any of the others? As they are, so it is, & as it is, so they are. Upon my word you are unfair to it – & I scratch my head, bewildered. 'Tis surely a graceful, ingenious, elaborate work – with too many pages, but with (I think) an interesting subject, & a good deal of life & style. There! *All* my works may be damnable – but I don't perceive the particular damnability of that one. However I feel as if it were almost gross to defend myself – for even your censure pleases & your restrictions refresh. I have this very day received from Mr. Bain your *Memories & Portraits* & I lick my chops in advance.[2] It is very delectable, I can see, & it has the prettiest coat & face of any of your volumes.

London is settling to its winter pace, & the cool rich fogs curtain us in. I see Colvin once in a while *dans le monde*, which however I frequent less & less. My love to your wife & mother – I miss you too sensibly. My greeting to the brave Lloyd. Ever yours very faithfully

H. James

P.S. I am unspeakably vexed at the Century's long delay in printing my paper on you – it is quite sickening. But I am helpless – & they tell me it won't come out till *March* – d–n 'em all.[3] I am also sorry – very – not to have any other prose specimens of my own genius to send you. I have really written a good deal lately – but the beastly periodicals hold them back: I can't make out why. But I trust the dance will begin before long, & that then you may glean

1. Stevenson had written: 'I must break out with the news that I can't bear *The Portrait of a Lady*.' (LRLS VI, 61.)
2. James Bain (1829–94) and his brother Thomas (1835–1921) were both HJ's and Stevenson's regular booksellers at No. 1 Haymarket, London. *Memories and Portraits* came out on 21 November 1887 from Chatto & Windus and on 2 December from Scribner's.
3. Stevenson had seen a proof of the article – which was fated not to appear till April 1888 – at Newport, Rhode Island, in September.

some pleasure. I pray you, *Do* write something yourself for one who *knows* & yet is famished: for there isn't a morsel here that will keep one alive. I won't question you – 'twere vain – but I wish I knew more about you. I want to *see* you – where you live & *how* – & the complexion of your days. But I don't know even the name of your habitat nor the date of your letter: neither were on the page. I bless you all the same.

December 5*th*: D. V. Gdns. W.

97. To Edmund Gosse
24 December [1887]

Leeds MS   Published SLHJEG, 50

In his letter to WJ of 1 October 1887, HJ remarked: 'I am productive, & in the course of this autumn shall have sent off the 8th or 9th fiction of about the length of "Daisy Miller" since I quitted England on the 1st December last.' (CWJ II, 73.) But inconveniently, as he told Stevenson, 'the beastly periodicals hold them back': in all of 1887, only one piece of fiction by HJ ('Cousin Maria') was published.

It therefore seems likely that HJ's 'plaintive accents' to Gosse, mentioned in this letter, refer to his difficulties as a professional author. '[T]he celebrated "clique"' he has complained of may be the group of successful authors, publishers and editors who in the late 1880s were engaged in the sweeping commercialization of literary culture deplored by George Gissing in his novel New Grub Street *(1891).*

My dear Gosse –

An impulse not morbid I trust, leads me to send you three words on this (supposedly) genial Xmas eve, in correction of my plaintive accents of last night. Let them serve as a Xmas greeting, & a friendly cheer, to my own address as well as, particularly, to yours. I feel as if I had whined, & am ashamed of it – having, as I am resolved, a considerable future in my (as your friend O. B. Frothingham's critic would say,) guts![1] So have you – don't doubt of that! It is a good thing from time to time, in the floundering gallop of existence, to have to take a fence: let us therefore, at these moments, exchange jovial & stimulating cries. There is in all difficulties an excitement which it

1. Octavius Brooks Frothingham (1822–95), Boston Unitarian clergyman and hymn-writer, was author of *The Religion of Humanity* (1873), *Transcendentalism in New England* (1876) and many biographies of New England figures.

would be poor to be without. So, in short, I still propose to succeed, & let me have the pleasure of observing that you do the same. Even this dim morning is garish enough to flout, as I recall them, my lamplit remarks on the celebrated "clique." What I meant was so little that it was scarcely worth meaning at all; – the tongue magnifies things as it wags, & it is all accidental. Heaven bless them all, I wish them, vague as I am about their identity, every compliment of the Season. The same, my dear Gosse, to your intelligent & virtuous house – Greet your wife for me, end the year with me on a fine rich note, & believe me ever much-intendingly yours

Henry James

P.S. If you *should* speak to Besant I don't mind, after all your telling him it is for me you do it.[2] If I profit, in fact, by any suggestion of his, it is better that he should know I owe it to him.

34 D. V. G. W.
Dec. 24*th*

98. To William Dean Howells
2 January 1888

Houghton MS   Published HJL III, 208–10; LFL, 265–7

34 De Vere Gardens W.
January 2d 1888

My dear Howells.

Your pretty read book (that is a misprint for *red* – but it looks well, better than it deserves; so I let it stand:) the neat & attractive volume, with its coquettish inscription and its mystifying date, came in to me exactly as a new-year's gift.[1] I was delighted to get it, for I had not perused it in the pages of Harper, for reasons that you will understand – knowing as you must how little the habit of writing in the serial form encourages one to read in that odious way, which so many simple folk, thank heaven, think the best. I was

2. Walter Besant (1836–1901), the successful novelist to whose lecture of the same title HJ's 'The Art of Fiction' was a response, established the Society of Authors in 1883, to assert the professional rights of authors against publishers.
1. Howells's *April Hopes* was in *Harper's Monthly* (February–November 1887); then came out as a book from Harper's in December 1887 (but dated '1888').

on the point of getting *April Hopes* to add to the brave array of its predecessors (mine by purchase, almost all of them,) when your graceful act saved me the almost equally graceful sacrifice. I can make out why you are at Buffalo almost as little as I believe that you believe that I have "long forgotten" you.[2] The intimation is worthy of the most tortuous feminine mind that you have represented – say this wondrous lady, with the daughter, in the very 1st pages of April Hopes, with whom I shall make immediate & marvelling acquaintance. Your literary prowess takes my breath away – you write so much & so well. I seem to myself a small brown snail crawling after a glossy antelope. Let me hope that you *enjoy* your work as much as you ought to – that the grind isn't greater than the inevitable (from the moment one really tries to *do* anything.) Certainly one would never guess it, from your abounding page. How much I wish I could keep this lonely new year by a long personal talk with you. I am troubled about many things, about many of which you could give me, I think (or rather I am sure,) advice & direction. I have entered upon evil days – but this is for your most private ear. It sounds portentous, but it only means that I am still staggering a good deal under the mysterious & (to me) inexplicable injury wrought – apparently – upon my situation by my 2 last novels, the *Bostonians* & the *Princess*, from which I expected so much & derived so little. They have reduced the desire, & the demand, for my productions to zero – as I judge from the fact that though I have for a good while past been writing a number of good short things, I remain irremediably unpublished. Editors keep them back, for months & years, as if they were ashamed of them, & I am condemned apparently to eternal silence. You must be so widely versed in all the reasons of things (of this sort, to-day,) in the U.S. that if I could discourse with you a while by the fireside I should endeavour to draw from you some secret to break the spell. However, I don't despair, for I think I am now really in better form for work than I have ever been in my life, & I propose yet to do many things. Very likely too, some day, all my buried prose will kick off its various tombstones at once.[3] Therefore don't betray me till I myself have given up. That won't be for a long time yet. If we could have that rich conversation I should speak to you too of your monthly polemics in

2. The Howellses were in Buffalo to be near the sanatorium in Dansville, New York, where Winifred Howells was being treated.
3. The year 1888 would see the tombstones kicked off to startling effect: 'Louisa Pallant' (February); 'The Reverberator' (February–July); 'The Aspern Papers' (March–May); 'The Liar' (May–June); 'Two Countries' (June); 'A London Life' (June–September); 'The Lesson of the Master' (July–August); and 'The Patagonia' (August–September). HJ's sister would comment in November, 'He seems like the "buttony-boy" to have broken out all over stories' (DLAJ, 149).

Harper & tell you (I think I should go so far as that) of certain parts of the business in which I am less with you than in others. It seems to me that on occasions you mix things up that don't go together, sometimes make mistakes of proportion, & in general incline to insist more upon the restrictions & limitations, the *a priori* formulas & interdictions, of our common art, than upon that priceless freedom which is to me *the* thing that makes it worth practising.[4] But at this distance, my dear Howells, such things are too delicate & complicated – they won't stand so long a journey. Therefore I won't attempt them – but only say how much I am struck with your energy, ingenuity & courage, & your delightful interest in the charming questions. I don't care how much you dispute about them if you will only remember that a grain of example is worth a ton of precept & that with the imbecillity of babyish critics the serious writer need absolutely not concern himself. I am surprised some times, at the things you notice & seem to care about. One should move in a diviner air.

Two or three nights ago Edmund Gosse came to share my solitude & my beefsteak, & we talked, al solito, of you. He has I think quite recovered from the immediate effects of his horrid imbroglio of a year & a half ago – out of which he came very well; but not from some of its remoter ones.[5] Nor will he do this, I fear, so long as he continues to hold his Cambridge professorship. I shall be glad when that is over, as I think he will then be in a much freer, sounder, position. He is the only man of letters I ever see here – to speak of, or to speak to. I have many good friends here, but they are not in that class, which strikes me as mostly quite dense & puerile. I even confess that since the *Bostonians*, I find myself holding the "critical world" at large in a singular contempt. I go so far as to think that the literary sense is a distinctly waning quality. I can speak of your wife & children only interrogatively – which will tell you little – & me, I fear, less. But let me at least be affirmative to the extent of wishing them all very affectionately, & to Mrs. H. in particular the happiest

4. On 1 October 1887 HJ had written to WJ about Howells's 'Editor's Study' pieces in *Harper's Monthly*, especially 'Civilization and Barbarism, Romance and Reality: the question of modern civilization', which praises *The Princess Casamassima* as exceeding Balzac in scope: 'I hadn't seen the latter's "tribute" in the September *Harper*, but I have just looked it up. It gives me pleasure, but doesn't make me cease to deplore the figure that Howells makes every month in his critical department of *Harper*. He seems to me as little as possible of a critic & exposes himself so that I wish he would "quit," & content himself with writing the novel as he thinks it should be and not talking about it: he does the one so much better than the other.' (CWJ II, 75.)

5. In the *Quarterly Review* of October 1886 John Churton Collins (1848–1908), hitherto a friend of Gosse, violently attacked the scholarly errors in *From Shakespeare to Pope* (1885), which collected lectures Gosse had given as Clark Lecturer (not 'professor') in Cambridge, a post he held from 1884 to 1889.

New Year. Go on, my dear Howells, & send me your books always as I *think* I send you mine. Continue to write only as your admirable ability moves you & believe me ever faithfully yours

Henry James

99. *To William James*
[20 February 1888]

Houghton MS   Published CWJ II, 81–3

The first eight pages of this letter, which a pencilled annotation by Henry James III says concerned AJ's health, are missing; the fragment starts with the conclusion of that discussion. AJ had been in Leamington since the summer of 1887.

In this letter HJ records what seems to have been the result of his approach to Walter Besant through Gosse. Besant was represented by the Glasgow-born Alexander Pollock Watt (1834–1914), one of the first literary agents (since at least 1878), and ultimately Besant's literary executor. On 3 January 1888 HJ thanked Gosse for 'your quick, kind action in the matter of Mr Watt' (SLHJEG, 51).

... The manner in which she bears the dulness, isolation & solitude of Leamington are almost beyond my conception.[1] Fortunately the worst is over: the longer days, the spring & summer will bring much more brightness & variety. And next winter, I surmise, she will spend in London. She told me some time ago that she didn't mean to – but I gather from something she has said since that she has changed her mind. She is very political & more strenuously sure of certain things – the baseness of the Unionists &c, than I am able to be: but that would be corrected if she lived more in the world & her opinions were not formed so in private.[2] I will get you to-day the fotos. of A. Balfour & Morley.[3] I dined in company with the former & only one

1. AJ herself wrote to Sara Sedgwick Darwin from Leamington on 4 October 1887: 'Entire quiet & a reducing of myself, if possible, to a lower level of imbecility even than that already fixed by nature, has been decreed for me – intercourse with the bovine nature I find most conducive to that result.' (DLAJ, 131.)
2. AJ was a fierce supporter of Home Rule for Ireland, and had told WJ and his wife AHJ on 20 November 1887 that 'I am in a terrible ferment at moments over it all, desolate at not being in London, but glad too, because if I had to see my Unionist friends I should explode from blood-boiling.' (DLAJ, 136.)
3. Arthur Balfour (1848–1930), philosopher and Conservative statesman, future prime minister (1902–5), was in 1887 fierce chief secretary for Ireland ('Bloody Balfour'). John Morley, M.P.,

other man (2 other women) about a week ago; & was struck afresh with the degree to which in spite of his extremely pleasant, lazy and apparently sincere manner he is the type of latent aristocratic insolence & scorn, of the extremely refined & intellectual sort. He is extremely witty, & a master of persiflage & badinage &, at the same time is of the cold, ascetic & unfleshly type, not liking English sports & brutalities – only lawn-tennis, reading & conversation: purely virginal & cerebral. There is something painful to me in seeing a man of his extremely fine intellectual quality associated so intensely with the purposes of all the dense & brutal clan – I mean, the stupid thousands of "society," the cast of whose minds is in a measure the shame of the English race. *Aussi*, he today is the darling, the adored of London – they have never before had such a pure brain, & such a flexible wit (in talk at least – less so in the H. of Commons) at their service & ils ne se connaissent plus. I met yesterday, at a call, George Shaw-Lefevre, who apparently sincerely considers that Arthur Balfour is a deeply, coldly & deliberately *cruel* nature approaching the *infernal*: absolutely destitute of heart or sensibility.[4] I spent 2 days, in the autumn, at a country house with B. & Wilfrid Blunt & have feared since that I shld. be called upon to testify in regard to that visit – what passed between them – Blunt's allegations having since made it historical.[5] Blunt is a humourless madman & a very disagreeable person. Balfour I should think indeed a prodigy of amiable heartlessness. It all comes back to *race* – high Scotch Tory ancestry, lands & dominions. The lands, ancestry & Toryism give the insolence, & Scotland the *mind*[.]

I am having a very good winter & working steadily. But *don't* read any of my things in periodicals – unless I send them to you, till they come out as books. I have good reasons for this. I shall publish 2 or 3 vols in the next six months.[6] I have just written a longish article on Guy de Maupassant for the Fortnightly Review (it comes out in this next number) & have agreed to do

---

associated with Macmillan's when HJ began publishing with them, had been chief secretary for Ireland in 1886 in the Liberal government and in 1887 was important in the Round Table Conference on Irish policy.

4. George John Shaw-Lefevre (1831–1928), Baron Eversley, Liberal statesman.

5. The country house in question was Clouds in Wiltshire. Wilfrid Scawen Blunt (1840–1922), politician, poet and anti-imperialist, supporter of the Irish cause, publicly accused Balfour of saying Irish nationalist leaders did not speak for their people and should be ruthlessly treated – the heated dispute occupied space in *The Times*.

6. *Partial Portraits*, a collection of literary essays, appeared on 8 May; *The Reverberator* in June; *The Aspern Papers* in September, all from Macmillan. The long Maupassant essay HJ published in the March *Fortnightly* (he 'received but £23 for it' (HJL III, 229)) was included in *Partial Portraits*.

for them three more on French subjects.[7] The Maupassant will then go into a small volume of essays that the Macmillans are soon to put forth for me, uniform with Fredk. Harrison's *Choice of Books*. I am to run a novel through the *Atlantic* next year, & meanwhile to produce 2 or 3 more short fictions – in addition to those I have written during the last year & which even yet have not burst forth, save one which has begun in *Macmillan* (the "Reverberator") & which is to run 5 more months. (Don't read it till it's finished.) I have lately put my literary affairs (so far as they are connected with magazines) largely into the hands of an *agent*, one Mr. A. P. Watt, who places & arranges for all the productions of Walter Besant, Rider Haggard, W*m* Black, Bret Harte, James Payn & Wilkie Collins.[8] He appeared eager to undertake *me*, and am promised remarkably good results from it. He is to make one's bargains & take charge of one's productions generally – but especially over here. He takes 10 percent. of what he gets for me, but I am advised that his favourable action on one's market & business generally more than makes up for this – & that even if it didn't the relief & comfort of having him take all the mercenary & *selling* side off one's mind is well worth the cost. I debated a long time, but the other day he came to see me, & after a talk seemed so much impressed with the fact that I have done much less well for myself than I ought to be done for, that I entered into relations with him. There is nothing hard & fast in them & they can be terminated at any moment if they don't do.

I haven't said anything about the news Alice tells me she has got from New York & which you of course know all about, though you didn't mention it in your letter: Aunt Kate's acceptance of functions in regard to Henry W &c, & the large sums of money that are concerned.[9] These are so bewildering to me that I don't yet embrace the situation & am waiting & wishing to hear from her. I am delighted that if she is to have the burden of Henry she is to have ample compensation for it. But oh, what will become of all his

7. HJ only (ever) published two more *Fortnightly* essays on French subjects: 'Pierre Loti' (May 1888); 'The Journal of the Brothers Goncourt' (October 1888).

8. William Black (1841–98), bestselling Scots novelist published by Macmillan (his *Macleod of Dare*, reviewed by HJ in 1878, seems a source for *The Tragic Muse*); James Payn (1830–98), popular novelist and editor of the *Cornhill Magazine* from 1883 to 1896 (about whom HJ wrote a memorial essay); Wilkie Collins (1824–89), friend of Dickens and foremost sensation novelist of the period, best known for *The Moonstone* (1868) and *The Woman in White* (1860).

9. Aunt Kate was in New York looking after the rich but helpless Henry Wyckoff, sketched by WJ in his reply to this letter on 19 April as 'Henry, 72 years old, with the plasticity of nature of a box tortoise, so deaf that you must *write* to him half the time, with his irreproachable correctness and essential goodness, his dense obstinacy and dislike to obey suggestions from others . . . his five-cent ideas, and his $40000 dollar income' (CWJ II, 84).

money? It makes me *ache* to think of its flowing all away from people who are poor.

I keep up my *fencing*: a great boon. Ever your

H.J.

100. To Thomas Bailey Aldrich
3 March 1888

Houghton MS   Published HJL III, 223

HJ had begun The Tragic Muse *as a short novel in the summer of 1887, but put it aside to write* The Reverberator. *It seems to have been Aldrich who persuaded him to expand it; not perhaps anticipating that it would eventually run for seventeen instalments.*

34 De Vere Gardens W.
March 3d 1888.

My dear Aldrich.

I succumb to your arguments & will undertake to manage a serial for the full twelvemonth of 1889. It shall be of 17 or 18 pages – with the option of rising, *au besoin*, to 20 – & shall be paid for at the same rate as the Princess – i.e. $15 per page. And you shall have the opening chapters – numbers – by Oct. 1st.

To compass this end (I mean the end of giving you a longer rather than a shorter serial) – I shall probably run two stories (i.e. two subjects I have had in my head) together, interweaving their threads. But equally probably the thing will bear the name I gave you: "The Tragic Muse." She is an actress. But there will be much other richness, and the scene will be in London, like the *Princess* – though in a very different *monde*; considerably the "Artistic". There you are. It won't be improper; strange to say, considering the elements.

Yes, I have always thought Sargent a great painter. He wd. be greater still if he had one or two little things he hasn't – but he will do.[1] Ever yours

Henry James

1. In October 1887 HJ had published an appreciation of Sargent in *Harper's Magazine*, which praises his talent but distrusts his facility. It ends by asserting that 'There is no greater work of art than a great portrait', but 'the highest result is achieved when to this element of quick perception a certain faculty of brooding reflection is added' (PE, 228).

101. To Mary (Mrs Humphry) Ward
[March or April 1888]

Virginia MS   Unpublished

Lizzie Boott Duveneck died in Paris of pneumonia on 22 March 1888 – as HJ told Henrietta Reubell, 'an unspeakable shock to me' (HJL III, 230).

Mary Augusta Ward (née Arnold, 1851–1920), granddaughter of Thomas Arnold, the great headmaster of Rugby, niece of Matthew Arnold, and married to Thomas Humphry Ward (1845–1926), art critic of The Times, *made HJ's acquaintance in 1882. On 24 February 1888 she published her most popularly successful book, a much worked-over novel of religious questioning,* Robert Elsmere. *AJ reported on 5 April to a friend that the novel was 'one of the most beautiful books for purity & moral elevation I have ever read' (DLAJ, 98). HJ told his friend the controversial sensation novelist Rhoda Broughton (1840–1920) on 23 March, 'It is artistically – physically helpless, as it were – but morally & intellectually fine.' (Unpublished Cheshire MS DDB/M/J/1/6.)*

Dear Mrs. Ward.

I owe you an explanation of my long silence about your beautiful book – but I am afraid my explanation will only fill you with deeper contempt for my want of intellectual energy. I have read 2 volumes of it & then have just had to send the 3d off to my sister (to follow its predecessor,) both because she clamours for it & because I have just instantly to plunge into some very incongruous reading engendered by a promise to write immediately an article on Pierre Loti, & don't want to *touch* Robert Elsmere before that is brushed away.[1] I have to re-read the said Pierre from beginning to end, & I don't want to mix the said Robert up with him. Directly this episode is over I shall fall upon your 3d volume. But I *have* read the first 2 (all but the 40 last pp. of the 2d,) & I have done so with extreme admiration. The book has great & rare beauty, & interest of a high order: it is, I think, a very distinguished & remarkable production – large & rich & full of the feeling of human life, & of a most refreshing acquaintance (amid the vulgar fashions of the hour) with the things of the mind and the soul. The things you attempt in it are all so

1. HJ's essay on Pierre Loti (pseudonym of L. M. Julien Viaud, 1850–1923), naval officer and author of exotic fiction, appeared in the *Fortnightly Review* in May 1888. On 27 March HJ told Theodore Child he was to do the Loti essay, as well as other French studies – then came to 'Mrs. Humphry Ward's long religious novel. It is quite remarkable – but *voyez la différence!*' (HJL III, 229.)

interesting & the intelligence you bring to bear upon them so great – the view so wide – the horizon so full of blue distance & suggestion. The criticism I shld. make of you is almost only that your conceptions – so fine as conceptions – are not quite always *representations*, your people not simply enough seen & planted on their feet. But the book abounds in life – & that is the great thing. And as for knowledge – what a lot you know! But your head carries it like a garland of flowers, – and you have the truth of view of the interesting novel, that it's a history of our moral life & not simply of our physical accidents.[2] But this is only provisional & I shall have much more to say to you. I shall return to the charge. The book is immensely suggestive – it dashes from me the mantle of shame in which "in the eyes of Europe" – the greater part of current English fiction has lately plunged us. Ever faithfully & hurriedly yours

Henry James

102. To Daniel Connor Lathbury
9 June [1888]

Houghton TC   Unpublished

Daniel Connor Lathbury (1831–1922), was editor of the Guardian *from 1883 to 1899, and of* The Pilot *during its existence (1900–1904). He was married to Bertha Lathbury (née Price), and edited Gladstone's* Correspondence on Church and Religion *(1910). The Reverberator had just appeared in book form. Its caricature-villain Mr Flack is the European correspondent of an American society-paper, 'not a specific person', as the novella says, but full of 'the quality of the sample or advertisement, the air of representing a "line of goods" for which there is a steady popular demand'.*

34 De Vere Gardens, W.
June 9th [1888].

Dear Mr. Lathbury,

Your benevolence almost begets, on my part, the monstrosity of being a little glad of your having been forced to pause, in the rush of life, long enough

2. On 3 July 1888 HJ wrote a fuller letter to Mrs Ward, expanding this praise: 'The interesting thing to me, in your book (& its great success) as I think I have hinted before, is that you have seen a personal history in the richest & most interesting way – the way that yields most fruit – seen the adventures of the real being, the intensely living inner nature & seen them (rendering them too) so vividly that they become exciting, thrilling, strongly attaching as a 'story' & hold one's curiosity & suspense to the end.' (HJL III, 235.) He also expressed a number of reservations.

to read me – though indeed a short moment suffices for my little history of the newspaper-man. I am sorry for the reason of that check and hope you are going freely again – but I frankly rejoice that you obeyed the friendly impulse to write to me. That gives me the greatest pleasure – and I rise into the pure ether of refreshed ambition when I hear that acute people have found the thrill, the glow of life, as dear Matthew Arnold says, in any of my little creations. Mr. Flack is a conscientious study of a great reality (I don't of course mean of any individual) and he seemed to me to be worth attempting. But he won't like it: so little is conscience appreciated! Thank you for thinking the American character "inexhaustible" – that *does* give me a push, so afraid am I, generally, of having played all my cards. I hope Mrs. Lathbury has left the sofa to which I lately saw her chained and I am most truly yours and hers –

Henry James.

103. To Theodora Sedgwick
2 July [1888]

Houghton MS   Unpublished

Theodora Sedgwick (1851–1916), who never married, was of the eminent Cambridge family, connected to the Ashburners. Her elder sister Susan, who died in 1872, had been the wife of Charles Eliot Norton.

HJ sent off 'The Liar' to Robert Underwood Johnson on 28 October 1887, for the Century Magazine *(April 1888). It was partly inspired, as his later Preface to the story tells us, by his meeting at a London dinner-party a gentleman 'in whom I recognised the most unbridled colloquial romancer the "joy of life" had ever found occasion to envy' – and the gentleman's wife, who admirably carried off her husband's exaggerations. The painter who narrates the tale is still in love with the woman who rejected him twelve years before, and who is now married to the raconteur Colonel Clement Capadose, 'a thumping liar'. This narrator, morbidly jealous, contrives to paint the colonel, to execute 'a masterpiece of subtle characterisation, of legitimate treachery', in search of a tacit confession from the wife that 'with him her life would have been finer'. But the portrait's cruel accuracy reduces her to tears, the painting is destroyed, and her loyalty to her husband is demonstrated.*

34 D. V. G. W.
July 2d

My dear Theodora.

Your note about *The Liar* is a great little excitement, not at all diminished by the fact that I collapse before it as I do before any criticism addressed to any production of mine. I can't explain or defend them – & after they are written I can't in the least even remember why I wrote them in one way rather than in another. This doesn't prevent my being delighted with any remonstrance that is a sign of interest. Anent poor Mrs. Capadose – let's see: I think you are rather hard on the painter & his quite ineffectual experiment. – But even here I perhaps advance too much; I am too out of the mood in which I wrote the tale. And infinitely various are the views which different people take of the same representation. Haven't I been blown up by two or three ladies here for making such a woman as Mrs. C.? – as if she could exist! They declare it is monstrous to have represented her as *not* taking the artist into her confidence – & *as* sticking to her husband. We move, my dear Theodora, in dim & tortuous labyrinths & we sit in eternal darkness. Everything is in the way a thing strikes you – & yet that, after all, is nothing.

I saw Arthur the other day for 10 minutes & found him massive & "settled;" yet recalling the light of other days.[1] He was in London but for a day or two – but promises to reappear. The hated Season wanes & the summer is cold & wet. That consoles one a little for being in London now – not being in the sodden country. But it is the time when I love my love least. Let it bring you back some year, however, & I shall like it better! My friendliest greeting to Aunts – my love to nieces & nephews.

Ever most faithfully yours
Henry James

104. To Grace Norton
30 September 1888

Houghton MS   Unpublished

On 31 July 1888, HJ wrote to Stevenson that when The Tragic Muse, *which he had just started, was finished, he would turn to shorter fiction: 'I want to leave a*

1. Theodora's brother Arthur Sedgwick, brother also of Charles Eliot Norton's late wife Susan and of Sara Sedgwick Darwin, had been with Godkin at the New York *Nation*, for which HJ had written 220 pieces between 1865 and 1880. In 'Oft in the Stilly Night' by Thomas Moore (1779–1852), 'Fond Memory brings the light / Of other days around me; / The smiles, the tears, / Of boyhood's years, / The words of love then spoken . . .'

multitude of pictures of my time, projecting my small circular frame upon as many different spots as possible and going in for number as well as quality, so that the number may constitute a total having a certain value as observation and testimony.' (HJL III, 240.)

One such picture, 'The Lesson of the Master', HJ's teasing quasi-fable about the artist and marriage, appeared in the British Universal Review *(16 July and 15 August). (Grace Norton had always shown an interest in HJ's feelings about marriage.) HJ did not go away in the summer of 1888, confessing to Macmillan in July his 'need for a considerable sum' (CHJHM, 145).*

34 De Vere Gardens W.
Sept. 30*th* 1888

My dear Grace.

It is horrible, the way I don't write to you. A charming letter & two delightful notes from you have I had since last I wrote. I seem to myself to live with my pen in my hand, & to be writing notes and letters in *all* the time that I am not writing for the printers, & yet what I leave undone is ever the uppermost mass, weighing down the scales as against what I do. Your note about the "Lesson of the Master" was especially pleasant to me – for you appeared to have been not inconsiderably interested. This is so much gained & thrown in, as it were, in the case of a friend – for I have told you before, I think, how little it seems to me the usual law that one's friends, especially one's old friends, should be the people to care for one's "work" – especially when it is of the sort that I do. I send you my things, in general, not in the least as an appeal, but as a compliment, as it were, & if you happen to like one almost as well as if you didn't know me – so much the better. Besides, a "story" is so essentially a thing to take or to leave – experimental, adventurous and contingent, that one shrinks even from desiring a judgment where a defence is so out of the question. You write to me from Cambridge, without allusion to any absences or wanderings – & so I write to you from *my* poor equivalent to your territorial home, from which I have not strayed, these 14 months, for more than a day or two at a time. I have taken no holiday, as they say here, where the "holiday," for most people, occupies the biggest part of life. We have had an infamous summer of cold, darkness & rain – plastered over a little, indeed, with a smoother September; & I have been very content to crouch by my own fireside (literally.) I love "visiting" less & less & hate seaside or other lodgings more & more; & so, as it has not been on the cards that I should go abroad I have cheerfully shared the empty London of August & September with the unfashionable. I expect, however, to cross the Channel, for a month (probably little further than Paris,) at the end of another fortnight. Alice is at Leamington, where she has just decided, with a serenity which excites my admiration, to live for another year – having already lived there for a year and a quarter. I spend a day with her, or rather a few hours, all she will permit, every month. I have lately had plenty of occupation in getting launched in a long novel I am writing for next year's *Atlantic*: it begins in January & you may see it there for a twelvemonth, but I hope you won't read it till that fitful fever is over. It is an attempt to do an all-English subject – & the name of the U.S. doesn't even occur. I am getting to know English life better than American, of which to day I see nothing – & to understand the English character or at least the *mind*, as well as if I had invented it: which indeed I think I could have done without any very extraordinary expenditure of ingenuity. I have seen little of people of late, for there have been no people to see – a blessed halt, on the whole. I dined last night with Lowell, the only other guest being Lady Pomeroy-Colley (young, pretty & coquettish, & delighting in L.) & Mrs. Walter Clifford, the widow of the famous mathematician & philosopher.[1] Lowell was very young & very "clever" – he is a charming host – & the occasion was sufficiently agreeable. He has just returned from Whitby, St. Ives, & various visits, & says he means to stay in town till November *1st*, when he sails for home – but I doubt if he can stand the pressure of the social desolation. However he takes things much as they come – & pipes & books (interspersed with Mrs. Smalley!) content him when there are not other solicitations.[2] A couple of months ago he was so ill with gout & so gloomy about himself, that I hoped he would come back here no more – alone disabled & forlorn – seeing almost a want of dignity in his dragging his impaired latest years across the sea & to heartless London dinners. But now I rather wish he didn't have to go home – so bright & capable & gay does he appear. He is the oddest mixture of the loveable & the annoying, the infinitely clever & the unspeakably simple, the delightful *convive* & the almost impossible one. I have, however, become *very* fond of him – he is inexhaustibly friendly to me, & it is hardly fair of me to talk of him with the pen – so much better justice one could do him with the quick allowances, qualifications & pleas of the tongue. I gather from your

1. Lady Pomeroy-Colley, born Edith Altha Hamilton, daughter of a general, was the widow of Sir George Pomeroy-Colley, who had been Governor of Natal in 1880 (and killed in battle against the Boers in 1881), and who, in the 1870s, had been one of Sir Garnet Wolseley's 'Wolseley ring'. Sophia Lucy Clifford (née Lane) (1846–1929), widow of William Kingdon Clifford, was a professional novelist and a good friend of HJ, as she had been of George Eliot. 2. Phoebe Garnaut Smalley (1838–1923) was the adopted daughter of Wendell Phillips, the American abolitionist, and was married – till their legal separation in 1898 – to HJ's London-based American friend George Washburn Smalley (1833–1916).

allusions to him that he appears to less advantage in America than in England – or to you personally, at least; while, oddly enough, some people here, (mainly those who don't like him,) suppose that he appears to less advantage in England than in America!

I am going in half an hour (this is a decent Sunday afternoon,) to pick up a very nice & accomplished little man, of whom I have lately seen a good deal, Jusserand, the French Chargé d'Affaires, in order to go with him up to Hampstead.[3] We often do this of a Sunday afternoon when we are in town, & having scaled the long hill which used to be so rural & pretty, & now is all red brick & cockney prose, we go and see Du Maurier & he comes out & takes a longish walk with us – usually, or sometimes, with his pretty daughters (one of them is very pretty indeed) & his 2 little dogs.[4] Then we go home & dine with him à la bonne franquette, & walk back to London at 10 o'clk. Du Maurier is an old & good friend of mine & has a charming Anglo-French mind & temper. His work has grown weak & monotonous (narrow) with time, but he is personally & conversationally the pleasantest creature, & I am very fond of him. Jusserand is a little prodigy of literary & diplomatic achievement effected at an early age. He is only 33 & he has written admirably on early English literature & manners & made his way wonderfully in the French foreign-office. Perhaps you have his 1st rate volume on "La Vie Nomade & les Routes en Angleterre au Moyen Age": a most valuable & interesting little book. He is alive to his very small finger-tips, ambitious, capable & charming – & if he were a few inches less diminutive I should believe that Europe would hear of him as a diplomatic personage. But he is too short! Up to a certain point, or rather down to it, shortness, I think, constitutes a presumption of greatness; but below that point not. What shall I tell you more, my dear Grace? I have lately led so quiet a life that I feel very bare of bright patches. I had six weeks ago a seizure of deafness, which became very bad – almost complete; but which proved to be catarrhal & curable; & is already almost wholly dissipated & abolished. It was rather a pleasant rest while it lasted – though I had to spend tiresome moments in the aurist's hands & still more tiresome hours in his waiting-room. Arthur Sedgwick has been here all summer, I believe, & came to see me once (a couple of months ago,) sitting exactly four minutes. I have seen nothing more of him, & what I saw in those moments

3. Jean Jules Jusserand (1855–1932) met HJ while working at the French Embassy in London. He wrote on the history of English literature, and was later to become French Ambassador in Washington.
4. George Louis Palmella Busson Du Maurier (1834–96), Paris-born satirical writer and artist, was one of the great late-Victorian contributors to *Punch* and in 1894 author of the bestseller *Trilby*.

was so blank & inexpressive that it was like a tête à tête with a man of straw. What is the matter with him? Nothing at all, I suppose. (I hope you don't keep my letters.) When I return from abroad, after a very short absence, it will be to spend a winter of foggy, business-like work in London. I expect to do lots & lots for the next five years, or say ten, to make the stupid world think me more important than it supposed. After that, late in the spring, I shall flee – somewhere, to Italy if I can – before the Season. I don't apologise for this deluge of egotism – because I know you magnanimously like it like that. But unless you soon give me, freely, more of your own news think, my dear Grace, what a fool this desire to serve you to your taste will have made of yours ever affectionately

Henry James

105. To Frederic William Henry Myers
20 October [1888]

Wren MS   Unpublished

Having sent two (overlength) instalments of The Tragic Muse *to the* Atlantic, *about 10 October HJ went directly to Geneva, to the Hôtel de l'Ecu, for his 'very short absence'. On 27 October he sent a third, for March 1890.*

Myers (1843–1901), a poet and essayist, Fellow of Trinity College, Cambridge, was a friend of WJ through his interest in spiritualism and mesmerism; he was one of the founders of the Society for Psychical Research. His wife was a remarkable amateur photographer. Partial Portraits *had come out on 8 May 1888. On 27 March 1888 HJ had told Theodore Child he was to write 'a Daudet's Later Novels', but he never did (HJL III, 229). He did, however, after this translate Daudet's final Tartarin novel,* Port Tarascon, *published in 1890; and was Daudet's host on his visit to England in 1895.*

Hotel de l'Ecu: Geneva.
October 20*th*.

My dear Myers.

I greatly appreciate your good letter, which finds me, as you see, in foreign lands – for a few weeks. I shall be back by December 1*st* – or before. I wish to thank you without delay for your excellent thought of sending me the photograph of E. Gurney, which I shall not see till I return to London, as I prefer it should not encounter the dangers of following me, but which I shall certainly deeply value.[1] I much applaud your spontaneous action. Let me also say how much I welcome your remarks about Daudet & about my absence of stricture, in *Partial Portraits*. I was perfectly conscious of all that my article failed to say today – of its incompleteness as a picture of the actual Daudet. It *was* fairly complete as an account of the Daudet of several years ago, when it was published – allowing for a certain *voulu*, & I think legitimate, or at any rate generous & responsive insistence (on my part) on the agreeable side. The agreeable side of Daudet was then, to my sense, quite immense, and none of his late *base* productions – for they *are* base – had been put forth. His later "evolution" has been of the ugliest – but the bad part of it was to come. It has qualified my appreciation of him immensely – but I didn't hesitate, all the same, to republish my affectionate article of 6 or 7 years ago as it stood – inasmuch as it represented a state of mind which was frank at the time & which it appeared to me to savour of excessive caution to disavow. The poor man is a strange mixture – a *surface* of charm which he presented 1*st*, making it *chatoyer* in the sun[,] and an underside of foulness & poverty which he has now turned completely uppermost. But the beauty was real & I am not sorry to have expressed my sense of it, as one trying, in general, to do the same things. One must always do that, I think – & the reserves are not nearly so important. Silence covers them all – and that's the only criticism I shall ever have for Daudet's miseries. I shall like to talk of these things with you again in the Cambridge meads – we mustn't miss it.

Please to commend me kindly to your wife – & believe very faithfully yours

Henry James

P.S. I don't particularly recommend my article on the Goncourts. It isn't very good – & has the defect of seeming to have been written for French readers.

106. To William James
29 October 1888

Houghton MS   Published HJL III, 242–5; CWJ II, 94–8

About 25 October 1859 the James family had arrived at the Hôtel de l'Ecu in Geneva, where Wilky and Robertson were sent to the Pensionat Maquelin out of

---

1. Edmund Gurney, like Myers a fellow of Trinity and a member of the Society for Psychical Research, died mysteriously in June 1888, of a self-administered overdose of chloroform. He co-wrote with Myers and the Fabian Frank Podmore (1855–1910) *Phantasms of the Living* (1886), as well as other books.

town, WJ went to the Academy, and HJ to the Institution Rochette 'for preparing such boys as wish to be engineers, architects, machinists, "and the like" for other higher schools' (HJL I, 9). At the start of Notes of a Son and Brother *HJ says the hotel 'now erects a somewhat diminished head on the edge of the rushing Rhone' – and remembers the river as 'my own sole happy impression during several of those months'.*

Constance Fenimore Woolson was staying in a hotel a mile away across Lake Geneva, and she and HJ met in the evenings. AJ wrote to WJ, 'Henry is somewhere on the continent flirting with Constance' (DLAJ, 149).

> Hotel de l'Ecu: Geneva.
> October 29*th* 1888.

My dear William.

Your beautiful & delightful letter of the 14*th*, from your country home, descended upon me two days ago, & after penetrating myself with it for 24 hours I sent it back to England, to Alice, on whom it will confer equal beatitude; not only because so copious, but because so "cheerful in tone" & appearing to show that the essentials of health & happiness are with you.[1] I wish to delay no hour longer to write to you, though I am at this moment rather exhausted with the effort of a long letter, completed 5 minutes since, to Louis Stevenson, in answer to one I lately received from his wife, from some undecipherable cannibal-island in the Pacific.[2] They are such far-away, fantastic, bewildering people – that there is a certain fatigue in the achievement of putting one's self in relation with them. I may mention in this connection that I have had in my hands the earlier sheets of the *Master of Ballantrae*, the new novel he is about to contribute to Scribner, & have been reading them with breathless admiration. They are wonderfully fine & perfect – he is a rare, delightful genius.

I am sitting in our old family *salon* in this place & have sat here much of the time for the last fortnight, in sociable converse with family ghosts – father & mother & Aunt Kate & our juvenile selves. I became conscious, suddenly,

1. WJ's letter described the purchase and works on house and grounds at Chocorua, New Hampshire. 'I feel uncommonly hearty', he told HJ (CWJ II, 91).
2. Unfortunately there is no trace of this letter, which Stevenson, who was in the South Seas, may even not have received. Stevenson had begun *The Master of Ballantrae* late in 1887; had a pamphlet made up of the earlier chapters, which he had sent to Colvin (probably HJ's source); but had trouble with the ending, which he laboured at till May 1889. In March 1890 HJ would write to Stevenson that the book was 'a pure hard crystal, my boy, a work of ineffable and exquisite art' (HJL III, 273).

abt. Oct. 10*th*, that I wanted very much to get away from the stale dingy London, which I had not quitted, to speak of, for 15 months & notably not all summer – a detestable summer in England, of wet & cold. Alice, whom I went to see, on arriving at this conclusion, assured me she could perfectly dispense for a few weeks with my presence on English soil; so I came straight here, where I have a sufficient, though not importunate sense of being in a foreign country, with a desired quietness for getting on with work. I have had 16 days of extraordinarily beautiful weather, full of autumn colour as vivid as yours at Chocorua, & with the Mt. Blanc Range, perpetually visible, literally hanging, day after day, over the blue lake. I have treated myself, as I say, to the apartments, or a portion of them, in which we spent the winter of 59–60, & in which nothing is changed save that the hotel seems to have gone down in the world a little, before the multiplication of rivals – a descent, however, which has the *agrément* of unimpaired cleanliness & applies apparently to the prices as well. It is very good & not at all dear. Geneva seems both duller & smarter – a good deal bigger, yet emptier too. The Academy is now the University – a large, winged building in the old public garden below the Treille.[3] But all the old smells & tastes are here, & the sensation is pleasant. I expect, in three or four days, to go to Paris for about three weeks – & back to London after that.[4] I shall be very busy for the next three or four months with the long thing I am doing for the *Atlantic* & which is to run no less than 15 – though in shorter instalments than my previous fictions; so that I have no time for wanton travelling. But I enjoy the easier, lighter feeling of being out of England. I suppose if one lived in one of these countries one would take its problems to one's self also, & be oppressed & darkened by them – even as I am, more or less, by those which hang over me in London. But as it is, the Continent gives one a refreshing sense of getting *away* – away from Whitechapel & Parnell & a hundred other constantly thickening heavinesses.[5] Apropos of which I may say, in re[s]ponse to your speculation about Alice's homesickness

3. The Hôtel de l'Ecu de Genève was by a bridge where the Rhône meets Lake Geneva. La Treille is a shady promenade.
4. HJ went early in November to a torrentially rainy Genoa, where he spent a week before going on for two or three weeks to 'the delicious Monte Carlo'; he then spent 'the month of December in Paris' (HJL III, 249).
5. 'Jack the Ripper' sent letters to the police claiming responsibility for seven murders of women in the Whitechapel district between 7 August and 10 November 1888. The Phoenix Park murders in Dublin on 6 May 1882, of British officials by Fenian nationalists, seemed to have been privately excused, in a letter printed in *The Times* on 18 April 1887, by the Irish leader Charles Stewart Parnell, M.P. (1846–91), who had publicly denounced them. Beginning in September 1888 a commission examined the evidence and declared the letter a forgery; Parnell won a libel action.

(leaving her to answer the question directly for herself,) that she doesn't strike me as made *unhappy*, nostalgically, so much as occupied & stimulated, healthily irritated. She *is* homesick, but not nearly so much so as if she had a definite, concrete nest to revert to – a home of her own; & as if she had *not* a habitation which, materially & economically, happens to suit her very well in England. I don't think she *likes* England or the English very much – the people, their mind, their tone, their "hypocrisy" &c. This is owing partly to the confined life she leads & the partial, passive, fragmentary, unreacting way in which she sees them. Also to her seeing so many more women than men: or rather *only* women, so far as she now sees any one – & no men at all. Also to her being such a tremendously convinced home ruler. She *does* take a great interest in English affairs – & that is an occupation & a source of well-being (in the country) to her. It is always a great misfortune, I think, when one has reached a certain age, that if one is living in a country not ones own & one is of anything of an ironic or critical disposition, one mistakes the inevitable reflections & criticisms that one makes, more & more as one grows older, upon life & human nature &c, for a judgment of that particular country, its natives, peculiarities &c, to which, really, one has grown exceedingly accustomed. For myself, at any rate I am deadly weary of the whole "international" state of mind – so that I *ache*, at times, with fatigue at the way it is constantly forced upon one as a sort of virtue or obligation. I can't look at the English & American worlds, or feel about them, any more, save as a big AngloSaxon total, destined to such an amount of melting together that an insistence on their differences becomes more & more idle & pedantic & that that melting together will come the faster the more one takes it for granted & treats the life of the 2 countries as continuous & more or less convertible, or at any rate as simply different chapters of the same general subject. Literature, fiction in particular, affords a magnificent arm for such taking for granted, & one may so do an excellent work with it. I have not the least hesitation in saying that I aspire to write in such a way that it wd. be impossible to an outsider to say whether I am, at a given moment, an American writing about England or an Englishman writing about America (dealing as I do with both countries,) & so far from being ashamed of such an ambiguity I should be exceedingly proud of it, for it would be highly civilized. You are right in surmising that it must often be a grief to me not to get more time for reading – though not in supposing that I am "hollowed out inside" by the limitations my existence has too obstinately attached to that exercise, combined with the fact that I produce a great deal. At times I do read almost as much as my wretched little *stomach* for it (literally[)] will allow, & on the whole I get much more time for it as the months & years go by. I touched bottom, in the way of missing time, during the 1*st* half of my long residence in London – having traversed then a sandy desert, in that respect – where however I took on board such an amount of human & social information that if the same necessary alternatives were presented to me again I should make the same choice. One can read when one is middle-aged or old; but one can mingle in the world with fresh perceptions only when one is young. The great thing is to be *saturated*, with something – that is, in one way or another, with life; & I chose the form of my saturation. Moreover you exaggerate the degree to which my writing takes it out of my mind, for I try to spend only the interest of my capital.

I haven't told you how I found Alice when I last saw her. She is now in very good form – still going out, I hear from her, in the mild moments, & feeling very easy & even jolly about her Leamington winter. My being away is a sign of her really good symptoms. She was *wüthend* after the London police in connection with the Whitechapel murders, to a degree that almost constituted robust health. I have seen a great many (that is, more than usual) Frenchmen in London this year; they bring me notes of introduction – & the other day, the night before coming away, I "entertained" at dinner (at a club,) the French Ambassador at Madrid (Paul Cambon,) Xavier Charmes of the French Foreign Office, G. du Maurier, & the wonderful little Jusserand, the chargé d'affaires in London, who is a great friend of mine, & to oblige & relieve whom it was that I invited the 2 other diplomatists, his friends, whom he had, rather helplessly, on his hands.[6] *There* is the *real* difference – a gulf, from the English (or the American) to the French man, & vice-versa (still more;) & not from the English man to the American. The Frenchmen I see all seem to me wonderful the 1st time – but not so much, at all, the 2d. But I must finish this without having touched any of the sympathetic things I meant to say to you about your place, your work on it, Alice's prowesses as a country lady, the childrens' *vie champêtre* &c. Aunt Kate, after her visit to you, praised all these things to us with profusion and evident sincerity.[7] I wish I could see them – but the day seems far. I haven't lain on the ground for so many years that I feel as if I had spent them up in a balloon. Next summer I shall come here – I mean to Switzerland, for which my taste has revived. I am full of gratulation on your enlarged classes, chances of reading &c; & on your prospect of keeping the invalid child this winter.[8] Give my tender love to Alice. You are entering

6. Pierre-Paul Cambon (1843–1924); François-Xavier Charmes (1848–1916), formerly editor of the *Revue des Deux Mondes*.

7. On 6 March 1889 Aunt Kate would die in New York from what was called progressive mental paralysis.

8. WJ had written that 'There will probably be no migration to the South necessary' – i.e. no health problems necessitating avoidance of the Boston winter.

the period of keen suspense about Cleveland, & I share it even here.[9] I have lately begun to receive & read the *Nation* after a long interval – & it seems to me very rough. Was it *ever* so? I wonder about Bob. Ever your affectionate

Henry James

107. To Henrietta Reubell
23 March [1889]

Houghton MS   Unpublished

HJ met Henrietta Reubell (c.1839–1924), an American expatriate with a salon in Paris, in 1876. She was a friend of Sargent, Whistler and Wilde, the last of whom called her 'very ugly and very amusing' (LOW, 157). The painter William Rothenstein (1872–1945) recollected 'a striking figure, with her bright red hair crowning an expressive but unbeautiful face, her fingers and person loaded with turquoise stones. In face and figure she reminded me of Queen Elizabeth – if one can imagine an Elizabeth with an American accent and a high, shrill voice like a parrot's.'

Throughout this time HJ was occupied with The Tragic Muse.

34 De Vere Gdns W.
March 23d

Dear Miss Reubell.

I know it's very base of me not to have written to you before – but in truth my correspondence is a very fearful problem – & I am, little by little, totally sinking under it. Some of my friends I am condemned to love in absolute silence – to others I gasp a rare inarticulate greeting. I haven't free a spacious hour, like you – but come to the epistolary act with hand and brain worried by the perpetual grind of professional scribbling. Yet I long to exchange twenty words with you, & let them, now, be words of humility & affection. The weeks have gone fast since I last beheld you; & I have deplored my failure to write even while I noted it.[1] Then I have had very little to tell of, save a continuity of occupation. I have liked my winter (since Jan. *1st*,) because I have been busy & London has been mild & not too dark. I am staying on & on, & *near* dreams of going abroad again are far from me. When I *do* quit

9. The American president, Grover Cleveland, won a popular majority in the November elections but lost in the electoral college.

1. Presumably HJ had seen her in Paris in December 1888.

town it will be for some destination as yet undetermined. I shall fight it out to June 1st & then halt from the rush & crush. The exhibition will frighten me from Paris – such inventions & such monstrous wholesale quantity & number are a direct negation of everything I hold pleasant or, for myself, *possible* in life.[2] Sargent crosses to you, on (I believe) Tuesday next, after having painted an absolutely magnificent portrait of Ellen Terry as Lady Macbeth (she is beautiful as an image & abominable as an actress.)[3] She is clad in splendid peacock-blue robes, with a cobalt background, like an enamel or a figure in a missal or a mosaic, & with her wondrous open mouth, her iridescent garments, her huge, wild red braids (of dyed horsehair) hanging to her feet, her shining barbaric crown, which, with a grand movement of the arms, she is placing on her head – and with above all, her wondrous pale, fatal, painted, terrible face – half-Medusa, half-Rossetti, with light-coloured eyes & scarlet lips – she is a very distinguished person indeed & a very prodigious image. It is a *noble* picture – very strange, very hard, the result of a wonderfully vivid & direct vision of what he wanted to do & a still more wonderful ability to render it. People in general will stare & be idiotic & frightened, & not understand: but the thing will do him immense good with any one who *knows*. Fortunately that number doesn't diminish.

The young Von Glehn, mildly starchy & with (I *think*) new trousers, lunched with me the other day, in comp'y. with my very droll little friend Phil Burne Jones (the younger.)[4] He has "pupils" – hence perhaps the trousers. The King girls have been, & are still here – & I have tea'd & dined at M*me* Waddingtons & felt promoted, initiated & Affaires-Etrangèreish.[5] Don't *bouder* me, & give my love to Mrs. Boit.[6] Has she a nest yet for her brood? *Stia bene* & believe me affectionately yours

Henry James

2. In 1889 there was held in Paris the Exposition du Centenaire, for which the Tour Eiffel was built.

3. In Sargent's 1889 portrait, now in the Tate Gallery, Ellen Terry (1847–1928) was wearing an extraordinary costume designed by Alice Strettell Carr, wife of HJ's friend J. Comyns Carr (1849–1916).

4. Wilfred Von Glehn was a painter who married Jane Emmet, a cousin of HJ's. Philip Burne-Jones was the son of HJ's friend the painter Edward Burne-Jones (1833–98), and himself a painter (he painted a scene from HJ's story 'The Madonna of the Future').

5. Mary Waddington (née King), to whom 'the King girls' are presumably related, was wife of William Henry Waddington (1826–94), whose father was an English industrialist but who was a naturalized Frenchman. An archaeologist, he entered politics and was briefly prime minister of France. From 1883 to 1893 he was French Ambassador in London – hence the 'Foreign Affairs' in 'Affaires-Etrangèreish'.

6. Charlotte Louisa Cushing Boit, who had been painted late in 1887 by Sargent, was the wife of Edward Darley Boit (1840–1915), a rich American who had given up his law practice to

108. To Thomas Bailey Aldrich
2 November [1889]

Houghton MS   Unpublished

HJ remained in London working on The Tragic Muse, *visited by WJ in July. In September he went up to Whitby for four days to see Lowell, then to Dover for a fortnight, then had three days in Devonshire with Lord Coleridge and a week in London before crossing to Paris on 24 October, catching the last few days of the exhibition commemorating the centenary of the French Revolution. He stayed at the Hôtel de Hollande till 1 December, and as well as finishing* The Tragic Muse *translated Daudet's* Port Tarascon *from the printer's galleys. His big novel had been running in the* Atlantic *since January 1889, and would only finish in May 1890.*

Paris; November 2d
(*34 De Vere Gardens W.*)

My dear Aldrich.

I have just sent to London the first third of the last instalment of the *Muse*, to be type-copied. The instant it comes back to me it shall be dashed off to you – & the very ultimate & terminal pages shall follow with lightning speed.[1] The greater portion of the penultimate (February) part must have reached you just after your note to me quitted Boston. The first pages of that same instalment went three or four weeks ago. The others – the greater part of the – as I calculate – February number were posted in London Oct 19*th*. What I am now sending you is the very *finis*. Ever yours

Henry James

---

study painting in Paris with Couture. He also commissioned one of Sargent's most famous paintings, of his four daughters, in 1882.

1. On 2 December HJ was back in London and sent Aldrich 'the very last pages & words (6,980 of them alas!)' of *The Tragic Muse*; he had again had to divide the last chapter in two (Unpublished Houghton MS, bMS Am 1429 (2620)).

109. To Florence (Mrs Hugh) Bell
5 February [1890]

Texas MS   Unpublished

Florence Eveleen Bell (née Olliffe, 1851–1930), wife of the Northern ironmaster
Thomas Hugh Bell (afterwards second baronet), was a regular playgoing intimate
of HJ's during his four-year assault on the theatre from 1891. An admirer of the
Théâtre Français, she had a play, L'Indécis, *successfully acted by Coquelin in*
1887.

HJ's story 'The Solution' was published in the New Review *from December*
1889 to February 1890. A young English diplomat in Rome – who remorsefully
narrates the story years later – mischievously persuades a naïve rich American that
he has inadvertently 'compromised' the lovely but mercenary Veronica Goldie. The
chivalrous American instantly proposes; the appalled Englishman appeals to a clever
young widow he loves to prevent the marriage; the widow falls in love with the
American and he with her; some secret financial deal is made. American and widow
marry (unhappily). Neither the Englishman nor Veronica ever marries anyone.

February 5th
34, DE VERE GARDENS, W.

Dear Mrs. Bell

Your interest & sympathy are delightful: though they add tremendously to
my sense of responsibility. If you confess yourself "ingeniously fascinated"
what more can I desire? To fascinate is my highest ambition – I am a kind of
male literary Veronica. But, àpropos of her, the gentle reader evidently looks
instinctively (your remarks lead me to believe,) for something or other, in a
work of fiction – I don't quite know what it is – that is the last thing it occurs
to me, perverse, to put into it – & evidently the element which most makes
its interest for *me* (perverse as before) is something that is not indispensable
to the gentle reader. E.g., the interest of my little bêtise in the N.R. was not
in the least (for me) dependent on one's getting poor Veronica married. Rather
the reverse – that banality would surely have left the story much less individual,
much less challenging. But these are supersubtleties. What isn't is the grossness
(if I may be allowed the expression) of your putting off your advent till May
– when I fear I shall be gone. Do have little advents before, & do make them
clearly known to yours, dear Mrs. Bell, & all your house's, most truly

Henry James

110. To Florence (Mrs Hugh) Bell
7 February [1890]

Texas MS   Unpublished

Feb 7th
34, DE VERE GARDENS, W.

Dear Mrs. Bell.

Only just such a little *brin* of unacknowledgable acknowledgment as will prove me not a person who receiving "explanations" from a gracious & magnanimous lady, doesn't straightway hurl himself at her feet.

Certainly I must, as a peintre de moeurs & de caractères, be exasperating in my poor way – but it isn't – I think – in trying to give what the main public & the *gros* reader want that I shall seek the right remedy. They "want" simply bottomless niaiserie – look at Mr. Smith's bookstalls & you'll see.[1] Give them what one wants oneself – it's the only way: *follow* them & they lead one by a straight grand highway to abysses of vulgarity. Only the esprits d'élite – like you, however, take *gracefully* – your protests are simply a charming *manner*. Do have it always for yours most attentively

Henry James

111. To Frederick Macmillan
26 March 1890

BL MS   Published CHJHM, 159; HJL III, 274–5

Professionally, HJ now found himself in a tight corner. When it came to a contract for the book form of The Tragic Muse, *already sold for the American market to the* Atlantic*'s Boston publishers (Houghton, Mifflin & Co.), Macmillan was cautious: 'the commercial result of the last few books we have published for you has been anything but satisfactory' (CHJHM, 159). He offered instead of HJ's usual arrangement (an advance against profits), a more generous version of the high-Victorian half-profits contract – which would have deferred any remuneration.*

1. W. H. Smith & Sons began selling books at railway bookstalls in 1848, and later added town bookshops and circulating libraries to their operations.

March 26th 1890
34, DE VERE GARDENS, W.

My dear Macmillan

I am afraid I can't meet you on the ground of your offer in regard to the publication of "The Tragic Muse" in this country – two thirds profits in the future. That future is practically remote & I am much concerned with the present. What I desire is to obtain a sum of money "down" – & I am loth to perish without a struggle – that is without trying to obtain one. I gather that the terms you mention are an ultimatum excluding, for yourselves, the idea of anything down – which is why I make this declaration of my alternative. But I should be sorry to pursue that alternative without hearing from you again – though I don't flatter myself that I hold the knife at your throat. Yours ever

Henry James

112. To Frederick Macmillan
28 March 1890

BL MS   Published CHJHM, 160–61; HJL III, 275–6; SL2, 233

In response to HJ's request for a sum 'down', Macmillan calculated what two-thirds profits would come to on an edition of 500 copies.

March 28th 1890
34, DE VERE GARDENS, W.

My dear Macmillan.

I thank you for your note & the offer of £70. 0. 0 Don't, however, think my pretensions monstrous if I say that, in spite of what you tell me of the poor success of my recent books, I still do desire to get a larger sum, & have determined to take what steps I can in this direction. These steps I know will carry me away from you, but it comes over me that that is after all better, even with a due & grateful recognition of the readiness you express to go on with me, unprofitable as I am. I say it is "better," because I had far rather that in these circumstances you should *not* go on with me. I would rather not be published at all than be published & not pay – other people at least. The latter alternative makes me uncomfortable & the former makes me, of the two, feel least like a failure; the failure that, at this time of day, it is too humiliating to consent to be without trying, at least, as they say in America, to "know more about it." Unless I can put the matter on a more remunerative footing all round

I shall give up my English "market" – heaven save the market! & confine myself to my American. But I must experiment a bit first – & to experiment is of course to say farewell to you. Farewell then, my dear Macmillan, with great regret – but with the sustaining cheer of all the links in the chain that remain still unbroken.

Yours ever
Henry James

113. To Alexander Pollock Watt
2 April 1890

Berg MS   Unpublished

In spite of his 'farewell', HJ had already given Macmillan nearly all the revised copy of the novel. The pioneering agent Watt, probably reckoning Macmillan was committed to the book, proposed a new arrangement, £250 for exclusive rights in Britain and the dominions for five years and two months. The novel thus came out in July from Macmillan and in June in America from Houghton, Mifflin & Co.

April 2d 1890
34, DE VERE GARDENS, W.

Dear Mr. Watt.

I hear with pleasure from you that you have so promptly arranged the matter of the *Tragic Muse*: I am quite content with this result. I will sign the agreement as soon as Messrs. Macmillan send it, & am truly yours

Henry James

Mr. A. P. Watt.

114. To William James
16 May 1890

Houghton MS   Published CWJ II, 134–6; partly published LHJ I, 161–3

HJ went to Italy and was in Milan by 15 May 1890.

By 12 May 1889 he had engaged to write a dramatization of The American – *'Oh, how it must not be too good and how very bad it must be!' he told himself*

(N, 53) – for Edward Compton (1854–1918) and his American wife Virginia Frances Bateman (1853–1940) of the Compton Comedy Company, who had made an overture in December 1888. In February 1890 he had already sent the second act, and all four acts were written by April. HJ had told WJ on 9 March that he hoped for results 'profoundly pecuniary' (CWJ II, 131).

Hotel de la Ville, Milan.
May 16*th* 1890

My dear William.

I feel as if I were always owing you a letter tremendously but I have seldom felt so more than these many days past. I can't at last stand it any longer: so here goes a definite attempt at one which may do *me* some good, whether or not it does you. In fact it was with the conscious purpose of writing you as soon as I shld. have got to a breathing-place, well away from London, that, from day to day, for sometime past, I have been holding my hand – the more so as my hand had everything else to do. I have been both very busy & very bent on getting away this year without fail, for a miracle, from the oppressive London Season. I have just accomplished it; I passed the St. Gothard day before yesterday, & I hope to find it possible to remain absent till August 1*st*. After that I am ready to pay cheerfully & cheaply for my journey by staying quietly in town for August & September, in the conditions in which you saw me last year. I shall take as much as possible of a holiday, for I have been working carefully consecutively & unbrokenly for a very long time past – turning out one thing (always "highly finished") after another. However I *like* to work, thank heaven, and at the end of a month's privation of it I sink into gloom & discomfort – so that I shall probably not wholly "neglect my pen."

I spent a day with Alice just before I came away & left her girding her loins to try & begin to go out (in a chair) a little for the summer months. But she was to see a dentist first, (there is a goodish one at Leamington who comes to her,) and one of these efforts was to depend on the greater or less prostration consequent upon the other. She had up to the 14*th* (I have just got a note from her of day before yesterday,) received no news as to the probation of Henry W.'s will – & will probably remain in a state of inevitable tension until that matter, though it isn't an immense one, is settled.[1] It is immense enough, at

1. AJ was still at Leamington Spa. Henry Albert Wyckoff died on 23 February 1890. In her diary, on 25 March, AJ illustrates HJ's 'babe-like innocence' by mocking his optimism about Henry Wyckoff's will and his reluctance to believe that Albert, or rather the depraved Sarah (Mrs Albert) Wyckoff, would contest it. The will *was* contested, and the case ran on till autumn 1894.

any rate, to make me ardently hope, both for you & for her, that the vessel will have steered through the rapids. But I won't write more of it, after a fact probably now determined, though unknown to me. I go hence in a day or two to Florence for a week or two and then to Venice for the month of June. (I am suffering from a plague of bad pens – excuse therefore the different kinds of badness in my hand.) The Dan'l. Curtises have pressed me to stay with them in their marble palace & I shall probably go for ten days.[2] The strenuous Miss Wormeley is with them – but I don't mention that as a reason. I hope you will have received promptly a copy of *The Tragic Muse*, though I am afraid I sent my list to the publishers a little late. I don't in the least know, however, when the book is supposed to come out. I have no opinion or feeling about it now – though I took long & patient & careful trouble (which no creature will recognise) with it at the time; too much, no doubt; for my mind is now a muddled, wearied blank on the subject. I have shed & ejected it: it's over & dead – & my feeling as to what may become of it is reduced to the sordid hope it will make a little money – which it won't. Àpropos of such matters – both novels & money-making as I believe the book is through its big sale a source of lucre to the author – I have just been reading with wonder & admiration, Howells's last big novel, which I think so prodigiously good & able, & so beyond what he at one time seemed in danger of reducing himself to, that I mean to write him a gushing letter about it not a day later than tomorrow.[3] It seems to me to have an extraordinar[y] life & truth of observation & feeling, & to contain in old Dryfoos, a marvellous portrait. What one doesn't like in it doesn't in the least matter – it lives independently of all that. His abundance & facility are my constant wonder & envy – or rather not perhaps, envy, inasmuch as he has purchased them by throwing the whole question of form, style & composition overboard into the deep sea – from which, on my side, I am perpetually trying to fish them up. The matter you expressed a friendly hope about the success of & which for all sorts of reasons I desire to be extremely secret, silent & mysterious about, (I mean the enterprise I covertly mentioned to you as conceived by me with a religious & deliberate view of gain on a greater scale than the Book (my Books at least) can ever approach bringing in to me:) this matter is on a good & promising footing, but it is too

2. Daniel Sargent Curtis (1825–1908) and Ariana Randolph Wormeley Curtis (1833–1922) were rich Bostonians who lived and entertained at the Palazzo Barbaro in Venice. All three daughters of the British admiral Ralph Randolph Wormeley jointly wrote a volume of recollections of their father in 1879. The other sisters, Mary Elizabeth Wormeley (later Latimer) and Katherine Prescott Wormeley (1830–1908), the 'strenuous' one HJ mentions here, both published a number of works, including many translations from the French.

3. *A Hazard of New Fortunes*. HJ did: see next letter (115).

soon to say anything about it save that I am embarked in it seriously and with rather remarkably good omens. By which I mean that it is not to depend on a single attempt, but on ½ a dozen, of the most resolute & scientific character, which I find I am abundantly capable of making, but which, alas, in the light of this discovery, I become conscious that I ought to have made 10 years ago. I was then discouraged all round, while a single word or touch of *en*couragement wd. have made the difference.[4] Now it is late. But on the other hand the thing wd. have been then only an experiment more or less like another – whereas now it's an absolute necessity – imposing itself, without choice – if I wish a loaf on the shelf for my old age. Fortunately as far as it's gone it announces itself well – but I can't tell you yet how far that is. The only thing is to do a great lot.

By the time this reaches you I suppose your wife & children will have gone to recline under the greenwood tree.[5] I hope their gentle outlawry will be full of comfort to them. It's poor work – to me – writing about them without ever seeing them. But my interest in them is deep & large, & please never omit to give my great love to them: to Alice first in the lump, to be broken up & distributed by her. May you squeeze with a whole skin through the tight weeks of the last of the term – may you live to rest & may you rest to live. I shall not, I think, soon again, write to you so rarely as for the last year. This will be partly because the *Tragic Muse* is to be my last long novel. For the rest of my life I hope to do lots of short things with irresponsible spaces between. I see even a great future (10 years) of such. But they won't make money. Excuse (you probably rather will esteem) the sordid tone of your affectionate

Henry James

115. To William Dean Howells
17 May [1890]

Houghton MS   Published HJL III, 280–84; LFL, 275–8

As in December 1886, when he had followed the fortunes of Lemuel Barker in Howells's The Minister's Charge *(1886) on the train to Italy ('The beauties of nature passed unheeded' (HJL III, 148)), HJ wrote from Milan to praise Howells's*

4. HJ is referring to the rejection of *Daisy Miller: A Comedy in Three Acts* both by New York and London producers.
5. *As You Like It* II.v. 1–5: 'Under the greenwood tree, / Who loves to lie with me, / And tune his merry note / Unto the sweet bird's throat, / Come hither . . .' WJ stayed at Harvard while his family went ahead to Chocorua, New Hampshire.

latest, this time a remarkable New York social panorama, A Hazard of New Fortunes *(1890)*. *The family of the equable Basil March, who moves to New York as editor of a new magazine*, Every Other Week, *is based on the Howellses; but the most striking figure in the book, not appearing till nearly half-way though, is the magazine's backer, wealthy old Jacob Dryfoos, a corrupted Pennsylvania Dutch farmer whose land was bought by Standard Oil for drilling and whose 'moral decay began with his perception of the opportunity of making money quickly and abundantly'. In his 'gray business suit of provincial cut' and 'low, wide-brimmed hat of flexible black felt' Dryfoos, 'a Mammon-worshipper, pure and simple', is a tyrant: over his fretful rustic wife, who is uncomfortable in cosmopolitan New York because still spiritually among the sect of 'Dunkards' or 'Beardy Men' of her upbringing; over his two daughters, the elder of whom, the fiercely dominating Christine, is described as a 'leopardess'; and over his idealistic Christian son Conrad, whose wish to be a preacher he crushes in the attempt to make him 'a regular New York business man' by making him publisher of* Every Other Week.

> Hotel de la Ville Milan.
> May 17*th*
> 34, De Vere Gardens, W.

My dear Howells.

I have been not writing to you at a tremendous, an infamous rate, for a long time past; but I should indeed be sunk in baseness if I were to keep this pace after what has just happened. For what has just happened is that I have been reading the *Hazard of N.F.* (I confess I shld. have liked to change the name for you,) & that it has filled me with communicable rapture. I remember that the last time I came to Italy (or almost,) I brought your Lemuel Barker, which had just come out, to read in the train & let it divert an intensely professional eye from the most clamorous beauties of the way – writing to you afterwards from this very place I think, all the good & all the wonder I thought of it. So I have a decent precedent for insisting, to you, now, under circumstances exactly similar (save that the present book is a much bigger feat,) that, to my charmed & gratified sense, the *Hazard* is simply prodigious. I read the 1*st* vol. just before I left London – & the second, which I began the instant I got into the train at Victoria, made me wish immensely that both it & the journey to Bâle & thence were formed to last longer. I congratulate you, my dear Howells unrestrictedly, & give you my assurance – whatever the vain thing is worth – that, for me, you have never yet done anything so roundly & totally good. For, (after the flat-hunting business is disposed of) the whole thing is almost equally good – or would be, that is, if the Dryfooses were not so much better than even the best of the rest, & than even the best of S. Lapham, & the best of what has been your best heretofore.[1] I don't know whether you can bear to see the offspring of your former (literary) marriages sacrificed so to the last batch – but it is the sort of thing you must expect if you *will* practise so prolific a polygamy. The life, the truth, the light, the heat, the breadth & depth & thickness of the Hazard, are absolutely admirable. It seems to me altogether, in abundance, ease & variety, a fresh start for you at what I would call "your age" didn't I fear to resemble a Dryfoos – so that I'll say instead that to *read* the thing is a fresh start for me at mine. I should think it would make you as happy as poor happiness will let us be, to turn off from one year to the other, & from a reservoir in daily domestic use, such a free, full rich flood. In fact your reservoir deluges me, altogether, with surprise as well as other sorts of effusion: by which I mean that though you do much to empty it you keep it remarkably full. I seem to myself, in comparison, to fill mine with a teaspoon & obtain but a trickle. However, I don't mean to compare myself with you or to compare you, in the particular case, with anything but life. When I do that – with the life you see and represent – your faculty for rendering it seems to me extraordinary & to shave the truth – the general truth you aim at – several degrees closer than anyone else begins to do. You are less *big* than Zola, but you are ever so much less clumsy & more really various, and moreover you & he don't see the same things – you have a wholly different consciousness – *you* see a totally different side of a different race.[2] Man isn't at all *one* after all – it takes so much of him to be American, to be French, &c. I won't even compare you with something I have a sort of dim, stupid sense you might be and are not – for I don't in the least know that you might be it, after all, or whether, if you were, you wouldn't cease to be that something you are which makes me write to you thus. We don't know what people might give us that they don't – the only thing is to take them on what they do & to allow them absolutely & utterly their conditions. This alone, for the taster, secures freedom of enjoyment. I apply the rule to you, & it represents a perfect triumph of appreciation; because it makes me accept, largely, all your material from you – an absolute gain when I consider that I should never take it from myself. I note certain things which make me wonder at your form & your fortune (e.g. – as I have told you before – the fatal colours in which they let *you*, because you live at home – is it? – paint American life; & the fact that there's a whole

1. The book begins with the densely circumstantial domestic comedy of the Marches coming to New York from Boston and hunting for a flat.
2. In 1888 Howells had been attacked in the Boston *Post* for his declaration in the March 1888 'Editor's Study' in *Harper's Monthly* that Zola's *La Terre* was a book 'to be sought and seriously considered', 'filthy and repulsive as it is in its facts'.

quarter of the heaven upon which, in the matter of composition, you seem to me consciously – *is* it consciously? – to have turned your back;) but these things have no relevancy whatever as grounds of dislike – simply because you communicate so completely *what* you undertake to communicate. The novelist is a particular *window*, absolutely – & of worth in so far as he is one; & it's because you open so well & are hung so close over the street that *I* could hang out of it all day long. Your very value is that you choose your own street – heaven forbid I should have to choose it for you. If I should say I mortally dislike the people who pass in it, I should seem to be taking on myself that intolerable responsibility of selection which it is exactly such a luxury to be relieved of. Indeed I'm convinced that no reader above the rank of an idiot – this number is moderate I admit – can really fail to take any view that's really *shown* them – any gift (of subject) that's really given. The usual imbecillity of the novel is that the showing & giving simply don't come off – the reader never touches the subject & the subject never touches the reader: the window is no window at all – but only childishly *finta*, like the ornaments of our beloved Italy. This is why, as a triumph of *communication*, I hold the Hazard so rare & strong. You communicate in touches so close, so fine, so true, so droll, so frequent. I am writing too much (you will think demented with chatter;) so that I can't go into specifications of success. It is *all* absolutely successful, & if a part or two are better than the others it isn't that the others are not so good as they ought to be. These last have the deuce of an effect in making it appear that nothing ought *ever* to be less good than they. That is, you set a measure & example of the prehensile perception – & so many things, in future, will seem less good than they ever *could* be, for not coming up to such a standard. The Dryfooses are portraiture of the very first magnitude, the old man magnificent, without flaw or faintness anywhere, & the whole thing, in short, so observed, so caught, so felt, so conceived & created – so damningly & inexplicably American. How can they stand each other? (so many of them!) I asked as I read, reflecting that they, poor things, hadn't *you*, as I had, to make me stand them all. Or rather they *had* you, really – & that's the word of the enigma. You pervade & permeate them all, my dear Howells, just enough to save them from each other & from the unlimited extension of the movement of irresistible relief by which Christine D. scratches Beaton's face & even old Dryfoos smites his blank son (an admirable, *admirable* business, the whole of that).[3] Go on, go on, even if *I* can't – and since New York has

3. One of the contributors to *Every Other Week* is the artist Angus Beaton, a worthless young man who flirts with, then disappoints, Christine Dryfoos: 'with a scream of rage . . . she flashed at him, and with both hands made a feline pass at the face he bent toward her' (Pt IV, ch. XVII). Old Dryfoos has a history of violent strike-breaking, using armed Pinkerton agents, and

brought you such *bonheur* give it back to her with still larger liberality. Don't tell me you can't do anything now, or that life isn't luxurious to you, with such a power of creation. You live in a luxury (of that kind) which Lindau wd. reprehend, or at any rate have nothing to meet, & that I am not sure even poor March wd. be altogether easy about.[4] Poor March, my dear Howells – what tricks you play him – even worse than those you play Mrs. March! Just let me add that Conrad D. is a *1st class* idea, as the son of his father & a figure in the Dryfoos picture. But *all* the picture, I repeat, is of the highest worth. How the devil did you do it? You'll found a school – that of your "*3d* manner["] & I shall come to it.

I left London four days ago, with the cunning purpose of staying away from it for June & July & returning to it for August & September. I hope to spend June in Venice – July perhaps in some blue Giorgionesque background.[5] I continue to scribble, though with relaxed continuity, while abroad; but I cant talk to you about it. One thing only is clear that henceforth I must do, or ½ do, England in fiction – as the place I see most & to day, in a sort of way, know best. I have at last more acquired notions of it, on the whole, than of any other world, & it will serve as well as any other. It has been growing distincter that America fades from me, & as she never trusted me at best, I can trust *her*, for effect, no longer. Besides I can't be doing *de chic*, from here, when you, on the spot, are doing so brilliantly the *vécu*.

The *vécu* indeed reached me in a very terrible form, in London, just before I came away, in the shape of the news of the rejection at Washington of the International Copyright Bill.[6] That was the great news there, & it has made a very bad state of things – so that I was glad to come away, for a time at least, from the shame & discomfort of it. It seems as if this time we had said, loudly, that whereas we had freely admitted before that we in fact steal, we now seize the opportunity to declare that we *like* to steal. This surely isn't what we really *mean*, as a whole people – & yet apparently we do mean it enough not to care to make it clear that we mean anything else. It is a new sort of national profession, under the sun, & I am sorry the originality of it should belong to

---

when Conrad defiantly sympathizes with the New York transport strikers, his repressive father 'lifted his hand and struck his son in the face' (Pt IV, ch. IV).

4. Lindau is a high-minded Socialist German, a translator for the magazine, who has lost a hand fighting for the abolitionist cause in the Civil War; he lives in squalor in order not to forget the poor. March is a comfortable liberal *bourgeois* with an uneasy conscience.

5. The Venetian Giorgione (*c.*1476/8–1510) was one of the founders of modern painting, working for private collectors more than for institutions and producing ambiguous, intensely atmospheric pieces.

6. It was the twelfth time in HJ's lifetime that Congress had defeated a Bill which would have given copyright protection for foreign authors. It finally passed in 1891.

us. Of course however there will be another big fight before the civilization of the country accepts such a last word. I have lately seen much the admirably acute & intelligent young Balestier, who has been of much business use to me, & a great comfort thereby – besides my liking him so.[7] I think that practically he will soon "do everything" for me. Also your (also acute) young friend H. Harland, whom I had to fish out of a heaped-up social basket *as* your friend.[8] I shall be glad to make him mine if he'll be so – he seems a very clever fellow. But why won't you ever project these young stars into my milky way? If it's to "spare" me you don't, because I always – at last – discover them & then have to try to lavish myself on them the more to make up to them for the unnatural rigour with which you've treated them. Please give my love to Mrs. March & tell her I could "stand" *her* if she'd only give me a chance. Do come out again, with Tom & Bella, whom I press to my heart, & I will take you to a better hatter, in London, than Dryfoos did. Ever, my dear Basil, enthusiastically yours

Henry James

116. To Horace Elisha Scudder
30 August 1890

Houghton MS   Published AMRP, 77–8

HJ went on to Venice and the Curtises, who took him to Oberammergau for the Passion Play; then he returned to Italy – to Venice and then Florence, where he stayed and then travelled for a time with his friend the American doctor William Wilberforce Baldwin (1850–1910) – who gave him as they went the anecdote on which he based 'The Pupil'. He moved on to Siena, and then the home of Edith

7. The enterprising and engaging Charles Wolcott Balestier (1861–91), novelist, publisher and agent, born in Rochester, New York, and known to Howells as an *Atlantic* contributor, came to London – and quickly met HJ – in December 1888 as representative of the U.S. publisher John W. Lovell. He formed Heinemann & Balestier to publish English and American books on the Continent, rivalling Tauchnitz, and collaborated with Rudyard Kipling on *The Naulahka*. HJ placed 'the settlement of the money-question' with Compton in his hands, finding him 'the perfection of an "agent"' (HJL III, 286): HJ received a £250 advance on royalties, and if *The American* was successful in London could hope for £350 a month during its run.

8. Henry Harland (1861–1905), born in New York City, was a prolific writer, first in the U.S. as 'Sidney Luska', producing fiction about Jewish immigrants, then under his own name in Britain. Howells saw him in New York in 1888 and called him 'a delightful fellow and a most ardent convert to realism' (SLWDH III, 224). In 1894 he was founder-editor of *The Yellow Book*, with the artist Aubrey Beardsley (1872–98) and the publisher John Lane (1854–1925).

Peruzzi, William Wetmore Story's daughter, at Vallombrosa – till departing for London on 3 August.

The author and critic Horace Elisha Scudder (1838–1902) took over the Atlantic *in the summer of 1890 from Aldrich. Scudder's admiring, elaborate review of* The Tragic Muse *concludes: 'We can only advise students of literature and art who wish to see how a fine theme may be presented with a technique which, at first blush, would seem inconsistent with breadth of handling, but on closer scrutiny proves to be the facile instrument of a master workman who is thinking of the soul of his art, to read* The Tragic Muse.*'*

August 30th '90.
34, DE VERE GARDENS, W.

Dear Mr. Scudder

Your note of the 20*th* gives me great pleasure, especially as, the September *Atlantic* coming in with it, I have been able to read the pages of charming sympathy that you have therein dedicated to the *Tragic Muse*. They have really brought tears to my eyes – giving me a luxurious sense of being understood, perceived, felt. Your words are delightful & I thank you for them with all my heart: perhaps especially for those about the reader's never being "in any eddies of conversation, but always in the current."[1] That discovery is of a sort far beyond the compass of the usual Anglo-Saxon intelligence. Therefore I regard you still more as an acute than as a benevolent critic. Have you not achieved the miracle of suspecting there may be a *meaning* in what one writes? I don't notice that any one else ever has!

As regards your proposal to send you four short stories before 1892, I embrace it with enthusiasm. I am perhaps even capable of sending you five. *One* of them shall be a two-number tale; the others a single number, & I will very presently despatch you the first.[2] I will do the very best I can for you; I appreciate the friendly quality of your hospitality, & I am very truly yours

Henry James.

1. Scudder: 'Not for a moment does the reader find himself in any eddies of conversation; he is always in the current.'
2. HJ sent Scudder 'The Pupil' on 5 October 1890, only to have it rejected as 'lacking in interest, in precision and in effectiveness' – which gave him, he wrote back on 10 November, 'the shock of a perfectly honest surprise' (AMRP, 79).

117. To Florence (Mrs Hugh) Bell
9 October [1890]

Texas MS   Unpublished

On his return from Italy HJ threw himself into the theatre, rewriting The American
to fit Compton's and the company's requirements. Here – this letter went 'with a parcel',
the envelope says – he sends his confidante the latest version of the four-act play.

October 9th
34, DE VERE GARDENS, W.

Dear Mrs. Bell.

I will with pleasure come in tomorrow *Friday* – I fear (for you,) as early
as 4. 15 or 4. 30, about, as I have an engagement dans vos parages from 3 to
4. I am out of town Sunday p.m. Yes, Ste. Geneviève is very worthy indeed
in her Slough of Despond.[1] It is so graceful of you to take the interest of
re-glancing, & of hoping poor dear C–pt–on will be "up to" something (he
won't!) that je me décide d'en finir & to inflict the ponderous piece on you to
read; especially as I do think that, in spite of its formidable appearance, it may
beguile for you (gracious sympathy apart,) the passing hour. Therefore I
venture to send it *with* this, & a very earnest injunction, please, not to
communicate it to qui que ce soit. If I were to see you *1st* (I don't do that
because I wd. rather, humiliation apart, see you afterwards) there are 2 or 3
things I shld. like you to bear in mind in reading it. One of these is the simple
& essential fact that I accepted (for sufficient reasons,) as imposed from without,
the idea of squeezing into a play playable in 2 hours & forty minutes (without
entractes) a long & complicated novel, with its hard & fast conditions, never
intended for such forlorn hopes. I mean I didn't take it (the idea) up *myself*
nor regard it as intrinsically brilliant. Ergo, I think I can do better with a
subject that is a play-subject *from the 1st*.

2*d* On subjecting the play, the other day, to a more complete test of duration
– by very deliberate, histrionic reading – than it had met before, Compton's
optimistic measurements were found to have been fallacious to the tune of
about *20 minutes* having still to come out. Where they are to come from the

1. Geneviève Ward (1838–1922), who was born in New York, started as a singer in Paris in
1859, then acted in Britain and America till 1918. In 1880 HJ called her 'the most interesting
actress in London', praising in her 'a finish, an intelligence, a style, an understanding of what
she is about, which are as agreeable as they are rare' (SA, 154). 'Ste.' may refer to her regime
of cold baths and morning exercises.

deuce knows: it is such an absolute mosaic. But I prefer you to read it *with* the 20 minutes in. (Practically, they have already come out.)

3d Kindly remember there are to be a few verbal changes which happen not to be marked on this copy.

4th. Also note that there is a passage accidentally omitted in this copy, in the "great" scene of the *4th* act, a passage of four or five lines, spoken by Mrs. B. to Newman, which by re-italicizing a motive, dots an indispensable *i*, & which I have restored in the acting copies.[2]

5th. Do you *think* Ste. Geneviève *would*, in London, lend her high tone to act M*me* de Bellegarde? Elle y serait plus en scène, après tout, que dans le Strug.[3]

Perhaps – if you can snatch an hour or, d'ici là, so for secret – very secret – perusal, you will be able tomorrow to give your impression on this point to yours most theatrically

Henry James

118. *To Mrs Ariana (Wormeley) Curtis*
18 December 1890

Huntington MS   Unpublished

Even while preparing for the Southport première of The American, *HJ had written another play, as he told his Venetian hostess of the summer.*

December 18*th* 1890.
34, DE VERE GARDENS, W.

Dear Mrs. Curtis.

Strike but hear me. Don't judge my long & ugly silence too harshly till I tell you that at the very moment I received your last most delightful & beautiful

2. 'Mrs. B.' is Mrs Bread, the Bellegarde family's old English housekeeper, who befriends Newman and gives him access to the family's dark secret.

3. HJ is thinking beyond the provincial tour of the play, to begin with the première in Southport on 3 January 1891, to the later London run, which in the event began on 26 September 1891. The important Geneviève Ward was currently appearing at the Avenue Theatre to much critical acclaim as the Duchess Padovani in *The Struggle for Life*, an adaptation by Robert Buchanan and Frederick Horner of Daudet's *La Lutte pour la vie*. The male lead was George Alexander (1858–1915). On 20 October, to Mrs Bell, HJ called Geneviève Ward a 'GOOSE' for thinking *The American* had been dramatized before (Unpublished Texas MS). She didn't join *The American*, but he wrote another play for her.

letter, I found myself launched in an occupation so absorbing – a literary, or rather, to speak frankly, a dramatic job so imperative, that I turned cynic & brute on the spot & accepted, doggedly, the idea of neglecting my correspondence (as I saw I should have to, utterly,) until I had polished off the pressing task. I have done so, to a charm (the "charm" is a manner of speaking,) & now I can take breath. The 1st use I make of it, literally, is to thank you for your vivid & most interesting letter – which filled me with a sympathy for your general & particular circumstances & situation which my graceless silence has but ill expressed. Constantly have I wondered how the drama of the H. Huntington claim has gone forward – if it has moved at all – and whether you have obtained any relief or redress.[1] A more intolerable or iniquitous pressure I can't imagine – or a more bottomless trap opened beneath the feet of unsuspecting good nature. I have no right to ask you for more news or for more anything; but I participate deeply, at my clumsy distance, in your conceivable – & inconceivable – worry. What a far-reaching, reverberating scourge to all whom he touches such an irresponsible life as Henry Huntington's may become: he himself, all the while, probably suffering less than any one.

I hope you are finding Venice, this winter, a convenient & not too draughty restingplace. I would face its chilliest hour to escape from such a day as this in London – black darkness, universal lamplight & poisonous fog. Such has been our fate for the past month – a real extravagance of gloom, deepened by all sorts of public chaos; the weeks of alarm & imminent disaster in the city, the collapse of the bloated Barings, which, as you know much more fully than I, lodged us all, for days, on the edge of quite universal smash, the biggest financial disaster since finance was invented – a ticklishness apparently by no means yet allayed – & then the squalid Irish drama, made still more so by the effrontery & baseness of the newspapers.[2] *They* are, to my sense, high comedy now; & my only comfort in it all is a purely selfish one – the joy that *I* am neither a politician nor a journalist. Apropos of comedies it is delightful of you

1. On 15 March 1887 HJ had written to Francis Boott, another American living in Italy, of the horror of 'Henry H[untington]'s unmanageable madness' (the identification is Edel's), saying that 'Poor Mrs. Henry finds herself now, I fear, overwhelmed with demands for the payment of crazy debts contracted by her husband' (HJL III, 176). Francis Boott's sister was married to Henry Greenough, whose sister, Ellen Greenough Huntington, may be this 'Mrs. Henry' (she died in 1893). These Huntingtons lived in the Villa Castellani in Florence. HJ dined with the wife in February 1887.

2. The banking firm of Baring Brothers & Co., in London, invested heavily in Argentina and had great losses. There was a panic when the Russian government withdrew its funds from the bank in November 1890. The Irish drama was the case in which W. H. O'Shea sued his wife, Kitty O'Shea, for divorce on the ground of her adultery with Parnell. The divorce was granted in November 1890 and Parnell's leadership of the Irish party fatally weakened.

to take such an interest in *my* droll & dusky (as yet) stage-life. It has been broadening a goodish bit, inasmuch as the "absorbing occupation" mentioned above has been the composition at high pressure & with extreme rapidity of a *new* play (of which fortunately I had carried the subject & substance in my mind for years,) to meet a special contingency & "fit" a couple of actors – to whom I have been reading it act by act, with all the success I could have wished.[3] It is (this sort of thing) very difficult & exacting work – a mosaic of complicated calculations – & to have to do it on the gallop consumed all the vitality I had at my command, so that there was nothing left for anything else. The time & place of production of this particular masterpiece still hang in the balance; the only thing as yet definite is that it will be produced in London first, & not, like its predecessor of which I told you & of which the provincial "1*ere*" draws on, in the twilight of the country; & probably *before* the latter is acted here. *This* (I mean the provincial) comes off on Saturday night January 3ᵈ – & I have just been correcting the proof of the playbill – so you see I am seeing it through down to the small details. This is what I've been doing all the autumn – ever since you were here – & visiting all kinds of queer places & passing rheumatic hours on all sorts of draughty stages. I hope for a success & am presumptuous enough to almost believe in one; inasmuch as, battered, vulgarized, "cut", rendered only with humble zeal & without a ray of genius, the poor distracted play, when I see it rehearsed, appears to me to have, in spite of its misfortunes, inherent vitality, – to hold up its head and make a fight. But you must begin & pray for me *hard* about eight o'clk. on Saturday 3*rd*.

I am sticking fast to London this winter – save for the prospect of 3 or 4 weeks in Paris after the New Year. I shall spend the spring & depart if possible (from town,) about May 1*st*. But I am not sure I shall be able to go abroad this year as my sister's condition (she is spending the winter in London,) grows so steadily worse as to give me outlooks of nervousness at a distance. If I don't go to *your* country I shall go to Ireland, which is still more, indeed, abroad. But all that is far off yet. Sargent is de retour, with heaps of American gold, but unfortunately with only one picture (the rest are *là bas*, like the little Bopeep tails,) an admirable full-length of a yellow-satin Spanish dancer, fièrement campée, who is making the rain & the fine weather of New York.[4]

3. The two actors were Geneviève Ward and her frequent stage-partner W. H. Vernon, and the play HJ wrote in November–December 1890 was *Mrs Vibert*, which became *Tenants*. Geneviève Ward got it enthusiastically accepted by the actor-manager John Hare (1844–1921), who ran the Garrick Theatre from April 1889 to 1895, and who had asked HJ for a play as early as 1879. In 1880 HJ had praised Hare's 'quiet realism' (SA, 155). But casting difficulties delayed and finally prevented the play's production.

4. Sargent had painted the Spanish dancer La Carmencita in his *El Jaleo* in New York in the spring.

He goes, Sargent, to Egypt for the winter, for types to decorate (with religious subjects,) the big new public library of Boston, in pursuance of a large order conferred upon him and Abbey – who is to do, on another forty feet square of wall, the sources of Romance. The enterprise is interesting, and Sargent as Ary Scheffer is delightful.[5] He will beat the old Ary. Though I don't look like it – that is, my behaviour doesn't – I take the greatest interest in your Venetian winter existence – so romantic it seems, and such a picture it makes, from *this* point of view. I hear (I forget how) that Pen Browning & his wife perish amid their splendours – perish with the impossibility of warming up the same.[6] Is it even so? Mrs Bronson, I suppose, trusts as usual to the fuliginous cigarette. I hope, with all my heart, dear Mrs Curtis, that the New Year will clear off the clouds of the Italian judiciary – take pity on me, little as I deserve it, and let me know. I send you both the warmest wishes of the season & am ever most faithfully yours

Henry James

119. To William Archer
31 December 1890

BL MS   Unpublished

The Scot William Archer (1856–1924), who had spent some of his youth in Norway and already knew Ibsen's work, was the drama critic of the London weekly The World, *and wrote to HJ proposing to travel up from London and see the provincial première of* The American. *He was from 1880 a translator of Ibsen – the 1889 production, which HJ missed, of his translation of* A Doll's House *was controversial – and in 1891 he brought out five volumes of Ibsen in translation. (HJ's friend*

5. Sargent was asked to decorate the Boston Public Library by the remarkable and influential Europhile architect Stanford White (1853–1906), who had been apprenticed to H. H. Richardson. So was Edwin Austin Abbey (1852–1911), another American painter resident in London. In 1895 HJ wrote a note for the catalogue of Abbey's sequence, 'The Quest of the Holy Grail'. Ary Scheffer (1795–1858) was a Dutch-born historical painter who worked in France: 'In his second period Ary Scheffer sought inspiration from the greater poets and from the Scriptures' (*Bryan's Dictionary of Painters and Engravers* (1921)).
6. When in Venice in June, HJ had seen Robert Wiedemann Barrett Browning (1849–1912), known as 'Pen', the son of the poet, who had died on 12 December 1889 (HJ had written an anonymous commemorative essay, 'Browning in Westminster Abbey'). 'What Pen Browning has done here, through his American wife's dollars, with the splendid Palazzo Rezzonico, transcends description for the beauty, and, as Ruskin would say, "wisdom and rightness" of it.' (HJL III, 287.)

Gosse was his rival as an Ibsenist, and in January 1891 Gosse's translation of Hedda Gabler *was attacked by Archer.) The married Archer was to be the lover of HJ's friend the American actress Elizabeth Robins.*

Dec. 31st 1890.
34, DE VERE GARDENS, W.

Dear Mr. Archer –

I can't but feel greatly gratified that you should take enough interest in my experiment to contemplate so brave a step.[1] Southport, I believe, is a kind of more or less suburban Liverpool Brighton, & I should think you would get a train back to the latter place (I mean Liverpool,) *after* the play (which begins 7.30;) though as to this I am very vague – & the opposite sense (something late from Liverpool to Southport,) will be more likely. I will with pleasure see that a couple of stalls are kept for you; & pray meanwhile that we be not found stark & stiff by the wayside. I am rather nervous & depressed about the general conditions of the business & the rendering of my play by a company whose principal merit – I admit it's a great one – is that they sought me out & not I them. However, this is all in the day's work, & E. Compton, the most amiable & reasonable of men, has seemed to me a pearl among actor-managers. I'm afraid you won't find me, to begin with, startlingly "unconventional" – my notion having been to get well in the saddle *before* I begin to tickle my horse. I confess that with an untried hand, company & public, I have gone in above all for *safe* lines – look out for prancing & curveting later. But it's very good of you to look out for anything, & I am yours very truly

Henry James

120. To George du Maurier
8 January [1891]

Houghton MS   Unpublished

The Southport first night was a considerable success. AJ's diary, deriving from HJ's report, tells us William Archer invited himself to HJ's rooms afterwards, and having 'murmured some words of congratulation upon H's success', added '"I think it's a

---

1. HJ had at Archer's first overture written half-discouragingly on 27 December that 'The place is far, the season inclement, the interpretation, *extremely* limited, different enough, as you may suppose, from what I should count on for representation in London.' (HJL III, 309.)

play that would be much more likely to have success in the Provinces than in London"'; 'then he began, as by divine mission, to enumerate all its defects and flaws, and asked why H had done so-and-so, instead of just the opposite, etc.' Subsequently, Archer was found to have declared 'it was a most extraordinary and unheard-of, almost immoral thing, for a tyro to undertake to write a play without consulting a competent dramatic critic!' (DAJ, 162–3).

George du Maurier, who seems to have toasted the success of the play, was less grudging in his congratulations.

January 8th
34, DE VERE GARDENS, W.

Mon cher ami.

It was only the fear of seeming importunate & egotistical that kept me from wiring you on Sunday a.m. that the dire ordeal had blossomed into a complete & delightful success. We really did very well indeed & our triumph was as definitely affirmed as a tolerably obscure provincial town can affirm it. I had a very big, a very attentive & a very applausive audience – I was dragged forth at the end to receive their compliments – & my good Comptons were – to all appearance – quite radiantly content. There are more formidable tests in store, but I think that, essentially, ça y est. Your bumpers brought me luck, & I thank you all for the service. —

Dear old Keene – requiescat![1] I knew him personally scarcely at all, but, all the same, I shall be very glad to pay his admirable artistic personality the last homage by standing tomorrow, at the H.C., at 1, by his grave. I shall look out for you & find you & you must *come back to lunch with me here*: entendez-vous? Ever yours, mon bon,

Henry James

121. *To Elizabeth Robins*
1 June [1891]

BPL MS   Unpublished

On 6 February 1891 HJ told WJ he was committed to the drama, and 'just attacking my 4th!': 'I feel at last as if I had found my real form, which I am capable of

1. Charles Samuel Keene (1823–91) was a humorous illustrator, one of Du Maurier's colleagues on *Punch*. The 'H.C.' is the Highgate Cemetery.

carrying far, & for which the pale little art of fiction, as I have practised it, has been, for me, but a limited & restricted substitute.' (CWJ II, 168, 167.) HJ went to Paris from 19 February to 27 March – on an 'organized pot-boiling basis' (SLHJEG, 74), writing among other things the short story 'The Real Thing', based on an anecdote of du Maurier's.

The remarkable Kentuckyan actress and author Elizabeth Robins (1862–1952) had in the U.S. married, unhappily, another Boston actor, less successful than herself, George Richmond Parkes, who drowned himself in a suit of stage armour in the Charles River. The widow came to London in July 1888, staying with Louise Chandler Moulton, and helped by Oscar Wilde (before his success as a dramatist). Visiting Norway, she discovered a passion for Ibsen, and was first to play many of his heroines in London. It was calling on her senior colleague and supporter Geneviève Ward, on 12 January 1891, that HJ first met her; two weeks later he saw her in A Doll's House.

June 1st
34, DE VERE GARDENS, W.

Dear Miss Robins.

I am delighted to have heard from you & to know that there are *possibilities* of your hitting it off with Compton. I cling to the idea that you shld. do M*me* de C. I am moved to endeavour to say to you something that I might say more easily – that is more fully & clearly by word of mouth – yet which is, after all, vague & formless. It is – roughly speaking – that I enter fully into the difficulty & entanglement, the general worrying dilemma, of the questions that lie before you & of course shrink very much from any *responsibility* in throwing into the scale such weight, however slight, as I may possess. *But*, at the same time, I do *dream*, at least, that if you *do* play M*me* de C., & we make, as God grant & as the omens seem to indicate, a success of the play, it may very well be the beginning of a large career for – as it were – all of us. Compton has a theatre, & *I* have a resolute purpose of doing *everything* more that I can.[1] Your talent strikes me as so much more interesting than any that I see round me, that I shall ask nothing better than to work up to it & employ it & give it all the opportunity that it will rise to. It will be far more interesting & practically far more inspiring & helpful, to work with my eyes definitely on you than on nobody at all – which is what the other alternative amounts to. This is all that I am justified in saying – & of course it is very nebulous & irresponsible. But

---

1. At the beginning of February Compton had taken the Opera Comique in London on a long lease.

it *does* constitute, to a certain degree, a prospect – & a prospect without pledges demanded on your part – the terrible pledges, with such doors into inferiority opening out of them – by such proposals as Wyndham's.[2] Perhaps we can talk this over more – at any rate may *my* good star shine over your interview with Compton. Yours most truly

Henry James[3]

122. To Edgar Fawcett
7 June 1891

Princeton MS   Unpublished

Fawcett sent HJ two more novels, one of them his own, presumably A New York Family, A Romance of Two Brothers *or* Women Must Weep, *all published in 1891. The other work is possibly* A Diplomat's Diary *(1890),* A Puritan Pagan *(1891) or* Vampires & Mademoiselle Réséda *(1891) by the Paris-born American Mrs S. Van Rensselaer Cruger, subsequently Julie Grinnell (Mrs Wade) Chance, who wrote under the name of 'Julien Gordon'.*

June 7*th* 91.
34, DE VERE GARDENS, W.

My dear Fawcett

I should sooner have thanked you for your violet note of a month ago – such a sweet-tinted missive as Oberon might have addressed to Titania. But I am vile & vicious – or rather feeble & faltering, in matters correspondential. I live with my pen in my hand, but I don't get a tenth of my letters written. This is, too, the bafflingest month of the London year – & that is why I haven't yet, found leisure to read the three volumes of "transatlantic" fiction which your most liberal hand confers upon me. I regret it greatly as regards your

2. Charles Wyndham's proposal was probably for Elizabeth Robins to appear at the Criterion (from 30 April 1892) in an adaptation of *Le Demi-Monde* by Dumas *fils*, called *The Fringe of Society*.
3. 'À propos of actresses, he says Miss Robins is the most intelligent creature, next to Coquelin with whom he ever talked about her art.' So said AJ in her diary on 16 June 1891 (DAJ, 211). In April the actress had 'revealed herself, strikingly, here as Ibsen's *Hedda Gabler*', HJ told Isabella Stewart Gardner a few days after this letter: 'She is slightly uncanny, but distinguished and individual, and she is to do my heroine' (HJL III, 342) – Claire de Cintré in the London production of *The American*.

own goodly book, which however shall have my friendliest regard at the 1st calm hour. Mrs. Cruger is another affair, though I am willing to believe all the good you say of her. She labours under two (to me) weighty disadvantages – as regards claiming attention – in literature, in this short life, where the *important* unread is perpetually fixing one's conscience with eyes stern & reproachful & deep: she is a woman & she is an amateur. Isn't she distinctly silly in both capacities, & isn't her "vogue" in the U.S. but an ineffable example of the row which our inordinate, frantic system of publicity makes over the cheap & flimsy? Women aren't literary in any substantial sense of the term, & their being "fashionable" or "stylish" – nauseating words – doesn't make them so. However – next month, or in August – I shall vigorously try to inhale such fragrance as this importunate phenomenon may yield – thanking you meanwhile cordially for your good-natured trouble in showing me what they *do* happen to be chattering about in the home of my childhood. Don't give another thought to the missed dedication. Your intention was charming enough; & no fulfilments are ever as delicate as the radiant impulse. For *me* the book *is* dedicate. You say nothing about another spacious London August. Do lunch with me one of these dim days. I shall be here & always yours

Henry James

123. To Edmund Gosse
[27 September 1891]

Leeds MS   Published SLHJEG, 82

HJ went to Ireland at the end of June to get over influenza, returning to London on 11 August. At the Royal Marine Hotel, Kingstown, he wrote 'The Private Life' and 'The Chaperon', reflecting in his notebook that 'I must absolutely not *tie my hands with promised novels if I wish to keep them free for a genuine and sustained attack on the theatre'. He also told himself, 'Try everything, do everything, render everything – be an artist, be distinguished, to the last.' (N, 57, 58.)*

On 26 September 1891 The American *had a London première of great social éclat, despite opening before the start of the Season, but the critics were unenthusiastic: Arthur Symons asked: 'Is it conceivable that the play satisfied the author of the novel?'* The Era *felt that 'in adapting his novel he has been false to himself, and has thus fallen between two stools . . . The novel was a delicate water-colour. Mr. James has translated it into a third-rate wood-cut.' HJ was in considerable suspense as to how long the play's run would last.*

Sunday
34, De Vere Gardens, W.

My dear Gosse.

It is awfully late & I am awfully tired & jaded with sleepless nights & diurnal worry – but the strain is over – & the Rubicon crossed. I have had all the air of a success – even a great one. The papers, I believe, are very restrictive – very stingy, I call it – very stupid *you* must. But the play goes – it went last night in an indisputable fashion. I don't forecast the future, but it was – I am assured – a remarkably good 1ère. Compton had a very great personal success – & he is so charming, so delightful that I can't doubt he will keep & prolong & repercute it. I passed through hells of nervousness – but am in comparatively quiet waters now. I am, however, weary & sleepy exceedingly – & have 30 notes to answer. I will tell you all the rest & am ever yours & your wife's

Henry James[1]

124. To Dr William Wilberforce Baldwin
19 October 1891

Morgan MS   Unpublished

While HJ had been in Ireland in the summer, his American friend Baldwin, the Florentine doctor, with whom (and his friend Taccini) he had toured in central Italy in 1890, had been in London (on his way to Kansas). Constance Fenimore Woolson, who was living in Oxford, suggested Baldwin see AJ: he diagnosed the lump in her breast as cancerous, and prescribed morphine to kill the pain. AJ welcomed the prospective end of her long ordeal: 'It is the most supremely interesting moment in life,' she told WJ, and wrote of Baldwin's 'inspiring effect' (DLAJ, 186, 187).

Athenaeum Club, London

My dear Baldwin.

I will tell you immediately why I have delayed too many days to answer, & thank you for, your two beautiful & so graceful letters – but let me first tell you how glad I was to get them & what a delightful whiff of Florence &

1. The following day HJ cabled Gosse: 'Wrote you yesterday such things difficult immediately to interpret as to future bearings but every appearance of great and valid success great and I believe casting personal success for Compton Henry James.' (Unpublished Leeds MS telegram (carbon).)

Italy – & yourself (to say nothing of Taccini,) it always gives me to hear from you. You are a generous friend to take up valuable hours in so vividly covering paper for one who makes you such poor returns. When there isn't one reason for my epistolary feebleness, there is sure to be another – & this time I have, for the last three weeks, been infinitely preoccupied & worried. I am happy to say the phase is passing, but I have been learning what it is to bring out a play – for the 1st time – to take the plunge – the very formidable plunge of a dramatic author, at a time of the year when London is too empty of the upper-class of playgoers & when the "critics" have a free field to be stupidly cross with me for doing something totally different from all I have done before. This state of things – with some others begotten of inevitable inexperience, had given me plenty to bother my head & break my heart about – & you would have had a 2d nervous patient on your hands if (happily for you,) you had not been at a safe distance. To finish this subject let me say simply that though my drama is in its 4th week, it is still rather too early to say how it's going. What is apparent – seemingly – however is that each week it does better, that people are returning to town, & that, after a difficult infancy, better days, or rather nights, may very well be in store for it. It only wants to catch on; when it once does so it will *stay* on. Unfortunately much of the interpretation leaves to be desired. The rest of the acting is very good. C.F.W. has seen it, I believe, 5 times – there's friendship for you!

My sister grows weaker & weaker – but you have, thank heaven, put her pain very much into the background. Lately she has had a good deal of irregularity of the heart – a condition that Katherine Loring will have described to you. How good are your expressions of regret at our remoteness – & all your generous expressions of readiness to serve & help! I thank you, my dear Baldwin, a 1000 times. Very well do I picture to myself what a little painted paradise Florence must have seemed to you on your return – & how greasily-greenbacky much of American life must look to you in your retrospect. I don't know what is to become of us – we're too big & booming & brassy to live. It is true that the other nations are each too something else. You make me feel, in my own, the clammy & pudgy palm of the most unctuous one. He is as faithful as he's rotund & please tell him that I always cherish him. I hope your mother's initiation goes smoothly on. Please give her, & your wife & your dear little human animals of children my particular remembrance. To Mrs. W.W.B. I send a very especially grateful greeting. Don't pile up fatigue, my dear Baldwin – but thank your stars every night for Florence – & believe me always yours

Henry James

P.S. I send the two Independents & your letter of the 10th to my brother –

with great pleasure: it was too good of you to take so much trouble.[1] I have only been waiting for the right moment of time to read the 2 papers first. *Everything* sometimes seems to me a miracle – a miracle of commonplace.

We live in tornadoes & tempests here; & I gnash my teeth when I think of your golden Arnoside.

Oct. 19*th* 1891.

125. To Edwin Laurence Godkin
15 November 1891

Houghton MS   Unpublished

34, DE VERE GARDENS. W.
Nov. 15th 1891

My dear Godkin.

Too long – too shamefully long – have I delayed to answer, to thank you for your last so kind & sympathetic letter. I have been preoccupied, pressed & worried, & the happy hour has constantly failed me. It was delightful of you to judge the poor old play worthy of your friendly solicitude. Yet it *is*, worthy, after all – as it is now in its eighth week and it has celebrated its 50*th* night. It is probably – without vanity – as good a play as can ever be extracted from any novel not conceived from the 1*st* – *ab ovo* – from the scenic point of view – & I am very sure it is the best play now being performed in London. This is saying so little, however, that I don't blush for my swagger. Much of it is, unfortunately, badly acted – though very much better than at first: my inexperience & my good nature combined to consent to conditions of production that a more heart-hardened and initiated author would have declined. On the other hand some of it is very well acted indeed – & as a beginning it has done me great good. The great point is that if I hadn't made this particular beginning I shouldn't have made any at all; this one was pressed upon me – I did it for the sake of one big character – it was highly important to me that I *should* begin, & I am very glad to have done so. But a 1*st* play is at best but a 1*st* play, & a play taken from a book is at best but a play taken from a book. I

1. The *Independent* was an American weekly paper with a Congregationalist slant but noted for its literary articles. HJ's friend Lowell had died on 12 August, and the issues of 20 and 27 August carried respectively 'A Conversation with James Russell Lowell Twenty Years Ago' with a long editorial tribute, and 'Lowell's Home'.

HENRY JAMES: A LIFE IN LETTERS

am going at the drama in earnest and shall do things conceived & executed in
far happier conditions. Kindly say to Robinson (I mean if occasion & recollection
serve,) that the *American*, "goes" so much better – so *very* much better – now
than on the 1st night that it's quite a different thing.[1] And I have made an
important alteration in a part of the action – which has converted the 3d act
from the least successful (with the applausive audience) to the most successful.[2]
Excuse me for drenching you with this low information – your benevolence
has brought it upon you – & you see I have embraced a vulgar profession. I
talk of you both pretty often with Mrs. Sands – who communicates with me
with a certain regularity.[3] She has a charming house, & her life seems to me
to be, for the present, on a sufficiently cheerful & tranquil footing. She is,
however, a restless and fermenting spirit – but Ethel is a soothing & sensible
element – a very sweet & devoted girl.

Of my sister I can give you no good news – save in so far as it is good
news that the end of her long illness seems much nearer at hand than it has
ever done. Her weakness is so extreme that she is frequently unable to see me
– but I am happy to say she suffers less than she did a couple of months ago.
She fails week by week, but she is always most appreciative of any news of
you; & would send you both messages if she knew I am writing.

Dear Mrs. Godkin, please believe that this is partial response to your
charming letter as well – received more weeks ago than I venture to remind
you of. I build all kinds of splendid castles in the air of next summer, on the
foundation of your I sincerely hope not again to be postponed visit. But they
have rather a crazy architecture – inasmuch as I see *myself* inhabiting them far
from London, alas, where it already seems clear that I shall not find it possible
to spend next Season.[4] But as you – apparently have foreign plans too, I count
upon some preordained harmony. A wet windy fiercely tempestuous autumn
pursues us – but we are rather fogless & not quite so "filthy" as usual. The
London winter, however, has no great terrors for me – it is the summer that
tries my fortitude & my constitution. The flood of Americans has rolled by –

1. This is probably E. Randolph Robinson, a transplanted Virginian and prominent New York
lawyer, a close acquaintance of Godkin's and his ally in fighting civic corruption in New York
City.
2. The fiftieth night of the London run presented a play so significantly revised that some critics
called it a 'second edition'. Even so it closed after seventy performances.
3. Mary Morton (Hartpence) Sands (1853–96), an American beauty, knew the Prince of Wales,
who attended *The American* in the middle of October and briefly revived its fortunes. Her
daughter Ethel became a friend of HJ and an artist, later a Dame. Godkin's second wife was
Katherine Buckley Sands Godkin (d. 1907), sister of Mr Mahlon Sands (1842–88).
4. HJ went to Italy in June 1892, and then joined WJ in Switzerland, returning to London only
in mid August.

leaving only Mrs. Lockwood. Florence has the lordliest success – & lives in the lap of the *vieille noblesse*. Your pessimism, my dear Godkin, fills me with sorrow & credulity; & indeed if it weren't for the day's work what *would* one do?[5] I hear the cry under my own roof – to work, to work! I must obey it – farewell. I greet you both most heartily & am ever faithfully yours

Henry James

126. To Florence (Mrs Hugh) Bell
[23 February 1892]

Yale MS (Koch Collection)   Published HJL III, 372–3; SL2, 252–3

Lowell was dead, and AJ was known to be dying; on 6 December HJ's young friend and agent Balestier died of typhoid in Dresden – a blow to HJ's theatrical campaign and a personal loss (HJ wrote commemorating both Lowell and Balestier).

On 20 February 1892 HJ went to the first night of Lady Windermere's Fan *by Oscar Wilde at the St James's Theatre – at which Wilde, several of his friends and one of the cast, wore green carnations.*

Tuesday
34, DE VERE GARDENS. W.

Dear Mrs. Bell.

I am very sorry you are *not* here to mingle with these things – it would make them so much more interesting. In your absence they are, honestly, scarcely enough so to kindle in me the flame of the valued reporter. Still, I have seen them as through a glass darkly & you are welcome to the faint repercussion. Oscar's play (I was there on Saturday,) strikes me as a mixture that will run (I feel as if I were talking as a laundress,) though infantine, to my sense, both in subject and in form. As a drama it is of a candid & primitive simplicity, with a perfectly reminiscential air about it – as of things *qui ont traîné*, that one has always seen in plays. In short it doesn't, from that point of view, bear analysis or discussion. But there is so much drollery – that is "cheeky" paradoxical wit of dialogue, & the pit & gallery are so pleased at finding themselves clever enough to "catch on" to four or five of the ingenious – too – ingenious – *mots* in the dozen, that it makes

5. On 31 October AJ's diary records: 'A dreary letter to Harry from Mr. Godkin, set to the futile tune of which the old cow died so many centuries ago – "everything going to the dogs here."' (DAJ, 221.)

them feel quite "décadent" & raffiné & they enjoy the sensation as a change from the stodgy. Moreover they think they are hearing the talk of the *grand monde* (poor old *grand monde*,) & altogether feel privileged & modern. There is a perpetual attempt at *mots* & many of them *ratés*: but those that hit are very good indeed. This will make, I think, a success – possibly a really long run (I mean through the Season,) for the play. There is of course absolutely no characterization & all the people talk equally strained Oscar – but there is a "situation" (at the end of act III,) that one has seen from the cradle, & the thing is conveniently acted. The "impudent" speech at the end was simply inevitable mechanical Oscar – I mean the usual trick of saying the unusual – complimenting himself & his play.[1] It was what he was there for & I can't conceive the density of those who seriously reprobate it. The tone of the virtuous journals makes me despair of our stupid humanity. Everything Oscar does is a deliberate trap for the literalist, & to see the literalist walk straight up to it, look straight at it & step straight into it, makes one freshly avert a discouraged gaze from this unspeakable animal. The Mitchell–Lea affair was naturally, yesterday afternoon, before a fatally female & but languidly *empoignée* house, a very different pair of sleeves.[2] It is a perfectly respectable & creditable effort, with no gross awkwardness or absurdity in it, nothing in the least calculated to make the producer redden in the watches of the night. But it is too long, too talky, too thin & too colourless, rather flat & rather grey. I should think that it was capable of compressibility into a quite practicable three-act drama (there are *five*, just heaven,) which wd. produce an effect. Marian Lea was clever & pretty.

But come up to town & stir up the pot yourself. Miss Robins spoke a prologue, very well save that one couldn't hear her. I'm delighted the gallant boy is disrubescent.[3] May he soon release you to your natural duties. Thanks

1. Wilde spoke with a cigarette in his mauve-gloved hand. George Alexander (1858–1918), the leading actor, recalled it thus: 'Ladies and gentlemen: I have enjoyed this evening *immensely*. The actors have given us a *charming* rendering of a *delightful* play, and your appreciation has been *most* intelligent. I congratulate you on the *great* success of your performance, which persuades me that you think *almost* as highly of the play as I do myself.' (Ellmann, *Oscar Wilde*, 366.).

2. 'The Mitchell–Lea affair' is the production of *Deborah* at the Avenue Theatre, a play dealing with slave life in the U.S., featuring Marian Lea (1861–1944) and written by her new husband, American poet and playwright Langdon Mitchell (1862–1933). Elizabeth Robins: 'Miss Lea was a young Philadelphian of much natural distinction and cosmopolitan education, already [in 1891] favourably known on the London stage.' (TF, 29–30.) *The Era* complained that Marian Lea was 'lamentably indistinct' as Deborah, the leader of a slave-rebellion. She lived with her half-sister, Mrs Lea Merritt, a painter, in Tite Street, where HJ sometimes dined.

3. Mrs Bell's son seems to have had scarlet fever; on 7 January HJ had called him 'your little Scarlatino' (HJL III, 370).

for your kind attention to *Nona V.* – a very small & simple fantaisie of which the end is soon.[4] I greet all your house & am yours, dear Mrs. Bell, most truly

Henry James

127. To Robert Louis Stevenson
19 March 1892

Yale MS   Partly published HJRLS, 211–14; LHJ I, 188–90

Alice James died on 6 March 1892, and HJ writes on stationery with Gothic lettering and a thick black border.

34, De Vere Gardens, W.
March 19*th* *1892*

My dear Louis.

I send you today by bookpost, registered, a little volume of tales which I lately put forth – most of which however you may have seen in magazines.[1] Please accept at any rate the modest offering. Accept too, my thanks for your sweet & dateless letter which I received a month ago – the one in which you speak with such charming appreciation & felicity of Paul Bourget.[2] I echo your admiration – I think the Italian book one of the most exquisite things of our time. I am in only very occasional correspondence with him – & have not written since I heard from you; but I shall have an early chance, now, probably, to repeat your words to him, & they will touch him in a tender place. He is living much, now, in Italy, & I *may* go there for May or June – though indeed I fear it is little probable. Colvin tells me of the volume of some of your *inédites* beauties that is on the point of appearing, & the news is a bright spot in a vulgar world.[3] The vulgarity of literature in these islands at the present time is not to be said, & I shall clutch at you as one turns one's ear to music in the

4. 'Nona Vincent', a story about the theatre sketching a love triangle between an author, his married confidante (who has been identified with Mrs Bell) and an actress, was published in the *English Illustrated Magazine* in February–March 1892.
1. The book was *The Lesson of the Master*, published by Macmillan in February 1892.
2. HJ had sent Stevenson Bourget's *Sensations d'Italie* (1891): Stevenson told HJ in his 'sweet & dateless letter' (given by Mehew as 7 December [1891]) that in gratitude he 'wrote Bourget a dedication; no use resisting, it's a love affair' (LRLS VII, 211).
3. The volume of uncollected items, Sidney Colvin's conception, was *Across the Plains with Other Memories and Essays* (it was the work dedicated to Bourget). 'So shines a good deed in a naughty world' is *The Merchant of Venice*, v. i. 91.

clatter of the market-place. Yet, paradoxical as it may appear, oh Louis, I have still had the refinement not to read the *Wrecker* in the periodical page.[4] This is an enlightened & judicious heroism, & I do as I would be done by. Trust me, however, to taste you in long draughts as soon as I can hold the book. Then will I write to you again. You tell me nothing of yourself – so I have nothing to take up or take hold of, save indeed the cherished superstition that you enjoy some measure of health & cheer. You are, however, too far away for my imagination, & were it not for dear Colvin's friendly magic, which puts in a pin here & there, I shouldn't be able to catch & arrest at all the opaline iridescence of your legend. Yet even when he speaks of intending wars & the clash of arms it all passes over me like an old-time song.[5] You see how much I need you close at hand to stand successfully on the tiptoe of emulation. You fatigue, in short, my credulity, though not my affection. We lately clubbed together, all, to despatch to you an eye-witness in the person of the genius or the *genus*, in himself, Rudyard, for the concussion of whose extraordinary personality with your own we are beginning soon to strain the listening ear.[6] We devoutly hope that this time he will really be washed upon your shore. With him goes a new little wife – whose brother, Wolcott Balestier, lately dead in much youthful "promise" & performance (I don't allude, in saying that, especially to the literary part of it,) was a very valued young friend of mine. Kipling's "future" is, to me, to-day, utterly undecipherable; & his marriage only complicates my uncertainty. The main thing that has lately happened to myself is the death of my dear sister a fortnight ago – after years of suffering, which however, had not made her any less rare or remarkable a person or diminished the effect of the event (when it should occur,) in making an extreme difference in my life.[7] Of my occupations what shall I tell you? I have of late years left London less & less – but I am thinking sooner or later

4. Stevenson co-wrote *The Wrecker*, which appeared in *Scribner's Magazine* from August 1891 to July 1892, with his stepson Lloyd Osbourne. It came out as a book in June 1892.

5. Stevenson was writing long bulletins to Colvin of his life in Samoa, which Colvin edited after his death as *Vailima Letters* (1895).

6. On 21 March 1890 HJ had told Stevenson of Rudyard Kipling, now married, as HJ says, to Caroline Balestier (1865–1939), sister of his deceased American collaborator Wolcott Balestier: 'Rudyard Kipling – your nascent rival – he has killed one immortal – Rider Haggard – the star of the hour, aged twenty-four and author of remarkable Anglo-Indian and extraordinarily observed barrack-life – Tommy Atkins – tales.' (HJL III, 272.) Kipling never visited Samoa.

7. To Elizabeth Lewis HJ wrote on 11 March: 'You are right – the loss is absolute & many of the "consolations" merely verbal. One would be sorry indeed not to feel it to the full – sorry not to know that one will feel it always. It makes a great difference in my life – but I must live with the difference as long as I live at all.' (Unpublished Bodleian MS, Dep. c. 834, fols. 115–16.)

(in a near present,) of making a long foreign, though not distant, absence. I am busy with the *short* – I have forsworn forever the long.[8] I hammer at the horrid little theatrical problem, with delays & intermissions, but, horrible to relate, no failure of purpose. I shall soon publish another small storybook which I will incontinently send you.[9] I have done many brief fictions within the last year. In the way of published items here, from other & greater hands, Mrs. H. Ward's *David Grieve* holds the top of the pavement. It is a monument of uninspired industry & culture – full of ability, too, yet of a painful mediocrity at the same time.[10] The good little Thomas Hardy has scored a great success with *Tess of the d'Urbervilles*, which is chock full of faults & falsity & yet has a singular beauty & charm.[11] I will send you both of these books the moment they quit their 3 vol. form, or cease to cost 31/6. What we most talk of, here, however, is the day when it may be believed that you will come to meet us on some attainable southern shore. We will *all* go to the Mediterranean for you – let that not nail you to Samoa. I send every hearty greeting to your playfellows – your fellow-phantoms. The wife-phantom knows my sentiments. The dim ghost of a mother has my heartiest regard. The long Lloyd-spectre

8. On 5 February 1892 HJ had noted that 'I find myself wrenched away from the attempt to get on with the drama – wrenched only for the hour, fortunately – by the necessity of doing *au plus tôt* some short tales.' (N, 63.) He published seven short stories in the rest of the year.

9. *The Private Life* was a collection published in London by James R. Osgood, McIlvaine & Co. (Osgood having started again in Britain) on 3 June and by Harper in New York on 15 August.

10. HJ read Mrs Humphry Ward's *David Grieve*, a northern, working-class *Bildungsroman*, directly after its publication on 22 January 1892. She received £1,750 from Smith, Elder in England and sold the U.S. rights to Macmillan for an extraordinary £7,000. ('Prendre le haut du pavé' in French is 'to lord it'.)

11. On 5 December 1892 Stevenson wrote to HJ, '*Tess* is one of the worst, weakest, least sane, most *voulu* books I have yet read . . . so far as I read, James, it was (in one word) damnable. *Not alive, not true*, was my continual comment as I read; and at last – *not even honest!*' (LRLS VII, 450.) HJ replied on 17 February 1893: 'I grant you Hardy with all my heart & even with a certain quantity of my boot-toe. I am meek & ashamed where the public clatter is deafening – so I bowed my head & let "Tess of the D.'s" pass. But oh yes, dear Louis, she's vile. The pretence of "sexuality" is only equalled by the absence of it, and the abomination of the language by the author's reputation for style. There are indeed some pretty smells & sights & sounds. But you have better ones in Polynesia.' (HJL III, 406–7.) Violet Hunt's diary recorded on 3 January 1896 that 'Henry James expressed disapprobation, laboriously, of "Jude"' (HJVH, 5). On 23 August 1906, HJ told Sarah Butler Wister an article on Hardy in the *Revue des Deux Mondes* took 'a false & erratic point of view, with its putting his "passion" en première ligne – instead of his extraordinary rustic, rural, natural, earthy sense & smell, as of a weasel, a badger, a field mouse, or some other burrowing & watching animal. Of this the man made nothing – though it's the side on which H. has genius (the only side to my sense – for his human side always has seemed to me inferior!)' (Unpublished Congress MS.)

laughs an eerie laugh, doubtless, at my *ébauche* of an embrace. Yet I feel, my dear Louis, that I *do* hold you just long enough to press you to the heart of your very faithful old friend

Henry James

128. To Robert Underwood Johnson
27 August 1892

Virginia MS   Unpublished

HJ did visit the Bourgets in Siena for a month in June, before going via Venice to Switzerland to meet WJ and his family. He was back in London on 16 August, writing to Robert Underwood Johnson, a poet who was associate editor of the Century Magazine *under Richard Watson Gilder (1844–1909) from 1881 till 1909, when he became its full editor up to 1913.*

August 27th 1892.
34, DE VERE GARDENS. W.

Dear Mr. Johnson.

I was very sorry to have to cable so curtly, this morning, a negative to your proposal about the article on Dagnan-Bouveret.[1] I hate to decline anything you ask me, but the conditions that surround the task in question seem to me to make it particularly difficult. It is not that I don't know a little Dagnan's work, and thoroughly admire it, (I think it among the most exquisite of our time,) but I should require to *see* it all, afresh, & it's in Paris & scattered, & would have to be hunted up & visited, & you want the article quickly, & I don't know when I shall next find it convenient to *be* in Paris – & therefore shrink from committing myself, &c, &c.. All these reasons have forced me to feel that it is safest to say nay. Add that, alas, I've ceased to care to write about painters. I remember writing to you a few years back – àpropos of a little article about Daumier, that I liked to do so – & I did, then, & of old. But the taste has departed from me since then, & I am willing – more than willing – to leave them to their own people. I care more & more for literature – & that

1. On 16 August HJ had told Johnson, 'Perfect is Dagnan-Bouveret.' (Unpublished Houghton MS, bMS Am 1094.2 (16).) Pascal-Adolphe Jean Dagnan-Bouveret (1852–1929) studied with Gérôme at the École des Beaux-Arts, and also with Corot. With the influence of Bastien-Lepage, his style opened up and simplified. He painted many Breton subjects, but was also one of the favourite portraitists of the Parisian aristocracy.

crowds them out. I wish the *Century* did too, & that it wasn't so much of a picture book. There never ought, to my sense, to be pictures with a good text. Excuse these blasphemies against your beautiful woodcuts. I wrote to you on finding your letter here on my return from abroad – & I hope things have gone well with you since your own return. Please recall me kindly to Gilder & very particularly indeed to Mrs. Gilder if you should ever see her. Yours ever

Henry James

129. *To Edmund Gosse*
30 August [1892]

Houghton TC   Unpublished

In August HJ read a much-revised comedy, Mrs Jasper, *later retitled* Disengaged, *based on his own story 'The Solution', to the Irish-born American actress Ada Rehan (1860–1916), who was the leading figure in the London company of the American producer and playwright Augustin Daly (1838–99). To Daly on 1 September he would concede 'the slenderness of the main motive' (HJL III, 396), but with Daly's encouragement revised it again.*

Gosse had given HJ his medieval romance The Secret of Narcisse *(1892), which he summarized for Theodore Watts-Dunton (1832–1914), Swinburne's protector: 'What I meant to depict was the failure of sympathy between a girl of slight intelligence but very strong instincts and a man of comparatively feeble sexual powers, easily distracted by art. Her robust and fiery temper finds him cold, and she cannot understand it. So in a vague tumult of anger she brings the charge of witchcraft against him.' (EGLL, 311.)*

To Edmund Gosse Esq. The Mill, Dunster.
Metropole Hotel Brighton.
August 30th [1892]

My dear Gosse.

Please forgive the indecorous delay in returning you the sheets of your beautiful tale. I have been worried, absent and preoccupied (occupied, too, with a momentary flitting,) and haven't found till today a congruous hour for an act of such delicate appreciation. But now I have just read the story through at a charmed sitting and I restore you the precious pages herewith. They are very graceful, very easy, and the incident is curious, naturally, and picturesque;

but, to speak frankly, I am not sure that a weaker pen than yours mightn't, on the whole, were the publication anonymous, have carried off equally well the credit of having produced them. Perhaps – or rather surely – I am an unqualified witness in the case of this *kind* of fiction – prejudiced as I am in favour of all sorts of intense modernity of realism and observation – therefore I grant you, at the outset, my want of jurisdiction. But the old-fashioned, the *vieux jeu*, in your subject and treatment, constitute, for me, a bar to the last rapture; assuming, that is, that I am justified in applying these opprobrious epithets. What I am really struggling thus ungraciously to say is that I think it is a defect in the execution of the little problem to which you addressed yourself that it is not, as we say, more *personal*. There would have been – there were – two ways, I think, of dealing with it – the facile, the usual, and, as I have called it, *vieux jeu* way, the old-fashioned English "historical-tale" way (which for me, as a form, has ceased to have any interest – it is too cheap!) or the way of Gustave Flaubert in the *Trois Contes*, for instance, or of A. France in *Thaïs* or in *Baltasar* – the way of verbal magic and surface perfection and *ciselure* and infinite particularity – the way, in short, of renovation by *style*.[1] One asks one's self whether the former way is worth going in for at this time of day – I mean for battered *raffinés* and mature children of light like you and me. I doubt it! – yet perhaps, after all, the success of the thing should be prejudged only in the light of what it is that you expect. I don't think you should expect a success that will count much for *you*. You may think I do scant justice to the style that you *have* put into the work – but this is not so. It is that of a man with a pen – but you will be particularly challenged. The thing is extremely pretty and perhaps that is all you – or any one – wants. Still I am personal enough to repeat that it isn't "personal" enough. However, as no one will know it, no one will say so but your fidgetty old friend

Henry James

P.S. I will return you the eloquent *Shelley*, with another word, tomorrow – when I have acquired a wrapper for it.[2] I am spending a few days here (since yesterday only, however – but before that I paid a visit,) to get out of the London streets. I shall shortly return to them as those of Brighton are not

1. Flaubert's *Trois Contes* (1877) consisted of two elaborate historical tales, 'La Légende de Saint Julien l'Hospitalier' and 'Hérodias', and one set in modern Normandy, 'Un Coeur simple'. Anatole France (1844–1924; Anatole-François Thibault), a writer with an antiquarian's knowledge of the pagan world, intensely rendered sexual desire in *Thaïs* (1890) and *Baltasar* (1889).
2. The next day HJ wrote again, embarrassed: 'I managed to *lose* the paper containing your beautiful address on Shelley.' (SLHJEG, 88.) The address, given at Horsham on the centenary of Shelley's birth, was reprinted in Gosse's *Questions at Issue* (1893).

worth great sacrifices. I hope your castled crag is all (again,) that you left, remembered and described it. If you were here there are things I would put my finger upon – in Narcisse – often charming ones.

130. To Edward Compton
15 September [1892]

Texas MS   Published MLT II 294–5

*After their London season the Comptons were touring again with classic English comedies (*She Stoops to Conquer, The School for Scandal, The Rivals*), and at this point moving from a week in Dublin to another in the Isle of Man. They were again playing* The American *– but finding the audience, now happy with the first two and the revised third acts, 'droop over the fourth' because of its 'grimness' (with Valentin's death), as HJ told WJ (CWJ II, 243).*

34 De Vere Gdns. W.
Sept. 15th

Dear Compton.

It is very interesting to hear from you & I rejoice that there is so early a chance of your being in town. I presume Sunday Oct 2*d* will be one of the days you speak of – & also the 9*th*. I shall watch for you, & be glad to be notified a bit in advance. (The Tour cards are a luxury!) Within a day or two it seems as if I may be able to go on with the play I mentioned sooner than I said – & there is every prospect of my being able to read you an act or two next month.[1] I *dream* of having it done indeed by Nov. 15*th*. But as to the exactness of this I must see. Meanwhile what you hint as to the lingering vital spark of the *American* warms my chilled blood. I am fairly crackling with curiosity to know what your "magnificent idea" for Act 4*th* may be. If it is as

1. This play may have been *The Reprobate* or *The Album*, both three-act comedies designed for the Compton company to take on tour. HJ wrote to Gosse on their publication in *Theatricals: Second Series* in December 1894, thanking him for his praise. '*The Reprobate* indeed is much the better of the 2; but they both had an inferior origin (like *Disengaged*, in the former volume:) they were written to bolster up poor Edward Compton 3 years ago, when, after withdrawing my other play, he found himself (asininically) with a theatre on his hands & nothing successful to produce; & they were addressed much to the actual vulgar compass of his, & his company's, little powers. Then he would have none of 'em.' (Tuesday (4 or 11 December), Unpublished Huntington MS (HM 48047).)

good as the one for Act 3*d* we may do something with it yet. I feel, indeed, that if it hadn't been for the grave initial mistake & misfortune of keeping so much of the substance of the *novel* (the ostensibly identical story, the same *names*, the same figures, the same associations &c,) I should have had a greatly freer hand, from an early stage of the experiment, in the work of redemption – of altering & reshaping. If I had kept only the *general* idea – the situation of the hero – & *renamed* & re-*placed* you all, so that you wouldn't be still Newmans & Bellegrades & Nioches – I could have got *away* from the disastrous part of the story, perhaps, into safer waters. But this was an error that only experience could prove. We clung to title, names, identity as far as possible with the novel &c, for the positive benefit & advertisement of the association; but from the moment this association did, on trial, so little, in the way of "advertisement," for us (how, ye gods, could it have done *less*?) it only hampered me in the effort to reconstruct & keep afloat. I really feel tempted to rebaptize you all – for the freedom it wd. give me to try & invent, heroically, – oh *heroically*! – a wholly new (a *comedy*!!!) 4*th* act – in which there should never be a ghost of a chance for a ghost of a Moodie! – in which Moodie should even (delicious thought!) become a charming comic character![2]

However I shall be much interested in anything that has occurred to you. Bravo Monty![3] I am delighted Mrs. Compton is pugnacious – I will write her a fighting part.

Yours ever
Henry James

131. To Mr and Mrs Edward Compton
[20 November 1892]

Texas MS   Published MLT II, 297–8

On 15 November, not long before this letter, HJ wrote to WJ that the day before he had taken to Compton at Bath 'a completely rewritten & reconstructed (in a comedy-sense – heaven forgive me!) 4th act of the American'. The new ending

2. The veteran Miss Louise Moodie (1846–1934) played Mrs Bread in the London production of *The American*, and Mrs Solness in *The Master Builder* with Elizabeth Robins in February 1893 (to whom HJ commented that Miss Moodie was 'disappointing – entirely too monotonously and conventionally *tragic* – making poor Mrs S. a stale theatrical *category*, instead of a special person' (TF, 102).

3. The Comptons' son, Edward Montague Compton Mackenzie (1883–1972), later the successful novelist and friend of HJ, published this letter in his copious memoirs.

'will basely gratify their artless instincts & British thick-wittedness' (CWJ II, 243). Where Claire emerged from Valentin's sickroom with 'He's gone – he's gone!', now the doctor rejoices, 'Great news – great news! He's better!' The play was performed with the new fourth act (of which only a fragment survives) in Bristol late in the month.

Evidently the changed final act, 'a wholly new thing' as HJ told Compton it would be, involved altering the 'secret' of the Bellegardes, in such a way that Claire de Cintré knows her mother's 'improprieties' and Urbain, the Marquis, 'is no longer an asinine accomplice in a crime – but a dupe, pompous, pretentious etc.' (MLT II, 295, 301). Here HJ discusses further adjustments.

34, DE VERE GARDENS. W.
Sunday p.m.

My dear Comptons.

Three different parcels (for distinctness sake,) are posted to you this afternoon. May they arrive surely & swiftly. Each of them (constituting an individual alteration,) has a little explanation on the inner cover. But I think I may trust them to explain themselves. The promptbook goes by the 1st post tomorrow – I can't post it as a parcel today. Tomorrow also shall go to you – so far as I can achieve it – the alteration asked for by Mrs. Compton in the matter of some "nice things" said at the last by Claire to Newman. These words are the most difficult of all to place – for obvious reasons. There is a great awkwardness in making her say them *before* all the people present – & that is why I have felt her necessarily restricted to what I have made her *do* – & to dumb emotion, manner &c. I can't make her too publicly *sweet* to him. But what I can I will do – & will give her more words, & a longer message, to Urbain. That is a little easier. I have tried placing the "nice thing or two" in the short scene with Newman after she comes out of V.'s room, but this brings the thing very much back to the scene in Act III – the parting & the imploring & paying tribute even *while* she parts.

The change to making Claire absolutely and conspicuously *know* has been a far more complicated one to make than by the writing in of a few words. I defer to your conviction that it is the only way to be clear – & I have now *made* it clear; but to do so I have *rewritten* the Newman–Valentin scene (III) and the Newman–Mrs. Bread scene (IV,) to say nothing of the Claire–Mrs. Bread scene in the IV. In anything so *tight* & close one can't confine an alteration to one spot – it must extend, like a growing grease-spot, to save the whole from incoherency. I *meant* that Claire *didn't* know – to account for her attitude of submission to her mother. And I meant that at bottom she *did*, vaguely & uneasily, *suspect*, to account for her agitation on suddenly finding that Newman & Mrs. B. are to put their heads together. This too was the *shorter* way. But I accept your assurance that it strikes you so as evidence that this, undescribed, unexplained, is too subtle for a country audience, & have therefore changed her attitude & arranged as best I could the explanation of her subservience to her mother – making the explanation as *definite* as I could. Please look on p.4 of the parting of C. & N. in Act 3*d* when the promptbook reaches you. A dozen words are changed. I will write again tomorrow. Yours ever

Henry James

132. To Julian Russell Sturgis
[Early? 1893]

Houghton TC   Published LHJ I, 212

Percy Lubbock's 1893 dating corresponds to HJ's extreme ambivalence about the experimental and far from popular Ibsen at this time, when he was trying for financial success in the English theatre. In particular, Sturgis may be responding to 'Ibsen's New Play' in the Pall Mall Gazette *of 17 February 1893, where HJ wrote on the Elizabeth Robins production of* The Master Builder. *There HJ calls Ibsen a 'master'; 'he at any rate gives us the sense of life' as nothing else does; and one feels 'the hard compulsion of his strangely inscrutable art'.*

34 De Vere Gardens, W.
Sunday [1893]

My dear Julian,

I wish I had your gift of facile and fascinating rhyme: I would turn it to account to thank you for your note and your sympathy. Yes, Ibsen is ugly, common, hard, prosaic, bottomlessly bourgeois – and with his distinction so far *in*, as it were, so behind doors and beyond vestibules, that one is excusable for not pushing one's way to it. And yet of his art he's a master – and I feel in him, to the pitch of almost intolerable boredom, the presence and the insistence of life. On the other hand his mastery, so bare and lean as it is, wouldn't count nearly as much in any medium in which the genus was otherwise represented. In *our* sandy desert even this translated octopus (excuse my confusion of habitats!!) sits alone, and isn't kept in his place by relativity. "Thanks awfully" for having retained an impression from the few

Tales.[1] My intentions are mostly good. I hope to knock at your door this p.m.

Yours always
Henry James

133. To Robert Underwood Johnson
14 April [1893]

Horne MS   Unpublished

On 15 March 1893 HJ went to Paris, passing on early in May to Lucerne and returning to London in late May.

Hotel Westminster: Paris.
April 14th

Dear R. U. Johnson.

I wrote you my hideous confession about Dagnan-B. about a week before your justly-inquiring lines arrived. I have only to repeat my regret at the insurmountable obstacles – primarily that of the fewness of his things here (only 1 – & that of secondary importance – in the Luxembourg.) Moreover one (of this few,) is so evidently one that I should not be able to speak of as you would desire: that is I *can't* regard the Madonna as a success![1] Clarke, to whom you kindly addressed me, is a remarkably kind & charming man – & has been everything I could have asked.[2] I am only sorry I had to delay so long to put the matter to the test – by coming here. I was a prisoner in London all winter with gout & other fetters. This must have been why I was so unmannerly as to have failed to thank you for the little lyrical book, which I thought it most kind of you to send me – & in which I refound (as we say here) with pleasure some things I had seen elsewhere.[3] I think your verses sincere & charming. Yours most truly

Henry James

1. This might conceivably refer to the collection *The Real Thing*, published by Macmillan in March 1893, but 'retained' suggests *The Lesson of the Master*, published in February 1892.
1. One of the poems in Johnson's volume *The Winter Hour and Other Poems* (1891) is 'A Madonna of Dagnan-Bouveret', which begins 'Oh, brooding thought of dread! / Oh, calm of coming grief!'
2. This is probably William Fayal Clarke (1855–1935), who had been at school with Johnson and remained a close friend, working on the editorial staff at the children's magazine *St Nicholas*, 1873–1927, as editor-in-chief from 1905.
3. On 16 August 1892 HJ had written to Johnson that he had read some of Johnson's verses, which expressed HJ's feelings about the place, to the company in Mrs Bronson's house at Asolo

134. To Edmund Gosse
[21 April 1893]

Leeds MS   Published SLHJEG, 93–4; HJL III, 409–10

On 19 April John Addington Symonds died in Rome. Gosse had recently returned from Paris, where he had seen HJ. About 1890 Gosse seems to have written to the homosexual activist Symonds confessing his own sexual torments. On 7 January 1893 HJ had written to Gosse about Symonds's A Problem in Modern Ethics *(1891), a privately printed pamphlet on homosexuality, which he had borrowed: 'It's, on the whole, I think, a queer place to plant the standard of duty, but he does it with extraordinary gallantry . . . I think one ought to wish him more* humour *– it is really the* saving salt. *But the great reformers never have it.' (SLHJEG, 90.)*

Hotel Westminster
Friday

My dear Gosse.

I am very glad of the emotion that led you [to] write to me immediately about the sudden – the so brutal & tragic extinction, as it comes to one, of poor forevermore silent J.A.S. I had never even (clearly,) seen him – but somehow I too can't help feeling the news as a pang – & with a personal emotion. It always seemed as if I *might* know him – & of few men whom I didn't know has the image so much come home to me. Poor much-living, much-doing, passionately out-giving man! Various things, however, seem to me to have made – to have contributed to make – his death – in the conditions – fortunate & noble. The superabundant achieved work – I mean, the achieved maturity – with age & possibly aberration (repetition & feverish overproduction) what was mainly still to come; and now, *instead*, the full life stopped and rounded, as it were, by a kind of heroic maximum – and under the adored Roman sky. I hope he will be buried there – in the angle of the wondrous wall where the Englishmen lie – & not in his terrible Davos. He must have been very interesting – & you must read me some of his letters. We shall talk of him. *Requiescat*! I hope it isn't to the same "roundedness" – heaven save the

---

near Venice (unpublished Houghton MS, bMS Am 1094.2 (16)). Johnson's chief's wife, Mrs R. W. Gilder, was Mrs Bronson's sister and Johnson had visited Asolo just after the death of Browning, a regular visitor there, and had written 'Browning at Asolo': 'Yesterday he was part of it all . . .'

mark! – that R.L.S. is coming home, if his return be not again merely one of the lies in the dense cloud of mendacity in which *on se débat* – in these days. I wrote to you yesterday. The *heat* here is simply fierce! Do let me know of any *circumstance* about Symonds – or about his death – that may be interesting.

Yours always
Henry James

135. To Edward Compton
29 April [1893]

Texas MS   Published MLT II, 306–8

*In Paris HJ began a new, more serious play for the Comptons, based on a figure he had recorded in his notebook the previous August at Lausanne – 'that once-upon-a-time member of an old Venetian family . . . who had become a monk, and who was taken almost forcibly out of his convent and brought back into the world in order to keep the family from becoming extinct' (N, 71). On 25 March, swamped by proofs of three books all to be published in June (*Picture and Text, The Private Life *and *Essays in London and Elsewhere*)*, he postponed sending the promised play; but on 16 April sent the first act, typed by 'Miss Gregory, my little Hampstead copyist' (MLT II, 304), and a scenario of the other two. By 25 April, however, he was sadly writing to the Comptons that 'the "ending" that you express a dread of* is *the only ending I have ever dreamed of giving the play. I oughtn't to talk of "giving" it to the play – it* is *the play . . .' (HJL III, 411; where, following Compton Mackenzie, it is misdated 2 May). He told Compton to 'Be absolutely frank' on the situation (HJL III, 412).*

Hotel Westminster
April 29*th*

My dear Compton.

I am very glad you have written to me exactly as you have, & you need make no excuse for your frankness – which was the very thing I asked of you, & the only thing possible in the business. Above all is it well that it should have come sooner rather than later – for one feels that later it would have been too late for almost anything! Therefore be at ease about that. As for your melancholy & your disappointment I fully share them, for I had had as much confidence in my subject as you are so good as to say you had in *me*![1] The one shade of doubt I felt was in the Catholicity – but I had ended with thinking that that – relegated to the last century & tinted with distance & an old-world effect, would practically *not* count as a stumbling-block, but rather, on the contrary, as a novelty and a prettiness. And I thought my story *simple* and broadly interesting and just picturesque *enough* – I mean *romantic* enough – and not so picturesque or so romantic as to be strange; & genially human and touching in the right way – & in fact addressed to the simple-minded British public most directly and diplomatically. Above all I thought it *dramatic*! I accept of course completely your statement that, for your purposes (which are the only purposes in question,) I am in error. It's sufficient that you don't *like* the subject – we will drop it on the spot. I won't even defend it against some misconceptions that my meagre exposé of the remainder of the story has apparently led you to form about it – for they don't, now, practically matter. I shall only continue to love it & believe in it in secret & to hope that I may yet do something with it. What I feel to be a worse consequence than any other of my vision of this false start is that coming after some others & occurring in a case in which I had greatly *calculated*, – greatly counted – the thing has inspired me with a most discouraging scepticism as to my power, after all, to light on the particular subject that *will* suit you. My faith in this consummation drops terribly for the hour – though I daresay it will revive again. I have fortunately a great deal of fight in me & a general determination not to be beaten. I must give this plant time to flower again – but it will take a little watering. As *against* this, I have a general strong impression of my constitutional inability to (even in spite of intense & really abject effort) *realize* the sort of simplicity that the promiscuous British public finds its interest in – much more, after this indispensable realization, to *achieve* it. Even where I think I am dropping most diplomatically to the very rudiments & stooping, with a vengeance, to conquer, I am as much "out of it" as ever, & far above their unimaginable heads. That is the consciousness before which I falter and evidently the lesson of this poor wasted "Guy." (I picked myself up the day after writing you, & have been fondly triumphing, in dreams, for the last 48 hours, in my second act.) I agree with you wholly as to the wisdom of not attempting to treat for you any subject and any dénouement that I haven't definitely *shown* you. But I am too bewildered & too dispirited just now to be

1. On 25 April HJ had written that the subject was 'a case of "magnanimity." The idea of it is that Domville throwing up the priesthood to take possession of his place in the world etc. finds, in fact, that he comes into the world only to make himself happy at the *expense* of others . . . and in the face of this reality – ugly and cruel – turns back again to his old ideal, renounces his personal worldly chance, sacrifices himself and makes the others happy.' (HJL III, 411.)

ready with any *assurance*, general or particular. I shall pull round, however, and I will write to you again – in as few days as I can – telling you how the immediate future presents itself to me & whether I can hope to propose anything to you *soon*. If I do *that* I shall still require ample time to let you know *what* that proposal is. In other words I must look round me & draw breath & change horses. I have been living into the Domville story & can't from one day to the other live into another. Accept however, the assurance that what I *can* do I *will* do. The serious side of this mistake is the loss of valuable time – the other sides are not so serious; but I wish as little as you to lose any more than is necessary. I leave Paris on the 3d for Switzerland – *Hotel National, Lucerne*, where I join my brother & his wife who arrive from Italy. The escape from the worrying complications of Paris may bring with it some light & another prospect.[2] I have your card – for the rest of this tour. Please tell your wife that I am very sorry for both of you – I can measure your disappointment. But aren't we, after all, really mismated? Another disaster will seem a warning of that. However, we won't talk or think of "other" disasters – but guard elaborately against them. I shall be afraid, now, for a month, to ask you about your healths! Yours ever

Henry James

136. To Arthur Wing Pinero
28 May 1893

Pusey MS   Unpublished

On 7 May, in Lucerne, HJ confided to his notebook that 'Among the delays, the disappointments, the déboires of the horrid theatric trade nothing is so soothing as to remember that literature sits patient at my door, and that I have only to lift the latch to let in the exquisite little form that is, after all, nearest to my heart' (N, 77).

Soon after he returned to London, he saw George Alexander (1858–1918), popular actor-manager of the St James's Theatre from 1891 to 1918, in the first night (27 May) of an immensely successful play, The Second Mrs Tanqueray by

2. On 6 May, in Lucerne, HJ wrote again to Compton, who had proposed a closer collaboration, about which HJ was sceptical ('One has one's own way of working and one feels that it's either that or nothing . . . I am very willing to try to *be* willing but one must handle one's machinery gently.' (MLT II, 311).) He sent Compton from Switzerland the scenario of the first two acts of a three-act comedy; and, back in London, sent the scenario of the last act late in May.

*Arthur Wing Pinero (1855–1934), an ex-actor, knighted in 1909. He approached
Alexander and it was soon agreed HJ would write* Guy Domville *for him.*

*In Pinero's four-act tragedy Aubrey Tanqueray loves and marries a second wife,
Paula, despite his knowledge of her scandalous past (cohabiting with another man).
He trusts that their love can overcome prejudice and suspicion. In the third act, after
various complications with intercepted letters, Paula's former lover Major Hugh
Ardale arrives from Paris as the suitor of her vulnerable stepdaughter Ellean, who
has just returned from there; he is a threat to Paula's new home. She pleads with
him to tell Tanqueray of their past and to give up Ellean, but he refuses. She says
she will tell him herself. (In the last act, Paula realizes she has lost Tanqueray's
love and kills herself.)*

May 28*th* 1893.
34, DE VERE GARDENS. W.

My dear Pinero:

I shall not let the morning wane nor the impression fade without thanking
you again – after the fact & better than I was able to do when I wrote you
from Switzerland – for the pleasure you enabled me last night to enjoy. Such
occasions are momentous to me, & the evening was deeply impressive. It
sounds almost patronising to say it – but I was held, as in a strong hand, by
your play. I found it full of substance & full of art, and interesting from
beginning to end. If circumstances favoured (I mean favoured *me* – of course!)
I think I should contend with you on the question of the quantity of tragedy
– or even of gravity, so to speak – resident in the situation thrown up in the
third act. But it isn't for this that I write; it's only to congratulate you on the
happy talent that has won another so difficult victory & to express – as regards
the life, the skill & the brilliancy of your piece – the very cordial appreciation
of yours most truly

Henry James[1]

1. Pinero replied on 30 May, mentioning that '"The Real Thing" charmed and consoled me
at a moment of much worry and mental tribulation. You do not need me to tell you that in
The Chaperon you have the germ of a fine comedy for the theatre.' (Unpublished Houghton
MS, bMS Am 1094 (387).) Pinero's letter prompted HJ to several pages of speculation in his
notebook, beginning, '*Is* there a subject for comedy – for a pretty three-act comedy – latent in
The Chaperon?' (N, 247.)

137. To Mrs Elizabeth Lewis
1 June [1893]

Bodleian MS   Unpublished

Elizabeth Robins and others who had had a success with The Master Builder *earlier in the year now had an Ibsen Subscription series at the Opera Comique, adding to that play* Hedda Gabler *and* Rosmersholm. *Elizabeth ('Betty') Eberstadt Lewis (1844–1931) was the wife of George Henry Lewis (1833–1911), who was knighted in 1893, a 'society' solicitor for Wilde and Elizabeth Robins, as well as many other artists and writers. 'In England when one professional gentleman is traduced by another in print the injured party goes off at once to Mr. George Lewis' (*The Era, *16 December 1893). HJ had known them since at least 1879.*

June 1st.
34, DE VERE GARDENS. W.

Dear Mrs. Lewis.

Please believe that I shall do my best to cling to *Wednesday 21st* – at 8. 15. (Instead – I *fully* embrace the idea – of Friday 23*d*.) Oh yes, too, *Hedda Gabler* isn't "infinite" – in the least; is far from being one of the things one can see often. I have seen it *too* often – and am weary & worn with it. But I am braving *Rosmersholm* – with a heavy heart – this afternoon. It will be, I foresee, far too afternoony.[1] *That* will not be the fault of your dinner.

Yours, dear Mrs. Lewis, always
Henry James

138. To Henrietta Reubell
[5 June 1893]

Houghton MS   Unpublished

HJ had spent some days in Paris on his way back from Switzerland to London in May. The great Italian actress Eleanora Duse (1859–1924), preferred by some to

1. *Hedda Gabler* was played in Gosse's translation on Monday afternoon, 29 May, with Elizabeth Robins repeating her 1891 success as Hedda. *The Era* commented that 'The Ibsenites took their pleasure seriously and sadly.' Elizabeth Robins played Rebecca West in *Rosmersholm* on Thursday, 1 June, and, on Saturday, 3 June, Hilda Wangel in *The Master Builder*, as well as taking part in the fourth act of Ibsen's poetic drama *Brand* (1866).

the more forceful Sarah Bernhardt (1844–1923), appeared in London in 1893 and 1895.

> *Monday*
> IMPERIAL INSTITUTE, LONDON S.W.

Dear Miss Etta.

I'm glad to hear the little book reached you in safety. *Evelina* is well worth reading, as I remember it: it will change you from the Egerton Winthrops & d'autres choses encore![1] But I remember it, I confess, from many, many years agone. However the little volumes *are* pretty & *font bien* on little shelves. London is really lovely at present, & I am sorry you are not here to see it. Venez donc, chère mademoiselle & amie, before everything changes. My brother & sister-in-law have not come yet, so that I have des loisirs inattendus; my other relations being in Scotland.[2] The Duse is intensely interesting – not through force & what is vulgarly termed power, but through an exquisite delicacy & truth & naturalness.[3] The temperament of Sarah she hasn't – nor the vulgarity. But a pathos & finish & an absence of the tricks of the trade that are strangely touching & fascinating. No beauty – no wigs, no clothes, scarcely any paint – but a peculiar delicate refinement & originality. Also a little limp or lameness! The total is rare. I am trying to live quiet & keep clear of saloons – with some success. Oscar Wilde's play an *enfantillage* – a piece of helpless puerility.[4] Sargent very big, very red, very pleasant & nice & very great.[5] Paris looks in memory like a fairy-tale full of *eating*! That's right – be civil to the Dame – studiously, imperturbably, simplifyingly civil.[6] If I had

1. Frances (Fanny) Burney, Mme d'Arblay (1752–1840), published her first (epistolary) novel, *Evelina, or a Young Lady's Entrance into the World*, anonymously in 1778 – to widespread admiration, which launched her career.
2. WJ and his family arrived a few days later and stayed at 34 De Vere Gardens; on 22 June HJ decamped to Ramsgate, as he told Gosse, 'to save my life – that is my literary life – from the interruptions & embroilments of this horrible time' (SLHJEG, 96). The 'other relations' were sisters-in-law and families – Carrie James, widow of Wilky, with her two children, and Mary Holton James, wife of Robertson, with her mother and daughter.
3. The Duse season at the Lyric Theatre in May and June consisted of *Camille* (Dumas *fils*), *Fédora* (Sardou), *Cavalleria Rusticana* (Verga) with *La Locaderia* (Goldoni), *A Doll's House* and *Antony and Cleopatra*.
4. The author of *A Woman of No Importance*, which opened at the Haymarket Theatre on 19 April, was a friend of Henrietta Reubell's.
5. At this time Sargent was working on the large project of the murals for the Boston Public Library, as well as continuing his successful career as a society portraitist.
6. I have not identified 'the Dame' among the numerous nicknames of Henrietta Reubell's Parisian circle.

been there I wd. have gone to Whistler's with you.[7] I sent you another book last week – le mien propre.[8] Thank me when you come. Yours always mademoiselle & chère camarade

Henry James

139. To Edward Compton
8 June [1893]

Texas MS   Published MLT II, 314–16

HJ's new subject, sketched in scenario form, failed to suit the head of the Compton Comedy Company – as had that of Guy Domville, *which HJ still hoped, in his notebook on 6 June, 'can be improved with* reflection' (N, 252). (He was soon negotiating over Guy Domville with George Alexander.) The proposal in question here may possibly be 'the subject that I have been turning over as a theme for a play, and tackled very superficially the 1st act of, under the designation of* Monte Carlo' (N, 78; 30 August 1893) – of which not even a description survives.

June 8th
34, De Vere Gardens, W.

My dear Compton:

    You recommend me not to answer your letter – but I think it much better to do so without delay; much better not to wait till you come to town, that is, to say two or three things to which I am much prompted by what I hear from you this morning. Your remarks suggest to me afresh what I very definitely said to you on receiving the letter you wrote me after 1st getting the sketches of *all* the acts, viz: that I am afraid your objections to the story and your desire for new matter in it, mean really, in essence, simply that the story I have given you won't do. For I don't see how I can introduce so much new matter as I gather that you require, or judge necessary, & leave it what I intend it & desire

7. HJ had written from Paris to Isabella Stewart Gardner on 1 May, 'I went to tea yesterday with the Whistlers in their queer little garden-house of the rue du Bac, where the only furniture is the paint on the walls and the smile on the lady's broad face.' (CC, 168–9.) James McNeill Whistler (1834–1903), the controversial American artist, whom HJ had known since 1878, had married in 1888 Beatrix Goodwin, an architect's widow, and left London for Paris.
8. Presumably one of the three books HJ published in June 1893, and probably *The Private Life*, out on 3 June; since *Picture and Text* was published only in the U.S. and *Essays in London and Elsewhere* was advertised only on 17 June.

it to be. *What* I intend & desire it to be is a very *definite thing*, the idea of which I like and cling to. I don't exactly know what you mean by a "backbone" & a something *big* – but evidently you mean something that will differentiate, as it were, the play greatly from a play founded on the general lines I have hinted at. I don't see *how* the play can become so different & *remain* fundamentally my story – the story my scenario expresses, nor, I confess, do I understand what you see in my story *at all* – what is left of it – if something so much is still wanting to it. You speak of a backbone – but if it hadn't a backbone in the germ it won't get it at all. A backbone can't be thrust in after the fact. I like it myself well enough to see what I can do with it by treating it; therefore I am very loth to sacrifice or to spoil it. Trying to make another story of it, which the idea of which it was born would quite cease to fit, would to my sense spoil it utterly. Another story about another matter – *that* is perfectly conceivable; but not a strange surgical operation practised on this. I see a great deal *in* this – comedy & picture & pathos – a real comedy-idea; all sorts of things that I want to draw out. They are things that make it very full. I don't see how I *can* draw them out if another element of any magnitude is to be imported. This I definitely said in my 1*st* letter. Your objection to the end of the second act, & your proposal to substitute for it an *omnium gatherum* of the characters strikes me as a signal symptom of your appreciating my subject so differently from what I do myself that our divergence is probably unreconcilable. This, in fact, is what it seems to me important to say definitely before we take anything more for granted. The situation at the end of the 2*d* act is exactly the thing in the little story that I like best. With every desire to oblige you, it would be *impossible* to me to replace it with any such scene as the one which, if I rightly read your meaning, you have in view. Something depends upon what the scene would be about; but precisely my difficulty is in imagining that it should be about the relations which my subject establishes between my characters. To speak the entire truth, that you should ask for the suppression of the bit I speak of (I quite *love* it!) & for something of so wholly different an order instead, seems to me to constitute the strongest presumption that we shall not agree on the treatment of my theme, or on any lines for discussion. Moreover, now that you have seen my statement, approximate as it only pretends to be, I must candidly say that it is impossible for me to go into the business of "thinking out," very much, with any one but myself. I can do my own work only in my own way – and my play would be to take or to leave. But it is much better that you should leave it at this stage if you don't care enough for the subject. I would a thousand times rather you should say so frankly than try and imagine it possible to do something with it that will enable you to care. For one can do nothing with a subject but *treat* it – or leave it alone. It's what it is or it's nothing; in the latter case one must go on to the next. You will, I am sure, recognise that it's better to tell you this today than to wait till later in the month to tell you. Inacceptable to me is the mere thought of leaving you for instance under a wrong impression as to how radically we differ on the question of the 2d act ending. I may add, àpropos of that, that my hatred, in general, of assemblages, for assemblages' sake, of the characters at the end of the acts is extreme. I have done it for the *third* act – by a violent effort; but when you ask me to do it for the second – & instead, my dear Compton, of that *perfect* list! – I can only hastily sign myself yours ever

Henry James

140. *To Augustin Daly*
3 December 1893

Pusey MS   Unpublished

HJ was at the Kent coast, in Ramsgate, for much of July, working on the second act of Guy Domville *for George Alexander. While dealing with Compton, and now Alexander, HJ had also been waiting for the American manager Daly, who had built Daly's Theatre (opened on 27 June 1893), to produce* Mrs Jasper, *with his star Ada Rehan. Daly had accepted it – requiring months of adjustments by HJ – in 1892 (supposedly, at first, to produce it in New York). In August 1893 HJ had seen the designer's models of the sets. In September HJ was at another seaside town, Whitby, in the lodgings his now-dead friend Lowell used to take, writing it seems another three-act comedy (not extant) for the producer Joseph William Comyns Carr (1849–1916) – and Daly informed him the play was delayed till January. In late October Daly reread the play and asked for new cuts and changes – which five days later HJ declared himself unable to make in the already reduced text. Daly also demanded a new title, and accepted* Mrs Jasper's Way *out of dozens offered by HJ. On 15 November HJ wrote to WJ of Daly's losses through his company's 'very bad season' (CWJ II, 289) – two German adaptations, Tennyson's poetic drama* The Foresters *and* The School for Scandal. *Daly held rehearsals first without asking HJ, then invited him to attend one.*

34, De Vere Gardens, W.
Dec. 3d 1893

Dear Mr. Daly:
    I am very sorry, & not a little alarmed, to hear of the impression made on you by such rehearsal as has taken place. I will come on Wednesday at 12.30

without fail. I am afraid the effect you allude to – that of inadequacy of "story" – will, if it strikes me in the same manner, be too much of the very essence & texture of the play to be remedied, as you suggest, by any superficial patching-up. The subject, such as it is, is what it is, and the treatment of it fits it very tight. Nothing I can do to the play at this stage will make it other, and indeed to do anything *fundamental* seems to me impossible. If rehearsal lights up a dangerous weakness I shall not be slow – however regretfully – to recognise it. This makes me impatient – very – to see your judgment illustrated – & I shall be punctual on Wednesday. Yours very truly

Henry James[1]

141. To William James and Alice Howe Gibbens James
25 May [1894]

Houghton MS   Published CWJ II, 307–8; HJL III, 476–7

HJ's notebook for the winter of 1893–4 is full of subjects for plays and stories – including on 3 February that for 'The Death of the Lion', which he contributed to the first issue of Henry Harland's (and Aubrey Beardsley's) controversial new journal, The Yellow Book.

Constance Fenimore Woolson had died in Venice on 24 January 1894, falling from a window into the street. The newspapers soon reported the death as suicide – disturbing HJ so much he could not leave in time for her funeral as he had planned. On 2–14 February 1894 he wrote to Elizabeth Gaskell Norton of 'Miss Woolson's tragic death': 'What is very evident is that she was at the time absolutely out of her mind with fever & illness (had influenza;) but it's far the more miserably to be gathered that this had supervened on a condition of chronic & absorbing melancholy which was not the consequence of anything in her situation (though it was perhaps sharpened by loneliness,) but which those who knew her well (not merely encountering

---

1. On 29 December HJ gave WJ an account of the outcome: 'I *withdrew* my play from him after a single (absolutely humbugging) rehearsal, & in consequence of an attitude on his part of unmistakeable provocation to do so . . . He has so blundered & muddled away his whole season here that he has lost money appallingly – has had not a *single* success – pursuing with a third rate company an utterly 3*d* rate policy, which has landed him on the verge of ruin. Under these circumstances I became for him simply an author to whom he had the dreadful prospect of having "royalties" to pay – and he addressed himself crudely and odiously to getting rid of.' The rehearsal HJ had attended he called 'one ghastly make-believe, to the end that I might be disgusted' (CWJ II, 295–6). In June 1894 HJ published the play as *Disengaged* – a title perhaps reflecting his rupture with Daly.

her socially,) were painfully familiar with and always apprehensive, or at least anxious about.' (Unpublished Houghton MS, bMS Am 1193 (111).)

HJ left London on 18 March for Genoa, where on 29 March he met Miss Woolson's sister and niece, Clara (d. 1923) and Clare Benedict, later rejoining them in Venice to sort out the dead woman's affairs.

Ravenna, May 25th

Dearest brother & sister.

This letter is but a stopgap till I can (in 2 or 3 days,) write you both properly. A fine letter from each of you since last I wrote makes me feel how strangely long my silence will have seemed to you – especially in face of my receipt of Alice's magnificent diary.[1] It has been caused by insurmountable hindrances – mainly a pressure of work in Venice to make up for the dreadful interruptions & adversities in general of that place and in particular for the great hole bored in my time & my nerves by the copious aid & comfort I couldn't help giving to poor Mrs. Benedict – Miss Woolson's sister, who, staying there 5 weeks, made daily demands of me to help her in the winding-up of Miss W.'s so complicated affairs, all left, so far as Venice was concerned, at sixes and sevens. This proved a most devouring an almost fatal job, & as at the same time I had just promised a splendid work of art, in London, for the 2d number of the *Yellow Book* I had to *fight* for every hour to finish it by the promised date.[2] ¾'s of an hour ago I posted, in this place, the last of the covenanted 25,000 words to London, & though I am exhausted with the effort & the heavy heat I scrawl you these feverish lines to keep you in patience – till I can get a quieter hour. I leave in an hour for 5 days in Rome & 7 in Florence (with Baldwin;) after which I return to Venice till July 1st. Another reason I didn't instantly *sfogare* to you on the subject of Alice's wonderful Diary was that in addition to my immense *impressedness* by it, and, during the first days superseding even that, I was terribly scared and disconcerted – I mean alarmed – by the sight of so many private names & allusions in print. I am still terrified by this – as I partly feel responsible as it were – being myself the source of so many

1. The letters from WJ and AHJ are not known to survive. AJ's companion Katharine Loring had privately printed four copies of her diary.
2. The story in question was 'The Coxon Fund', sketched in Venice only on 17 April and begun about 25 April, suggested by Dykes Campbell's biography of Coleridge. On 28 May HJ told WJ he hadn't sent him the first number of *The Yellow Book* on purpose: 'I hate too much the horrid aspect & company of the whole publication. And yet I am again to be intimately – conspicuously – associated with the 2d number. It is for gold & to oblige the worshipful Harland (the editor.)' (CWJ II, 312.)

of the things told, commented on &c. This kept me from being, at first, able to express anything but my anxiety – & my regret that K.P.L. hadn't sunk a few names, put initials – I mean in view of the danger of accidents, some catastrophe of publicity. The book is rare – wondrous; & I will express *everything* from Rome – including all my sympathy with your melancholy illness – which I now feel that I must have looked "heartless" not to have poured forth about.[3] But my horrid predicament in Venice made me simply ferocious till my promise – in London – shld. be redeemed. God send you have been long ere this wholly well. I really wept for you. À bientôt.

Ever your
Henry

142. *To Edmund Gosse*
17 December 1894

BL MS   Published SLHJEG, 121–2; HJL III, 495; LHJ I, 223–4

HJ remained in Italy till mid July, suffering constant social embroilments and interruptions – 'these 3 months have been simple hell!' he told WJ on 29 June from Venice (CWJ II, 315). Back in England he spent two weeks of August at St Ives, near the Leslie Stephens.

On 7 September HJ told WJ he had spent two long mornings with George Alexander on Guy Domville, 'going . . . above all over the hideous supreme ordeal of the "cuts" – desired by the English manager on lines so abject, a theory of the play so beggarly in its meagreness & crudity, that it is absolutely nauseating' (CWJ II, 323–4).

On 29 September HJ was staying in Oxford, near the Anglophile Bourgets, at Constance Fenimore Woolson's last English address, and noted the idea for his story of creative mourning, 'The Altar of the Dead', whose hero, dwelling on the dead, 'is struck with the way they are forgotten, are unhallowed – unhonoured, neglected, shoved out of sight' (N, 98). Stevenson died in Samoa on 3 December 1894; his death was reported in the London evening papers on 17 December.

3. HJ told WJ on 28 May from Rome of his principle with AJ 'of always bringing in the world to her & telling her in her sick solitude everything I could scrape together'. Beyond his fear of the newspapers getting hold of the diary, 'I have been immensely impressed with the thing as a revelation & a moral & personal picture. It is heroic in its individuality, its independence – its face-to-face with the universe for-&-by herself – & the beauty & eloquence with which she often expresses this, let alone the rich irony & humour, constitute (I wholly agree with you,) a new claim for the family renown.' (CWJ II, 311.) WJ was recovering from a month in bed with a subcutaneous abscess.

Dec. 17*th* *1894*
34 DE VERE GARDENS. W.

My dear Gosse.

I meant to write you tonight on another matter – but of what can one think, or utter or dream, save of this ghastly extinction of the beloved R.L.S.? It is too miserable for cold words – it's an absolute desolation. It makes me cold & sick – & with the absolute, almost alarmed sense, of the visible material quenching of an indispensable light. That he's silent forever will be a fact hard, for a long time, to live with. Today, at any rate, it's a cruel, wringing emotion. One feels how one cared for him – what a place he took; & as if suddenly *into* that place there had descended a great avalanche of ice. I'm not sure that it's not for *him* a great & happy fate; but for us the loss of charm, of suspense, of "fun" is unutterable. And how confusedly & pityingly one's thought turns [to] those far-away stricken women, with their whole principle of existence suddenly quenched & yet all the monstrosity of the rest of the situation left on their hands! I saw poor Colvin to-day – he is overwhelmed, he is touching. But I can't write of this – we must talk of it. Yet these words have been a relief.

And I can't write, either, of the matter I had intended to – viz. that you are to rest secure about the question of June 5*th* – I will do everything for you.[1] *That* business becomes for the hour tawdry & heartless to me.

Yours always
Henry James

---

143. *To Henrietta Reubell*
31 December 1894

Houghton MS   Partly published LHJ I, 225–7

December 31*st* 1894
34, DE VERE GARDENS. W.

Dear Miss Etta.

This is to wish you a brand-New Year, & to wish it very affectionately – & to wish it of not more than usual length but of more than usual fulness. I have had an unacknowledged letter from you longer than is decorous. But I have shown you ere this that epistolary decorum is a virtue I have ceased to

1. A slip for 'January 5*th*', the first night of *Guy Domville*, rehearsals of which had begun on 10 December. HJ gave the Gosses complimentary seats.

pretend to. And during the last month I have not pretended to any other virtue either – save an endless patience & an heroic resignation, as I have been, & still am, alas, in the sorry position of having in Rehearsal a little play – 3 acts – which is to be produced on Saturday next – at the St. James's Theatre; as to which I beg you heartily to indulge for me, about 8 30 o'clk, on that evening, in very fervent prayer. It is a little "romantic" play of which the action is laid (in England,) in the middle of the last century, & it will be exquisitely mounted, dressed, &c; & very creditably acted, as things go here. But rehearsal is an *écoeurement* & one's need of heroic virtues infinite. I have been in the breach daily for 4 weeks, & am utterly exhausted. Tonight (the theatre being closed for the week on purpose,) is the *1st* Dress-rehearsal – which is here of course not a public, as in Paris, but an intensely private function – all for *me, me prélassant dans mon fauteuil*, alone like the King of Bavaria at the opera.[1] There are to be three nights more of this, to give them ease in the wearing of their clothes of a past time, and *that*, after the grind of the earlier work, is rather amusing – as amusing as anything *can* be, for a man of taste & sensibility, in the odious process of practical dramatic production. I may have been meant for the Drama – God knows! – but I certainly wasn't meant for the Theatre. C'est pour vous dire that I am much pressed and am only sending you *mes voeux très-sincères* in a shabbily brief little letter. You shall have a much better one when my painful ordeal is over. There are a number of interesting things in your last to which I want to respond. I send you also by post 3 or 4 miserable little (old) views of Tunbridge Wells, which I have picked up in looking, at rare leisure-moments, for the good one for you.[2] I haven't, alas, found that; but I think I am on the track of it, and you shall have it as soon as it turns up. Accept these meanwhile as a little stop-gap & a symbol of my New Year's greeting. Little Potter writes me that he has been to see you at last – & that his long silence was occasioned by his upset condition on his father's death.[3] He seems to think he must have made a very bad impression on you through shyness &c; but he is a very clean, pure, earnest little chap, – with, I think, a

1. Ludwig II, the mad King of Bavaria who built Bayreuth for Richard Wagner, notoriously had whole operas performed for himself alone.
2. During 1894 Henrietta Reubell had convalesced at Tunbridge Wells in Kent, 'the beneficent Tunbridge' as HJ called it on 5 November 1894 (Unpublished Houghton MS, bMS Am 1094 (1125)).
3. On 5 November HJ wrote to Henrietta Reubell that he had given a note of introduction to a young American artist working in Paris, whom he 'met last summer in Venice'. 'He has a very fine & charming talent de dessinateur (I think,) & his name is, very Americanly, John Briggs Potter – of the West. But he is so young, so clean, so sincere & ingenuous, with such a charm in his face, such a beauty of a curious sort, in his delicate talent, & such an absence of fortune at his elbow, that he interested me.' (Unpublished Houghton MS, bMS Am 1094 (1125).)

beautiful *drawing*-talent. Poor dear Harrison Ritchie – he's a figure you will miss: he was a genial, social, easy fellow, with his handsome roses and frost, and one felt he was a gentleman.[4] I have had some communication with the little Navarros; – he has been in anguish, but she is recovering happily.[5] I shall see them when *I* have recovered. He seems a rather pathetic clinging little chap. I hope you are in good case & good hope. We are having here an excellent winter; almost fogless and generally creditable. Write me a little word of hope & help for the 5*th*: I shall regard it as a happy influence for yours forever

Henry James

144. To Lady Lewis
1 January 1895

Bodleian MS   Unpublished

George Lewis had been knighted. HJ had declined an invitation to dine with the Lewises on New Year's Eve.

Jan. 1st *1895*
34, DE VERE GARDENS. W.

Dear Lady Lewis.

All thanks for the charity of your letter. This is a word to tell you how very far from well it would have been for me not to have minded my own business, as it were, last evening. There was a dress-rehearsal of my trembling little play at which my presence proved quite horribly indispensable & from which my absence wd. have been destructive – fatal. If the thing in short seems at all

4. Harrison Ritchie and his wife were Bostonians living in Paris. HJ had met them in 1876 at the same period as meeting Henrietta Reubell.
5. Mary Antoinette Anderson de Navarro (1859–1940) had been the American actress Mary Anderson, successful in 1880s London, a friend of Mrs Humphry Ward and HJ. She retired from the stage on marrying Antonio Fernando de Navarro (1860–1932), papal privy chamberlain, engineer and writer. On 26 November HJ told Henrietta Reubell of a visit from Navarro, 'who told me that his "Marie", round the corner, is still waiting for the baby that doesn't come ... the delay appears to be abnormal' (Unpublished Houghton MS, bMS Am 1094 (1126)). A son was born, but died shortly afterwards. Mary Anderson de Navarro: 'I was stricken ... Henry James's sympathy was unfailing during that time of illness and death ... His only mention of our little boy was: "We have both lost our first-born. I was very fond of *Guy Domville* too."' (*A Few More Memories* (1936).)

tolerable on Saturday it will be because – in company with several fat women connected with the clothes – I was there on Monday. Your indulgence has none the less greatly eased off the distracted spirit that illegibly scrawls these lines. I hope your feast prospered in every way – & I have every sense of what I lost. My great New Year's wish is for myself – may 1895 bring me some compensation! *Then* may it bring you, dearest Lady Lewis, & bring yours, every conceivable good thing. Do unite in family prayers for me on the 5*th*.[1] Yours forever

Henry James

145. To Henrietta Reubell
10 January 1895

Houghton MS   Published SL1, 153–5

The première of Guy Domville *did not go smoothly. As HJ told WJ, 'the delicate, picturesque, extremely human & extremely artistic little play, was taken profanely by a brutal & ill-disposed gallery which had shown signs of malice prepense from the 1*st *& which, held in hand till the end, kicked up an infernal row at the fall of the curtain. There followed an abominable ¼ of an hour during wh. all the forces of civilization in the house waged a battle of the most gallant, prolonged & sustained applause with the hoots & jeers & catcalls of the roughs, whose* roars *(like those of a cage of beasts at some infernal "Zoo") were only exacerbated (as it were!) by the conflict. It was a char[m]ing scene, as you may imagine, for a nervous, sensitive, exhausted author to face.' (CWJ II, 337.) For HJ had been led on to the stage in response to calls of 'Author!'*

HJ wrote to Lady Lewis on Monday, 7 January of 'the unspeakable theatre. I feel as if I mean to let it so much alone forever that abysses of silence will but poorly represent my detachment.' (Unpublished Bodleian MS, Dep. c. 834, fols. 127–8.)

Jan. 10*th* 1895
34, DE VERE GARDENS. W.

Dearest Miss Etta.

I rejoice in the warm glow of your friendship & of your indignation. Yes, I encountered on Saturday evening the most horrible hours of my life – *but*

---

1. HJ would be too nervous to watch his own première, and went to Wilde's new *An Ideal Husband*, returning to his own play just before the final curtain.

the demonstration didn't come from the audience in any real sense of the term – infinite members of whom have deluged me – even when complete strangers – with letters & visits to tell me they had been delighted with the play. An ill-disposed, vicious, brutish *gallery* +[1] was in the house, & bent, for particular & backstairs reasons, on mischief.[2] They made it effectually, & the newspapers in general, have by their vulgar stupidity & density increased the damage of the mob. I send you, however, Clement Scott in the *Telegraph*, & will send you W. Archer (in the *World*,) next week: these are the only 2 critics who in the least count.[3] Of course however the play has *du plomb dans l'aile*, & it remains to be seen what will become of it. I am prepared for the worst, & had no real illusions at any time. You can take my word for it that the piece is extremely charming & skilful – *je ne suis pas une bête*, either to write a silly play, or not to know it if I had. But when I stood in the presence of that yelling crew (gallery pure & simple – out-vociferating the applause, thanks to leathern lungs,) I felt with bottomless dismay how the atmosphere of *any* London theatre is in mortal danger of becoming a complete non-conductor of any *fine* intention or any really civilized artistic attempt – & I saw, in one sickened moment, (it wasn't pleasant,) the *effondrement* of my labour & my hope. *Are* they really effondrés? It is too soon to say; but this week will show. The *seconde*, on Monday, went admirably, to a full & enthusiastic house. But that was an inevitable manifestation, on the part of the public, of shame & remorse for the brutishness of an element on Saturday, & may mean nothing in relation to a "run." So I am prepared, as I say, for the worst, & am, thank God, absolutely philosophic. The only thing they understand, or want here, is *one kind* of play – the play of the same kind as the unutterable kind they already know. With anything a little more delicate they are like a set of savages with a gold watch. Yet God knows I had *tried* to be simple, straightforward & British, & to dot my i's as big as with targets. The subject doubtless is too far away – an episode in the history of an old English Catholic family in the last century – treated as I thought, at least, very ingeniously & humanly.[4] But the theatre is verily a black abyss – & one feels stained with vulgarity rien que

1. + 'The row was all the gallery, though much of the stupidity was elsewhere too.' [HJ's note.]

2. There were newspaper reports that there had been a conspiracy against Alexander.

3. Apart from William Archer and Clement Scott (1841–1904), *Telegraph* critic, 1871–98, also present were Herbert George Wells (1866–1946), new theatre critic of the *Pall Mall Gazette*, and George Bernard Shaw (1856–1950) of the *Saturday Review*, both of whom wrote appreciatively of the play. Enoch Arnold Bennett (1867–1931) was there too, for *Woman*. (He wrote as 'Cécile'.)

4. HJ wrote to John Hay on 9 February, 'The subject of my little play demanded that I shd. put Catholics en scène, & the British public won't stand Papists.' (HJJH, 113.)

d'y avoir passé. Thank heaven there is another art. I embrace you, dear Etta Reubell, for your prompt participation in my little *ennui*, & am yours more than ever

Henry James

146. To William Dean Howells
22 January 1895

Houghton MS   Published HJL III, 511–13; LFL, 297–9

HJ was quickly resolved to return to fiction; as he told WJ, 'you can't make a sow's ear out of a silk purse' (CWJ II, 338). His analysis was that 'The play has failed because it has been unfamiliar*' (CWJ II, 344).* Guy Domville *had thirty-one performances (bringing HJ $1,300) before closing on 5 February; nine days later Alexander opened Wilde's* The Importance of Being Earnest. *HJ's severance from the theatre was not instant or absolute, however: on 5 February he saw the actress Ellen Terry about the one-act comedy* Summersoft, *which he would post to her late in August 1895 (she paid £100 for the option, but never performed it).*

On Thursday, 10 January, HJ visited Addington, residence of Edward White Benson (1829–96), the Archbishop of Canterbury, whose son Arthur Christopher Benson (1862–1925) he had known since 1884 through Frederic Myers. The Archbishop told him the anecdote that would become 'The Turn of the Screw'.

January 22d *1895*
34, De Vere Gardens. W.

My dear Howells.

I have 2 good things – & have had them for some time – to thank you for. One is John's charming paper about the Beaux Arts which I was delighted you should have sent me – so lovely it is & young & fresh & vivid & in every way calculated to minister to the "fondness of a father" & the frenzy of a mother – to say nothing of the pride of an affectionate old friend.[1] The dear boy seems to have been born to invent new ways of being filially gratifying & generally delectable. Happy you – happy, even if you had *only* him! Surely, surely you *must* all come out this summer to visit him with your condign tenderness. Any other course will be utterly shabby of you. I regard this as quite settled.

1. John M. Howells's 'Architect at the Gates of the Beaux-Arts' appeared in *Harper's Weekly* on 22 December 1894.

Secondly (or firstly it shld. have been,) I am indebted to you for your most benignant letter of December last.[2] It lies open before me and I read it again & am soothed & cheered & comforted again. You put your finger sympathetically on the place & spoke of what I wanted you to speak of. I *have* felt, for a long time past, that I have fallen upon evil days – every sign or symbol of one's being in the least *wanted*, anywhere or by anyone, having so utterly failed. A new generation, that I knew not, & mainly prize not, had taken universal possession. The sense of being utterly out of it weighed me down, & I asked myself what the future wd. be. All these melancholies were qualified indeed by one redeeming reflection – the sense of how little, for a good while past (for reasons very logical, but accidental & temporary,) I had been producing. I *did* say to myself "Produce again – produce; produce better than ever, & all will yet be well"; and there was sustenance in that so far as it went. But it has meant much more to me since *you* have said it – for it *is*, practically, what you admirably say. It is exactly, moreover, what I mean to admirably do – & have meant, all along, about this time to get into the motion of. The whole thing, however, represents a great change in my life, inasmuch as what is clear is that periodical publication is practically closed to me – I'm the last hand that the magazines, in this country or in the U.S., seem to want. I won't afflict you with the now accumulated (during all these past years,) evidence on which this induction rests – & I have spoken of it to no creature till, at this late day, I speak of it to you. But, until, the other month (two mos ago,) Henry Harper, here, made a friendly overture to me on the part of his magazine, no sign, no symbol of any sort, has come to me from any periodical whatever – & many visible demonstrations of their having, on the contrary, no use for me.[3] I can't go into details – & they wd. make you turn pale! I'm utterly out of it *here* – & Scribner, the Century, the Cosmopolitan, will have

---

2. Howells had written to HJ on 13 December 1894, answering a letter of some weeks before which struck a 'note of unjustified discouragement', and which had half asked about ' "American chances and opportunities" ' (LFL, 296–7) (the letter is not known to survive). Howells had wished to assure him that 'so far as literary standing is concerned there is no one who has your rank among us', and to tell him that new magazines like the Chicago *Chap-Book* of Stone & Kimball would welcome contributions (in 1897 it would publish *What Maisie Knew*).

3. On 17 October 1894 HJ was at a 'gorgeous dinner' given at the Reform Club by the publisher Clarence McIlvaine, partner of the late J. R. Osgood (both were Harper representatives in London) in the firm of Osgood, McIlvaine (which published several books by HJ about this time). The dinner was for J. Henry Harper, head of Harper & Brothers. Harper 'brought me a kind of message from Alden of the *Magazine*, a message strongly backed up by himself, to the effect that they "wanted to see me in the Magazine again" ' (N, 100). Henry Mills Alden (1836–1919) was editor of *Harper's New Monthly Magazine*. Nothing by HJ appeared in the magazine till September 1897.

nothing to say to me – above all for fiction.[4] The *Atlantic*, & H. & M., treat me like the dust beneath their feet; & the Macmillans, here, have cold-shouldered me out of all relation with them.[5] All this, I needn't say, is for your segretissimo ear. What it means is that "production" for me, as aforesaid, means production of the little *book* pure and simple – independent of any antecedent appearance; &, truth to tell, now that I wholly *see* that, & have at last accepted it, I am, incongruously, not at all sorry. I am indeed very serene. I have always hated the magazine form, magazine conditions & manners, & much of the magazine company. I hate the horrid little subordinate part that one plays in the catchpenny picture book – & the negation of all literature that the insolence of the picture book imposes. The money-difference will be great – but not so great after a bit as at first; & the other differences will be so all to the good that even from the economic point of view they will tend to make up for that & perhaps finally even completely do so. It is about the distinctness of one's *book-position* that you have so substantially reassured me; & I mean to do far better work than ever I have done before. I have, potentially, improved immensely – & am bursting with ideas & subjects: though the act of composition is, with me, more & more slow, painful & difficult. I shall never again write a *long* novel; but I hope to write 6 immortal short ones – & some tales of the same quality. Forgive, my dear Howells, the cynical egotism of these remarks – the fault of which is in your own sympathy. Don't fail me this summer.[6] I shall probably not, as usual, absent myself from these islands – not be beyond the Alps as I was when you were here last. That way Boston lies, which is the deadliest form of madness. I sent you only last night messages of affection by dear little "Ned" Abbey, who presently sails for N.Y. laden with the beautiful work he has been doing for the new B. public library. I hope you will see him – he will speak of me competently & kindly. I wish all power to your elbow. Let me hear as soon as there is a sound of packing. Tell Mildred I rejoice in the memory of her. Give my love to your wife, & believe me my dear Howells yours in all constancy

Henry James

4. HJ had sent his essay on 'The Grand Canal' to Edward Livermore Burlingame (1848–1922), editor of *Scribner's Magazine* from 1887 to 1914, in August 1892, and the story 'The Middle Years' appeared there in May 1893. Scribner's other magazine, the *Century*, under R. W. Gilder and R. U. Johnson, published nothing by HJ between January 1890 and 'Broken Wings' in December 1900. Howells edited the *Cosmopolitan Magazine* for four months in 1892, managing to print an essay and two tales by HJ in that year; it took nothing by HJ thereafter.
5. HJ had had fictions in Horace Scudder's *Atlantic* (published by Houghton, Mifflin) in August, November–December 1891 and April 1892, but nothing since. There is a three-year gap in HJ's correspondence with Macmillan between 1893 and 1896.
6. Howells did not go to Europe till 1897.

147. To Edmund Gosse
[8 April 1895]

Leeds MS   Published SLHJEG, 126–7; HJL IV, 9–10; SL2, 290

The day after writing the previous letter, HJ entered in his notebook that 'It is now indeed that I may do the work of my life. And I will.' Three days later he sketched his story 'The Next Time': 'The idea of the poor man, the artist, the man of letters, who all his life is trying – if only to get a living – to do something vulgar, to take the measure of the huge, flat foot of the public' (N, 109).

In March HJ visited Dublin for more than a fortnight, staying first with the Lord Lieutenant of Ireland, Lord Houghton (son of his old friend), and then with the Wolseleys (Lord Wolseley was commander-in-chief of the British army in Ireland).

On 1 March Oscar Wilde had the Marquess of Queensberry, father of 'Bosie', Lord Alfred Douglas, arrested for libel (for the words 'To Oscar Wilde posing as a Somdomite [sic]'). When the case failed Wilde was arrested on 5 April for 'committing unnatural acts' and taken to Bow Street Police Station. Gosse was concerned because Wilde's ex-lover and supporter Robert Ross (1869–1918), whose epitaph on himself was 'Here lies one whose name was writ in hot water', was a friend of the Gosse family. WJ wrote HJ that, 'Time has given you your revanche over poor Oscar Wilde.' On 26 April HJ wrote back as Wilde's trial began that 'there are depths in London, & a certain general shudder as to what, with regard to some other people, may possibly come to light' (CWJ II, 356, 359).

Monday
34, De Vere Gardens. W.

My dear Gosse.

Yes, I will come with pleasure tomorrow, Tuesday. Yes, too, it has been, it is, hideously, atrociously dramatic & really interesting – so far as one can say that of a thing of which the interest is qualified by such a sickening horribility. It is the squalid gratuitousness of it all – of the mere exposure – that blurs the spectacle. But the *fall* – from nearly 20 years of a really unique kind of "brilliant" conspicuity (wit, "art," conversation – "one of our 2 or 3 dramatists &c,") to that sordid prison-cell & this gulf of obscenity over which the ghoulish public hangs & gloats – it is beyond any utterance of irony or any pang of compassion! He was never in the smallest degree interesting to

me – but this hideous human history has made him so – in a manner. À demain
– Yours ever

Henry James

Quel Dommage – mais quel Bonheur – que J.A.S. ne soit plus de ce monde![1]

148. To Horace Elisha Scudder
8 June 1895

Houghton MS   Unpublished

On 12 May 1895 (in the middle of acting as host for a three-week visit to England by the Daudets), HJ wrote to Scudder, with whom he had resumed contact in 1891 after the débâcle of 'The Pupil', agreeing to send him three short stories for the Atlantic. *One of them, 'The House Beautiful' was later to become* The Spoils of Poynton. *Scudder's word-limit was 10,000.*

On 15 May HJ's new publisher William Heinemann (1863–1920), an associate of his dead friend Balestier, brought out Terminations. *Heinemann had begun his firm in 1890 and had in September 1891 privately printed about twenty copies of* The American: A Comedy in Four Acts. *From 1895 to 1897 he was proprietor of the* New Review, *which serialized* What Maisie Knew *in Britain.*

34, DE VERE GARDENS. W.

Dear Mr. Scudder.

I am much obliged to you for your allowance of time – for the delivery of the 1st of my three Tales. I can certainly let you have it well *before* Oct. 15*th*. In fact it's ½ written & I have only a temporary impediment, which goes on, however, a while longer, to finishing it.[1] The name thereof is "The House Beautiful." I had also infinitely rather that there shld. be no cutting in two –

1. HJ wrote these words on the flap of the envelope. 'What a shame – but what a relief – that J.A.S. should be no longer of this world!' Wilde had reviewed Symonds's *Studies of the Greek Poets* in 1876, and in prison would ask for his *Introduction to Dante*; but it is probably Symonds's high-minded polemics for homosexual love HJ is thinking of. Gosse had lent HJ the pamphlet *A Problem in Modern Ethics* in January 1893, and HJ borrowed what he called further 'fond outpourings of poor J.A.S.' after Wilde's arrest (SLHJEG, 127).
1. The 'impediment' may have been the composition for Henry Harland's *Yellow Book* of the story 'The Next Time'. HJ was planning it in his notebook on 4 June 1895, and it appeared in the July issue.

in fact it's out of the question; & I shall send you nothing in *excess* of 15 000 words. But I am afraid that nothing I am likely to see my way to do will fail to creep *up* to that figure. Believe me yours most truly

Henry James

June 8*th* 1895.

149. To Robert Underwood Johnson
24 June 1895

Virginia MS   Unpublished

On 5 May HJ had declined to write for Johnson's Century *an article on the great Italian actress Eleanora Duse. He admired her, but, 'The truth is I can't write anymore about theatrical people – & I don't want to!' (Unpublished Yale MS, Koch 966.) In the event HJ did write about the actress Eleanora Duse for Johnson in 1895, albeit in passing, in an article on 'Dumas the Younger', where he mentions her Marguerite in* La Dame aux camélias *(SA, 263–4). But Johnson returned that article, HJ recorded in his notebook on 13 February 1896, 'as shocking to their prudery' (because of the mentions of adultery &c. unavoidable in plot-summaries). HJ satirized 'the whole loathesomely prurient & humbugging business' of Anglo-American Grundyism in 'John Delavoy' (1898) (N, 154).*

June 24*th* 1895
34, DE VERE GARDENS. W.

My dear Johnson.

I am very sorry about the Duse question – for it was my fault. However, when I 1*st* declined I had seen her so little. Now that she has been giving me chances I have made up that void, & I have felt rather prepared & inspired. She has been acting here, for 3 weeks, very exquisitely. But I don't in the least *want* to write about her – for I am, as I told you, woefully weary of the (today) all-invasive theatre, with its cheapness of criticism, its overestimated art, & vulgarity of air, & I am delighted to surrender the task to someone who probably *does* want to deal with it & whom I'm delighted you have found. Therefore n'en parlons plus.

I am very sorry to say, however, that I *can't* write the little article you are so good as to propose as a substitute – & as to my brief allusion to something that you appear to have taken for the subject of which (what a sentence! –

don't analyse it!) you have, I fear fallen into a misconception.[1] What I, by the way, dropped a reflection about was not the love of Notoriety in general (on which there wd. doubtless be much to say, but which is rather a big, vague, loose subject;) it was a very definite & *special* craze of the day, the ridiculous abandonment of all proportion & perspective in the worship of the *actor &* *actress*, the deification of their little 3*d*-rate personalities, the colossal inflation of them by the gigantic bellows of the Press – which, in our English-speaking countries, the total absence of dramatic authors (worth speaking of,) contributes to by establishing no measure of their relativity, their merely servile office. In France, where the drama is primarily the Author, the case is infinitely less bad: the actors are kept more in their places. (I shall not forget Alphonse Daudet's stupefaction, the other day, at seeing John Kemble & Mrs. Siddons – by statue – in Westminster Abbey.)[2] That *is*, if you like, a subject, & an excellent one; but *I* can't write it. I don't *care* to, for all sorts of reasons; &, I must add, I am no longer able to give time to the "little article," with which I desire less & less to be identified, especially in the case of a big manifesto like your Anniversary number. I must concentrate, & I only want henceforth to be associated with "creative work"! – excuse the priggish phrase. And of this my hands are already too full – & tied by too many pledges. So – I'm very sorry – I can't do anything – but wish you all increase & felicity.

Even London is so torrid that I fear the Gilders must be grilling in Venice.[3]

Yours most faithfully

Henry James

1. In declining to write about Duse, HJ had explained to Johnson that 'I think the whole periodical press takes a vastly disproportionate view of the importance & interest of mountebanks & mimes & that the immense resonance given by that vast machinery for publicity to their little "personalities" (as they like to call them,) is one of those features of our Terrible Time at the expense of which much – or most – profane mirth might be caused to flash. I think I could almost write an article about *that* if you like; yet it would even then – prohibitively – be about the theatre.'

2. John Kemble (1757–1823) and his sister Sarah Siddons (1755–1831) had been among the most eminent of British actors.

3. Richard Watson Gilder's wife Helena De Kay Gilder, formerly a close friend of Minny Temple, was the sister of Katherine De Kay Bronson, who lived in the Casa Alvisi in Venice, and the Gilders were there for the marriage of their niece into the Rucellai family.

150. To John Lane
13 August 1895

Texas MS   Unpublished

HJ was at Torquay, staying near his friend William Edward Norris (1847–1925),
a successful popular novelist, from mid July till mid August, and then again from 6
September to the end of October. He described it to Anne Thackeray Ritchie: 'This is
a little démodé "crescent" hanging over a green, green garden that hangs over a blue,
blue sea. Over all hangs my balcony – & over my balcony hangs a beautiful striped
awning. No sound but the waves licking the honey-coloured sands.' (Unpublished Eton
MS, 'Tuesday'.) It was at Torquay, HJ later recalled, he began to ride a bicycle.

   John Lane (1854–1925), who had founded the Bodley Head with Elkin Mathews
in 1887, was the publisher of The Yellow Book, *the sixth issue of which in July*
had printed HJ's 'The Next Time'. The firm was associated with fine books and
'advanced' writers (including Wilde and Harland) in the 1890s.

34, DE VERE GARDENS. W.
August 13*th 1895*

Dear Mr. Lane.
   Your cheque for £35. 0 0 reached me this a.m. – better late than never.[1] I
am much obliged to you for your hospitable expressions with regard to my
writings & am yours very truly

Henry James

John Lane esq.

151. To Horace Elisha Scudder
4 October 1895

Houghton MS   Published HJL IV, 22–3

'The House Beautiful' lengthened, and on 3 September HJ wrote to Scudder that
after a 'mortal struggle' it would be at least 25,000 words and 'must go elsewhere'.

1. HJ would write to Lane on 2 February 1896: 'it is impossible to me to contribute another
story to the Yellow Book at £35. I have only once, for many years, accepted that sum; viz: in
the case of the tale published in the Y.B. last July. I did so, much against the grain, because
Harland made me an appeal, on your behalf, as I understood him, to do so, for some special

He said he would 'put another attempt through by October 1st' (HJL IV, 18). On
8 September he resolved to tackle a subject he had noted on 26 June, which became
'Glasses', the story he sends here. It appeared in the February Atlantic.

HJ then resumed 'The House Beautiful', which became the novel called The
Old Things *when it first appeared in seven instalments in the* Atlantic *from April*
to October 1896 — Scudder proved flexible — and then as a book, The Spoils of
Poynton, *in February 1897.*

Torquay: Oct 4*th 1895.*

Dear Mr. Scudder.

I am in much humiliation & distress, for though I am sending you something
by this post I am not sending you what will satisfy you. This is not, heaven
knows, for want of time & labour — but because I *can't*, alas, even after renewed
heroic effort, which has made the job the most consuming, in all ways I've
ever tackled, keep within your limits of space. It seems absurd, with a little
twopenny subject, but so it is. I am not able to day to send you the whole of
the little story of which I despatch all but some three thousand words — I can
only send you, to catch this (tomorrow's,) steamer as much as I am able to
get back from the copyist. I have had it all copied once before & then cut into
that as I had cut into my MS.; this is the second copy, & hence the delay: that
is, in addition to *other* intrinsic causes. I will send you the final pages the hour
they come back to me; but the melancholy truth is that they will transcend
your measurement by 2 or 3 thousand words.[1] As I wrote you the other day,
I find, in my old age, that I have too much manner & style, too great &
invincible an instinct of completeness & of seeing things in all their relations,
so that *development*, however squeezed down, becomes inevitable — too much
of all this to be able to turn round in the small corners I used to. I select very
small ideas to help this — but even the very small ideas creep high up into the
teens. This little subject, — of an intense simplicity — was tiny at the start; but
in spite of ferocious compression — it has taken me a month — it has become
what you see. Of course, if it's absolutely too long for you — in spite of it's
high merit! — you will return it: I send it to make some decent — or indecent
— semblance of keeping my promise. But my failure, with such a thing as this,
makes me hopeless about the other two things as to which I have given you

reason, for that occasion only. At all events, my customary fee is more than double that amount.'
(SL2, 294.) He then cited the £87 he received for 'Glasses' from the *Atlantic* and £50 from
Chapman's Magazine of Fiction for the English rights alone of 'The Way It Came'.

1. HJ sent Scudder the rest on 10 October: 'You may say, "Who in the world cares for high
finish?"' (Unpublished Houghton MS, bMS Am 1094.1 (18).)

my assurance. I must candidly & cynically say that, rather than worry over them as I have worried over this, I shall have, if I find that worry inevitable – (& culminating even then in a failure to meet your conditions,) sadly to renounce the attempt. But I will *make* it, once more. Let me say that it would be simply fatal to this little "Glasses" to print it as two instalments – it wouldn't bear that at all; & if that is your alternative please, without hesitating, send it back to me. I am all the sorrier about my interminability, because I am obliged to say, in answer to your inquiry (of Sept. 13*th*) on the subject of *The House Beautiful* that that equally ill-starred fiction is disposed of – yet not even to a magazine. I have contracted with a publisher for a volume of tales which shall, mainly, not already have appeared; & it is settled that the *H.B.* shall form part of it.[2] Thus is engulfed also another thing – *The Awkward Age* – which I started, originally, to meet your invitation, but which it soon became obvious would fatally exceed that measure.[3] I am very sorry, I repeat, for all this, & can only ask you to believe that the fault is not in my not having taken my problem seriously. I hope very much to make the final pages of "Glasses" reach you in time to be used convenien[t]ly in case you do find the thing usable. Believe me yours most truly

Henry James

152. *To Alphonse Daudet*
10 November 1895

Houghton MS   Published HJL IV, 24

34, DE VERE GARDENS. W.
ce 10 Novembre *1895*.

Ah non, par exemple, mon très-cher Daudet – pas le moins du monde *oublieux*: tout au contraire – vivant bien tendrement dans le souvenir & dans l'arrière-goût,

2. On 9 November HJ would tell Scudder he had managed to arrange with Heinemann that 'The House Beautiful' could be serialized in a magazine before book publication; and sent the first 112 pages of it (Unpublished Houghton MS, bMS Am 1094.1 (20)). The volume of tales was presumably *Embarrassments*, published by Heinemann on 12 June 1896, containing 'The Figure in the Carpet', 'Glasses', 'The Next Time' and 'The Way It Came' (later retitled 'The Friends of the Friends').
3. HJ had sketched the idea of *The Awkward Age* on 4 March 1895, and thought of it at first as one of the three tales for Scudder; by 21 December it was in a list of '*sujets de roman*', ideas for full-length novels (N, 146).

et cela d'autant plus que je me sentais plus rivé à mon pieu. Il m'a été, croyez-le bien, je vous en supplie, materiellement impossible, tout l'été, de passer la Manche. C'est une longue et lugubre histoire, que je ne vous infligerai pas, d'obligations accumulées, devant lesquelles j'ai dû baisser la tête & plier le dos. Elles me tiennent encore – très sensiblement – jusqu'à me rendre douteux, pendant bien des semaines à venir, la douce liberté d'aller vous voir.[1] Je suis moins libre, hélas, que je ne vous le parais peutêtre – & je suis certes beaucoup moins infidèle. Non, je suis tout simplement dans une période *d'arrièrages* comme je n'en ai jamais connue. Si vous me trouviez ou me croyiez mal disposé, rien ne manquerait à ma tristesse. Cette tristesse se dissipe à mesure que le travail se solidifie; & aussitôt que le trou sera comblé & le ciel balayé, vous m'entendrez frapper à votre porte. En attendant j'ai plus besoin de patience que vous – c'est à dire de cette égoïste espèce. Je suis depuis quelques jours à peine de retour de la campagne où je suis allé m'enterrer dans les 1ers jours de juillet – pour n'en bouger qu'en rentrant, la semaine passée, dans la brume et la bousculade où je vis trop. J'ai passé presque 4 mois dans le midi de l'Angleterre, au fond de ce charmant Devonshire qui est un peu notre Provence, avec le doux Torquay pour lui servir de Cannes ou de Nice. J'y ai bien travaillé – sans voir presque personne – dans une station d'hiver complètement abandonnée l'été. Le 23 de ce mois je verrai Meredith – & aussi – j'espère – le 24, puisque je passe ces deux jours à la campagne chez sa fille – tout exprès pour me trouver près de lui.[2] Je ne l'ai pas vu depuis le mois de juin & je crains bien que sa surdité ne l'ait complètement englouti. Son nouveau roman – *Le Mariage Ahurissant* – est sur le point de paraître, mais n'aura pas la fabuleuse fortune de la *Trilby* de Du Maurier, dont il s'est vendu dans ce pays & en Amérique, plus de 250 mille exemplaires – avec dessins de l'auteur – à 7 frs. 50. le volume.[3] On vient d'en tirer une pièce, au théâtre du Haymarket,

1. Daudet died at the end of 1897, and HJ did not get to Paris till March 1899.
2. HJ had on 16 May taken the Daudets down to dine with the francophile George Meredith (1828–1909). The author of *The Egoist* (1879) lived at Box Hill, near Dorking in Surrey. From 1885 he was increasingly disabled by a spinal complaint. *The Amazing Marriage*, an extravagant study of female sacrifice set in 1840s Europe, was serialized in *Scribner's Magazine*, January– December 1895; the book was published by Constable.
3. The success of George du Maurier's *Trilby* (1894) preoccupied HJ, partly because du Maurier had offered him the topic in the late 1880s only for HJ to urge him to write it himself. It became 'possibly the bestselling single novel of the century' (LCVF, 634). On 24 February 1895 HJ wrote to the Boston novelist Alice Wellington Rollins (1847–97), who had reported on her charitable activities exploiting the craze: 'the whole phenomenon, the strange *Trilby* madness – the destiny of the book, among you, as a topic – its incredible fortune in the U.S. &c. – & its operation as platform to your beneficent efforts – all reads, from here, where none whatever, of these wonderful consequences have occurred, as a weird story of another planet, the picture of a far-away state of being.' (Unpublished Princeton MS, General MSS.)

& cette pièce s'annonce comme devant durer – "courir" comme nous disons ici – pendant 2 ou 3 ans! Ce que c'est que de "prendre mesure du pied" – comme nous disons encore – du bon gros public anglosaxon! Le rare Meredith n'est pas ce cordonnier-là – ni le pauvre James non plus.

J'ai reçu ce matin des nouvelles du pitoyable Wilde – par la visite d'un homme politique qui dans le dernier gouvernement était membre (je crois même qu'il l'est encore,) de la commission sur la question de la réforme des prisons – & qui a vu le malheureux, il y a quelques semaines, dans un état d'abattement complet, physique & moral – au point qu'on a dû beaucoup relâcher – lui alléger – la discipline & même le mettre à l'infirmerie – où probablement il fera le reste de son temps, dans des conditions relativement aisées.[4] Il ne lui a trouvé (mon ami) aucune faculté résistante ni récupérative. S'il l'avait, seulement, cette faculté, quel chef d'oeuvre il pourrait faire encore! Mais je vous entretiens de trop tristes choses. J'ose à peine vous demander de vos nouvelles & celles de tous les vôtres, puisque c'est vous engager à m'écrire – & que je ne le mérite pas. Des nouvelles de cet "ahurissant" Léon, j'en ai & de remarquables, par le volume de lui que j'ai trouvé sur ma table en rentrant de la campagne, que je suis en train de lire, dont je suis très-frappé, & dont, d'ici à très-peu de jours, je compte écrire le remercier.[5] Rappelez moi, je vous prie, au souvenir très indulgent de Mme Daudet – & croyez moi, mon cher ami, votre très affectueusement dévoué

Henry James

[TRANSLATION: 'Ah no, upon my word, my dearest Daudet – I was not in the slightest way *forgetful*: quite the contrary – dwelling most tenderly in memory and savouring the after-taste, and all the more so, given that I felt myself increasingly riveted to my stake. It was for me, I beg you to believe, physically impossible all summer to cross the Channel. It is a long and lugubrious story, which I won't inflict on you, of accumulated obligations, before which I had simply to get my head down and put my shoulder to the wheel. These obligations retain me still – very palpably – to the point of making me doubt

4. Daudet had met Wilde in 1883. The 'homme politique' is almost certainly Robert Burdon Haldane (1856–1928), Liberal M.P. from 1885 and later Viscount Haldane, who visited the stricken Wilde in Wandsworth Gaol on 12 June, obtained books for him, and advised him that 'misfortune might prove a blessing for his career, for he had got a great subject'. It was Haldane who persuaded the home secretary to transfer him to Reading.
5. No such letter is known to survive. Léon Daudet (1868–1942), eldest son of Alphonse, had divorced Victor Hugo's daughter Jeanne after frequent public quarrels 'for horrors', as HJ told WJ on 1 June, and had published *Les Morticoles* (1894). He was to become a notorious right-wing activist; on the day of *Guy Domville*'s première he was beside Maurice Barrès to watch the 'dégradation' of Captain Dreyfus. 'I don't like Léon,' HJ noted (CWJ II, 362).

whether, for many weeks to come, I shall be able to have the freedom to take the pleasure of coming over to see you. I am less free, alas, than I may perhaps seem to you – and I am certainly much less unfaithful. No, I am simply in a period of *arrears* such as I have never known. If you were to judge me or think me ill-disposed to you, my sadness would indeed be complete. This sadness is being gradually dissipated as my work takes shape; & as soon as the hole is filled in and the sky is clear once again, you will hear me knocking at your door. In the meantime, I have greater need of patience than you have – that is to say, of this egotistical kind. I came back only a few days ago from the country, where I went to bury myself in the first days of July – not leaving it until I returned last week to the fog and the bustle in which I live all too much. I spent nearly 4 months in the South of England, in the depths of the charming Devonshire, which is in some ways our Provence, with delightful Torquay serving as its Cannes or its Nice. I worked well there – and saw virtually no one – in a winter resort which is completely empty in the summer. On the 23rd of this month I will be seeing Meredith – and also – I hope – on the 24th, as I'm to spend those two days in the country at his daughter's house – with the main intention of being near him. I haven't seen him since June & I fear his deafness may have completely swallowed him up. His new novel – *The Amazing Marriage* – is about to appear, but will not have the fabulous success of du Maurier's *Trilby*, of which there have been sold, in this country & in America, more than 250 thousand copies – with drawings by the author – at 7 francs 50 a volume. A play has just been made of it, at the Haymarket theatre, & this play looks as if it is going to last – to 'run' as we say here – for 2 or 3 years! What it is to 'take the measure of the foot' – as we also say – of the good big Anglosaxon public! The exquisite Meredith is not such a cobbler – and neither is the unfortunate James.

This morning I had news of the pitiable Wilde – as a result of a visit from a politician who in the last government was a member (in fact, I think he still is one,) of the commission looking into the question of prison reform – & who saw the unhappy man, a few weeks ago, in a state of complete physical & moral collapse – to the point at which they have had to moderate – to lighten – his régime & even put him in the infirmary – where he will probably serve out the rest of his time, in relatively easy conditions. My friend found in him no capacity for resistance or recuperation. If he only had such a capacity, what a masterpiece he could still write! But I am conversing to you about topics that are too depressing. I hardly dare ask for news of you & your family, since that would commit you to writing to me – & I don't deserve it. News of that 'amazing' Léon I have, & remarkable news it is, by means of the volume by him which on coming back from the country I found on my table, which I am in the process of reading, by which I am very struck, & for which, in a very few days, I mean to write and thank him. Ask Mme Daudet, please, to remember me indulgently – & know that I am, dear friend, your very affectionately devoted / *Henry James*']

153. To Horace Elisha Scudder
3 March 1896

Houghton MS   Unpublished

On 18 December 1895 HJ told Scudder he was 'earnestly finishing' 'The House Beautiful'; but the title had become a problem. 'I think the title of Clarence Cook's book is *an objection to the retention of the "H.B." Therefore I will re-christen the thing on sending you the next copy. I* may *call it "The Great House" – or something better.' (Unpublished Houghton MS, bMS Am 1094.1 (21).)* The House Beautiful *(1878) was by the art critic Clarence Cook (1828–1900). HJ subsequently wired that* The Old Things *would be a better title. By this point HJ's story – which we know as* The Spoils of Poynton – *had greatly expanded.*

March 3d 1896.
34, DE VERE GARDENS. W.

Dear Mr. Scudder.

My XIV goes to you to-day & my XV on the 7*th*. Two more will go next week – & that will be I *hope*, within *one* chapter of the end. However, I will say one or *two*, to be sure. You catch me, as you have done before, in the act of finding my problem irreducible to *all* the brevity that my optimism has originally deluded itself into a belief in. My subject always refuses, I find, to be scraped down beyond a certain point – stiffens & hardens itself like iron. In this particular thing the very simplicity of my action forces me, I feel, to get everything out of it that it *can* give – as the real way, & the best way, to be interesting: if I *am* interesting – which I hope. However, I am close to port, & a spurt on the oars will bring me. There will, in other words be 18 or 19 chapters if I don't throw in a 20*th* to make the round number.[1]

Yours
Henry James

1. On 21 May 1896 HJ would write to Scudder that he had bundled off the final pages of the work the day before, and that symmetry had demanded a twenty-second chapter (Unpublished

154. To Sidney Colvin
[April–May 1896]

Yale MS   Unpublished

Stevenson's literary remains continued to be posthumously published. Reviewing Colvin's collection of Stevenson letters in 1900, HJ would write: 'There is no absolute privacy – save of course when the exposed subject may have wished or endeavoured positively to constitute it; and things too sacred are often only things that are not perhaps at all otherwise superlative . . . Stevenson never covered his tracks, and the tracks prove perhaps to be what most attaches us.' (LC I, 1257–8.)

This letter probably refers to Colvin's 'Editorial Note' to Weir of Hermiston, *which was published on 20 May 1896. Colvin's 'Note', acceding to the wishes, he says, of readers, editors and publishers, recounts Stevenson's projected ending 'so far as it was known at the time of the writer's death to his step-daughter and devoted amanuensis, Mrs. Strong'. It also cites many of his letters in a detailed discussion of his sources and intentions.*

34, DE VERE GARDENS. W.
Wednesday

My dear Colvin.

I don't see that in this admirable Epilogue, there is a line to alter – either by subtraction or addition. You have said what you *had* to, & said it with great tact. It is curious & it will "help" the book; but I'm not sure I don't regret the obligation – which, at the same time (for Mrs. Fanny, &c,) I fully recognise. I have a little pain at seeing a great man so *emptied* – so pursued to his innermost lair; the *sac* so *vidé*, the mystery, the backshop, the personal – i.e. the intellectual – loneliness of the artist so invaded as the hungry booksellers & newspapers insist more & more on its being. But one is face to face with a public that gobbles as well as bullies – & it's all difficult, & nothing could be more considerate & adroit than your hand. I hope all the rest of you – other & baser organs & members, more matches it – in perfection. Vale.

Ever yours
Henry James

Houghton MS, bMS Am 1094.1 (25)). In February 1897 Heinemann published the book in Britain and Houghton, Mifflin in America.

155. To John St Loe Strachey
6 May [1896]

King's MS   Unpublished

HJ left London on 1 May; he told John Hay that 'I have taken a hovel for the summer down in Sussex' (HJJH, 114). Point Hill, which he rented for three months from the architect Reginald Blomfield, was a hilltop bungalow, and HJ bicycled in the country around. At the end of May HJ wrote to WJ he had been till very recently in 'a fearful funk about some overdue "serial" work (for the Illust: London News – beginning July 4th, but à peine started in MS.)' (CWJ II, 399). This was The Other House – *placed in an unusually popular paper through the intervention of Lucy Clifford – which he had to start before he had (on 20 May) finished sending off* The Old Things.

   John St Loe Strachey (1860–1927), cousin of the more famous Giles Lytton Strachey (1880–1932), was at this time editor of the Cornhill Magazine *(he became proprietor and editor of* The Spectator, *1898–1925).*

Point Hill Playden. *Rye*. Sussex.
May 6*th*

My dear St. Lo Strachey.

   Many thanks for your note. I would say without reserve that I shall be very glad to give you a short story for the *Cornhill* were it not for a couple of little considerations that have to be taken into account. The first of these is that I shouldn't be able to do it immediately; – the second is that I fear I shouldn't be able quite to meet your conditions of space. Even 15 of your pages make less than 7000 words – & I find myself in my old age unable to turn round or to do anything interesting in so small a compass. As one grows older one's manner inevitably becomes more complicated – one's reach, or embrace, ampler; & the form (of brevity) you mention grows therefore a terrifically difficult & expensive process (unsuccessful even then,) of working on the *done* thing – re-boiling-down, re-elimination, in which the subject (*my* subject at least,) perishes. I have too much to say about it – *see* too much *in* it. I can't treat *any* worth treating at all in less than *10,000* words. That is the length of the thing in the May *Chapman*. Oswald Crawfurd told me his average was from 5000 to 7000; but that for *me* (!) ten thousand would be all right.[1] In *that*

   1. Oswald John Frederick Crawfurd (1834–1909), who wrote as 'John Dangerfield', had been British consul at Oporto, 1866–90 (HJ had in 1875 reviewed his *Travels in Portugal*), but was

space I will write you something with pleasure addressed to a public "not very intelligent" (inspiring thought!) – as soon as I have time: si le coeur vous en dit.[2] I am just for the present very busy. It would have to be 2 or 3 months hence – that I should do it.[3] All thanks for the "London" suggestion. I'm afraid my day is past for that. I can only write romantically, aesthetically – & with the dear old place I am now too wearily (& affectionately) *familiar*. I can't pump up a freshness! I am down here – peacefully – for all the Season. Believe me yours ever

Henry James

156. To Edmund Gosse
[8 November 1896]

Leeds MS   Published SLHJEG, 152

The Old Things *had not finished its run in the* Atlantic *(to October 1896) when HJ's other serial,* The Other House, *finished in the weekly* Illustrated London News *on 26 September. The Other House was published as a book on 1 October, and (as* The Spoils of Poynton*)* The Old Things *had to wait till February 1897 (both were from Heinemann). At the end of July HJ had to vacate Point Hill, but – 'this little corner of the land endears itself to me', he told WJ (CWJ II, 405) – took the Vicarage in Rye for two more months, returning to town only at the end of September. By mid September he was launched on* What Maisie Knew. *At the end of September he told WJ of the particular success of* The Other House: *'If that's what the idiots want, I can give them their bellyful.' (CWJ II, 416.)*

Walter Pater had died at fifty-five, from a weak heart, on 30 July 1894. HJ had responded in December 1894 to a memorial essay by Gosse: 'Well, faint, pale, embarrassed, exquisite Pater! He reminds me, in the disturbed midnight of our actual literature, of one of those lucent matchboxes which you place, on going to

now editor of *Chapman's Magazine of Fiction*, published by Chapman & Hall, of which he was a director. He was one of the lovers of Violet Hunt. HJ's story in the May issue of the magazine was 'The Way It Came', which he had written in January.

2. Nothing came of this discussion while Strachey was at the *Cornhill*. 'Miss Gunton of Poughkeepsie' (about 5,000 words) appeared in the *Cornhill* in May 1900 for £13 13s.; and 'The Two Faces' (about 7,600 words) in June 1901 for probably a little more.

3. HJ was busy with *The Other House*, turning it into a novel for the *Illustrated London News* from the scenario of a play intended for Compton (entitled *The Promise*, and first conceived at Christmas 1893).

bed, near the candle, to show you, in the darkness, where you can strike a light:
he shines in the uneasy gloom – vaguely, and has a phosphorescence, not a flame.'
(SLHJEG, 120.) Pater's Gaston de Latour: An Unfinished Romance, *set in*
sixteenth-century France, was to have been the second part of a trilogy beginning
with Marius the Epicurean *(1885).*

34, De Vere Gardens, W.

My dear Gosse.

All thanks for the little grey, pretty Pater, of which I have tasted fully the
faint, feeble sweetness. Of course it's casual work, but it gives one that odd,
peculiar sense that reading him always gives – that kind of little illusion that
some refined, pathetic object or presence is *in the room* with you – materially
– & stays there while you read. He has too little point, & a kind of wilful
weakness; but he's divinely uncommon. I went, by the way, yesterday to see
his sisters, my neighbours; & found them in a state of subdued flourish &
chaste symmetry which I hope means all manner of solid comfort.[1] But why
do I speak of the chaste, the weak & the feminine while I am still prostrate
beneath the impression of *Rudyard's* supreme deviltry?[2] As Du Maurier once
said in a note, "The little beast is Titanic."[3] The talent, the art, the hellish
cunning of this last volume (& all exercised in its amazing limitations, which
only makes the phenomenon more rare,) have *quite* bowed me down with
admiration. I ween they have you too. We must talk of him soon. And Norris
– strange collocation! – will tell us of him.[4] Ever your

Henry James

Sunday p.m.

---

1. After 1885 Pater had divided his time between Brasenose, his Oxford college, and his sisters'
house in London.
2. Kipling's most recent volume, *The Seven Seas*, a collection of verse, came out in October
1896. On 5 November HJ had written to his invalid friend Jonathan Sturges (1864–1911): 'I
am laid low by the absolutely uncanny talent – the prodigious special faculty of it. It's all *violent*,
without a dream of a *nuance* or a hint of "distinction"; all prose trumpets and castanets and
such – with never a touch of the fiddle-string or a note of the nightingale. But it's magnificent
and masterly in its way, and full of the most insidious art.' (HJL IV, 40.)
3. Du Maurier had died in October.
4. W. E. Norris knew Kipling.

157. To Henry Craik
30 May 1897

Virginia TS   Unpublished

What Maisie Knew was serialized in the American Chap-Book *from 15 January to 1 May 1897, and the British* New Review *from February to September.*

In February HJ's trouble with his rheumatic wrist forced him to take on a shorthand stenographer, William MacAlpine, for some letters as well as professional work (he had discussed the pros and cons of dictation with Mrs Humphry Ward as early as 1887). He abandoned a plan to spend three months in Italy: on 7 June he told his old Boston friend Fanny Morse that 'the click of the typewriter' now occupied in his life 'a place too big to be left vacant for long periods of hotel and railway life' (HJL IV, 47).

The volume 'of Elegant Extracts' to which HJ refers in the following letter is most probably English Prose Selections, *vol. V (1896), edited by Henry Craik (1846–1927), which includes passages, introduced by Craik himself, from Benjamin Disraeli (1804–81), novelist, political thinker and twice Conservative prime minister. Craik, son of a Glasgow clergyman, and later knighted, was a civil servant and Conservative politician concerned with education, as well as a man of letters.*

HJ was closer to Liberal prime ministers – Gladstone, Rosebery and Asquith – than to Conservatives. Here he amplifies his 1870 verdict on Disraeli's Lothair, *that 'Power enough there has been to arouse in [the reader's] mind the feeling of attention, but not enough to awaken a single genuine impulse of satisfaction' (LC I, 859). In 1880 Disraeli's novel* Endymion *'almost fatally disgusted me with the literary form to which it pretends to belong'.*

34, DE VERE GARDENS, W.
30th May, 1897

Dear Mr. Craik,

I have shamefully delayed to acknowledge your kindness in sending me the volume of Elegant Extracts – the genial sequel to our talk after Barrie's dinner.[1] Let this vulgar machinery, please, explain and attenuate my omission. I am reduced by infirmity to dictating altogether, and to using only at rare scraps of time such facilities as this leaves me for keeping abreast of a demoralised

---

1. Sir James Matthew Barrie (1860–1937), born in Scotland, started as a novelist before becoming a playwright in 1891, the same year as HJ. His greatest success was *Peter Pan* (1904).

correspondence. But I have read over the Beaconsfield morsels – with I won't pretend to say *all* the softening of the heart that I should like to be able to exhibit to you. Don't think me either stupid or perverse if I say that I don't find the sort of thing that, when I do find it, strikes me as *great* distinction in the specimens attached to your persuasive Notice. On the other hand, I don't deny that distinction of a sort there is; only it isn't to me of that clarified and final kind, hasn't that happy intensity and sincerity, that makes a literary thing stick to the mind – abide with it and feed it and amuse it. But there are doubtless sympathies in these matters, and humours and moods, congruities and affinities of taste. I am so fond of the thing its very self – I mean the Literary Thing – that I confess to a perhaps unsocial offishness from those who have mixed it up with other forms and tried to carry it off by their aid. This mistrust I particularly have of the admixture of politics, which drag with them so much – at any rate to my possibly too contracted vision – that is inferior in sincerity, in logic, in expression, and above all in beauty. But I am returning you – I mean I look as if I were doing so – a volume for your volume. Don't mind me; I am a mass of benighted artistic passion. Let me thank you also for giving me the chance to dip into a lot of other refreshers of memory and of taste. The solid volume is a deep sea of good reading. Believe me, dear Mr. Craik, yours most truly,

Henry James

158. To William Blackwood
15 October 1897

Scotland MS   Unpublished

At the end of June HJ went to Bournemouth and stayed till about 25 July, working and cycling with his typist MacAlpine. After two days of jury service and a visit to the Godkins in Surrey, on 6 August he went to Dunwich on the Suffolk coast and stayed near Minny Temple's younger sister Ellen Temple (1850–1920). He remained in the area till a week into September. On his return to London he found that the lease of Lamb House, Rye – he had first admired it in a painting by his architect friend Edward Warren (1856–1937) – was available for £70 a year. He signed, on 25 September, with Warren's advice and support, taking it for twenty-one years.

William Wetmore Story had died in October 1895; HJ wrote to Francis Boott of having seen him in Rome sixteen months before – 'the ghost, only, of his old clownship – very silent and vague and gentle' (HJL IV, 24). His son Thomas Waldo Story (1855–1915) and his son's wife Maud Broadwood Story (c.1860–1932) (from

whom Waldo separated in 1898 and whom he later divorced) asked HJ to write his
biography. In June 1896, busy with other work, HJ offered to withdraw, and again
in June 1897, but the Storys held firm. In October 1897 they were staying in London,
at the Savoy.

Oct: 15th 1897.
34, DE VERE GARDENS, W.
W*m* Blackwood Esq.

My dear Sir.

Mr. & Mrs. Waldo Story approached me some time ago on the question of
my undertaking some literary memorial of the late Mr. W. W. Story; but the
matter made for a year or two – I mean the matter of my entertaining the idea
– through various obstacles & complications – very little progress. It appears,
however, to be so strongly their wish that, in a conversation with them a
fortnight ago, I told them that I *should* be disposed to attempt a biographical
volume, for which materials seem to be considerably abundant & interesting
– *subject* to the results of two or three inquiries that I shld. like to address to
yourself – as I have gathered from them that you have expressed your desire
to publish some such record.

The statement most urgent for me to make in relation to the question is
that my time is too valuable, much, for me to write Mr. Story's Life, even on
the restricted scale on which alone I shld. be willing to proceed, as a mere
friendly & unremunerated task. I shld. be able to do it only at a sacrifice of
time – & yet the "business" side of the affair is one that I find it awkward to
break ground on with his children. Let me add moreover, that, as I have very
distinctly stated to them, I shld. not be able – I do not now see my way to this
– to promise to perform within a fixed limit of time. I shld. be able to do
nothing for several months; nothing before next summer.[1] Lastly, I should not
desire to consider the matter as more than a one-volume book. There appears
to me to be material for one very charming & interesting volume, but not for
more; & that a volume of medium size. This indeed, I think, is quite the view
of the family.

May I, at your convenience, hear from you directly on the matter?

It would be possible for me to do the book only for a definite *fee* on its
completion – which shld. exhaust my interest in it.[2]

1. From September till late November 1897 HJ dictated to MacAlpine 'The Turn of the Screw';
which was published in the New York *Collier's Weekly* from 27 January to 2 April 1898.
2. HJ wrote to Blackwood again on 23 October 1897 that 'A fee of £250 for all rights up to a
sale of 7000 – & then £100 for each additional 2000 – is the sum that, on the production of a

And I shld. have to be quite free as to time & form: though of course perfectly conscious of the undesirableness of undue delay.

Believe me, my dear Sir, yours very truly

Henry James

159. *To Arthur Christopher Benson*
11 March 1898

Bodleian MS   Published LHJ I, 278–80

In November 1897, through another intervention by Howells after his meeting with an anxious HJ in London at the end of October, Henry Loomis Nelson (1846–1908), editor of Harper's Weekly, *1894–8, proposed to HJ to serialize a novel –* The Awkward Age *– in the magazine. It would in the event run from 1 October 1898 to 7 January 1899. HJ told Howells of his relief and gratitude: 'I felt myself, somehow perishing in my pride or rotting ungathered, like an old maid against the wall & on her lonely bench.' (LFL, 304.)*

Arthur Benson (1862–1925), who had met HJ in 1884 through Frederic Myers, wrote a good deal as well as being a successful master and housemaster at Eton till 1903; he became a Fellow of Magdalene College, Cambridge, in 1904 and its Master in 1915.

March 11*th* *1898.*
34, DE VERE GARDENS, W.

My dear Arthur.

I suppose that in the mysterious scheme of providence & fate such an inspiration as your charming note – out of the blue! – of a couple of days ago, is intended somehow to make up to me for the terror with which my earlier – in fact *all* my past – productions inspire me, & for the insurmountable aversion I feel to looking at them again or to considering them in any way. This morbid state of mind is really a blessing in disguise – for it has for happy consequence that such an incident as your letter becomes thereby extravagantly pleasant and gives me a genial glow. All thanks & benedictions – I shake your hand very hard – or *would* do so if I could attribute to you anything so palpable,

---

volume on W. W. Story, I have in mind. I mean it, of course, to cover all American & colonial as well as British rights.' (Unpublished Scotland MS, 30690.) On 28 October HJ acknowledged Blackwood's acceptance of his terms (HJL IV, 59).

personal & actual *as* a hand. Yet I shall never write a sequel to the *P. of an L.* – admire my euphonic indefinite article.[1] It's all too faint & far away – too ghostly & ghastly – & I have bloodier things *en tête*. I can do better than that!

But à propos precisely, of the ghostly & ghastly I have a little confession to make to you that has been on my conscience these three months & that I hope will excite in your generous breast nothing but tender memories & friendly sympathies. On one of those 2 memorable – never to be obliterated – winter nights that I spent at the sweet Addington, your Father, in the drawingroom by the fire, where we were talking a little, in the spirit of recreation, of such things, repeated to me the few meagre elements of a small & gruesome spectral story that had been told *him* years before & that he could only give the dimmest account of – partly because he had forgotten details & partly – & much more – because there had *been* no details & no coherency in the tale as he received it – from a person who also but ½ knew it.[2] The vaguest essence only was there – some dead servants & some children. This essence *struck* me & I made a note of it (of a most scrappy kind) on going home. There the note remained till this autumn, when, struck with it afresh, I wrought it into a fantastic fiction which, 1*st* intended to be of the briefest, finally became a thing of some length & is now being "serialised" in an American periodical. It will appear late in the spring (chez Heinemann) in a vol. with *one* other story, & then I will send it to you.[3] In the meanwhile please think of the *doing* of the thing on my part as having sprung from that kind old evening at Addington – quite gruesomely hideous as my unbridled imagination caused me to see the inevitable development of the subject. It was all worth mentioning to you.

I am very busy & very decently fit & very much yours always, my dear Arthur,

Henry James

---

1. *The Portrait of a Lady* (1881).
2. To Gosse HJ wrote on 12 October 1898: 'To think of the good old Addington Archbishop (by a vague fragment of a tale he ineffectually tried to tell me) having given me the germ of anything so odious & hideous!' (SLHJEG, 164.)
3. 'The Turn of the Screw' appeared in *Collier's Weekly* (27 January to 2 April). In fact *The Two Magics*, pairing it with 'Covering End', only appeared in October 1898.

160. To Mrs John Chandler Bancroft
21 March 1898

Yale TS (Koch Collection)   Unpublished

*HJ knew John Bancroft (1835–1901), European-trained artist son of the eminent
American historian George Bancroft (1800–91), from Newport. Bancroft became a
good friend after 1862, when HJ took meals with him and WJ at Miss Upham's
Harvard boarding-house (as recalled in ch. x of* Notes of a Son and Brother*).
John Bancroft already knew, from Dusseldorf, George du Maurier, whose widow
is mentioned here. Mrs Bancroft (d. 1906), who visited London in the summer of
1897, was the sister of George Abbott James, HJ's old Boston friend from Harvard
Law School. In June 1897 HJ wrote to another old Boston friend, Fanny Morse,
that 'Mrs. J. B. I have liked from ancient days' (HJL IV, 46). What Maisie
Knew had come out as a book in October 1897 from Heinemann in London and
Herbert S. Stone in Chicago.*

34, DE VERE GARDENS, W.
21st March, 1898.

Dear Mrs. Bancroft,

Forgive this brutal way of acknowledging a sympathy expressed by yourself
in a manner so much more personal. But it is my inexorable fate to have, now,
to dictate almost altogether; for whenever I intermit it and return to the use
of my hand, which I moreover hate, I pay for it, collapse again and have to
fall back on Remington. The sight of *your* hand hooks on to the remembrance
of the autumn afternoons and the snug little corner on the edge of Piccadilly.
If you were still in that snug little corner and I on the other side of the fire,
perhaps I should be able to make you believe a little how very much I don't
know of what Maisie "became". I'm afraid I told all I *can* tell – for the money!
Send me another five dollars. Seriously, the case seems to me to illustrate the
marked difference between that which is in old-fashioned parlance a "story"
and that which has the distinctive characteristics of what *I* call a Subject. The
story, in the old-fashioned sense, isn't, I dare say, told – told to the end that
is, – in the book. But what the end – *where* the end, in that sort of thing, ever
is, I feel that I can never say: the place, the point, the limit seem to me so
arbitrary. Whereas, as regards the Subject of the poor little wretch, somehow
– isn't it so? – *that* is treated. There would doubtless be another Subject later
– but my mind, as yet, refuses to tackle it; for the reason, after all, I think,
that it can only be essentially less interesting. The situation certainly didn't

stay where I left it – the edifying step-parents didn't probably, for very long, make a very good thing of it together. Sir Claude and the lone infant bumped again against each other – and heaven only knows what *may* have occurred. Only, whatever it was, the best of it, for Art – forgive the vulgar expression – was over. The best of it was in other words all the *worst* of it – it must have been, though still doubtless curious and queer, less interesting after-wards. The subject was girl's childhood – it was the fact of that that was the whole note of the situation; and my climax, arrived at, was marked *by*, and consisted *of*, the stroke of the hour of the end of that childhood. Voilà. I'm afraid I haven't told you much – but all thanks for the interest expressed in your inquiry.

The quiet grey soft winter on the threshold of which you left me opened out – or perhaps I should say closed in – on quite that same mild and manageable key. Nothing particular, thank heaven, has happened to me; I've only been busy and decently well and decently humdrum. I stick to London till some time in May – then I leave it for six months. I don't think I've been up to tea and buttered buns in those uncanny topmost saloons of the Grosvenor Club since you and Miss Hester so soothed my nerves there.[1] I have taken great, though too infrequent, pleasure in G. T. Lapsley, whom you made known to me, and for whom I have conceived a lively affection – which he must have thought I have desperately concealed.[2] He dined with me the other night, however, and I took him to the play – only to learn, by the same stroke, that he is too soon departing. I have seen Mrs. Beaumont a couple of times – the soft white wreck that I find her somehow fearfully saddens me.[3] But all the same, in the teeth of it, I am going to see her – on a promise I but the other day made her – this very week if possible. George has written me of the engagement of his boy – which has, for me, at this distance, not knowing the

1. On 2 February 1906 HJ wrote to Mrs Yates Thompson that he 'came up to poor Mrs. Bancroft's meagre obsequies – & felt indeed again within the zone of the uncanny Hester's blighting influence. What a strange little pathetic struggle in its awkwardness & *vainness*, Mrs. Bancroft's efforts to *place* herself – having no possible place apparently anywhere (& least of all in her daughter's life) except where she has now found it!' (Unpublished Yale MS, uncatalogued material (gift of Mrs Donald G. Wing), ZA MS 262 920617–bl.)
2. The American Gaillard Thomas Lapsley (1871–1949), also a friend of Edgar Fawcett, Isabella Stewart Gardner and Edith Wharton, was a medieval historian who taught at Stanford, then at Cambridge University. HJ called him to Mrs Gardner 'a gallant, delightful, quite heroic being' (CC, 232; 20 April 1914). The play, to which HJ and Lapsley went on 12 March, was *Julius Caesar* at Her Majesty's Theatre, produced by and starring Herbert Beerbohm Tree.
3. In June 1897 HJ had met Mrs Bancroft and her daughter at Mary Beaumont's in London. He saw Mrs Beaumont 'with pain, or at least with pity', because of her illness, and because her past great beauty survived only in traces. But 'otherwise I judge her blissful, and she told me her husband is about to become an admiral' (HJL IV, 46).

boy and powerless to focus the maiden, only a somewhat legendary and mythical, or pictorial apprehensibility.[4] The only criticism my imagination makes of it is the general one that I always rather deprecate the marriage of two Bostonians! I always think that such a one should marry a Louisianian, or a native of San Antonio, Texas; just as I infallibly think that a Texan should marry a Bostonian. But when Lathrops and Lodges get at it together – well, one can't finish one's sentence! But I'm delighted at whatever rose-tint the event may suffuse withal the existence of your brother and his wife.

How jolly for John Bancroft to have gone and got so beautifully lacquered over in brown and gold – a delightful refreshment to your sense in manipulating him! I am decidedly too far away. I should like immensely to talk with him and to see his belles choses – if they *have* got out of the custom-house. The less I travel – and I have quite given it up – the more I want my friends to; though what's the use, after all, in cases when one gets so little good? Give my love to him, please, and the extremity of my envy.

I see dear Mrs. du Maurier now and again – whom her situation makes only more gentle and loveable. She has just, to my regret, taken the rather comfortless step of giving up her pleasant house, which she finds big and expensive, and preparing to squeeze into a flat near to her daughter May – which latter, I am sorry to say, though but a year married, and very happily so, seems to be somewhat invalidically constituted. Did I tell you, in the autumn, that I have taken a little old house in the country for a longish stretch, so that when I do get out of town I shall have a fixed habitation? I am at present, however, only in the grubbing and sparsely-furnishing stage, and my fruition is all to come. But these are old experiences to you, who sit under your palms in your isle of the blest and smile at clumsy navigators as they flounder among the reefs.

Goodbye again. I hope Miss Hester has had a happy winter's work, I recall those watercolours with much applause. Yours and hers and everyone's very constantly,

Henry James.

4. George Abbott James, Mrs Bancroft's brother, had in 1864 married Elizabeth Cabot Lodge, whose brother Henry (1850–1924) became Senior Senator for Massachusetts. The 'Lathrops' below may refer to the family of George Parsons Lathrop (1851–98), whom HJ disliked, son-in-law of Nathaniel Hawthorne through his marriage to Hawthorne's daughter Rose (1851–1926), and the author of *A Study of Hawthorne* (1876), which James used for his own *Hawthorne* (1879).

161. To Mary (Mrs Humphry) Ward
24 May 1898

Virginia MS   Unpublished

At this time HJ was working on The Awkward Age *– 'the whole "job" . . .*
wonderfully amusing and delightfully difficult from the first' as he recalled in the
Preface. He was also expensively preparing Lamb House for occupation at the end
of June (Edward Warren helped with the house, Lady Wolseley with the furniture).
Also, HJ had signed up with a new literary agent, James Brand Pinker (1863–
1922), formerly an editor at Pearson's Magazine, *by 7 May 1898, when he sent*
him a story, 'The Given Case', for 'placing' with a magazine (it appeared in
Collier's Weekly *in December 1898). On 20 April HJ told WJ that 'this year, &*
next, thank heaven, my income will have been much larger than for any year of
my existence' (CWJ III, 30).

In Helbeck of Bannisdale *(1898), often ranked as her highest achievement, Mrs*
Ward deals with a love tragically thwarted by doctrinal differences. Her religiously
sceptical heroine, Laura Fountain, comes to Bannisdale in the Lake District and falls
passionately but impossibly in love with her Catholic ascetic step-uncle, Alan Helbeck.
The anxious Mrs Ward, who on 3 May told her husband 'Sometimes I have dreadful
nightmares and depression about the book' (MHW, 157), had the proof-sheets of her
work sent to HJ for comment before its publication on 10 June.

34, DE VERE GARDENS, W.
May 24*th 1898*

Dear Mrs. Ward.

I don't know what horrors I may have inspired you to think of me by
waiting so long to acknowledge the advent of *Helbeck* – to give you some sign
of my having read the beautiful book. But I *do* give you that sign as soon as
I have laid down the precious sheets – I was able to enter into possession but
two days since & finished them but two or three hours ago. (They are already
in Mrs. Green's hands.)[1] They arrived at a moment when I was so inexorably
occupied that I couldn't for days & days give them the unreserved attention
which alone I desired for them – & for which no "dipping" could be a
substitute. So I just had to wait & seem unmannerly. I have suffered – to
myself – thereby. But here I am, safe & sound. I have been full to the brim

1. This is probably Alice Stopford Green (1847–1929), Irish widow of one of Mrs Ward's
patrons, the English historian John Richard Green (1837–83).

of interest & admiration – & that you shld. take hold to that extent of a reader with so abnormally little theological imagination & theological curiosity is, I think, by itself (even allowing for sensibilities of said reader in other directions,) a proof of great power. The whole thing is done in a way to make the book run an immense chance of being pronounced the finest of the lot – with all the splendid profit of its big subject – *secured* & gripped by the beauty of the personal drama that presents the case. I am too special & too technical a reader, I feel – I *do*, myself, if I can read a novel at all, the subject over (as I go) as *I* see it artistically conditioned; & there are things that, from this point of view, I said to myself, which are probably of no value to any one *but* myself – as for instance in regard to the greater intensity the picture would have got by getting an *exclusive* unity, as it were, from the consciousness of the girl – presenting only, that is, *her* vision & 'going behind' nothing & no one else, least of all Helbeck. But that is probably mere aesthetic superstition, & few persons, certainly, in the millions who will read you will miss any possible intensity whatever. No more, really, have I – I remained under the completest charm & coercion, full of the sense of the wealth you have brought to your subject. The fine, free, high way you walk round & over the big question, Laura's question, does you the greatest intellectual honour. And as a 'love-story,' heaven help it, the thing is rarely beautiful & noble – apart from the other complexity of the situation. This is all I can write tonight – but I shall come in & see you, unless insuperably prevented, on Thursday. Yours dear Mrs. Ward, more than ever

Henry James

162. To Paul Bourget
19 August 1898

Unknown TS   Published LHJ I, 286–90

HJ moved into Lamb House late in June 1898 and there completed In the Cage, *a short novel. It was published in August 1898 by Duckworth in London, without prior magazine use, and in September Stone of Chicago followed suit. On 1 October* The Awkward Age *began to appear in* Harper's Weekly.

The Bourgets had cut short an English visit, on the advice of Dr William Bezly Thorne, a heart specialist and author of The Treatment of Chronic Diseases of the Heart by Baths and Exercises According to the Method of the Doctors A. and T. Schott *(1894). Thorne sent them to Nauheim, a German spa, for Minnie Bourget's heart.*

Dictated.
Lamb House, Rye.
19th August, 1898.

Mon cher Ami,

I have hideously delayed to acknowledge your so interesting letter from Paris, and now the manner of my response does little to repair the missing grace of my silence. I trust, however, to your general confidence not to exact of me the detail of the reasons why I am more and more *asservi* to this benevolent legibility, which I so delight in on the part of others that I find it difficult to understand their occasional resentment of the same on my own – a resentment that I know indeed, from generous licence already given, you do not share. I have promised myself each day to attack you pen in hand, but the overpowering heat which, I grieve to say, has reigned even on my balmy hilltop, has, by really sickening me, taken the colour out of all my Gallo-latin, leaving very blanched as well the paler idiom in which I at last perforce address you.

I have been entering much more than my silly silence represents into the sequel of your return to London, and not less into the sequel of *that*. Please believe in my affectionate participation as regards the Bezly Thorne consultation and whatever emotion it may have excited in either of you. To that emotion I hope the healing waters have already applied the most cooling, soothing, softening douche – or administered a not less beneficent draught if the enjoyment of them has had in fact to be more inward. I congratulate you on the decision you so speedily took and, with your usual Napoleonic celerity when the surface of the globe is in question, so energetically acted upon. I trust you are, in short, really settled for a while among rustling German woods and plashing German waters. (Those are really, for the most part, my own main impressions of Germany – the memory of ancient summers there at more or less bosky Bäder, or other Kur-orten, involving a great deal of open air strolling in the shade and sitting under trees.) This particular dose of Deutschland will, I feel, really have been more favourable to you than your having had to swallow the Teuton-element in the form of the cookery, or of any other of the manifold attributes, of the robust fausse anglaise whom I here so confoundingly revealed to you. Let it console you also a little that you would have had to bear, as well, with that burden, a temperature that the particular conditions of the house I showed you would not have done much to minimise. I have been grilled, but I have borne it better for not feeling that I had put you also on the stove. Rye goes on baking, this amazing summer, but, though I suppose the heat is everywhere, you have a more refreshing regimen. I pray for the happiest and most marked results from it.

I have received the *Duchesse Bleue*, and also the Land of Cockaigne from Madame Paul, whom I thank very kindly for her inscription.[1] I had just read the Duchess, but haven't yet had leisure to attack the great Matilda. The Duchess inspires me with lively admiration – so close and firm, and with an interest so nourished straight from the core of the subject, you have succeeded in keeping her. I never read you sans vouloir me colleter with you on what I can't help feeling to be the detrimentary parti-pris (unless it be wholly involuntary) of some of your narrative, and other technical, processes. These questions of art and form, as well as of much else, interest me deeply – really much more than any other; and so, not less, do they interest you: yet, though they frequently come up between us, as it were, when I read you, I nowadays never seem to see you long enough at once to thresh them comfortably out with you. Moreover, after all, what does threshing-out avail? – that conviction is doubtless at the bottom of my disposition, half the time, to let discussion go. Each of us, from the moment we are worth our salt, writes as he can and only as he can, and his writing at all is conditioned upon the very things that from the standpoint of another method most lend themselves to criticism. And we each know much better than anyone else can what the defect of our inevitable form may appear. So, though it does strike me that your excess of anticipatory analysis undermines too often the reader's curiosity – which is a gross, loose way of expressing one of the things I mean – so, probably, I really understand better than anyone except yourself why, to do the thing at all, you must use your own, and nobody's else, trick of presentation. No two men in the world have the same idea, image and measure of presentation. All the same, I must some day read one of your books with you, so interesting would it be to me – if not to *you*! – to put, from page to page and chapter to chapter, your finger on certain places, showing you just where and why (selon moi!) you are too prophetic, too exposedly constructive, too disposed yourself to swim in the thick reflective element in which you set your figures afloat. All this is a clumsy notation of what I mean, and, on the whole, mal àpropos into the bargain, inasmuch as I

1. *La Duchesse bleue: récit d'un peintre* (1898) by Paul Bourget, dedicated to Matilde Serao, deals with the psychology of the artist through a study of the relations between a manipulative, womanizing playwright, Jacques Molan, his painter friend (the book's narrator) Vincent La Croix, and the actress Camille Favier, who is Molan's mistress and plays the Blue Duchess in Molan's play but whom Vincent loves (and paints). Camille's rival for Molan is a ruthless society woman, Mme de Bonnivet. *Paese di Cuccagna* (1890) is by the Italian novelist Matilde Serao (1856–1927) (whom HJ had met in Rome in 1894 and called 'a wonderful little burly Balzac in petticoats' (HJL III, 474), and about whom he wrote in 1901). A realist novel focusing on the obsession with gambling in Neapolitan life, it was translated into French by Madame Bourget, whom HJ called to Baldwin on 29 June 1892 'a polyglot (½ Belgian ½ Greek & all French)' (Unpublished Morgan MS, Baldwin Collection).

find in the Duchess plenty of the art I most like and the realisation of an admirable subject. Beautifully done the whole episode of the actress's intervention in the rue Nouvelle, in which I noted no end of superior touches. I doubt if any of your readers lose less than I do – to the fiftieth part of an intention. All this part of the book seems to me thoroughly handled – except that, I think, I should have given Molan a different behaviour after he gets into the cab with the girl – not have made him act so *immediately* "in character." He takes there no line – I mean no deeper one – which is what I think he would have done.[2] In fact I think I see, myself, positively what he would have done; and in general he is, to my imagination, as you give him, too much in character, too little mysterious. So is Mme. de Bonnivet – so too, even, is the actress. Your love of intellectual daylight, absolutely your pursuit of complexities, is an injury to the patches of ambiguity and the abysses of shadow which really are the clothing – or much of it – of the *effects* that constitute the material of our trade. Basta!

I ordered my year-old "Maisie" the other day to be sent to you, and I trust she will by this time have safely arrived – in spite of some ambiguity in the literation of the name of your villa as, with your letter in my hand, I earnestly meditate upon it. I have also despatched to Madame Paul myself a little volume just published – a poor little pot-boiling study of nothing at all, qui ne tire pas à conséquence.[3] It is but a monument to my fatal technical passion, which prevents my ever giving up anything I have begun. So that when something that I have supposed to be a subject turns out on trial really to be none, je m'y acharne d'autant plus, for mere superstition – superstitious fear, I mean, of the consequences and omens of weakness. The small book in question is really but an exercise in the art of not appearing to one's self to fail. You will say it is rather cruel that for such exercises the public also should have to pay. Well, Madame Paul and you get your exemplaire for nothing.

I have not seen La Femme et le Pantin – I see nothing in the way of books here; but what you tell me disposes me to send for it – as well as my impression of the only other thing that I have read by the same hand.[4] Only, on the

2. In the episode in question, the actress Camille has happened to be trapped in her and Molan's love-nest when he brings Mme de Bonnivet there. She hears their sexual intercourse and afterwards sees the '*lit défait*', the rumpled bed. Returning later to confront her rival, she finds Mme de Bonnivet's murderously jealous husband waiting outside, and nobly goes up to warn the pair, taking the faithless Molan into her cab to save him. He at once shamelessly tries to kiss her.

3. *In the Cage*.

4. On 7 August Bourget had recommended '*La Femme et le Pantin*, du jeune Pierre Louÿs. C'est une histoire d'une sensualité presque horrible, mais supérieurement contée. Avant de connaître cet écrivain, je n'aurais pas cru qu'un artiste moderne peut avoir cette perversion

question of talent and of effect produced, don't you forget, too much, with such people, that talent and effect are comparatively easy things with the licence of such gros moyens? They are a great short-cut – the extremities to which all these people proceed, and anyone can – no matter who – be more or less striking with them. But I am writing you an interminable letter. Do let me know – sans m'en vouloir for the quantity and quality of it – how Nauheim turns out, and receive my heartiest wishes for all sorts of comfortable results. Yours both always constantly,

Henry James.

163. To Mary (Mrs Humphry) Ward
[22 September 1898]

Virginia MS   Unpublished

An Alsatian Jewish officer in the French army, Alfred Dreyfus (1859–1935), was in October 1894 court-martialled and sent to Devil's Island for supposedly spying for the Germans. In 1896 a new chief of intelligence found secrets were still being betrayed by a spy whose handwriting matched that on the earlier letters. His efforts to reopen the Dreyfus case blocked, he was transferred to Tunisia. In 1897, Dreyfus's brother made a similar discovery and accused a Major Esterhazy of the spying; Esterhazy was cleared by a military court. Liberals and radicals (including Zola) were aroused by what seemed extreme antisemitic prejudice, and throughout 1898–9 France was torn by ugly conflicts. HJ, a 'dreyfusard', followed the 'Affaire' intently; Bourget was an 'anti-dreyfusard'.

---

morale avec une telle beauté de fortune.' (Unpublished Houghton MS, bMS Am 1094.) (TRANSLATION: '*The Woman and the Puppet*, by young Pierre Loüys. It is a story of almost horrible sensuality, but exquisitely told. Before knowing this writer I wouldn't have believed a modern artist capable of combining such moral perversity with such innovative creation of beauty.') On 26 September HJ would reply with his verdict on the *Lolita*-like novel, in which a man buys a Spanish child-bride and is taunted into beating her before sex: 'Cette idée du pathétique, de se plaindre à ce point, d'avoir toujours à rouer de coups la sale négrillonne (car elle n'est que cela – et à moitié racoon! comme chez Ferdinand) qu'on a prise pour maîtresse, avant de la posséder – ne voilà-t-il pas ce qu'on a encore trouvé de plus compliqué comme "états d'âme"? Beaucoup de talent, un grand sens littéraire, oui, mais quelle aridité pittoyable et quelle ignorance crasse de la vie!' (HJL IV, 80.) (TRANSLATION: 'This idea of pathos, of grievance carried to such a point, that he has constantly to rain blows upon the grimy piccaninny (which is all she is – and half racoon! as in Ferdinand) that he has taken as his mistress, before possessing her sexually – isn't this the most complicated thing yet discovered in the way of "psychological states"? Much talent, a great literary instinct, yes, but what pitiful aridity and what a crass ignorance of life!')

LAMB HOUSE, RYE.
Thursday

Dear Mrs. Ward.

It is delightful to hear from you – but I am very sorry to say it will not be possible to me to leave home – even under the great allurement of your invitation – for October 8th, & I am afraid not any other day in the month. It is a month of necessary immobility here – for reasons too many to inflict on you. One of them is that though I have been very immobile since coming down here the fruits of that state (a considerable quantity of necessary production) have been to a certain extent blighted by the rather unexpected presence, under my roof, of a good many irrepressible sojourners – the consequence of which has been that I've not had all the concentration I settled myself in this supposedly sequestered spot in search of.[1] But concentration is doubtless not of this horrid *époque*. If nothing else prevented it, the newspapers would. Instead of shutting myself up in a little temple of the Muses that I have here, detached from my house, I sit in the garden & read l'Affaire Dreyfus. What a bottomless & sinister *affaire* & in what a strange mill it is grinding the poor dear French. You do well to frequent them in happier days of their history. I am just making arrangements to have my Sainte-Beuve – au complet – moved down here: oddly enough I too, this summer, have been reading Chateaubriand – to the extent of the Mémoires d'Outre-Tombe – of which the literary talent seems to me immense, but the earlier portions the best.[2] Mrs. Fields & Miss Jewett did come – & Mrs. Fields took me back to my far-away youth & *hers* – when she was so pretty & I was so aspiring.[3] Read, if you haven't, Miss Jewett's *Country of the Pointed Firs* (I will send it you if you possess it not) for the pleasure of something really exquisite. I am very, very sorry, dear Mrs. Ward that I see my way so dimly to respond to your hospitality. The worst is that

1. The sojourners included Gosse, the Warrens, and WJ's son Henry (1879–1947) and HJ's young cousin Rosina Emmet (b. 1873), who was studying painting in France.
2. Vicomte François-René de Chateaubriand (1768–1848), Romantic writer and Christian apologist, who was exiled to America by the French Revolution, and on his return wrote *Atala* (1801) and *René* (1802), both immense successes. *Mémoires d'outre-tombe* (published posthumously in 1849–50) starts with a striking picture of his melancholy childhood. Mrs Ward was to base the plot of her next novel, *Eleanor*, on Chateaubriand's love affair in 1800 with his intellectual helper on *Le Génie du christianisme* (1802), Pauline de Beaumont, and his subsequent abandoning of her for a more beautiful woman.
3. After the death of James T. Fields in 1881, Annie Fields became the inseparable companion of Sarah Orne Jewett (1849–1909), the Maine-born author of New England fictions, most famously of *The Country of the Pointed Firs* (1896). She edited Miss Jewett's letters in 1911. They came down for the day on 13 September, and HJ, 'intent on the largest hospitality' as Mrs Fields recorded in her diary (HJAH, 89), lunched them and took them on an excursion to Hastings before they caught the London train.

it is questionable if I be in London at all this winter. It will depend on the temperature of this house whether I am able to remain *here* till Xmas; but if I have to bolt it will probably then be straight across the Channel. This is ungracious talk & it doesn't preclude a few dashes up to town. Mesdames F. & J. spoke of you as *recently* unwell – but I trust they were only "mixed."[4] I heartily pray you be in good case & comfort. I think often of your brother – & for him I pray. And I bless all your house & am, dear Mrs. Ward very interrèdly but very constantly yours

Henry James

P.S. The 2 glasses are the glory of my home & the wonder & envy of all the country-side.[5]

164. To James Brand Pinker
19 October 1898

Yale MS   Unpublished

Pinker, who only began his agency in January 1896, is described by a historian of the subject as 'perhaps the most impressive of all the early agents', successfully representing Arnold Bennett and Joseph Conrad, H. G. Wells and Ford Madox Ford, Stephen Crane and HJ. He was described by Frank Swinnerton as 'short, compact, a rosy, round-faced clean-shaven grey-haired sphinx with a protrusive under-lip, who drove four-in-hand, spoke distinctly in a hoarse voice that was almost a whisper, shook hands shoulder-high, laughed without moving, knew the monetary secrets of authors and the weaknesses of publishers . . .' (AEP, 57). He made a point of cultivating the American market as well as the British.

LAMB HOUSE, RYE.
October 19*th* 98.

Dear Mr. Pinker.

Consternation has definitely settled upon me as the weeks & the months have gone round without my hearing from you that you have been able to do

---

4. After the huge convulsion of finishing a novel like *Helbeck*, Mrs Ward, whose nervous and physical health was precarious, and who would alternate sleeping draughts and cocaine lozenges, used to collapse completely and require a long convalescence.
5. Mrs Ward had sent HJ a pair of 'glasses' (presumably pier-glasses) for Lamb House in the first half of June.

anything with the three Tales of mine actually in your hands, & this is a word to confess to you that, as my nerves are really giving way under the tension of so much appearance that my work has, save in rare cases, for some reason I can't fathom, ceased to be serially placeable, I shall be relieved – as I doubt not you yourself will be as well – if you will kindly return to me the unfortunate wanderers.[1] It's their wandering so far, in vain – I mean the *consciousness* of it – that upsets me, & if they are again safe in my table-drawer I shall at least be able to feel that, by adding 3 or 4 others which I won't, naturally, this time, serially offer, I can still make a book of them.[2] You will, I am sure, fully enter into my despair, which doesn't in the least diminish my appreciation of your efforts in my behalf or my being yours most truly

Henry James

Mr. James B. Pinker

165. To James Brand Pinker
23 October 1898

Yale MS   Published HJL IV, 85

LAMB HOUSE, RYE.
October 23 1898.

Dear Mr. Pinker.

By all means keep my three things if you do see any chance for them – or possibility of one – still: I wouldn't suppose that you had any remaining faith. Moreover, the episode has been, for me, a horrible unprecedented *scare*, the effect of which on my nerves, as it were, is – with the vision of my things declined on every side, unfavourable to work, & it seemed to me desirable to put an end to the suspense connected with the whole magazine question. I'm afraid I shouldn't be able to bear very much more of it. It comes to me late –

1. On 7 May 1898 HJ had sent 'The Given Case' (9,650 words), which was published in *Collier's Weekly* (December 1898–January 1899). On 24 May he sent another tale, probably 'The Great Good Place', of 10,500 words; and on 6 June a third of 7,400 words, probably ' "Europe" ', noted as a subject on 7 May (N, 169), and published in *Scribner's Magazine* in June 1899.
2. All three of the stories mentioned in the previous note were included in HJ's next collection, *The Soft Side*, published by Methuen on 30 August 1900, and in the U.S. by Macmillan in September 1900.

one can take that in youth. But this is mainly a word to say that I shall be very glad indeed if you will come down to see me – I should like extremely to talk with you. *This* week would be rather bad for me, by reason of my happening to be taken up with some relations who are to be with [me] for several days; but *next* I hope you will come & I will in a few days write you again, giving you your choice of days & times. Believe me yours very truly

Henry James[1]

166. To Herbert George Wells
9 December 1898

Bodleian MS   Published HJL IV, 85–7; SL1, 181–3; SL2, 313–15; HJHGW, 55–7

All this autumn HJ had been continuing to write The Awkward Age *– "about 135,000 words arranged as a fable of superior quality" (HJL IV, 89), as he told Bourget – which had been appearing in* Harper's Weekly *since 1 October. HJ's polio-crippled, witty American writer-friend Jonathan Sturges (1864–1911), whom he had known at least since 1889 when he wrote a preface for a Maupassant translation by Sturges, stayed with him at Lamb House for the two months up to Christmas.*

HJ seems to have met H. G. Wells (1866–1946) when he and Gosse, on their bicycles, visited the young writer in August 1898 after Wells collapsed with a fever on a cycling holiday. Wells moved to Sandgate this summer, not far from Rye over Romney Marsh. With The Time Machine *in 1895, he had successfully launched a line of "scientific romances", including* The Island of Dr Moreau *(1896),* The Invisible Man *(1897) and* The War of the Worlds *(1898).*

LAMB HOUSE, RYE.

My dear H. G. Wells,

Your so liberal & graceful letter is to my head like coals of fire – so repeatedly for all these weeks have I had feebly to suffer frustrations in the matter of trundling over the marsh to ask for your news & wish for your continued amendment. The shortening days & the deepening mud have been at the bottom of this affair. I never get out of the house till 3 o'clock, when

1. On 23 November HJ was to acknowledge receipt from Pinker of £46 6s. from *Scribner's* for 'The Great Good Place'; and on 14 December returned corrected proofs of 'The Given Case'.

night is quickly at one's heels. I would have taken a regular day – I mean started in the a.m. – but have been so ridden, myself, by the black care of an unfinished and *running* (galloping, leaping & bounding,) serial that parting with a day has been like parting with a pound of flesh. I am still a neck ahead, however, & *this* week will see me through: I accordingly hope very much to be able to turn up on one of the ensuing days. I will sound a horn, so that you yourself be not absent on the chase. Then I will express more articulately my appreciation of your various signs of critical interest, as well as assure you of my sympathy in your own martyrdom. What will you have? It's all a grind & a bloody battle – as well as a considerable lark, & the difficulty itself is the refuge from the vulgarity. Bless your heart, I think I could easily say worse of The T. of the S., the young woman, the spooks, the style, the everything, than the worst any one else could manage.[1] One knows the *most* damning things about one's self. Of course I had, about my young woman, to take a very sharp line. The grotesque business I had to make her picture & the childish psychology I had to make her trace & present, were, for me at least, a very difficult job, in which absolute lucidity & logic, & singleness of effect were imperative. Therefore I had to rule out subjective complications of her own – play of tone &c.; & keep her impersonal save for the most obvious & indispensable little note of neatness, firmness & courage – without which she wouldn't have had her data. But the thing is essentially a pot-boiler & a *jeu d'esprit*.

With the little play, the absolute creature *of* its conditions, I had simply to make up a deficit & take a small *revanche*.[2] For three mortal years had the actress for whom it was written (utterly to try to *fit*,) persistently failed to produce it, & I couldn't wholly waste my labour. The B.P. won't read a play with the mere names of the speakers – so I simply paraphrased these & added such indications as might be the equivalent of decent acting – a history & an evolution that seem to me moreover explicatively and sufficiently smeared all over the thing. The moral is of course Don't write one-act plays. But I didn't mean thus to sprawl. I envy your hand your needle-pointed fingers. As you

1. Wells's letter or letters before this date are not known to survive. On 16 January 1899 he would write to HJ that, unable to think of a better way of doing 'The Turn of the Screw', he had concluded that 'The story is not wrong – I was' (HJHGW, 58). In December 1898 Wells was writing *When the Sleeper Wakes*, then being serialized in the *Graphic* and published as a book in 1899 by Harper in the U.S. and Britain.
2. The other tale in *The Two Magics*, 'Covering End', was the unperformed one-act comedy *Summersoft*, written in 1895 for Ellen Terry, 'reclaimed a little for literature – & for my pocket – by being simply turned, on the absolutely same Scenic lines, into narrative', as HJ told Gosse (SLHJEG, 164). The 'B.P.' is the British Public.

don't say that you're *not* better I prepare myself to be greatly struck with the same, & send kind regards to your wife. Believe me yours ever

Henry James

Dec. 9*th* 1898.

P.S. What's this about something in some newspaper? — I read least of all — from long & deep experience — what my friends write about me, & haven't read the things you mention.[3] I suppose it's because they know I don't that they dare!

167. To Frederic William Henry Myers
19 December 1898

Wren MS   Published HJL IV, 87–8

Myers's letter to HJ about 'The Turn of the Screw' is not known to survive, but as a founder-member of the Society for Psychical Research the Cambridge don may have had a special interest in the tale.

Dec 19*th* 1898.
LAMB HOUSE, RYE.

My dear Myers.

I don't know what you will think of my unconscionable delay to acknowledge your letter of so many, so very many days ago, nor exactly how I can make vivid to you the nature of my hindrances & excuses. I have, in truth, been (until some few days since) intensely & anxiously busy, finishing, under

3. On a Sunday soon after this in December 1898, the day before finishing *The Awkward Age*, HJ wrote to Fanny Stevenson's friend the young American humourist Frank Gelett Burgess (1866–1951), editor of *The Lark*, 1895–7, and inventor of words like 'blurb' and 'goop'. Burgess had written in apology; HJ reassured him, 'I haven't seen the article you tell me of, & haven't heard the lightest echo of it. I never see the I.L.N. &, to speak frankly — very frankly — shouldn't, had I come across the No[.] in question, have read the sketch — or whatever it was: I don't quite gather from your allusion — from the moment I perceived it to belong to the species of what is called personal journalism — of which I won't pretend to deny to you my horror.' (Unpublished Bancroft MS, C–H 52 B.) (The 'I.L.N.' seems not to be the *Illustrated London News*, which had no items on HJ in the period.) HJ warned Burgess to keep 'utterly *out*, for God's sake, even of such pen-play as it takes only the treachery of some unscrupulous editor to convert into a thing of offense' (ibid.); then invited him to Rye for the following weekend.

313

pressure, a long job that had from almost the first – I mean from long before I had reached the end – begun to be (loathsome name & fact!) "serialized" – so that the printers were at my heels & I had to make a sacrifice of my correspondence *utterly* – to keep the sort of cerebral freshness required for not losing my head or otherwise collapsing. But I won't expatiate. Please believe my silence has been wholly involuntary. And yet, now that I *am* writing I scarce know what to say to you on the subject on wh. you wrote, especially as I'm afraid I don't quite *understand* the principal question you put to me about "The Turn of the Screw." However, that scantly matters; for in truth I am afraid I have on some former occasions rather awkwardly signified to you that I somehow can't pretend to give any coherent account of my small inventions "after the fact." There they are – the fruit, at best, of a very imperfect ingenuity & with all the imperfections thereof on their heads. The one thing & another that are questionable & ambiguous in them I mostly take to be conditions of their having got themselves pushed through at all. The *T. of the S.* is a very mechanical matter, I honestly think – an inferior, a merely *pictorial*, subject & rather a shameless pot-boiler[.] The thing that, as I recall it, I most wanted not to fail of doing, under penalty of extreme platitude, was to give the impression of the communication to the children of the most infernal imaginable evil & danger – the condition, on their part, of being as *exposed* as we can humanly conceive children to be. This was my artistic knot to untie, to put any sense or logic into the thing, & if I had known any way of producing *more* the image of their contact & condition I should assuredly have been proportionately eager to resort to it. I evoked the worst I could, & only feel tempted to say, as in French: "Excusez du peu!"

I am living so much down here that I fear I am losing hold of some of my few chances of occasionally seeing you. The charming old humble-minded "quaintness" & quietness of this little brown hilltop city lays a spell upon me. I send you & your wife & all your house all the greetings of the Season & am, my dear Myers, yours very constantly

Henry James

168. *To William Leon Mead*
27 March 1899

Virginia MS   Unpublished

In late December HJ let his London flat, 34 De Vere Gardens, for six months, and planned three months in Europe – including the performance of what in March

1899 he called to Warren 'a very serious obligation on me, long shirked, in Rome'
– an examination of the Story papers (Unpublished Huntington MS, 'Tuesday',
HM 40261). Delayed a fortnight by a fire at Lamb House in the small hours of
27 February, he left Jonathan Sturges there and in mid March reached Paris, where
he spent sixteen days seeing his young Emmet cousins. He also finished there the
page proofs of The Awkward Age, *which came out as a book from Heinemann*
on 25 April, and from Harper's in the U.S. on 12 May. On his way to Italy and
its social entanglements, HJ stayed just over a week with the Bourgets at their
estate in the South of France.

The American Mead (b. 1861), writer of poems and stories, also produced How
Words Grow *(1897), republished in 1902 as* Word-Coinage. *Later in life he*
wrote much on Napoleon and lived in Hollywood.

Strictly Private
Leon Mead esq.
LE PLANTIER COSTEBELLE HYERES.
March 27. 1899.

Dear Sir.

I am afraid I am wholly unable to aid you in collecting words either of my
own invention or of any one's else.

I have attempted only to write in a language already existing & consecrated,
& have found *that* a literary task abundantly, & superabundantly, difficult by
itself. Complicated, further, by extemporized & imported substances, it would,
I fear, have got the better of me altogether. In short I have never had anything
to say to which some word or other already forming a part of human speech
has not had, to my sense, something to contribute of its own, & I am yours
very truly

Henry James

169. To Mary (Mrs Humphry) Ward
[23 July 1899]

Unknown MS or TS   Published LHJ I, 320–23

HJ was in Venice in the last part of April, writing a story, 'The Great Condition',
till 3 May in response to an urgent request from Lady Randolph Churchill (1854–
1921), the former American Jennie Jerome, for the first issue in June of her luxurious,
short-lived Anglo-Saxon Review. *One of HJ's many social engagements in Italy*

— apart from seeing various Storys — was a stay at the Villa Barberini in Rome,
for a few days up to 20 June. He wrote to Warren from there: 'The irrepressible
Humphry Wards have taken (that she may do an "Italian" novel,) this wondrous
place for 3 months (nearly at an end,) & I am spending 3 or 4 days with
them. The villa vast, rambling, bare, shabby & uncomfortable; but the position,
circumstances, views, walks, drives, sensations of every aesthetic order, ravishing
& inexpressible.' (Unpublished Huntington MS, HM 40268.) At the Roman studio
of the American artist John Elliott (1858–1925), HJ met and became friendly with
the young Norwegian-American sculptor Hendrik C. Andersen (1872–1940), who
had grown up in Newport. (Elliott's wife Maude Howe Elliott was daughter to
Julia Ward Howe.) HJ was back at Rye on 7 July.

Mrs Ward did not complete Eleanor *till March 1900, and it was not published*
till 1 November 1900; what she sent HJ were proofs of the early chapters. Edward
Manisty, a handsome Catholic High Tory politician who has quarrelled with the
government, has come to Rome to write a book, helped by the frail young English
widow Eleanor Burgoyne. She loses him to Lucy Foster, a provincial and idealistic
American Protestant girl, and dies of it, nobly nursed by her rival.

Lamb House, Rye.
Sunday.

Dear Mrs. Ward,

I return the proofs of *Eleanor*, in a separate cover from this, and as I think
it wise to *register* them I must wait till to-morrow a.m. to do that, and this,
therefore, will reach you first. Let me immediately say that I don't light (and
I've read carefully every word, and many two or three times, as Mr. Bellasis
would say — and is Mr. B., by the way, naturally — as it were — H.J.???!!!) on
any peccant particular spots in the aspect of Lucy F. that the American reader
would challenge.[1] I do think he, or she, may be likely, at first, to think her
more English than American — to say, I mean: "Why, this isn't *us* — it's English
'Dissent.'" For it's well — generally — to keep in mind how very different a
thing that is (socially, aesthetically &c.) from the American free (and easy)
multitudinous churches, that, practically, in any community, are like so many
(almost) clubs or Philharmonics or amateur theatrical companies. I *don't* quite
think the however obscure American girl I gather you to conceive would have
any shockability about Rome, the Pope, St. Peter's, kneeling, or anything of

---

1. Mr Bellasis is a vain English poet and playwright, unlike HJ in appearance, who comments
of his own latest, 'my friends tell me in Rome that the book cannot be really appreciated except
at a second or third reading'. When he leaves, Manisty mutters, 'Intolerable ass!'

that sort – least of all any girl whose concatenations *could*, by any possibility of social handing-on, land her in the milieu you present at Albano. She would probably be either a Unitarian or "Orthodox" (which is, I believe, "Congregational," though in New England always called "Orthodox") and in either case as Emersonized, Hawthornized, J. A. Symondsized, and as "frantic" to *feel* the Papacy &c, as one could well represent her. And this, I mean, even were she of any provincial New England circle whatever that one could conceive as ramifying, however indirectly, into Villa Barb. This particularly were her father a college professor. In that case I should say "The bad clothes &c, oh yes; as much as you like. The beauty &c, *scarcely*. The offishness to Rome – as a spectator &c. – almost not at all." All this, roughly and hastily speaking. But there is no false note of surface, beyond this, I think, that you need be uneasy about at all. Had I looked over your shoulder I should have said: "*Specify*, localise, a little more – give her a *definite* Massachusetts, or Maine, or whatever, habitation – imagine a country-college-town – invent, if need be, a name, and stick to that." This for smallish, but appreciable reasons that I haven't space to develop – but after all not imperative. For the rest the chapters you send me are, as a beginning, to my vision very charming and interesting and pleasing – full of promise of strong elements – as your beginnings always are.

And may I say (as I *can* read nothing, if I read it at all, save in the light of how one would *one's self* proceed in tackling the same *data*!) just two other things? One is that I think your material suffers a little from the fact that the reader feels you approach your subject too *immediately*, show him its elements, the cards in your hand, too bang off from the first page – so that a wait to begin to guess *what and whom the thing is going to be about* doesn't impose itself: the ante-chamber or two and the crooked corridor before he is already in the Presence. The other is that you don't give him a positive sense of dealing with your subject from your logical centre. This centre I gathered to be, from what you told me in Rome (and one gathers it also from the title,) the consciousness of Eleanor – to which all the rest (Manisty, Lucy, the whole phantasmagoria and drama) is presented by life. I should have urged you: "Make that consciousness full, rich, universally prehensile and *stick* to it – don't shift – and don't shift *arbitrarily* – how, otherwise, do you get your unity of subject or keep up your reader's sense of it?" To which, if you say: How then do I get *Lucy's* consciousness, I impudently retort: "By that magnificent and masterly *indirectness* which means the *only* dramatic straightness and intensity. You get it, in other words, by Eleanor." "And how does Eleanor get it?" "By *Everything*! By Lucy, by Manisty, by every pulse of the action in which she is engaged and of which she is the fullest – an exquisite – register. Go behind *her* – miles and miles; don't go behind the others, or the subject – *i.e.* the unity of

317

impression – goes to smash." But I am going too far – and this is more than you will have bargained for. On these matters there is far too much to say. This makes me all the more sorry that, in answer to your kind invitation for the last of this month, I greatly fear I can't leave home for several weeks to come. I am in hideous backwardness with duties that after a long idleness (six full months!) have awaited me here – and I am cultivating "a unity of impression!" In *October* with joy.

Your history of your journey from V.B., your anxieties, complications, horrid tension and tribulation, draws hot tears from my eyes. I blush for the bleak inn at the bare Simplon. I only meant it for rude, recovered health. Poor Miss Gertrude – heroine partout et toujours – and so privately, modestly, exquisitely.[2] Give her, please, all my present benediction. And forgive my horrid, fatigued, hieroglyphics. Do let me have more of "Eleanor" – to re-write! And believe me, dear Mrs. Ward, ever constantly yours,

Henry James

P.S. I've on reflection determined that as a *registered* letter may not, perhaps, reach Stocks till Tuesday a.m. and you wish to despatch for Wednesday's steamer, it is my "higher duty" to send the proofs off in ordinary form, apart from this, but to-night.[3] May it be for the best!

H.J.

170. To Mary (Mrs Humphry) Ward
26 July 1899

Virginia MS   Published HJL IV, 109–12

Mrs Ward's reply to the previous letter is not known to survive. HJ's '2 or 3 words' of rejoinder – in fact about 1,300 – help us reconstruct it.

LAMB HOUSE, RYE.
July 26*th* 1899.

Dear Mrs. Ward.

I beg you not to believe that if you elicit a reply from me – to your so interesting letter just received – you do so at any cost to any extreme or

2. Gertrude Ward, Mrs Ward's sister-in-law, had served as her amanuensis, confidante and housekeeper till 1891, when her conscience drove her to become first a district nurse in London and then from 1895 a missionary nurse in Zanzibar.

3. In the summer of 1892 the Wards had bought Stocks, an estate in Hertfordshire, under an hour by train from London's Euston Station.

uncomfortable pressure that I'm just now under. I am always behind with
everything – & it's no worse than usual. Besides, I shall be very brief.+[1] But
I *must* say 2 or 3 words – not only because these are the noblest speculations
that can engage the human mind, but because – to a degree that distresses me
– you labour under 2 or 3 mistakes as to what, the other day, I at all wanted
to express. I don't myself, for that matter, recognise what you mean by any
"old difference" between us on *any* score – & least of all when you appear to
glance at it as an opinion of mine (if I understood you, that is,) as to there
being but *one general* "hard & fast rule of presentation." I protest that I have
never had with you any difference – consciously – on any such point & rather
resent, frankly, your attributing to me a judgment so imbecile. I hold that there
are five million such "rules" (or as many as there [are] subjects in all the world
– I fear the subjects are *not* 5000000!) only each of them imposed, artistically,
by the particular case; – involved in the writer's responsibility to it & each
then – & then only – "hard & fast" with an immitigable hardness & fastness.
I don't see, *without* this latter condition, where any work of art, any artistic
question is, or any artistic probity. Of course, a 1000 times, there are as many
magnificent & imperative cases as you like of presenting a thing by "going
behind" as many forms of consciousness as you like – all Dickens, Balzac,
Thackeray, Tolstoy, (save when they use the autobiographic dodge,) are huge
illustrations of it. But they are illustrations of extreme & calculated selection,
or singleness, too, whenever that has been, by the case, imposed on them. My
own immortal works, for that matter, if I may make bold, are recognizable
instances of *all* the variations. I "go behind" right and left in "The Prss.
Casamassima," "The Bostonians," "The Tragic Muse," just as I do the same
but singly in "The American" & "Maisie," & just as I do it consistently *never
at all* (save for a false & limited *appearance*, here & there, of doing it a *little*,
which I haven't time to explain,) in *The Awkward Age*. So far from not seeing
what you mean in *Pêcheur d'Islande*, I see it as a most beautiful example – a
crystal-clear one.[2] It's a picture of a *relation* (a *single* relation) & that relation
isn't given at all unless given on both sides, because, practically, there are no
other relations to make *other* feet for the situation to walk withal. The logic
jumps at the eyes. Therefore acquit me, please, *please*, of anything so abject

---

1. +'Later – !!!! Latest. Don't "rejoin!" – *don't!*' [HJ's note.]
2. HJ's 1888 essay on 'Pierre Loti', to write which he had delayed finishing Mrs Ward's *Robert
Elsmere*, had praised *Pêcheur d'islande* (1886), a tragic love story, as 'one of the very few works
of imagination of our day completely and successfully beautiful', 'the history of a passion, but
of a passion simplified, in its strength, to a sort of community with the winds and waves, the
blind natural forces hammering away at the hard Breton country where it is enacted' (LC II,
500, 501).

as putting forward anything at once specific & *a priori*. "Then why," I hear you ask, "do you pronounce for <u>my book</u> à *[sic] priori*?" Only because of a mistake, doubtless, for which I do here humble penance – that of assuming too precipitately, & with the freedom of an inevitably too-foreshortened letter, that I was dealing with it à *posteriori*! – and *that* on the evidence of only those few pages & of a somewhat confused recollection of what, in Rome, you told me of your elements. Or rather, – more correctly, – I was giving way to my irresistible need of wondering how, *given* the subject, one could best work oneself into the presence of it. And, lo & behold, the subject isn't (of course, in so scant a show & brief a piece) "given" at all – I have doubtless simply, with violence & mutilation, *stolen* it. It is of the nature of that violence that I'm a wretched person to *read* a novel – I begin so quickly and concomitantly, *for myself*, to write it, rather – even before I know clearly what it's about! The novel I can *only* read, I can't read at all! And I had, to be just with me, one attenuation – I thought I gathered from the pages already absorbed that your *parti pris* as to your process with "Eleanor" was already defined – and defined as "dramatic" – and that was a kind of *lead*: the people all, as it were, phenomenal to a particular imagination (her's) and that imagination, with all its contents, phenomenal to the reader. I, in fine, just rudely & egotistically thrust forward the beastly way *I* should have done it. But there is too much to say about these things – & I am writing too much – & yet haven't said ½ I want to – *and*, above all, there *being* so much, it is doubtless better not to attempt to say pen in hand what one can say but so partially. And yet I *must* still add one or two things more. What I said above about the "rule" of presentation being in each case, hard & fast, *that* I will go to the stake & burn & burn with slow fire for – the slowest that will burn at all. I hold the artist must (infinitely!) know how he is doing it, or he is not doing it at all. I hold he must have a perception of the interests of his subject that grasps him as in a vise, and that (the subject being of course formulated in his mind,) he sees *as* sharply the way that most presents it, & presents most of it, as against the ways that comparatively give it away. And he must there choose & stick & be consistent – & that is the hard-&-fastness & the vise. I am afraid I *do* differ with you if you mean that the picture can get any *objective* unity from any other source than that; can get it, from, e.g., the "personality of the author." From the personality of the author (which, however enchanting, is a thing for the reader only, & not for the author himself, without humiliating abdications, to my sense, to count in at all,) it can get nothing but a unity of execution & of tone. There is no short cut for the subject, in other words, out of the process, which, having made out most what it (the subject) is, *treats* it most, handles it, in that relation, with the most consistent economy. May I say, to exonerate myself a little, that when, e.g. I see you make Lucy "phenomenal" to Eleanor (one has to express it briefly & somehow,) I find myself supposing completely that you "know how you're doing it," & enjoy as critic, the sweet peace that comes with that sense. But I *haven't* the feeling that you "know how you're doing it" when, at the point you've reached, I see you make Lucy phenomenal, even for one attempted stroke, to the little secretary of embassy.[3] And the reason of this is that Eleanor counts as presented, & thereby *is* something to go behind. The secretary *doesn't* count as presented (& isn't he moreover engaged, at the very moment – *your* moment – in being phenomenal, himself, to Lucy?) & is therefore, practically, *nothing* to go behind. The promiscuous shiftings of standpoint & centre of Tolstoi & Balzac for instance (which come, to my eye, from their being not so much big dramatists as big *painters* – as Loti is a painter,) are the inevitable result of the *quantity of presenting* their genius launches them in. With the complexity they pile up they *can* get no clearness without trying again & again for new centres. And they don't *always* get it. However, I don't mean to say they don't get enough. And I hasten to add that you have – I wholly recognise, – every right to reply to me: "Cease your intolerable chatter & dry up your preposterous deluge. If you will have the decent civility to *wait*, you will see that *I* 'present' also – *anch'io!* – enough for *every* freedom I use with it!"[4]

And with my full assent to that, & my profuse prostration in the dust for this extravagant discourse, with all faith, gratitude, appreciation & affection, I *do* cease, dear Mrs. Ward; I dry up! & am yours most breathlessly

Henry James

3. In ch. III the American Lucy is sitting in the garden: her hostess Eleanor Burgoyne solicitously sends out a young diplomat: 'Lucy looked up to see a charming face, lit by the bluest of blue eyes, adorned moreover by a fair moustache, and an expression at once confident and appealing. / Was this the "delightful boy" from the Embassy Mrs. Burgoyne had announced to her? No doubt. The colour rose softly in her cheek . . . / Her companion looked at her with approval. / "My word! She's dowdy" – he thought – "like a Sunday-school teacher. But she's handsome."'

4. *'Anch'io!'*, 'I too!', which HJ puts in as an afterthought, alludes to the famous phrase said by Vasari to have been uttered by the young Correggio (Antonio Allegri, 1494–1534) in front of a work by Mantegna: 'Anch'io son pittore!', 'I too am a painter!'

171. To Edward Prioleau Warren
13 August 1899

Huntington MS   Unpublished

When with Warren's support HJ had in 1897 signed a twenty-one-year lease on Lamb House, its new owner Arthur Bellingham was going to the Klondyke goldfields. In August 1899 HJ learned that Bellingham had died and his mother was offering HJ the freehold for £2,000 (in fact, for £750 and an undertaking to pay the interest on £1,250 in mortgages). WJ was initially sceptical, but HJ protested on 9 August: 'My whole being cries out aloud for something that I can call my own – & when I look round me at the splendour of so many of the "literary" fry my confrères (M. Crawfords, P. Bourgets, Humphry Wards, Hodgson Burnetts, W. D. Howellses &c,) & I feel that I may strike the world as still, at 56, with my long labour & my genius, reckless, presumptuous & unwarranted in curling up (for more assured peaceful production,) in a poor little $10,000 shelter – once for all & for all time – then I do feel the bitterness of humiliation, the iron enters into my soul, & (I blush to confess it,) I weep!' (CWJ III, 78–9.) Encouraged by Warren, though, he went ahead, letting 34 De Vere Gardens for a year. (He got rid of the lease and in due course managed to find a bed-sitting room in the extension to the Reform Club.)

The hard-working Warren, who was architect of many buildings in Oxford and Cambridge, and his wife Margaret (sister of Philip Morrell, who married Lady Ottoline Bentinck), had a London home in Cowley Street, and also a place in the country near Abingdon. Warren knew HJ's invalid friend Jonathan Sturges and also Ethel Sands, artist daughter of the late Mrs Mahlon Sands.

LAMB HOUSE, RYE
Aug. 13. 1899.

My dear Edward.

All thanks for your little document, which belongs to the class of little documents it is not always so delightful to receive as it is in this particular case, with *you* at the other end. I am always astounded at your moderation. Please, at any rate find herein a cheque, for the £29. 16. 3 in question.

I am happy to say I *have* closed with Mrs. Bellingham's offer – though it comes at a moment when I was a little depleted & unexpecting. If I had known it was so near at hand the 1st of Jan. last, I would have arranged my little affairs – as bearing on a purchase – a little differently (by which I don't in the least mean the chimney & office affairs – the *being* done of which is nothing but a pure blessing to me.)[1] On the other hand the conditions are so very reasonable & comfortable that I shall find it all convenient & manageable. I have only to sit close the next 6 months & attend to my business – which, heaven knows, is all I *want* to do.

Meanwhile it is a great blessing to have the question at rest: it makes me love dear little L.H. more than ever. I have arranged to get rid, at a *probably* early date, of 34 De Vere Gardens – and the only drawback to that is that the things I shall thereby have on my hands to bring down here are biggish & crowdingish for the place – besides endless prints & photos. (*all* the latter valued for association &c,) & 5,000 books! I'm afraid poor little L.H. won't look the better for them. But à la guerre comme à la guerre. It is lovely here now & blissfully quiet. I hope you are getting more of Abingdonshire than your Cowley St. date superficially denotes. I hope also that Sturges's presence in London is connected with no collapse, on his part, in the country. I hope, in October, to get him down here for 2 or 3 weeks. I *shall* want *you* when I begin to stick in more furniture. But I am counting on you & M. for some moment in the early autumn – if *with* J.S. it would be good. I've heard from Ethel Sands, most responsively, & written to her again – but she had not yet seen Margaret. Love to that lady. Yours ever

Henry James

P.S. I believe you *would* be damned if you were to buy the *Awkward Age*. I am writing to Heinemann – *now* to send it you. My delay is all my shyness – not to Heinemann – to *you*.

172. To William Dean Howells
25 September 1899

Houghton MS   Published LFL, 351–3

Howells wrote to HJ on 10 September from a rented summer house at Kittery Point, Maine, apologizing for his long silence and explaining he still had not read The

---

1. After the fire on 27 February in the Lamb House Green Room and dining-room, Warren had handled the insurance claim (for £28) and the reconstructions, installing three new fireplaces. On 22 May HJ wrote to Warren, 'What a state of general fireplace villainy you must have discovered – & how I rejoice in every abolished & annihilated danger that you have dealt with . . . I . . . desire no money spared for any *complete & total* rectification study & east bedroom fire-traps [*sic*].' (Unpublished Huntington MS, HM 40265.) Warren evidently did a good deal more than make good the damage.

Awkward Age *(whose Harper's serialization he had helped to bring about by intervening with the editor Nelson in November 1897).*

Sept. 25th. 1899.
LAMB HOUSE, RYE.

My dear old Friend.

I take your genial letter from Kittery's Point as a great kindness & a great charity. Let us not, at this late day, have any question of "turns," in such communication, & communion, as may still contrive to enhance the comparatively contracted remnant of our years. I am quite capable, I warn you, (& even not improbable,) of following up this with other utterance even should temporary silence be your own necessity. *Giusto*, I was (one says those things, but to this I'll swear,) on the point of writing to you to ask you to post to me the benefit of the *Ragged Lady*, your novel that you mentioned to me so long as nearly 2 years ago as then finished, that has since then, I gather, been put forth as a book, & that I yearn to read in a copy not bought with vulgar gold but having my name in it as from your hand.[1] Will you do this? – definitely? My articulate thanks will then be, *as* definitely, your portion. Àpropos of which matters I confess I'm sorry to hear from you that you've not read that much-battered (I'm told) *Awkward Age* that you so kindly (&, you may feel, so blindly,) godfathered: all the more that you won't ever, now – for it's one of those things that, if not done at the time, as it were, get fatally out of hand.[2] On the other hand, I'm very glad you didn't read the thing serially, for I feel that it's only as a book that it compactly exists – that it isn't read *at all* unless so read. This, of course, was not my intention, but just the opposite: what happened was that I found the subject had much more to *give*, was still more curious & rich than it had first struck me as having & being, & that in short it grew & rounded itself on my hands. This made it longer, much, than the

1. *Ragged Lady* (1899), started in 1896 and written (with interruptions) by the end of 1897, was serialized in *Harper's Bazar* from 2 July to 5 November 1898 and appeared as a book in February 1899.
2. Howells did read *The Awkward Age*, for in his essay promoting 'Mr Henry James's Later Work' in the *North American Review* of January 1903 he comments approvingly on the book's method: 'What he does is simply to show you these people mainly on the outside, as you mainly see people in the world, and to let you divine them and their ends from what they do and say.' It was 'much-battered' by the critics, though they acknowledged and sometimes admired HJ's skill: 'we are inexpressibly wearied by it' (*The Dial*); 'the reader's interest in the fortunes of its characters is in danger of waning to extinction before its close' (*Literature*); 'So much rarefied psychology, paralysis of will, and general bloodlessness has, after a time, a stultifying effect on the mind' (*Athenaeum*).

70,000 words intended – &, I'm afraid, awakened the disgust, thereby, of Editor & Publishers; at least I never heard from them, at all definitely that it *didn't*: so that I've sat in darkness ever since, under the dreadful sense of having failed (as if I were 25 again,) in the chance you had got for me. And yet, to my own perverse perception, nothing I've ever done is better – firmer, fuller, more unbrokenly sustained; in every way more expert & mature. *That* I only want to say to justify my regret at your not having been able to tackle it. But now wait for the next! I'm only sorry there is at present no track laid *for* a next – & I labour under the drawback that the *book* brings me still so little money that I can't afford to take the time to write one in the absence of *some* presumption of being able to serialize it. However, I shall fight this out better now that I'm really settled in the country – & meantime I didn't mean to afflict you afresh with my ignoble secrets. I'm doing a good deal in brevities – trying to learn to write "short stories" again as in the old days of the "Galaxy." The devil is that no periodical will *take* now anything of anything *like* the length of "The Extraordinary Case," your kind words about which, after long years, so greatly touch me.[3] To be mature in 5000 words is rather, *for* the mature, (25 years can do it, doubtless,) a sickening effort.

Very strange, but less "intimate" to me, naturally, than to you, the transformation of the Harper business, periodicals &c. – very obscure also, so long as unexplained & unvivified.[4] Also, further, somehow, rather saddening & crushing, as representing moves farther & farther away from "literature" – if indeed any move in any such direction have been, for a long time, left to be made. I hadn't realized the proportions of the particular abyss, which your letter seems to send a red spark fluttering down into. I had, just before it arrived, dropped (through my "literary agent,") a small packet of MS. into the black gulf;

3. Howells had found some old *Atlantic*s in their rented house, 'and found in one a brave early story of yours, which I had never forgotten, called A Most Extraordinary Case. I don't believe you've any idea how good it is; it is masterly, with an amazing grip on "cultivated American" character, which made me feel you ought never to have relaxed that hold.' (LFL, 349.) The story appeared in April 1868.

4. Howells had written: 'There have been cataclysmal changes at Franklin Square. The earth there has opened and taken in McClure and his company, where never was anything but Harpers before. Really I lost half a night's sleep in surprise and grief, and well-nigh forgot the shame of the Phillipine war. The magazine goes down to $3 a year, but the quality will keep up, and the opportunities will remain the same; certainly they will be no worse. The new house will publish six periodicals.' (LFL, 350.) Harper & Brothers had been deeply in debt, and was reorganized in 1899 by the financial house of J. P. Morgan. In the event S. S. McClure (1857–1949), founder-editor of the McClure Syndicate and partner in Doubleday & McClure, was to have purchased a controlling share but withdrew in October 1899 due to lack of funds. Then George B. Harvey (1864–1928), owner and editor of the *North American Review*, was asked to take over the firm.

addressed, that is, in spite of the *A.A.*, a short fiction (about 8000 words,) to "Harper" – or addressed, rather, I believe, an inquiry as to whether they would care for it. Should you, by any remote chance, hear any of the now, (isn't it?) so strangely commingled company, wondering if they *do* care for a small masterpiece called "The Beldonald Holbein," throw out a hint to them that they are quite probably enchanted with it.[5] Can you in any way reveal to me who is the new (or actual) editor of *The Atlantic*?[6] It's queer to be coming to you at this time of day with such questions – but I'm in the grossest darkness, & have been for a long time, at the hands of that periodical, & yet it *may* come to pass that my "literary agent," though not of much use for anywhere but this country, shall find himself approaching the cold theatre of my early triumphs as a supplicant. But a truce to these sordid images.

I'm infinitely interested in your personal & paternal news. How you make me yearn for a walk with you on the Maine rocks, or through the Maine woods, or by the Maine sea. Your summer history sounds delightful – & to have *all* that "& Heaven too" (by which I mean California too, & its golden crowns, in the forms of the victorious John,) must indeed have warmed your innards.[7] I rejoice immensely over what you tell me of John's career & the rate at which it moves. Please transmit to him my blessing & tell him that I pat him on the back till he chokes. Oh, I remember, too, "Wassons" & things.[8] But they seem very ghostly. I have had a very quiet, solitary & extremely rural summer (since July 10*th*, when I came back from 4 months in Italy,) & I cultivate this prospect for the months to come – save that I am now looking, from week to week, for the advent of my brother W*m* & his wife & daughter – he fresh (if fresh that can be called,) from a long cure at Nauheim where an evil *heart* has most woefully forced him to seek amelioration. He has in some degree found it, I

5. HJ had sent it to Pinker on 8 September for forwarding to the Harpers. It was published in *Harper's New Monthly Magazine* only in October 1901. Since returning from the Continent HJ had been working his way through a list of fourteen subjects in his notebook. He had also written – to judge by his letters to Pinker – 'Paste', 'Winchelsea, Rye and *Denis Duval*', 'The Present Literary Situation in France', 'Broken Wings' and 'The Special Type'. He continued till the year's end with an unnamed tale of '5,182' words (perhaps 'The Tree of Knowledge'), 'The Faces' (later 'The Two Faces'), 'Miss Gunton of Poughkeepsie' and 'The Third Person'.
6. Bliss Perry (1860–1954), novelist and critic, was editor of the *Atlantic* for ten years from 1899.
7. 'All this and heaven too' entered the language from the *Life of Philip Henry* by Matthew Henry (1662–1714). The architectural firm of Howells's son John (Howells, Stokes & Hornbostel) had won second prize in the California University Buildings competition for the design of the Berkeley campus.
8. D. A. Wasson (1823–87) was a well-known Transcendentalist poet and essayist, an *Atlantic* contributor, whom Perry had attacked in April 1864 in the *Harvard Magazine*. The Howellses were renting a house from his painter son, George Savary Wasson (1855–1931).

believe, but he spends the winter on this side of the sea.[9] I remain here till January or February – I find the country more & more a source of profit & even of rejuvenescence – a simplification to good ends. I send *Tanti saluti* to Mrs. Howells & I keep tight hold of the memory of Mildred. *Don't* forget the Ragged Lady – & believe, my dear Howells, in the perfect fidelity of your very old friend, the Ragged Gentleman

Henry James

173. To James Brand Pinker
9 November 1899

Yale MS   Unpublished

The complicated autumn of 1899 saw HJ extremely productive and full of projects, probably writing a scenario for The Sense of the Past *and an early scenario of* The Ambassadors. *This letter most likely refers to the early* Ambassadors *scheme, which was sent first to Bliss Perry of the* Atlantic; *the version of the scenario which survives is dated 1 September 1900 and was sent to Harper's then (N, 541–76).* The Ambassadors *would thus appear, after delays, not in the* Atlantic, *which rejected it, but in a Harpers journal, the* North American Review, *from January to December 1903. HJ was also negotiating (through Pinker) with the new Harper firm, proposing 'the delivery early in the year 1900 . . . of a novel in 80,000 words, calculated to appear in a reputable American periodical in ten instalments of 8000 words each' (Unpublished Yale MS, 4 October, Za James 1, vol. 1). Later in October, at the Kiplings' in Rottingdean, HJ met Frank Nelson Doubleday (1862–1934), the American publisher, at the time associated with Harpers, who encouraged him to think of more ghostly fiction like 'The Turn of the Screw'. On 23 October HJ told Pinker he had written to Doubleday's employee Cornford 'in relation to* two *separately serialisable stories of about 40,000 words apiece' (Unpublished Yale MS, Za James 1, vol. 1). One of these was to be 'The Sense of the Past', which as HJ wrote to Howells on 29 June 1900 'was to have been supplied to a certain Mr. Doubleday who was then approaching me . . . as the most outstretched arm of the reconstructed Harpers' (Doubleday's arm was then 'drawn in again, or lopped*

9. WJ was to have given the Gifford lectures at Edinburgh, starting on 15 January 1900, on 'The Psychology of Religious Experience'. With postponements due partly to his health problems, they would not begin till 16 May 1901. WJ had been sent to Nauheim by the heart specialist Dr William Bezly Thorne. The William Jameses stayed in HJ's London flat from about 10 October till 1 December when WJ took a fortnight at Malvern; then he spent a month with HJ at Rye before departing again for the Continent.

off . . . Doubleday simply vanished into space' – presumably because of his partner McClure's collapse). These 'two Tales – each tales of "terror"', were to make 'another duplex book' like The Two Magics *(LFL, 355).*

Lamb House, Rye.
Nov. 9*th* 1899.

Dear Mr. Pinker.

I send you to-day, separately, the Project for a Novel, as yet unchristened, that I promised you. I finished it a week ago, but my typist in London asked, for a particular reason, for a special allowance of time – which I gave; & I have but just got the copy. I have another, of course, if you want a second. The thing so speaks for and explains itself that I have nothing to add with it. I could do it – only *long* to go on with it – <u>soon</u>; though if my idea for Doubleday (through Cornford) is met, I should prefer to do those things (as each shorter,) first. One or the other, at all events, I am quite languishing, quite *sick*, to be warranted & secured in getting at! Yours very truly

Henry James[1]

174. To Henrietta Reubell
[12 November 1899]

Houghton MS   Published SL2, 315–17; partly published LHJ I, 333–5

HJ wrote to Henrietta Reubell on 25 October that 'Ça ne m'est pas égal du tout – je vous prie de croire – what you may have thought of "The Awkward Age." I only wish you had expressed yourself more fully – if you had anything in mind – about it. It is too satiric, too ironic, to be understanded of the many; & too touffu, *closepacked, complicated & architectural (in form) – if you know what that means! – to be, I fear, easy reading. But it is some re[s]pects the best thing I've done. I am working rather steadily & abundantly – & shall be having, before too long – other things to send you.' (Unpublished Houghton MS, bMS Am 1094 (1139).)*

---

1. On 13 December Bliss Perry, editor of the *Atlantic*, wrote to HJ to say, as HJ told Pinker, 'that he has seen the Synopsis of my novel & is much taken with it – but is uncertain & will write you "in a day or two"; offering, I infer, a price (for serialization.)' HJ says the projected story is to be 80,000 words. The *Atlantic* did not in the event take any more HJ novels: the paper's business-manager MacGregor Jenkins begged the editor in 1900 'with actual tears in his eyes' not to print another 'sinker' by James lest the *Atlantic* be thought 'a "high-brow" periodical' (Bliss Perry, *And Gladly Teach: Reminiscences* (1935), 178).

LAMB HOUSE, RYE.
Sunday midnight

Dear Etta Reubell.

I have had great pleasure of your last good letter & this is a word of fairly prompt reconnaissance. Your bewilderment over *The Awkward Age* doesn't on the whole surprise me – for that ingenious volume appears to have excited little *but* bewilderment – except indeed, *here*, thick-witted denunciation. A work of art that one has to *explain* fails, in so far, I suppose, of its mission. I suppose I must at any rate mention that I had in view a certain special social (highly "modern" & actual) London group & type & tone, which seemed to me to *se prêter à merveille* to an ironic – lightly & simply ironic! – treatment, & that clever people at least would know who, in general, & what, one meant. But here, at least, it appears, there are very few clever people. One must point with finger-posts – one must label with *pancartes* – one must explain with *conférences!* The *form*, doubtless, of my picture is against it – a form all dramatic & scenic – of presented episodes, architecturally combined & each making a piece of the building; with no going behind, no *telling about* the figures save by their own appearance & action & with explanation reduced to the explanation of everything by all the other things *in* the picture. Mais il parait qu'il ne faut pas faire comme ça: personne n'y comprend rien: j'en suis pour mes frais – qui avaient été considérables, *très*-considérables! [TRANSLATION: "But it seems one must not do it this way; nobody understands anything by it: I''ve had all my trouble for nothing – and my trouble was considerable – *very* considerable!"] Yet I seem to make out you were interested – & that consoles me. I think Mrs. Brook the best thing I've ever done – & Nanda also much *done*. Voilà. Mitchy marries Aggie by a calculation – in consequence of a state of mind – delicate & deep, but that I meant to show on his part as highly conceivable. It's *absolute* to him that N. will never have him – & she *appeals* to him for another girl, whom she sees him as "saving" (from things – realities – she sees.) If he does it (& she shows how she values him by wanting it,) it is still a way of getting & keeping near her – of making for *her*, to him, a tie of gratitude. She becomes, as it were, to him, responsible for his happiness – they can't (*especially if the marriage goes ill*) *not* be – given the girl that Nanda is – more, rather than less, together. And the *finale* of the picture *justifies* him: it leaves Nanda, precisely, with his case on her hands. Far-fetched? Well, I daresay: but so are diamonds & pearls & the beautiful Reubell turquoises! So I scribble to you, to be sociable, by my loud-ticking clock, in this sleeping little town, at my usual more than midnight hour.

I'm so glad you saw & liked Mrs White: she's far & away one of the most charming women I've ever known.[1] Yet I see her rarely – one can't live in her world & do any work or save any money or retain control of 3 minutes of one's time. So a gulf separates us. I'm too poor to see her! She has extraordinary harmony & grace.

Well, also, I'm like you – I like growing (that is I like, for many reasons, *being*) old: 56! But I don't like growing *older*. I quite love my present age & the compensations, simplifications, freedoms, independences, memories, advantages of it. But I don't keep it long enough – it passes too quickly. But it mustn't pass *all* (good as that is,) in writing to *you*! There is nothing I shall like more to dream of than to be conveyed by you to the Expositionist Kraals of the savages & haunts of the cannibals.[2] I surrender myself to you de confiance – in vision & hope – for that purpose. Jonathan Sturges lives, year in, year out, at Long's Hotel, Bond St. & promises to come down here & see me, but never does. He knows hordes of people, every one extraordinarily likes him, & he has tea-parties for pretty ladies: one at a time. Alas, he is ¾'s of the time ill; but his little spirit is colossal. Sargent grows in weight, honour & interest – to *my* view. He does one fine thing after another – & his crucifixion (that is big crucifié with Adam & Eve under each arm of cross catching drops of blood) for Boston Library is a most noble, grave & admirable thing.[3] But it's already tomorrow & I am yours always

Henry James

175. To Katharine Prescott Wormeley
28 November 1899

Yale MS   Unpublished

This is 'the strenuous Miss Wormeley' (1830–1908), sister of Ariana Curtis of Venice, who had once been T. S. Perry's Sunday-school teacher and lived in

1. The former Margaret (Daisy) Stuyvesant Rutherford (1854–1916) was the wife of Henry White (1850–1927), First Secretary of the U.S. Embassy in London in 1900 and from 1908 U.S. Ambassador in Paris.
2. HJ had written to Henrietta Reubell on 25 October, 'Is Paris autumnally pretty – or does the Exhibition (which, please God, I shan't see,) too effectually build out the sunset?' (Unpublished Houghton MS, bMS Am 1094 (1139).)
3. The work mentioned is part of Sargent's 'Judaism and Christianity' (1895–1916), a sequence of mural decorations, and is described in the library's guide: 'On the cross is the figure of the dead Christ, with the figures of Adam and Eve, typifying Humanity, kneeling on either side. They are closely bound to the body of Christ, since all are of one flesh, and each holds a chalice to receive the Sacred Blood.'

Jackson, New Hampshire. Her Memoir of Honoré de Balzac, *which came out in 1892, takes issue with HJ's 1875 'Honoré de Balzac' about Balzac's idea of women. She slightly misquotes HJ on Balzac's attitudes: 'It seems to us that his superior handling of women is both a truth and fallacy . . . There is not a line in him that would not be received with hisses at any convention for giving women the suffrage or admitting them to Harvard College . . . He takes the old-fashioned view of woman as the female of man, and in all respects his subordinate.' She treats this account, disapprovingly, as reflecting only HJ's own view: 'It is not likely,' she says, 'that many could be found to endorse the views just quoted, because, in the first place (and without touching upon the question of Balzac at all) the tone of these remarks is contemptuous of womanhood. They belong to a period of ideas on which is written* passagère.*' (*Memoir, 260, 261.*)*

LAMB HOUSE, RYE.

Dear Miss Wormeley.

I wrote you the other day; but this is a fresh line to thank you for the so interesting vol. the Balzac biography, which has come since, & for your not less interesting elucidative letter, accompanying it. I turned, immediately, with excitement to the invidious, the incriminated pages that you name to me, & I was really disappointed to find them so almost divinely gentle in their animadversions. I'll tell you what they *are* a monument to – the beautiful tenderness of your conscience: if you could let such a mild & doubtless deserved rap on my knuckles weigh (a hair's-weight) on it. "Ill-nature" nil: "acerbity" less than nil. Yes, I'll put it that I merited worse. I won't even defend myself. I *could*, if [I] could take the time; but I prefer to give that to saying something else to you. (My article on Balzac, par parenthèse, was, moreover, written long years ago – in 1874 – though printed, I believe in '75 or '76; & seems to me now to belong to a very primitive critical state. I was young – that is I was 31. That seems to me now infantile!) *The* interesting thing is your wondrous labour over, & possession of, him – for the use, so mystifying to me, of an alien race in an alien air.[1] The mystery of a possible *relation* to Balzac (of your readers,) which doesn't take in that prime condition his *tongue* is a phenomenon on which I won't linger: what I am lost in admiration of is your service to him & your mastery of him. These things are beautiful – magnificent. Be sure he knows it all, in some mansion in the skies, & looking down on snow-bound

---

1. HJ wrote to her a couple of months after this letter that she was 'in danger of tending or desiring too much to reconstruct a B.[alzac] in conformity with Anglo-Saxon ideals' (Unpublished Yale MS, Za Cortissoz; 8 February 1900).

Jackson N.H., finds more – more romance & profundity & variety – in the Human Comedy, than ever he put on paper. I greatly value both of your volumes, & note everything you say of the tortuous Louvenjoul. I shall profit by you yet – & so far as I can, publicly commemorate you.[2] And to think how you *might* have staid with me! Oh, it was a morbid stroke! I regret you afresh; I thank you, otherwise, not less renewedly, & I am, dear Miss Wormeley yours quite unscathedly & more than ever cordially

Henry James

Nov: 28: 1899.

176. To Sarah Orne Jewett
24 December 1899

Huntington MS   Unpublished

The Queen's Twin, and other stories, *Jewett's latest collection of New England tales, was published in 1900. Britain had suffered a series of setbacks in the Boer War, which had begun in October; on 12 November HJ had told Gosse, 'I find S. Africa a nightmare & need cheering.' (SLHJEG, 172.)*

LAMB HOUSE, RYE.
Dec. 24 *1899*

Dear Sarah Jewett.

I sit in one of the little old rooms you wot of, on Christmas eve, & I thank you very kindly indeed, very rejoicingly, for the precious "Queen's Twin". It is in fact almost Xmas Day – so late the night waxes & so still, huddled on its hilltop under the winter stars, the little old black town sleeps. I snatch the

2. The Viscount A. C. J. de Spoelberch de Lovenjoul (1836–1907) – HJ misspells his name here – was the author of several *Études balzaciennes*, including *Un Roman d'amour* (1896) about Balzac's relations with Mme Hanska. The British Library copy bears Miss Wormeley's increasingly wrathful purple marginalia, pointing out Lovenjoul's errors of fact or 'pure speculation' (28). On page 66 she says Lovenjoul had offered to sell her Balzac's letters to Hanska without revealing the literary property in them was not his. On page 77 she suggests Lovenjoul is printing a partly forged letter. On page 106, 'All this is shameful.' In 1902 HJ's introduction to a translation of Balzac's *The Two Young Brides*, perhaps the public commemoration mentioned here, calls her 'the devoted American translator, interpreter, worshipper, who in the course of her own studies has so often found occasion to differ from M. de Lovenjoul on matters of fact and questions of date and appreciation'.

small backwater of an hour – of a quarter of an hour, from complications & preoccupations. I recall, in the pitiless quietude that murmurs me no relief & stretches me no perch of excuse, my deep dark guilt in having had other volumes from you, last spring, all unacknowledged &, (save by fond perusal & reperusal,) much less honoured as they deserve. They came while I was in Italy, & I found them on my return. I revelled in them – I lived into them – but I didn't turn & *chatter* to you about them! Well, after all, it was graver and nobler so. Let me put it that I feel too much about them. *No one*, at any rate, I firmly believe, squeezes more of the whole fragrance out of your exquisite work than I do. The sense & the sound, the colour & the taste, the meaning of every stroke & the felicity of every – felicity: these things I am at home in as in the very lap of the Muse. I find in The Queen's Twin all of everything I so luxuriously count on with you; & most, perhaps, in the Coon Dog (perfection!) & Aunt Cynthy Dallett.[1] Don't intermit – don't languish – don't *not* do anything that ever occurs to you: for I desire & require you with the revolving season. I wish I had something, myself, to send you. Well, I shall have before long. I've done a goodish many short things, all these months, & am doing more, & a volume – a couple of volumes – are brewing.[2] I had lately a most kind note from Mrs. Fields, which shall have an early & direct response.[3] My brother William & his wife are with me – he rather gravely ill; yet, I am happy to say, promising at last to improve – within limits. I fear, however, his great activity will be hereafter broken-winged. But it's a case – a serious affection of the heart – to be grateful for small mercies. Forgive, dear Miss Jewett, my long, lame silence & my short, lame speech; believe in my constant attention & affection; & take from me the heartiest wishes for the great dimly-looming, formidably-bulking, ambiguously-scowling New Year: I mean for your own terms of life & work with him. England is sad, England is rubbing

1. In 'The Coon Dog' two old New England villagers leave behind Rover, an aged hunting dog, borrowing instead a poor old neighbour's inherited and reputedly 'very val'able coon dog' Tiger to hunt racoons one night. But Tiger runs away and Rover, reappearing, trees a racoon for them. In the morning they allow the neighbour to believe Tiger lives up to his name, and she goes off to sell him. In the understated 'Aunt Cynthy Dallett', a kindly old widow living in a house on the mountain is visited one New Year's Day, according to old custom, by her desperately impoverished niece and a friend. There is some discussion of the informal etiquette of New England country visits. The niece offers her enfeebled aunt accommodation in her own house; Aunt Cynthy, declaring herself too old to move, invites the niece to come and live with her.
2. *The Soft Side*, containing twelve stories, was published in August 1900 by Methuen in Britain and Macmillan in America. HJ had already written at least four of the stories that would appear in *The Better Sort* (1903).
3. The letter promised here is not known to exist.

her eyes – but she profits by discipline, & I love her better bruised than purely & simply bruising. Good night!

Yours very constantly,
Henry James

177. To James Brand Pinker
17 January 1900

Yale MS   Unpublished

On New Year's Day 1900 HJ explained to Rhoda Broughton his protracted absence from London: 'I've been the victim, among other things, of an economic crisis' (HJL IV, 128). In negotiations for the new collection of stories, Pinker's involvement as agent caused difficulties with HJ's existing publishers, who had previously dealt with HJ directly. HJ moved from Heinemann to Methuen for The Soft Side *partly because of Heinemann's fierce campaign against literary agents. On 15 January 1900 HJ wrote to Pinker of Heinemann's 'rejoinder': 'ıst: that he tells me he shall not even answer your letter! & 2d, that I have written to him repeating that I have placed the disposal of the book in question definitely in your hands & that it must remain in them. That point is therefore settled.' (Unpublished Yale MS, Za James 1, vol. 1.) To Lucy Clifford on 24 January HJ spoke of 'a lively row (temporarily calmed) with Heinemann – over Pinker!' (HJL IV, 130.)*

Lamb House, Rye.
January 17*th* 1900.

Dear Mr. Pinker

Both the arrangements you write me of under date of yesterday – that with Methuen & that with *Punch* – are highly satisfactory.[1] I will send you in a very few days the 6000 words for *Punch*, divided so as to make two instalments. And I will as quickly as possible send you the arranged copy for the volume. Will you, when the arrangement for the volume is concluded – as to approximate date, &c – (*I* prefer an early one) write on the subject of the American book-rights to *Mr. George P. Brett*, Macmillan Company, 66 Fifth Avenue, New York – arranging with him for simultaneity of publication. I shall

---

1. Methuen paid an advance of £100 for *The Soft Side*. The story for *Punch* was 'Mrs Medwin', sent to Pinker on 30 January 1900 and published in August–September 1901, for which HJ was paid £66 3s. (after deduction of Pinker's 10 per cent).

meanwhile myself have written him – & I regard the book as promised to him. But I don't expect him to give as much "down" as Methuen gives – to give more than £100. He *will*, I daresay, give that.[2]

I must tell you that I have broken down on the subject of "The Sense of the Past," the thing I wrote you that I had begun (for 50,000–60,000 words:) I mean as to that particular idea.[3] It is admirable, but it proves diabolically, tormentingly *difficult* except for some very spacious occasion, when I can give large leisure to it. So I am laying it aside – with a little time wasted; & would say that I would do, in the same compass, another & different thing immediately were it not that if I do take upon myself to do some more short tales (on your arranging, if you can, with "Truth" N.Y. & with Collier – & such chances as this thing for *Punch*,) I think I had better keep myself free for *them* & for getting on with the thing of which I sent you the Synopsis.[4] Without delaying too much *that*, this combination will be probably as much as I can manage. So let us consider "The Sense of the Past" or its equivalent postponed. Yours ever

Henry James

2. George Platt Brett (1858–1936) was president till his death of the Macmillan Company of New York, a separate entity from the London firm since 1896. In November 1897 Brett had obliged HJ by bringing out a pre-publication copyright edition of 'John Delavoy', one of the stories in *The Soft Side* (which HJ at first wanted to call after 'The Great Good Place'). On 2 January HJ had told Pinker to offer the volume first to Brett in New York and Heinemann in London, saying: 'I should wish it to go naturally, to the people whose "sum down" would be largest. Could I get £100 in London & the same in N.Y. – £200 altogether – I should be content.' Pinker proposed to Brett on 5 January terms including an advance of £150; but by 22 February HJ was writing to Pinker in embarrassment that 'it was not a case in which I felt that I have a free hand', and that Brett had insisted on the same terms as for the last HJ book he had published – *The Two Magics*, for which the advance was £50. 'Please now let him have it – the present volume – on these terms. It will terminate, in all probability, my relations with him (for the future).' (Unpublished Yale MSS, Za James 1, vol. 1.)

3. On 2 January HJ had written: 'I am well started on the short novel (50,000 to 60,000 words) that I named to you recently & if all goes well could finish it by March *1st* – deliver it, I mean. It wd. possibly be called "The Sense of the Past." But it's not "abstract"! – it's thrilling!'

4. *Truth* (New York) published 'Miss Gunton of Poughkeepsie' in May–June 1900; *Collier's Weekly* published 'The Special Type' on 16 June 1900. 'The thing of which I sent you the Synopsis' may be *The Ambassadors*, or *The Wings of the Dove*: on 30 January HJ told Pinker, 'I want to get at my longer novel if the *Atlantic* wants it, & even whether the *Atlantic* wants it or not.' (Unpublished Yale MS, Za James 4.)

178. To Violet Hunt
1 April 1900

Virginia MS   Unpublished

After sending off complete copy for the volume of tales on 25 January, HJ kept up his rate of production. On 22 February he told Pinker, 'I am doing half-a-dozen short stories – four of which are practically ready to send you.' On 25 February he sent 'The Tone of Time', with three others due back from the typist soon to be forwarded: 'The Story in It' was sent on 27 February. When HJ sent 'Flickerbridge' on 2 March, he told Pinker, 'I am keeping back a little The Sacred Fount, *the 4th of this little group I spoke of sending you; because I am not yet satisfied with it – but you shall have it soon.' (Unpublished MSS Yale, Za James 1, vol. 1.) HJ spent 10–27 March in London, staying at his rooms in the Reform Club, having let 34 De Vere Gardens for a year.*

HJ had known the novelist Violet Hunt (1866–1942) since she was a girl, having visited her father, the painter Alfred Hunt. She led an active love-life – even Oscar Wilde had proposed to her about 1880 – and had an affair with the diplomat, writer and editor Oswald Crawfurd, who had an invalid wife and gave her syphilis, as well as with Somerset Maugham and H. G. Wells. In 1908 she would meet another friend of HJ's, Ford Madox Hueffer, and start a conspicuous decade-long liaison. Pinker was also her agent. She became an energetic advocate of female suffrage. Her 1899 novel The Human Interest: A Study in Incompatibilities *is a mock* Madame Bovary*: a shallow unhappy wife from Newcastle, self-consciously imitating Nora in* A Doll's House *('I am a great Ibsenite!'), throws herself into London artistic circles and at a serious painter, and ends in farcical desperation by taking what she thinks is poison.*

LAMB HOUSE, RYE.

Dear Violet Hunt.

Let me not delay longer to thank you more intelligently for *The Human Interest*, which I have now absorbed in its totality. I am extremely struck with its cleverness & expertness – your acuteness of mind & skill of hand. Of course I don't, in my battered & wrinkled stage of life & reflection, read any fiction *naivement* & unquestioningly – the eternal critic within me insists on his rights & takes his ease, or his fun, as he goes – & he, precisely, was set in motion, – which he isn't on every occasion, by any means. He made, in short, his account of the affair. But I have no right whatever to thrust him on you – that was by no means what your graceful offering invited. Besides, he *talks* – or *would* talk – his impression: he *will* indeed talk it to you, if you'll then let him, on his first chance. For the present please believe me under the charm of your wonderfully observant talent & singularly neat execution. I haven't alas, absorbed your young Irish friend yet. But I will take an early hour.[1] Believe me yours always

Henry James

April 1. 1900.

179. To James Brand Pinker
12 June 1900

Yale MS   Unpublished

On 12 May HJ, who was still expanding The Sacred Fount, *reported to WJ that 'I have totally shaved off my beard, unable to bear longer the increased hoariness of its growth: it had suddenly begun these 3 months since, to come out quite white – & made me feel, as well as look so old. Now, I feel* forty *– & clean & light.' (CWJ III, 119.)*

In July 1901 HJ told Pinker he had 'well started' The Wings of the Dove *'more than a year ago'; which suggests he made a beginning on it during the period of creative flux in the first half of 1900.*

The Doubleday–McClure Harper connection having collapsed, Doubleday joined with Walter Hines Page (1855–1918) in 1899 to form Doubleday, Page & Company.

Lamb House, Rye.
June 12*th* 1900.

Dear Mr. Pinker.

I have no objection whatever to Mr. Doubleday's having *The Sacred Fount* if he should wish to do so.[1] But it isn't the thing, in the least, I planned to give

---

1. The 'young Irish friend' is probably Ethel Colburn Mayne (1870–1941), born in Cork, who shared Violet Hunt's feminist sympathies and wrote stories in *The Yellow Book* as 'Frances E. Huntley'. If so, HJ read her first book *The Clearer Vision* (1900), and judged its author 'did not cut the cord' (HJVH, 8).

1. *The Sacred Fount*, which was not serialized in a magazine, was published on 6 February 1901 by Scribner's in New York and on 15 February 1901 by Methuen in London.

him when that negotiation dropped, in the autumn. It's quite another matter. *That* particular thing (a wonderful terrible story to have been called *The Sense of the Past*) I can't write *now* (the idea is too damnably difficult.) But I shld. have magnificently risen to it *then*, – was doing so; I believe, if the negotiation hadn't dropped. If Doubleday doesn't care for *The Sacred Fount* & wd. care for *another* thing of 50,000 or 60,000 words, my idea would be something "International." *That's* what I want more & more to do, & I have ½ a dozen subjects in my head. I have just received the (intended-to-be) final type-copy of *The Sacred Fount*, with the exception of the last sixth, which I am intensely finishing, & *shall* have finished in a very few days. Meanwhile I am sending back my copy for reproduction with embodied new inspired last touches. But the whole thing will take very few days. You shall then have it all. Believe me yours ever

Henry James

180. To William Dean Howells
9 and 14 August 1900

Houghton TS and MS   Published HJL IV, 157–62; LFL, 358–62; partly published LHJ I, 354–60

It was not till 25 July that HJ sent Pinker the completed MS of The Sacred Fount, *which he admitted was recognizably 'a thing planned as a very short story, & growing, on my hands, to a so much longer thing, by a force of its own – but a force controlled & directed, I believe, or hope, happily enough. It is fanciful, fantastic – but very close and sustained, & calculated to minister to curiosity.' (HJL IV, 154–5.) On 10 July he had told Jonathan Sturges he was "on the point of sitting down to the 50,000 of another (an international tale of terror, bespoken from a respectable source)" (HJL IV, 153). This was another attempt on* The Sense of the Past.*

On 29 June HJ had responded enthusiastically to a letter – not extant – Howells had sent from Annisquam, Cape Ann, about a syndication enterprise he was floating, the International Association of Newspapers and Authors, to put out a number of novels. HJ declared himself ready to provide a 50,000-word novel by December 1900: "I can get at the book, I think, almost immediately and do it within the next three or four months." Howells had suggested "an international ghost", and HJ was struck by the promising coincidence that this had been his difficult subject in The Sense of the Past. *But "I'm not even sure that the international ghost is what will most bear being worried out." Uncertain about* The Sense of the Past, *HJ*

mentions a second possible subject (conceived for Doubleday) in the same category:
"I had only, when the project collapsed, caught hold of the tip of the tail of this
other monster", which he would do for Howells if "I can at all recapture him, *or*
anything like him" (LFL, 355–6).

    On 15 July Howells wrote back to HJ, slightly alarmed, emphasizing "how
conditional the enterprise is" (LFL, 356). (It soon collapsed because Howells
distrusted the publisher James Clarke.)

Read P.S. (Aug. 14th) first!

Lamb House, RYE.

August 9, 1900.

My dear Howells,

    I duly received and much pondered your second letter, charming and vivid,
from Annisquam; the one, I mean, in reply to mine dispatched immediately
on the receipt of your first. If I haven't since its arrival written to you, this is
because, precisely, I needed to work out my question somewhat further first.
My impulse was immediately to say that I wanted to do my little stuff at any
rate, and was willing therefore to take any attendant risk, however measured,
as the little stuff would be, at the worst, a thing I should see my way to dispose
of in another manner. But the problem of the little stuff itself intrinsically
worried me – to the extent, I mean, of my not feeling thoroughly sure I might
make of it what I wanted and above all what your conditions of space required.
The thing was therefore to try and satisfy myself practically – by threshing
out my subject to as near an approach to certainty as possible. This I have
been doing with much intensity – but with the result, I am sorry to say, of
being still in the air. Let the present accordingly pass for a provisional
communication – not to leave your last encompassed with too much silence.
Lending myself as much as possible to your suggestion of a little "tale of
terror" that should be also International, I took straight up again the idea I
spoke to you of having already, some months ago, tackled and, for various
reasons, laid aside.[1] I have been attacking it again with intensity and on the
basis of a simplification that would make it easier, and have done for it, thus,
110 pages of type. The upshot of this, alas, however, is that though this second
start is, if I – or if *you* – like, magnificent, it seriously confronts me with the
element of *length*; showing me, I fear, but too vividly, that, do what I will for
compression, I shall not be able to squeeze my subject into 50,000 words. It

---

1. *The Sense of the Past.*

will make, even if it doesn't, for difficulty, still beat me, 70,000 or 80,000 – dreadful to say; and that faces me as an excessive addition to the ingredient of "risk" we speak of. On the other hand I am not sure that I can hope to substitute for this particular affair *another* affair of "terror" which *will* be expressible in the 50,000; and that for an especial reason. This reason is that, above all when one has done the thing, already, as I have, rather repeatedly, it is not easy to concoct a "ghost" of any freshness.[2] The want of ease is extremely marked, moreover, if the thing is to be done on a certain scale of length. One might still toss off a spook or two more if it were a question only of the "short-story" dimension; but prolongation and extension constitute a strain which the merely *apparitional* – discounted, also, as by my past dealings with it, doesn't do enough to mitigate. The beauty of this notion of "The Sense of the Past" of which I have again, as I tell you, been astride, is precisely that it involves without the stale effect of the mere bloated bugaboo, the presentation, for folk both in and out of the book, of such a sense of gruesome *malaise* as can only – success being assumed – make the fortune, in the "literary world," of everyone concerned. I haven't, in it, really (that is save in one very partial preliminary and expository connection,) to make anything, or anybody, "appear" to anyone: what the case involves is, awfully interestingly and thrillingly, that the "central figure", the subject of the experience, has the terror of a particular ground for feeling and fearing that *he himself* is, or may be, may at any moment become, a producer, an object, of this (for you and me) state of panic on the part of others. He lives in an air of *malaise* as to the *malaise* he may, woefully, more or less fatally, find himself creating – and that, roughly speaking, is the essence of what I have seen. It is less gross, much less *banal* and exploded, than the dear old familiar bugaboo; produces, I think, for the reader, an almost equal funk – or at any rate an equal suspense and unrest;

---

2. On this day, 9 August 1900, seemingly after writing this letter, HJ worried in his notebook at the possibility of 'some possible *alternative* to the 50,000 words story as to which I've been corresponding with Howells'. He recalled that 'I *had* a vague sense, last autumn when I was so deludedly figuring out *The S. of the P.* for "Doubleday," that, as a no. 2 thing (in "Terror") for the same volume, there dwelt a possibility in something expressive of the peculiarly acute Modern, the current polyglot, the American-experience-abroad line ... *The Advertiser* is an idea – a beautiful one, if one could happily fantasticate it.' *The Advertiser*, when first mentioned on 21 December 1895, was not described: '*The Advertiser* (Hall Caine): The idea, as I hinted it, the other night when I was dining with the former, to Colvin and Barrie (it came to me on the spot roughly and vividly), strikes me as really magnificent.' (N, 146.) HJ goes on: 'I see the *picture* somehow – saw it, that night, in the train back from Brighton – the picture of the 3 or 4 "scared" and slightly modern American figures moving against the background of three or four European *milieux*, different European conditions, out of which their obsession, their visitation is projected.' (N, 189–91.)

and carries with it, as I have "fixed" it, a more truly curious and interesting drama – especially a more human one. *But*, as I say, there are the necessities of space, as to which I have a dread of deluding myself only to find that by trying to blink them I shall be grossly "sold," or by giving way to them shall positively spoil my form for your purpose. The hitch is that the thing involves a devil of a sort of prologue or preliminary action – interesting itself and indispensable for lucidity – which impinges too considerably (for brevity) on the core of the subject. My one chance is yet, I admit, to try [to] attack the same (the subject) from still another quarter, at still another angle, that I make out as a possible one and which may keep it squeezable and short. If *this* experiment fails, I fear I shall have to "chuck" the supernatural and the high fantastic. I have just finished, as it happens, a fine flight (of eighty thousand words) *into* the high fantastic, which has rather depleted me, or at any rate affected me as discharging my obligations in that quarter. (But I believe I mentioned to you in my last "The Sacred Fount"+[3] – as to the title of which kindly preserve silence.) The *vraie vérité*, the fundamental truth lurking behind all the rest, is furthermore, no doubt, that, preoc[c]upied with half a dozen things of the altogether human order now fermenting in my brain, I don't care for "terror" (terror, that is, without "pity") so much as I otherwise might. This would seem to make it simple for me to say to you: "Hang it, if I can't pull off my Monster on *any* terms, I'll just do for you a neat little *human* – and not the less International – fifty-thousander consummately addressed to your more cheerful department; do for you, in other words, an admirable short novel of manners, thrilling too in its degree, but definitely ignoring the bugaboo." Well, this I *don't* positively despair of still sufficiently overtaking myself to be able to think of. *That* card one has always, thank God, up one's sleeve, and the production of it is only a question of a little shake of the arm. At the same time, here, to be frank – and above all, you will say, in this communication, to be interminable – that alternative is just a trifle compromised by the fact that I've two or three things begun ever so beautifully in such a key (and only awaiting the rush of the avid bidder!) – each affecting me with its particular obsession, and one, the *most* started, affecting me with the greatest obsession, for the time (till I can do it, work it off, get it out of the way and fall with still-accumulated intensity upon the *others*) of all.[4] But alas, if I don't

3. +'This has been "sold" to Methuen here, & by this time, probably, to somebody else in the U.S. – but, alas, not to be serialized (as to which indeed it is inapt.)' [HJ's MS note.]
4. *The Ambassadors* may be this '*most* started' fiction; it may also be *The Wings of the Dove*, which he had begun by October 1899. (See Sister Stephanie Vincec, ' "Poor Flopping *Wings*": The Making of Henry James's *The Wings of the Dove*', *Harvard Library Bulletin*, 24 (1976), 60–93.)

say, bang off, that *this* is then the thing I will risk for you, it is because "this", like its companions, isn't, any way I can fix it, workable as a fifty-thousander. The scheme to which I am *now* alluding is lovely – human, dramatic, International, exquisitely "pure," exquisitely everything; only absolutely condemned, from the germ up, to be workable in not less than 100,000 words. If 100,000 were what you had asked me for, I would fall back upon it, ("Terror" failing,) like a flash; and even send you, without delay, a detailed Scenario of it that I drew up a year ago; beginning then – a year ago – to *do* the thing – immediately afterwards; and then again pausing for reasons extraneous and economic.[5] (Because – now that I haven't to consider my typist – there was nobody to "take" it! The *Atlantic* declined – saying it really only wanted "Miss Johnson"!)[6] It really constitutes, at any rate, the work I intimately want actually to be getting on with; and – if you are not overdone with the profusion of my confidence – I dare say I best put my case by declaring that, if you don't in another month or two hear from me either as a Terrorist or as a Cheerful Internationalist, it will be that intrinsic difficulties will in each case have mastered me: the difficulty in the one having been to keep my Terror down by *any* ingenuity to the 50,000; and the difficulty in the other having been to get, for the moment, in close quarters with any *other* form of Cheer than the above-mentioned obsessive hundred-thousander. I only wish you wanted *him*. Yet I have now in all probability a decent outlet for him.[7]

Forgive my pouring into your lap this torrent of mingled uncertainties and superfluities. The latter indeed they are properly not, if only as showing you how our question does occupy me. I shall write you again – however vividly I see you wince at the prospect of it. I have it at heart not to fail to let you know how my alternatives settle themselves. Please believe meanwhile in my very hearty thanks for your intimation of what you might perhaps, your own quandary straightening out, see your way to do for me.[8] It is a kind of intimation that I find, I confess, even at the worst, dazzling. All this, however, trips up my response to your charming picture of your whereabouts and present conditions – still discernible, in spite of the chill of years and absence, to my eye, and eke to my ear, of memory. We have had here a torrid, but not wholly

5. The purchase of Lamb House in August 1899.
6. This bracketed insertion is handwritten. 'Miss Johnson' may refer to Mary Johnston (1870–1936), whose romance *To Have and to Hold* was a current bestseller.
7. *The Ambassadors* was in due course serialized in the *North American Review*, one of the Harpers' magazines.
8. 'If you like,' Howells had said, 'I will myself do your bargaining with the enterpriser; perhaps I can get better terms still, and at any rate I believe I can get better terms than you could.' (LFL, 357.)

a horrid, July; but are making it up with a brave August, so far as we have got, of fires and floods and storms and overcoats. Through everything, none the less, my purpose holds – my genius, I may even say, absolutely thrives – and I am unbrokenly yours,

Henry James

14th August.

P.S. The hand of Providence guided me, after finishing the preceding, to which the present is postscriptal, to keep it over a few days instead of posting it directly: so possible I thought it that I might have something more definite to add – and I was a little nervous about the way I had left our question. Behold then I *have* then to add that I have just received your letter of Aug. 4 – which so sim[pl]ifies our situation that this accompanying stuff becomes almost superfluous.[9] But I let it go for the sake of the interest, the almost top-heavy mass of response, that it embodies. Let us put it then that all is for the moment for the best in this worst of possible worlds: all the more that had I not just now been writing you exactly as I am, I should probably – and thanks, precisely, to the lapse of days – be stammering to you the ungraceful truth that, after I wrote you, my tale of terror *did*, as I was so more than half fearing, give way beneath me. It *has*, in short, broken down for the present. I am laying it away on the shelf for the sake of something that *is* in it, but that I am now too embarrassed and preoccupied to devote more time to pulling out. I really shouldn't wonder if it be not still, in time and place, to make the world sit up; but the curtain is dropped for the present. All thanks for your full and prompt statement of how the scene has shifted for you. There is no harm done, and I don't regard the three weeks spent on my renewed wrestle as wasted – I have, within three or four days, rebounded from them with such relief, vaulting into another saddle and counting, D.V. on a straighter run. I have *two* begun novels; which will give me plenty to do for the present – they being of the type of the "serious" which I am too delighted to see you speak of as lifting again, "Miss Johnson" *permettendolo*, its downtrodden head. I mean, at any rate, I assure you, to lift *mine*! Your extremely, touchingly kind offer to find moments of your precious time for "handling" something I might send you is altogether too momentous for me to let me fail of feeling almost ashamed that I haven't something – the ghost or t'other stuff – in form, already, to enable me to respond to your generosity "as meant". But heaven only knows what may happen yet! For the moment, I must peg away at what I have in hand – biggish

9. Howells's letter of 4 August, presumably announcing the collapse of the syndication scheme, is not known to survive.

stuff, I fear, in bulk and possible unserialisability, to saddle you withal.[10] But thanks, thanks, thanks. Delighted to hear of one of your cold waves – the newspapers here invidiously mentioning none but your hot. We have them all, moreover, *réchauffées*, as soon as you have done with them; and we are just sitting down to one now. I dictate you this in my shirt-sleeves and in a draught which fails of strength – chilling none of the pulses of yours gratefully and affectionately,

Henry James

181. To Alice Howe Gibbens James
1 October 1900

Houghton MS   Published HJL IV, 166–8

HJ produced a new version of the scenario of The Ambassadors, *dated 1 September 1900, which was then sent to Harper's. The editor of* Harper's Magazine, *Henry Mills Alden (1836–1919), a friend of Howells, commented in a memorandum: 'The story (in its mere plot) centres about an American youth in Paris who has been captivated by a charming French woman (separated from her husband) and the critical situations are developed in connection with the efforts of his friends and relatives to rescue him. The moral in the end is that he is better off in this captivity than in the conditions to which his friends would restore him. I do not advise acceptance. We ought to do better.' (NHJ, 372.) None the less, by October HJ was working on* The Ambassadors *for serialization in a Harper magazine, as well as arranging for* The Wings of the Dove.*

AHJ, who had been staying with HJ at Rye, had just over a week before rejoined WJ, who was again at Nauheim for his heart. She and WJ then spent the autumn in Italy – not going to Egypt.

LAMB HOUSE, RYE.
October 1st 1900.

Dearest Alice.

I have your good letter of Friday last & two postcards, one from each of you since – yours to tell me you were not going to Geneva & W*m*'s to ask for boots &c. Two pair of boots went to-day by parcel-post, both *new*, as the new ones seemed to pack into closer compass. They are in *one* parcel. May

10. *The Ambassadors.*

they safely & swiftly arrive. Your letter tells me much of what Sir J. Scott tells you about going to Egypt – the preferable post-boats &c, & makes me feel with hope & cheer that you're really thinking of it.[1] I heartily conjure you to do so – quite apart from the question of whether *I* can go. Believing as I do that it's the very best thing William can attempt, & yet being, alas, *very* sceptical about myself, I am *angoissé* to think of this benefit for him standing or falling at all by my frail possibilities. My case is partly economical – but also partly, even largely, embarrassed in another way. I this day at 3 o'clk., in Walter Dawes's office, at last solemnly & triumphantly "completed the purchase" of this house, which is now therefore, beneficently mine, (subject to a mortgage which I can certainly pay off easily in 2 or 3 years:) that is, I paid to Mrs. Bellingham upwards of half the value of the house.[2] The rest resides in 2 annual payments of interest on a mortgage, of £25 apiece – which the holder is but too glad to keep going. This disbursement has given me a sense of temporary depletion – not at all to the point of inconvenience so long as I stay quiet, but making me considerably shrink from plans of Eastern travel. In expectation & view of it, moreover, I a short time since covenanted for the delivery of a novel (to Constable & Co. here & Ch. Scribner's Sons in the U.S.) for publication in the autumn of 1901; & this novel will *have* to be written during 6 or 7 of the prior months of next year.[3] I can't write it *now*, for I am writing now a novel to begin serialisation in Harper also next autumn (the other one is to come *straight* out as a book;) & this I am devoutly (as to regularity of "daily stint") now proceeding with & hoping to finish soon after the New Year. I can *put off* the Constable & Scribner book to 1902; but I quite awfully don't *want* to – there are reasons, as to order, intervals, dates of subsequent work, &c, so cogent as to keeping it just where it *is*. I feel as if the ghost of the unwritten book would interpose between me & all the pyramids & temples, & as if I shld. rather "eat my heart out" over the delay. Now that after such previous years of dropping out & languishment – by my own dire detachment from *ways* – the excellently effective Pinker is bringing me up, & round, so promisingly that it really contains the germs of a New Career, I don't want (at 57!) to sacrifice any present & immediate period of production – however brief – that I can stiffly (*and* joyously!) keep in its place. Such is the manner in which I am at present moved, for safety's & lucidity's sake, to

1. Probably Sir John Scott (1841–1904), judicial adviser to the khedive (the viceroy or ruler of Egypt), 1891–8, who had re-created and simplified the Egyptian legal system.
2. Walter Dawes was the Rye solicitor who had handled HJ's original lease of Lamb House.
3. On 9 October HJ wrote to WJ and AHJ that 'I've just, this p.m. signed the final, formal contract with Constable & Co. for a novel to be delivered by *Sept. 1st, 1901*' (CWJ III, 139). This would be *The Wings of the Dove*.

put the case; but there will be time for us still to talk of it further: (though the finishing of my *serial* book, now on the stocks (150,000 words,) is truly also by itself a prospect requiring margin.) What I *yearn* to hear of is some *quand même* attitude towards Cairo & the Nile on William's & your part. Cultivate it, embrace it, cherish it.

It's extremely sweet to me, now that it's done, this sense of real possession of L.H. – it brings a deep peace. (The house was, by the way, bought (after some years of hiring) by Francis Bellingham from Davis Lamb only in *1893* – so that it has been almost as recently Lamb as possible.) Many thanks for Billy's second letter – almost as delightful as the *1st*. I'm sending it to Peg.[4]

Baldwin *doesn't* come down for a night – can't: rather to my relief.[5] Gosse has been & gone & I walked him out to tea with Elly & Leslie (he being delighted with the whole impression,) yesterday p.m.[6] The 2 Warrens come down for a Sunday & Monday before the end of the month – then, for a while, I ween, *plus personne*. I shall get your *2d* lecture-copy (William,) from McA., in case you want it, & myself register & post it to you.[7] He will, in response to your postcard, give you details, today, I suppose as to how he sent it. He tells me he put into an envelope left with him, directed by you, for the purpose; but didn't register it. I should think you had better have the *2d* copy without delay. But it's more than midnight. Goodnight. Much love,

Henry.

4. Billy is HJ's nephew, WJ's son William (1882–1961), later a painter. Peg is Billy's sister, Margaret Mary (1887–1950).
5. In the summer of 1899 Baldwin had been with WJ and AHJ in Nauheim, and when HJ wrote announcing his opportunity to buy Lamb House, Baldwin was reported by the discouraging WJ as saying 'it's a bad speculation anyhow' (CWJ III, 71). HJ replied, stung, that 'I allow no weight whatever to Baldwin's judgment' (CWJ III, 73).
6. Gosse had written to HJ 'sadly & sternly', complaining of neglect, such a letter as, HJ told W. E. Norris, 'had I been such another, would have, vulgarly speaking, put the fat on the fire'; but HJ invited him down for Saturday, 29 September (SLHJEG, 178, 180n.). Elly Hunter, widowed and then unhappily remarried to a Scot called George Hunter (1847–1914), and her daughter Edith Leslie Emmet (b. 1877), were cousins through the Temple connection. The Warrens came down on 27 October.
7. HJ's amanuensis William MacAlpine had been typing WJ's Gifford Lectures (which became *The Varieties of Religious Experience*). Although some seem to have gone astray, there were duplicate copies.

182. To Edith Wharton
26 October 1900

Yale MS   Published HJEWL, 32–3; HJL IV, 170–71

HJ met Edith Newbold Jones Wharton (1862–1937) first in Paris (at the Boits')
around 1887, and subsequently at the Curtises' in Venice, but without establishing
any literary connection. She was friendly with his friends the Bourgets from 1893,
but only in 1899 with her first collection, The Greater Inclination, *did HJ start*
to follow her early career – through her New York sister-in-law Mary Cadwalader
Jones (1850–1935), whom HJ had known through Godkin since 1883. In April–
May 1900 a short novel, The Touchstone, *appeared in* Scribner's. *Mrs Wharton*
was eager for a closer acquaintance, and sent HJ a story, 'The Line of Least
Resistance', on its publication in Lippincott's Magazine *in October 1900.*

The tale sardonically traces the failure of a representative American upper-class
marriage, following the passive, dyspeptic millionaire businessman Mr Mindon in
his dissatisfaction with the life of conspicuous consumption in his Newport mansion
and with his neglected display-wife Millicent. He finds evidence of her affair with
a young man, and briefly asserts himself by leaving her a letter threatening divorce,
but at the end of the story is persuaded by a panel of elders to return home 'for the
children'.

LAMB HOUSE, RYE.
October 26*th* 1900

Dear Mrs. Wharton.

I brave your interdiction & thank you both for your letter & for the brilliant little tale in the Philadelphia repository. The latter has an admirable sharpness & neatness, & infinite wit & point – it only suffers a little, I think, from one's not having a *direct* glimpse of the husband's provoking causes – literally provoking ones. However, you may very well say that there are two sides to that; that one can't do everything in 6000 words, one must narrowly choose (& à *qui* le dites-vous?) & that the complete non-vision of Millicent & her gentleman was a less evil than the frustrated squint to which you would have been at best reduced. Either *do* them or don't (directly,) touch them – such was doubtless your instinct. The subject is really a big one for the canvas – that was really your difficulty. But the thing is *done*. And I applaud, I mean I value, I egg you on in, your study of the American life that surrounds you. Let yourself go in it & *at* it – it's an untouched field, really: the folk who try, over there, don't come within miles of any civilized, however superficially, any "evolved" life. And use to the full your remarkable ironic & satiric gifts; they form a most valuable, (I hold,) & beneficent engine. *Only*, the *Lippincott* tale is a little *hard*, a little purely derisive. But that's because you're so young, &, with it, so clever. Youth *is* hard – & your needle-point, later on, will muffle itself in a little blur of silk. It *is* a needle-point! Do send me what you write,+[1] when you can kindly find time, & do, some day, better still, come to see yours, dear Mrs. Wharton, most truly

Henry James

183. To Mary (Mrs Humphry) Ward
22 November 1900

Virginia MS   Unpublished

The Soft Side *was published by Methuen on 30 August 1900, and in New York by Macmillan in September. On the day of this letter HJ sent Pinker complete corrected proofs of* The Sacred Fount, *for forwarding to Scribner in New York, where it came out on 6 February 1901 (in London Methuen published it on 15 February).*

   Eleanor *was published on 1 November 1900. Mrs Ward's father, Tom Arnold (1823–1900), son of Thomas Arnold of Rugby and brother of Matthew Arnold, a Catholic convert who had quarrelled with his daughter in Rome in 1899 about the Boer War, fell ill on 7 November and died in Dublin on 12 November. HJ had read his* Passages in a Wandering Life *(1900).*

LAMB HOUSE, RYE.
November 22d 1900.

Dear Mrs. Ward.

   I have had, these last days, two impulses: one to write to you as soon as I heard of your Father's death – & the other to let a little time pass – & it's the latter that has got itself obeyed. I had just begun *Eleanor* & was absorbing it in deep & quiet draughts when I became aware that that so marked hour in your life had struck – to the reverberation of which, in all your consciousness I think I can do full justice. They are the pair all by themselves – the two hours of the parental extinctions, & whenever they come there is nothing like them. I think, at least, people are to be pitied when there *is* anything. So at

1. +'Oh, I'll do the same by you!' [HJ's note.]

any rate I let myself be guided by the sense of being glad that I should presently have, when I had finished your book, words to utter to you more of a nature to heal wounds than to be harsh to them. I have reflected for you too that your Father has passed away in the serenity of his accomplished age, after many mutations &, assuredly after seeing himself magnificently justified of *you*. What a gladness to you to be able to think of the pleasure & pride you must have filled his life with! I hope he had been able to read *Eleanor*. I never met him, but I read, with a great impression of his loveability the volume of personal recollections he published a year or two ago. And what a date his death in the already so much unrolled Arnold family cycle!

For your letter of three, or more, weeks ago, as well as for the book, please be heartily thanked. *The Soft Side* is but a little bundle of sordid potboilers – of a sort which I am forced to write because no demand for anything else on the part of any living editor or publisher (so far as I am concerned,) appears to exist – I mean for anything of a larger or more inspiring order. So I've done also lately the stuff of another volume of similar snippets – even while cordially conceding that I'm old enough to know better.[1] I've done much longer things too – which lurk, as yet, in back-shops, but not with such public triumph as not to leave me glad of the chance to overflow into my favourite occupation of re-writing, as I read, such fiction as – I *can* read! I took this liberty in an inordinate degree with *Eleanor* – & I always feel it the highest tribute I can pay: I recomposed & reconstructed her from head to foot – which I give you for the real measure of what I think of her. I think her, – less obscurely – a thing of rare beauty, a large & noble performance; rich, complex, comprehensive, deeply interesting & highly distinguished. I congratulate you heartily on having mené à bonne fin so intricate & difficult a problem & on having seen your subject so wrapped in its air & so bristling with its relations. I should say that you had done nothing more homogeneous, more hanging & moving together. It has beauty, the book, theme & treatment alike, in magnificent measure, & is really a delightful thing to have done – been *able* to do – under the appeal – to have laid at the old golden door – of the beloved Italy.[2] You deserve well of her. I can't "criticise" – though I *could* (that is I *did* – but can't do it again,) rewrite! The thing's infinitely delightful & distinguished & that's enough. The success of it, specifically, to my sense is Eleanor; admirably

1. HJ had already written at least eight of the eleven stories published in *The Better Sort* on 26 February 1903. (The other three, 'The Beast in the Jungle', 'The Birthplace' and 'The Papers', were published without prior magazine use.)
2. Mrs Ward's novel was dedicated to the Italian nation: 'To Italy, the beloved and beautiful, Instructress of our past, Delight of our present, Comrade of our future: – the heart of an Englishwoman offers this book.'

sustained in the "high-note" way, without a break or a drop. She is a very exquisite & very *rendered* conception. I won't grossly pretend to you that I think the book hasn't a weakness – rather a grave one, or you will doubt of my intelligence. It *has* one, & in this way, to my troubled sense: that the antithesis on which your subject rests isn't a *real*, a valid, antithesis. It was utterly built, your subject, by your intention, of course *on* one, but the one you chose seems to me not efficiently to have operated – so that if the book is so charming & touching even *so*, that is a proof of your affluence. Lucy has, in respect to Eleanor – that is the image of Lucy that you have tried to teach yourself to see has – no true, no adequate, no logical antithetic force. And this is not only, I think, because the girl is done a little more *de chic* than you would really have liked to do her, but because the *nearer* you had got to her type the less she would have served that particular condition of your subject. You went too far for her – or, going so far, should have brought her back – roughly speaking – stranger. [Irony (& various things!) should at its hour have presided.][3] But I throw out that more imperfectly, I recognise, than I should wish; – it doesn't matter, & not a solitary reader in your millions – or critic in your hundreds – will either have missed or have made! And when a book's beautiful, nothing *does* matter! I hope greatly to see you after the New Year. Goodnight! – it's my usual 1.30 a.m.! Yours, dear Mrs. Ward, always

Henry James

184. To Mrs Mary (Humphry) Ward
15 March 1901

Virginia MS   Published HJL IV, 185–6

HJ spent most of his time from mid December to early April in London, suffering from lumbago and working on The Ambassadors, *which in October 1900 he had been 'hoping to finish soon after the New Year'. The* Sacred Fount *had come out in February, and HJ's story of emotional vampirism was received with puzzlement: the* Boston Evening Transcript *said 'it seems insane'; the British* Academy *called it 'an elaborate satire on himself'; the* Independent *judged that 'He kicks up too much literary dust for the size of his caravan'; the* Critic *asked, 'It is wonderful, but is it worth while?' Privately, Edith Wharton declared 'I could cry over the ruins of such a talent' (LEW, 45).*

Queen Victoria died in January 1901, and the Prince of Wales ascended the

3. HJ's use of square brackets.

throne; as HJ said to Oliver Wendell Holmes, 'We grovel before fat Edward – E. the Caresser, as he is privately named' (HJL IV, 184).

REFORM CLUB, PALL MALL. S.W.
March 15. 1901.

Dear Mrs. Ward.

Most kind your letter, most kind your invitation. In the face of all this benevolence I feel I need all my courage – or rather all my caution – not to be fully & immediately responsive. But the stern & sordid truth is that it is, alas, impossible to me to go abroad this spring. I am not free but bond, very intensely & inexorably. I've a terrible unfinished & belated book on my hands, which I can't get away from for a day, & which alone is a roaring lion in my path. But in addition to this my brother & his wife arrive precisely *from* Italy to find me in England at Easter & to come down & spend a month with me, & to have left them there unvisited all winter in order to go just as they depart, crossing them on the way, would really disgrace me forever.[1] However, I sufficiently rattle for you my chains. I talked only yesterday with a lady who knows your villa well (Mrs. Peter Harrison, who used to be Alma Strettell,) & she made my mouth water for the thought of it.[2] But I must, woe is me, wipe my mouth hard & sit down again to my task. Let me not however do so without expressing my liveliest appreciation of your remarks on the *Sacred Fount* – as to which I almost blush to have made you suppose that, for the thing that it is, any at all were necessary. I say it really in all sincerity – the book isn't worth discussing. It was a remarkably accidental one, & the merest of *jeux d'esprit*. You will say that one mustn't write accidental books, or must take the consequences when one does. Well, I do take them – I resign myself to the figure the thing makes as a mere tormenting trifle. The subject was a small fantasticality which (as I *have* to write "short stories" when I can,) I had intended to treat in the compass of a single magazine instalment – a matter of 8 or 10 thousand words. But it *gave* more, before I knew it; before I knew it

1. Mrs Ward may have been going to the Villa Bonaventura at Cadenabbia on Lake Como, which became her favourite resort. WJ and AHJ had spent the winter in Rome, and came to England in April, to prepare for WJ's Gifford Lectures in Edinburgh, which began on 16 May 1901.
2. Alma Strettell (1853–1935) – sister of Alice Carr, who designed Ellen Terry's costume as Lady Macbeth, painted by Sargent – had been in the 1880s part of the circle of American artists (Sargent, Abbey, Millet) in the Cotswold village of Broadway: Sargent painted her four times. In 1890 she married the painter L. A. ('Peter') Harrison. She collected and published folk-songs, and from the 1900s lived in Cheyne Walk, Chelsea.

had grown to 25 000 & was still but a third developed. And then, in the hand-to-mouth conditions to which I am condemned with my things, (which I can scarcely place anywhere,) I couldn't afford to sacrifice it; my hand-to-mouth economy condemned me to put it through in order not to have wasted the time already spent. So, only, it was that I hatingly finished it; trying only to make it – the one thing it *could* be – a *consistent* joke. Alas, for a joke it appears to have been, round about me here, taken rather seriously. It's doubtless very disgraceful, but it's the last I shall ever make! Let me say for it, however, that it has, I assure you, & applied quite rigorously & constructively, I believe, its' own little law of composition. Mrs. Server is *not* "made happy" at the end – what in the world has put it into your head? As I give but the phantasmagoric I have, for clearness, to make it *evidential*, & the Ford Obert evidence all bears (indirectly,) upon Brissenden, supplies the motive for Mrs. B.'s terror & her re-nailing down of the coffin. I had to testify to Mrs. S.'s sense of a common fate with B. & the only way I could do so was by making O. see her as temporarily pacified. I had to give a meaning to the vision of Gilbert L. out on the terrace in the darkness, & the *appearance* of a sensible detachment on her part was my imposed way of giving it. Mrs. S. is back in the coffin at the end, by the same stroke by which Briss is – Mrs. B.'s last interview with the narrator being all an ironic *exposure* of her own false plausibility, of course. But it isn't worth explaining, & I mortally loathe it! Forgive my weariness over my deadly backward present book, which *isn't* a joke – unless I don't know the difference. But I am miswriting for dizziness. May your villa be an Eden without the least little serpent! Yours, dear Mrs. Ward, very constantly

Henry James

185. To Maud Broadwood (Mrs Waldo) Story
13 June 1901

Texas MS   Unpublished

On 19 April, a fortnight after returning to Rye, HJ wrote to Pinker of a shocking proposal from Harvey, editor both of Harper's Weekly *and the* North American Review, *the latter of which was to serialize* The Ambassadors, *still unfinished: 'I am staggered by the unexpected barbarity of his asking me at this time of day to take* 70,000 *words out of a thing of* 150,000.' *(Unpublished Yale MS, Za James 4.) On 22 May HJ signed an agreement with the Harpers, despite its conditions: payment 'down' of only half the serialization fee and 'the relegation of publication to any vague hereafter that suits them' (to Pinker, Unpublished Yale MS, Za James 4).*

HJ's Scots amanuensis MacAlpine moved on to better-paid employment, and in April 1901 Mary Weld, daughter of a British judge in India and product of Cheltenham Ladies College and a Berlin 'finishing-school', started work as HJ's secretary-typist. She comments: 'He dictated beautifully. He had a melodious voice and in some way he seemed to be able to tell if I was falling behind. Typewriting for him was exactly like accompanying a singer on the piano.' His routine: 'After working all morning [from 10 till 1.45], he would read in the afternoon, then after tea go for a walk, and then in the evenings he'd make notes on the next day's work, planning an outline.' (HJAH, 152, 154.)

LAMB HOUSE, RYE.
June 13*th 1901.*

Dear Mrs. Waldo.

It is a very great joy &, as it were, relief to me to hear from you – as it gives me a chance to break the spell of silence that has weighed on me so long – so horribly long – like an unnatural pall, & which I have never succeeded in flinging off, repeatedly as I have desired to. I am greatly touched by your long patience with me, – & Waldo's – & ask you to believe that in spite of the way I must seem to be letting time go by, I shall really justify it. I had some correspondence (of the most amicable sort) with Mr. Blackwood a few months since, & as he then told me he was writing to Waldo I asked him to say something special & definite to you *for* me – to repeat, that is, something I had said to him.[1] I don't know whether he has ever done this – ever *did* write to you: if not I must have struck you as more damnably & brutally soundless even than I have feared. But it has all been a most regrettably inevitable business – beginning in a long hindrance that I had immediately after coming back last year from Rome & when I was in the very act [of] sitting down to put my Volume through. Let it suffice I should mention that this hindrance was sternly *economical* & that I had absolutely to take it into account. An unexpected turn in my modest domestic affairs, in other words, had made it imperative that I should make for a couple of years (& without

1. This seems to refer to a letter replying to an inquiry by William Blackwood of 14 October 1900, in which HJ told him he had intended to write the Story book on his return from Italy in 1899 – 'Unfortunately it befell, however, as soon as I got back, that circumstances unexpected & urgent absolutely compelled me to fall upon other work'; on 22 November he had written again with the Storys' address, which he had forgotten to give (Unpublished Scotland MS, 4702, ff. 27–30).

delay) as much *money* as I could – & this was only achievable by doing certain definite things. I make very little at the best & I work very slowly & can only do one thing at a time, & am in every way a very discouraging & disappointing producer even to myself. But the situation that turned up for me directly after I last saw you I had to accept on the spot – & as it represented more delay about the book I was very much ashamed of myself: too much so to have any comfort in writing to you. I hadn't the heart to tell you my wretched little tale of postponement – which I hoped wd. be a much shorter story than it has proved &, I am sorry to say, is yet a certain time longer proving. What I wrote to William Blackwood (some time last year) was that I had then contracted to do two novels & that I couldn't touch the Volume till these were completely off my hands; but that as soon as they *were* I would fasten tight upon it. One of the novels in question *is*, thank heaven, finished, but I am in the midst of the other – though proceeding as steadily as my native meticulosity permits.[2] The day it is done I shall instantly give myself to the volume & probably then finish it in 3 or 4 months. *That*, my dear Mrs. Waldo, is my plain unvarnished tale. I am sorry it isn't a more brilliant one, & I repeat that I much appreciate the admirable way you & Waldo have let me alone. I have let *you* far too much so – but I hated to write as I am reduced to writing now, & of the two evils I drifted into the gracelessness of following up my so happy sojourn in Rome 2 years ago, & my enjoyment of all your kindness to me there, by this total absence of signs & portents. Let me say *this* – that I will, when I fairly get my hand on it, do my utmost to make the little book charming enough to show that I *deserve* forgiveness. Of course you feel that so long a delay after Mr. Story's death has already been a disadvantage. Yet it is a disadvantage perhaps, after all, to *me* mainly – & if such a volume doesn't follow the death of a distinguished man *immediately*, I don't know that the somewhat more or somewhat less time deliberately taken very greatly signifies. Likewise you may be moved to wonder why, even though committed to do other important things I shouldn't have worked in this minor undertaking *along* with them, as many another man in my shoes would. To that I can only reply that such, unfortunately for you from the first, has been my poor little literary constitution. I *can't* do 2 things at once – of however different kinds, one in the morning & one in the evening; I can only do one at a time & that with difficulty. However, I *do* succeed, for the most part in doing each thing in its order – so that I wind up with thanking you once more for such patience as that statement will enable you further to show me.

And now I rejoice to hear you are coming to England. It will not only

2. Strictly speaking, even *The Ambassadors* seems not yet to have been absolutely finished.

give me extraordinary satisfaction to see you down here, but will give me extraordinary distress *not* to do so. I am not quite suburban, but I am not really far from town, & the thing – the little journey is very manageable. Only, please, give me your London address, so that I may know how to get at you & where. I am keeping intensely out of town while the Season rages. Please give my love to Waldo – to whom this long-winded epistle is of course also largely addressed. I hope his health is wholly re-established. May his American pilgrimage be blessed to him. Yes, I am shorn & shaven, & I wish I could be sure it makes me "look younger." It almost, however, makes me feel so. I am obliged, for want of any other certainty to direct this to the Barberini, whence, I fear, it will have wild wanderings in search of you.[3] Let it at any rate take you the assurance of the affectionate constancy of yours always

Henry James

186. To James Brand Pinker
31 June [1 July] 1901

Yale MS   Published HJL IV, 193

HJ had still not quite finished preparing The Ambassadors *for serial publication.*

LAMB HOUSE, RYE.
June 31st 1901.

Dear Mr. Pinker.

Yes, it *is* the case, to my very great regret, in respect to my Constable– Scribner book. I have already had a word of inquiry from W*m* Meredith, in answer to which I was obliged to write him that I must ask for a delay to the end of the year – say *Dec. 31st*.[1] He has taken this very kindly – I've just heard from him; & I shld. have immediately written to you even if I had not got your note. It is simply because from one of these last days to the other (absolutely,) I was expecting to send you the last three Instalments of my Harper novel, that I hadn't communicated with you on the Constable question

3. The Storys lived in part of the same Palazzo in Rome where HJ had visited Mrs Humphry Ward in 1899 when she was writing *Eleanor*.

1. The contract HJ had signed in October 1900 for *The Wings of the Dove* with Constable's William Maxse Meredith (1865–1937), son of the novelist and poet, specified delivery by 1 September 1901.

before. I hated to write without accompanying my letter with my packet of finally-finished fiction – as I am after all doing even now. Yesterday, to-day, tomorrow (literally) has it seemed certain this business would have had *Finis* – & it *will*, veraciously, in all probability have it tomorrow. Then the stuff will instantly go to you – Parts Ten & Eleven being all ready. It has been a long, long job – & not from interruptions (of late,) or disasters, for I've kept steadily & intensely at it. It's simply that the thing itself has *taken* the time – taken it with a strong & insistent hand.

This Constable one will, for intrinsic reasons, take less; besides being already well started. (I did *that* more than a year ago.) It is of high importance to me to delay it as little as possible – I hate the delay actually inflicted; & within the time I shall now positively work it. Constable & Co, as I say, are humane to me – & for those who are humane to me I will do anything. But will you very kindly write to Scribner on the subject of the inevitable delay & my regrets at it – & giving them the fresh date of the end of the year?

I shall be writing you again within the week. Yours very truly

Henry James

187. *To William Dean Howells*
10 August 1901

Houghton MS   Published HJL IV, 198–200; LFL, 366–8

'Within the week', on 6 July, HJ wrote to Pinker that 'I have finished my novel, thank goodness' (Unpublished Yale MS, Za James 4), and on 10 July, once it was copied, sent him 'the too-long retarded Finis of "The Ambassadors"' (HJL IV, 194). Mary Weld's diary records the novel HJ soon told William Meredith would be called The Wings of the Dove *as being begun – that is, taken up again – on 9 July 1901, and completed on 21 May 1902, and as taking 194 days of dictation.*

LAMB HOUSE, RYE.
August 10*th 1901.*

My dear Howells.

Ever since receiving & reading your elegant volume of short tales – the arrival of which from you was affecting & delightful to me – I've meant to write to you, but the wish has struggled in vain with the daily distractions of a tolerably busy summer.[1] I should blush, however, if the season were to melt away without my greeting & thanking you. I read your book with joy & found in it recalls from far, far away – stray echoes and scents as from another, the American, the prehistoric existence. The thing that most took me was that entitled A Difficult Case, which I found beautiful & admirable, ever so true & ever so *done*. But I fear I more, almost, than anything else, lost myself in mere envy of your freedom to do &, speaking vulgarly, to place, things of that particular & so agreeable dimension – I mean the dimension of most of the stories in the volume. It is sternly enjoined upon one here (where an agent-man does what he can for me,) that everything – every hundred – above 6 or 7 thousand words is fatal to "placing"; so that I do them of that length, with great care, art & time (much re-boiling,) & then, even then, can scarcely get them worked off – published even when they've been accepted. *Harper* has had a thing for nearly two years which it has not thought worth publishing – & Scribner another for some 15 months or so; & my agent-man has others that he can't place anywhere.[2] So that (though I don't know why I inflict on you these sordid groans – except that I haven't any one else to inflict them on – & the mere affront – of being unused so inordinately long – is almost intolerable,) I don't feel incited in that direction. Fortunately, however, I am otherwise immersed. I lately finished a tolerably long novel, & I've written a third of another – with still another begun & two or three more subjects awaiting me thereafter like carriages drawn up at the door & horses champing their bits.[3] And àpropos of the 1st named of these, which is in the hands of the Harpers, I have it on my conscience to let you know that the idea of the fiction in question had its earliest origin in a circumstance mentioned to me – years ago – in respect to no less a person than yourself. At Torquay, once, our young friend Jon. Sturges came down to spend some days near me, and, lately, from Paris, repeated to me five words you had said to him one day on his

1. *A Pair of Patient Lovers* came out from Harper's on 23 May 1901. HJ's notebook for 15 June records an idea he got for a (never written) story from 'Reading in a small vol. of tales of Howells's a thing called a *Circle in the Water*' (N, 196).
2. In October 1901 *Harper's Monthly* published 'The Beldonald Holbein', which HJ had sent them via Pinker in September 1899. *Scribner's Magazine* published 'Flickerbridge' in February 1902, which HJ had given Pinker on 2 March 1900. Three long stories in *The Better Sort* (1903), 'The Beast in the Jungle', 'The Birthplace' and 'The Papers', were published without prior magazine use; while 'The Story in It' was much rejected and eventually given to a magazine *gratis*.
3. The 'tolerably long novel' just finished is *The Ambassadors*; the other, of which a third has been written, is *The Wings of the Dove*, for Constable and Scribner; the 'still another begun' may be *The Sense of the Past* or *The Golden Bowl*; HJ's 'two or three more subjects', presumably for novels, seems to refer to others never realized.

meeting you during a call at Whistler's.[4] I thought the words charming – you have probably quite forgotten them, & the whole incident – suggestive – so far as it was an incident; &, more than this, they presently caused me to see in them the faint vague germ, the mere point of the *start*, of a Subject. I noted them, to that end, as I note everything; & years afterwards (that is 3 or 4,) the Subject sprang at me, one day, out of my notebook. I don't know if it be good; at any rate it has been treated, now, for whatever it is; & my point is that it had long before – it had in the very act of striking me as a germ – got away from *you* or from anything like you! had become impersonal & independent. Nevertheless your initials figure in my little note; & if you hadn't said the 5 words to Jonathan he wouldn't have had them (most sympathetically & interestingly) to relate, & I shouldn't have had them to work in my imagination. The moral is that you are responsible for the whole business. But I've had it, since the book was finished, much at heart to tell you so. May you carry the burden bravely!

I hope you are on some thymy promontory & that the winds of heaven blow upon you all – perhaps in that simplified scene that you wrote to me from, with so gleaming a New England evocation, last year.[5] The summer has been wondrous again in these islands – 4 or 5 months, from April 1*st*, of almost merciless fine weather – a rainlessness absolute & without precedent. It has made my hermitage, as a retreat, a blessing, & I have been able, thank goodness, to work without breaks – other than those of prospective readers' hearts.

It almost broke mine, the other day, by the way, to go down into the New Forest (where he has taken a house,) to see Godkin, dear old stricken friend. He gave me in a manner, news of you – told me he had seen you lately. He was perhaps a little less in pieces than I feared, but the hand of fate is heavy upon him. He has mitigations – supremely in the admirable devotion of his

4. HJ recorded his conversation with Sturges in his notebook the next day (31 October 1895): 'Sturges said [Howells] seemed sad – rather brooding; and I asked him what gave him (Sturges) that impression. "Oh – somewhere – I forget, when I was with him – he laid his hand on my shoulder and said *à propos* of some remark of mine: 'Oh, you are young, you are young – be glad of it: be glad of it and *live*. Live all you can: it's a mistake not to. It doesn't so much matter what you do – but live. This place makes it all come over me. I see it now. I haven't done so – and now I'm old. It's too late. It has gone past me – I've lost it. You have time. You are young. Live!' " ' (N, 141.) The meeting in Whistler's garden in the rue du Bac took place in June 1894, when Howells was visiting his son John, who was studying architecture at the Beaux Arts. Howells was called home when his father had a stroke, and wrote his son that July: 'Perhaps it was as well I was called home. The poison of Europe was getting into my soul. You must look out for that. They live much more fully than we do. Life here is still for the future, – it is a land of Emersons – and I like a little present moment in mine. When I think of the Whistler garden!' (LLWDH II, 52.)

5. In 1901 the Howellses spent the summer at York Harbor, Maine.

wife. And he is quartered for the time in the Forest of Arden. I am alone here just now with my sweet niece Peggy, but my brother & his wife are presently to be with me again for 15 days before sailing (31*st*) for the U.S. He is immensely better in health, but he must take in sail hand over hand at home to remain so. Stia bene, caro amico, anche Lei (my Lei is my joke!) Tell Mrs. Howells & Mildred that I yearn toward them tenderly. Yours always & ever

Henry James

188. To Sarah Orne Jewett
5 October 1901

Houghton MS   Published HJL IV, 208–9; SL2, 332–3

President William McKinley was fatally shot on 6 September 1901 and Theodore Roosevelt replaced him; HJ told Jessie Allen on 19 September: 'I don't either like or trust the new President, a dangerous and ominous Jingo – of whom the most hopeful thing to say is that he may be rationalized by this sudden real responsibility.' (HJL IV, 202.) On 23 September HJ suffered the climax of a domestic upheaval: his alcoholic servants the Smiths departed, in what he described to Gosse as 'a whirl-wind determining the violent elimination from my life, in the course of 48 hours, of the pair of old servants, man & wife, whom you know & who had been with me – the mainstay, with qualifications & titubations, of my existence – for 16 years' (SLHJEG, 187).

Sarah Orne Jewett had sent HJ her historical novel The Tory Lover *(1901), set in Maine during the American Revolution. HJ had recently wrestled with the representation of the historical consciousness in his attempts on* The Sense of the Past.

Lamb House, Rye, Sussex.
October 5*th* 1901.

Dear Miss Jewett.

Let me not criminally, or at all events gracelessly, delay to thank you for your charming & generous present of *The Tory Lover*. He has been but 3 or 4 days in the house, yet I have given him an earnest, a pensive, a liberal – yes, a benevolent attention, & the upshot is that I should like to write you a longer letter than I just now (especially as it's past midnight) see my way to doing. For it would take me some time to disembroil the tangle of saying to you at once how I appreciate the charming touch, tact & taste of this ingenious exercise, & how little I am in sympathy with experiments of its general (to my sense) misguided stamp. There I am! – yet I don't do you the outrage, as a fellow craftsman & a woman of genius & courage, to suppose you not as conscious as I am myself of all that, in these questions of art & truth & sincerity, is beyond the mere twaddle of graciousness. The "historic" novel is, for me, condemned, even in cases of labour as delicate as yours, to a fatal *cheapness*, for the simple reason that the difficulty of the job is inordinate & that a mere *escamotage*, in the interest of ease, & of the abysmal public *naïveté*, becomes inevitable. You may multiply the little facts that can be got from pictures & documents, relics & prints, as much as you like – *the* real thing is almost impossible to do, & in its absence the whole effect is as nought; I mean the invention, the representation of the old <u>consciousness</u>, the soul, the sense, the horizon, the vision of individuals in whose minds half the things that make ours, that make the modern world were non-existent. You have to *think* with your modern apparatus a man, a woman – or rather fifty – whose own thinking was intensely-otherwise conditioned, you have to simplify back by an amazing tour de force – & even then it's all humbug. But there is a shade of the (even then) humbug that *may* amuse. The childish tricks that take the place of any such conception of the real job in the flood of Tales of the Past that seems of late to have been rolling over our devoted country – these ineptitudes have, on a few recent glances, struck me as creditable to no one concerned.[1] You, I hasten to add, seem to me to have steered very clear of them – to have seen your work very bravely & handled it firmly; but even you court disaster by composing the whole thing so much by sequences of speeches. It's when the extinct soul talks, & the earlier consciousness airs itself, that the pitfalls multiply & the "cheap" way has to serve. I speak in general, I needn't keep insisting, & I speak grossly, summarily, by rude & provisional signs, in order to suggest my sentiment at all. I didn't mean to say so much without saying more; & now I have douched you with cold water when I only meant just lightly & kindly to sprinkle you as for a new baptism – that is a *re*-dedication to altars but briefly, I trust, forsaken. Go back to the dear country of the Pointed Firs, *come* back to the palpable present *intimate* that throbs responsive, & that wants,

1. In one of the 'American Letters' for *Literature* in 1898, for instance, HJ had commented crushingly on J. A. Altsheler's *A Soldier of Manhattan*, set in the mid eighteenth century: 'The knowledge and the imagination, the saturation, perception, vigilance, taste, tact, required to achieve even a passable historic *pastiche* are surely a small enough order when we consider the feat involved – the feat of completely putting off one consciousness before beginning to take on another . . . A single false note is a sufficient betrayal – by which I do not mean to imply, on the other hand, that the avoidance of many is at all possible. Mr. Altsheler, frankly, strikes me as all false notes.' (LC I, 679.)

misses, needs you, God knows, & that suffers woefully in your absence.[2] Then I shall feel perhaps – & do it if only *for* that – that you have magnanimously allowed for the want of gilt on the gingerbread of the but-on-this-occasion-*only* limited sympathy of yours very constantly

Henry James

P.S. My tender benediction, please, to Mrs. Fields.

189. To James Brand Pinker
6 November 1901

Yale MS   Unpublished

On 27 February 1900 HJ had sent Pinker his ironic tale of emotional sacrifice and sexual hypocrisy, 'The Story in It'. By late 1901 it had undergone many rejections. The enigmatic literary entrepreneur Fernand Ortmans, editor of the defunct Cosmopolis: An International Monthly Review *(1896–8), was asking for help in the launch of a new organ, in the event called* The Anglo-American Magazine. *On 21 January 1902, although in fact the magazine* had *published the tale that month, HJ would write to Violet Hunt of meeting to talk 'of the beautiful Ortmans, the beautiful, the perfidious. No glimpse have I had of the AngloAmerican Mag: yet; & mystery surrounds the same. He wrote me that Simpkin & Marshall dispense (issue) it here – but S.M. write that they have never heard of it!' (Unpublished Penn State MS.) By 19 February 1902 HJ was writing to Pinker of 'the unspeakable Ortmans' (Unpublished Yale MS, Za James 1, vol. 1).*

Lamb House, Rye, Sussex.
Nov: 6: 1901.

Dear Mr. Pinker.

I have received the enclosed from the unhappy former editor of *Cosmopolis*, & for particular reasons I am disposed to give him – literally *give*! – the magazine use of something. Only I can't break off from pressing work now to do anything for the purpose – & it comes over me that you must still have in

---

2. On 25 January 1902 HJ wrote to Howells that, 'The *little* American tale-tellers (I mean the two or three women,) become impossible to me the moment they lengthen . . . dear Sara Jewett sent me not long since a Revolutionary Romance, with officers over their wine &c, & Paul Jones terrorizing the sea, that was a thing to make the angels weep.' (LFL, 370.)

your hands a little tale that I placed there quite a year & ½ ago ("*The Story in It*",) & that you have, I judge, not found it possible to dispose of. I understand now (I wonder I ever blinked it,) the difficulty – the amiable freedom of the *subject*, & the extremely unamiable & otherwise abject prudery of the usual Anglo-Saxon Editor. I feel that the difficulty will be *permanent*, & if you haven't very lately lodged the thing somewhere I am moved to ask you to let me sacrifice it on the altar of sentiment – that is of compassion (&, a little, of gratitude,) to the afflicted Ortmans, who, so long as he was not afflicted, treated me honourably enough – came to me for contributions to his *1st* number & paid me very decently for it, paid me again my price for a second story at a time when the waters must have been closing over him, & banquetted me (& others) with fatal luxury at the Savoy![1] I think it's better that the tale, moreover, shld. at last be printed & read than await some impossibly brave editor who will never turn up. Ortmans *is* brave (!!) & will swallow it without winking (I judge he has a free hand as far as shockability goes;) & if the periodical has sufficient reality to print & pay for other short things of mine afterwards, it is an opening the more.[2] (I only want to do enough more to make up a full new vol. of short stories – in addition to the others published since *The Soft Side*.[3] This will take, of very short ones, 5 or 6 more; of longer but 2 or 3.) Will you therefore kindly *wire* me if *The Story in It* be, as I take for granted, still at large? I have a duplicate of it here.

I am happy to say I am going very steadily & straight with the novel I am finishing for *Constable*.[4] And how, when I've done it, I shall want to engage for another! Yours very truly

Henry James

1. The Bourgets were also present at this dinner in August 1896. The multi-lingual *Cosmopolis* had printed two of HJ's stories of literary life, 'The Figure in the Carpet' and 'John Delavoy'.
2. The New York Preface to the tale recalled its multiple rejections, and took mild rueful pleasure in the collapse of Ortmans's venture: 'finally an old acquaintance, about to "start a magazine," begged it in turn of me and published it (1903 [1902]) at no cost to himself but the cost of his confidence, in that first number which was in the event, if I mistake not, to prove only one of a pair. I like perhaps "morbidly" to think that the Story in it may have been more than the magazine could carry.' (LC II, 1285.)
3. HJ's next collection would be *The Better Sort* (1903).
4. *The Wings of the Dove*.

190. To Lucy (Mrs William Kingdon) Clifford
[9 May 1902]

Houghton TC   Unpublished

The Wings of the Dove *kept extending. The original deadline of 1 September 1901 had passed; then the renegotiated one of 31 December. On 25 January 1902 HJ told Howells, 'I've had a workful autumn & early winter, finishing a novel which* should *have by this time been published – that is been ready to be – but on which, as it is long, I fear too long, I've still several weeks' work . . . It's . . . of a prettyish inspiration – a "love-story" of a romantic tinge, & touching & conciliatory tone.' HJ seems to have been hoping for magazine publication: 'no publishers, alas (& they've had a mass of it for some time in their hands,) have told me that it has "taken their fancy."' (LFL, 371, 372.) On 29 January in London he fell seriously ill with inflammation of the bowels, and after a week in bed retreated to Rye on 11 February, only gradually recovering. On 12 March, convalescing, he went to Torquay for ten days near the Godkins. On 21 March, from there, he told Pinker that if Constable 'give me till* May 15th *(not "end of April,") to hand them the remainder of my ms. for "Wings of the Dove" I assent to their proposal to publish in July'; they were in possession of a revised proof up to p. 355, but HJ had to provide a hundred pages more (Unpublished Yale MS, Za James 1, vol. 1).*

On 13 May he reported to Gosse from Rye: 'Here I am in the throes of finishing – by a date, *May 20th – a long & awfully retarded novel, which* must *be published by July 1st, & the final, terminal process of which (while 4/5's, printed, wait for the remainder,) leaves me not a little spent.' (SLHJEG, 195.)*

Lamb House, Rye.
Friday night.

Dearest Lucy C.

I have criminally delayed to answer your note or thank you for the precious volume it accompanied.[1] And now you will be whirling away to Venice, and this will barely avail to catch you in a lucid hour before you distractedly start. I rejoice that you *do* start, but deplore the brevity, and otherwise hover, in spirit, about you. Go to the *Luna* – an excellent, moderate, sympathetic, non-smart, but quite genial hotel (on grand canal.) The reason of all my dumbnesses is that I fled hither many days ago under a very special anxious

---

1. Presumably her novel *Woodside Farm* (1902), mentioned below. Her letter is not known to survive.

pressure (not at all, primarily, of health,) and that pressure has held, and is still holding, my head down under the water – so that, till the strain is over I can't lift it (to call lifting,) even for a moment. Quite apart from recurrent torment of shoeless Gout, which hounded me hither, I've been having, and have still got, my awfully belated Book to finish by the 15th (May) – having sworn by all that's sacred that it *shall* at last come out by July 1st. Four fifths of it are set up, printed and ferociously waiting for this remainder, which I am now gouging out of me and which leaves me spent and voided[,] while the tension lasts, for everything else. I can't distil quality, form and fable for some 4 hours on end a day, in a sustained and clock-watching, calendar-watching way, and not be a poor creature the rest of the time. So, dear Lucy, the days have shamelessly gone. But I've read *W.F.* and have wished we might talk of it – as a better business than this weary writing – which I won't now pretend to go into. There are too many things to say, for me to try for them here, and we will talk of them when you come back (for I shall be in town a little again.) The book has life, like all your books, and moves and goes, and is full; but there is perhaps a want of deliberation about it – I will tell you, by your fire, what I mean. I talk of fire by reason of this Arctic May, which I hope you will leave behind you here. Take my blessing with you – and share it with Ethel.[2] Yours and hers mid-nocturnally and constantly

Henry James

191. *To Owen Wister*
7 August 1902

Congress MS   Published HJL IV, 232–4

On 17 June HJ told Violet Hunt the newspaper rumours were wrong: 'it's not a bit true that I've been unable to finish a book & obliged to postpone it indefinitely. I had – for a while – to postpone it, but I've finished it all the same, & it's printed, & comes out as soon as possible.' (Unpublished Virginia MS, 6251 #294.)

On 20 June HJ sent Pinker, who was to negotiate with publishers, the eight recent stories not included in The Soft Side, *amounting to 60,000 words and under the proposed title of* The Better Sort. *On 24 June HJ and Pinker were considering withdrawing* The Ambassadors *from Harper altogether because of their delay in serializing it since receiving it in September 1901 (and thus delaying also, under*

2. Lucy Clifford's daughter Ethel, later Lady Dilke, also wrote verses, and some fiction early in the new century.

the contract, paying the other half of the £1,000 due to HJ). On 1 July HJ made a start on the story which became 'The Beast in the Jungle'; then turned to three other stories, one of them (called in Mary Weld's diary 'The Beautiful Child') never completed.

Owen Wister (1860–1938), a novelist since 1882, was Fanny Kemble's American grandson, son of HJ's old friend Sarah Butler Wister, and a friend of Theodore Roosevelt. The Virginian (1902), dedicated to Roosevelt, was by far his most successful work. Its cowboy hero the Virginian, viewed by the admiring Eastern narrator, displays his taciturn courage, skill and wits, cunning humour and chivalrous good nature – then in the end marries a schoolteacher from Vermont by whom he has many children.

Lamb House, Rye, Sussex.
August 7th 1902

My dear Owen.

I have been reading *The Virginian* & I am moved to write to you. You didn't send him to me – you never send me nothing; as to which, heaven knows, you're not obliged, &, conscious of your probably multitudinous preoccupations, I mention the matter only from the sense of my having felt, as I read, how the sentiment of the thing would have deepened for me if I *had* had it from your hands. The point is that the sentiment of the thing so appealed to me, interested me, convinced me, that I thus unscrupulously yield to the pleasure of making an however ineffectual sign of the same to you across the waste of distance & darkness. Signs are, in this vast, poor things, & to talk with you would be the real delirium; still, I want it to pass as dimly discernible to you that what I best like in your book deeply penetrates even my weather-beaten, my almost petrified old mind. What I best like in it is exactly the fact of the *subject* itself, so clearly & finely felt by you, I think, & so firmly carried out – the exhibition, to the last intimacy, of the man's character, the personal & moral complexion & evolution, in short, of your hero. On this I very heartily congratulate you; you have made him *live*, with a high, but lucid complexity, from head to foot & from beginning to end; you have not only intensely seen & conceived him, but you have reached with him an admirable objectivity, & I find the whole thing a rare & remarkable feat. If we *could* only palaver (ah, miserable fate!) & you were to give me leave, there are various other awfully interesting things I shld. like both to say & to sound you on; these same, & connected, questions, elements of the art we practise & adorn, being, to my judgment, the most thrilling that can occupy the human mind. I won't deny that I have my reserves, – perverse perhaps & merely personal – in respect to some sides of your performance; but in the first place they don't touch the Essence; in the second they would take space (tremble at what you escape!) & in the third you haven't asked me for them – an indispensable condition, I hold, of offering such observations. The Essence, as I call it, remains – the way the young man's inward & outward presence builds itself up, fills out the picture, holds the interest & charms the sympathy. Bravo, bravo. *I* find myself desiring all sorts of poetic justice to hang about him, & I am willing to throw out, even though you don't ask me, that nothing would have induced me to unite him to the little Vermont person, or to dedicate him in fact to achieved parentage, prosperity, maturity, at all – which is mere *prosaic* justice, & rather grim at that. I thirst for his blood, I wouldn't have let him live & be happy; I should have made him perish in his flower & in some splendid sombre way – as e.g. Loti makes Yann (with whom your friend has points in common,) do so invaluably in *Pêcheur d'Islande*.[1] But I am letting myself loose among my reserves & I pull myself up. I only wanted to pat you officiously, & both violently & tenderly, on the admirably assiduous back. Bend this last possession again to – ah, not to the Virginian. *Don't* revive him again, at your peril, or rather at his: I have an impertinent apprehension that you're promising yourself some such treat for his later developments. Damn his later developments – & yet I can't say Write me another Wild West novel, all the same. For I believe the type you've studied & dismissed to be, essentially (isn't it?) ce qu'il y a de mieux in the W.W. But write me something equally American on this scale & with this seriousness – for it's a great pleasure to see you bringing off so the large & the sustained.[2] How I envy you the personal knowledge of the W.W., the possession of the memories; that *The V.* must be built on, & the right to a complete romantic feeling about them. But it's one o'clock in the morning, & I am too long-winded. And I have made myself too late for inquiries or messages. Yet I involve you all, your wife, your mother, your children, your every circumstance (including your next book,) in a common benediction, & am yours, my dear Owen, very delightedly

Henry James

1. This is presumably the point HJ refers to in a letter to Wister's mother, Sarah Butler Wister, on 21 December: 'his reply to an objection that I had made to his treatment of his subject in one particular . . . left me stubbornly unconvinced' (HJL IV, 261).
2. Wister's next substantial work was *Lady Baltimore* (1906), not a Western.

192. To Edith Wharton
17 August 1902

Yale MS   Published HJEWL, 33–5; HJL IV, 234–6

Edith Wharton's The Valley of Decision, *which came out in February 1902 and is dedicated to the Bourgets, is a densely researched novel of ideological conflict (between liberal reform and Catholic conservatism), set in a ducal court in eighteenth-century Italy.*

August 17*th 1902*
LAMB HOUSE, RYE, SUSSEX.

Dear Mrs. Wharton.

I have just asked the Scribners to send you a rather long-winded (but I hope not hopelessly heavy) novel of mine that they are to issue by the end of this month (a thing called *The Wings of the Dove*,) and I find myself wishing much not to address myself to you to that without doing so still more. This has been made especially the case, I assure you, by my lately having read *The Valley of Decision*, read it with such high appreciation & received so deep an impression from it that I can scarce tell you why, all these weeks, I have waited for any other pretext to write. I think in truth I have waited simply because, really, your book gives one too much to say, & the number of reflections it made me make as I read, the number of remarks that, in the tone of the highest sympathy, highest criticism, highest consideration & generally most intimate participation, I articulated, from page to page, for your absent ear, have so accumulated on my consciousness as to render me positively helpless. I can't discharge the load by this clumsy mechanism. The only possible relief would be the pleasure of a talk with you, & that luxury, thanks to the general perversity of things, seems distant & dim. I greatly regret it – I seem to have the vision of our threshing out together, if chance only favoured, much golden grain. But I gather indeed from your admirable sister-in-law & niece, who have been so good as to come & pay me a little visit, that chance *may* favour your coming hitherward – within the next few months.[1] I shall pray for some confirmation of this – i.e. for your being able to be for a little in England.[2] Even, however,

1. Edith Wharton's older brother Frederick Rhinelander Jones (1846–1918) had briefly married Mary Cadwalader (Rawle) Jones (1850–1935); their daughter Beatrix (1872–1959) was later a famous landscape gardener.
2. In January 1903 Edith and Teddy Wharton sailed for Genoa. They did not visit England, however.

were I prepared to chatter to you about *The Valley*, I think I should sacrifice that exuberance to the timely thought that the first duty to pay to a serious & achieved work of art is the duty of recognition *telle quelle*, & that the rest can always wait. In the presence of a book so accomplished, pondered, saturated, so exquisitely studied & so brilliant & interesting from a literary point of view, I feel that just now heartily to congratulate you covers plenty of ground. There is a thing or two I should like to say – some other time. You see what reasons I have for wishing a Godspeed to that talk. *The* particular thing is somehow mistimed while the air still flushes with the pink fire of the Valley; all the more that I can't do it any sort of justice save by expatiation. So, as, after all, to mention it in 2 words does it no sort of justice, let it suffer the wrong of being crudely hinted as my desire earnestly, tenderly, intelligently to admonish you, while you are young, free, expert, exposed (to illumination) – by which I mean while you're in full command of the situation – admonish you, I say, in favour of the *American Subject*. There it is round you. Don't pass it by – the immediate, the real, the ours, the yours, the novelist's that it waits for. Take hold of it & keep hold, & let it pull you where it will. It will pull harder than things of more *tarabiscotage*, which is a merit in itself. What I would say in a word is: Profit, be warned, by my awful example of exile & ignorance. You will say that *j'en parle à mon aise* – but I shall have paid for my ease, & I don't want you to pay (as much) for yours. But these are impertinent importunities – from the moment they are not developed. All the same <u>*Do New York*</u>![3] The 1st-hand account is precious. I could give you one, by the way, of Mrs. Cadwalader & Miss Beatrix, very fresh & accented, if it were not past midnight. We renewed & augmented our friendship & I rejoiced to see your sister-in-law always so brave & beneficent. She made me fairly feel that I *need* her here. There you have the penalty of the dispatriated. And the Bourgets are paying again one of their inexplicable little visits to England – spending three or four weeks at Bournemouth. Non comprenny! – I who know Bournemouth. But it gives me the chance to hope for them for a day or two here; as I should be so glad some day to hope for you. Believe me, with kind regards to your husband, yours, dear Mrs. Wharton, most cordially

Henry James

3. Three days later HJ wrote to Mary Cadwalader Jones of Edith Wharton's latest works that 'they've made me, again, as I hinted to you other things had, want to get hold of the little lady and pump the pure essence of my wisdom and experience into her. She *must* be tethered in native pastures, even if it reduce her to a back-yard in New York.' (HJL IV, 237.)

193. To Lucy (Mrs William Kingdon) Clifford
8 September 1902

Houghton TC   Unpublished

The Wings of the Dove *was issued by Scribner on 21 August and by Constable
on 30 August.*

Lamb House, Rye.
September 8th, 1902.

My dear Lucy C.

Don't, I beseech you, be cross if I *do* thank you for your generous letter today received. I want, if nothing else, to rejoice with you over the happy find of the subject for a novel which visited you, as you say, so lately, in the watches of the night.[1] These are the great dates of life and I hope with all my heart that you may have turned up a trump card. But you must tell me more of it.

Also I must bow my head in the dust to Ethel for having, in my desire to serve the mother, lost sight for the moment of my promise to her child. Tell her, please, I but too well remember it and that I become, with the thought, a perfect Peony of Shame. But I have two more forthcoming (more or less) works – that is all finished and only awaiting publication; one a volume of tales, the other a longish novel, much better than *The Wings*, and less long.[2] She shall, I vow by all that's sacred, have *both*, and you none at all. So serve you write. I am touched by your just discriminations about the book – of the truth of which I am but too conscious. I have been through them all myself and exhaustively read the moral (of its manner, size and muchness.) A special accident operated, a series of causes conspired, to make it write itself that way – but they won't, absolutely they won't, conspire again. I have got them under. This particular thing must pass for what it is worth, and though it won't vulgarly succeed, it will have done me a certain good. It's so much money in my pocket, meanwhile, to think of you and Ethel (as I trust she continues to be) so sweetly housed and gardened, and so baked and boiled and swept and garnished for. Do drain the wholesome cup to the dregs. I am housed and gardened as usual, but the spell – of the *hush* – is broken and I now bake and boil for three female cousins![3] The Bourgets haven't come; she was ill and they

---

1. Lucy Clifford's next novels were *The Getting Well of Dorothy* and *The Way Out* (both 1904).
2. Respectively *The Better Sort* and *The Ambassadors*.
3. There were many Emmets in Europe in 1902, as well as Elly Temple Emmet Hunter.

have fled to Paris. But you are in error – I haven't lost, in *him*, a source of vivifying commerce. I really don't *communicate*, with him; but I will explain.[4] Goodnight – from your affectionate old friend

Henry James.

194. To Ford Madox Hueffer (Ford)
9 September 1902

Houghton MS   Published HJL IV, 239; SL2, 341–2; FMFSCHJ, 40–41

The extraordinary novelist, poet, editor, biographer and critic Ford Madox Hueffer (1873–1939), later Ford Madox Ford, first called on HJ in Rye in 1896, through the offices of their common friend Lucy Clifford. He moved to Winchelsea (where his wife's father had been mayor), across the Romney Marsh from Rye, in 1901. Accounts of their relations differ: HJ's typist Mary Weld evidently disliked him, recalling interrupted walks to Winchelsea: 'unfortunately his literary flatterer Ford Madox Hueffer who lived at Winchelsea used to waylay him, and this annoyed Mr James. Once we actually jumped a dike to avoid meeting Hueffer who was looking out for us.' (HJAH, 154.) Hueffer said that Merton Densher in The Wings of the Dove *was based on him.*

September 9th 1902
LAMB HOUSE, RYE, SUSSEX.

My dear Hueffer.

I thank you ever so kindly for your letter, which gives me extreme pleasure & almost for the moment makes me see the *Wings*, myself, not as a mass of mistakes, with everything I had intended absent & everything present botched![1] Such is the contagion of your charming optimism. There is something, I

4. On 11 June 1900 HJ had written about him to Urbain Mengin (1869–1955), a young French friend of the Bourgets working on English Romantic poets in Italy: 'The manner in which his imagination, his admirable intelligence and his generous and sensitive soul have been led captive by a certain abnormal vision of "high life" remains for me one of the oddest and most indescribable facts with which literary, with which moral criticism, just now, has to deal.' (HJL IV, 148.)

1. To Mary Cadwalader Jones on 23 October HJ gave a fuller account: 'The thing in question is, by a complicated accident ... too inordinately drawn out and too inordinately rubbed in. The centre, moreover, isn't in the middle, or the middle, rather, isn't in the centre, but ever so much too near the end, so that what was to come after it is truncated. The book, in fine, has too big a head for its body.' (HJL IV, 247.)

suppose, by way of leaven in the lump; but I feel – have *been* feeling – mainly as if I had deposited in the market-place an object chiefly cognisable, & evitable, *as* a lump. Nothing, all the same, is ever more interesting to me than the consideration, with those who care & see, or want to, of these bottomless questions of How & Why & Whence & *What* – in connection with the mystery of one's craft. But they take one far, &, after all, it is the *doing* it that best meets & answers them. The book had of course, to my sense, to be composed in a certain way, in order to come into being at all, & the lines of composition, so to speak, determined & controlled its parts & account for what is & what isn't there; what isn't, e.g., like the "last interview" (Hall Caine wd. have made it large as life, & magnificent, wouldn't he?) of Densher & Milly. I had to make up my mind as to what was my subject & what wasn't, & then to illustrate & embody the same logically. The subject was Densher's history with Kate Croy – hers with him, & Milly's history was but a thing involved & embroiled in that. But I fear I even thus let my system betray me, & at any rate I feel I have welded my structure of rather too large & too heavy historic bricks. But we will talk of these things, & I think I have a plan of getting over [to] Winchelsea some day next week, when I shall no longer have 3 American cousins staying with me, & 2 others at the Mermaid![2] But I will consult you telegraphically first. I am hoping you *have* been able to pass the book on to Conrad.[3] Yours most truly

Henry James

195. To Mary (Mrs Humphry) Ward
23 September 1902

Virginia MS   Published HJL IV, 242–3

Mrs Ward was close to the end of her new novel, Lady Rose's Daughter *(1903). By this time HJ deliberately avoided seeing reviews of his work; those of* The Wings of the Dove *were generally respectful – a mixture of admiration, bafflement and resentment.*

2. The Mermaid Inn, supposedly an old haunt of smugglers, was near Lamb House.
3. Joseph Conrad (Teodor Josef Konrad Korzeniowski, 1857–1924) was living at Pent Farm, Stanford, near Hythe, in Kent. He and Hueffer were close at the time, and had been collaborating since 1898 on a succession of novels (they had written *The Inheritors* (1901), and were finishing *Romance*). HJ met Conrad in 1897 after his Polish admirer had sent him a flattering letter and a copy of *An Outcast of the Islands* (1896).

September 23*d* *1902.*
LAMB HOUSE, RYE, SUSSEX.

Dear Mrs. Ward.

All thanks for your kind & generous letter. I think I see the faults of my too-voluminous fiction exhaustively myself: indeed when once my thing is done I see nothing *but* the faults. There are three or four major ones (or rather 2 maximum ones in particular) in the book that I think of very ruefully. Neither of them, I may say, however, is the objection you raise – as to Kate's understanding with Densher, for that understanding was *in its explicitness* simply the subject of the book, the idea without which the thing wouldn't have been written. The subject is a *poor* one, I unaffectedly profess – the result of a base wish to do an amiable, a generally-pleasing love-story. But such as it is, it's *treated*, & it wouldn't have been treated if my pair hadn't *met* on the subject of Milly's money. The thing is essentially a Drama, like everything I do, & the drama, with the logic, the progression, the objectivized presentation of a drama, is all *in* their so meeting. The main field of it is, as the book is composed, in Densher's consciousness; that composition involves, for us, largely, the closing of Kate's, & there is no torment worth speaking of for Densher; there's *no* consciousness – none, I mean, that's at all dramatic – if their agreement hasn't been *expressed* & this expression, above all, been <u>the</u> <u>thing</u> he has subscribed to. Everything in Kate, meanwhile, has from the first led up to it by innumerable marks – or been meant to: her offer to her Father, in particular, being of course but the appeal to be protected – against herself (*in general*) by rupture with the danger of what she foresees in the *other* life. But it's long past midnight & my lamp burns low. I didn't mean to expatiate. What's done is done, & what isn't, alas, isn't: Kate is a very limited success, Mrs. Stringham is a charming idea not carried out, & Mrs. Lowder (& these are not the maximum faults, either!) has slipped away altogether. Milly & Densher are decent – at most.

And I, dear Mrs. Ward, am not even *that*; for I can't, I am very sorry to say, come to you next month. It won't be possible for me to leave home at present – I mean next month, at all – too many things keep me here. But I come up to town on Jan. 10*th* – to stay till May, & then I hope with all my heart to make up a little. But it *is* 1.15 a.m. Good night, good morning. Yours very constantly

Henry James

196. To Viscount Field-Marshal Garnet Joseph Wolseley
15 October 1902

Hove MS   Unpublished

On 30 September HJ reported to Pinker his progress with The Better Sort, *his collection of tales for Methuen. 'What has been happening is that, after starting and, for the most part, nearly finishing, some weeks ago, no less than four supplementary tales for the volume, I suddenly found the screw put on . . . in respect to a short volume, of a biographic sort, that I a good while ago spoke to you of as a botheration hanging over me – as to which, in short, I have been these several years under pledges to Blackwood. I was meaning to do it, finally, this autumn, at any rate, but the appeal (from B. – and small blame to him!) suddenly became so sharp that it made me nervous, and to assuage my nervousness (which upset for the moment my application to the little tales) I broke off and instantly began to write the other book. The consequence is that now I have got him well started, and got my mind free to return to the three or four fictions in question, polish them off and transmit them to you at, as I say, the earliest possible moment.' (Unpublished Yale TS, Za James 1, vol. 1.) As his typist recorded, he finished 'The Birthplace' on 10 October, 'The Beast in the Jungle' on 16 October and 'The Papers' on 13 November.*

Sir Garnet Wolseley (1833–1913) was 'the victor of the Ashantees' in the first Ashanti War of 1873–4, author of The Decline and Fall of Napoleon *(1895), and from 1895 to 1899 Commander-in-Chief of the British army; his cultivated wife was the former Louisa Erskine (1843–1920). HJ met them in 1877 at the Dugdales' in Warwickshire (HJL II, 130). He told WJ in 1878 Wolseley was 'a very handsome, well-mannered & fascinating little man – with rosy dimples and an eye of steel', but that he knew the wife better – 'who is pretty, & has the air, the manners, the toilets & the taste, of an American' (CWJ I, 296).*

On 9 September 1900 HJ wrote to Edward Warren of visiting the Wolseleys at Glynde, walking 'on those wondrous circumambient Downs – & with a good deal of envious & surprised perception . . . of the way the little house, originally so thankless, justifies itself when peopled with the proprietors & their treasures' (Unpublished Huntington MS, HM 40276).

Lamb House, Rye, Sussex.
Oct: 15th 1902

Dear Lord Wolseley.

Most kind your letter about Hudson's book – for which it was very good of you to take time.[1] I'm glad you felt the charm of the volume, & I echo the reflections, gloomy though they be, that the subject moves you to make; the only branch of it that is not gloomy being the probable safety (from ravage,) of our own poor residue of time. *We* shall see no change, no; & goodness knows that the next time I have the joy of alighting at Farm House I *want* to see none, of any sort whatever. But I can believe anything, or at any rate fear anything, of the Downland of the hereafter. However, we must dash away the image, & plunge the more into the actual, still, after all, so wonderfully undamaged. What an England it will be that will sacrifice it! The thought makes me even the more yours & Lady Wolseley's & the Miss Lawrence's – even, sooth to say, Admiral Brand's.[2] I renew all my sentiments to your house & am yours, dear Lord Wolseley, very constantly

Henry James

197. To Herbert George Wells
15 November 1902

Bodleian MS   Published HJHGW, 83–5

On 13 November HJ had nearly finished sending Methuen the extra stories – 'The Beast in the Jungle', 'The Birthplace' and 'The Papers' – for The Better Sort; *he confessed to Pinker that '"THE BETTER SORT" will be of quite maximum length for a vol. of "short" stories; the extra things I've been sending straight to Methuen amounting to* very *much more than the original 60,000 words on the basis of which we originally approached him. The last story in the list is in fact by itself of about 40,000: almost the matter alone of a sweet little book. This is my usual bad economy in respect to the* Quid pro quo *– or rather in respect to the "quo" pro quid.' (Unpublished Yale TS, Za James 1, vol. 1.) The three new stories totalled 73,000 words.*

1. On 18 August 1901 HJ wrote to Robert Bontine Cunninghame Graham (1852–1936), writer, South American traveller and anti-imperialist, about this work, *Nature in Downland*, by the Argentine-born nature-writer and novelist William Henry Hudson (1841–1922), whose American parents were of English descent: 'A delightful, admirable, sumptuous work *Downland* promises to be – & now my brother & his wife, who are with me, know Hudson's other works.' (Unpublished Scotland MS, Acc. 11335/73 (i).) On 12 October Wolseley had thanked HJ for the book: 'Those Downs will last my time, but I can see that their end is not far distant. No railway should ever have been allowed to penetrate here. Hideous towns & jerry-built villas now cover what was not many years ago that sheep-loved turf of a generation back. The vulgarity of irredeemably vulgar citizens from London pours in here daily by train to rob this beautiful Downland of all its greatest charms.' (Unpublished Houghton MS, bMS Am 1094.)
2. A Mrs Lawrence was a friend of the Wolseleys; Admiral Brand could not be identified.

HJ and Wells had apparently been discussing the craft of writing: on 7 October HJ wrote to Wells, a fellow Pinker client, of his habit of rewriting other people's fiction in his head, asking jocularly to 'be put in possession of your work in its occult and pre-Pinkerite state' (HJHGW, 82).

LAMB HOUSE, RYE, SUSSEX.
November 15*th*, *1902.*

My dear Wells,

It is too long that I have neglected an interesting (for I can't say an interested) inquiry of yours – in your last note; & neglected precisely *because* the acknowledgment involved had to be an explanation. I have somehow, for the last month, not felt capable of explanations, it being my infirmity that when "finishing a book" (and that seems my chronic condition) my poor enfeebled cerebration becomes incapable of the least extra effort, however slight & simple. My correspondence then shrinks & shrinks – only the least explicit of my letters get themselves approximately written. And somehow it has seemed highly explicit to tell you that (in reply to your suggestive last) those wondrous & copious preliminary *statements* (of my fictions-that-are-to be,) don't really exist in any form in which they can be imparted. I think I know to whom you allude as having seen their semblance – & indeed their very substance; but in 2 exceptional (as it were) cases. In these cases what was seen was the statement drawn up on the basis of the *serialization* of the work – drawn up in one case with extreme detail & at extreme length (in 20,000 words!)[1] Pinker saw that: it referred to a long novel, afterwards (this more than a year,) written & finished, but not yet, to my great inconvenience, published; but it went more than 2 years ago, to America, to the Harpers, & there it remained & has probably been destroyed. Were it here I would with pleasure transmit it to you; for, though I say it who should not, it *was* the statement, full & vivid, I think, as a statement could be, of a subject as worked out. Then *Conrad* saw a shorter one of the *Wings of the D.* – also well enough in its way, but only ½ as long & proportionately less developed. *That* had been prepared so that the book might be serialized in another American periodical, but this wholly failed, (what secrets & shames I reveal to you!) & the thing (the book) was then written, the subject treated, on a more free & independent scale.[2] But *that* synopsis too has been destroyed; it was returned from the U.S., but I had then

1. For *The Ambassadors*.
2. There is no record of Conrad's comments on this statement; which if produced *before* the book's main period of composition, as HJ's phrasing here suggests, would date from before July 1901.

no occasion to preserve it. And evidently no fiction of mine can or *will* now be serialized; certainly I shall not again draw up detailed & explicit plans for unconvinced & ungracious editors; so that I fear I shall have nothing of that sort to show. A plan for *myself*, as copious & developed as possible I always do draw up – that is the 2 documents I speak of were based upon, & extracted from, such a preliminary *private* outpouring. But this latter voluminous effusion is, ever, so extremely familiar, confidential & intimate – in the form of an interminable garrulous letter addressed to my own fond fancy – that, though I always, for easy reference, have it carefully typed, it isn't a thing I would willingly expose to any eye but my own. And even *then*, sometimes, I shrink! So there it is. I am greatly touched by your respectful curiosity, but I haven't, you see, anything coherent to produce. Let me promise however that if I ever do, within any calculable time, address a manifesto to the dim editorial mind, you shall certainly have the benefit of a copy. Candour compels me to add that that consummation has now become unlikely. It is too wantonly expensive a treat to them. In the first place they will none of me, & in the second the relief, & greater intellectual dignity, so to speak, of working on one's own scale, one's own line of continuity & in one's own absolutely independent *tone*, is too precious to me to be again forfeited. Pardon my too many words. I only add that I hope the domestic heaven bends blue above you. Yours, my dear Wells, always

Henry James

198. To William Dean Howells
11 December 1902

Houghton MS   Published HJL IV, 250–52; LHJ I, 407–10; LFL, 379–81

American comment on the new novel was arriving. On 25 October WJ wrote to HJ: 'I have read the Wings of the Dove (for which all thanks!) but what shall I say of a book constructed on a method which so belies everything that I acknowledge as law? You've reversed every traditional canon of story-telling (especially the fundamental one of telling the story, wh. you carefully avoid) and have created a new genre littéraire which I can't help thinking perverse, but in which you nevertheless succeed, for I read with interest to the end (many pages, and innumerable sentences twice over to see what the dickens they could possibly mean) and all with unflagging curiosity to know what the upshot might become.'

HJ replied on 11 November: 'Your reflections on the W. of the D. . . . *greatly interest me; yet, after all, I don't know that I can very explicitly meet them. Or rather, really, there is too much to say. One writes as one can – & also as one sees, judges, feels, thinks. And I feel & think so much on the ignoble state to which in this age of every cheapness, I see the novel, as a form, reduced, that there is doubtless greatly, with me, the element of what I would as well as of what I "can." At any rate my stuff, such as it is, is inevitable – for me.' (CWJ III, 220, 222.)*

Howells also wrote a letter, which unfortunately does not seem to survive.

LAMB HOUSE, RYE, SUSSEX.

December 11*th 1902*

My dear Howells.

Nothing more delightful, or that has touched me more closely, even to the spring of tears, has befallen me for years, literally, than to receive your beautiful letter of Nov. 30*th*, so largely & liberally anent *The W. of the D*. Every word of it goes to my heart & to "thank" you for it seems a mere grimace. The same post brought me a letter from dear John Hay, so that my measure has been full.[1] I haven't known anything about the American "notices," heaven save the mark! any more than about those here (which I am told, however, have been remarkably genial;) so that I have *not* had the sense of confrontation with a public more than usually childish – I mean had it in any special way. I confess, however, that that is my chronic sense – the more than usual childishness of publics; & it is (has been,) in my mind, long since discounted, & my work definitely insists upon being independent of such phantasms & on unfolding itself wholly from its own "innards". Of course, in our conditions, doing anything decent is pure disinterested, unsupported unrewarded heroism; but that's in the day's work. The *faculty of attention* has utterly vanished from the general anglosaxon mind, extinguished at its source by the big blatant *Bayadère* of Journalism, of the newspaper & the *picture* (above all) magazine; who keeps screaming "Look at *me*, *I* am the thing, & I only, the thing that will keep you in relation with me *all the time* without your having to attend *one minute* of the time." If you are moved to write anything anywhere about the *W. of the D*. do say something of that – it so awfully wants saying.[2] But we live in a

1. HJ replied gratefully to Hay on 16 December that his praises 'give me extraordinary joy' and 'nerve me, as the phrase is, to fresh efforts!' (HJJH, 128).
2. In January 1903 Howells's 'Mr. Henry James's Later Work' in the *North American Review* praised *The Wings of the Dove* as giving a vivid sense of London, Venice and New York, though without discovering any figure in HJ's carpet: 'What I feel sure of is that he has a meaning in it all, and that by and by, perhaps when I least expect it, I shall surprise his meaning.' On *The Sacred Fount* the essay asked, apparently without satirical intention, 'why should not a novel be written so like to life, in which most of the events remain meaningless, that we shall never quite know what the author meant?' (WDHAC, 406–18, 413, 415.)

lonely age for literature or for any art but the mere visual. Illustrations, loud simplifications & *grossissements*, the big Building (good for John;) the "mounted" play, the prose that is careful to be in the tone of, & with the distinction of, a newspaper or bill-poster advertisement – these, & these only, meseems "stand a chance."[3] But why do I talk of such chances? I am *melted* at your reading *en famille The Sacred Fount*, which you will, I fear, have found chaff in the mouth & which is one of several things of mine, in these last years, that have paid the penalty of having been conceived only as the "short story" that (alone, apparently,) I could hope to work off somewhere (which I mainly failed of,) & then *grew* by a rank force of its own into something of which the idea had, modestly, never been to be a book. That is essentially the case with the *S.F.*; planned, like the Spoils of Poynton, What Maisie Knew, The Turn of the Screw & various others, as a story of from "8 to 10 thousand words" (!!) & then having accepted its bookish necessity or destiny in consequence of becoming already, at the start, 20,000; accepted it ruefully & blushingly, moreover, since, *given the tenuity of the idea*, the larger quantity of treatment hadn't been aimed at. I remember how I would have "chucked" *The Sacred Fount* at the 15*th* thousand word, if in the 1*st* place I could have afforded to "waste" 15 000, & if in the second I were not always ridden by a superstitious terror of not finishing, for finishing's and for the precedent's sake, what I have begun. I am a fair coward about *dropping*, & the book in question, I fear, is, more than anything else, a monument to that superstition. When, if it meets my eye, I say to myself, "You know you *might* not have finished it," I make the remark not in natural reproach, but, I confess, in craven relief.

But why am I thus grossly expatiative on the very carpet of the bridal altar? I spread it beneath Pillar's feet with affectionate jubilation & gratulation & stretch it out further, in the same spirit, beneath yours & her mother's.[4] I wish her & you, & the florally-minded young man (he *must* be a good 'un,) all joy in the connection. If he stops short of gathering samphire it's a beautiful trade, & I trust he will soon come back to claim the redemption of the maiden's vows. Please say to her from me that I bless her – *hard*.

Your visit to Cambridge makes me yearn a little, & your walking over it with C.N. & your sitting in it with Grace.[5] Did the ghost of other walks (I'm

3. 'John' here is Howells's son, the architect.
4. 'Pillar' or 'Pilla' was Mildred, Howells's daughter, who became engaged in October 1902 to David G. Fairchild (1869–1954), a botanist, but broke it off by January 1903.
5. Howells, now living in New York, visited the Nortons on 22 November. Saddened by the hostile American reception of *The Kentons*, he confessed to Norton a 'literary weariness of myself', an avowal for which he later apologized (SLWDH V, 40). In the 1860s HJ and Howells had often taken long literary walks in Cambridge, and Fresh Pond (a small lake) was a favourite place.

told Fresh Pond is no longer a Pond, or no longer Fresh, only Stale, or something,) ever brush you with the hem of its soft shroud? Haven't you lately published some volume of Literary Essays or Portraits (*since* the Heroines of Fiction) & won't you, munificently send me either that *or* the Heroines – neither of which have sprung up in my here so rustic path?[6] I will send you in partial payment another book of mine to be published on Feb: 27*th*.[7] Good night, with renewed benedictions on [y]our house & your spirit. Yours always and ever

Henry James

199. To Maud Broadwood (Mrs Waldo) Story
6 January 1903

Texas TS and MS   Partly published LHJ I, 411–13

HJ was now working on William Wetmore Story and his Friends. *On 21 December 1902 he told Sarah Butler Wister that 'I hope to finish in six weeks, or perhaps less' (HJL IV, 260). In the event the book seems to have been delivered to Blackwood in March. On 29 December 1902 he confided to Houghton, Mifflin, the U.S. publishers of the book – declining to treat J. R. Lowell for them as a 'real Biographic subject' – what 'diabolical art' he was driven to use in his 'actual difficult job of trying to treat W. W. Story as one' (HJL IV, 263).*

On 5 January 1903 he told Pinker that 'I hear from the Harpers, all of a sudden, that they are serializing "The Ambassadors", after all, in the North American Review' (Unpublished Yale TS, Za James 1, vol. 1); in fact the first of the twelve monthly instalments was that of January 1903. The magazine had never before published a work of fiction, in nearly a century.

Lamb House, Rye Sussex.
Jan. 6th, 1903.

Dear Mrs. Waldo.

Let my first word be to ask you to pardon this vulgar machinery and this portentous legibility: the fruit of dictation, in the first place (now made absolutely necessary to me;) and the fruit, in the second place, of the fact that, pegging away as I am at present, in your interest and Waldo's (and with the end of

6. Since *Heroines of Fiction* (1901) Howells had published *Literature and Life* (1902).
7. *The Better Sort.*

our business now, I am happy to say, well in sight) I so live, as it were, from day to day and from hour to hour, by the aid of this mechanism, that it is an effort to me to break with it even for my correspondence. I had promised myself to write you so that you should receive my letter on the very Capo D'Anno; and if I had *then* overcome my scruple as to launching at you a dictated thing, you would some time ere this have been in possession of my news. I have delayed till now, because I was every day hoping to catch the right moment to address you a page or two of my own proper hieroglyphics. But one's Christmastide burden (of writing) here is heavy; I didn't snatch the moment; and *this* is a brave precaution lest it should again elude me; which, in the interest of lucidity, please again forgive.

So much as that about a minor matter. The more important one is that, as you will both be glad to know, I have (in spite of a[n] almost damnable interruption of several weeks, this autumn, a detested compulsion to attend, for the time, to something else,) got on so straight with the Book that three quarters of it are practically written and 4 or 5 weeks more will see me, as I calculate, at the end of the matter.[1] After that, Blackwood ought to publish as promptly as possible, and will probably desire to do so. This question, however, must wait till he has the whole thing in his hands; then it will be easily settled, and I will immediately let you know more. The Book has proved difficult to do – which was what I expected; only it has proved rather *more* so and it has also insisted on being longer. It will make, I estimate, a tolerably thick octavo; whereas if it had remained of the size in which I originally, in my mind's eye, saw it, I should probably at this date have been writing to you that it was finished. The difference of a month, or thereabouts, after all this time, is nothing; and I may as well say, in the connection, that, given the manner in which, alone, I have seen my way to do the volume, our long wait has turned out, to my sense, a positive advantage. You will see later on, I think, what I mean. All the material I received from you has been of course highly useful – indispensable; yet, none the less, all of it put together was not material for a Biography pure and simple. The subject itself didn't lend itself to *that*, in the strict sense of the word; and I had to make out, for myself, what my material *did* lend itself to. I *have*, I think, made out successfully and happily; if I haven't, at any rate, it has not been for want of a great expenditure of zeal, pains, taste (though I say it who shouldn't!) and talent! But the Book will, without doubt, be an agreeable and, in a literary sense, really artistic and honourable one. I shall not have made you all so patiently, amiably, admirably wait so long for nothing.

1. The 'almost damnable interruption' may have been the writing of the extra stories for *The Better Sort*.

The advantage I just hinted at – that of the Book's appearing now rather than three years ago – will be, provisionally, explained to you by this: that the title I must give it describes it, and that a record so described is inevitably better for the free hand given by delay: each year enabling one to handle the *past* with something more of freedom, something less of the fear of treading on ancient or too-recently defunct toes. WILLIAM WETMORE STORY AND HIS FRIENDS: FROM LETTERS, DIARIES AND RECOLLECTIONS – *that* is what I feel I shall best call the volume, and you will feel what that suggests in the way of such old-time retrospect as is glad to profit by every added inch or ell at which contemplation and description (I mean of course predominantly of the Friends!) can stand off. I have looked at the picture, as it were, given me by all your material, *as* a picture – the image or evocation, charming, heterogeneous, and a little ghostly, of a great cluster of people, a society practically extinct, with Mr. and Mrs. Story, naturally, all along, the centre, the pretext, so to speak, and the *point d'appui*. This course was the only one open to me – it was imposed with absolute logic. The Book was not makeable at all unless I used the Letters of other people, and the Letters of other people were usable with effect only in so far as I could more or less evoke and present the other people. I shall have used – by which I mean I shall have bodily printed – almost *all* the Letters I had from you, with the exception of a few of those from W.W.S. to Edith late in life.[2] Everything that could give the Book variety and substance has been absolutely imperative; so, as I say, I have worked the Letters for all they are worth. And it is exactly in this connection that I have wanted to ask you a particular question or two. There have been many things, many moments, indeed, that have made me wish the Barberini were within call; but I have managed in one way and another to tide over, I hope without gross error, most doubts and difficulties. *The* little matter, however, is just this: am I correct in having got from you the impression that you had communicated with the Miss Gaskells, of Manchester, about their mother's letters? There are some dozen from *her*, considerable parts of which I am printing – passages that contain, however, nothing whatever of a private, delicate or possibly unpublishable nature. I shall feel, all the same, *completely* at ease, if I hear from you that they *have* said "All right." If you have had *no* word, I will write to them myself, and their sanction, I am sure, will not fail.[3]

2. Story's daughter Edith, now the Countess Peruzzi.
3. It did fail. On 14 June HJ wrote to Mrs Story that 'The Miss Gaskells' absolute veto about their mother's letters made a horrid little cavity which I felt I could ill afford' (Unpublished Texas MS). Elizabeth Cleghorn Gaskell (1810–65) had joined the Storys in Rome in February 1857 (meeting and befriending also a young Charles Eliot Norton), and that summer the middle one of her three daughters, 'Meta' (Margaret Emily Gaskell, 1837–1913), had become fiancée

381

All other sanctions (of relatives) seem a matter of course; I find, for instance, Lady Betty Balfour's letter to you about her father's; in short it is plain sailing.[4]

But I am writing you at hideous length – and crowding out all space for matters more personal to ourselves. When once the Book is out I shall want, I shall need, exceedingly, to see you all; and I don't think that, unless some morbid madness settles on me, I shall fear to. But that is arrangeable and shall be arranged. I hope peace reigns meanwhile at the Barberini; that you and Waldo are both sound and serene, and that the young ones bloom as they should. My blessing on all of you. Yours, dear Mrs. Waldo, most faithfully

Henry James

P.S. I go to London, in a few days, till May – & my address there is always *Reform Club, Pall Mall. S.W.*

200. *To Frederick Macmillan*
17 June 1903

BL MS   Published CHJHM, 204–5

HJ was mostly in London from mid January till mid May 1903. On 25 March he formally agreed with Methuen, through Pinker, to supply 'Two Novels' in 1904. On 17 April he specified dates and lengths: 'I am ready to engage to deliver complete, in November next the first of the novels for Methuen, and then to deliver the second in six months from the time of the delivery of the first . . . They will, neither, be of less than 125,000 words, but I intend that they shall not be of more.' On 18 April he supplied the titles: first The Golden Bowl *and then* The Sense of the Past *(Unpublished Yale MSS, Za James 1, vol. 1). Work on* The Golden Bowl *seems to have started at once.*

On 21 December 1902 HJ had told Sarah Butler Wister he wanted to revisit America: 'my native land, in my old age, has become, becomes more and more, romantic to me altogether' (HJL IV, 259). But he was unsure when or how he could go. On 10 April he set out the position to WJ: 'my dilemma is rather tragic.

---

to a Captain Charles Hill, who proved unrespectable – so that the engagement was painfully broken off, perhaps causing the 'veto' applied to HJ. There are some passages from Mrs Gaskell's letters in the published book, however.

4. In 1887 Lady Betty, daughter of the poet and statesman Robert Lytton (1831–91), first Earl of Lytton (who was a friend of the Storys and whose correspondence is quoted in *William Wetmore Story and His Friends*), married Gerald William Balfour, second Earl of Balfour (1853–1945), brother of Arthur Balfour the Conservative statesman and prime minister.

It is all economic. It is more & more important I should go, to look after my material (literary) interests in person, & quicken & improve them, after so endless an absence . . . But the process itself *is so damnably expensive – 6 mos. of American hotels . . . I should wish to write a* book *of "impressions["] (for much money)' (CWJ III, 231).* WJ's *discouraging reply provoked HJ to restate his determination on 24 May: 'Simply and supinely to shrink – on mere grounds of general fear and encouraged shockability has to me all the air of giving up, chucking away without a struggle, the one chance that remains to me in life of anything that can be called a* movement: *my one little ewe-lamb of possible exotic experience, such experience as may convert itself, through the senses, through observation, imagination and reflection now at their maturity, into vivid and solid* material, *into a general renovation of one's too monotonised grab-bag.' (CWJ III, 237.)*

The economic motive – sharpened by the unavoidable expense (£200) of buying land adjoining Lamb House to prevent unsightly development – seems to have motivated HJ's protracted campaign of production and contractual commitment.

LAMB HOUSE, RYE, SUSSEX.
June 17*th 1903*

My dear Macmillan.

I am much obliged to you for your letter of the date of yesterday.

I think I *am* ready to accept your proposal in respect to the book on London for the series containing Crawford's *Ave Roma* &c; so please consider that I hereby do so. The size & general character of Crawford's 4 volumes (in all) commend themselves to me, &, as the subject appeals to me, I am not without a confidence of being able, on the basis in question, to do something successful.[1] I certainly shall not be able to treat my subject in *less* than 150 000 words – which as a maximum, I gather, you would even prefer to 120,000. [sic] And I will combine & arrange with Pennell for the best advantage of each of us.[2] Last not least, I am obliged to you for your statement of terms – a royalty of 20 per cent. & an advance of one thousand pounds on account. The only shade on the picture, a little, for me is that a plan I have for next year may prevent my putting the book through as early, in time, as I should otherwise have been disposed to do. I am thinking, rather definitely, of going to America for 6 or 8 months (some time in 1904) & that won't contribute to a study of London

1. Francis Marion Crawford (1854–1909), another Macmillan author, published *Ave Roma Immortalis* (1898), *The Rulers of the South* (1900) and *Salve Venetia* (1905) in the same series.
2. HJ's 1888 essay on 'London' in the *Century* had been illustrated by Joseph Pennell (1857–1926), the well-known American illustrator, who had also illustrated the 1900 reissue of *A Little Tour in France* and would do *English Hours* (1905) and *Italian Hours* (1909).

– though it *may* (eventually,) contribute to the subsequent leisure for dealing with it. However, with the margin you mention, I don't think that need alarm me.[3] I must do, as I reflect with pleasure, a good deal of fertilizing reading, besides other prowling & prying; but once these things get themselves adequately done, I think I shall be able to *write* the book in some eight months.[4] And perhaps, after all, I shall be able to read – a little – even in America – even on a return there after 20 years of absence! Moreover I shall not start, even at the earliest, for a goodish many months. So on the whole, as I say, I am not afraid! Believe me, my dear Macmillan, yours always

Henry James

201. *To James Brand Pinker*
1 November 1903

Yale MS   Unpublished

The Ambassadors *was published by Methuen on 24 September and by the Harpers on 6 November.*

HJ had originally promised delivery of The Golden Bowl *by the end of November; but although he had reported the book to Pinker on 8 September as something he was 'getting on with steadily' (Unpublished Yale TS, Za James 1, vol. 1), he had to break off for ten days to write a promised essay on 'Gabriele D'Annunzio' for the* Quarterly Review *(published in April 1904), and by 25 October he had to admit that despite his 'gouging away at it with great constancy ever since the date of that vow, [i.e. April] . . . I am not now as far toward completion as I should like – and being overpressed maddens me and destroys my work'. He had completed 'some 110,000 of the (about) 170,000 words of which it is my plan that the Book shall consist' (HJL IV, 285); and initially offered to give Methuen three quarters of the novel by the deadline.*

3. Macmillan replied on 19 June that, while the contract specified nothing about date of publication, they looked forward 'to being able [to] bring the book out early in the autumn of 1906' (CHJHM, 206). On 22 June HJ signed and returned the contract for *London Town* (Walter Besant had written a *London* in 1892).

4. HJ put together a small library for this projected book, which he never wrote, including Besant's *London*, Stow's *Survey of London* and Loftie's *History of London*. He did explore London for it, filling thirty-six and a half pages of a notebook between August 1907 and October 1909.

Nov. *1st 1903*
LAMB HOUSE, RYE, SUSSEX.

Dear Mr. Pinker.

If I have delayed two or three days to answer your note conveying Mr. Methuen's offer of a delay of some three or four months for the publication of *The Golden Bowl*, it has been in order to take full counsel with myself on the matter. The result is that I *accept* the offer with thanks, as on the whole it will ease me off and contribute to the higher perfection, so to speak, of the book. Will you therefore kindly say that I appreciate the proposal & will consider the time definitely fixed for *August* 1904.[1] I shall nevertheless be able to send them the whole copy with an only moderate extension of time – in some 10 or 12 weeks from now – & the second book by the moment *The Golden Bowl* is published.[2] My only regret will be in having, alas, to wait so long for my money – but we will talk of that later on. Yours very truly

Henry James

202. *To Brander Matthews*
16 November 1903

Columbia MS   Unpublished

Brander Matthews (1852–1929) was a professor of English and drama at Columbia, 1891–1924, but also a playwright.

Lamb House Rye
Nov. *16th 1903*

Dear Brander Matthews.

All thanks for the Sainte-Beuve, which I shld. not have known how to come by save with your help.[1] I am sending him back to you (in a separate envelope from this) revised, embellished & slightly abbreviated. I couldn't forbear to tidy him up a little & rap his knuckles here & there; for verily he made me say to myself with humiliation "How vilely I used to write!" The corrections

1. By the end of November 1903 HJ was planning to leave for America in August 1904.
2. The second book was to have been *The Sense of the Past*.
1. The previously uncollected essay on Sainte-Beuve, from the *North American Review* of January 1880, was not published by Matthews; on 30 May 1904 HJ sent it, at Matthews's request, to another U.S. educator, William Morton Payne (1858–1919), who included it in *American Literary Criticism* (1904).

will require a little careful proof-reading, but they are, I think, straight & clear. I would ask to *see* a proof if I didn't fear to worry you – so do in this matter as you must. Only, please, at any cost, leave the *date* – 1880.

I am much moved by your remembering anything of mine in the far-away ghostly *Parisian*. You are a true bibliographer. I shouldn't know where to look for *that* now, but I remember a matter concerning it & concerning poor (*as* ghostly) Theodore Child.[2] Yours very truly

Henry James

203. To Howard Overing Sturgis
18 November 1903

Houghton MS   Unpublished

Julian Sturgis's younger brother, Howard Overing Sturgis was also wealthy and also a writer: he had written a boys' book, Tim, *in 1891 and a short novel,* All That Was Possible, *in 1895. He lived at Queen's Acre, otherwise Qu'Acre, the Sturgis family home near Windsor, with his mustachioed companion, 'The Babe', William Haynes Smith, who commuted to work in the City. In 1899 he had written to HJ about* The Awkward Age, *and HJ had replied, 'I greatly applaud the tact with which you tell me that scarce a human being will understand a word, or an intention, or an artistic element or glimmer of any sort, of my book.' (HJL IV, 106.)*

Now Sturgis, a friend of HJ, Rhoda Broughton, A. C. Benson and Edith Wharton, was sending him the proofs of a novel, Belchamber, *whose martyred hero Sainty is a Marquis. On 8 November HJ commented encouragingly on the first batch, but noted that 'you have a great deal increased your difficulty by screwing up the "social position" of all your people so very high' (HJL IV, 286).*

November 18*th* 1903.
LAMB HOUSE, RYE, SUSSEX.

My dear Howard.

I have too much delayed – partly because I've been up to town for four or five days & that has made a hole in my time. But I have had your last good letter, as well as your copious last proofs (161–224) which I gratefully return

---

2. HJ only published two items in Child's *The Parisian*: 'A Bundle of Letters' (18 December 1879, promptly pirated in America) and a review of Zola's *Nana* (26 February 1880).

– just as I do full justice to your (amiably superfluous) explanations of grounds, logic &c. in respect to your hero's social position &c. I think that as the thing goes on, these grounds, this logic &c, speak more for themselves – so that the reader will see your wherefore & your concatenations. You *keep up* the whole thing bravely – & I recognise the great difficulty involved in giving conceivability to your young man's marriage.[1] I am not sure you have taken *all* the precautions necessary – but one feels, in general, that Sainty's physiology, as it were, ought to be definitely & authoritatively established & focussed: one wants in it a *positive* side, – all his own – so that he shall not be *all* passivity & nullity. The thing is at any rate always interesting, observed, felt, ironized – copious & various. Send along the rest – I won't again delay so long.

I went up to town for 24 hours & staid eighty or ninety or whatever, caught in the *engrenage*. All that was wanted to make the whirl complete was that I should have gyrated to Windsor. But this I only want, ever, to do, with the necessary protocols & solemnities – after preliminary gloatings. Now I'm very much back here in deep *receuillement* – modified by an elegant brochure of Arthur Benson's which he has sent me & for which I mean to thank [him] – I mean his official announcement of departure.[2]

Let me add that you will see that I have *marked* nothing at all in your proofs – not because I haven't here & there made my observation, but because it's late for any such interposition – & only & vainly worrying to you – & also not urgent. Votre siège est fait – & will take the town. But morning dawns, & I am yours, my dear Howard, always & ever

Henry James

204. To Henry Adams
19 November 1903

Mass. Hist. Inst. MS   Published HJL IV, 288–9; SL2, 349–50; CHJHA, 62–3; partly published LHJI, 431–2

On 18 November Henry Adams wrote from Paris of the powerful impact on him of William Wetmore Story and His Friends, *published in October. 'The painful truth is that all of my New England generation, counting the half-century, 1820–*

1. In the novel Cissy Eccleston's scheming mother Lady Eccleston traps the eligible but innocent Sainty (Lord Belchamber), who, apart from his rank, lacks 'all that women most prized in man, strength, courage, virility' (ch. xv), into marrying her equally cynical daughter.
2. Benson gave up his post as a housemaster at Eton in 1903 and went to live in Cambridge, where he became a fellow of Magdalene College in 1904 (and Master in 1915).

1870, were in actual fact only one mind and nature; the individual was a facet of Boston ... Type bourgeois-bostonien! A type quite as good as another, but more uniform ... So you have written not Story's life, but your own and mine, – pure autobiography, – the more keen for what is beneath, implied, intelligible only to me, and half a dozen other people still living ... You make me curl up, like a trodden-on worm. Improvised Europeans, we were, and – Lord God! – how thin!' (CHJHA, 60.)

> November 19*th* *1903*
> LAMB HOUSE, RYE, SUSSEX.

My dear Adams.

I am so happy at hearing from you *at all* that the sense of the particular occasion of my doing so is almost submerged & smothered. You did bravely well to write – make a note of the act, for your future career, as belonging to a class of impulses to be precipately obeyed &, if possible, even tenderly nursed. Yet it has been interesting, exceedingly, in the narrower sense, as well as delightful in the larger, to have your letter, with its so ingenious expression of the effect on you of poor *W.W.S.* – with whom, & the whole business of whom, there is (yes, I can see!) a kind of *inevitableness* in my having made you squirm – or whatever is the proper name for the sensation engendered in you! Very curious, & even rather terrible, this so far-reaching action of a little biographical vividness – which did indeed, in a manner, begin with me, myself, even as I put the stuff together – though pushing me to conclusions less grim, as I may call them, than in your case. The truth is that <u>any</u> retraced story of bourgeois lives (lives other than great lives of "action" – *et encore!*) throws a chill upon the scene, the time, the subject, the small mapped-out facts, & if you find "great men thin" it isn't really so much their fault (& least of all yours) as that the art of the biographer – devilish art! – is somehow practically *thinning*. It simplifies even while seeking to enrich – & even the Immortal are so helpless & passive in death. The proof is that I wanted to invest dear old Boston with a mellow, a golden glow – & that for those who know, like yourself, I only make it bleak – & weak! Luckily those who know are indeed but three or four – & they won't, I hope, too promiscuously tell. For the book, meanwhile, I seem to learn, is much acclaimed in the U.S. – a better fate than I hoped for the mere dissimulated-perfunctory. The Waldo Storys absolutely *thrust* the job upon me five, six, *seven* years ago – & I had been but dodging & delaying in despair at the meagreness of the material (*every* – documentary – scrap of which I have had thriftily to make use of.) At last I seemed to see a *biais* – of subjective amplification – by which something in the nature of a *book* might be made, & then I could with some promptness work my little oracle. Someone has just written to ask me if the Family "like it," & I have replied that I think they don't know whether they like it or not![1] They are waiting to find out, & I am glad on the whole they haven't access to *you*. I wish I myself had – beyond *this*.[2] But even this, as I tell you, has been a great pleasure to yours, my dear Adams, always & ever

Henry James

205. To Howard Overing Sturgis
[28 November 1903]

Houghton MS   Unpublished

On 23 November HJ wrote to Sturgis about the next part of Belchamber, *containing the wedding night of Sainty and the scornful Cissy: 'I am perhaps just a wee bit disappointed in the breadth of the celebrated nuptial night scene.' He also wished he could have influenced Sturgis 'in the interest of a Sainty with a constituted & intense imaginative life of his own, which would have been to be given (given more than any thing else,) out of which all relations with people would have come as baffled & tragic excursions – mangled & bewildering days (or nights,) "out"' (HJL IV, 294). He consolingly mentioned 'the humiliating difficulty I am having here over my own stuff' – The Golden Bowl; and in any case, as he says in the following letter, the 'B.[ritish] P.[ublic]' won't share HJ's qualms.*

Lamb House[1]
Saturday

My dear Howard.

I am again, in returning you the enclosed, but too aware of how little "comments" have their place, in any suggestive or supervisory sense, in regard to a finished & accomplished thing. I think then the thing continues very interesting & animated & *soutenu*, very vivid & clear, never for a moment dull

---

1. On 17 March 1911 HJ wrote to Howells that Story's 'foolish, or rather reprobate, progeny didn't like the book – though they could help me with nothing but a few, the very fewest, stray grains of trash toward doing it' (LFL, 446).
2. HJ and Adams had not seen each other since the summer of 1898, when HJ visited Surrenden Dering in Kent, which the widower Adams was renting with Senator Donald Cameron and his wife Elizabeth Cameron (1857–1944), to whom Adams was attached.
1. But see the last sentence.

or flat. It suffers, (as I have already said this it may not – or may it just the more? aggravate you that I shld say it again?) – it suffers from Sainty's *having no state of his own* as the field & stage of the vision & drama – so that the whole thing doesn't seem to be happening *to* him; but happening at the most round him; & one says: "To whom *is* it happening?" This is particularly sensible in the matter of his life, on the essentially *bafoué* terms, under the same roof, day by day, with his wife – which would be really for him an experience of *some* kind of Intensity. There was something in him (at the worst!) to wh: this was to be *shown as happening* – horribly, tormentedly, strangely, – in some way or *other* – happening; & "the shyness with her which was the beginning of dislike" – on p. 284 – strikes me as a phrase of an almost giving-away (of *him*) inadequacy.[2] "Beginning of dislike?" – *end*, rather, of something-or-other-else! *What* was for you to find. *And* I wish his failure to conjoin with her about 2 a.m. that night on the drawing-room sofa, could for his sake have been a stand-off *determined* by some particular interposing, disconcerting, *adequate* positive fact – of impression, suspicion, alarm: something not so merely *negative* for him.[3] He couldn't afford there (for interest,) to fail without a reason – & the reason était à trouver. I don't undertake now to find it for you – but I *could* before! I repeat all the same that nothing of this – all this will be missed by the B.P., who will degustate much that you have given & find the scene of temp[t]ation quite delightfully *scabreuse*. But enough – save that I want more, & am always too hurryingly (through this one day in town,) yours

Henry James

206. To Mary (Mrs Humphry) Ward
16 December 1903

Virginia MS   Published RRR, 122

In his next letter to Sturgis on 2 December HJ had to respond to 'your too lamentable letter, in which you speak of "withdrawing" your novel . . . If it springs from

2. At the beginning of ch. XXI, the gentle, confused Belchamber and his mercenary, reckless, egotistical wife Cissy, who is (as yet unknown to him) pregnant by another man, are increasingly alienated from each other: 'On the rare occasions when they met, he was conscious in his wife's manner of a more thinly veiled contempt, while on his side he felt a shyness with her which was the beginning of dislike.'
3. Cissy in fact sits only on chairs, not sofas, in the scene, during which she tells him 'you are repulsive to me', and to 'Keep away. Don't touch me' (ch. XVII) – saying her worldly mother forced her into the marriage.

*anything I have said to you I must have expressed myself with strange and deplorable clumsiness.' This prevented withdrawal, but on 7 December – still in mid-*Golden Bowl *– HJ disputed Sturgis's description 'of the book after Sainty's marriage as the part in which "nothing happens to him." Why, my dear Howard, it is the part in which* most *happens! His marriage itself, his wife* herself, *happen to him at every hour of the twenty-four – and he is the only person to whom anything does.'* (HJL IV, *295, 296.) In April 1904 Arthur Benson's diary records HJ talking at the Athenaeum about his shock at their friend's treatment of a promising idea in the now-published novel: 'Good Heavens, I said to myself, he has made nothing of it! . . . Good God, why this chronicle, if it is a mere passage, a mere ante-chamber, and leads to nothing?'*

Reactions began to arrive to The Ambassadors, *whose publication had been long delayed by the Harpers after HJ had handed it over to Pinker in July 1901.*

LAMB HOUSE, RYE, SUSSEX.
Dec: 16th *1903*

Dear Mrs. Ward.

Please believe in the very great pleasure given me by your kind & generous letter. It belongs to the order of acts that touch deeply, & of which the remembrance abides. I felt a good deal of despair after "The Ambassadors" were launched, & said to myself "What can be expected for a novel with a hero of 55, & properly no heroine at all?" But I have slowly felt a little better, & the book is, intrinsically, I daresay, the best I have written – in spite of a fearful, though much patched over, fault or weakness in it (which, however, I seem to see no one has noticed, & which nothing will induce me *now* ever to reveal – or at least till some one does spot it!)[1] It is, in general, meritorious for its conformation & composition – *that* I make bold to say. But it was written 4 years ago, & I feel myself rather away & "off" from it. What gives me particular pleasure is your feeling that one is in a fresh & a larger period – which I really hope & believe (D.V., absit omen, unberufen, &c, &c.!) may prove to be the case. Yet I find it all a *too* damnably difficult art – & have so to *pretend* that it isn't! However, we pretend life isn't, either – & toward *that* such good friends as you exceedingly help. I rejoice to think of finding you before very long in town & I am, dear Mrs. Ward, yours very constantly

Henry James

1. In the essay as an appendix to which Jerome McGann prints his text of this letter, he ingeniously argues that the supposed 'reversed chapters' (28 and 29) of *The Ambassadors* in the November Harper first edition, the subject of much controversy since 1950, are not in fact reversed. He bases this claim partly on a reading of this letter in which the 'fault or weakness'

207. To Millicent, Duchess of Sutherland
23 December 1903

Yale MS (Koch Collection)   Published HJL IV, 302–3

Lady Millicent Fanny St Clair-Erskine (1867–1955), eldest daughter of the fourth
Earl of Roslyn, also a friend of the Bourgets, wrote fiction and plays.

LAMB HOUSE, RYE, SUSSEX.
December 23d *1903.*

My dear Duchess.

I fear there is little chance this will reach you on Xmas day in your remote
stronghold, but let it take you none the less my warmest Xmas greeting & my
lively appreciation of the kindness of your charming letter about poor dear
W.W.S., & my effort to perform in that record, in a manner, the operation of
making bricks without straw & chronicling (sometimes) rather small beer with
the effect of opening champagne. Story was the dearest of men, but he wasn't
massive, his artistic & literary baggage were of the slightest, & the materials
for a biography *nil.* Hence (once I had succumbed to the amiable pressure of
his children,) I had really to *invent* a book, patching the thing together & eking
it out with barefaced irrelevancies – starting above all *any* hare, however small,
that might lurk by the way. It is very pleasant to get from a discriminating
reader the token that I have carried the trick through. But the magic is but
scantly mine – it is really that of the beloved old Italy, who always *will* consent
to fling a glamour for you, whenever you speak her fair. It's ill news, however,
that you have been ill, though if I brightened an hour of that I shall not have
laboured, as they say, in vain. I don't know that you make in Scotland as much
of Xmas as we make, – say, at Rye – perhaps because if you *did* make much
your machinery of mirth (by which I mean your war-dances & frolic pipings
generally) might bring down the vault of heaven. But I trust you are able to
face, by this time, bravely, whatever demonstrations the discretion of the
national character permits. Take, meanwhile, pray, the *Ambassadors* very easily
& gently: read five pages a day – be even as deliberate as that – but *don't break
the thread*. The thread is really stretched quite scientifically tight. Keep along
with it step by step – & then the full charm will come out. I *want* the charm,
you see, to come out for you – so convinced am I that it's there! Besides, I

is the reversal of the chapters in the September Methuen first edition: he takes 'much patched
over' as referring to HJ's putative correcting of the Methuen error in the Harper first edition.

find that the very most difficult thing in the art of the novelist is to give the impression & illusion of the real *lapse of time*, the *quantity* of time, represented by our poor few phrases & pages; & all the drawing-out the reader can contribute helps a little perhaps the production of that spell. I am delighted meanwhile to hear that you are to be in town a little later on. I go up next month – some time – to stay a goodish many weeks, & nothing will make me feel more justified of my adventure than the great pleasure of seeing you. Perhaps you will then even tell me more about the composition you have been busy with – there are literary confidences that I am capable of rejoicing in.[1] But I shall rejoice more to know that health & strength possess you & that they dedicate you to a secure & prosperous new Year. I invoke a friendly benediction on all your house, & am, my dear Duchess, yours very cordially & constantly

Henry James

208. To William Dean Howells
8 January 1904

Houghton TS   Published LFL, 397–9; partly published LHJ II, 8–10

Howells was acting as an intermediary for HJ with the Harpers, to whom he was literary adviser. On the basis of his return to the U.S., HJ was planning to write a novel on an American subject again – for the Harpers. (He began work on it in autumn 1907, but postponed it because of the burden of work for the 'New York Edition of the Novels and Tales of Henry James' – the monumental project negotiated during his visit.)

Lamb House, Rye, Sussex.
Jan. 8th, 1904.

My dear Howells.

I am infinitely beholden to you for two good letters, the second of which has come in to-day, following close on the heels of the first and greeting me most benevolently as I rise from the couch of solitary pain. Which means nothing worse than that I have been in bed with odious and inconvenient gout, and have but just tumbled out to deal, by this helpful machinery, with dreadful

---

1. In 1904 she published a book edited by herself, *Wayfarer's Love: Contributions from Living Poets*, and in 1905 a play, *The Conqueror*.

arrears of Christmas and New Year's correspondence. Not yet at my ease for writing, I thus inflict on you without apology this unwonted grace of legibility.

It warms my heart, verily, to hear from you in so encouraging and sustaining a sense – in fact makes me cast to the winds all timorous doubt of the energy of my intention. I know now more than ever how much I want to "go" – and also a good deal of why. Surely it will be a blessing to commune with you face to face, since it is such a comfort and a cheer to do so even across the wild winter sea. Will you kindly say to Harvey for me that I shall have much pleasure in talking with him here of the question of something serialisable in the North American, and will broach the matter of an "American" novel in *no* other way until I see him. It comes home to me much, in truth, that, after my immensely long absence, I am not quite in a position to answer in advance for the quantity and quality, the exact form and colour, of my "reaction" in presence of the native phenomena. I only feel tolerably confident that a reaction of some sort there will be. What affects me as indispensable – or rather what I am conscious of as a great personal desire – is some such energy of direct *action* as will enable me to cross the country and see California, and also have a look at the South. I am hungry for Material, whatever I may be moved to do with it; and, honestly, I think, there will not be an inch or an ounce of it unlikely to prove grist to my intellectual and "artistic" mill. You speak of one's possible "hates" and loves – that is aversions and tendernesses – in the dire confrontation; but I seem to feel, about myself, that I proceed but scantly, in these chill years, by those particular categories and rebounds; in short that, somehow, such fine primitive passions *lose* themselves for me in the act of contemplation, or at any rate in the act of reproduction. However, you are much more passionate than I, and I will wait upon *your* words, and try and learn from you a little to be shocked and charmed in the right places. What mainly appals me is the idea of going a good many months without a quiet corner to do my daily stint; so much so in fact that this is quite unthinkable, and that I shall only have courage to advance by nursing the dream of a sky-parlour of some sort, in some cranny or crevice of the continent, in which my mornings shall remain my own, my little trickle of prose eventuate, and my distracted reason thereby maintain its seat. If some gifted creature only wanted to exchange with me for six or eight months and "swap" its customary bower, over there, for dear little Lamb House here, a really delicious residence, the trick would be easily played. However, I see I must wait for all tricks. This is all, or almost all, to-day – all except to reassure you of the pleasure you give me by your remarks about the A's and cognate topics.[1] The "International" is very presumably indeed,

1. *The Ambassadors.*

and in fact quite inevitably, what I am *chronically* booked for, so that truly, even, I feel it rather a pity, in view of your so-benevolent colloquy with Harvey, that a longish thing I am just finishing should not be *disponible* for the N.A.R. niche; the niche that I like very much the best, for serialisation, of all possible niches.[2] But "The Golden Bowl" isn't, alas, so employable – being contracted for, with Methuen here and the Scribners in New York, as a volume only, and on no brilliant terms. Fortunately, however, I still cling to the belief that there are as good fish in the sea – that is in *my* sea – ! I am sorry you failed of the sight of Harland, if only that he might have pleased you (for he has greatly matured and solidified with Success!) more than his recent inspirations can have done. They truly are "rum" phenomena – scarcely less rum than the Success in question. And I speak of his gain of ripeness even in the face of a most unutterable Interview journalistically had with him in N.Y. and transmitted me by some importunate hand – in which I seem to have been sacrificed with the best good faith in the world on the most fantastic altar.[3]

But *non ragionam'* of these luridities; the fruit, so absolutely and so strangely, of conscientious devotion on dear H.'s part.[4] Such are the slings and arrows of the truest loyalty! You mention to me a domestic event – in Pilla's life – which interests me scarce the less for my having taken it for granted.[5] But I bless you all. Yours always

Henry James

2. Howells's novel *The Son of Royal Langbrith* began a run in the *North American Review* in January 1904, following *The Ambassadors*.
3. Michael Anesko has located this item, 'A Pinch from *The Cardinal's Snuff-Box*', in the *New York Herald* of 31 December 1903, in which Harland, now a successful novelist, told his interviewer, 'Be sure to put in a lot of James, and let me out of it, because, you know, when we talk of him we speak, as you are doubtless aware, of the very greatest mind that has ever been devoted to the writing of fiction in any language since the beginning of created literature.'
4. In the *Inferno*, canto III, Dante bursts into tears on a dark plain at the dismal sounds coming from the punished spirits of the blankly selfish. Virgil, his guide, tells him, 'Questo misero modo / tengon l'anime triste di coloro, / che visser senza infamia e senza lodo.' (ll. 34–6: 'This miserable mode of being is obtained by the dreary souls who lived without blame and without praise.') These cannot die, and envy all others. 'Fama di loro il mondo esser non lassa, / misericordia e giustizia gli sdegna: / non ragionam di lor, ma guarda e passa.' (ll. 49–51: 'Report of them the world does not permit to exist; Mercy and Justice disdains them: let us not speak of them; but look, and pass.')
5. The breaking of Mildred Howells's engagement.

209. To Alice Stopford Green
10 January 1904

Virginia TS   Unpublished

The historian Alice Stopford Green, a friend of Mrs Humphry Ward, had known HJ and followed his writings, as he read hers, since at least the early 1880s.

Lamb House, Rye, Sussex.
Jan. 10th, 1904.

Dear Mrs. Green,

Please don't take this grey result of dictation as the measure of the delight given me by your vivid letter about the poor dear Ambassadors. Take it rather simply for evidence of my having been most inconveniently laid up, for many days, with gout, at first in bed and now, this day or two, in a hampered and depressed condition of "sitting up" in my room. I find it, on experiment, no condition for pen and ink and for exemplary attitudes; so that I avail myself, without scruple or shame, and in a measure consolingly, of all the resources of civilization and of the grace of an unwonted legibility. The end (of my confinement) is unfortunately not yet, though I hope I am nearer to it; and I don't want to delay longer thanking you. For you give me exceeding pleasure, and I rejoice, without reserve, to have done in any degree for you that which is perhaps as good a thing as we poor mortals can do for each other – administered the anodyne of a tolerably intense alternative or vicarious experience, a beguiling interruption to the dire familiarities of self. To do that, to do it at all persuasively, convincingly, attachingly, or, as it were, charmingly – by the *operation* of some charm in the other, the suggested or imposed, vision, contact, company, or whatever one may call it – this I suppose is really the most decent "good" one can do, and there is much sustaining comfort in being helped to feel that one has somehow mastered the secret of it. This secret one then, naturally, swells with the hope of being able again to draw happy effects from. I think that the more one goes on the more one sees that the creation, the projection and evocation by hook or by crook, of some human and personal *good company*, for the mind and imagination of one's readers – beset as we all are, at the best, with much bad and indifferent – is as kind a turn as one can render, and really no more than a proper return for any generous intellectual confidence. I am moved, at any rate, by this confidence of yours to say to you boldly "Look out then in future for 'charming people' – neither more nor less!" It's a good deal to ask you to keep perpetually looking out; but I mean that, whenever you do at all, that's the sort of thing that I shall try to have ready for you. Meanwhile, I repeat, you greatly cheer me for keeping at it. And your so benevolent reference to the *parts*, several of them, of the A's comes straight home to me. I only think you wrong about one little matter – viz. the harm done by Maria's temporary flight. She went away to escape the putting of a straight question to her, about Mme. de V. and Chad – as to which she saw her way neither to tell the truth nor to falsify, both courses presenting difficulties (for her kind of interest, and imagination of possibilities, in Strether and his drama.) She felt that when she came back the need for her speaking would more or less have blown over – that he would have got on by himself. He *had* got on, but I don't know that by that he had necessarily got away from her. He was never sufficiently *with* her, in a manner, to call it getting "away" – and yet also in a manner never sufficiently away not to feel her there. But she is really (poor thing!) functional, convenient as it were, for the presentation and exhibition of the facts themselves, the "story" – she is more that than (for S. at least) something nearer and dearer: a luxury of his luck rather than a need of his soul. But these are fine shades to be discussing with one's foot in the air. Very soon after I have got the wretched member to the earth again I shall hobble up to town and stay for as many weeks as possible. I don't know when this may be – for I have other loose ends here to tuck in. But then, at all events, I shall come straight to see you. Believe me meanwhile yours always

Henry James

210. *To Violet Hunt*
16 January 1904

Virginia MS   Published HJL IV, 220–21

LAMB HOUSE, RYE, SUSSEX.
My dear Violet.

No, I am not yet in the field; but I come up to town on Feb. 1*st*, when I will immediately make you overtures for one of those so pleasant little talks in Sackville St. – which I like to "place," periodically. All thanks meanwhile for your so graceful remarks about the poor dear old "A.'s" by which I am touched, but which I was not writing when you were here.[1] The A.'s were finished 3, or more, years ago (before the *W. of the D.* were written,) & had

1. Violet Hunt had visited HJ at Lamb House for the weekend of 8 August 1903.

a long serialization in an American Review. (Hence the XII so marked "parts.")
You are right about Mme de Vionnet's visit to Mrs. P. – it gave her away &
was intended to have for the reader that indirectly revealing virtue. Maria G.
is, dissimulatedly, but a *ficelle*, with a purely functional value, to help me to
expose Strether's situation, constantly, in the dramatic & scenic way, without
elementary explanations & the horrid novelists' "Now you must know that –"[2]
She is not *of the subject*. Mme de V. *is*, of course, "of" the subject. But Strether
is the subject, the subject itself. But we will talk of these interesting things. As
for the already great bouncing *teething* New Year, je vous la souhaite bonne
& douce. Yours always

Henry James

Jan: 16: 1904

211. To Mrs Eveleen Tennant (Frederic William Henry) Myers
8 April 1904

Wren MS   Unpublished

*Eveleen Myers, the widow of the Cambridge poet and psychical researcher, and
herself a remarkable photographer, was the daughter of the somewhat bohemian
Mrs Gertrude (Collier) Tennant, who knew Flaubert and Daudet; in February 1900
WJ and AHJ had stayed in France with Myers and his wife, and found her difficult.
WJ had called her 'perfect "white trash," but with a certain foundation of animal
good humour that makes one not take her too severely'. HJ had explained her more
sympathetically by 'the queer Tennant milieu, &c' (CWJ III, 103, 101). She was
now thinking about an edition of her late husband's letters.*

REFORM CLUB, PALL MALL. S.W.

Dear Mrs. Myers.

It is most interesting to receive such an inquiry from you, as it is most
interesting to me to be in *any* sort of communication with you again. But, as
the case stands, I doubt if I have anything very substantial to send you. I never

2. HJ develops this account in the Preface to the novel: 'She is the reader's friend ... in
consequence of dispositions that make him so eminently require one; and she acts in that
capacity, and *really* in that capacity alone, with exemplary devotion, from beginning to end of
the book. She is an enrolled, a direct, aid to lucidity; she is in fine, to tear off her mask, the
most unmitigated and abandoned of *ficelles*.'

had *many* letters from your husband – I can almost remember, individually, now, the few occasions, & until I go home to the country (about a fortnight hence – I am spending, or *have* been, some weeks in town,) I can't be sure whether or no I am still possessed of these relics.[1] I will then immediately look, & assure myself; but I have a certain amount of doubt. When, some 2 or 3 years before his death, I broke up my London existence, I committed to the flames a good many documents, as one does on the occasion of the great changes & marked dates & new eras, closed chapters, of one's life.[2] I had nothing of Myers's that wasn't *brief*, & what I found *may* have gone the way of a great collection of other letters; up to which time I had kept everything, for years. But, as I say, you shall hear from me again. I should be delighted to think you *were* intending some *partage* with those of us all – the many of us too – who would *most* care. As for your own relics of him, they must absolutely not be lost to the world – *the* world; by wh: I mean the few hundred, of the future, who may be left to feel & discriminate, & keep the light of beauty & distinction from going utterly out. Yet I understand, too, that *time* must pass over such things, blow upon them with cooling, chilling, generalising lips – though I don't, either, think the Browning case to be lamented.[3] The interest of the people & the passion makes it right. Sometimes this happens – sometimes this fails – but when it does happen the rightness consecrates. I wish I saw you less drearily seldom. I have had great pleasure in two or three happy chances of seeing your so happy & so sympathetic children. Believe me your very faithful old friend

Henry James
Apr: 8: 1904.

1. In 1904 Eveleen Myers published *Fragments of Prose and Poetry* by her late husband; her Preface says she has collected 'many beautiful letters of my husband's both to myself and to friends'; 'some day they may possibly be printed, but they are of too personal a nature for present publication'. No edition of his letters ever was published.
2. On 2 January 1910, when Annie Fields inquired about the letters of Sarah Orne Jewett, who had died, HJ recalled that, 'I kept almost all letters for years – till my receptacles would no longer hold them; then I made a gigantic bonfire and have been easier in mind since – save as to a certain residuum which *had* to survive.' (HJL IV, 541.)
3. In 1899 the Brownings' son Robert Wiedemann Barrett Browning ('Pen') had controversially published *The Letters of Robert Browning and Elizabeth Barrett Browning, 1845–1846*, soon known as 'the Browning love letters'.

212. To James Brand Pinker
20 May 1904

Yale TS   Partly published LHJ II, 15–16

On 13 April HJ wrote to WJ that 'I have been pressing hard toward the finish of a long book, still unfinished (but not very much, thank heaven!) which I am doing with such perfection that every inch is done over & over: which makes it come expensive in the matter of time.' (CWJ III, 268.) HJ returned to Rye about 25 April, with The Golden Bowl *still unfinished.*

LAMB HOUSE, RYE, SUSSEX.
May 20*th*, 1904

Dear Mr Pinker.

I will indeed let you have the whole of my MS. on the very first possible day, now not far off; but I have still, absolutely, to finish, and to finish right, and Methuen's importunity does meanwhile, I confess, distress me. I have been working on the book with unremitting intensity the whole of every blessed morning since I began it, some thirteen months ago, and I am at present within but some twelve or fifteen thousand words of Finis. But I can work only in my own way – a deucedly good one, by the same token! – and am producing the best book, I seem to conceive, that I have ever done. I have really done it fast, for what it is, and for the way I do it – *the* way I seem condemned to which is to *overtreat* my subject by developments and amplifications that have, in large part, eventually to be greatly compressed, but to the prior operation of which the thing afterwards owes what is most durable in its quality. I have written, in perfection, *200,000* words of the G.B. – with the rarest perfection! – and you can imagine how much of that, which has taken time, has had to come out. It is not, assuredly, an economical way of work in the short run, but it is, for me, in the long; and at any rate one can proceed but in one's own manner. My manner however is, at present, to be making every day – it is now a question of a very moderate number of days – a straight step nearer my last page, comparatively close at hand. You shall have it, I repeat, with the very minimum further delay of which I am capable. I do not seem to know, by the way, *when* it is Methuen's desire that the volume shall appear – I mean after the postponements we have had. The best time for me, I think, especially in America, will be about next October, and I promise you the thing in distinct time for that. But you will say that I am "over-treating" this subject too! Believe me yours ever

Henry James[1]

213. To Joseph Pennell
23 June 1904

Congress MS   Unpublished

On 1 June W. D. Howells, who had been in England since March, was staying with HJ at Lamb House, and was mediating with the Harpers – Colonel George Harvey and Elizabeth Jordan, editor of Harper's Bazar *– for arrangements about lectures HJ might give in the U.S. to 'deserving Women's Clubs': 'He would lecture on Balzac, or on the Novel generally.' (SLWDH V, 102, 103.) HJ had engaged with Harvey not long before to write a book about America – which became* The American Scene.

HJ was to collect his English travel pieces for Heinemann as English Hours, *to be illustrated by Pennell.*

June 23d 1904.
LAMB HOUSE, RYE, SUSSEX.

My dear Pennell.

I knew you were off, for a deep immersion, with Hewlett; & I have been very patient about the "English book" – slim stuff as it is – that we discussed a few months ago.[1] I am glad you can now conveniently get at it – but oh, I

1. On 11 June HJ wrote to Pinker that he didn't need to postpone *The Golden Bowl* till the spring: '*It is so all but finished* that I can promise you the whole, I think, by the 1st July.' On 28 June he had 'but one more chapter of my interminable book to write' (Unpublished Yale MS, TS, Za James 1, vol. 1). On 29 June HJ responded enthusiastically to Pinker's news of possible American serialization (in the *Century*), offering to spend up to a fortnight cutting it for the purpose. The very next day, after hearing from Pinker, he sent eleven out of twelve parts, 'various heartbreaking excisions having been ruthlessly practised', and 'three priceless gems of chapters' in particular having been omitted (they were later restored). (Unpublished Yale TS, Za James 1, vol. 1.) HJ delivered the last part in mid July; but on 27 July was 'a little prostrate' to hear the possibility had come to nothing (Unpublished Yale MS, Za James 1, vol. 1).
1. Maurice Henry Hewlett (1861–1923), who had been the government's expert on medieval law (1896–1901), gave it up for full-time writing with the success of his historical novel *The Forest Lovers* (1898). The work by Hewlett illustrated by the curmudgeonly Pennell was *The Road in Tuscany* (1904).

must absolutely *revise* & tidy up the <u>text</u> – as I did that of the L.T. in France, before it goes to the Printers! I shall send you in a day or two 2 small additions I should like made to the same – a paper on this place & one on Suffolk.[2] I think you could find a picture or two for each.

Yes, I go to the U.S. (D.V.,) on Aug. 24*th*; & a month ago, Harvey being here, I arranged with him for a book of Impressions, for the Harpers, to be serialized in the North American Rev. That limits it (that is limits *that* book) to the non-pictorial; which my stuff must also largely, *in itself*, be. But I have a sort of foreboding of finding within me *more* (independent) stuff that *would* be pictorial. Of this, however, I can't be sure till I *see* the blessed, or accursed, place or places. I am afraid that is an indispensable preliminary condition. After 22 years of absence I am too much in the dark.[3] The book I arranged for – this I *had* to, in advance, to see my way to go at all – is a thing about social & human aspects &c. Yours very truly

Henry James

214. To Charles Scribner's Sons
17 September 1904

Princeton MS   Unpublished

In July HJ wrote a short story, 'Fordham Castle', for Harper's Magazine, *who published it in December. He seems not to have even attempted further work on* The Sense of the Past, *his promised second novel for Methuen.*

On 24 August HJ sailed from Southampton on the Kaiser Wilhelm II *for New York. Arriving on 30 August at Hoboken, he noted, as* The American Scene *would report, 'the unregulated traffic, as of innumerable desperate drays charging upon each other with tragic long-necked, sharp-ribbed horses'; and immediately obeyed the invitation of Colonel Harvey of Harpers for thirty-six hours at his New Jersey*

2. The two additional essays were the only ones not to have been previously collected: 'Old Suffolk' (*Harper's Weekly*, 25 September 1897) and 'Winchelsea, Rye and "Denis Duval"' (*Scribner's Magazine*, January 1901).

3. Pennell's reply made HJ write again on 27 June, to say that 'the possibility of three or four American papers of the pictorial order, *as things by themselves*, finds me, in spite of the fact mentioned in my last, very responsively disposed. It is by no means inconceivable to me that, once on the spot, I should quite yearn to do something of the kind – over and above, as it were, the other stuff. Because, if the spectacle over there says anything to me at all, it ought to say more than a mere meagre measureful – and probably will. It is difficult for me to be positive, none the less, before the facts – I must be *in presence* before I can be at all sure.' (Unpublished Congress TS.) HJ's absence from America, since August 1883, was in fact twenty-one years.

'cottage', where he found the lately widowed Mark Twain 'beguiles the session on the deep piazza' (CWJ III, 278). Then HJ went straight up via Boston to join WJ and his family at Chocorua in New Hampshire.

A journalist from the New York Herald came with a letter from Scribner's, and asked if his novel-endings didn't leave the question of 'moral purpose' open for his readers. HJ replied: 'Ah is not that the trick life plays? Life leaves you with a question – it asks you questions.' On 10 November 1904 the Scribner edition of The Golden Bowl came out in two volumes. Methuen's, on 10 February 1905, was set up from HJ's corrected Scribner proofs.

(95 Irving St., Cambridge *Mass.*)
Sept 17*th* 1904

Dear Sirs.

I return you corrected the galley proofs 1–6 of *The Golden Bowl* received here *yesterday* p.m; & I also return the corresponding copy, separately. (Will you kindly make a point of ordering that copy, which is superfluous for my correcting, be *not* sent me?) I shall not expect to see Revise. I greatly rejoice to learn from your letter of the 13*th*, which I have been waiting to answer till proof had come, that you are able to set up the whole of the book so promptly. I will match your promptitude by my alacrity in dealing with the proof, & will adjure my English publishers to do the same. I entirely agree with you as to the urgency of as early an issue as possible. I am at this writing still in New Hampshire, but I leave this place today for others more quickly accessible to the post, & I have put at the head of my letter the address to which I beg you now to direct.[1] Anything sent me before you get this will be sent immediately after me.

As to the enquiry you make about your reproducing the estimate of the *G.B.* (my own – in relation to my other things,) that I expressed to you, I feel that I must leave the matter to your discretion & tact – in which I have faith.[2] I may add, however, that my remark embodied the plain truth of my personal sense of the comparative value & quality (let alone quantity!) of the book. It is distinctly, in my view, the most *done* of my productions – the most composed & constructed & completed, and it proved, during long months, while it got itself, step by step, endowed with logical life, only too deep & abysmal an artistic trap. By which I don't mean an abyss without a bottom, but a shaft

1. 95 Irving Street is WJ's Cambridge address. HJ was still at Chocorua.
2. On 9 September 1904, also from Chocorua, HJ had written to Scribner's 'promising never again to write so long a novel – & this on many grounds. The best work of my life has, however, I think, gone into the G.B.' (Unpublished Princeton MS, Scribner's Archives 81: 2.)

sunk to the real basis of the subject – which was a real feat of engineering. Therefore I shamelessly repeat – &, yes, *you* may, why not? – I hold the thing the *solidest*, as yet, of all my fictions.

Many thanks, further, for your offer to send *me* the cheque – the amt. of the advance "down" – concerning which Mr. Pinker has written you.[3] I appreciate this, but there are reasons, as it happens, why this cheque *should* go to him, & I beg you therefore to be so good as to address it to him in London.

Permit me to add here a word as to the setting-up of the G.B. – accidentally omitted on my proof, which is now addressed & stamped. Please when the thing is paged have the title of the whole, "The G.B.," only on the left-hand top, keeping the opposite for (in Vol I) "Book First: The Prince", & (in Vol. II) "Book Second: The Princess." This is very important – that the reader should have the latter before him at each turn of the leaf.

Finally, kindly don't fail of *duplicates. I depend on them for Methuen & Co.* Believe me yours very truly

Henry James

Messrs. Ch. Scribner's Sons.

215. To James Brand Pinker
22 October 1904

Yale MS   Unpublished

During 17–31 October HJ was staying with Edith Wharton at what on his arrival he told Howard Sturgis, who was to join them, was a 'delicate French chateau mirrored in a Massachusetts pond (repeat not this formula)' (HJL IV, 325). (He told Jessie Allen on 22 October that in Lenox 'everyone is oppressively rich . . . "a million a year" (£200,000) seems to be the usual income' (HJL IV, 329).) On 21 October he wrote to Colonel Harvey of the Harpers declining a New York banquet in his honour on the ground of 'that constitutional infirmity, a rooted panic dread of banquets, toasts, speeches – any sort of personal publicity'. He assured Harvey that 'I shall be able not only to write the best book (of social and pictorial and, as it were, human observation) ever devoted to this country, but one of the best – or why "drag in" one of, why not say frankly the Best? – ever devoted to any country

3. Presumably not the advance for *The Golden Bowl*, since before leaving London on his way to the U.S., HJ had already acknowledged on 5 August 1904 in a letter to Pinker the receipt of £450 by his bank, representing the money for that novel from Scribner's and Methuen, minus Pinker's 10 per cent (Unpublished Yale MS, Za James 1, vol. 1).

at all ... I have been bethinking myself much of my necessary kind of form and tone and feeling, how it must *be absolutely personal to myself and proper to my situation. If Thomas Hardy hadn't long ago made that impossible I should simply give the whole series of papers the title of* The Return of the Native. *But as that's out of the question I have found myself thinking of, and liking even better –* The Return of the Novelist.' *(HJL IV, 326–8.)*

STATION: LEE. TELEGRAMS: LENOX.

October 22d 1904.

THE MOUNT, LENOX, MASS.

Dear Mr. Pinker.

I have had for some days your good letter of Sept 30*th*; which I speak of as "good" in especial by reason of its having set my mind at rest about your coming over.[1] I was uneasy, for my responsibility, so long as that was at all in the air. You decided wisely – very much so; & I feel that I myself, here, have work cut out for a good while to come. My state is most prosperous, & I feel the whole thing exceedingly interesting & suggestive, quite inspiring in fact, in respect (in the 1*st* place,) to doing my book of Impressions; that as far as seeing, observing, collecting material &c, goes – for all of which I am in possession, evidently, of the very best advantages. I have spent seven admirable weeks – of the most glorious, golden autumnal beauty – all here in New England & a dozen different places.[2] But the conditions – of life, space, time, opportunity, number & quantity &c, – are all so complex & formidable that I am still asking myself where & when & how the time to produce, *while here*, can come in – & asking still more in respect to the much greater complications & formidablenesses of the future. The mere lengths of all journeys & movements are a devourer of time, & the kindness, hospitalities, & other good offices of people, are an element of the overwhelming as well as an element of furtherance. I want to *see* all of all this I can, to miss no possible impression – that is the very basis; but I can't knock off pages of prose like a war-correspondent writing

1. Pinker was to come to America to negotiate on HJ's behalf in various quarters, especially for 'the matter of the collective edition'. HJ had written to him on 14 September that there was no urgency in his coming: 'my book of Impressions, opening out very wide before me, will *by itself* give me plenty to do' (HJL IV, 323).
2. On 16 September HJ visited Katherine Wormeley Prescott at Jackson, New Hampshire. He also went to Cotuit on Cape Cod where Howard Sturgis was staying with his half-sister, and to the Barack-Matiff Farm at Salisbury, Connecticut, home of HJ's Emmet cousins (Mrs George Hunter, Rosina, Leslie and Bay). He also spent a good deal of time in Cambridge and Boston, visiting, notably, Concord, Salem, the Boston Public Library and Isabella Stewart Gardner's Venetian palace.

on his knee or his hat, & I want to do a really artistic & valuable book. That part of my work must wait a good deal, I fear, upon the fulness of my observations. This I foresaw, in advance, as my difficulty – & I am in fact face to face with it. However, I shall worry out my problem somehow – that I am taking impressions on board by the bushel is the essential. Harvey is meanwhile all consideration in spite of my having absolutely (& on the best & most lucid grounds) declined to be entertained by him at a public banquet next month in N.Y. His advertising makes me wince & "squirm" – but I bow my head; only I must draw the line somewhere. I am rather puzzled meanwhile by your inquiry as to the *where*, of publication, of my articles – that is whether they go in the magazine or the *N.A. Review*. Am I mistaken in having thought it was definite that they (eight of them at least,) were to appear in the Review – the question being open only as to the whereabouts of serialization of the *Novel*?[3] I don't know that with identity of payment for both places, the question greatly matters for me – but I can't but think that the Review [is] a place in which they (the Papers) will make much more show. You imply indeed that there will be more pay if, through their being in the Review, you shall be able to make use of them in England. If the question *is* open I imagine the Harpers won't be able to decide till I have given them a first Paper – & I hope, in spite of all obstacles, to be able to give them a preliminary "New England" (I mean an article with that title.)[4] I have sent Methuen & Co. all the copy for the Golden Bowl – twice over; first in corrected galley-proofs, then in paged revises, also corrected. The Scribners will doubtless, in due course, be rather straining to appear – & Methuen ought not to delay more than is absolutely necessary. Seeing the whole American book set up will show them, I surmise, that it really *waits*. Scribners are making me *two* very pretty volumes, in the congruous page of which, for my stuff, I delight.

I am wondering if you have kindly arranged for the price of *Fordham Castle*, the "Harper" Xmas story – & paid the money to Brown Shipley & Co –?[5]

I wish I could think you have been having, or *are*, as magnificent an autumn as the last 2 months here – a revelation of weather. But I hope you are well. Yours ever

Henry James

3. Two of the parts of *The American Scene* did appear in *Harper's Magazine*, as well as eight in the *North American Review*. HJ's undertaking to do a new novel for Harper's was never realized, though they made a small book of the novella *Julia Bride* in 1908.
4. The three-part 'New England: An Autumn Impression' appeared in the *North American Review* (April–June 1905).
5. The price was $437.

216. To Colonel George Harvey
25 January 1905

Congress MS   Unpublished

HJ returned to Cambridge, Massachusetts, on 1 November, staying for a month (except for a four-day visit to Newport in mid November). Visiting the family grave-plot at dusk in late November, 'I seemed then to know why I had come . . . Everything was there, everything came; the recognition, stillness, the strangeness, the pity and the sanctity and the terror, the breath-taking passion and the divine relief of tears.' (N, 240.) On 4 December he went to New York to stay with Mary Cadwalader Jones for five days. He returned to Cambridge and Boston on 11 December; but ten days later went back to New York, staying again with Mrs Jones and with Edith Wharton (3– 9 January). On 9 January he was in Philadelphia, lecturing on 'The Lesson of Balzac'; then went down to Washington to stay with Henry Adams and attend dinners given on 10 January by John Hay, now Secretary of State, meeting President Roosevelt, and then two nights later by 'Theodore Rex' himself (HJL IV, 337). On 16 January he dined with the French Ambassador – his old friend Jusserand.

Going back up to lecture at Bryn Mawr College, the high-toned university for young ladies, he stayed in Philadelphia with Dr William White, and then with Sarah Butler Wister at Butler Place. To WJ he wrote of Philadelphia on 22 January, 'I am overdone with monotonous people – all the people so of the same kind & same kindness – alas, alas!' (CWJ III, 281.) Throughout his American visit HJ was repeatedly dealing with dentists; at Butler Place, he told WJ on 26 January, 'My poor right-hand upper front tooth has come out, & I look like a "fright," but I am cynical, indifferent, desperate – I don't mind it.' (CWJ III, 282.)

> Butler Place. Logan Station. Philadelphia.
> Jan: 25: 1905

Dear Colonel Harvey.

I have been inordinately long in sending you a first instalment of "American" copy, – but I beg you to believe that only good & valid, anxious & earnest reasons (connected mainly with the very *excess* of my interest in the general job) have had to do with this delay. If I were face to face with you I should be able to make this plea more vivid than in this poorer way. I am sending you herewith (in 2 envelopes, for greater ease,) a *first paper*, finished many weeks since, but kept back for many reasons; reasons, partly, of my finding that I was having, in a manner, *too much* to say & fearing to let these pages go till I had tried, by squeez-ing, to fuse portions of them with what was to follow. But what 1st followed, for me, was that I had, imperatively *had*, to write a literary Lecture, for lucre, & deliver it in 2 or 3 places (as I've done, & shall do in 2 or 3 more;) all of which took troubled *time* & worry – & left me (much circulation aiding,) with my unforwarded & undetermined quantity of MS. on my hands. The delay, however, has had the great advantage that I can now go straighter & (save for the drawback of too much concomitant *motion*) essentially faster – with a path cleared of the absurdly formidable lion of the Lecture-*making*. It has all made for my seeing & learning a great deal more than I could have felt myself possessed of sooner – & thereby having more impressions & visions, more confidence & competence. With *these* qualities I feel that I now magnificently bristle. But to return to what I am actually sending you. It's a *long* paper – as to which I can only hope that its intrinsic beauty shall strike you as carrying it off. I have so much of the "New England" material that I shall have to take at least one other (but shorter) paper to it; & indeed I think I shall not be able to do so with less than *three*. I let the present one stand as it is – though it covers but part of the "Autumn" ground; because, on earnestly & prayerfully hanging over it again, I find it all so knitted together & cared for & *done*, that there is nothing I shouldn't bleed to sacrifice; not even the first pages about my 1*st* hours in New York & at Deal Beach: which make a desirable beginning.[1] There are two more things. One is that I think the question of the *general* or Book *title* needn't come up at all now – but may wait *for* the Book, – as I see it hasn't come up for Howells's foreign sketches in Harper – & *is* so waiting. Secondly I shall greatly rejoice if you judge the North American Review to be the best place for my papers. As to this you will freely judge – but in that case (of the N.A.R.) I shall be able to have them placed, somehow, independently, in England.

I have been for a while in Washington & came up from there 5 days ago to pay a pair of promised & inevitable visits here; after which I go straight to the South, to see as much of that much-beckoning zone as I can. I expect to be here till Monday a.m. next, & then for some days at George Vanderbilt's Biltmore House, Biltmore, N.C. but 95 Irving St. Cambridge Mass, always reaches yours most truly

Henry James[2]

1. Deal Beach was where HJ had visited Harvey's New Jersey 'cottage' on his first arrival in the U.S.
2. George Washington Vanderbilt (1862–1914), the youngest son of the railroad tycoon, built in 1890 a $3,000,000 mansion in North Carolina. HJ suffered there both from an 'explosion of gout in my left foot', as he told his nephew Henry on 4 February, and from the 'huge freezing spaces' of the house; he spoke of his host's 'wondrous deludedness (though now, I think on poor George Vanderbilt's part, waked up from) as to what *can* be the application of a colossal French château to life in this irretrievable niggery wilderness' (HJL IV, 344).

217. To James Brand Pinker
6 March 1905

Yale MS   Unpublished

After Biltmore HJ went on to Charleston, South Carolina, then on down to Florida – Jacksonville, Palm Beach and St Augustine – having to relinquish the idea of Cuba in order to get back to Cambridge, Massachusetts, on 24 February. On 5 March he took a train west.

Washington Hotel *St. Louis.*
March 6*th* 1905.

Dear Mr. Pinker.

A word to say, only, that I have just returned to the *N.A.R.*, corrected, the proof of *Part Second* of "New England: an Autumn Impression" – of which I despatched you Part First a few days ago.[1] I expected to have received a duplicate, & thought I had made this clear; so as to have been able to send it you myself. But I have requested Mr. Munro, very strenuously & urgently, to post you off one immediately – which he will do.[2] Also, as I wrote you the other day, I have requested that payment for these 2 instalments be made to you. It ought to come to £160. Will you – thereafter – I think I already mentioned it – pay in the money to my acct. with Messrs. *Brown, Shipley & Co; 123 Pall Mall, S.W.* – letting me know you have done so?

I came on here, by a 40 hours journey (from Boston) last night – of which the enclosed document is a sign.[3] *Pray* for me – in these drearinesses – & believe me yours ever

Henry James

1. No English magazine published the three-part 'New England: An Autumn Impression', which HJ had now completed, the first section of *The American Scene.*
2. David Alexander Munro (d. 1910), who had been trained in Harper's publishing house, was editor of the *North American Review*, 1896–9, and then assistant till his death to Harvey, who was its editor from 1899 to 1926 and also edited *Harper's Weekly*, 1901–13.
3. A rough arrow probably points to an enclosed lecture ticket, which HJ has inscribed 'St. Louis', and which begins: 'THE Thirty-second Regular Meeting of the Contemporary Club will be held at the new WASHINGTON HOTEL, corner of Kingshighway and Washington Ave., Tuesday, March 7th, at 6:45 p.m. / ADDRESS BY ... / Mr. Henry James, / The Distinguished American Author. / SUBJECT: – "The Lesson of Balzac." ' HJ wrote to WJ the next day: 'I spouted my stuff last night "successfully" (the cheque slipped into my hand *coram publico* & almost before I had said my last word) – in the large room of this hotel, crowded to suffocation & with the exhaustion of a long preliminary dinner preceded in *its* turn by 150

P.S. Let this P.S. put it more frankly & crudely that I *have* done very well, for my material, my "literary" situation & reputation, by my presence here these few months. That is very clear indeed. In fact it is sadly clear that if I were but to come back & abide I should find things probably profitable enough to enable me to live in (comparative!) affluence: my being here makes such a difference. But I would rather *starve* at Lamb House than abide here. However, I – I dare sa[y] I shall even go *back* to better conditions. I *think* the G.B. is in its *4th* edition – but I'm not sure, & am afraid to ask too many questions. But what bewilders me is my little "lecture" boom (all before "Social" & "Ladies'" Clubs;) at all events a great financial convenience. They seem positively to *rejoice* to give me £*50* for 50 minutes (20/ a minute,) & Indianapolis gives me on the 16*th* next £*80* for the same (almost as if I were Patti:) I give the "Lesson of Balzac" at St. Louis on the 7*th*, & then – 10*th* – 15*th* – 4 times in all at Chicago (to different associations,) making £200 for the 4 hours.[4] If I had only known this in advance – that is more about it, & realized that I *can* lecture, very prettily, & could have taken more time to prepare a more popular subject &c – if I could have done all this I might be doing it to very "big business" indeed. Each of my Philadelphia audiences were of 6 & 7 hundred people (large, very, for "club" audiences) & if I would do it for $150 I could have far more engagements. But I can't go to the small places – it's impossible; & the no. of the £50 ones is of course limited. But I repeat in San Francisco in April, & perform in Brooklyn N.Y. on May 10*th*. It is my 2 Philadelphia evenings that have "boomed" all these other bookings. But what greedy talk! However, you will understand! I shall ask the Harpers to send *you* the money for the 2 N.A.R. papers already in their hands. Will you kindly pay it into the hands of Messrs. Brown, Shipley & Co, 123 Pall Mall, for me? And if you get something for the English rights will you pay *that* money into my account at *Lloyds Bank Rye*?

"presentations," well nigh undoing me. I got through, however, honourably, but more & more feeling that my lecture is too special & too literary – too critical – for these primitive promiscuities.' (CWJ III, 289.)

4. HJ doubtless compared £50 for a lecture to the £80 he received for the magazine publication of an instalment ('New York Revisited') of *The American Scene*. That piece records his being reminded of the famous soprano Adelina Patti by seeing again New York's Castle Garden, formerly a concert-hall: 'there outlives for me the image of the infant phenomenon Adelina Patti, whom (another large-eyed infant) I had been benevolently taken to hear: Adelina Patti, in a fan-like little frock and "pantalettes" and a hussar-like red jacket, mounted on an armchair, its back supporting her, wheeled to the front of the stage and warbling like a tiny thrush even in the nest'.

Don't judge of these *1st* 3 papers too much by themselves. They should be read together – & they are a mere getting into the subject.

H.J.

218. *To James Brand Pinker*
6 June 1905

Yale TS and MS   Unpublished

From St Louis, HJ went on to Winnetka, Illinois, and then Chicago, which gave him, as he told Edward Warren on 19 March, 'the sense of power, *huge and augmenting power (vast mechanical, industrial, social, financial) everywhere! This Chicago is huge,* infinite *(of potential size and form, and even of actual;) black, smoky, old-*looking, *very like some preternaturally* boomed *Manchester or Glasgow lying beside a colossal lake (Michigan) of hard pale green jade, and putting forth railway antennae of maddening complexity and gigantic length.' (LHJ II, 31–2.)*

After a pair of lectures in Indianapolis, arranged by Booth Tarkington (1869–1946), later author of The Magnificent Ambersons *(1918), HJ took the train on to Los Angeles, and went down to the Hotel del Coronado at San Diego 'to write, in extreme urgency, an article', as he told AHJ, the third part of 'New England: An Autumn Impression', which was about Cambridge. California 'has completely bowled me over', he said. '(I speak of course all of nature and climate, fruits and flowers; for there is absolutely nothing else, and the sense of the shining social and human inane is utter.)' (HJL IV, 356–7.) He lectured in San Francisco, called in Portland and Seattle, then regretfully took the train back East in time to lecture on 27 April in New York; on 29 April in Washington; and on 6 May at Smith College, Northampton, Massachusetts. He then spent about a month exploring New York, staying first with Mary Cadwalader Jones (making a trip to lecture at Harvard on 23 May).*

Pinker came over on the Caronia *to negotiate with the Scribners the basic arrangements for the New York Edition of HJ's novels and tales.*

36 West 10th Street.
Tuesday, June 6th, 1905.

Dear Mr. Pinker –

I received yesterday your letter of May 26th – just after I had gone to ask of the Scribners' if they knew anything about your probable whereabouts; and it completes comfortably, the good news of your cable, which I promptly answered.[1] I hope everything may be as "comfortably" completed (or be in course of being) for *you* too; as comfortably, that is, as the temperature that I fear you will find may permit of. (This rather horrid heat began but yesterday; however, it's no worse than I have known it in dear muggy old London.) I am rather in the dark as to the usual run of the Caronia – though it comes over me that she is the new Cunarder which hasn't had time to establish a tradition: at any rate I am leaving this note to-day at the Cambridge, as you instruct me, in the hope that your arrival will quickly follow it. There is a sad little state of things, however; arising from my perverse necessity to leave New York to-morrow, Wednesday, for some three days at least, I fear. I have been contracted these many weeks to deliver an address (well paid for, I desire you should know) at the Commemoration of Bryn Mawr College, which is off in the country near Philadelphia – and I am obliged to repeat the thing (for another fee) at Baltimore on Saturday.[2] All this, southward, means much fiery furnace; but if I survive it I *hope* to get back here Saturday night. I shall strain every nerve to do so, for I want to have Sunday to talk with you. If, unfortunately, it should prove more difficult to get free than I reckon I will be with you on Monday afternoon at latest, and shall have wired you from Baltimore or Philadelphia meanwhile.[3] I greatly hope that you won't find the two or three days wasted, and that if you have any definite view about anything, by which I mean about the Edition in particular, you may be able to break ground about it even before seeing me. Only remember, please, that my idea is a Handsome Book, distinctly, not less so than the definitive RLS, or the ditto GM; and also that I have made up my mind not to let it include absolutely *everything*.[4] It is best I think, that it should be selective as well as collective; I want to quietly disown a few things by not thus supremely adopting them. Likewise I cherish the idea of the *Scribners'*, preferentially; there is another firm we wot of, the idea of which I rather *don't* cherish.[5] But I shall see you, after all, before you have had time to turn round very fast. I hope your voyage has refreshed you, and that this whole job will. I am on the telephone here –

1. Neither Pinker's cable nor HJ's reply is known to survive.
2. HJ delivered 'The Question of Our Speech' at Bryn Mawr on Thursday, 8 June, and at Baltimore on Saturday, 10 June.
3. On Monday, 12 June, HJ wrote to Pinker from Philadelphia that 'I return to N.Y. as early in the afternoon as possible, tomorrow Tuesday'; hoping to see him at 5 p.m. (Unpublished Yale MS, Za James 1, vol. 1).
4. The collected edition of Robert Louis Stevenson was the posthumous Edinburgh Edition, edited by Sidney Colvin (twenty-eight volumes, 1894–8). That of George Meredith, not posthumous, was in fact Constable's reissue (1902–5) of 'The New Popular Edition' in eighteen volumes.
5. This other firm was probably Houghton, Mifflin; but might possibly have been the Harpers.

staying with my friend Lawrence Godkin, at the above address, and his "phone" number is 234 Gramercy. Yours ever,

Henry James

219. To Frederick Allen King
2 July 1905

Virginia TS   Published HJL IV, 359–60

In June, for his last weeks in the U.S., HJ visited Howells at Kittery Point, Maine, and Sarah Orne Jewett near by; and revisited Newport (with Hendrick Andersen, who was from there), and Edith Wharton at Lenox. She drove him to Ashfield, Massachusetts, where he saw Charles Eliot Norton for the last time.

HJ had written a new lecture for Bryn Mawr, 'The Question of Our Speech', his tour de force *on elocution as a mark of civilization (on 2 July he hoped to incorporate WJ's suggested examples: '"vurry," "Amurrca," "tullugram," Phulladulphia etc.' (CWJ III, 293)).*

Frederick Allen King (1865–1934), later literary editor of the Literary Digest, *1909–33, wrote to HJ asking the Master for details of his apprentice work. On 8 September 1904, HJ had already put off a bibliographer, Le Roy Phillips (b. 1870), whose* Bibliography of Henry James *appeared in 1906, saying: 'authors in general do not find themselves interested in a mercilessly complete resuscitation of their writings – there being always, inevitably, too many that they desire to forget and keep buried' (HJL IV, 320).*

95 Irving Street, Cambridge, Mass.
July 2, 1905.

My dear Sir:

I have been perpetually occupied and moving about since receiving your letter of June 23rd on the matter of the bibliography of my writings, which you tell me you are at the trouble of preparing; and I am now reduced to answering your questions very briefly and with this needful aid to expedition.[1]

I feel that I almost answer them, with completeness, in frankly telling you that I quite abhor bibliographies, so far as I myself, at least, may be the subject

---

1. A bibliography by King appeared in the first book-length study of *The Novels of Henry James* by Elisabeth Luther Cary in 1905. (HJ's 'aid to expedition' is the typewriter; the letter is dictated.)

of them, and that my principle (already more than once put into practise) is to find it impossible to give them any furtherance. I always think it over-much to ask of an author, for instance, that he shall help to divest his early aberrations, his so far as possible outlived and repudiated preliminary, of any blessed shelter of obscurity or anonymity that may luckily have continued to cover them. With this sentiment on my part, you may judge how little use your altogether flattering (I admit) but too misguided undertaking can make of my befogged memory.

Since you mercifully ask me if your unearthing early unsigned reviews (or at least the attribution of them) in The Atlantic, The North American, "meets my approval," I brace myself to answer frankly that it fills me only with the bitterness of woe. I would much rather myself, with my own hand, heap mountains of earth upon them and so bury them deeper still and beyond *any* sympathetic finding-out.

Of articles contributed to the "Balloon Post", Boston, 1871, I have, quite candidly, no recollection whatever, and think you must be here on some false scent.[2]

Almost the only thing I *can* tell you without anguish is that "Cousin et Cousine" in the R. des 2 M. Oct. 1, 1876, must have been simply a translation of a little tale called "Four Meetings", contributed to I forget what American periodical, and afterwards gathered into some volume of "short stories", but which particular volume I can't recall.[3] With the differences of distribution, title, etc., between the American and the English issues of these various collections, I am nowadays quite at sea.

Let me add that your great good-will in the matter almost brings to my eyes tears of compassionate remonstrance for misapplied effort. You inquire for instance where the English subjects in "Transatlantic Sketches" originally appeared in serial form? – whereat any ability I might possess to brood over that point for revival of remembrance quite loses itself in wonder as to why and how any such wretched little question can matter, at this hour, to any human being endowed with the responsibility of intelligence. *Help* no intelligence to feed itself on such twaddle (millions of miles removed from any real *critical* play of mind) and believe me

Yours very truly,
Henry James

2. HJ's closet-drama 'Still Waters' was published in the *Balloon Post* (12 April 1871), a publication in aid of French relief after the Siege of Paris.
3. 'Four Meetings' was not published till November 1877; 'Cousin et Cousine' was a translation by Lucien Biart of 'A Passionate Pilgrim'.

220. *To Robert Herrick*
7 August 1905

Chicago MS   Published HJL IV, 370–71

HJ sailed from Boston on 5 July and landed at Liverpool nine days later. By the middle of July he was back in Lamb House.

On 30 July HJ wrote to Scribner's, who were to publish the New York Edition, that the revision of Roderick Hudson *and* The American *demanded 'extreme (and very interesting) deliberation'; on 7 August he was thanking Pinker for having the pages of* Roderick Hudson *'so beautifully put into condition for revision for me' – that is, pasted on to larger sheets with broad margins (HJR, 330). He was writing* The American Scene *and revising his earlier works for the New York Edition at the same time.*

Robert Herrick (1868–1938), a novelist who taught in the English Department at the University of Chicago, had published The Common Lot, *about a Chicago architect's loss of integrity, in 1904, and having visited HJ at Rye on 17–18 July, was presently in France.*

LAMB HOUSE, RYE, SUSSEX.
August 7*th* 1905.

Dear Robert Herrick.

It has been charming to hear from you – but I am always miles & miles behind all proper forms of correspondence. When I have done a day's stint of work – that is of "literary composition" – with any intensity, any power to write further – in *any* manner – dreadfully abandons me; I am depleted and exanimate, and letters come off as they can – the larger proportion of them never coming off at all. But I must thank you for the gentle gift of *The Common Lot* too, which I want to read & *shall* read: it rests on my table only till I shall have got into the traces again, for dragging my cart along in its customary ruts.[1] I have been since my return from the U.S. much *de*railed – but things are running more smoothly. I rejoice heartily that your Breton conditions prove so charming to you, & envy you the romantic experience.[2] Why do you speak of "sparing" me the expression of your "unregenerate enthusiasm" for them? I shouldn't have supposed that at this time of day j'en étais encore at

1. I have come across no evidence of HJ having read the novel, nor Herrick's next, *The Memoirs of an American Citizen* (1905).
2. Herrick and his wife Harriet (his first cousin, five years his senior) spent the summer in France: June in Paris, then August and part of September at Beg-Meil on the Breton coast.

having to prove *my* haunting preoccupation with the things of France. You didn't even come – you told me – to my fanatical Balzac lecture! – All thanks at any rate, for your so serious & urgent remarks on the matter of my revisions, in respect to some of the old stuff I spoke of to you in connection with the plan of an édition définitive. I am greatly touched by your having felt & thought strongly enough on the matter to take the trouble to remonstrate at the idea of my retouching. The retouching with any insistence will *in fact* bear but on one book (the *American* – on *R. Hudson* & the *P. of a Lady* very much less;) but in essence I shouldn't have planned the Edition at all unless I had felt close revision – wherever seeming called for – to be an indispensable part of it. I do every justice to your contention, but don't think me perverse or purblind if I say that I hold myself really right & you really wrong. Its *raison d'être* (the edition's) is in its being selective as well as collective, & by the mere fact of leaving out certain things (I have tried to read over Washington Square, & I *can't*, and I fear it must go!) I exercise a control, a discrimination, I treat certain portions of my work as unhappy accidents. (Many portions of many – of all – men's work are.) From that it is but a step further – but it is 1 o'clk a.m., & I've written 7 letters, & I won't attempt to finish that sentence or expand my meaning. Forgive my blatant confidence in my own lucid literary sense! If I had planned not to retouch – that is revise closely – I would have reprinted *all* my stuff and that idea is horrific. You, also, will be ravished! Trust me – & I shall be justified. But good night, and pardon my untidy scrawl & my belated incoherence. Recall me kindly to your wife and believe me yours always

Henry James

221. *To Elinor Mead (Mrs William Dean) Howells*
14 August 1905

Houghton MS   Unpublished

LAMB HOUSE, RYE, SUSSEX.
August 14*th* 1905.

Dear, dear Mrs. Howells.

Infinitely touched & delighted am I at your sweet letter just received, which ministering angels prompted you to write. I like to think – I *revel* in the thing – of you 2 intelligent twain sitting there in the summer nights & sipping the

Golden Bowl in that delicate gustatory fashion. Well, I'll be brazen & say, that so it is, I think, it should be read. Never, also, I believe, was a Subject, a Situation, pumped so dry as that one – striking you as so pumped & left so thirsty for any remaining shade of mystery – by the time the last page is reached. It is *over-treated* – but that is my ruinous way & why I have never made my fortune. No matter – if I have made yours! We are thinking of you all, in your neighbourhood, immensely, in Europe, just now, as accessories to Portsmouth Drama, & I should be able to swagger, immensely, also, before a larger Gallery than this little place, were I disposed, by saying that I had *almost* seen the Wentworth Hotel, while with you, & the Navy Yard, & the rest of the Scene of Action.[1] But I keep all this romantic consciousness quite tenderly to myself, as part of my memory of those 2 wondrous days at Kittery Point & at Sara Jewett's place – so wondrous has everything become to me since my return here – in such iridescence does it all shine as seen from the re-entered, contracted tent of the Pilgrim at rest.[2] The Pilgrim is going to immortalize you in his own particular ruinous way however – overtreat & pump you dry till you will gasp for a drop of neglect. I find a beautiful summer here & the sense of the return to private life & the resumption of literary labour most sustaining. But all the things I didn't say to Howells, while I was with you, still whirl about the room like importunate bats – tormenting me overmuch. Tell him, please, that I just love his new London chapters & wish they wd. go on & on.[3] Also please that I love *him* & constantly hang about him, & am firm in the faith that we shall have you here again. There is distinctly room for you, always. And believe, again, that your letter was a joy, dear Mrs. Howells, to your affectionate old friend

Henry James

1. Theodore Roosevelt had interceded in the Russo-Japanese War (1904–5), with the result that a peace conference was held at the Portsmouth Navy Yard, situated in Kittery Point, Maine. The delegates were staying at the Wentworth Hotel. A treaty was concluded on 5 September, and Roosevelt received the Nobel Peace Prize.
2. Sarah Orne Jewett's place in Maine was at South Berwick; HJ and Howells had visited her in mid June from Kittery Point.
3. Howells's *London Films*, which he had finished by 25 June 1905, was being serialized intermittently in *Harper's Monthly* (December 1904; March 1905; June–August 1905). The book was published in 1906.

222. To Edith Wharton
8 November 1905

Yale MS   Published HJEWL, 52–6; HJL IV, 373–6

Scribner's progress with the 'New York Edition of the Novels and Tales of Henry James' was held up in September when Houghton, Mifflin, who retained the rights to many of HJ's books, made it a condition of release that their Riverside Press print the edition.

On 7 October The Question of Our Speech: The Lesson of Balzac: Two Lectures *was published in Boston by Houghton, Mifflin. On 9 October HJ sent 'New York: Social Notes' to the* North American Review. *On 18 October* English Hours *came out in London from Heinemann; and on 28 October from Houghton, Mifflin in Boston. On 7 November HJ sent 'Boston' to Munro of the* North American Review.

Edith Wharton's The House of Mirth, *the grim story of a proud but impoverished upper-class New Yorker, Lily Bart, whose decline is ambivalently observed by her wavering admirer Gilbert Selden, had been running in* Scribner's Magazine *from January till November 1905. Mrs Wharton's unstable husband Edward was increasingly subject to nervous collapses and bouts of eccentric behaviour.*

LAMB HOUSE, RYE, SUSSEX.
November 8*th 1905.*

Dear Mrs. Wharton.

You cannot say that I have bombarded you with letters, & I should be very sorry if I had put any such statement into your power. I have had, had perhaps to excess, a conscience about writing to you, having become aware, for myself, more & more, as I grow older, of the several things – interests – that life would be more fully, more needfully applicable to, if it were not for its letters. So many of them are not *fair*! And I have wanted immensely, where you are concerned, to *be* fair. So I have measured what I was doing – as well as what I wasn't – & have said again & again "No, no – not yet!" The limit I fixed myself was when the final number of the House of Mirth should have come out: "when I've read that," I said to myself, "I'll write." Half an hour ago, or less, I laid down the November *Scribner*, & now I have no scruple. Let me tell you at once that I very much admire that fiction, & especially the last three numbers of it; finding it carried off with a high, strong hand & an admirable touch, finding it altogether a superior thing. There are things to be said, but they are – some of them – of the essence of your New York donnée – &

moreover you will have said them, to a certainty, yourself. The book remains one that does you great honour – though it is better written than composed; it is indeed throughout *extremely* well written, & in places quite "consummately." I wish we could talk of it in a motor-car: I have been in motor-cars again, a little, since our wonderful return from Ashfield; but with no such talk as that. There are fifty things I should like to say – but, after so long an interval there are so many I want to, in general; & I think that my best way to touch on some of the former would be by coming back to the U.S. to deliver a lecture on "The question of the *roman de moeurs* in America – its deadly difficulty." But when I do that I shall work in a tribute to the great success & the large portrayal, of your Lily B. She is very big & true – & very difficult to have *kept* true – & big; & all your climax is very finely handled. Selden is too *absent* – but you know that better than I can make you. I hope you are having a boom. Have you read Les Deux Soeurs? – & have you read the amazing little Mme Tynaire's "Avant l'Amour"?[1] You are sure to have done both; so oh, for an hour of the motor again. The French, in the Tinayre light, are *impayables*; & so is our poor P.B., frankly, I think, in the *poncif* light – & even in the "Amour" light too – this Amour light of his latest manner. But as a surrender to the *poncif* in all the force of the term, the thing – his last book – is, I think, for a man of his original value, one of the strangest literary documents conceivable. Not that the poncif was not always in some degree – in a great degree – present in his fiction (though never in his criticism &c;) but the way it has now invaded his "morality," as well as his form, deprives me of any power to acknowledge his so inveterate, & so generous, gifts of his volumes. It affects me as a painful *End*. So I have no news whatever of that couple – they haven't come (as usual) to England this summer, & the tidings you brought home were my last.

I despatched Mrs. Jones & Beatrix back with as much Impression as their two brief little stations in London (during which I went up to attend them,) permitted me to stuff into them. Beatrix I thought less well than she ought to be – but every ill would fade from her if she would give up Doctors & Waters & really & sacrificially commit herself to the divine Fletcher (who, now that I have got back to my own good conditions, here, for worshipping him,) has renewed the sources of my life.[2] I have made a few short absences, but the

1. Paul Bourget's short novel *Les Deux Soeurs* (1905), and *Avant l'amour* (1897) by Marguerite Suzanne Marcelle Tinayre (1872–1948), who had briefly visited England a couple of years before and knew Mrs Humphry Ward. The novel concerns women's emancipation.
2. On New Year's Day 1904 WJ had sent HJ *The New Glutton or Epicure* (1903) by the nutritionist Horace Fletcher, which recommended thorough chewing of every bite. When HJ got it he excitedly read it through and, he told WJ on 23 February 1904, asking for more (*The*

pax britannica of this (to me,) so amiable & convenient retreat, awaited me, on my return from my American adventure, with such softly-encircling arms that I have, for the most part, sunk into it deep, & shall be here for two or three months to come. I go to spend a couple of days, in a week or two, with Mrs. Humphry Ward – & I haven't even yet read *Wm Ashe*, which she has handsomely sent me, as a preparation. But I have had practically to *tell* her that all power to read her has abandoned me – though I have put it as the power to read *any* fiction.[3] But she will extract from me when I see her that I *have* read Mrs. Wharton, & what I think of that – being very gentle about it, though, for she also greatly admires Mrs. Wharton. Of this, however, you will have personal evidence, as she appears to be really intending to go over & see you in the course of the winter. What a prodigious drama it will be – her tumbling herself bodily into the circus of her millions, & how little either the millions or she will make the other party out.[4] *Pourvu qu'elle en réchappe*! You must give me news of the commotion, into which I foresee you inevitably dragged & engulfed. But news of Walter Berry I greatly want too, who, after having greatly endeared himself to me, in the summer, par son naturel, ses dons & ses malheurs, vanished from my sight on his mad Italian errand – & has left me since a prey to wonder & fear.[5] I have – I *had* – heard of, & wept over, his "ill-luck", the guignon pursuing him – but I see it now to be in the consummate art with which he invokes that goddess. I tried to save him – hard; but he rushed (full of fractures,) on his fate – & I don't know at all what has become of him (in what *gargote* he sank by the wayside;[)] & I still lie awake at night thinking of it – that being the force of the impression he made on me.

I am very busy "in my poor way", trying to make my 10 months in America the subject of as many *Sensations d'Italie* as possible, & finding, strangely, that I have more impressions than I know what to do with or can account for – & this in spite of finding that, also, they tend exceedingly to melt & fade & pass

---

A.B.–Z. of Our Nutrition), was 'disposed to swallow *him* at least whole – without mastication' (CWJ III, 262).

3. On 8 August HJ had written to Mrs Ward confessing that he had not yet read her new novel *The Marriage of William Ashe* (1905), which had been serialized in *Harper's Magazine* from June 1904 to May 1905.

4. John Sutherland, in *Mrs Humphry Ward: Eminent Victorian, Pre-eminent Edwardian* (1990), has shown that in 1904 she was making five sixths of her literary income from American sales. Mrs Ward did not go to North America till March 1908.

5. Walter Van Rensselaer Berry (1859–1927), much-travelled American lawyer and diplomat, was a very close friend of Edith Wharton. He and HJ and Elizabeth Robins had sailed back to England on the s.s. *Ivernia* together.

away, flicker off like the shadows from firelight on the wall.[6] But I shall draw a long breath when I have worked them off – which it looks as if it would take me perhaps *two* (separate) volumes (*of* Impressions, pure & simple) to do: whence I fear that it may be very fantastic & irrelevant stuff I am producing – for I don't see, I repeat, where it all comes from. And the queerest part of the matter is that, though I *shall* rejoice when it is over, I meanwhile quite like doing it. *Entre temps* my thoughts wing their way back to Pagello & his precious freight (have you read the luridly interesting little vol. *George Sand & sa Fille*, by the way?) & hover about him as he so greatly adventures & so powerfully climbs, m'attachant à ses pas, to his flights & his swoops, & even more to his majestic roll in the deep valleys, with a wistfulness in which every one of those past hours lives again.[7] Most of all lives, I think, perversely, & even a little hauntingly, that leave-taking of ours at the Ashfield door last June – & poor dear Charles's unforgettable fixed smile of farewell (here below) to *me*, & poor Margaret's pathetic glare.[8] But I wouldn't for anything not have had that experience, so beautiful, of our whole going & coming, or not have rendered them that visitation, & I thank you again, even at this distance of time, for having made it so exquisitely possible to me.

I know about your shock & your pang in connection with poor Miss Crane's strange & terrible annihilation, but I can't speak of it, any more than I can of those unhappy overdarkened Dixeys (with my impression of the boy in the pride of his youth, (a great ornament & *panache* to them,) & of their existence there, as I saw it, all of such innocent *un*ironic comedy.[9] Heaven help us all!

The Pagello-sense has been with me a little, here, again, this autumn – notably during 4 or 5 splendid October days spent with Ned Abbey (& his wife – R.A.!) in Gloucestershire, who have a wondrous French machine & who, in the insolence of their net-gains, want to buy some fine old Jacobean

6. Bourget's travel book, *Sensations d'Italie*, seems to have been the work by Bourget HJ admired with least reservation. HJ's image recalls Book Seven of Plato's *Republic*.
7. Dr Pietro Pagello was the Venetian surgeon who attended Musset in 1834, then replacing him as lover of George Sand: it was the name HJ and Edith Wharton had for her automobiles. *George Sand et sa fille d'après leur correspondance* (1905) by Samuel Rocheblave (1854–1944) dealt with the complex relations between George Sand and her daughter Solange.
8. Norton was old and frail, but did not die till 21 October 1908. Margaret (b. 1870) was the youngest of his three daughters. HJ commented to WJ on 2 July, three days after the Ashfield visit: 'the impression of the poor girls there, in the dull unpeopled void, out of which the years have taken all interest for them, was saddening exceedingly' (CWJ III, 295).
9. I have been unable to identify Miss Crane. HJ had met 'that handsome clever young Arthur Dixey' at Lenox in the autumn of 1905 and was '*sickened*' by the news of his death (HJEWL, 57n.).

(or other) house & estate.[10] I roamed with them far over the land to look at three or four, & found it a most interesting & charming pursuit: in fact in a capacious luncheon-stocked car, the very summit of human diversion! This absurd old England is still, after long years, so marvellous to me, & the visitation of beautiful old buried houses (as to "buy" – seeing them *as* one then sees them,) such a refinement of bliss. Won't you come out with Pagello, & a luncheon-basket, & feign at least an intention of purchase – taking me with you to do the lying? I will show you all the Abbeys haven't yet bought. Submit this programme to Mr. Edward, please, with my very cordial regards. I hope his health & "form" are, in all his splendid applications of them, of the best.

But it's long past midnight, while I write – past 1 a.m., & I bid you at once good night & good morning. Don't be morbid, *you*, in the matter of our postal relation, please, & believe me yours, dear Mrs. Wharton, very constantly

Henry James

223. To Herbert George Wells
19 November 1905

Bodleian MS   Published HJHGW, 102–7; HJL IV, 377–80

In 1905 Wells published both A Modern Utopia, *one of his controversially speculative disquisitions on society, and* Kipps: The Story of a Simple Soul, *whose shy but resilient shopboy hero Artie inherits money and rises uncomfortably through the English class system.*

LAMB HOUSE, RYE, SUSSEX.
November 19*th* 1905.

My dear Wells

If I take up time & space with telling you why I have not *sooner* written to thank you for your magnificent bounty, I shall have, properly, to steal it from my letter, my letter itself; a much more important matter. And yet I *must* say, in 3 words, that my course has been inevitable & natural. I found your first munificence here on returning from upwards of 11 months in America, toward

10. Abbey became a full member of the Royal Academy in 1898. His wife Mary Gertrude Mead was also a painter and also a fellow of the Royal Academy. They bought Morgan Hall in Gloucestershire, and had a London home in Tite Street.

the end of July – returning to the mountain of Arrears produced by almost a year's absence & (superficially, thereby,) a year's idleness. I recognized, even from afar (I had already done so) that the Utopia was a book I should desire to read only in the right conditions of *coming* to it, coming with luxurious freedom of mind, rapt surrender of attention, adequate honours, for it of every sort. So, not bolting it like the morning paper & sundry, many, other vulgarly importunate things, & knowing moreover I had already shown you that though I was slow I was safe, & even certain, I "came to it" only a short time since, & surrendered myself to it absolutely. And it was while I was at the bottom of the crystal well that Kipps suddenly appeared, thrusting his honest & inimitable head over the edge & calling down to me, with his note of wondrous truth, that he had business with me above. I took my time, however, there below (though "below" be a most improper figure for your sublime & vertiginous heights,) & achieved a complete saturation; after which, reascending and making out things again, little by little, in the dingy air of the actual, I found Kipps, in his place, awaiting me – & from his so different but still so utterly coercive embrace I have just emerged. It was really well he was there, for I found (& it's even a little strange,) that I could read *you* only – *after you* – and don't at all see whom else I could have read. But now that this is so I don't see either, my dear Wells, how I can "write" you about these things – they make me want so infernally to talk with you, to see you at length. Let me tell you, however, simply, that they have left me prostrate with admiration, & that you are, for me, more than ever, the most interesting "literary man" of your generation – in fact the only interesting one. These things do you, to my sense, the highest honour, & I am lost in amazement at the diversity of your genius. As in everything you do (and especially in these 3 last Social Imaginations) it is the quality of your intellect that primarily (in the Utopia) obsesses me and reduces me – to that degree that even the colossal dimensions of your Cheek (pardon the term that I don't in the least invidiously apply,) fails to break the spell. Indeed your Cheek is positively the very sign & stamp of your genius, valuable to-day, as you possess it, beyond any other instrument or vehicle – so that when I say it doesn't break the charm, I probably mean that it largely constitutes it, or constitutes the force: which is the force of an irony that no one else among us begins to have – so that we are starving, in our enormities and fatuities, for a sacred satirist (the satirist *with* irony – as poor dear old Thackeray was the satirist without it,) & you come, admirably, to save us. There are too many things to say – which is so exactly why I can't write. Cheeky, cheeky, cheeky is *any* young man at Sandgate's offered Plan for the life of Man – but so far from thinking that a disqualification of your book, I think it is positively what makes the performance heroic. I hold, with you that it is only by our each contributing Utopias (the cheekier the better,) that anything will come, & I think there is nothing in the book truer & happier than your speaking of this struggle of the rare yearning individual toward that suggestion as one of the certain assistances of the future. Meantime you set a magnificent example – & of *caring*, of feeling, of seeing, above all, & of suffering from, & with, the shockingly sick actuality of things. Your epilogue tag in italics, strikes me as of the highest, of an irresistible & touching beauty. Bravo, bravo, my dear Wells![1]

And now, coming to Kipps, what am I to say about Kipps but that I am ready, that I am compelled, utterly to *drivel* about him? He is not so much a masterpiece as a mere born gem – you having, I know not how, taken a header straight down into mysterious depths of observation & knowledge, I know not which & where, & come up again with this rounded pearl of the diver. But of course you know yourself how immitigably the thing is done – it is of such a brilliancy of *true* truth. I really think that you have done, at this time of day, two particular things for the 1st time of their doing among us. 1/ You have written the first closely & intimately, the 1st intelligently & consistently ironic or satiric novel. In everything else there has always been the sentimental or conventional interference, the interference of which Thackeray is full. 2/ You have for the very 1st time treated the English "lower middle" class &c, without the picturesque, the grotesque, the fantastic & romantic interference, of which Dickens, e.g., is so misleadingly, of which even George Eliot is so deviatingly full. You have handled its vulgarity in so scientific & historic a spirit, & seen the whole thing all in its *own* strong light. And then the book has, throughout, such extraordinary life; everyone in it, without exception, & every piece & part of it, is so vivid & sharp & *done*. Kipps himself is a diamond of the 1st water, from start to finish, exquisite & radiant; Coote is consummate, Chitterlow magnificent (the whole 1st evening with Chitterlow perhaps the most brilliant thing in the book – unless that glory be reserved for the way the entire matter of the *shop* is done, including the admirable image of the boss.) It all, in fine, from cover to cover, does you the greatest honour, & if we had any other than skin-deep criticism (very stupid, too, at [th]at,) it would have immense recognition. I repeat that these things have made me want greatly to see you. Is it thinkable to you that you might come over at this ungenial season, for a night, – some time before Xmas? Could you, would you? I should immensely rejoice in it. I am here till Jan. 31*st* – when I go up to London for 3 months. I go away, probably, for 4 or 5 days, at Xmas – &

1. The book ends with a four-page passage in italics, addressing the reader about the fragmentary dialogic form of the work and the limits of the Utopian imagination.

I go away for next Saturday–Tuesday.[2] But apart from those dates I wd. await you with rapture.

And let me say just one word of attenuation of my (only apparent) meanness over the *Golden Bowl*. I was in America when that work appeared & it was published there in 2 vols & in very charming & readable form, each vol. but moderately thick & with a legible, handsome, large-typed page. But there came over to me a copy of the London issue, fat, vile, small-typed, horrific, prohibitive, that so broke my heart that I vowed I wouldn't, for very shame, disseminate it, & I haven't, with that feeling, had a copy in the house or sent one to a single friend. I wish I had an American one at your disposition – but I have been again & again depleted of all ownership in respect to it. You are very welcome to the British brick if you, at this late day, will have it. I greet Mrs. Wells & the Third Party very cordially & am yours, my dear Wells, more than ever

Henry James[3]

224. To William James
23 November 1905

Houghton MS   Published CWJ III, 303–6; HJL IV, 380–83; partly published LHJ II, 42–4

On 22 October, WJ had written bringing HJ up to date with his Harvard lecturing (he taught the beginnings of two philosophy courses), and of the unlikeliness of his lecturing at the Sorbonne; as well as with his children's doings: Henry's law office, William's studies at the Art School of the Boston Museum of Fine Arts, Alexander's schooling and Peggy's dress-making.

He also commented: 'I read your Golden Bowl a month or more ago, and it put me, as most of your recenter long stories have put me, in a very puzzled state of mind. I don't enjoy the kind of "problem," especially when as in this case it is treated as problematic (viz. the adulterous relations betw. Ch.[arlotte] & the P.[rince]), and the method of narration by interminable elaboration of suggestive reference (I don't know what to call it, but you know what I mean) goes agin the grain of all my own impulses in writing; and yet in spite of it all, there is a brilliancy and cleanness of effect, and in this book especially a high toned social atmosphere

---

2. Probably the visit to the Wards mentioned in the next letter.
3. The 'Third Party' was Wells's son George Philip Wells, by his second wife Amy Catherine (Robbins) Wells (d. 1927).

that are unique and extraordinary. Your methods & my ideals seem the reverse, the one of the other – and yet I have to admit your extreme success in this book. But why won't you, just to please Brother, sit down and write a new book, with no twilight or mustiness in the plot, with great vigor and decisiveness in the action, no fencing in the dialogue, no psychological commentaries, and absolute straightness in the style? Publish it in my name, I will acknowledge it, and give you half the proceeds.' (CWJ III, 301.)

LAMB HOUSE, RYE, SUSSEX.
November 23d 1905

Dearest William.

I wrote not many days since to Aleck, & not very, very many before to Peggy – but I can't tonight hideously further postpone acknowledging your so liberal letter of Oct 22d (the one in which you enclosed me Aleck's sweet one,) albeit I have been in the house all day without an outing, & very continuously writing, & it is now 11. p.m. & I am rather fagged: my claustration being the result 1st, of a day of incessant bad weather, & 2d of the fact that Grenville Emmet & his Indian bride spent yesterday & last night here, much breaking into my time, & 3d that I go tomorrow up to town, to proceed thence, under extreme & cogent pressure, to pay a 36 hours' visit, in the country, to the Humphry Wards.[1] She & Humphry go to America after the New Year, & I think she wants me greatly to indoctrinate & *avertir* her. She will in sooth be lionized limb from limb. But don't you & A. think it necessary to lift a finger. *I* am not in any degree "beholden" to them – I regard it quite as the other way round; & she, amiable & culture-crammed woman as she is, is strangely stupid. (*Burn* & repeat not this – such reverberations – of imbecillity – come back to me from the U.S.!) Grenville's Squaw is much better than I thought she wd. be – facially ugly, but vocally & intelligently good & civilized, & with a certain "air"; & he (in addition to being in his way a "dear",) is, for a lawyer, almost fabulously ingenuous. One gets such strange *bouffées*, from those young people, of the general blankness of the homes over which the

---

1. The letter to his nephew Alexander James (1890–1946) is not known to survive. The one to his niece, of 3 November, asks her to tell her Dad that 'all the time I haven't been doing the American Book, I have been revising with extreme minuteness three or four of my early works for the Edition Définitive. And 'still other tracts of my time, these last silent weeks, have gone, have *had* to go, toward preparing for a job that I think I mentioned to him while with you – my pledge, already a couple of years old to do a romantic-psychological-pictorial "social" *London*' (LHJ II, 36–7). Grenville Temple Emmet (1877–1937), son of Minny Temple's elder sister Kitty, was on his honeymoon with Pauline Anne Ferguson (b. 1879).

Kitty T. of our youth later presided. I am having a very good & peaceful autumn – (the best one I have ever had here, with *enormous* profit from Fletcher,) & shall prolong my present phase till February 1*st*, going then up to town till (probably) May. I am working off my American book very steadily (absit omen!) – or rather the stuff which is taking, irresistibly & inevitably, the form of 2 moderately-long books (separate, of course, not 2 vols., which wouldn't at all do, but a sort of First & Second Series, with an interval between, the 1*st* winding up with Philadelphia & Washington & the 2*d* beginning with 2 papers on the South & going on with all the rest of my so unaccountably-garnered matter.)[2] I have practically *done* the 1*st*, & serial publication of it begins in December.[3] I shall be mightily glad to have tapped it all off, for the effort of *holding rather factitiously on* to its (after all virtual) insubstantiality just only to convert it into some sort of paying literature is a very great tension & effort. It would all so melt away, of itself, were it not for this artificial clutch! But I am hoping to have made the whole thing, really, a short job (for the way it will have been done.) You tell me what is good of yourself & your more or less disposed-of College lectures, & of your probably not going to France next year ('faudra voir!') but you say nothing about California, & I am much puzzled by a mystery & ambiguity in all your Sequences – Peg's admission to Bryn Mawr, mixed up with her simu[l]taneous social début & your California absence &c.[4] When do you go there, anyhow, & when does she go to B.M., & does she go to California with you, & if she doesn't who takes her out, at home &

2. On 26 September HJ had written to Munro of the *North American Review* mentioning chapters intended for *The American Scene* which were never written, including 'The Middle West: an Impression', 'California and the Pacific Coast', 'The Universities and Colleges: an Impression', and 'Manners: an Impression' (presumably his articles for *Harper's Bazar* on 'The Manners of American Women' cover much of the material of this last). HJ would tell Morton Fullerton on 2 December that 'I shall have uncannily hived enough acrid honey to make, probably, a couple of books (of social notes, &c) – instead of the scant *one* I had very timidly planned' (Unpublished Princeton MS, General MSS, Misc.).

3. On 24 November HJ sent F. A. Duneka of *Harper's Magazine* 'The Bowery and Thereabouts' and 'Salem and Concord' (later 'Concord and Salem'), saying also that he had done 'The Sense of Newport' but was keeping it back. 'New York and the Hudson: A Spring Impression' appeared in the December 1905 *North American Review*, followed in 1906 by two parts of 'New York: Social Notes' (January–February); 'Boston' (March); 'Philadelphia' (April); 'Washington' (May–June); and 'Baltimore' (August). Other chapters appeared elsewhere: in *Harper's Magazine* 'New York Revisited' (February–March, May 1906) and 'The Sense of Newport' (August). 'Richmond, Virginia' appeared only in the British *Fortnightly Review*, which had previously carried three chapters simultaneously with the *North American Review*. Four chapters in the finished book were previously unpublished.

4. WJ was to have lectured at Stanford from January till May 1906, but the San Francisco earthquake on 18 April closed the university before he finished. Peggy went to Bryn Mawr in the autumn of 1906.

with whom does she abide? However, I shall write to Alice for information – all the more that I deeply owe that dear eternal Heroine a letter. I am not "satisfied about her," please tell her with my tender love, & should have testified to this otherwise than by my long cold silence if only I hadn't been, for stress of composition, putting myself on very limited contribution to the post. The worst of these bad manners are now over, & please tell Alice that my very next letter shall be to her.[5] Only *she* mustn't put pen to paper for me, nor so much as dream of it, before she hears from me. I take a deep, a rich & brooding comfort in the thought of how splendidly you are all "turning out," all the while – especially Harry & Bill & especially Peg, &, above all, Aleck – in addition to Alice & you. I turn you over (in my spiritual pocket,) collectively & individually, & make you chink & rattle & ring; getting from you the sense of a great, though too-much (for my use) tied-up fortune. I have great joy (tell him with my love,) of the news of Bill's so superior work, & yearn to have some sort of a squint at it. Tell him, at any rate, how I await him, for his holidays, out here – on this spot. And I wish I realized more richly Harry's present conditions. But I am probably *incapable* of doing it – & he must judge me so. I await him here not less.

I mean (in response to what you write me of your having read the *Golden B.*) to try to produce some uncanny form of thing, in fiction, that will gratify you, as Brother – but let me say, dear William, that I shall greatly be humiliated if you *do* like it, & thereby lump it, in your affection, with things, of the current age, that I have heard you express admiration for & that I would sooner descend to a dishonoured grave than have written. Still, I *will* write you your book, on that two-&-two-make-four system on which all the awful truck that surrounds us is produced, & *then* descend to my dishonoured grave – taking up the art of the slate pencil instead of, longer, the art of the brush (vide my lecture on Balzac.)[6] But it's, seriously, too late at night, & I am too tired, for me to express myself on this question – beyond saying that I'm always sorry when I hear of your reading anything of mine, & always hope you won't – you seem to me so constitutionally unable to "enjoy" it, & so condemned to look at it from a point of view remotely alien to mine in writing it, & to the

5. HJ wrote to AHJ on 15 December, saying he was to spend Christmas with Manton Marble (1834–1917), born in Worcester, Massachusetts, editor and owner of the New York *World* from 1862 to 1876, and now resident in Brighton. HJ had visited the Marbles from 9 to 12 October.
6. In 'The Lesson of Balzac', HJ praises Balzac's art of composition, contrasting it with 'the method now usual among us, the juxtaposition of items emulating the column of numbers of a schoolboy's sum in addition. It is the art of the brush, I know, as opposed to the art of the slate-pencil; but to the art of the brush the novel must return, I hold, to recover whatever may be still recoverable of its sacrificed honor.' (LC II, 136.)

conditions out of which, *as* mine, it has inevitably sprung – so that all the intentions that have been its main reason for being (with *me*,) appear never to have reached you at all – & you appear even to assume that the life, the elements, forming its subject-matter deviate from felicity in not having an impossible analogy with the life of Cambridge. I see nowhere about me done or dreamed of the things that alone for me constitute the *interest* of the doing of the novel – & yet it is in a sacrifice of them on their very own ground that the thing you suggest to me evidently consists. It shows how far apart & to what different ends we have had to work out, (very naturally & properly!) our respective intellectual lives. And yet I can read *you* with rapture – having 3 weeks ago spent 3 or 4 days with Manton Marble at Brighton & found in his hands ever so many of your recent papers & discourses, which having margins of mornings in my room, through both breakfasting & lunching there (by the habit of the house,) I found time to read several of – with the effect of asking you, earnestly, to address me some of those that I so often, in Irving St. saw you address to others who were not your brother. I had no *time* to read them there. Philosophically, in short, I am "with" you, almost completely, & you ought to take account of this & get me over altogether.

There are 2 books by the way (one fictive) that I permit you to *raffoler* about as much as you like, for I have been doing so myself – H. G. Wells's *Utopia* & his *Kipps*. The *Utopia* seems to me even more remarkable for other things than for his characteristic cheek, & *Kipps* is quite magnificent. Read them both if you haven't – certainly read Kipps.

There's also another subject I'm too full of not to mention the good thing I've done for myself – that is for Lamb House & my garden – by moving the greenhouse away from the high old wall near the house (into the back garden – setting it up better against the *street* wall) & thereby throwing the liberated space into the front garden to its immense apparent extension & beautification. The high recaptured wall is alone worth the job – though the latter has been proving far more abysmal & long-drawn than I intended. But hot-water pipes & a radiator fed from the new greenhouse stove, or boiler, pass straight into the garden room now & warm & dry it beautifully & restore it to winter use. But oh, fondly, goodnight! Ever yr

Henry.

225. *To Auguste Monod*
17 December 1905

Unknown MS or TS   Published HJLACBAM, 100—101

On 5 December HJ sent Munro and the North American Review *'Philadelphia',
and as he told Pinker had decided on* The American Scene *as a title; 'which won't
perhaps be catchpenny enough altogether to please the Harpers, but which, to my mind,
will represent the book better than anything else' (Unpublished Yale TS, Za James
1, vol. 2). He was planning to call his second volume* The Sense of the West. *He
would send Duneka 'The Sense of Newport' on 21 December (HJR, 332).*

*Auguste Monod (b. 1855) was the brother of Henry Adams's old friend Professor
Gabriel Monod (1844–1912), who was editor of the* Revue Historique. *When
Auguste, who later translated* Beauchamp's Career *by Meredith, wrote asking
HJ's permission to translate* Madame de Mauves *and* The Siege of London, *HJ
replied on 1 November suggesting different works, and avowing, discouragingly,
that he had 'never been eager to be translated, holding that one's form and style
are a part of one's value; that essence and thereby that value is terribly liable to
evaporate in the process. And I have had a very few disconcerting adventures in
French with all my poor* real *little notes replaced by the most shameless* clichés *and
failures to render.' (HJLACBAM, 97–8.)*

LAMB HOUSE, RYE, SUSSEX.
December 17*th*, 1905

Dear Mr Monod,

Pardon my accidental delay in thanking you for your letter of a few days
ago. I imagined in general that I wasn't particularly easy to translate, for the
possession in any degree of a form and colour of one's own opposes an obstacle
always to any but a very approximate rendering into another tongue and the
other tongue may even forbid its being approximate enough! But evidently I
am in the strange predicament of defying the genius of the French language
altogether, I who adore that genius, who have always found myself irresistibly
sacrificing to it, and who pass in this benighted country for an unbridled
Gallicist. The impossibility of my longer fictions I quite recognise – but I had
fancied that some of my shortest might be manipulated and that the fact of
their being so essentially by my intention, at least, studies in *composition*, (which
so few English things are) in condensation and in foreshortening, might already
recommend them. But I have evidently underestimated their unmanageability
(irreductibility) of surface, of which your yet so comparatively mild a specimen

(of the unparaphrasable) from *Paste* is a prompt example. Et moi qui m'imaginais que *Paste* se laissait lire à peu près comme une traduction libre (ou plutôt moins libre que l'original) de Maupassant . . . au point qu'il serait facile même de le remettre en français. Il est vrai que je ne l'avais pas moi-même soumis à cette épreuve. N'y perdez pas votre temps, cela n'en vaut pas la peine: ou ne persistez que si cela vous paraît mieux aller. Des nouvelles que j'ai marquées c'est je crois la moins considérable. [TRANSLATION: 'And there I was thinking that *Paste*[1] could be read pretty much as a free translation (or rather less free than the original) of Maupassant . . . to the point where it would even be easy to put it back into French. It is true that I myself had not put it to this test. Don't waste your time at it, it isn't worth it: or persist only if it seems to you to be going better. Of the novellas I marked it is I think the least valuable.'] But there are no holes to pick in the short specimen passage in your letter: that is all right and I am

Yours truly
Henry James[2]

226. To Mary Cadwalader Jones
25 March 1906

Houghton MS   Unpublished

In early 1906 HJ was concurrently finishing The American Scene *and revising and writing prefaces to his early novels. In February he moved up to town, to his flat at the Reform Club, returning to Lamb House late in April. The revised* Roderick Hudson *was sent off to Scribner's in mid March.*

H. G. Wells sailed for America on 27 March in order to write The Future in America *(1906). HJ also gave him a note of introduction to the New York poet Witter Bynner.*

THE ATHENAEUM, PALL MALL. S.W.
March 25*th 1906*

Dear Mrs. Cadwalader Jones.

I have written to you already on behalf of H. G. Wells — whose significant name I thus find myself no more garnishing than I should that of Charles

---

1. 'Paste' (1899) gives an English twist to the premise of Maupassant's famous story 'La Parure'.
2. Monod published translations of 'Perle Fausse' (*Revue bleue*, January 1908) and 'La Conquête de Londres' (*Mercure de France*, November–December 1912).

Dickens. He is more than half known to you already, moreover – by everything he has so potently done, & especially by *Kipps* – the admirable, the rare. But I don't know that I had told you before how much he is my friend & how almost my near country neighbour. He is capable of *seeing*, in New York, & I have said to you in my other note how I shall rejoice in anything you may find it possible kindly to help him to see.[1] You know your New York so beautifully & he will be to you so earnest & so grateful an *élève*, as Walt Whitman says.[2] Likewise he will carry you the benediction of yours most faithfully

Henry James

227. *To Charles Scribner's Sons*
12 May 1906

Princeton MS   Unpublished

At the end of April HJ met Edith Wharton and her husband at Dover and motored with them for three days in the West of England, leaving them at Malvern.

Roderick Hudson was to be the first volume of the intended twenty-three – in the event twenty-four – of the New York Edition.

May 12. *1906*.
Lamb House *Rye. Sussex*[1]
Messrs. Ch. Scribner's Sons.

Dear Sirs.

This is but a brief postscript to my letter of two or three days ago: to say what I am afraid I there omitted, but what I assume you are taking for granted – that I count on your kindly sending me Proof of *Roderick H.* & the rest – which I feel I must see for the full security of the text.[2] This will not be to *work over* the latter in any degree – I shall thoroughly & finally have established

1. On 18 June HJ wrote to Mrs Jones of Wells's gratitude for her kindness to him.

2. The word occurs in *Leaves of Grass* (1891–2): 'Eleves, I salute you! come forward! / Continue your annotations, continue your questionings.' ('Song of Myself', 38.)

1. Headed paper, with 'The Athenaeum, / Pall Mall. S.W.' crossed through. HJ was briefly in London.

2. On 9 May HJ had written to Scribner's concerning the compositors' difficulties with the MS revisions on the pages of *Roderick Hudson*, offering to have the whole retyped. The letter also discussed a specimen page for the New York Edition, the total number of volumes, the number of words per volume, and the deferral of inclusion of *The Bostonians* (HJL IV, 402–4).

it in Copy; but to ensure that absolutely supreme impeccability that such an Edition must have & that the Author's eye alone can finally contribute to. It makes for consistency & Harmony – as I needn't tell you! I beg the Compositors to *adhere irremoveably* to my punctuation & *never* to insert death-dealing commas.

> Yours most truly
> *Henry James*

228. To Arthur Christopher Benson
[31 May 1906]

Bodleian MS   Unpublished

Arthur Benson's study of Walter Pater in the 'English Men of Letters' series appeared in 1906.

LAMB HOUSE, RYE, SUSSEX.

My dear Arthur.

I am much moved to write to you; so, hang it, I let myself go! This beautiful crisis has risen from my perusal of your infinitely interesting & accomplished volume on Pater, under the charm of which, as I lay it down, I so feel myself – the charm of a wrought nearer proximity to you as well as to W.H.P. – that I can no more *not* write than I could turn my back on you in silence after a personal hour. It has been an admirable way of being *with* you – even though doubtless not the very best – & there is no moment of the experience that hasn't had its fine value for me. I am not writing you at length – there is too much to say (things we must talk about at some easier hour!) but the book is one on which I want affectionately to congratulate you. It affects me as with the great distinction of your having a critical passion for your admirable subject (since admirable, as a subject, Pater assuredly is,) & got & kept extraordinarily & exquisitely near to it. I think you have got more sentimentally than scientifically near (as I may say,) & there is some final formulation of his case (for he was a *case* if there ever was one!) that has somehow escaped you, & that leaves one's appetite for ultimate definition a little unsatisfied.[1] But this isn't what I wish to say at all insistently: *that* is, on the contrary, how the

1. On 7 September 1894 HJ had written to Arthur Symons declining to contribute to a memorial volume for Pater on the ground that the appropriate tone of eulogy would prevent 'absolute

whole performance does you honour & how happily & tenderly & eloquently you have rendered & expressed the most difficult & elusive parts of the subject – pressing it so intelligently hard, *le serrant de si près*, & playing all over it such fine penetrating restless finger-tips! You have highly served his memory & you have made a singularly saturated & initiated book – as literary as he deserved, full of all the references of the matter & the admirable opposite of *thin*! You have done in especial *this* delightful & interesting thing – that you have ministered to that strange, touching, edifying (to me quite thrilling) operation of the whirligig of time, through which Pater has already, in these few years, & little as he seemed marked out for it, become in our literature that very rare & sovereign thing a Figure: a figure in the sense in which there are so few! It is a matter altogether independent of the mere possession of genius, or achievement even of "success," I think – it's a matter almost of tragic or ironic (or even comic) felicity; but it comes here & there to the individual – unawares – & it leaves hundreds of the eminent alone. Well, I feel that it has come to dear, queer, deeply individual & homogeneous W.H.P., crowning his strong & painful identity – & that your study of him, in which many of your observations go so deep, will really quite have settled the thing. Therefore it is that I am patting you so tenderly & applausively, & so presumptuously on the back. I detest meanwhile seeing you so little. It was horrible to me to have to lapse from a scheme I had almost elaborated with dear G.T.L. of Trinity – of coming to Cambridge for 2 or 3 days of this past month.[2] But it was inevitable. Have patience, my dear Arthur, with yours always & ever

Henry James

P.S. I am "going through" you – quite impudently – vol. by vol; & even my impudence finds you thus singularly agreeable & attaching to live with.[3] But it, (the impudence,) is laying up such a store of belated questions to broach – ever so delicately – with you! Heaven send me & them relief!

---

freedom of literary portraiture': 'uttered in the real spirit of criticism, there might be a single line that wd. be a false note in a collection of the kind you mention – & yet that line might be the very one to which one wd. hold most' (PPLGB, 80–81).

2. The American historian Gaillard Thomas Lapsley, who was now teaching at Cambridge. HJ explained to Lapsley on 1 May that he had fallen behind with his work through the visit of the Whartons and '*fidgets*' about the safety of WJ and AHJ in the San Francisco earthquake (Unpublished Houghton MS, bMS Am 1094.4 (35)).

3. Benson kept a copious diary, extracts from which were published after his death. In 1897 he had shown it to HJ, and he appears to have done so again.

229. To James Brand Pinker
27 June 1906

Yale MS   Unpublished

On this day HJ also wrote to Elizabeth Jordan of Harper's Bazar, *organizer of his American lecture-tour, agreeing to write 'a little* explicit trio *on the subject of our Women's Speech – entitled "The Speech of Our Women," "A Talk on Tone" (I, II, III) or something of that sort . . . But there are other cognate questions – on manners, address, the Public Behaviour of our Girls &c, which ferment in my mind & at which I should like to have a go' (HJL IV, 411). The first 'trio' was written by 17 July.*

LAMB HOUSE, RYE, SUSSEX.
June 27th 1906

Dear Mr. Pinker.

All thanks for both your letters – the "holograph" of this morning & the typed one of yesterday (or rather the other way round.)

This is my idea about the "second" American Book – seeing it, that is, as a volume open to containing both the subordinate, or minor, remainder of my "Impressions" *and* such little papers as there is thus a question of my giving to Miss Jordan. I am now very much aware that after I have sent Munro *one* more "long" paper ("Florida") for the N.A.R. I shall have done all the possible or advisable that way – so that my first Book will very conveniently wind up with the inclusion of the "Florida."[1] The second must consist of *shorter* things – things of 5000 & 3000 words. I shall be very glad to give Miss Jordan as many in the 3000 words form as she may care for, & to make these consist of what one has to say about Speech, Manners, Forms & cognate matters – especially as illustrated by the women. I don't think I can make a *book all about* these phenomena (engage, that is, beforehand to make it,) but I can do so by letting half the contents consist of them, & the rest of my other *local* Impressions (after the fashion of those already done, only – as I say – shorter.) I can thus work off in the 2 vols *all* my American material. I shall be wholly content with (& proud of!) £50 apiece for the Bazaar papers; but don't ask even that if you in the least think it too much! Decidedly yes – the question of issuing *here* the American vol. containing the Bazaar articles (speech, manners &c) had much

---

1. It was not till 27 September that HJ told Pinker he had the 'Florida' ready to send Munro; neither it nor 'Charleston' was published in a magazine before appearing in *The American Scene*.

better remain, at any rate for the present, in abeyance. When I have sent Munro the "Florida" he will have 4 ("Baltimore," "Richmond," "Charleston," & the said "Florida") still to publish & conclude with.

I have returned one Vol. of corrected proof of R.H. to the Scribners – but they send a special statement that they desire the revised *Copy* also back with the proof. So I am embarrassed to give it to you. What I *can* do will be to give you with pleasure as a curiosity of literature (at least of *my* literature,) the revised Copy of the *American*, which is to be *all* typed for transmission to N.Y.; so that I shall preserve the original revised sheets & let you have them.[2] I'll tell you about the garden – poor old garden! – the next time I write, or rather when I see you, as I hope to about July 10*th*. (I must then be 3 days in town.)[3] The Spanish irises are doing however (as we here innocently suppose!) beautifully.

Also, I am happy to say, I have a very good & right (& beautifully done) photographic portrait, at last, which I will bring you when I come. The gifted youth comes down next week again to do the House.[4] Yours ever

Henry James

230. *To Frederick A. Duneka*
28 August 1906

Yale TS   Unpublished

Frederick A. Duneka (d. 1919), formerly editor of the New York World, *was from 1900 an editor at* Harper's Monthly *and involved in the firm's publishing of books.*

2. Pinker had the revised text of *The American* bound; in 1928 his son Eric Pinker gave it to Henry James III, HJ's nephew, for presentation to the Houghton Library. In 1976 a facsimile was published.
3. HJ told Edward Warren on 6 July that he was to do 'a dozen accumulated things in & beyond London', then hastening back to Lamb House because he had 'never been more pressed with urgent occupation' (Unpublished Huntington MS, HM 40303). On 11 July he visited Howard Sturgis at Queen's Acre, Windsor, and on 13 July saw Coburn in town to inspect the photographs of Lamb House taken on Coburn's visit.
4. The talented Boston-born Alvin Langdon Coburn (1882–1966) had photographed HJ for the *Century* magazine in New York in April 1905. He had taken portraits of many notable English literary and artistic figures, and early in 1906 had a one-man show, of landscapes and cityscapes as well as of portraits, at the Royal Photographic Society, with a catalogue introduced by George Bernard Shaw. Coburn noted in his autobiography that the portrait mentioned here 'evidently satisfied' HJ, 'for he subsequently suggested that I should make photographs to be used in all the other volumes of the forthcoming collected edition: and thus began our friendship' (*Alvin Langdon Coburn, Photographer* (1966; repr. 1978), 52).

On 4 August 1906 HJ wrote to Pinker that he would soon 'send Duneka the 5,000 words tale. I have an excellent little idea through not having slept a wink last night all for thinking of it, and must therefore at least get the advantage of striking while the iron is hot.' (Unpublished Yale TS, Za James 1, vol. 2.)

LAMB HOUSE, RYE, SUSSEX.
28th August, 1906.

Dear Mr. Duneka,

I am sending you with this a short story, "The Second House;" over which, in respect to brevity, I have had a big and desperate struggle – with the final effect of my being worsted. The thing is very much longer than you like, as I know; and yet, after taking earnest counsel with myself – to say nothing of desperate pains with *it* – I am still sending it, on the chance that, after all, you will feel it to have been worth your seeing – as a miraculous masterpiece in the line of the fantastic-gruesome, the supernatural-thrilling, or anything else of that sort it may best be called. I think the real reason I send it you, with all its length on its head, or rather at its tail, is that it is the best thing of this sort I've ever done; and that, as I wholly undertook it for your use, with my too fond and false estimate of the compass I could keep it down to – well, I just desperately pack it off. It is as short, by every sacrificed inch, as its magnificent subject permits![1]

But, as I have not been able to keep to the letter of my bond, I have at heart to send you another really Short one – though of course on a subject less magnificent – which I will despatch to you, in 6,000 words at most, within these next very, very few days: counting on your being meanwhile sufficiently beguiled with the present one to mercifully wait.

Yours very truly
Henry James.

1. This disturbing story, of an American expatriate returning to New York and being haunted by a ghost of his past, was about 13,000 words long and Duneka did not use it. Its title became 'The Jolly Corner' and it first appeared in Ford Madox Hueffer's *English Review* in December 1908.

231. To Frederick A. Duneka
14 September 1906

Yale TS   Unpublished

LAMB HOUSE, RYE, SUSSEX.
14th September, 1906.

Dear Mr. Duneka,

This is a word, following up my last, and in conformity with it, to say that I have struggled hard to be able to send you a fiction of the small dimensions you prefer, but that, alas, again, I have been worsted in the battle; and the story I post to you to-day is as long as its predecessor, the one I despatched to you with my last letter. It seems no use! – unless I can take more time. It takes me a great deal of time, and a very complicated process, to keep things down and down, that way – and this makes it come very expensive. But the real difficulty is that the subject so slight and small as to be *easily* short doesn't interest me or seem worth my doing; whereas the subject that does interest me, and does seem worth my doing, refuses to be treatable in so few words. Yet I am sending you, all the same, what I have done – as I sent you "The Second House," to which it is in no degree inferior – on the chance of your still being able to do something with it for the sake of its merit! So I make it over to you, and shall be glad to hear what, if anything, is possible.

Believe me yours very truly
Henry James.

F. A. Duneka Esq.

P.S. The thing in question is entitled: "Julia Bride" & ought to knock "Daisy Miller" into a cocked hat![1]

1. This P.S. is a hand-written addition by HJ. 'Julia Bride' was again about 13,000 words. On 4 September HJ had told Pinker that, 'It is the deuce to make these things short enough, if I take hold of a little idea that shall be at the same time interesting enough (for me to have anything to do with)!' (Unpublished Yale TS, Za James 1, vol. 2.) It was again rejected by Duneka – at first. However, Colonel Harvey, the head of Harper's, took an interest, and it appeared in *Harper's Magazine* in March–April 1908, then in the Scribner New York Edition (vol. XVII), then (only in the U.S.) in September 1909 as a small elegant Harper's book.

232. To Joseph Conrad
1 November 1906

Berg MS   Published HJL IV, 418–19; SL1, 188–9; SL2, 367–8; TLHJJC
[unnumbered]

In early October Coburn went to Paris to photograph frontispieces for The American,
The Princess Casamassima, The Reverberator, The Tragic Muse *and* The
Ambassadors.

   Conrad sent HJ The Mirror of the Sea: Memories and Impressions *in October
with an elaborate French inscription, concluding,* 'Votre oeil ami saura distinguer
dans ces pages cette piété du souvenir qui a guidé la phrase tâtonnante et une plume
toujours rebelle.' ('Your friendly eye will be able to distinguish in the pages that
piety of remembrance which has directed the groping sentences and an ever-rebellious
pen.') This is one of few surviving letters from HJ to Conrad.*

November 1st 1906.
LAMB HOUSE, RYE, SUSSEX.

My dear Conrad.

   I have taught you that I am lumbering & long, but I haven't, I think, yet
taught you that I am base, & it is not on the occasion of your beautiful sea-green
Volume of the other day that I shall consent to begin. I read you as I listen to
rare music – with deepest depths of surrender, & out of those depths I emerge
slowly & reluctantly again, to acknowledge that I return to life. To taste you
as I do taste you is *really* thus to wander far away & to decently thank you is
a postal transaction (quite another affair,) for which I have to come *back*, &
accept with a long sad sigh the community of our afflicted existence. My silence
is thus – after your beautiful *direct* speech to me too – but that I [have] been
away *with* you, intimately & delightfully – & my only objection to writing to
you in gratitude is that I'm not reading you, but quite the contrary, when I do
it. But I *have* you now, & the charm of this process of appropriation has been
to me, with your adorable book for its subject, of the very greatest. And I am
touched in the same degree by the grace of your inscription, all so beautifully
said & so generously felt. J'en suis tout confus, my dear Conrad, & can only
thank you & thank you again. But the book itself is a wonder to me really –
for its so bringing home the prodigy of your past experience; bringing it home
to me more personally & directly, I mean, the immense treasure & the
inexhaustible adventure. No one has *known* – for intellectual use – the things
you know, & you have, as the artist of the whole matter, an authority that no

one has approached. I find you, in it all, *writing* wonderfully, whatever you may say of your difficult medium & your *plume rebelle*. You knock about in the wide waters of expression like the raciest & boldest of privateers – you have made the whole place your own & vous y avez, en même temps que les droits les plus acquis, les plus rares bonheurs. Nothing you have done has more in it the root of the matter of *saying*. You stir me in fine to amazement & you touch me to tears, & I thank the powers who so mysteriously let you loose, with such sensibilities, into such an undiscovered country – *for* sensibility. That is all for tonight. I want to see you again. Is Winchelsea a closed book? Are the Ford Madoxes still away?[1] (What a world they must then have been let loose into!) I am looking for some sign of them, & with it perhaps some more contemporary news of you. I hope the smaller boy is catching up, & your wife reasserting herself, & your "conditions favourable."[2] Ah, one's conditions! But we must *make* them, & you have, on every showing, de quoi! I pat you, my dear Conrad, very affectionately & complacently on the back & am yours very constantly

Henry James

P.S. Mille amitiés at the fireside & the crib!

233. *To Herbert George Wells*
8 November 1906

Bodleian MS   Published HJHGW, 113–15; HJL IV, 420–22

Wells's The Future in America, *the book of his U.S. tour earlier in the year, appeared just as 'Richmond, Virginia', the last instalment of HJ's American book to be published in a magazine, came out in November's* Fortnightly Review.

LAMB HOUSE, RYE, SUSSEX.

My dear Wells.

I came back last night from 5 days in London to find your so generously-given "America," & I have done nothing today but thrill & squirm with it & vibrate to it almost feverishly & weep over it almost profusely (this last, I mean, for intensity of mere emotion & interest.) But the difficulty is that I am too dazzled

1. In May Hueffer had dedicated *The Heart of the Country* to HJ. Conrad told Pinker on 11 October that 'Ford's Back' (CLJC III, 365) – he and his wife Elsie had been to Germany and then the U.S. They were based in London after their return, with weekends in Winchelsea.
2. On 2 August Jessie Conrad had given birth to John Alexander, younger brother to Borys.

by your extraordinary, your (to me) fascinating, intellectual energy for all the *judgment* of you that I should like to be able to command. The mere sight & sense & sound of your prodigious *reactions* before the spectacle of all actualities, combined with your power of making all those actualities – by a turn of the hand – consist of amazing, fermenting, immeasurable passionate "questions" & social issues, comes near affecting me as the performance of a "strong man" or a conjurer, (juggler;) seems to show you playing with your subject & its parts as with the articles those *virtuosi* cause to rebound & fly about.[1] This amounts to saying that what primarily flies in my face in *these* things of yours is *you* & your so amazingly active & agile intellectual personality – I may even say your sublime & heroic cheek – which I can't resist for the time, can't *sufficiently* resist, to allow me to feel (as much as I want to,) that you tend always to simplify overmuch (that is as to large *particulars* – though in effect I don't think you do here as to the whole.) But what am I talking about, when just this ability & impulse to simplify – so vividly – is just what I all yearningly envy you? – I who was accursedly born to touch nothing save to complicate it. Take these fevered lines tonight then simply for a sign of my admiring, panting, more or less gasping impression & absorption of your book. When I think of the brevity of the process, of the direct & immediate experience, from which it springs, the intensity & superiority of the projection, of the realization, leave me, I confess, quite wonderstricken, & I ask myself if such a quantity of *important* observation – so *many* of such – have ever before sprung into life under so concentrated a squeeze. I think not, & your vividness & your force & your truth, & your caught & seized images, aspects, characteristics & conditions are infinitely remarkable, for all your precipitation. I seemed to see, for myself, while I was there, absolutely *no* profit in scanning or attempting to sound the future – the present being so hugely fluid & the direction (beyond mere space & quantity & motion so incalculable – as to the *whole*;) & yet here you come & throw yourself *all* on the future, & leave out almost altogether the America of my old knowledge; leave out all sorts of things, & I am gripped & captured & overwhelmingly beguiled. It comes of your admirable communicative passion for the idea, & from your wealth of ideas, and from your way of making intensely interesting each one that you touch. I think you, frankly, – or think the whole thing – too *loud*, as if the country shouted at you, hurrying past, every hint it had to give & you yelled back your comment on it; but also, frankly, I think the right & the only way to utter many of the things you are delivered of *is* to yell them – it's a yelling country, & the voice

1. The chapters of Wells's book are thematically arranged: 'The Economic Process', 'Corruption', 'The Immigrant', 'The Tragedy of Colour', 'Culture' and so on.

must pierce or dominate; & *my* semitones, in your splendid clashing of the cymbals (& *theirs*,) will never be heard. But there are still more things to say than I can so much as glance at, & I've only wanted to put to you, before I go to bed, that your book is, to my vision, extraordinarily full & rich & powerful & worthy, for all its fine fury of procedure – or perhaps just by reason of the same – of the vast uncomfortable subject. How glad you must be to have cast it from you! I don't know where this will find you – amid what blooming of citrons – but *may* it find you safely & assure you both that I am, as by communication, breathlessly yours

Henry James

NOV: 8: 1906

234. *To Mrs Alice Dew-Smith*
12 November 1906

Houghton TC   Published HJL IV, 422–3; LHJ II, 55–6

HJ's Rye neighbour Alice Dew-Smith was an eccentric author of works including the novel The Diary of a Dreamer *(1900). She later held Women's Suffrage meetings at her house which HJ would attend with his secretary Theodora Bosanquet. On 16 December HJ would tell their common friend Fanny Prothero that Mrs Dew-Smith had joined a rifle club '& lies for hours on her stomach in the Marsh (awaiting her prey)' (Unpublished Houghton MS, bMS Am 1094.3 (10)). Mrs Dew-Smith had written objecting to HJ's revision of* Roderick Hudson, *which was to be the first volume of the New York Edition.*

Lamb House, Rye.
November 12*th* 1906.

Dear Mrs. Dew-Smith!

Very kind your note about the apples and about poor R.H.! Burgess Noakes is to climb the hill in a day or two, basket on arm, and bring me back the rosy crop, which I am finding quite the staff of life.[1]

As for the tidied-up book I am greatly touched by your generous interest in the question of the tidying-up and yet really think your view of that process erratic, and – quite of course – my own view well inspired! But we are really

1. Burgess Noakes (1884–1975), a Rye local, was HJ's house-boy at Lamb House.

both right, for to attempt to retouch the *substance* of the thing would be as foolish as it would be (in a *done* and impenetrable structure) impracticable. What I have tried for is a mere revision of surface and expression, as the thing is positively in many places quite *vilely* written! The essence of the matter is wholly unaltered – save for seeming in places, I think, a little better brought out. At any rate the deed is already perpetrated – and I do continue to wish perversely and sorely that you had waited – to re-peruse – for this prettier and cleaner form. However, I ought only to be devoutly grateful – as in fact I am – for your power to re-peruse at all, and will come and thank you afresh as soon as you return to the fold; as to which I beg you to make an early signal to

Yours most truly
Henry James.

P.S. I am letting your tenants of course religiously alone.[2]

235. To Alvin Langdon Coburn
11 December 1906

Virginia MS   Unpublished

Coburn went to Venice in mid December ('Never before or since have I felt so miserably cold and damp,' he recalled in his memoirs), carrying elaborate instructions from HJ about photographs for 'The Aspern Papers' and The Wings of the Dove.

Dec. 11th 1906
LAMB HOUSE, RYE, SUSSEX.

My Dear A.L.!

I rejoice in your good news & yearn over your visible results. Hooray for your fine day, your nine exposures, & the effect of your 2/6 (a postal order for which I by the way enclose.)[1] Make your Mother dress you warmly for the journey to Venice – which I think (I am in fact sure) you will, with the

2. Mrs Dew-Smith's tenants at the Steps were the Henn Collinses. The following summer she let to the young Stephens: HJ reported to Fanny Prothero on 19 August 1907 that, 'The longest, leanest, dumbest of Virginias & Adrians now glower at me & at my conscious inadequacies from the Steps.' (Unpublished Houghton MS, bMS Am 1094.3 (17).)
1. On the preceding day, a Monday, Coburn had gone, by arrangement with HJ's friend the keeper Claude Phillips (1846–1924), to photograph an ornate chimneypiece with elaborate gilt clock and mirror in Room 21 of the Wallace Collection for the frontispiece to *The Spoils of Poynton*. On the Sunday HJ had told him: 'please give the attendant, as a tip, 2/6 for me: (I will send you a postal order for same in the morning . . .)' (HJL IV, 431).

elasticity of youth, really enjoy. Do make me a postal sign (5 words on a picture postcard only,) when you have got to work. It will be a thrill to see the developed series of Hampstead, Room 21, & these Venetian triumphs (which I pray all the powers to forward.) I enclose also the note for Miss Fletcher – go with it in the a.m. early – I mean by ten o'clock – not *before* – & take a look, outside, – *all round* – ! *well*, if possible, while waiting for her to see you.[2] (A good *gondolier* & his boat by the way – or even – & *better* at this season – a good one without his boat – will be a great general help & practical furtherance to you. Make him your "tipped" ally – for looking, finding &c.) And give me news as soon as you heave in sight again. Also keep an eye on corner – or at least *postal* – groceries, on the *chance*.[3] There is no knowing how the *picturing* of the vols. may not be made to work out with two or three extras (extra *choices*) to help. Ever yours

Henry James

236. To Charles Scribner's Sons
15 February 1907

Princeton MS   Unpublished

HJ was in London and then Brighton for Christmas with the Manton Marbles, returning to Rye on 2 January. The American Scene *came out in London on 30 January from Chapman & Hall, and in New York on 7 February from Harper's. About this time too HJ must have been writing his introduction to* The Tempest, *vol.* XVI *of the Renaissance Edition, published by subscription in March 1907.*

LAMB HOUSE, RYE, SUSSEX.

Dear Sirs.

The whole of the Second Half of the minutely-revised "American," (in complete type-copy) is forwarded you this week by Mr. Pinker, & I am to-day

2. Julia Constance Fletcher (1858–1938), American novelist and author of *Kismet* (1877), lived with her aged mother and the painter Eugene Benson, her mother's second husband, on the Rio Marin in the Palazzo Capello – a house with a garden, 'the old house I had more or less in mind for that of the Aspern Papers' (HJL IV, 426).

3. On 7 December HJ had told Coburn, 'There will be then another thing that I haven't mentioned, for "In the Cage": a London corner, if possible, with a grocer's shop containing a postal-telegraph office.' (HJL IV, 429.)

mailing you the Preface to accompany it. Please pardon my long delay – which must have been discouraging to you – over *The American*; it has all been the fruit of the intrinsic difficulty of happy & right & *intimate* revision – which defied considerations of time: the process has had to be so extremely deliberate. But it is, thank goodness, ended; the aspect of the book is essentially improved, its attraction augmented, &, above all, I am now "out of the wood." Everything else will henceforth, let me repeat, go fast & straight, & I shall quickly send you the Princess C., the Tragic Muse & the Awkward Age.[1] Mr. Coburn moreover goes to New York a week hence with photographs for *all* the illustrations save, I think, one or two at most – to be taken over there.)[2] Believe me yours very truly

Henry James

Messrs: Scribner's Sons New York City
Feb: 15*th* 1907.

237. To Elizabeth Jordan
5 March 1907

NYPL MS   Published HJBL, 47–9

In the spring of 1906 Howells had suggested to Elizabeth Jordan, editor of Harper's Bazar, *the troubled collaborative project that became* The Whole Family: A Novel by Twelve Authors *(1908). Each writer was to narrate a chapter from the point of view of one of the Talbert family of Eastridge, New England. HJ's ch. VII, told by the refined, perhaps pretentious Charles Edward, 'The Married Son', which he posted off on 25 January, is an indirect ironic review of the preceding chapters.*

LAMB HOUSE, RYE, SUSSEX.
March 5*th* 1907.

Dear Miss Jordan.

It has come over me that I made no reply to your interesting inquiry, on behalf of the House, as to the idea of a pretty little *Book* formed by the eight

1. HJ sent Scribner's the last pages of the revised *Princess Casamassima* from Rome on 22 May; of *The Tragic Muse* from Lamb House on 6 August; and of *The Awkward Age* on 9 September.
2. The New York photographs used in the New York Edition are the exterior of the Metropolitan Museum for 'Julia Bride', and Fifth Avenue house fronts for 'Lady Barberina'.

Manners & Speech articles in the "Bazaar" – made none, that is, five or six weeks ago, when you wrote, & when we were so busy discussing the Whole Family. But I have since had more freedom of mind to think of the matter, & shld. be very glad [to] have the small Book put forth – if you will say so to the House, for me – but with a modification that I desire to propose; or rather, as I should call it, an extension. The Book wd. be very small – & it would be one (composed *simply* of those extremely critical Speech & Manners papers) that I should *not* entertain the idea of publishing simultaneously in this country. On the other hand I have still a good many *other* American notes & impressions unused, & if you would care for a further series in the Bazaar of papers of the same length – say even six or eight – I should greatly like to undertake *that* little job. I am thinking of special episodes, pictures, vignettes – such e.g. as my little visit to Notre Dame Indiana, another to Smith College Northampton Mass., another to Indianapolis itself, another to the coeducative Berkeley Cal, another to that extraordinary place Point Loma, Southern California, the neo-Bhuddist (educational) paradise of the amazing lady who runs it, (Mrs. Tingley) & who "runs" Mrs. Eddy, in a manner, "so close"; together with other matters of a similar sort mainly Western – a wonderful school at St. Louis which gave me much to think &c.[1] I shld like to "do" these things – they would have a harmony & I think I could make the little vignettes & so forth of them – of 3,500 words – have a charm. The result would be a more graceful as well as a more substantial little book; & one I could then (the other things *with* the 8 you already have) consider the issue of here as well. When I think of the Pacific Coast, of San Francisco before the convulsion &c, of Coronado & Seattle & various other bits, I think I could certainly undertake *eight*. Should you care for them? If so I will set to work at them as soon as I come back from a short little trip to the continent for which I start tomorrow.[2] The Book would then be of *twice* the size of a volume consisting of the present papers alone, but wd. still be a small book, & I should like nothing better than that

1. HJ did not mention the 'wonderful school' when he wrote from St Louis to WJ on 8 March 1905: 'This vast gray, smoky, extraordinary *bourgeois* place seems to offer, in a ceaseless mild soft rain, no interest & no feature whatever.' (CWJ III, 289.) He lectured at Notre Dame, Indiana, on 14 March 1905, and at Indianapolis on 16 March. He visited Point Loma, Southern California, in late March or early April; in 1904 Katherine A. Tingley, successor to Madame Helena Petrovna Blavatsky in charge of the Theosophical Movement, had established there her Râja-Yoga College. Mrs Mary Morse Baker Glover Eddy (1821–1910) was the founder of the Church of Christ Scientist. HJ was then in San Francisco on 11–15 April, and paid a short visit to Berkeley across the Bay. He lectured on 6 May at the all-female Smith College, where he was memorably photographed by Elizabeth McClellan.

2. HJ set off for Paris on 7 March, staying first with the Whartons at 58 rue de Varenne, and seeing his old friend T. S. Perry, who was there for the winter.

it should be *pretty*. I would then, on your assent ask Mr. Pinker to write to the House about it.[3]

I sent you quickly back three or four days ago the corrected proofs of the *Married Son*. If you desire to omit the "Chataway part" (as you are perfectly free to do,) please make the chapter terminate then on the words (just *before* C.E. mentions his taking the night express for N.Y.) "strike for freedom." The person whom I have imagined presenting in *her* recital what C.E. did in N.Y. – did with Eliza & H.G. – is the Mother herself (his whole reference to his mother *prepares* for that;) & ah me how *I* shld like to "do" the Mother – verily! – (under a false, an extemporized name!!)[4] Yours abominably

Henry James

P.S. *The American Scene* has had such a "remarkable" & genial reception, apparently, in this country – beyond any that anything of mine has had here before – that it increases my desire not to put forth a volume that I wouldn't issue here. (And, as I say, I wouldn't the 8 Bazaar papers alone.)

H.J.

238. To Colonel George Harvey
6 September 1907

Congress MS   Unpublished

After a fortnight in Paris HJ and the wealthy Whartons left on about 20 March for a motor tour in their Panhard down to the Pyrenees (HJ called it to Jessie Allen 'an expensive fairy-tale' (HJL IV, 441)). On 11 May he travelled south to Turin

3. On 3 May HJ had received Elizabeth Jordan's answer, and replied from Paris. The *Bazar* would take three of the 'short American "impressionist" papers' HJ had proposed – if 'specificially addressed to Women'. He said he would send them 'only if they come out specifically right'. Nothing came of the idea; perhaps because at this period HJ and Pinker were increasingly indignant at the treatment of *The American Scene* by the Harpers (who left off the page headings HJ had provided and claimed – apparently in error – already to have paid for 'Charleston').

4. Once HJ's character Charles Edward has tracked the wildly romantic 'Old-Maid Aunt', Eliza, to the home of her dingy friends the Chataways in New York, he goes on to Central Park, where he finds his young sister's feeble fiancé Harry Goward. The cut mentioned, which was not made, would have left Charles Edward in Eastridge. 'The Mother' was ch. IX, and was written by Edith Wyatt (1873–1958), whose first effort had been rejected. HJ told Elizabeth Jordan on 2 October 1907 that the completed work gave him 'the feeling of a competent cook who sees good vittles messed' (HJBL, 53).

and then on to Rome, where his nephew Bill was working in Julian Story's studio and where he sat to Hendrick Andersen for a bust. He called with Howard Sturgis near Vallombrosa, and then spent just over a week with the Curtises in Venice before returning to Rye a week into July for what he later called the 'beastliest, wettest, windiest, cruellest summer known here for six centuries' (HJL IV, 461).

On 22 August HJ found a replacement for Mary Weld, who had got married in 1905 during his American absence, in another secretary-typist from Miss Pether-bridge's Secretarial Bureau – Theodora Bosanquet, a graduate of University College London and an admirer of HJ's work. Her diary: 'He wore green trousers & a blue waistcoat with a yellow sort of check on it & a black coat – that was rather a shock. I'd imagined him as always very correctly dressed – in London . . . His eyes, grey I think, are exactly what I should expect – but the rest of his face is too fat. He talks slowly but continuously . . .' (Houghton, bMS Eng 1213.1.)

HJ's resentment of his treatment by the Harpers was finally appeased by a letter from Harvey, not explaining what had happened but asking HJ, as HJ told Pinker on 8 September, to ' "fling the mantle of charity over it" ' (Unpublished Yale MS, Za James 1, vol. 2).

LAMB HOUSE, RYE, SUSSEX.
September 6th 1907.

Dear Colonel Harvey.

I am much obliged for your letter – & hope to have my Novel ready by the winter's end.[1] It has been much hindered for months past by my having had to devote precious time & labour to the revision of my old books & the writing of Prefaces for a Definitive Edition; but I am out of the woods as regards that & shall now get on. The book will moreover be shorter than "The Ambassadors" – 120,000 words as against 170 000 (or upwards.) But you shall have more news of it on the earliest day & I am yours very truly

Henry James

---

1. On 28 August HJ had told Owen Wister that, 'I am getting at a Wanton Tale (though no more Wanton than usual) with some of the keenness of frustration overcome. As it is to be a shorter Novel (& of Moeurs Américaines) than either of my three longest & latest, I have good hopes of no very distant port.' (Unpublished MS, Congress.) This seems to have been the American novel HJ signed for with Harvey and Harper's at the same time as *The American Scene*; probably what became *The Ivory Tower*.

239. To Mary Frances (Mrs Fanny) Prothero
18 October [1907]

Houghton MS   Unpublished

HJ went up to Scotland in mid September for some days at the Forfarshire grouse-moor hired by the husband of Mary Cadwalader Jones, returning via Swinford Old Manor, from where, as he told Fanny Prothero on 24 September, he was motored through 'the absolutely saccharine Kentish landscape' by his friends the Charles Lawrences (Unpublished Houghton MS, bMS Am 1094.3 (20)). On 18 October he had recently finished the Preface to The Tragic Muse *and was dictating that for* The Awkward Age *to the anxious Theodora Bosanquet ('The nervous tension of the situation when he is "agonising" for a word is appalling').*

Mary Frances Prothero (née Butcher, daughter of a bishop), was the lively wife of George Walter Prothero' (1848–1922), a Cambridge historian who edited the Quarterly Review. *They lived when in London at Bedford Square and when in Rye at Dial Cottage, where their loyal housekeeper was Mrs Bryan. They were friends of the Mrs Humphry Wards and the Gosses, and with Alice Dew-Smith were part of HJ's close Rye community, intimates to the point where HJ could relax into self-parody.*

LAMB HOUSE, RYE, SUSSEX.
Oct: 18*th p.m.*

Dear Mrs. George!

Just as black despair was seizing us – that is 10 minutes ago – the Devotee to the interests of the Idol (though we won't say who the Idol in this case *is*) arrived with an "I hope you don't mind me coming" & a nice little fat-faced boy. I said "Oh dear no, Mrs. Bryan: always so glad to talk with you about them" & then she broke it that she had just had a postcard & that they would be with us tomorrow. You could have knocked me down with a feather – the revulsion was so violent. For you see we had, the others of us, met of late in such at last almost deathly tension. It had been, it had *become*, more & more *this* kind of thing.

"Have you heard – ?["]

"Oh yes – one 'hears': that's the bitterness of it. She is clearly indisposed –"

"Indisposed? Don't tell me!"

"Indisposed, I mean" – this very gravely indeed – ["]to *come*."

"Oh, *that*? Don't call it indisposed. Call it firmly resolved, call it fundamentally determined."

"Well – since you go straight to the terrible truth of it – *there* we are. But she professes – !"

"Oh, she dresses it with ribbons & gardens: you know her enchanting way – !"

"Ah yes, her enchanting way *is* the bitterness of it. She *does* deck it out – !"

"As with streamers & a band of music! But all the while –"

"Yes – but don't too awfully *say* it – !"

"I *must* – for we must face the worst! *She has cooled.*"

"*Aïe!*" – as of a nerve in anguish. "Not *cooled*, put it – only just a little (in this weather) lowered her temperature."

"Oh, weather me no weather! She has frozen!"

"Let us then *melt* her!"

"We can't – all our tears won't. It's the icy smile."

"Yes, that smile! It muddles, but it means –"

"It 'means' – ?" (hanging on one's lips.)

"*That she will never come again.*"

"Aïïee!" – the shriek of ten thousand wincing nerves – a piercing wail, a heavy fall & silence; from my gloomy gaze on the prostrate presence of which imagine the revulsion, as I say, of Mrs. Bryan's breathless approach to yours in ecstasy

Henry James

240. To Elizabeth Robins
20 October 1907

Princeton MS   Unpublished

Elizabeth Robins was a novelist and playwright as well as an actress. Her play Votes for Women!, *about which she had consulted HJ, and its novel version* The Convert *both appeared in 1907. Late in 1907 she went back to the U.S. intending to write a book on the 'Colour Question', and HJ recommended her to WJ, who knew W. E. B. DuBois, Booker T. Washington and other black leaders, as an ardent Suffragist, 'but not in the obstreperous, police-prodding or umbrella-thumping way of many others' (CWJ III, 352). Her feminist address 'Woman's Secret' was first published as a pamphlet by the Pankhursts' Women's Social and Political Union, then collected in* Way Stations *(1913), where it served as a preface.*

October 20*th 1907*
LAMB HOUSE, RYE, SUSSEX.

My dear E.R.!

The brilliant little manifesto has arrived & I have read it with great attention, admiration & interest. It *compels* attention, so desirous is the reader, from the first, to see what you would be at, & your idea of the Secret is really, I think – or *was* – a great card to play.[1] Indeed this is so much the case that I even think *more* (in the same compass) might have been made of it, as an *image* (of the long history of the matter,) & with my infernal preoccupation as to the form & presentation of a case, always, just *such* a portentous image (of your general contention) strikes me as susceptible of still intenser, exploiting. It is almost as good – & very *like*, in value (forgive my levity) a really happy idea for a play. And this apart from the absolute truth – I mean the question of it – of your *position* about the secret & the silence; which I can't help thinking not wholly void of a fallacy. *Directly*, women *have* been, no doubt, through the ages, keeping their card up their sleeve, their "great" card, call it; but indirectly they were in the game, through an effect upon men; & through a limit to their separateness from them ("truckling" again quite apart,) to which I suggest you don't do justice. However, on the whole I am immensely *with* you, for you say it in places admirably, & I do believe that you have a card up your sleeve that *is* much of a mystery & also of a value. But all my "opinion" on your advent & its desirability is merged in the simple intimate conviction that it's absolutely going to take place, that it is part & parcel of the whole current drift of things, & that above all, when it becomes complete (as complete as it *can* become, for I believe too in inevitable limits,) the thing will be enormously *interesting*. Only all the novels will become *bad* thereby – all yours & mine, or at least all the novelists; & the new ones, poor things, will have to learn a new trade altogether. You *are*, already, *partly* a new one – & your particular "Secret" is doubtless that you're going to become more of one yet: for you probably will be there to see – & to *do*! I *shan't* – which simplifies. Miss me then a little, & remember that I wrote you tonight that your pamphlet

1. The secret in question is that of woman's *real* equality with man in thought and feeling. In the barbaric origins of human society, Robins argues, woman, till then equal, voluntarily accepted an unequal position for the sake of the advancement of civilization, out of 'the female's instinct to provide the best possible environment for her young'. For the man to maintain the role of defender and food-gatherer, as the same instinct required, he had to be flattered and protected from 'the long-suppressed truth': 'No douche of cold criticism or shaft of wit must be turned on him.' This arrangement has become outworn, though; women must learn to speak their minds frankly and without bitterness. 'Our brothers must therefore try to see through our imperfections of presentment something of that truth we have so long and religiously withheld.'

is the first sharp "ting" on a particular tense chord that will then be vibrating
– well, terrifically. I wish I saw you oftener & that our counties weren't of
such different sexes![2] Lucy Clifford has asked me to go up to her Play on the
29th (afternoon,) & I am taking my courage in both hands to go – but I fear
you will have escaped that coercion & that we shall miss that chance of
meeting.[3] But I shall invoke others, & am yours with hopes for you of a
100 000 sixpences for the cause, very constantly

Henry James

P.S. I go up on Friday to see Julia Marlowe – very privately![4] I am "*that*
theatrical –"! – & more so too!!!!

241. To Edmund Gosse
10 November 1907

Berg MS   Published SLHJEG, 230–31

*On 23 October, having been approached a second time by the 'very decent and
reasonable' actor-manager Johnston Forbes-Robertson (1853–1937), HJ began to
dictate a redramatized version of his 1898 story 'Covering End', originally intended
as a one-act play for Ellen Terry (HJL IV, 464). He sent off* The High Bid *on
12 November, now in three acts; it was produced at Edinburgh on 26 March 1908
with Forbes-Robertson and his wife the American actress Gertrude Elliott (1874–
1950). On 25 October 1907 HJ sent Scribner's the Preface to* The Awkward
Age.*

   On 30 October HJ received a copy of Gosse's masterpiece, his memoir* Father
and Son, *published anonymously five days earlier and detailing his painful spiritual
struggles with his extraordinary father, a biologist but also a member of the Plymouth
Brethren, an austere Protestant sect. Gosse wanted his book to be 'a call to people
to face the fact that the old faith is now impossible to sincere and intelligent minds,*

---

2. The envelope is addressed to Elizabeth Robins at 'Blyth / *Woldingham* / Surrey'.
3. As a novelist, Lucy Clifford's greatest popular success was *Aunt Anne* (1892). On 12 August
1907 HJ had written to her agreeing to read over her new comedy, *Hamilton's Second Marriage*,
and on 20 October had confirmed he would go up to town for its première at 2.30 on the 29th,
at the Court Theatre.
4. The actress Julia Marlowe (1866–1950) was born in Cumberland, but went to the U.S. in
1870, and from the age of twelve had a successful American career. She first appeared in London
in April 1907. In December 1907, back in the U.S., she appeared in a new play at the head of
her own company.

and that we must consequently face the difficulty of following entirely different ideals in moving towards the higher life'.

LAMB HOUSE, RYE, SUSSEX.
November 10*th* *1907*.

My dear Gosse.

I shall greatly rejoice to see you on Saturday next 16*th* by the 4. 28 from Charing Cross – as I have these last days been so leaving you to infer. I have been reading you meanwhile with deep entrancement – spell-bound from cover to cover. *F. & S.* is extraordinarily vivid & interesting, beautifully done, remarkably *much* done, & deserving to my sense to be called – which I hope you won't think a disparagement of your literary & historic, your critical achievement – the very best thing you have ever written. It has immense & unfailing *life*, an extraordinary sort & degree, quite, of vivacity & intensity, & it *holds* & entertains from beginning to end – its *parti-pris* of absolute & utter frankness & objectivity being, it strikes me, brilliantly maintained – carried through with rare audacity. You have thus been in a position to write a book that must remain a document of the 1*st* importance – *à consulter* – about the pietistic passion & the religious rage; unique, surely, as a detached & ironic yet a so perfectly *possessing* portrayal of these things – from so very near. No one who has seen them from so very near has ever had your critical sense or your pictorial hand, & thus been able to write about them in any manner to be *called* writing: which is what your manner almost inordinately *is*! Your wonderful detachment will, I daresay, in its filial light, incur some animadversion – but this is to my mind the very value & condition of the book; though indeed there are perhaps a couple of cases – places – in which I feel it go too far: not too far, I mean, for truth, but too far for filiality, or at least for tenderness. On the *whole*, however, let me add, I think the tenderness of the book is, given the detachment, remarkable – as an intellectual, reflective thing: I can conceive the subject treated with so much more uneffaced a bitterness. I can conceive it treated too, on a side, I may further add, with a different shade of curiosity, a different kind of analysis – approached, as it were, at another angle – but at one that is a bit difficult to express – so that I must wait till I see you; when I shall have various other things to say about it – as well as to pressingly ask. Suffice it for the present that you have had, immensely, the advantage of a living, intimate subject, & that cela vous a porté bonheur & caused you to produce a real work of art: which the theological world (even not the mere besotted) will moreover instinctively hate – to your great credit & advantage. Let me subjoin lastly that I think you have been of an excellent discretion, &

produced a real effect of vivid candour, about your infant Self. But you break off at a point too interesting – I could have (literally) done beautifully with as much again. That "lastly" just now isn't my last, either: this is, rather, that, as a fact, your picture will have *this* to reckon with – that it's whole evocation is somehow of visible *ugliness*: a very interesting & pathetic truth & value about the facts themselves, & quite a part of the importance of your record. But it colours your page, it becomes the note of your material – a study of the *consistently* ugly. (I speak of the suggested *visibilities* – the whole key of aspect & association.) The charming pages about the old Babbacombe seaside beauty (they are lovely) come as a blessing.[1] But I want awfully to *talk* of these things. Therefore fail me not. These last have been beautiful days here; I pray for something, a week hence, *like*. Good-night: *tanti saluti*!

Yours always
Henry James

242. *To James Brand Pinker*
31 December 1907

Yale MS   Unpublished

On 14 November HJ started dictating a rough statement for a three-act dramatization of his 1891 story 'The Chaperon', praised by Pinero in 1893 as apt for the theatre. During 22–4 November he had to go to Liverpool to accompany Lawrence Godkin to the burial of his stepmother in Hazelbeach, Northamptonshire. Back at Lamb House he abandoned 'The Chaperon' and on 1 December began dictating notes for a new play, a version of the 1892 story 'Owen Wingrave' called The Saloon, *first intended as a one-act opener for the Forbes-Robertsons; he finished it on 31 December. On 12 December he dispatched to Scribner's the Preface to* The Spoils of Poynton *volume.*

On 17 December Scribner's had sent both HJ and Pinker the first two volumes of the New York Edition, Roderick Hudson *and* The American.

LAMB HOUSE, RYE, SUSSEX.
New Year's Eve *1907*.

Dear Mr. Pinker.

I write you, on the stroke of midnight, the first letter of my 1908. I've a friend with me (who has gone to bed, leaving me to keep the vigil alone,) &

1. The Devon village where Gosse and his father lived is renamed 'Oddicombe' in the book.

his presence, all day, has with other complications baffled till this moment my constant inclination to answer, & thank you for, your delightful letter this morning received.[1] I rejoice that you are in as punctual possession as I am of the two beautiful volumes (for beautiful I hold them to be,) in which I quite agree with you that we may take pleasure & pride. They are in every way felicitous, they do every one concerned all honour, & the enterprise has now only to march majestically on. I have but to glance over the books to feel, I rejoice to say, how I have been a thousand times right to revise & retouch them exactly in the manner & in the degree in which I proposed to myself to do it. My effort has taken effect & borne excellent fruit – I have, I feel sure, surer than ever, *immensely* bettered & benefitted them. I am sorry the length of the Prefaces has demanded type a little too small, but I "guess" they make up for that defect in other ways. So it *is*, really, a brave beginning of our New Year!

When I see you next week I shall ask you when Constable & Co. are going to take action in the matter.[2] I hope that hasn't dropped! I expect to go up for 3 or 4 days *about* the 8*th* or 9*th*; & will communicate with you then. Perhaps you wd. let me lunch with you one of these days – but I will make you a further sign. I wish you & your House all peace & prosperity for this coming time & am yours most truly

Henry James

P.S. I don't think I've said with half due emphasis how much the 2 purple volumes make me value all that ingenious effort & patience & temper of yours, 3 years ago &c, without which they would be so far, at this hour, from reposing gloriously on our tables!

H.J.

243. To William Ernest Norris
30 January 1908

Yale MS   Unpublished

HJ finished The Saloon *on New Year's Eve and soon afterwards showed it to the playwright and producer Harley Granville-Barker (1877–1946). He then began*

1. The friend was G. T. Lapsley.
2. Scribner's had sent Pinker with the first two volumes a quotation for the prices of sheets of the New York Edition for English publishers. On 16 January Will Meredith of Constable rejected the price as outlandish; Pinker next tried John Murray, who declined in late February; but by June 1908 Scribner's themselves had an agreement with Macmillan. (See AACCI.)

dictating the Preface to What Maisie Knew, *which he sent Scribner's on 22 January, immediately going on to those for* The Wings of the Dove *(starting on 19 January and dispatching it to Scribner's on 30 January) and* The Ambassadors *(starting on 27 January). He was also revising the texts for the New York Edition.*

LAMB HOUSE, RYE, SUSSEX.
January 30*th* 1908

My dear Norris.

Had I obeyed the impulse of the hour I should have acknowledged your last interesting letter the day I received it; but I stayed my hand intentionally, I saw & felt you oppressed & submerged with letters – after having been already fairly worn out with them at the Xmastide; so that abstention seemed to me the better part of kindness. Only the consequence has been that *now* too many days have elapsed – a consequence made rather inevitable by the fact, highly injurious to all my correspondence (& to all my repute for decency in that matter just now,) that I sit here this winter more continuously busy, on the whole, I think, than ever in my life before. I am occupied with a very hard nut to crack in the way of a novel on one hand, & with the fact that I am bringing out a "handsome" (very handsome!) & intensely revised & selected Edition (collective & definitive, with large & most discreet omissions at the same time) of my novels & tales, & that the labours connected with the 23 volumes of this, & their intimate revision & proof-reading to say nothing of their enhancement each, or almost each – for some books are in 2 – with everlasting prefaces of 7000 words each: this perpetual business, I saw, added to the appeal of the current Muse somehow makes up a "drain on me" that leaves me rather voided & spent for other play of the pen. So my prospect is graced by a pyramid of letters unanswered these many, many weeks or even months that hangs over my scene of action very much as the pyramid of Caius Cestius dominates the Protestant Cemetery in Rome.[1] But the end of all this, I may say, is in sight; the issue of the monstrous series has begun in America – it is delayed by some temporary hitch apparently in London – & it *may* make a little money for me – the consummation sordidly aimed at. If it doesn't I shall be the most "sold" (or unsold) of men. But I brush away that horrible possibility – yet a perfectly thinkable one – & I tell you all these things my

1. HJ had visited Constance Fenimore Woolson's grave there the year before. In 1873 he had written: 'The past is tremendously embodied in the hoary pyramid of Caius Cestius, which rises hard by, half within the wall and half without, cutting solidly into the solid blue of the sky and casting its pagan shadow upon the grass of English graves – that of Keats among them – with an effect of poetic justice.' (CTW: C, 468.)

dear Norris partly because I want you [to] know why I'm rather jaded & faded (though otherwise "well," absit omen!) & proportionately inarticulate; & partly because I want to talk with you, simply – & I have talked *1st* of what is, all prosaically enough, at *my* end of the line. To wonder about you much, ever so faithfully & yet ever so inconclusively, has been meanwhile perfectly compatible with everything else – my most definite vision of you, however, being that of your having had to turn, round wearily & drearily enough, to face the *post* after the subsidence – if one can speak of subsidence – of that miserable black wave of a month ago.[2] For God's sake face *this* only at your utter ultimate ease & convenience – I feel I *almost* vividly know all your sad *essence* without your having to project the picture. The temporary fever & strain of all great mutations, which make a kind of uplifting or at least supporting excitement while they last, must have dropped – & when *in* the drop I see you & your brother-in-law face to face with each other, it wouldn't take much, I assure you, to make me cry out for pain. Which isn't at all a profitable remark to treat you to. But I'm afraid I can't pretend to make, about your great incurable & absolute sorrow & losses, profitable remarks. They are what they *are*, & we drink the cup to the dregs. What does come to me is that you are probably all-important & all-helpful to Sir Arthur Havelock & that *that* probably keeps you in a manner going. But what questions must loom before *him* now – & what grimnesses probably confront! – problems, evidently, of which you have all the benefit. I wish I weren't on the other side of the kingdom & *were*, for the time, as much your neighbour as occasionally of old – I should thrust my company on you every afternoon of the week. I go up to town for 10 days on Feb *3d* – for on top of everything else (you will scarcely credit your ears,) I have to attend the rehearsals of a Play – an *old* one written 13 years ago (mainly in Hesketh Crescent by the way) & never acted – only in a manner printed – but now dragged to the light (after old insistences *then* resisted but actually at last, & most sordidly, yielded to) by Forbes Robertson & his wife.[3] But I hold *those* things almost indecent to mention – & don't you mention them when you write to me, as some day or other you all patiently & stoically will. Good night now, my dear Norris. Yours very constantly

Henry James

2. Norris's sister Anne and her husband since 1871, Sir Arthur Elibank Havelock (1844–1908), ex-governor of several British colonies, had recently moved to Torquay, where Norris lived, only for her to die on 6 January 1908. Havelock only survived her till June.
3. Hesketh Crescent, Torquay, is where HJ stayed at the Osborne Hotel, near Norris's home, in 1895. He had posted the one-act play *Summersoft* (the basis of *The High Bid*) to Ellen Terry from there late in August that year.

244. To Dr Charles E. Wheeler
25 March 1908

UCL MS   Unpublished

In March—April 'Julia Bride' appeared in Harper's Magazine. *On 13 March HJ sent Scribner's the Preface to the* Aspern Papers *volume of the New York Edition.*

After joining Forbes-Robertson's company at Manchester on 21 March for rehearsals, HJ travelled with them to Edinburgh on 23 March for the première of The High Bid *at the Royal Lyceum Theatre on the 26th. Wheeler (1868–1949), a homoeopathic physician married to an actress, translated at least one German play and was with Harley Granville-Barker on the Council of Management of the Incorporated Stage Society, which put on subscription performances of deserving plays refused a licence by the censor, including some by Maeterlinck, Shaw and Barker himself.*

ROXBURGH HOTEL EDINBURGH

Dear Dr. Wheeler.

Your very interesting letter finds me in this place & a little breathless over rehearsals of a little Play (a 3-act comedy) that Forbes Robertson & his wife bring out tomorrow night here. The flurry & worry (as it to some extent is) of Preparation leaves me short of time & "steam" to say all I want – till after that ordeal is over; but I can even now assure you that your observations about what the little "Saloon" still needs are absolutely in the right direction, & that I feel the importance of further explicitness & clarification – in the highest degree. Thank heaven I also see, I think, my way to render the piece that benefit (& one or two others) & shall proceed to the work of doing so as soon as I get away from this place & am restored to nearer normal conditions. That will probably be on Saturday – when I shall have to spend 3 days in town on my way to the country. I should greatly like to *see* you on that occasion – whereby would it be possible to you to dine with me either on Monday or on Tuesday night – at the Reform Club Pall Mall at 8?[1] May I have a word *there*

1. HJ had dinner with Wheeler, and afterwards, on 2 April, had to reassure him that he had understood their talk as 'thoroughly a tribute to H.[arley] G.[ranville] B.[arker], to whom I am, I think, almost as kindly & engagingly & as confidently affected as yourself. One makes nothing & nobody one's *own* save by criticism – which is appreciation – which is criticism! I yearn to get at the Saloon again. I shall absolutely better it.' (Unpublished UCL MS.) On 22 April HJ wrote he would soon send Wheeler 'a fresh copy of "The Saloon" embodying my effort to clarify the *crux* of the Situation as much as I see my way to – as *yet*!' (Unpublished Virginia MS, 6251–a #517, Box 6.)

– as safest? Your appreciation of the Saloon greatly touches & delights me –
& I strongly feel that I can clarify & improve. But pray for me meanwhile
here – at 8.30 tomorrow. Yours most truly

Henry James

March 25*th* *1908.*

245. To Frederick Macmillan
5 April 1908

BL TS   Published CHJHM, 209–11

*Back from Edinburgh and London, on 3 April HJ wrote to his nephew Harry of
the 'Nightmare of the Edition': 'The printers and publishers tread on my heels, and
I feel their hot breath behind me.' (LHJ II, 96.) On that same day Macmillan
wrote to HJ reminding him of his long-standing contract to write* London Town,
mentioning that Pennell had 'produced an enormous mass of illustration'.

April 5th: 1908
LAMB HOUSE, RYE, SUSSEX.
Frederick Macmillan Esq., St. Martin's St., W.C.

My dear Macmillan

   Mr. A. H. Hyatt, of whom your letter of the 3rd: contains mention to me,
has himself written me about his appropriating the three or four pages out of
"The Princess Casamassima"; and I have answered him, but have had to do
so in the negative.[1] Mrs Laurence Binyon many months ago appealed for my
leave to include just the same morsel in a volume of specimen extracts of
English Style, English Prose, or whatever; and I, having applied to your house
for assent, wrote her she might do so – to which she proceeded with such
effect that the book has been now for some time out.[2] I don't therefore muddle
the matter by renewing the license for a quite different publication; and this I
have made Mr Hyatt duly understand – so there need be no further trouble
for you.

   As for the other and much greater question, the 'London' book, I don't

1. The anthologist Alfred H. Hyatt was preparing *The Charm of Venice* for Chatto & Windus.
2. Mrs Laurence Binyon (née Cicely Margaret Powell) married in 1904 the prolific poet and
critic Robert Laurence Binyon (1869–1943), an associate of Colvin's in the British Museum's
Department of Prints and Drawings. Her *Nineteenth Century Prose* appeared in 1907.

wonder at your enquiry; only do wonder, rather, that some thunderbolt of reprobation hasn't descended upon me long before this. I have expected it very often, and crouched and grovelled, burying my head in the sand, whenever I could fancy the faintest distant mutter. How can I tell you coherently, or inspire you with any patience to hear, what a long train of fatality and difficulty and practical deterrence, has attended my connection with that (none the less cherished and unrelinquished) promise. Things kept going damnably against my performance of it, going practically, I mean, and perversely and pertin-aciously, from very soon after my making it to you: this frustration and delay took the form of my having to keep as hard as possible at (more or less immediately productive) fiction, which I had near chances to serialise, and which with my lean ability to do but one good job at once, took all my weeks and months and – I blush red to write the word! – years, wretched years! Then came the immense distraction of my going for a year to America – which raised an immense barrier, that of a different, an opposite association and interest; and from which I returned saddled, inevitably, with too portentous complications: very good in themselves, but awful from the point of view of buckling down to a book about London and putting it through. One of these engagements was to begin immediately (immediately, that is, after I had written a great fat book of Impressions, the first of two vols. of such, the second of which will now, however, not appear) the publication of an elaborately revised and retouched and embellished and copiously prefaced and introduced Collec-tive, and *se*lective, Edition of my productions, in 24 Volumes – which I have been putting through, and which has proved a task of the most arduous sort, such as I can't but be glad of, but such as I at the same time wouldn't have had the courage to undertake had I measured all the job was to cost me. It is still going on, my own part of it, though I draw to a close. The beautiful vols. have begun successively to appear in New York – though arrangements for them here have been difficult, complicated and delayed.[3] I mention all this to account for my burdened and tied-up and apparently (in respect to "London") thankless and perfidious state. The worst is, however, that the Edition represents but half the burden I assumed in respect to New York: I came away pledged to supply two Novels for serialisation – and even the first of these (with which alone, perhaps, however, I shall be able to get off) has been most inconveniently and disgracefully delayed.[4] The Edition has smothered me, in other words,

3. In the event, through the intervention of Scribner's London agent Lemuel Bangs, HJ was to sign on 13 July an agreement with the Macmillans themselves for the British publication of the New York Edition.

4. Possibly *The Sense of the Past*, though I know no evidence that he was yet actively thinking of returning to work on it.

like an enormous featherbed – and I have scarce breathed outside of it: indeed either outside or in! This is my sorry tale, and I scarce expect you to be able to take it for anything but a virtual, though deeply unintentional and most rueful, trifling with your honourable hopes! The case remains that, all the while, I haven't, for myself, "gone back" on the idea of the book at all, but have kept it constantly in view, making a great deal of preparation for it, I have been able fortunately to read a great deal (I've even bought a good many books) and roamed and poked and pried about in town when I have had leisure moments on being "up".[5] I feel still strongly, that I should like to do it; I feel that having known the subject, having sounded and cared for it, on certain sides, so well and so long, I shall quite have lost one of the opportunities of my life if I don't do it. But there remain[s] the fact that I have absolutely to finish both my Edition and a longish Novel first; and that I am perfectly conscious of my little right to expect of you more waiting and postponing. If any other idea – by which I mean if any other image of "attractive" authorship – for getting the book done should hover before you, you certainly owe me no consideration; and I shouldn't look to you for any but definite notice! I hope still it won't come to that, and I feel that if I once clear away my Novel (the first to be done – I can manage for the time with that) the ground will be more disencumbered than it has been for a long time, and a good deal of additional reading which I want to put in will have been managed. Don't answer this on the spot, but let me come to see you the next time I'm in town, when there are various other things I shall be able to say to you that may mitigate a little the disgrace, and still keep alive a little the hope, of yours ever faithfully

Henry James

P.S. All thanks for your reference to the as yet but provincial, though apparently in spite of that definitely "successful", Play![6] It only needed a fresh plunge into the theatre – absolutely necessary at a time of long and laborious Editions with their fruit all in the future – to make my confusion worse confounded! It is a homely fact, however, that nothing can possibly conduce more to my having a real free and deliberate and leisurely hand for "London" than a definitely good and sustained success or two at the box-office! I haven't published a Novel, alas, since just before I went to America! The play Forbes

5. For instance, on 22–4 August and 8 October 1907, when HJ had made in a little red book notes of his wanderings and observations (see N, 273–80).

6. *The High Bid* was not, however, successful enough to justify a full London run, partly because judged by the critics to give Forbes-Robertson himself an insufficiently large role.

Robertson has produced was *written* a dozen years ago; the re-preparation and rehearsing of it, however, has been a dire trap to one's weeks!

246. To William Dean Howells
17 August 1908

Houghton TS   Published LFL, 425–9; partly published LHJ II, 98–104

Throughout 1908 HJ continued to revise his works for the New York Edition. About 25 April he went to Paris to stay a fortnight with Edith Wharton, where he sat for his portrait to the fashionable Jacques-Émile Blanche (1861–1942), returning to England to attend one of the Oxford Hibbert lectures being given by an increasingly fatigued WJ on 'The Present Situation in Philosophy' (they became A Pluralistic Universe *(1909)). WJ, AHJ, and their children Alexander and Peggy spent much of the summer with HJ, visiting Ethel Sands and Lady Ottoline Morrell at Newington, with a trip to Europe in mid August.*

Howells and his family spent the winter in Italy, writing the pieces later collected as Roman Holidays and Others *(1908), then came in June to London, where HJ saw them. On 2 August Howells sent a typed letter from Kittery, fearing 'something I had said about your prefaces . . . might not be so wholly pleasing as I meant it . . . We especially enjoyed you where you rounded upon yourself, and as it were took yourself to pieces, in your self-censure . . . I remember so well your telling me, on such a Sunday afternoon as this, when we were rowing on Fresh Pond, what R.H. [Roderick Hudson] was to be.' (LFL, 422–3.)*

LAMB HOUSE, RYE, SUSSEX.
17th: August 1908

My dear Howells.

A great pleasure to me is your good and generous letter just received – with its luxurious implied licence for me of seeking this aid to prompt response; at a time when a pressure of complications (this is the complicated time of the year even in my small green garden) defeats too much and too often the genial impulse. But so far as compunction started and guided your pen, I really rub my eyes for vision of where it may – save as most misguidedly – have come in. You were so far from having distilled any indigestible drop for me on that pleasant *ultimissimo* Sunday, that I parted from you with a taste, in my mouth, absolutely saccharine – sated with sweetness, or with sweet reasonableness, so to speak; and aching, or wincing, in no single fibre. Extravagant and licentious, almost, your delicacy of fear of the contrary; so much so, in fact, that I didn't remember we had even spoken of the heavy lucubrations in question, or that you had had any time or opportunity, since their "inception", to look at one. However your fond mistake is all to the good, since it has brought me your charming letter, and so appreciative remarks you therein make. My actual attitude about the Lucubrations is almost only, and quite inevitably, that they make, to me, for weariness; by reason of their number and extent – I've now but a couple more to write.[1] This staleness of sensibility, in connection with them blocks out for the hour every aspect but that of their being all done, and of their perhaps helping the Edition to sell two or three copies more! They will have represented much labour to this latter end – though in that they will have differed indeed from no other of their fellow-manifestations (in general) whatever; and the resemblance will be even increased if the two or three copies *don't*, in the form of an extra figure or two, mingle with my withered laurels. They are, in general, a sort of plea for Criticism, for Discrimination, for Appreciation on other than infantine lines – as against the so almost universal Anglo-Saxon absence of these things; which tends so, in our general trade, it seems to me, to break the heart. However, I am afraid I'm too sick of the mere doing of them, and of the general strain of the effort to avoid the deadly danger of repetition, to say much to the purpose about them. They ought, collected together, none the less, to form a sort of comprehensive manual or *vade-mecum* for aspirants in our arduous profession. Still, it will be long before I shall want to collect them together for that purpose and furnish *them* with a final Preface. I've done with prefaces forever. As for the Edition itself, it has racked me a little that I've had to leave out so many things that would have helped to make for rather a more vivid completeness. I don't at all regret the things pretty numerous, that I've omitted from deep-seated preference and design; but I do a little those that are crowded out by want of space and by the rigour of the 23 vols., and 23 only, which were the condition of my being able to arrange the matter with the Scribners at all. Twenty three do seem a fairly blatant array – and yet I rather surmise that there may have to be a couple of supplementary volumes for certain too marked omissions; such being, on the whole, detrimental to an at all professedly comprehensive presentation of one's stuff. Only these, I pray God, without Prefaces! And I have even, in addition, a dim vague view of re-introducing, with a good deal of titivation and cancellation, the too-diffuse but, I somehow feel, tolerably full and good "Bostonians" of nearly a quarter

1. On 25 August HJ would send off the Preface to the *Author of 'Beltraffio'* volume (XVI); on 25 September that for the *Altar of the Dead* volume (XVII); on 5 January 1909 that for *The Ambassadors*, and soon after 8 March that for *The Golden Bowl*.

of a century ago; that production never having, even to my much-disciplined patience, received any sort of justice. But it will take, doubtless, a great deal of artful re-doing – and I haven't, now, had the courage or time for anything so formidable as touching and re-touching it. I feel at the same time how the Series suffers commercially from its having been dropped so completely out. *Basta pure – basta*!

I am charmed to hear of your Roman book and beg you very kindly to send it me directly it bounds into the ring. I rejoice moreover, with much envy, and also a certain yearning and impotent non-intelligence, at your being moved to-day to Roman utterance – I mean in presence of the so-bedrenched and vulgarised (I mean more particularly *commonised*) and transformed City (as well as, alas, more or less, Suburbs) of our current time. There was nothing, I felt, to myself, I could *less* do than write again, in the whole presence – when I was there some fifteen months agone. The idea of doing so (even had any periodical wanted my stuff, much less bid for it) would have affected me as a sort of give-away of my ancient and other reactions in presence of all the unutterable old Rome I originally found and adored. It would have come over me that if those ancient emotions of my own meant anything, no others on the new basis could mean much; or if any on the new basis should pretend to sense, it would be at the cost of all imputable coherency and sincerity on the part of my prime infatuation. In spite, all the same, of which doubtless too pedantic view – it only means, I fear, that I am, to my great disadvantage, utterly bereft of any convenient *journalistic* ease – I am just beginning to re-do (on a meagre understanding with Houghton & Mifflin, re-attenuated by the involvement of Pennell) certain little old Italian papers, with titivations and expansions, in form to match with a volume of "English Hours" re-fabricated three or four years ago on the same system.[2] In this little job I shall meet again my not much more than scant, yet still appreciable, old Roman stuff in my path – and shall have to commit myself about it, or about its general subject, somehow or other. I shall trick it out again to my best ability, at any rate – and at the cost, I fear, of your thinking I have re-titivation on the brain. I haven't – I only have it on (to the end that I may then have it a little consequently *in*) the flat pocket-book. The system has succeeded a little with "English Hours;" which have sold quite vulgarly – for wares of mine; whereas the previous and original untitivated had long since dropped almost to nothing. In spite of which I could really shed salt tears of impatience and yearning to get back, after so prolonged a blocking of traffic, to too-dreadfully postponed

2. *Italian Hours*, which contained four new essays, was published by Heinemann on 28 October 1909, and by Houghton, Mifflin on 20 November.

and neglected "creative" work; an accumulated store of ideas and reachings-out for which even now clogs my brain.

We are having here so bland and beautiful a summer that when I receive the waft of your furnace-mouth, blown upon my breakfast-table every few days through the cornucopia, or improvised resounding trumpet, of The Times I groan across at my brother William (now happily domesticated with me:) "Ah why *did* they, poor infatuated dears? why *did* they?" – and he always knows I mean Why did you three hie home from one of the most beautiful seasons of splendid cool summer, or splendid summery cool, that ever was, just to swoon in the arms of your Kittery *genius loci* (genius of perspiration!) – to whose terrific embrace you saw me four years ago, or whatever terrible time it was, almost utterly succumb. In my small green garden here the elements have been, ever since you left, quite enchantingly mixed; and I have been quite happy and proud to show my brother and his wife and two of his children, who have been more or less collectively and individually with me, what a decent English season can be. I stayed on in town a little after that sad sweet Sunday with you – and there kept itself up still, for a few weeks, a certain overdone swing of the pendulum (I mean hither and yon; but always back hither again with renewed glee) and yet I had but that *one* pleasant séance with the good Scotch Member – through the conjunction you and Mildred had so suddenly, and almost violently, precipitated.[3] I greatly liked my tea on the Terrace with him (though with three or four others too whom he gathered in;) and thought him a very kindly and honest and sturdy, and above all *native*, Scotch Member indeed. That's as far as I went – and I thought I descried the limits of the ground I should ever be moved to cover (rapturously) at the best. However, I shall be sure to see him again – perhaps in the autumn (for there's to be an autumn Session, beginning Oct. 12th:, Mildred may be interested to know; if indeed she doesn't already know, and by profuse communication, a great deal more about it all than I can pretend to.) Perhaps even at an October Tea there will be a chance of my meeting her afresh in person: though, more seriously, I regard this as too much either to hope or to fear. Only tell her, please, with my love, that she really did, by the mere indirect whisk of her skirt, before she left, (she and the Scotch Member together – he by the mere imposition of his large parliamentary hand) improve my social position inordinately. I had never before, in the almost half-century, had tea on the Terrace at all; but immediately thereafter it so befel I had it twice, from different entertainers; though unfortunately without again encountering our friend. I like him, on the whole, indeed, more than I fear

3. The Howellses had met in a Roman hotel John Sutherland (1854–1918), Liberal M.P. for Elgin and chairman of the Scottish Temperance and Social Reform Association.

him – and shall not let him escape my further analysis. Tell Mildred, please, that, rather than this, I'm prepared to perish by Tea!

Let me thank you again for your allusion to the slightly glamour-tinged, but more completely and consistently forbidding and forbidden, lecture possibility.[4] I refer to it in these terms because in the first place I shouldn't have waited till now for it, but should have waked up to it eleven years ago; and because in the second there are other, and really stouter, things, too definite ones, I want to do with which it would formidably interfere, and which are better worth my resolutely attempting. I never have had such a sense of almost bursting, late in the day though it be, with violent and lately too much repressed creative (again!) intention. I *may* burst before this intention fairly or completely flowers, of course; but in that case, even, I shall probably explode to a less distressing effect than I should do, under stress of a fatal puncture, on the too personally and physically arduous, and above all too gregariously-assaulted (which is what makes it *most* arduous) lecture-platform. There is one thing which may conceivably (if it comes within a couple of years) take me again to the *contorni* of Kittery; and on the spot, once more, one doesn't know what might happen. *Then* I should take grateful counsel of you with all the appreciation in the world. And I *want* very much to go back for a certain thoroughly practical and special "artistic" reason; which would depend, however, on my being able to pass my time in an ideal combination of freedom and quiet, rather than in a luridly real one of involved and exasperated exposure and motion.[5] But I may still have to talk to you of this more categorically; and won't worry you with it till then. You wring my heart with your report of your collective Dental pilgrimage to Boston in Mrs Howells's distressful interest. I read of it from your page, somehow, as I read of Siberian or Armenian or Macedonian monstrosities, through a mercifully attenuating veil of Distance and Difference, in a column of The Times. The distance is half the globe – and the difference (for me, from the dear lady's active afflictedness) that of having when in America undergone, myself, so prolonged and elaborate a torture – in the Chair of Anguish, that I am now on t'other side of Jordan altogether, with every ghost, even, of a wincing nerve extinct and a horrible inhuman acheless void installed as a substitute. Void or not, however, I hope Mrs Howells, and you all, are now acheless at least, and am yours, my dear Howells, ever so faithfully

Henry James

4. Howells's letter: 'When you parted with me you forbade my doing anything for you in the lecturing way, and so I have attempted nothing, though I should have been so glad to try.' (LFL, 424.)

5. This 'special "artistic" reason' seems likely to be connected with one or both of the American novels HJ was pledged to write.

P.S. With all of which I catch myself up on not having told you, decently and gratefully, of the always sympathetic attention with which I have read the "Fennel and Rue" you so gracefully dropped into my lap at that last hour, and which I had afterwards to toy with a little distractedly before getting the right peaceful moments and right retrospective mood (this in order to remount the stream of time to the very Fontaine de Jouvence of your subject-matter) down here.[6] For what comes out of it to me more than anything else is the charming freshness of feeling of it, and the general miracle of your being capable of this under the supposedly more or less heavy bloom of a rich maturity. There are places in it in which you recover, absolutely, your first fine rapture. You confound and dazzle me; so go on recovering – it will make each of your next things a new document on immortal freshness! I can't remount – but can only drift on with the thicker and darker tide: wherefore pray for me, as who knows what may be at the end?

247. To James Brand Pinker
13 October 1908

Yale MS card   Unpublished

On this day HJ replied to Edith Wharton's distressed confession of her affair with their friend Morton Fullerton and of the deterioration of her marriage: 'Only sit tight yourself & go through the movements of life. That keeps up our connection with life – I mean of the immediate & apparent life; behind which, all the while, the deeper & darker and the unapparent, in which things really happen to us, learns, under that hygiene, to stay in its place.' (HJEWL, 101.)

Before the New York Edition HJ had always received unlimited author's copies from Macmillan.

LAMB HOUSE, RYE, SUSSEX.
October 13*th* 1908.

My dear Pinker.

Your word from the Macmillans makes me feel I might have sooner let you know that before I left town – the last thing – I *called* there (in urgent need of a copy or two) to see whether in my absence any had been sent down here. This inquiry brought an appeal – urgent – from Fred: M., that I would see

6. Howells's story *Fennel and Rue* (1908).

him; with whom I had a talk to the effect that as they only bought from the Scribners they couldn't give me any – but would let me have what I wanted for a "very small" payment! Thus it has been settled – I of course assenting – & I buy from them what I want at the price they pay Scribners for them. It all adds to my sense of literature being for me, somehow, ever only an *expensive* job – but I won't go into that now. I shall "have" copies! Yours ever

Henry James

248. To James Brand Pinker
20 October 1908

Yale MS   Unpublished

On 16 September Pinker had written pointing out to Scribner's that HJ's work on the New York Edition 'means that I have received practically nothing for him for the last twelve months' – in fact HJ's literary income in 1908 was his lowest for twenty-five years – but on 6 October Charles Scribner replied, enclosing the account, 'I wish very much that the sale of the New York Edition of Mr. James's books justified a substantial remittance.' (Unpublished Princeton TS, Scribner Archive: AM 19189 d (4).) The complicated deals made with the other publishers who held the rights to HJ's books diminished HJ's royalties and involved payments which came out of initial profits.

LAMB HOUSE, RYE, SUSSEX.
October 20*th* *1908*.

My dear Pinker.

I return you the Scribners' documents – which have knocked me rather flat – a greater disappointment than I have been prepared for; & after my long & devoted labour a great, I confess, & a bitter grief. I hadn't built *high* hopes – had done everything to keep them down; but feel as if comparatively I have been living in a fool's paradise. Is there *anything* for me at all? I don't quite make out or understand. If there be, will you please send it to me here straight – not to my bankers?

I shall pick myself up, but I must take a day or two; & then I shall write to you or want to see you.

Believe me yours ever

Henry James

249. To James Brand Pinker
3 December 1908

Yale MS (Za James 1, vol. 2)   Unpublished

On 22 October HJ had to reply to another disappointing letter – from Gertrude
Elliott, telling him that the Forbes-Robertson company, who had a hit on their
hands with Jerome K. Jerome's The Passing of the Third Floor Back, *had no*
immediate plan to perform The High Bid *in London, as he had hoped. The next*
day he told Pinker, 'The non-response of both sources has left me rather high &
dry . . . aching in every bone to get back to out-&-out "creative" work, the long
interruption of which has fairly sickened & poisoned me.' (HJL IV, 498.) On 21
October Charles Eliot Norton died, and on 19 November HJ began a memorial
essay on him (published in the Burlington Magazine *in January 1909).*

Theodora Bosanquet, 28 October: 'Mr James depressed – nearly finished "Golden
Bowl" preface – bored by it – says he's "lost his spring" for it.' But on Saturday,
14 November: 'Mr James recommenced work – after a week's break – "breaking
ground" on a new fiction which opens splendidly. Mrs Wharton is staying with
him . . .'

LAMB HOUSE, RYE, SUSSEX.
December 3*d 1908.*

My dear Pinker.

I acknowledge with thanks your cheque for £8. 3. 1, today received &
representing certain small royalties on various books, & from various sources,
less your commission.

And there's another matter. H. M. Alden has lately written to ask me for a
Tale in 5000 words – one of their terrible little shortest of short stories – for
Harper's Magazine, & I have answered him with a promise of the same. In
fact I got, promptly, at the job – but with the usual & inevitable result that I
shall have to do two or three – too irreducibly & irredeemably long, – in order
to pull off the really short enough. In fact I *have* done one with infinite anguish
of trying to keep it down; but the subject, the motive, has *had* to be expressed
& I shall ruin it if I now attempt to mutilate it further.[1] I shall do at least – &
immediately another, in my effort to arrive at something that will *go* in 5000
words; but meanwhile I don't want to waste the thing, "The Top of the Tree,"

1. The diary of Theodora Bosanquet records on 26 November 'a frenzied morning of stirring
to "boil down" "The Tree Top"'.

already, with infinite labour, produced (*reduced* from something done before & given up, but kept on hand,) & am wondering if Hueffer wouldn't care for it, yet again, for his Magazine.[2] He is welcome to it (*cheap*, I suppose, inevitably??!!) if he would – & will you very kindly make the inquiry &c for yours very truly

Henry James

250. To James Brand Pinker
3 January 1909

Yale MS   Unpublished

On 14–15 December HJ had to face a 'serious complication' with the New York Edition, discovered by the Scribners: the volumes of tales would be unprofitably overlength, so a twenty-fourth was added and his careful groupings disturbed, requiring adjustments to the Prefaces.

Theodora Bosanquet, 17 December: 'Wet. Mr James going on with "short" story for Harpers which extends mightily – & is, I think, dull.' (Probably 'Crapy Cornelia', about 11,000 words, published in Harper's Magazine, *October 1909.) HJ told Howells on New Year's Eve that 'I have fortunately broken ground on an American novel' – perhaps the one for Harper's (LFL, 430). Looking back on 16 January 1910, HJ would tell Pinker of his explanation to Harper's of 'why last winter, my Edition at last done, I didn't tackle the job of a serial for them . . . I had a troublesome, though superficial, heart-ailment, which has wholly subsided, & it made me nervous and anxious about undertaking a* long winded *thing.' (Unpublished Yale MS, Za James 1, vol. 2.)*

Theodora Bosanquet, 2 January 1909: 'Mr James at work on another short story – which promises very well indeed'. And on Sunday, 3 January, 'Mr James had done a lot of his story last night & we raced along. He says he wants to do three or four – & finds his only plan is to write them himself – it keeps him more within bounds – and then dictate them. Hope he'll remember to pay me for copying them! He forgot the last. He is so kind in providing chocolates for me!'

---

2. The title of 'The Top of the Tree', an ironic story of a writer exploited by a 'Princess', a dazzling but ambitious woman novelist, is a barely veiled reference to Edith Wharton's *The Fruit of the Tree* (1907). HJ sent it to Pinker the next day and it became 'The Velvet Glove' in the *English Review*, edited by Ford Madox Hueffer (another Pinker client), in March 1909.

LAMB HOUSE, RYE, SUSSEX.
January 3d 1909.

My dear Pinker.

Receive my thanks for your cheque for £10. 7. 1 – representing royalties from Scribner's Sons on old books &c.

I hope you have been able to place "The Velvet Glove" with "The English Review" – on possible terms!

It is absurd, the labour I have incurred by trying to produce 5000 words of fiction – detestable number! – for Alden, (Harper) as I wrote you some time since I had engaged, or promised, to do. I have one consequent thing of 10 000 finished, another of about 8,000 almost finished & two others started which, or one of which, *will* be a true 5000. But all of them will be too good & too *done* to sacrifice – & the *two* shortest shall presently go to Alden; in fact all 4 ought to. It will make *five* (with the "Velvet Glove,") started for his benefit – a most ridiculous commentary on my ruinously expensive mode of work, & the annoyance of his asking me for things of a form that I can't but assent to for the money's sake (so pressed am I now for that article) & of which the interrupting botherment is yet so much greater than the chance or the glory – or the larger profit.[1] But I will write you again, very soon, when I have the thing or things ready to despatch with some word about the question of the fee. Believe me, with all good wishes for the abysmal 1909, yours always

Henry James

251. To George Bernard Shaw
20 January 1909

Unknown TS   Published, CP, 643–6; HJL IV, 510–14; SL2, 376–80

Theodora Bosanquet noted on 8 January, 'Mr James began another story'; on 13 January, 'Slow progress with a "short story"'; and on 14 January, 'Mr James finds it very *difficult to get to the point with this story – which has spread about 4000 words too far already.' On 17 January: 'Mr James unwell (heart trouble).'*

After HJ's consultations with Charles Wheeler about The Saloon, *he was invited late in 1908 to submit it to the Incorporated Stage Society. The board rejected it on 12 January 1909, and Shaw, who was also on the executive committee of the Fabian*

1. The other stories were 'Mora Montravers' (*English Review*, August–September 1909); 'The Bench of Desolation' (*Putnam's Magazine*, October 1909–January 1910); and 'A Round of Visits' (*English Review*, April–May 1910).

Society, wrote an idiosyncratic letter on 17 January urging HJ to write a new ending and demanding, 'In the name of human vitality WHERE is the charm in that useless, dispiriting, discouraging fatalism which broke out so horribly in the 1860's at the word of Darwin, and persuaded people in spite of their own teeth and claws that Man is the will-less slave and victim of his environment?'

Theodora Bosanquet had no morning work on 20 January: 'Mr James dictated a letter to Bernard Shaw after tea – explaining his grounds for having "perpetrated" The Saloon – very interesting.'

Lamb House, Rye
20*th* January 1909

My dear Bernard Shaw.

Your delightful letter is a great event for me, but I must first of all ask your indulgence for my inevitable resort, to-day, to this means of acknowledging it. I have been rather sharply unwell and obliged to stay my hand, for some days, from the pen. I am, thank goodness, better, but still not penworthy – and in fact feel as if I should never be so again in presence of the beautiful and hopeless example your inscribed page sets me. Still another form of your infinite variety, this exquisite application of your ink to your paper! It is indeed humiliating. But I bear up, or try to – and the more that I *can* dictate, at least when I absolutely must.

I think it is very good of you to have taken such explanatory trouble, and written me in such a copious and charming way, about the ill-starred Saloon. It raises so many questions, and you strike out into such illimitable ether over the so distinctly and inevitably circumscribed phenomenon itself – of the little piece as it stands – that I fear I can meet you at very few points; but I will say what I can. You strike me as carrying all your eggs, of conviction, appreciation, discussion, etc., as who should say, in one basket, where you put your hand on them all with great ease and convenience; while I have mine scattered all over the place – many of them still under the hens! – and have therefore to rush about and pick one up here and another there. You take the little play "socialistically," it first strikes me, all too hard: I use that word because you do so yourself, and apparently in a sense that brings my production, such as it is, up against a lion in its path with which it had never dreamed of reckoning. Yes, there literally stands ferocious at the mouth of your beautiful cavern the very last formidable beast with any sop to whom I had prepared myself. And this though I thought I had so counted the lions and so provided the sops!

But let me, before I say more, just tell you a little how The Saloon comes to exist at all – since you say yourself "WHY have you done this thing?" I may not seem so to satisfy so big a Why, but it will say at least a little How (I came to do it;) and that will be perhaps partly the same thing.

My simple tale is then that Forbes Robertson and his wife a year ago approached me for the production of a little old one-act comedy written a dozen years or so previous, and that in the event was to see the light but under the more or less dissimulated form of a small published "story."[1] I took hold of this then, and it proved susceptible of being played in three acts (with the shortest intervals) – and was in fact so produced in the country, in a few places, to all appearances "successfully"; but has not otherwise yet affronted publicity. I mention it, however, for the fact, that when it was about to be put into rehearsal it seemed absolutely to require something a little better than a cheap curtain raiser to be played in front of it; with any resources for which preliminary the F.R.'s seemed, however, singularly unprovided. The matter seemed to me important, and though I was extremely pressed with other work I asked myself whether I, even I, mightn't by a lively prompt effort put together such a minor item for the bill as would serve to help people to wait for the major. But I had distractingly little time or freedom of mind, and a happy and unidiotic motive for a one-act piece isn't easy to come by (as you will know better than I) offhand. Therefore said I to myself there might easily turn up among all the short tales I had published (the list being long) something or other naturally and obligingly convertible to my purpose. That would economise immensely my small labour – and in fine I pounced on just such a treatable idea in a thing of many years before, an obscure pot-boiler, "Owen Wingrave" by name – and very much what you have seen by nature. It was treatable, I thought, and moreover I was in possession of it; also it would be very difficult and take great ingenuity and expertness – which gave the case a reason the more. To be brief then I with consummate art lifted the scattered and expensive Owen Wingrave into the compact and economic little Saloon – very adroitly (yes!) but, as the case had to be, breathlessly too; and all to the upshot of finding that, in the first place, my friends above-mentioned could make neither head nor tail of it; and in the second place that my three-act play, on further exploitation, was going to last too long to allow anything else of importance. So I put The Saloon back into a drawer; but so, likewise, I shortly afterwards fished it out again and showed it to Granville Barker, who was kind about it and apparently curious of it, and in consequence of whose attention a member of the S.S. saw it. That is the only witchcraft I have used! – by which I mean

1. *The High Bid* was adapted from the story 'Covering End', itself adapted from the 'little old one-act comedy' *Summersoft*.

that that was the head and front of my undertaking to "preach" anything to anyone – in the guise of the little Act – on any subject whatever. So much for the modest origin of the thing – which, since you have read the piece, I can't help wanting to put on record.

But, if you press me, I quite allow that this all shifts my guilt only a little further back and that your question applies just as much, in the first place, to the short story perpetrated years ago, and in the re-perpetration more recently, in another specious form and in the greater (the very great alas) "maturity of my powers." And it doesn't really matter at all, since I am ready serenely to answer you. I do such things because I happen to be a man of imagination and taste, extremely interested in life, and because the imagination, thus, from the moment direction and motive play upon it from all sides, absolutely enjoys and insists on and incurably leads a life of its own, for which just this vivacity itself is its warrant. You surely haven't done all your own so interesting work without learning what it is for the imagination to *play* with an idea – an idea about life – under a happy obsession, for all it is worth. Half the beautiful things that the benefactors of the human species have produced would surely be wiped out if you don't allow this adventurous and speculative imagination its rights. You simplify too much, by the same token, when you limit the field of interest to what you call the scientific – your employment of which term in such a connection even greatly, I confess, confounds and bewilders me. In the one sense in which The Saloon *could* be scientific – that is by being done with all the knowledge and intelligence relevant to its motive, I really think it quite supremely so. That is the only sense in which a work of art can be scientific – though in that sense, I admit, it may be so to the point of becoming an everlasting blessing to man. And if you waylay me here, as I infer you would be disposed to, on the ground that we "don't want works of art," ah then, my dear Bernard Shaw, I think I take such issue with you that – if we didn't both *like* to talk – there would be scarce use in our talking at all. I think, frankly, even, that we scarce want anything else at all. They are capable of saying more things to man about himself than any other 'works' whatever are capable of doing – and it's only by thus saying as much to him as possible, by saying, as nearly as we can, all there is, and in as many ways and on as many sides, and with a vividness of presentation that "art," and art alone, is an adequate mistress of, that we enable him to pick and choose and compare and know, enable him to arrive at any sort of synthesis that isn't, through all its superficialities and vacancies, a base and illusive humbug. On which statement I must rest my sense that all *direct* "encouragement" – the thing you enjoin on me – encouragement of the short-cut and say "artless" order, is really more likely than not to be shallow and misleading, and to make him turn on you with a vengeance for offering him some scheme that takes account but of a tenth of his attributes. In fact I view with suspicion the "encouraging" *representational* work, altogether, and think even the question not an *a priori* one at all; that is save under this peril of too superficial a view of what it is we have to be encouraged or discouraged *about*. The artist helps us to know this, – if he have a due intelligence – better than anyone going, because he undertakes to represent the world to us; so that, certainly, if *a posteriori*, we can on the whole feel encouraged, so much the better for us all round. But I can imagine no scanter source of exhilaration than to find the brute undertake that presentation without the most consummate "art" he can muster!

But I am really too long-winded – especially for a man who for the last few days (though with a brightening prospect) has been breathing with difficulty. It comes from my enjoying so the chance to talk with you – so much too rare; but that I hope we may be able before too long again to renew. I am comparatively little in London, but I have my moments there. Therefore I look forward – ! And I assure you I have been touched and charmed by the generous abundance of your letter. Believe me yours most truly,

Henry James

252. To George Bernard Shaw
23 January 1909

Unknown TS   Published CP, 646–7; HJL IV, 514–15

On 21 January Shaw retorted, 'You cannot evade me thus. The question whether the man is to get the better of the ghost or the ghost of the man is not an artistic question: you can give victory to one side just as artistically as to the other.'

Lamb House, Rye
23rd January 1909

My dear Bernard Shaw.

This is but a word to say No, I am not "evading," the least little scrap; though alas you will think I am when I say that I am still worried with work and correspondence put into sad arrears by my lately having been unwell and inapt. I am only conscious, I think, that I don't very well even *understand* your contention about the "story" of The Saloon – inasmuch as it seems to me a quarrel with my subject itself, and that I inveterately hold any quarrel with the subject of an achievable or achieved thing the most futile and profitless of demonstrations.[1] Criticism begins, surely, with one's seeing and judging what the work has made of it – to which end there is nothing we *can* do but accept it. I grant of course that we may dislike it enough neither to criticise it nor to want to – only that is another matter! With which, too, I seem not to understand, further, what you mean by the greater representational interest of the "man's getting the better of the ghost," than of the "ghost's getting the better of the man"; for it wasn't in those "getting the better" terms on one side or the other that I saw my situation at all. There was only one question to me, that is, that of my hero's within my narrow compass, and on the lines of my very difficult scheme of compression and concentration, getting the *best of everything*, simply; which his death makes him do by, in the first place, purging the house of the beastly legend, and in the second place by his creating for us, spectators and admirers, such an intensity of impression and emotion about him as must promote his romantic glory and edifying example for ever. I don't know what you could have more. He wins the victory – that is he clears the air, and he pays with his life. The whole point of the little piece is that he, while protesting against the tradition of his "race," proceeds and pays exactly like the soldier that he declares he'll never be. If I didn't shrink from using the language of violence I would say that I defy you to make a man in a play (that shall not be either a comedy or an irony, that is a satire, or something like) proceed consistently, and go all lengths, as a soldier, and do his job, and *not* pay with his life, – not do so without exciting the execration of the spectator. My young man "slangs the ghost" in order to start him up and give him a piece of his mind; quite on the idea that there may be danger in it for him – which I would again defy you to *interest* any audience by any disallowance of. Danger there must be therefore, and I had but one way to prove dramatically, strikingly, touchingly, that in the case before us there *had* been; which was to exhibit the peril incurred. It's exhibited by the young man's lying there gracefully dead – there could be absolutely no other exhibition of it scenically; and I emphasise "gracefully"! Really, really we would have howled at a *surviving* Owen Wingrave, who would have embodied for us a failure – and an ineptitude. But enough – I think it is, really; and I don't and won't use the language of violence. You look at the little piece, I hold, with a luxurious perversity; but my worst vengeance shall be to impose on you as soon as possible the knowledge of a much longer and more insistent one, which I may even put you in peril of rather liking. But till then I am yours most truly

Henry James

1. In 'The Art of Fiction' (1884), HJ had declared: 'We must grant the artist his subject, his idea, his *donnée*: our criticism is applied only to what he makes of it.'

253. To Charles Scribner's Sons
8 March 1909

Princeton MS card   Unpublished

On 18 February The High Bid *was put on by Forbes-Robertson's company in London for the first of five matinée performances, which received excellent reviews. On 25 February HJ saw Dr James Mackenzie (1853–1925), a heart specialist, who was encouraging and urged HJ to exercise and lose weight.*

From late January HJ had been mailing off batches of revised copy for The Golden Bowl *– the final work (in his lifetime) in the New York Edition.*

> Messrs. Charles Scribner's Sons:
> LAMB HOUSE, RYE, SUSSEX.
> March 8th 1909

Dear Sirs.

I mail you herewith my last instalment – for the Edition – of revised Copy – that for the End of The Golden Bowl. The Preface goes to you by the next mail – or the next after that. It has been written these many weeks, but I am making an alteration in it.[1]

> Believe me yours very truly
> *Henry James*

254. To James Brand Pinker
1 April 1909

Yale MS   Unpublished

> LAMB HOUSE, RYE, SUSSEX.
> *April 1st 1909.*

My dear Pinker.

I am obliged to you for your cheque for £7. 14. 2, representing Scribner's Sons' remittance on the Edition royalties &c. This first instalment of a

---

1. On 22 January HJ had replied to Coburn's complaint that he was uncredited for his photographic contribution to the New York Edition: 'I shall commemorate it myself, charmingly and appreciatively, in the last Preface of the lot; that of "The Golden Bowl" . . . I shall, by a

"realization" on that exhausting enterprise is very agreeable – as a sign of a probable More – to yours, in his destitution, very truly

Henry James

255. To Violet Hunt
6 April 1909

Virginia MS card   Unpublished

In November 1909, when public scandal loomed, HJ would rescind – probably out of loyalty to Elsie Hueffer – a Lamb House invitation to Violet Hunt, who had become Ford Madox Hueffer's mistress that summer. Hunt, a member of the W.S.P.U. and a founder of the Women Writers' Suffrage League, had also been published by Hueffer in the English Review, *and wrote asking HJ to autograph a copy of the* Review *containing 'The Velvet Glove' for a suffragist fund-raising campaign.*

LAMB HOUSE, RYE, SUSSEX.
April 6th 1909.

My dear Violet.

I will with pleasure "sign" the numbers of the English Review that you may send me – by which I suppose you mean something of mine – "The Velvet Glove?" *in* those numbers. No – I confess I am not eager for the *avènement* of a multitudinous & overwhelming female electorate – & don't see how any man in his senses *can* be; I am eager at present only for dreadnoughts & aeroplanes & people to man – not to woman – them![1] But *qu'à cela ne tienne!* I will autograph at your discretion, & your affair will be what the poor scratch shall avail you. Yours ever

Henry James

---

happy inspiration, change those three or four pages into a little friendly and felicitous recital of our hunt about for illustrative subjects; that is for mine, H.J.'s, in company with his gallant and gifted young friend A.L.C., without whom he couldn't have tackled the business for a moment; and with whom, at moments of exhaustion, he consumed bath buns by the dozen.' (Unpublished Virginia TS, 6251–g #202.)

1. *The Times* the previous day had covered the build-up of the German navy under Admiral von Tirpitz, as well as carrying the second part of a long article, 'The Case against the Admiralty', about the scrapping of ships.

256. *To William James*
18 July [1909]

Houghton MS (bMS Am 1094 (2213))   Published CWJ III, 391–4

HJ went up to London in mid May, returning to Lamb House early in July. During 11–14 June he was entertained by various young admirers at Cambridge, among them Rupert Brooke (1887–1915). During 13–15 July HJ had a motor-tour with Edith Wharton and Fullerton, whose affair was at its peak.

In June 1909, approached by the poet, playwright and impresario Frederic Herbert Trench (1865–1923) for a play in his planned repertory season at the Haymarket, HJ took up for dramatization the scenario he had dictated in September 1908 from The Other House *(1896), itself based on a sketch towards a play meant for Edward Compton. HJ received in late June a £90 advance from Trench, but after cuts, casting problems, disagreements and so forth the play was unproduced. HJ had also spoken to J. M. Barrie on 12 May as representative of the American producer Charles Frohmann, about writing a play for another new repertory season. On 2 July HJ, emphasizing his financial worries about unremunerative work, was telling Pinker 'I feel rather demoralized and nervous' (Unpublished Yale MS, Za James 1, vol. 2).*

WJ's A Pluralistic Universe, *based on his Oxford lectures, had recently come out.*

LAMB HOUSE, RYE, SUSSEX.

Dearest William.

Horribly silent have I too long been in spite of two most generous letters from you – the first from Salisbury Conn., as long ago (hideous for me to relate,) as the end of May, & the 2d from Silver Lake, N.H., of comparatively the other day.[1] I received both of them in town, from which I lately returned after a stay of a couple of months; a stay on from week to week (for it seemed good for me) during which I kept promising myself to write as soon as ever I should get back to these more peaceful shades – remarkably dense just now as an effect of too long a turn of cold & torrential rain (which made also for my hanging on in town, where the weather can more or less be flouted.) But you spoil me – that is the real truth – by your unreckoning munificence. Now

1. WJ had written from the Barack-Matiff Farm at Salisbury, home of Henrietta Temple Pell-Clarke, on 31 May to say that he had decided not to go to Europe and Nauheim for his heart. On 23 June he wrote from Silver Lake reporting on the family summer.

that I *am* back here dear little old L.H. reasserts its value & its charm as almost never before; the garden is thick & blooming – & withal (thanks to inveterate George) beautifully neat; today is a delightfully mild & soft sun-dappled, shade-flickering, west-windy Sunday, full of rustle & colour; & I have just tried to express to Harry how "unhandsome" (as Father used to say) it is that I should be piggishly keeping, or at least having, it all to myself – to the exclusion of my near & dear.[2] Nurse at least & keep firm on its feet the project of your *all* coming out to me next summer. The years fearfully lapse & it won't do to miss another. Yet I am counting on Bill for September – & *all* September – at furthest, if so be it he can't come sooner. I am, however, immediately writing him about this. I am really better – ever so much better – than I have been at any time since I began to grow too fat & move too little; my clothes hang loose upon me, & I must soon begin to have some of them "taken in"; a delicious prospect after years of letting out. In short I am *easy*, & will say no more about it – save that I feel myself to have profitted enormously by getting renewedly into touch with dear Horace Fletcher, during a few days he spent with me in town.[3] His physiology is priceless to me, & his example ditto – though I have no use for his general bland & boresome idealisms & christian endeavourings – on which, however, we don't have to touch at all – having a most beautiful & successful relation without it. I feel that physiologically & on *that* Fletcherizing basis he knows *absolutely* where he is; & we thrashed things out together in a way that will have really been of great use to me for the rest of my days – of this I am confident. I don't despair of returning to & leaning on dear Mother Nature even to within almost measurable distance of dear – of almost *as* dear – H.F. himself, who visibly before me, during ten days, partook of one very simple dish (& of only about a 3*d* of that – frequently a Welsh Rabbit!) not more than once in 48 hours – & with the effect of remaining but the *more frais & dispos* & active all the while. I see now – with the effects (*local doctor-produced*) of my 1*st* bewilderment of some months ago cleared up – effects of "more *meat* & really a glass of good port-wine after dinner," eventuating 1*st* in a bilious attack here & then, in town, in the 1*st* fit of gout, in my *right* foot this time, for years – with those consequences intelligibly outlived, & forever, I say, I am more full of resource, on a more intimately understood Fletcher basis, for the rest of my days, than ever before.[4] But enough of that – which may be summed up, as I say, in the statement that

2. George Gammon was HJ's gardener, who won many prizes in 1909 (as usual) at the local horticultural show.
3. In the event, WJ's son Bill did not go to Europe but remained in the U.S. studying at the Museum of Fine Arts, Boston. HJ lunched with Fletcher on 9 June.
4. The local doctor in Rye was Ernest Skinner of Mountsfield.

I am *easier* than for a long time past, & that I know, I feel, a great deal more than I had done before, about remaining so. Also I have lots of interesting work before me – two jobs that are for the moment a little conflicting. I am having at last to come to the point of doing for the Macmillans the "London" – more or less impressionistic & with drawings by Joseph Pennell – that I long ago contracted with them for & that it has been ever since convenient, & necessary, for me to hold off from (the agreement as to *time* I having made from the 1st an easy one.) I shall enjoy doing it when once I buckle down, & the terms being very good, & the possibility of tourist &c sale big, the profit *may* be very great. Only meanwhile the Theatre has been loudly knocking in my door, & my reasons both intrinsic & extrinsic for listening to it exceedingly strong & valid & urgent. Therefore as the New "Repertory" Theatre (Haymarket – in the person of Herbert Trench,) & the later-to-be-opened one in the person of Frohmann – but acting (on *me*) through J. M. Barrie – have both applied to me for plays at an early date, I am for this summer pegging away for *them*, all the more that from Trench I have already received my advance of money "down". All of which facts, however, are *only* for family consumption. I hang about you all in imagination & wonder, & hope, ardently, that you are most – save the heroic Harry, I fear – to whom I have just written – among your various woods & lakes & orchards & piazzas, & above all that Alice & Peggy to whom I send my tenderest love, haven't too monstrous a social situation to face.[5] When I image *those* resources of yours in their large romanticism, I look out of my window at my so rosy & so mulberried & so swarded garden with a more consoled sense of its small contractedness – that is of its snugness combined with its emptiness – in respect to your presence; & heaven send that you be all making in your various ways a successful & manageable summer of it. Your own movements – through space – seem to me to testify for you; as for myself, "better" as I am, *déplacements* less & less appeal – save the always interesting one (after sufficient intervals,) of going hence up to town & reverting back here again. That oscillation will simply suffice me for the remainder of my life – but of course it is a very good one. Also it has "come my way" to motor – or rather to be motored – a good deal these last weeks, & that, when not overdone, & in this admirable county of Sussex in particular – as for that matter anywhere in England – I find, if *contemplatively* done (& only then,) immensely suggestive, interesting & inspiring. Mrs. Wharton has been these 2 months in & near London, with an admirably conceived & guided Panhard – & was *here*, just after my return,

5. Harry was now working as a partner in the law firm of Warren, Hague, James & Bigelow. Peggy had left Bryn Mawr after a nervous collapse and was living at home.

for 3 or 4 days; during all of which, fine weather occasionally favouring, she whirled me admirably about – notably from London down to Dorsetshire (to Frampton, the Sheridans', near Dorchester, where we spent the night;) & the other day hence to the west extremity of the County – Chichester – & then the next day otherwise back through absolute enchantments of scenery & association. I find I get a good deal out of it.[6]

All this time I'm not thanking you in the competent way for your "Pluralistic" volume – which now I can effusively do. I read it, while in town, with a more thrilled interest than I can say; with enchantment, with pride, & almost with comprehension. It may sustain & inspire you a little to know that I'm *with* you, all along the line – & can conceive of no sense in any philosophy that is not yours! As an artist & a "creator" I can catch on, hold on, to Pragmatism, & can work in the light of it & apply it; finding, in comparison everything else (so far as I know the same!) utterly irrelevant & useless – vainly & coldly parallel![7] Sydney Waterlow told me a day or two ago that he had had a very interesting & beautiful letter from you – the spirit of which he seemed greatly – immensely – to appreciate.[8] Awfully interesting what you tell me of Plutarch – whom I reopened – with extreme interest, to the extent of 3 or 4 Greek Lives – a year or two ago; not having looked into him since old Newport days.[9] But I can for this year only go on reading *London* books – of which

6. On 28 June HJ motored with Edith Wharton and Howard Sturgis from Windsor to Andover, had tea at Salisbury and 'dined and slept at Frampton Court Dorchester' (N, 303). Clare Frewen Sheridan (1885–1970), sculptress daughter of HJ's Rye neighbours the Moreton Frewens, was married to Wilfred Sheridan, who was killed at Loos in 1915. Wharton said she had bought her car on the proceeds of her last novel. HJ: 'With the proceeds of *my* last novel I purchased a small go-cart, or hand-barrow, on which my guest's luggage is wheeled from the station to my house. It needs a coat of paint. With the proceeds of my next novel, I shall have it painted.' (Percy Lubbock, *Portrait of Edith Wharton*, 69–70.)

7. On 17 October 1907 HJ had written to WJ explaining his delay in writing to him about his *Pragmatism: A New Name for Some Old Ways of Thinking* (1907) by 'the very fact of the spell itself (of interest & enthrallment) that the book cast upon me: I simply sank down, under it, into such depths of submission & assimilation that *any* reaction, very nearly, even that of acknowledgment, would have had almost the taint of dissent or escape. Then I was lost in the wonder of the extent to which all my life I have (like M. Jourdain) unconsciously pragmatized. You are immensely & universally *right* . . .' (CWJ III, 347.)

8. Sydney Waterlow (1878–1944), a former Cambridge contemporary of Leonard Woolf with political interests, was at this time a frequent Rye walking companion of HJ's, being (unhappily) married to Alice Pollock, daughter of Sir Frederick Pollock (1845–1937), a former professor of jurisprudence at Oxford who lived next door to Alice Dew-Smith. WJ's letter is not known to survive.

9. In the 23 June letter WJ had written: 'I have just finished 3 vols. of Plutarch's lives – great stuff to read, more everlasting human business, more "rammed with life" than in any book I know. I recommend it.' (CWJ III, 390.)

there are far too many. But the best interest me. I pray for Aleck & embrace you all.[10] Ever your fond

Henry
July 18.

257. To James Brand Pinker
21 July 1909

Yale MS   Unpublished

On 2 July HJ wrote to Pinker of 'the wild dream of your having been able to do something *or other with the accursed two other short stories that I did in the winter for the fond vision of immediate profit & for the belief that the false Alden, with his complimentary letter to me, would like them' (Unpublished Yale MS, Za James 1, vol. 2). Pinker had managed to place 'The Bench of Desolation' with* Putnam's Magazine *and, finally, 'A Round of Visits' in the* English Review *for April–May 1910.*

LAMB HOUSE, RYE, SUSSEX.

My dear Pinker.

I am greatly obliged to you for what you have done, with Putnam, for the "Bench of Desolation," & am quite content, as a *pis aller*, with the £75. But clearly I have written the last short story of my life – which you will be glad to know!

Yours ever
Henry James

July 21*st* 1909.

258. To William James
31 October 1909

Houghton MS   Published CWJ III, 402–5; partly published LHJ II,
140–42

On 29 July HJ posted to Elizabeth Jordan, for a symposium in Harper's Bazar,
*'Is There a Life After Death?' (published January–February 1910), a speculative
two-part essay twice as long as those of other contributors ('I didn't seem to make
it at all worth while except by saying what I wanted and what I seemed to* have
*to' (HJBL, 55)). On 23 September, not having received the promised novel from
HJ, Harper's published the tale* Julia Bride *as a small book.*

*HJ was away from Rye, in London and elsewhere, much of September. During
6–11 September he went to the Three Choirs Festival, failing to relish Elgar's*
Apostles *and staying with Fanny Kemble's daughter and her husband the Dean of
Hereford. He returned to London via the Abbeys in Fairford, Gloucestershire.*

Back in Rye from 2 October, and troubled with gout, HJ was working on The
Outcry, *a comedy about American money threatening British cultural treasures,
for Frohmann, who with J. M. Barrie was also commissioning plays for his repertory
season from Harley Granville-Barker (*The Madras House*), Shaw (*Misalliance*)
and Galsworthy (*Justice*) among others. On 14 October HJ told Pinker, 'I . . . find
myself very ardent & interested; feeling, the more I get into it – into the whole
thing – that* that *way, for me the Future (what is left me of it!) lies.' (Unpublished
Yale MS, Za James 1, vol. 2.)*

> LAMB HOUSE, RYE, SUSSEX.
> *October 31st 1909.*

Dearest William.

I have beautiful communications from you all too long unacknowledged &
unrequited – though I shall speak for the present but of two most prized letters
from you (from Cambridge & Chocorua respectively – not counting quaint
sequels from Franconia, 'autumn-tint' postcards &c, a few days ago, or
thereabouts, & leaving aside altogether, but only for later fond treatment,
please assure them, an admirable one from Harry & an exquisite from Bill.)[1]
To these I add the arrival still more recently of your brave new book, which

---

1. WJ wrote from Chocorua on 6 October, and from Franconia Notch, New Hampshire, on 9
October. No WJ letters to HJ from Cambridge in this period appear to survive. WJ had also
sent HJ his new book, *The Meaning of Truth*.

I fell upon immediately & have quite passionately absorbed – to within 50 pages of the end; a great number previous to which I have read this evening – which makes me late to begin this. I find it of thrilling interest, triumphant & brilliant, & am lost in admiration of your wealth & power. I palpitate as you make out your case, (since it seems to me you so utterly do,) as I under no romantic spell ever palpitate now; & into that case I enter intensely, unreservedly, & I think you would allow almost intelligently. I find you nowhere as difficult as you surely make everything for your critics. Clearly you are winning a great battle & great will be your fame. Your letters seem to me to reflect a happy & easy summer achieved – & I recognize in them with rapture, & I trust not fallaciously, a comparative immunity from the horrid human *incubi*, the awful "people" fallacy, of the past, & your ruinous sacrifices to that bloody Moloch. May this luminous exemption but grow & grow! & with it your personal & physical peace & sufficiency, your profitable possession of yourself. Amen, amen – over which I hope dear Alice hasn't *lieu* to smile! I came back here a month ago from a month's absence, & should have, especially for this last month, a pretty fair account of myself to give weren't it for the curse of our abominable Season, a summer & autumn of the most blighting, the most cruel, inclemency. This whole October has capped the climax with diluvian & unceasing rains (they've been going on since May;) horrible roaring tempest & brutal polar cold! One doesn't know how one "is" in such conditions – one is simply beaten & laid low by the elements. And still it goes on. This blessed old house helps me to endure – is, if possible, even a *growing* boon to me, with its singular little secret of being favourable to life, & in respect to my heart-trouble of upwards [of] a year ago (as to its bad *crisis*) I am very distinctly & confirmedly better & better; in spite of anginal tendencies, which lapse, practically, even as they come – & which I can in a measure control or accommodate myself to.) Movement, ambulation & circulation, continue as markedly good for me as Mackenzie guaranteed, & it is a question, only, of getting, conveniently *enough* of them; which I do better in London than here, unfortunately, during these oncoming days of waning light & increasing mud. I haven't felt the need to see Mackenzie again – that fact will give you by itself a good deal, the measure. There are other things, or mainly *one* other – which I might sum up as being at last, again, *definitely & unmistakeably*, the finally proved *cul de sac* or defeat of literal Fletcherism – might so sum up if I could go at all into the difficult & obscure subject by letter. I *can't* do so – though I will return to it on some future writing, & after more results from my of late – that is these last 3 months' very trying experience – which has abated since queer lights (*on* too prolonged Fletcherism) have more & more distinctly & relievingly come to me. But meanwhile communicate nothing distressful to poor dear H.F. if he is in America – his malady of motion, a perfect St. Vitus's Dance of the déplacement-mania, make me never know *where* he is. I am worrying out my salvation – very interesting work & prospects, I think, much aiding – & "going into" the whole fearsome history intelligibly *this* way is an effort from which I recoil.

November 1st I broke this off last night & went to bed – & now add a few remarks after a grey soft windless & miraculously rainless day (under a most rainful sky,) which has had a rather sad hole made in it by a visitation from a young person from New York, addressed to [me] by poor Ida Smalley there as her bosom friend (Helen Fiske by name, daughter of vice-president of Metropolitan Insurance Company) who, arriving from town at 1. 30, to luncheon, remained New Yorkily conversing till 6. 30, when I got her off to Hastings, where she was – & I trust *is* – to sleep.[2] She stole from me the hour or two before my small evening feed in which I hoped to finish "The Meaning of Truth"; but I have done much toward this since that repast, & with a renewed eagerness of inglutition. You surely make philosophy more interesting & living than any one has *ever* made it before, & by a real creative & undemolishable making; whereby all you write plays into *my* poor "creative" consciousness & artistic vision & pretension with the most extraordinary suggestiveness & force of application & inspiration. Thank the powers – that is thank *yours*! – for a relevant & assimilable & *referable* philosophy, which is related to the rest of one's intellectual life otherwise & more conveniently than a fowl is related to a fish. In short, dearest William, the effect of these collected papers of your present volume – which I had read all individually before – seems to me exquisitely & adorably cumulative &, so to speak, consecrating; so that I, for my part, feel Pragmatic invulnerability constituted. Much will this *suffrage* help the cause!

Not less inspiring to me, for that matter is the account you give, in your beautiful letter of Oct *6th*, from Chocorua, of Alice & the offspring, Bill & Peggot in particular, confirming so richly all my precious observations of the son & letting in such rich further lights upon the daughter. I shall write soon to Bill & tell him all I believe of him & count on from him; & I languish for the sequel of the Medea-performance plan & for further news of Peg's connection with it.[3] I wd. almost cross the wintry ocean to see my gifted niece in the "title rôle." But I mean really & truly, soon to write her straight & supplicate her for a letter. Poor dear Aleck – his "parts" have evidently to grow more

2. Ida Smalley was the daughter of HJ's old Paris friend George Washburn Smalley, Helen Fiske (later Evans) the daughter of Haley Fiske (1852–1929).

3. Bill had painted a portrait of WJ this summer, and Peggy was to take part in a production of *Medea* by the Bryn Mawr Club of Boston (she ended up in the chorus).

successively than simultaneously, & each as a distinct & independent proposition; but I am convinced that they will still, together make a fair, a coherent
& beautiful sentence. But we mustn't try too much to hurry it up – to the risk
of loss of part of the good meaning. I send him his faithful old Uncle's love.
And àpropos of Uncles, though not so much of love, I had Bob's Ned here
again for a day 3 weeks ago, on his way back from London to Paris – improved
as to manners & even appearance & the general tinge, faint though it be, as
of civilization; but so indescribably *Naught*, as regards anything like content
or character or value or possession of anything to give, or perception of
anything to take, that the result is almost uncanny +.[4] I got oddly enough at
the same time a short letter from Bob – tacked on to one of Mary's; the 1st
word I have had from him for years & which I immediately & rejoicingly
answered. Humorous & fairly friendly, but queer & latently vicious or invidious
– all, however, in a harmless & sad & imaginable way (as out of the bitter
depths of a consciousness of comparative failure & obscurity – comparative
to you & me, with our "literary talent" &c!) which moves me to nothing but
tender & unexpressible (not quite *in*expressible!) compassion for the image of
narrowed-down savourless life that he presents. Little has he too reduced
himself to having either to give or to take! Another thing which just lately
made a grudged hole in a couple of days was my having consented at the
gentle Florence Pertz's instance to read the voluminous type-copy of a Life of
J. J. G. Wilkinson – done by a cousin, a Dr. Clement Wilkinson of Windsor
– but done so drearily & artlessly & impossibly, & on a subject really most
thankless & arid & dead, that I had no hesitation in saying that publication is
wholly hopeless & unprocurable – a verdict in which she entirely concurs; so
that, visibly, the thing will blush unseen – after the poor cousin's most
well-meaning & uninspired & unreadable toil.[5] But good-night again – as my
thoughts flutter despairingly (of attainment) toward your farawayness, under
the hope that the Cambridge autumn is handsome & wholesome about you. I
yearn over Alice to the point of wondering if some day before Xmas she *may*
find a scrap of a moment to testify to me a little about the situation with her

---

4. + 'He has the merit, on the other hand of being wholly un-importunate & un-boring, & of
certain practical discretion in relations – or non-relations.' [HJ's footnote.] Edward Holton
James (1873–1954), son of HJ's brother Robertson, was a quixotic socialist with a Harvard
legal training and a wife who had $12,000 a year. HJ had seen Mary Holton James, wife of
Bob, in St Augustine, Florida, in 1905.

5. In London on 1 October HJ saw Florence Pertz, a serious musicologist who was granddaughter
of Henry James Senior's British Swedenborgian friend James John Garth Wilkinson (1812–
99), a homoeopathic physician. Her mother Florence had been a friend of AJ's in England.
James John Garth Wilkinson was in fact published in 1911.

now too unfamiliar pen. Oh if you only *can* next summer come out for 2 years! This house shall be your fortress & temple & headquarters as never, never, even, before. I embrace you all – I send my express love to Mrs. Gibbens[6] – & am your fondest of brothers

Henry James

P.S. I have read both your Hodgson report & your Am. Magazine article – thanks! The former depressing; the latter most interesting & uplifting![7]

---

259. To Elizabeth Jordan
14 November 1909

NYPL, RBMS MS   Published HJBL, 55

After 'Is There a Life After Death?' HJ was asked for another Bazar *paper for a series of six, probably after a conversation with Howells between 20 and 30 September. He made a start – four typed pages about his abandonment of the Harvard Law School – but in the event only Mark Twain's and Howells's own appeared (in February and March 1910). In ch. x of* Notes of a Son and Brother *HJ would write more amply about his time at the Law School, including 'a black little memory' of 'the fierce light of a "moot-court"', where he publicly dried up attempting to argue a case, 'quavered away into mere collapse and cessation, . . . so that I liken it all to a merciful fall of the curtain on some actor stricken and stammering'.*

LAMB HOUSE, RYE, SUSSEX.
November 14*th 1909.*

Dear Miss Jordan.

I will with pleasure do my best with Howells's good example before me to

---

6. Eliza Putnam Webb Gibbens (1827–1917) was WJ's mother-in-law.

7. In the spring of 1906 WJ was attempting to communicate with another (recently dead) psychical researcher, Richard Hodgson – through Leonora Evelina Piper, a medium who had twice given AHJ a message which deeply impressed HJ, as coming from his mother: 'Mary repeats her message to Henry. He must be anxious no more for the end shall be as he desires.' (CWJ III, 309.) In the 1909 *Proceedings* of the Society for Psychical Research, WJ published an unconvinced 'Report on Mrs. Piper's Hodgson-Control'. In the *American Magazine* (October 1909) WJ's 'Confidences of a "Psychical Researcher"' were frankly inconclusive, but he admitted his conviction of 'a continuum of cosmic consciousness, against which our individuality builds but accidental fences, and into which our several minds plunge as into a mother-sea or reservoir'.

become conscious, first of What the Turning Point of my Life may have been – if it – my Life – ever had any; & then to give you as vivid account of it as possible.[1] But I am obliged to make the Proviso that my Fee be $300 – I find it, commercially speaking, impossible to get under way & turn round, in article, for less. I work very expensively artistically speaking, to myself – to begin with. But I shall *always* be glad to do a gentle paper for the Bazaar for the sum I name.

Will you, if my condition can be met, let me know *when* my contribution may be wanted?

And will you further, please, be very sure to send me a Proof of the "Life after Death" paper? Believe me

Yours very truly
Henry James

260. To James Brand Pinker
6 January 1910

Yale TS and MS   Unpublished

HJ posted the third and final act of The Outcry *to Granville-Barker (for Frohmann's repertory) on 16 December, though he had already starting cutting the first two.*

On 17 December he made a start on sketching 'the "K.B." (Venice) idea', about a youngish New York widow and her predicament, based on his and Browning's old friend Katherine de Kay Bronson, which would become his unfinished novel The Ivory Tower. *On that day he went on to note: 'The receipt of a letter from Duneka (F.A.) about a serial Fiction for Harpers comes in at an odd psychological moment and with an odd psychological coincidence today – when I have been literally in the very act of sitting down to a statement of the little idea that I have for these few years past carried in my brooding brain.' (N, 258.) This was a further attempt to realize the novel HJ had contracted for with Harper's years before. (It turned out HJ had misunderstood: Duneka had no idea of serialization.)*

Already on 30 December HJ was writing to Granville-Barker in pencil that he was unwell: it was the beginning of a long period of nervous depression and illness.

1. The fragment HJ wrote is reproduced in N, 437–8 (misdated there as 1900–1).

Lamb House, Rye.
January 6th: 1910

My dear Pinker.

This is to say, in appreciative response to yours this morning received, that – yes – the thing will be, I think, to await the approach of the Frohman business people a week or two before invoking their attention; which I dare say will be given, at furthest, before the end of next week. I have reason to suppose that a particular circumstance will by that time have occurred to *determine* it.[1]

As for the Duneka matter I think there will be no difficulty about time; inasmuch as I have, for the thing I wrote him about, absolutely arranged to keep myself, as by the operation of an immutable ring-fence of steel down to the comparative brevity of the 100,000 words. My thing is so planned, that is, as to be *organically* confined to that number – four Books of two instalments each, and each instalment 12,000 and a small fraction; and on this basis, with a strong motive, moreover, intensely operating, I shall be able to promise them the whole quite in time for the first number to appear in July, if that is likely to be what they want; and if it will be any use to them I can let them have the first half by three months hence, and the second a few weeks later. In other words I am casting the thing into such form that I shall be able, my necessities assisting, to do it rapidly. On the other hand I doubt whether they will consider that this particular thing quite squares with the old agreement your letter refers to. This is indeed to be a Novel, of 100,000 words; but making, as I say, 8 instalments instead of the ten or twelve more or less implied in the other matter; and with each instalment so constructed *as* an instalment that this will preclude chopping up and stretching out into any series of shorter snippets. That may make a difference to them, but even *with* a difference (that is with a part of the figure, the old figure, knocked off) it will still be all eminently worth my while. But as to this you must judge on Duneka's reply – which won't be due, however, for some ten or twelve days more. I may mention to you further, in the Harper connection, that the Bazaar lately applied to me for another Paper on the same terms as the last, which I am immediately proceeding to send.[2] They make really a very good bargain with me, as I am always irresistibly impelled to do more – their proposed space is so meagre; and they *use* all my More – rejoicingly it would seem, and making two instalments of it. However, it's my little way, and I don't mind.

1. This circumstance may have been HJ's sending of a cut version of Act Three of *The Outcry* to Barker, or more likely the question of casting – as Barker thought ' "vital" ' – the eminent actor Sir John Hare as Lord Theign (HJL IV, 543; Hare turned the part down about the end of January).
2. 'The Turning Point of My Life', which illness seems to have prevented HJ's completing.

I *hadn't* understood your having disposed of the last outstanding thing to Putnam, & am sorry it has had to go for so little; it is a great "come down."[3] However, I could bear it – & will try to bear it from now on – if Putnam will pay me that sum (the £45) as the other American magazines do, now that of the possible £1500 on the basis of the terms offered to – or, rather, secured by! – or *for* – ! – the author of *The Inner Shrine*.[4] I'll be hanged if each of my instalments won't be worth as much as each of his – or even (if it's a She,) Hers!

You probably know as well as I – I only knowing through G. Barker – that he (G.B., Shaw & Galsworthy) are each having a new play produced by Frohman's Repertory undertaking – & are in possession of material for some conclusion of what ones are the best possible for yours ever

Henry James

P.S. When you next write will you kindly mention for what *time* Herbert Trench has my 4-act play in his hands?[5] – if it's for more than a year? I *forget* the time! – & though I am, for a reason, letting him utterly alone, as heaven knows

261. To Hugh Walpole
13 May 1910

Texas MS   Published HJL IV, 551–2; SL2, 384–6

HJ's illness continued worryingly; he described it to Gosse on 13 February as 'a very bad & obstinate & rather obscure gastric, stomachic crisis – making food repulsive & nutrition proportionately difficult (damnably so at times – with conse-quent weakness, prostration, depression &c, as much as you like)' (SLHJEG, 249). WJ and AHJ came over to be with him, arriving on 7 April, despite WJ's own worsening heart-condition.

3. From 'the last outstanding thing to Putnam' the rest of the letter is handwritten. *Putnam's Magazine* was absorbed in 1910 by the *Atlantic Monthly*, but having apparently already accepted 'A Round of Visits' for publication in a single instalment. They paid HJ $218 for it before folding and, set from Putnam proofs, the story appeared in the *English Review* (April–May), edited from December 1909 by Austin Harrison (1873–1928), who paid HJ 40 guineas.
4. The Canadian novelist William Benjamin Basil King (1859–1928) was the author of *The Inner Shrine: A Novel of Today* (1909).
5. A pencilled annotation above the line, possibly by Pinker himself: 'for five years from date of production'.

On 6 May 1910 Edward VII died and the Frohmann season collapsed with the closing of the theatres – the final nail in the coffin of The Outcry, *already severely compromised by HJ's continuing illness (though he was sending Barker cuts up to 11 May). On 5 May HJ sent Pinker complete copy for a final gathering of short stories,* The Finer Grain, *published by Scribner's on 6 October and Methuen on 13 October, the dust-jacket bearing the author's own gloss on the cryptic title: 'a peculiar accessibility to surprise, to curiosity, to mystification or attraction – in other words, to moving experience'.*

Hugh Walpole (1884–1941), just starting as a novelist and man of letters, had written introducing himself to HJ in December 1908 with recommendations from A. C. Benson and Percy Lubbock, and an affectionate friendship began. HJ's writing is shaky.

LAMB HOUSE, RYE, SUSSEX.
May 13th 1910

Dearest, Dearest Hugh.

I have been utterly, but necessarily silent – so much of the time lately quite too ill to write. Deeply your note touches me, as I needn't tell you – & I would give anything to be able to have the free use of your "visible & tangible" affection – no touch of its tangibility but would be dear & helpful to me. But, alas, I am utterly unfit for visits – with the black devils of Nervousness, direst, damnedest demons, that ride me so cruelly & that I have perpetually to reckon with. I am mustering a colossal courage to try – even to-morrow – in my blest sister-in-law's company (without whom & my brother, just now in Paris, I couldn't have struggled on at all) to get away for some days by going to see a kind friend in the country – in Epping Forest.[1] I feel it a most precarious & dangerous undertaking – but my desire & need for change of air, scene & circumstances after so fearfully overmuch of these imprisoning objects, is so fiercely intense that I am making the push – as to save my life – at any cost. It *may* help me – even much, & the doctor intensely urges it – & if I am able, afterwards (that is if the experiment isn't disastrous,) I shall *try* to go to 105 Pall Mall for a little instead of coming abjectly back

---

1. WJ was again on his way to Bad Nauheim for heart treatment. Mary Smyth (Mrs Charles) Hunter (1857–1933), wealthy wife of a Northern coal owner and Tory M.P. (they divorced in 1913), was the sister of the composer Ethel Smyth (1858–1944). Her recently acquired Jacobean house, Hill Hall in Essex, was often full of artists and musicians: including her friend John Singer Sargent, a musician as well as a painter, the Australian composer and pianist Percy Grainger (1882–1961), the composer Roger Quilter (1877–1953), the painter Wilfred Von Glehn (husband of Jane Emmet, one of HJ's Emmet cousins) and Auguste Rodin.

here.[2] Then I shall be able to see you – but all this is fearfully contingent. Meanwhile the sense of your personal tenderness to me, dearest Hugh, is far from not doing much for me. I adore it.

I "read," in a manner Maradick – but there['s] too much to say about it, & even my weakness doesn't alter me from the grim & battered old *critical* critic – no *other* such creature among all the "reviewers" do I meanwhile behold. Your book has a great sense & love of life – but seems to me nearly as irreflectively juvenile as the Trojans, & to have the prime defect of your having gone into a subject – i.e. the marital, sexual, bedroom relations of M. & his wife & the literary man & his wife – since these *are* the key to the whole situation – which have to be tackled & faced to mean anything. You don't tackle & face them – you *can't*.[3] Also the whole thing is a monument to the abuse of voluminous dialogue, the absence of a plan of composition, alternation, distribution[,] structure, & other phases of presentation than the dialogic – so that *line* (the only thing *I* value in a fiction &c,) is replaced by a vast formless featherbediness – billows in which one sinks & is lost. And yet it's all so loveable – though not so *written*. It isn't written *at all*, darling Hugh – by which I mean you have – or, truly, only in a few places, as in Maradick's dive – never got expression *tight* & in close quarters (of discrimination, of specification) with its subject.[4] It remains loose & far. And you have never made out, recognised, nor stuck to, the *centre of your subject*. But can you forgive all this to your fondest old reaching-out-his-arms-to you

H.J.?

262. To Theodora Bosanquet
1 August 1910

Houghton MS   Published HJAD, 239–40

On 25 May, stuck at Hill Hall where he had suffered a relapse, HJ told Pinker his illness prevented his making engagements for future work, in particular the novel

2. 105 Pall Mall was HJ's small flat in Reform Club Chambers, just round the corner from the club itself.
3. Walpole's first novel, published as *The Wooden Horse* (1909), had been started under the title *The House of the Trojans* while he was still a schoolmaster. *Maradick at Forty* (1910), his second, is a suburban comedy of manners whose dull hero James Maradick, married for fifteen years to a dull, pretty wife, Emmy, flirts with Milly Lester, wife of a 'literary man'. HJ's 'you *can't*' may refer to the restrictions of censorship, or to Walpole's ignorance, as a romantic, homosexual young man, about heterosexual goings-on.
4. In ch. VIII Maradick and young Tony Galt go for an exhilarating Cornish swim: 'They flung

for Harper's. Having booked a passage with WJ and AHJ back to America, he returned to Lamb House on 2 June, then set off with AHJ to join the ailing WJ at Nauheim, arriving on 9 June. On 13 June HJ wrote to Gosse that 'black depression – the blackness of darkness & the cruellest melancholia – are my chronic enemy & curse' (SLHJEG, 252). They went down to Switzerland in July, and in what HJ's diary called 'dark troubled sad days' (N, 317) heard of the death of Robertson James on 3 July, of heart-failure in his sleep. They returned to London on 12 July, and went to Rye on 23 July with WJ to make final arrangements.

LAMB HOUSE, RYE, SUSSEX.
August 1st 1910

Dear Miss Bosanquet.

I sail, with my brother & sister, for America on August 12*th* – & am very sorry to have no prospect of seeing you before I leave. I am better, but my brother is very ill (we came back from the continent 16 days ago,) & I fear I can't be in town save for the night before our embarking. Besides, you are certainly not there now, I take it – and, lastly, though exceedingly better, I am not yet on an absolutely firm plane – & am liable to bad days (like, I am sorry to say, this one.) I called at the Bradleys, in spite of it, this afternoon, to get, among other things, news of you – but found a cold welcome, "the house let," in short a sad drop of my hope.[1] I of course don't know what you are now doing – & heartily trust all is well & convenient with you; but am also wondering if *this* wd. be possible. 'The Outcry' utterly gave way under my illness & complete inability to superintend & carry on rehearsal – as I knew it would; & Frohmann paid a substantial forfeit & I recovered my rights in the play. I don't see clearly at all, yet, its future – but want a copy of it in which the *last* awful cuts (thousands & thousands of words slashed out, loathingly, by me in May, sick & suffering, & under Barker's & Barrie's even then urgent requisition) shall be embodied. I am waiting anxiously to have the copy containing these cuts back from Granville Barker – it hasn't yet come. It *must* come, I think, this week, & I wonder if you could then make a fresh copy for me & send it to me in the U.S. I mean send the leaves – sheets –

---

off their clothes with an entire disregard of possible observers. A week ago Maradick would have died rather than do such a thing . . . As Maradick felt the water about his body his years fell from him like Pilgrim's pack . . . As he cleaved it with his arm it parted and curled round his body like an embrace.'

1. Theodora Bosanquet's best friend and companion – HJ called her 'a pal & second-self of hers (a lady-pal)' (HJEWL, 130) – was Miss Ellen ('Nelly') Bradley, whose family lived in Rye and were acquaintances of HJ.

loose of course, without binding. It will be a comparatively light job – the Acts have each been so ignobly shortened.[2] May I hear from you about this? I could give you *time* – a month or two. And do tell everything else of your news, & Miss Bradley's, that will interest him (& *all* will) to yours & hers all faithfully

Henry James

263. *To Sydney Waterlow*
10 September 1910

Yale MS (Koch Collection)   Unpublished

After a calm voyage HJ, WJ and AHJ reached Quebec on 18 August and came down to Chocorua on 19 August. After 'a heartbreaking unforgettable week' (HJEWL, 169) WJ died on 26 August.

*On 11 September, HJ described to Fanny Prothero 'the drearily-drawn-out pilgrimage to Cambridge', where 'Harvard, meagre mother, did for him – the best that Harvard can. The spirit & the demonstration were of the tenderest – but starved & thin & cold here (*there*) the scene, the background & the rite.' (Unpublished Houghton MS, bMS Am 1094.3 (49).)*

Sydney Waterlow had met WJ in Rye and corresponded with him about A Pluralistic Universe.

My dear Sydney.

Please believe that your word of friendship, of close participation in what we have lately been through is anything but "inopportune" & that I am much touched by it. Dark & dismal enough have things been for us – & the sense of what they might *really* mean was with me, intimately, even during my brother's last three weeks in England; which was why I was too oppressively preoccupied, & too wretchedly anxious, to make the attempt to see you or in any way to take leave of you. We could think but of one thing – the helping him to such a condition that we could embark for home & reach it without the worst disaster. This we did (with Skinner's aid he was encouragingly "better" at the moment of our sailing;) but, in spite of a wonderfully fair &

2. In the U.S., later on, HJ converted *The Outcry* into a novel, published by Methuen and Scribner's on 5 October 1911.

easy voyage, he lost ground swiftly day by day, suffered heartbreakingly, & struggled to his very threshold here (to which we came by one long, dreadful day of rail & motor, straight from Quebec, only to sink &, at the end of seven days, still more heartbreakingly succumb. For though he had wanted for some time before the last only to have it all over, he had previously to that immensely desired to live & do 2 or 3 things that his heart & mind were deeply in – being as he was, to my conviction, in the very plenitude of his noble genius & his admirable intellectual life. The loss of him, to me, personally, pulls to pieces the whole aspect of things (of life & the world;) so far as they *relate* to me.[1] But we must always keep on fighting – & I am, in spite of everything, thank heaven, more & more leaving behind me those miserable months of my own from last January to last mid July; when (at the latter date,) the situation cheered up for me so that I have the unutterably precious memory of having been able to give myself to my beloved brother, helpfully, to the end. And we had admirable help on reaching here (& not counting my sister-in-law's unweariable devotion) to the end. I stay with *her* & her children for some months to come; & *here* in wondrous golden weather – all of which has a kind of saturation of my Brother's presence – for some weeks.[2] I greet your wife ever so faithfully & I am, my dear Sydney, affectionately yours

Henry James

Chocorua, N.H.
Sept. 10. 1910

264. *To Gertrude Kingston*
31 January 1911

King's MS   Unpublished

On 12 December HJ wrote to Pinker from Irving Street about a recent Harper's proposal, which he had declined: 'Duneka's letter anent the "London recollections"

1. HJ told H. G. Wells on 11 September that, 'He had an inexhaustible authority for me, and I feel abandoned and afraid, even as a lost child.' (HJHGW, 125.)
2. Except for a trip to Boston to see Grace Norton and T. S. Perry on 25–9 September (once he had corrected and returned the proofs of *The Finer Grain*), HJ stayed on, 'living here more & more', as he told Edith Wharton, '*into* the difference in the world & the whole aspect of life [made] by the extinction of his so cherished & dominant presence' (HJEWL, 170). On 3 October he told Pinker he was 'well at work' on his conversion of *The Outcry* into a book for

– heaven save the mark, when I think of the treacherous tell-tale personalities, the exploitations of old & intimately interesting & private relations with trusting individuals, that they (he & Harvey) must fondly want & take for granted!' (Unpublished Yale MS, Za James 1, vol. 3.) He later told WJ's widow, though, *'it was in talk with you in that terrible winter of 1910–11 that the impulse to the whole attempt came to me'* (HJL IV, 707) – the impulse, that is, to write a book of recollections about the James family. On 12 January 1911 he sent Pinker the first two of the three books of The Outcry, now a novel which he hoped would be serialized.

Still unwell, he was finding the U.S. uncongenial, writing to Fanny Prothero on 30 December 1910 that, *'Everything* but *the immediate interest & attachment & absorptions of this house is unspeakably flat & unprofitable to me here – the whole face of life (or almost,) frankly & confidentially speaking, affects me as repulsive & appalling.'* (Unpublished Houghton MS, bMS Am 1094.3 (52).) HJ was in New York from mid January 1911 staying with Mary Cadwalader Jones – but became ill again and returned to Cambridge, Massachusetts, on 6 February.

In mid November HJ had posted Pinker a copy of The Saloon from Cambridge, Massachusetts, for possible use by the established actress-manager Gertrude Kingston (d. 1937), who was probably aware of it through HJ's young theatrical neighbour Jack (Sir Frederick John) Pollock (1878–1963), a brilliant historian who had attended Harvard Law School. She built the Little Theatre in London in 1910, and used HJ's play as a curtain-raiser to Cicely Hamilton's Just to Get Married on 17 January 1911. It had a mixed reception; most critics deplored in particular the yelling and screaming towards the climax.

TELEPHONE, 2750 STUYVESANT.
21, EAST ELEVENTH STREET. *New York.*
Jan. 31st 1911

Dear Miss Kingston.

I thank you kindly for your interesting letter – which gives me news of *The Saloon* for which I have naturally not a little yearned. It was with an effort of course that I, after much searching of the heart, resigned myself to the production of the play in my so remote & helpless absence from rehearsals, but your invitation greatly tempted me, & I got all the comfort I could – on deciding to assent – from the fact of my so extremely detailed & numerous expressional & representational indications & aids; with which my Copy fairly bristled &

---

possible serialization; but on 10 October he returned to Boston and went on to New York – not to impose on his grieving sister-in-law – after suffering a slight relapse.

of which I rejoice to hear that so careful account has been taken. I have had time to hear from three or four friends as to the effect of the thing – as to its quality making a way through the interpretation; though none of them (of these private reporters,) I am sorry to say, has spoken of Mr. Vanderlip as adequate, in type or talent, to the rendering of Owen W.[1] By the way that very intellectual & ardent & concentrated young man *should* be rendered I felt that the little play would more or less stand or fall – & I am especially sorry not to have been present enough to deal with that particular question. My friends speak well of Miss Dora Barton & Mr. Halliwell Hobbes (of the latter particularly,) & I beg you to express to each of them my grateful appreciation. I see no newspapers on these occasions – having long since learnt *à quoi m'en tenir* on the general poverty of critical intelligence of the people who "do" the theatres in their columns; but I gather with real dismay that at the final crisis of The Saloon & during the momentary rush of black darkness, some object or figure *appears* on the stage – there is an attempt at the *showing* of the presence or monster that "walks." There is absolutely no warrant or indication for this in my text, & I view any such introduction with the liveliest disapproval. I considered that question (in writing my play,) only to dismiss it – that is to settle it in the sense that the complete & utter dense darkness, lasting only what the fullest flash of *light* would last, represents & covers the whole ground (of the apparition) & that if it is only real & effective darkness what takes place within it (that is the seeing, for the bare but sufficient & deadly instant, of the sudden presence by Owen,) remains invisible & inscrutable, only intensely presumable & *felt*, by the audience. Let me very earnestly request you then to suppress the "figure" – if the darkness is right the figure is utterly wrong.[2] For I hope the little play will have some life – is in fact having it. I don't return to England for three or four months yet, alas, but when I do I shall have the pleasure of seeing you, & I am yours most truly

Henry James

1. Gertrude Kingston's cast included Miss Dora Barton (who had been in many productions by the Incorporated Stage Society) as Kate Julian, and Mr Everard Vanderlip as Owen Wingrave. H. M. Walbrook of the *Pall Mall Gazette* saw the play on 17 January: 'If Miss Dora Barton and Mr. E. Vanderlip had played their little scene with a little more quiet intensity and a little less uproar, they would have got a good deal nearer to the emotional centre of the audience.' (*Nights at the Play* (1911), 116.)

2. The text of *The Saloon* at this point asks for 'a great quick Blackness of deeper Darkness, completely obscuring the cold light from the high window, which passes, like the muffling whirlwind of an Apparition, and has come and gone even as a great flash of light. Out of it has sounded, like a ringing cry of Battle, an immense, recognising "A — a — h!" the last breath of Owen's gasping throat.'

265. To Herbert George Wells
3 March 1911

Bodleian MS   Published HJHGW, 126–9; LHJ II, 180–82

From 4 March HJ sat for his portrait to his nephew Bill – immediately following a protracted series of encounters with Roberts, his Boston dentist.

On WJ's death Wells had sent a touching letter of condolence to HJ and his sister-in-law. He had now sent HJ a copy of his latest novel, The New Machiavelli *(1911), a study of the conflict between politics and sexual passion prompted by the new importance of women. His politically ambitious Liberal, then young Tory eugenicist hero, Dick Remington, leaves his wife Margaret for his mistress Isabel.*

95 IRVING STREET CAMBRIDGE MASSACHUSETTS
March 3d 1911.

My dear Wells.

I seem to have had notice from my housekeeper at Rye that you have very kindly sent me there a copy of the New Machiavelli – which she has forborne to forward me to these Tariff-guarded shores; in obedience to my general instructions. But this needn't prevent me from thanking you for the generous gift, which will keep company with a brave row of other such valued signs of your remembrance at Lamb House: thanking you all the more too that I hadn't waited for gift or guerdon to fall on you & devour you, but have just lately been finding the American issue of your wondrous book a sufficient occasion for that. Thus it is that I can't rest longer till I make you some small sign at last of my conscious indebtedness.

I have read you then, I need scarcely tell you, with an intensified sense of that life & force & temperament, that fulness of endowment & easy impudence of genius, which make you so extraordinary & which have long claimed my unstinted admiration; you being for me so much the most interesting & masterful prose-painter of your English generation (or indeed of your generation unqualified,) that I see you hang there over the subject scene practically all alone; a far-flaring even though turbid & smoky lamp, projecting the most vivid & splendid golden splotches, *creating* them about the field – shining scattered innumerable morsels of a huge smashed mirror. I seem to feel that there can be no better proof of your great gift – *The N.M.* makes me most particularly feel it – than that you bedevil & coerce to the extent you do such a reader & victim as I am; I mean one so engaged on the side of ways &

attempts to which yours are extremely alien & for whom the great interest of the art we practise involves a lot of considerations & preoccupations over which you more & more ride roughshod & triumphant – when you don't, that is, with a strange & brilliant impunity of your own, leave them to one side altogether (which *is* indeed what you now apparently incline most to do.) Your big feeling for life, your capacity for chewing up the thickness of the world in such enormous mouthfuls, while you fairly slobber, so to speak, with the multitudinous taste – this constitutes for me a rare & wonderful & admirable exhibition, on your part, in itself, so that one should doubtless frankly ask one's self what the devil, in the way of effect & evocation & general demonic activity, one wants more. Well, I am willing for today to let it stand at that; the whole of the earlier part of the book, or the first half, is so alive & kicking & sprawling! – so vivid & rich and strong – above all so *amusing* (in the high sense of the word;) and I make my remonstrance – for I do remonstrate – bear upon the bad service you have done your cause by riding so hard again that accurst autobiographic form which puts a premium on the loose, the improvised, the cheap & the easy. Save in the fantastic & the romantic (Copperfield, Jane Eyre, that charming thing of Stevenson's with the bad title – "Kidnapped"?) it has no authority, no persuasive or convincing force – its grasp of reality & truth isn't strong & disinterested. R. Crusoe, e.g., isn't a novel at all. There is, to my vision, no authentic, & no really interesting & no *beautiful*, report of things on the novelist's, the painter's part unless a particular detachment has operated, unless the great stewpot or crucible of the imagination, of the observant & recording & interpreting mind in short, has intervened & played its part – & this detachment, this chemical transmutation for the aesthetic, the representational, end is terribly wanting in autobiography brought, as the horrible phrase is, up to date. That's my main "criticism" on *The N.M.* – & on the whole ground there would be a hundred things more to say. It's accurst that I am not near enough to you to say them in less floundering fashion than this – but give me time (I return to England in June, never again, D.V., to leave it – surprise Mr. Remington thereby as I may!) & we will jaw as far as you will keep me company.[1] Meanwhile I don't *want* to send across the wintry sea anything but my expressed gratitude for the immense impressionistic & speculative wealth & variety of your book. Yours, my dear Wells, ever

Henry James

1. Remington finally leaves England with his mistress Isabel, repudiating in particular its sexual hypocrisy: 'I was never given a light, never given a touch of natural manhood by all this dingy, furtive, canting, humbugging English world. Thank God! I'll soon be out of it!'

P.S. I think the exhibition of "Love" *as* "love" – functional Love – always suffers from a certain inevitable & insurmountable flatfootedness (for the reader's nerves &c;) which is only to be counterplotted by roundabout arts – as by tracing it through indirectness & tortuosities of application & effect – to keep it somehow interesting & productive (though I don't mean *re*productive!) But this again is a big subject.[2]

P.S. 2 I am like your hero's forsaken wife: I know *having* things (the things of life, history, the world,) only as, & by, *keeping* them. So, & so only, I *do* have them![3]

266. To Lady Victoria Welby
[August? 1911]

Unknown MS or TS   Published OD, 341–2

HJ went down to New York on 15 March to stay with Mary Cadwalader Jones, returning to Cambridge on 20 April after a relapse. He travelled to Connecticut on 20 May to stay with Theodate Pope Riddle (1868–1946) (she was an architect and collector of Impressionist paintings) at Farmington, and with his Emmet cousins at Salisbury, then moved on via Cambridge on 5 June to George Abbott James's house on a breezy promontory at Nahant, where he stayed, with visits to Chocorua and Edith Wharton at Lenox, till going down to New York on 1 August to board the Mauretania.

Victoria Alexandrina Maria Louisa Stuart Wortley, afterwards the Honourable Lady Victoria Alexandrina Maria Louisa Welby Gregory (1837–1912), was Queen Victoria's god-daughter and a philosophical, even mystical, theorist of language (e.g. What is Meaning? Studies in the Development of Significance *(1903)). On 2 September 1892 HJ sent WJ 'the "Semantic" lucubrations of the tiresome*

2. HJ's postscript may have been suggested by Remington's rhetorical questions about his rapturous love for Isabel: 'But here I come to untellable things ... What can a record of contrived meetings, of sundering difficulties evaded and overcome, signify here? Or what can it convey to say that one looked deep into two dear, steadfast eyes, or felt a heart throb and beat, or gripped soft hair softly in a trembling hand?'

3. HJ is perhaps answering Remington's set of contrasts between himself and his wife Margaret: 'She was loyal to pledges and persons, sentimental and faithful; I am loyal to ideas and instincts, emotional and scheming. My imagination moves in broad gestures; hers was delicate with a real dread of extravagance ... I like the facts of the case and to mention everything; I like naked bodies and the jolly smells of things. She abounded in reservations, in circumlocutions and evasions, in keenly appreciated secondary points.'

though most sweet & beautiful Lady Welby, who sends me them for that purpose
& desires to know you. I think she is crazy – though a lovely type.' (CWJ II, 230.)
On 20 September, possibly after reading Witnesses to Ambiguity *(1891), WJ*
replied that 'She is a monster of erudition as well as a person of a great deal of
sense and acuteness' (CWJ II, 233); he corresponded with her, 1905–8.

This suggestive fragment of a letter can be dated as after Macmillan's publication
in June of her Significs and Language: The Articulate Form of our Expressive
and Interpretative Resources *(1911); and probably after HJ's return to England.*

I take it most kindly of you to have caused my name to figure with honour
on the title-page of *Significs* and then to have sent me that so deeply suggestive
and interesting volume, which I have read with earnest attention and rich
profit.[1] You have so many ideas, and you launch and start so many, that mere
recognition of your freighted vessel seems but a poor form and yet any
overhauling of the cargo a formidable job. I must content myself with assuring
you, all responsively, that nothing in the world appeals to me more than the
question of expression or leaves me more dismally wonder-struck than the
neglect and dishonour in which it languishes – at the same time that as a
would-be artist I am oppressed with the difficulties (distraught and half-paralysed
by a sense of them) with which all "ideal" and extensions of the matter bristle
– and the sweep of your extensions is sublime. The universe so seems to me
to strain its expression itself to breaking that I ask myself how such a cockle-boat
of a compromise as art can pretend to live in such a sea. For *there* is the hitch
– that one somehow feels (at least I in my feebleness do) that expression is, at
the most insurmountably, a compromise. Has it not, in the interest of finite
form, to *keep* compromising, ever; for the sake of certain effects that our
precious *quand même* – our poor, human, limping, fallacious associational *quand
même* – values? That is, I mean, in the said – so very ambiguous after all –
world of art; which isn't the greatest of all things, I seem to make out, but
only the second greatest! Poetry strains expression to the cracking-point. I

1. Victoria Welby had taken as her epigraph the passage from *The Question of Our Speech*
beginning: 'All life therefore comes back to the question of our speech, the medium through
which we communicate with each other . . .' Her preface: 'Significs may be briefly and provisionally defined as the study of the nature of Significance in all its forms and relations, and thus of
its working in every possible sphere of human interest and purpose.' She advocates reforms of
language to combat 'our contented subjection to the tyranny of misfitting Expression'. A
respectful anonymous short review in *The Times Literary Supplement* (8 June) asks, 'What, after
all, are exactly "the forward step," "the undreamt-of height," the rebirth of language, over
which Lady Welby waxes almost dithyrambic?'

mean the greatest has done so; with Dante and Shakespeare it cracks and splits perpetually, and yet we like it so tortured and suffering. Does not that mean that its very weaknesses (with the great waves and winds of reality beating upon it – upon *them*) may have a beauty, or a value for life, or a power for interest, that would make of the adequate or infinite reflector – comparatively – a great splendid sterile victory?

However I mustn't venture on too deep waters – further than thus to show you how brilliantly you attract pursuit there. I feel the matter but as an intensely ingenious proser who adores the medium – it is impossible to adore it more – but for whom that precious property resembles rather a vast box of relics and heirlooms and old wondrous stamped ducats and doubloons than – what shall I say? a bank-book of blank cheques signed for me with whatever solvency! . . .

267. To Henry James III (nephew)
26 November 1911

Houghton MS   Unpublished

HJ returned from America having corrected Scribner's proof of The Outcry, *which was published in Britain and America on 5 October, to friendly reviews. On 19 November he told Edith Wharton, who had written to him about it, that, 'You speak at your ease, chère Madame, of the interminable & formidable job of my producing à mon âge another Golden Bowl – the most arduous & thankless task I ever set myself . . . I shld. have to go back & live for 2 continuous years at Lamb House to write it (living on dried herbs & cold water – for "staying power" – meanwhile;) & that would be very bad for me, wd. probably indeed put an end to me altogether. My own sense is that I don't want, & oughtn't to try, to attack ever again anything* longer *(save for about 70 or 80 pages more,) than The Outcry. That is déjà assez difficile – the "artistic economy" of that inferior little product being a much more calculated & ciphered, much more cunning & (to use your sweet expression) crafty one than that of five G.B.'s.' (HJEWL, 197.)*

After his illness in Lamb House, he told Theodora Bosanquet on 25 October, he found Rye 'unmistakeably too dreary & unpropitious again' – 'London proves extraordinarily good for me & there I am getting back to work'. And on 11 November he declared, 'what I really want most is just to get back to the dear old Remington tick' (Unpublished Houghton MSS, bMS Eng 1213 (38 & 41)). On 13 November he told WJ's widow he had arranged to dictate to Miss Bosanquet in her and Miss Bradley's Chelsea flat, a taxi-ride from Pall Mall – a sign of 'the yearning effort really to get, more surely & swiftly now, up to my neck into the book about WJ &

the rest of us'. Continuing that letter on 19 November, he also promised to write to Harry, who was to edit WJ's letters, to 'tell him how I am entirely at one with him about the kind *of use to be made by me of all these early things, the kind of setting they must have, the kind of encompassment that the book, as* my *book, my play of reminiscence & almost of brotherly autobiography, & filial autobiography not less, must enshrine them in. The book I see & feel will be difficult & unprecedented & perilous – but if I bring it off it will be exquisite & unique; bring it off as I inwardly project it & oh so devoutly desire it.' (Unpublished Houghton MS, bMS Am 1094 (1722).)*

> Telephone: 21 Epping. Station & Telegraph Office: Epping 3 miles.
> Hill   Theydon Mount   Epping.
> Nov. 26th *1911*

Dearest Harry.

I'll be hanged if I don't use this Sunday a.m. here to acknowledge your so fine long letter of – I haven't it with me, alas, & forget the date, but the one accompanying your last most precious packet of your Dad's younger letters typecopied.[1] I am putting in the "week-end" here, under earnest pressure – here where I spent that strange three weeks with your Mother a year & ½ ago (after your Dad had gone off from Lamb House to Paris & to Nauheim, where we presently joined him.) It would in spite of its immense hospitality & kindness – that is its ever-wonderful hostess's; who is as strenuously & overwhelmingly munificent *as* ever – be rather haunted with the sense of that tragic time for me, were it not that under the spell of your mother's devotion I then took the signal *turn* of my miserable illness in her company here, consciously & measurably began to get better & be of some use again, even eventually, during the following weeks to your Dad, & came away hence quite different from the state in which I had arrived: all of which gives me a certain kindness to the scene *quand même* – by which I mean even a little too in spite of the fact that Mrs. Hunter's fine bright & rather intense remindingness, her urgency to me to come, to come often, to come always, didn't rather rise as a menace to future peace & ease in town; the place being so near London as to make pretexts & facilities & motor-lifts immensely workable. I am on such good terms with London now (in spite of *its* too much & too many of everything – of every one,) & am so fond of the dear old Victorian Sunday, just as it

---

1. On 13 November HJ had told his sister-in-law, 'I have written to Harry to ask him for certain of the young, youthful letters (copies of them) which I didn't bring away with me.' (Unpublished Houghton MS cited *supra*.)

used pleasantly to be in my earlier years there, that the recurrent week-end of the present intense modernness, with its specious motor-car, its fevered & overshadowed Saturday & its blighted & sacrificed Monday forenoon, most precious part of the day, easily becomes too much of a good thing & really cuts down the real value of the week. However, one has only to sit firm & do what one conveniently can & no more – the remedy is in one's own hands. It's very lovely here today, which is radiant & mild, & though the smallish party isn't very interesting it is very easy, & Sargent, of whom I am fond, comes down in an hour for the rest of the day. (Helleu, the brilliant French portrait-draughtsman – a great friend of S. – is here with his curious black & hairy & so-called beautiful young daughter.)[2] But it isn't of all *these* things I wished to write you, but of the interest & pleasure I take in your response to my asking for more – from your Dad; & in my understanding that you have still something more to send me. I am absolutely at one with you as to your idea of the atmosphere & setting that should flow round & encircle all these things – and that should (& shall) be filled with all the evocations that I can summon up of the old figures & feelings & times, all the personal & social & subjective (& *ob*jective) furniture of our family annals. Seen this way & in the light of my own "genius", the whole subject-matter opens out to me most appealingly & beguilingly, & if you will but trust me so to *keep* seeing it & doing it, I think something altogether beautiful & interesting & remarkable & rare will be the issue – for I now have got thoroughly into the vein & the current; so much so that I hope really to go very straight & uninterruptedly & quite swiftly. There are things I shall have to communicate with you about, things I shall have to ask you – but minor & accessory matters all, & easy & not numerous. After a little I shall put you some of these questions. Is it possible to you meanwhile to send me by book-post two of your Grandfather's volumes that were in your Dad's possession: *Lectures & Miscellanies* & *The Church of Christ &c.*[3] I want to *do* your Grandfather so beautifully & tenderly. I rejoice to say that my renewal of co-operation with Miss Bosanquet is bearing steady fruit & seems most propitious, & that my so reasonable & convenient little arrangement with her for the 2 small (yet amply sufficient) rooms annexed to her own & Miss Bradley's premises makes an admirable footing for quiet forenoon labour, off & away from the central flurry of the town. The blest

2. Paul César Helleu (1859–1927) studied with Gérôme and at the Académie Julien; and received encouragement and help from Sargent at a vital stage in his career. Percy Grainger was also present.

3. Henry James Senior's *Lectures and Miscellanies* (1852) is mentioned in *Notes of a Son and Brother*, unlike *The Church of Christ Not an Ecclesiasticism: A Letter to a Sectarian* (1854) (an attack on formalistic institutional religion).

London taxi makes my whole relation to them highly possible & convenient, & I regard the situation in short as giving me all I could at present require. The only shadow on the picture is the desolation of Lamb House – I mean in the persons of Kidd, Burgess & Joanna; but with this, for the present & under my great need & profit, I must make my account.[4] They are on very reasonable board-wages – but it's their boredom over nothing to do that preys on them. However, I go down to see them when I can, & I shall not let that part of the case poison my now so much more salubrious cup. I most yearningly hope that Peg's improvement continues & send her, & to your Mother, to whom I rather lately wrote, the tenderest love. So do I hope that Bill's engagement has ceased now to prevent his working & is in fact making him work but the more nobly.[5] If dear Aleck would make me happy – but I must write to tell him how he can do it. May your own great life go on meanwhile to greater greatness, as your greatness of soul will carry you through anything & everything.

Ever your fond old Uncle
Henry James

268. To Henry Mackinnon Walbrook
5 January 1912

Houghton TC   Published TULM, 493–5

After his London autumn HJ went down to Rye on 30 December. Henry Mackinnon Walbrook (1865–1941), dramatic critic of the Pall Mall Gazette *(1906–15), had praised* The Saloon *in a review reprinted in his* Nights at the Play *(1911), which HJ found at Lamb House on his arrival. He wrote in thanks in 'the last half-hour of 1911' to remark that Walbrook's judgements 'tend to sin a little, to my sense, by excess of geniality . . . deserting the question of the play, and what is to be said on all that ground, for the question of the actors' (TULM, 492).*

4. Minnie Kidd was the house-parlour maid, Burgess Noakes the butler-valet, and Joan Anderson the cook-housekeeper.
5. Peggy James had suffered from severe depression in the aftermath of her father's death; then had an appendectomy in May. HJ's painter-nephew, Bill, got engaged to Alice Runnells in September 1911 and they married in January 1912. Aleck was training as a painter at the Boston Museum School.

Lamb House, Rye.
January 5th, 1912.

Dear H. M. Walbrook,

I have troubled your spirit, I fear, more than lighted your path, and this mustn't be. I quite understand your consciousness of what the hungry histrions *want* in the way of adulation – following as they do the most personal, the most self-exhibitional of trades, the one that makes the men as vain and jealous and touchy as the women, and the women still more of all those things than nature had already made them. Largely that fact is the great *désagrément* and drawback of your own office – that you have to say personal things about intense and importunate and irritable persons, and that you greatly shrink from unfavourably affecting their value to the theatres that enable them to live &c. I agree with you that to the mere natural man (and gentleman) that kind of good-nature and delicacy about them much imposes itself – so much more imposes itself than anything else does, that for my own part the "false position" involved in the matter would make, in London, such posts as yours impossible to me – once the ingenuous flush of youth had gone by. It hasn't, with you, gone by – so *stick* to your post. *For* one must care for the Theatre and the Drama as the late inimitable and incorruptible Francisque Sarcey did, in Paris, for his Forty Years; one must take it with his ferocious seriousness and with his intensity of conviction; to let the care for individuals, as compared with the care for the art and the Truth and the Right, and the rigour of the high standard, and the critic's critical honour and integrity, matter as little, and as not one farthing's worth, as he systematically did.[1] The real relief, in your case, seems to me to be in this, that, comparatively speaking, the actors matter so little – so little compared with the interest and dignity of the question of the play itself – that very little attention need be given to them at all. If you follow up the questions raised, critically, by the play, follow them up further than (if you'll very amiably let me – also very amiably! – say so) you strike me as on the whole inclined to do, I think you will find the actor-questions fall very naturally into their normal modest relation (to the others) and take care of themselves. *And*, dear young man, you will thereby nobly *help the great cause* – that of righting and overhauling the monstrous disproportion, *false* proportion, that has come, in this country, to get established between the drama itself, the responsible originating sources of it, the matters at issue in the play, the authority of the author &c, and the wretched ruck of the interpretation.

1. Francisque Sarcey (1827–99) was dramatic critic of *Le Temps* from 1867 and the arch-defender of the technical traditions of the Théâtre Français. His *Quarante ans de théâtre: feuilletons dramatiques* appeared posthumously in 1900.

That has produced the state of things in which the actor-manager is so grotesquely possible, and in which he and his train are so tremendously cocks of the walk. America makes it still worse – in America no one but the actor is regarded as of the theatre at all; with results of a colossal vulgarity. Of course such a condition couldn't have been created here at all but for the ineptitude and inferiority of the playwrights themselves, pretty well up to our own hour – their poor dissociation from the intellectual life of the country.[2] This has deprived them utterly of authority and *position* – or at least it very effectually had up to day before yesterday. If they are intelligent enough and able enough they can *recover* their place and proportion (or in the case of most of them, the actual ones, it would have to be, quite primarily, gain it.) The point is that the critic can there greatly *aid* them – from outside; though of course the thing must be essentially and fundamentally done from inside. I commend to you the high emprise – I sound the trumpet for your charge. May I even go a little further while I am about it? – moved as I am to illustrate by a case or two what I mean by re-establishing the proportions and getting *into* the question of the play. Some of the performances in your book I happen to have been present at, and I am rather possessed of the sense of where your chance, in these connections, would have been, and where you seem not to have quite seen your way to take it. As to "Don", the "Chorus Girl", "The Mollusc", "Irene Wycherley" there were, e.g., oh *such* desirable and urgent and edifying and interesting things to say and points to make and discriminations to drive home, that if I had been near you on those occasions I would have taken the liberty of tenderly seizing and holding you and saying to you: "No, my dear boy, you shall *not* chuck those happy chances for a righteous criticism, those peculiar intensities of appeal by reason of perpetrated ineptitude, you shan't turn your back so quickly and squarely upon them and address yourself almost only to the actor-people, for that simply shirks all the responsibilities and begs all the questions. Therefore only over my prostrate form – !"[3] However, I overwhelm you with words, and you will ask yourself *why*, and what you have

---

2. In August 1909, in a letter sent to John Galsworthy for reading out before a Joint Select Committee of Lords and Commons looking into the licensing of plays, HJ had asserted another cause of the same effect: 'I *do* consider that the situation made by the Englishman of letters ambitious of writing for the stage has less dignity – thanks to the Censor's arbitrary rights upon his work – than that of any other man of letters in Europe, and that this fact may well be, or rather *must* be, deterrent to men of any intellectual independence and self-respect.' (HJL IV, 532.)

3. The plays in question are: *Don: A Comedy in Three Acts* (1909) by Rudolf Besier; *The Chorus Lady* (1909) by an unnamed playwright (HJ seems to confuse it with *The Chorus Girl* (1907) by Arthur Applin); *The Mollusc* (1907), a comedy by Hubert Henry Davies; and *Irene Wycherley* (1909) by Anthony P. Wharton.

done to draw down such an invidious avalanche. Were it not for this I should almost have been capable of telling you what *I* should portentously have said in the particular cases I have named almost at hazard. So you see what you lose! And I should have put before you how such critics as Jules Lemaître and Emile Faguet, in their admirable series of "Impressions" and "Propos" de Théâtre respectively, have reprinted *all* their notices with the space *all* given to the pieces themselves and the questions raised by them and the points of interpretation either relegated to the very fewest words or dropped altogether.[4] They have the excellent position thus that justice to the play, in each case, and attention to the claims of the drama, have *demanded* that. I have even the impression that Faguet, for the reprinted Propos, *cut out* any allusion to the actor-people that might sometimes have tagged a little at his ends; on the ground that the Play was the thing, *the* thing; whereby the Propos are a rounded record of the Drama in France during the particular years (playhouse or no playhouse;) and proportionately complete and serious in consequence.

But you have long since called a halt – my zeal (for "the Drama in England"!) *is* distinctly excessive; and the moral of the whole thing is that you must absolutely come to tea with me one day, as soon as I get back to town – as to which I shall make you an earnest sign.[5] Yours all faithfully,

Henry James

P.S. Kindly feel that I have delivered myself in the foregoing after a fashion that is really "private and confidential!"

269. To Herbert George Wells
25 March 1912

Bodleian MS   Published HJHGW, 161–3; HJL IV, 608–10

In 1910 Edmund Gosse had succeeded in establishing 'An Academic Committee of English Letters', to match the Académie Française, under the aegis of the Royal Society of Letters, including to begin with Conrad, Hardy, Andrew Lang, Pinero, Yeats and HJ. Kipling and Shaw refused membership. In March 1912 Wells was elected but refused to join, and Gosse and HJ attempted to change his mind. HJ wrote on 20 March to Gosse – 'Wells's attitude is indeed tiresome' (SLHJEG,

4. Jules Lemaître (1853–1914) and Émile Faguet (1847–1916) were both dramatic critics for the *Journal des débats*. Lemaître published ten volumes of *Impressions de théâtre* (1888–98); Faguet's *Propos de théâtre, etc.* came out in 1903.
5. HJ's diary shows that Walbrook did not come to tea till 11 May.

263) – and to Wells: 'Don't make too much of rigours & indifferences, of consistencies
& vows; I have no greater affinity with associations & academies than you – a priori;
& yet I find myself glad to have done the simple, civil, social easiest thing in
accepting my election – touched by the amenity and geniality of the thought that
we shall probably make something collectively – in addition to what we may make
individually.' (HJL IV, 608.) On 25 March HJ had back, as he told Gosse, a
letter written that day from Wells 'very amiable to us in general & to H.J. in
particular, but I think inexorable & immutable' (SLHJEG, 264). Wells declared
'an insurmountable objection to Literary or Artistic Academies as such, to any
hierarchies, any suggestion of controls or fixed standards in these things . . . This
world of ours, I mean the world of creative and representative work we do, is I am
convinced best anarchic.' (HJHGW, 160.)

105, PALL MALL, S.W.
March 25*th 1912*

My dear Wells.

Your letter is none the less interesting for being what, alas, I believed it
might be; in spite of which interest – or in spite of which belief at least – here
I am at you again! I know perfectly what you mean by your indifference to
Academies & Associations, Bodies & Boards, on all this ground of ours; no
one should know better, as it is precisely my own state of mind – really caring
as I do for nothing in the world but lonely patient virtue, which doesn't seek
that company. Nevertheless I fondly hoped that it might end for you as it did,
under earnest invitation, for me – in your having said & felt all those things
& then joined – for the general amenity & civility & unimportance of the thing,
giving it the benefit of the doubt – for the sake of the good-nature. You will
say that you *had* no doubt & couldn't therefore act on any; but that germ, alas,
was what my letter sought to implant – in addition to its not being a question
of your acting, but simply of your *not* (that is of your not refusing, but simply
lifting your oar and letting yourself float on the current of acclamation.) There
would be no question of your being entangled or hampered, or even, I think,
of your being bored; the common ground between all lovers & practitioners
of our general form would be under your feet so *naturally* & not at all out of
your way; & it wouldn't be you in the least who would have to take a step
backward or aside, it would be *we* gravitating toward you, melting into your
orbit as a mere more *direct* effect of the energy of your genius. Your plea of
your being anarchic & seeing your work as such isn't in the least, believe me,
a reason against; for (also believe me) you are essentially wrong about that!
No talent, no imagination, no application of art, as great as yours are is able

not to make much less for anarchy than for a continuity & coherency much bigger than any disintegration. There's no representation, no picture (which is your form,) that isn't by its very nature preservation, association, & of a positive associational *appeal* – that is the very grammar of it; none that isn't thereby some sort of interesting or curious *order*: I utterly defy it in short not to make, all the anarchy in the world aiding, far more than it unmakes – just as I utterly defy the anarchic to express itself representationally, art aiding, talent aiding, the play of invention aiding, in short *you* aiding, without the grossest[,] the absurdest inconsistency. So it is that you are *in* our circle anyhow you can fix it, & with us drawing always more around (though always at a respectful & considerate distance,) fascinatedly to admire & watch – all to the greater glory of the English name & the brave, as brave as possible, English array; the latter brave even with the one American blotch upon it. Oh *patriotism*! – that mine, the mere paying guest in the house, should have its credit more at heart than its unnatural, its proud & perverse son! However, all this isn't to worry or to weary (I wish it *could*!) your ruthlessness; it's only to drop a sigh on my shattered dream that you might have come among us with as much freedom as grace. I prolong the sigh as I think how much you might have done for *our* freedom – and how little we could do against yours![1]

Don't answer or acknowledge this unless it may have miraculously moved you by some quarter of an inch. But then oh *do*! – though I must warn you that I shall in that case follow it up to the death!

Yours all faithfully
Henry James.

270. *To Arthur Christopher Benson*
9 *May 1912*

Bodleian MS   Published HJLACBAM, 82

On 7 May the Browning Centenary was commemorated at Caxton Hall, London, with Edmund Gosse chairing proceedings for the Academic Committee of the Royal Society of Literature. After sitting through an overlong paper by Pinero on Browning

1. The next day HJ told Gosse that Wells had found him at the Reform Club 'at luncheon-time' and convinced HJ 'that he is right about himself & that he wouldn't at all do among us from the moment our whole literary side – or indeed any literary side anywhere – is a matter of such indifference to him as I feel it to be today – to an extent I hadn't been aware of. He has cut loose from literature clearly – practically altogether: he will still do a lot of writing probably – but it won't be *that*.' (SLHJEG, 265.)

as a dramatist, HJ delivered to a rapt audience 'The Novel in "The Ring and the Book"', emphasizing Browning's 'exhibition of the great constringent relation between man and woman at once at its maximum and as the relation most worth while in life for either party' (LC I, 809). Two days earlier he had written to Pinker about the planned collection it would become part of (Notes on Novelists): 'a considerable array of critical papers etc. which have accumulated on my hands during these latter years and which I have always meant to gather in. But I must take some free little time to go over them much again for revision and titivation.' (Unpublished Yale TS, Za James 1, vol. 3.)

105 Pall Mall, S.W.
May 9th *1912*.

My dear Arthur.

It's beautiful of you to have breathed upon me so balmily as to that rather abortive occasion (so far as I was concerned,) of Tuesday.[1] My intensely literary & quasi-technical subject (the only approach possible to the big bristling Browning *total*, which would have been wholly unmanageable,) was inordinately thankless, & my large, promiscuous and so predominantly female & frumpy audience disconcertingly unreachable.[2] (I had taken for granted a company of men of letters – on my own comparatively private premises.) So I lost heart & voice & almost consciousness – lost everything (almost too) but your esteem & confidence, & that of a few other children of light – with Percy L. as the most torch-waving.[3] In this I rejoice – to the effect of being therefore on my side but the more & more affectionately yours,

Henry James

1. To Jessie Allen HJ remarked on 12 May: 'Don't regret having missed the Browning address – I really clucked to no great purpose *there* (owing to conditions which I won't, can't, rehearse to you – and the omelette into which the elements resolved themselves had got cold and clammy by the time it was served.)' (Lettere, 122.)

2. Accepting Gosse's invitation on 5 February, HJ was still hesitating between subjects: 'I shall make up my distracted mind between 2 things: a shy at the subject of (as who should say) "The Browning of one's Youth"; or, quite differently, a go at "The Ring & the Book as a Novel" (or perhaps better "The Novel in the Ring & the Book.") I predominate toward the latter.' (SLHJEG, 261.)

3. Percy Lubbock and Howard Sturgis were present in support.

271. To Hugh Walpole
14 August 1912

Texas MS   Partly published LHJ II, 244–6

On 26 June an honorary doctorate of letters at Oxford was conferred on 'Henricum James'. On 11 July he went down to Lamb House, and on 16 July told his nephew Harry of his work on the 'Family Book': 'in doing this book I am led, by the very process and action of my idiosyncrasy, on and on into more evocation and ramification of old images and connections, more intellectual and moral autobiography (though all closely and, as I feel it, exquisitely associated and involved,) than I shall quite know what to do with – to do with, that is, in this book' (LHJ II, 240). On 7 August, back in Lamb House after a whirlwind motor tour with Edith Wharton from 21 July to 4 August which had culminated in a recurrence of HJ's angina, he told Pinker that, 'What I really make out is that I seem to have sufficient material, quite, for two *books, two distinct ones, taking the place of the one multifarious and comprehensive one that I originally saw.' At first he saw these as to begin with a two-volume (Early and Late) Letters of William James, which he would 'duly and vividly* biographise'*, and then a larger book (Unpublished Yale TS, Za James 1, vol. 3).*

Walpole had published Mr Perrin and Mr Traill: A Tragi-Comedy, *a novel of paranoid fixation drawing on Walpole's schoolmastering experience at Epsom College, with Mills & Boon in January 1911. HJ had introduced Walpole to the widowed Lady Lovelace, formerly Mary Wortley, who had married Byron's grandson in 1880, and the two novelists had recently spent a weekend (6–8 July 1912) at her Ockham Park in Surrey with other guests including Wilde's ally Robert Ross and Lady Florence Bell. Walpole's diary: 'Such a day! H.J. talking all the time. Described Daudet's meeting with Meredith, smashed Mrs. Tanqueray, argued with Robbie about the drama, long walk with me during which I told him about* Fortitude *and he approved. Final summing-up of everyone to me in the small hours of the morning.' (HWB, 94.)*

LAMB HOUSE, RYE, SUSSEX.

Dearest little Hugh.

When is it not a wonder & a joy to me to hear from you, whatever your news – that is your good news – may be?[1] Your best is certainly that of my living still in your faithful affection, as you, darling boy, live in that of your

---

1. HJ complained of the brevity of Walpole's notes to him, and preserved few of them. This one is not known to survive.

fondest Methusaleh. I rejoice that you wander to such good purpose – by which I mean nothing more exemplary than that you apparently live in the light of curiosity & cheer. I'm very glad for you that these gentle passions have the succulent scene of Munich to pasture in. I haven't been there for long years – was never there but once at all, but haven't forgotten how genial & sympathetic I found it.[2] Drink deep of every impression & have a lot to tell me when the prodigal returns. I love travellers' tales – especially when I love the traveller: therefore have plenty to thrill me & to confirm that passion withal. I travel no further than this, & never shall again; but it serves my lean purposes, or most of them, & I'm thankful to be able to do so much & to feel even these quiet & wholesome little facts about me. We're having in this rude clime a summer of particularly bad & brutal manners – so far the sweetness of the matter fails; but I get out in the lulls of the tempest (it does nothing but rain & rage,) & when I'm within my mind still to me a kingdom is, however dismembered & shrunken. I haven't seen a creature to talk of *you* with – but I see on these terms very few creatures indeed; none worth speaking of, still less worth talking to. Clearly *you* move still in the human maze – but I like to think of you there; may it be long before you find the clue to the exit. You say nothing of any return to *these* platitudes, so I suppose you are to be still a good while on the war-path; but when you are ready to smoke the pipe of peace come & ask *me* for a light. It's good for you to have read Taine's English Lit.; he lacks saturation, lacks *waste* of acquaintance, but sees with a magnificent objectivity, reacts with an energy to match, expresses with a splendid amplitude, & has just the critical value, I think, of being so off, so *far* (given such an intellectual reach,) & judging & feeling in so different an air.[3] It's charming to me that the Ambassadors have again engaged & still beguile you; it *is* probably a very *packed* production, with a good deal of one thing within another; I remember sitting on it, when I wrote it, with that intending weight & pressure with which you probably often sit in these days on your trunk to make the lid close & *all* your trousers & boots go in. I remember putting in a good deal about Chad & Strether, or Strether & Chad, rather; & am not

2. HJ was there for two days in September 1872, escorting AJ and his Aunt Kate. He told his parents then: 'It's a singular place and one difficult to write of with a serious countenance. It has a fine lot of old pictures, but otherwise it is a nightmare of pretentious vacuity: a city of chalky stucco – a Florence and Athens in canvas and planks.' (SL2, 94.)
3. Reviewing an English translation of Taine's *History of English Literature* in the *Atlantic Monthly* in April 1872, HJ had commented that Taine 'writes from an avowedly foreign stand-point', and that 'his treatment of the subject lacks that indefinable quality of spiritual initiation which is the tardy consummate fruit of a wasteful, purposeless, passionate sympathy' (LC II, 842, 843).

sure that I quite understand what in that connection you miss – I mean in the way of what *could* be there. The whole thing is of course, to intensity, a picture of relations – & among them is, though not on the first line, the relation of Strether to Chad. The relation of Chad to Strether is a limited & according to my method only implied & indicated thing, sufficiently there; but Strether's to Chad consists above all in a charmed & yearning & wondering sense, a dimly envious sense, of all Chad's young living & easily-taken *other* relations; other not only than the one to him, but than the one to Mme de Vionnet & whoever else: this very sense, & the sense of Chad, generally, is a part, a large part, of poor dear Strether's discipline, development, adventure & general history. All of it that is of my subject seems to me given – given by dramatic projection, as all the rest is given: how can you say I do anything so foul & abject as to "state"? You deserve that I should condemn you to read the book over once again! However, instead of this I only impose that you come down to me, on your return, for a couple of days – when we can talk better.[4] I hold you to the heart of your truest old

H.J.

Aug. 14*th*. 1912.

272. *To Mrs Humphry Ward*
24 October 1912

Virginia TS   Published LHJ II, 265–7

On 9 September HJ reported to Pinker that 'in going over more searchingly my work of the past winter I can't help recognizing in it – that is in a mere portion of it, for the moment – the stuff, already highly finished and, as it were, deliverable – of a beautiful little book of about 70000 words, complete in itself, carrying the record concerned in it up to my twelfth *year (!!!) and of the most enchanting effect!' This would become* A Small Boy and Others, *a title which he told Pinker on 29 September 'exactly describes the volume' (Unpublished Yale TS, MS, Za James 1, vol. 3). On 9 October Pinker told Scribner that HJ now intended to defer using WJ's letters, and* A Small Boy and Others *(sent by the same post, complete but for twenty or twenty-five pages) was published in the spring of 1913. On 15 November*

4. Walpole came down to Rye, 19–21 September. His diary records HJ as saying: 'I've had one great passion in my life – the intellectual passion. What that has been for me I cannot say. Make it your rule to encourage the impersonal interests as against the personal – but remember also that they are interdependent.' (HWB, 94.)

Pinker specified that Notes of a Son and Brother *(originally* Memories ...*) would use WJ's early letters and appear in the autumn of 1913.*

Theodora Bosanquet found HJ a possible flat at 21 Carlyle Mansions in Cheyne Walk, Chelsea, and he viewed and took it on 2 October, returning unwell to Rye next day. On 4 October he noted in his diary: 'Possibility of Shingles *– confirmed on going to bed by appearance of body, left side, of vivid red welts – sores – blisters. Unmistakeable shingles – and relief to know it.' (N, 368.) The illness was to last into 1913. On 8 October HJ told Pinker he was dazzled by but suspicious of an offer from Scribner's of an $8,000 advance for a novel to be serialized and then added to the New York Edition, with a lowering of the royalty to 10 per cent. In fact, as Edith Wharton, who had nominated HJ for the Nobel Prize in 1911, noted later, it was a charitable conspiracy: 'I gave Mr. Scribner this $8000 from the earnings of* The House of Mirth *to encourage H.J. to go on writing, as he was so despondent about his work.' (R. W. B. Lewis,* Edith Wharton: A Biography, *342.)*

Mrs Humphry Ward wrote sympathetically on 23 October that 'I do know the pain & grief of shingles – horrid thing', saying also she wanted to hear him about Wells's Marriage *'and a score of other things!' (Unpublished Honnold MS, Mrs Humphry Ward Collection, Special Collections).*

Dictated.
LAMB HOUSE, RYE, SUSSEX.
October 24th., 1912.

My dear Mary Ward.

I feel I *must* really thank you afresh, even by the freedom of this impersonal mechanism, for your renewed expression of kindness – very soothing and sustaining to me in my still rather dreary case. I am doing my utmost to get better, but the ailment has apparently endless secrets of its own for preventing that; an infernal player with still another and another vicious card up his sleeve. This is precisely why your generous accents touch me – making me verily yearn as I think of the balm I should indeed find in talking with you of the latest products of those producers (few though they be) who lend themselves in a degree to remark. I have but within a day or two permitted myself a modicum of remark to H. G. Wells – who had sent me "Marriage"; but I should really rather have addressed the quantity to you, on whom it's not so important I should make my impression.[1] I mean I should be in your case comparatively

1. On 18 October HJ had written to Wells telling him that he was less interested in the characters and action of *Marriage* than in Wells's own narration: 'the ground of the drama is somehow most of all in the adventure for *you* – not to say *of* you, the moral, temperamental, personal, expressional, of your setting it forth' (HJHGW, 167).

irrelevant – whereas in his I feel myself relevant only to be by the same stroke, as it were, but vain and ineffectual. Strange to me – in his affair – the co-existence of so much talent with so little art, so much life with (so to speak) so little living! But of him there is much to say, for I really think him more interesting by his faults than he will probably ever manage to be in any other way; and he is a most vivid and violent object-lesson. But it's as if I were pretending to talk – which, for this beastly frustration, I am not. I envy you the quite ideal and transcendent jollity (as if Marie Corelli had herself evoked the image for us) of having polished off a brilliant *coup* and being on your way to celebrate the case in Paris.[2] It's for me to-day as if people only did those things in Marie – and in Mary! Do while you are there re-enter, if convenient to you, into relation with Mrs. Wharton; if she be back, that is, from the last of her dazzling, her incessant, braveries of far excursionism. You may in that case be able to appease a little my always lively appetite for news of her. Don't, I beseech you, "acknowledge" in any manner this, with all you have else to do; not even to hurl back upon me (in refutation, reprobation or whatever) the charge I still persist in of your liking "politics" because of your all having, as splendid young people, the perpetual good time of being so intimately *in* them.[3] They never cease to remind me personally, here (close corporation or intimate social club as they practically affect the aged and infirm, the lone and detached, the abjectly literary and unenrolled alien as being,) that one must sacrifice all sorts of blest freedoms and immunities, treasures of detachment and perception that make up, and more than make up, for the "outsider" state, on any occasion of practical approach to circling round the camp; for penetration into which I haven't a single one of your pass-words – yours, I again mean, of the splendid young lot. But don't pity me, all the same, for this picture of my dim exclusion; it is so compatible with more *other* initiations than I know, on the whole, almost what to do with. I hear the pass-words given – for it does happen that they

2. Marie Corelli was the pseudonym of Mary Mackay or Mills (1855–1924), bestselling Victorian author of mystical novels of psychic travel. Mrs Ward, whose popularity was waning and whose poor health drove her to an excessive use of drugs, had just completed a first draft of *The Mating of Lydia*; her doctor sent her to Paris for two weeks of recuperation. Mrs Wharton had recently returned to Paris from a motor tour down to the Pyrenees.

3. Mrs Ward had written: 'I don't sympathise with you about politics, for they are to me the salt & sauce of every day – & a pretty sharp & stimulating sauce just now!' Her next novel, *The Coryston Family*, was to deal with 'the tyrannical sway of a political woman over her husband to whom she denies all freedom of action' (MHW, 324). On 28 February HJ had been in Humphry Ward's box at the Albert Hall for a meeting of Mrs Ward's Anti (Female) Suffrage League, in which she was wearyingly active. When Howells quizzed him about it, he denied on 27 March supporting her side: 'The question simply overwhelmingly bores me – & I resent being hustled into *concluding* about it at all.' (LFL, 457.)

sometimes reach my ear; and then, so far from representing for me the "salt of life", as you handsomely put it, they seem to form for me the very measure of intellectual insipidity. All of which, however, is so much more than I meant to be led on to growl back at your perfect benevolence. Still, still, still – well, *still* I am all harmoniously yours

Henry James

273. To Henry James III (nephew)
24 April 1913

Houghton TS   Unpublished

The first proofs of A Small Boy and Others *arrived in Rye on 19 December 1912. On 23 December HJ told the Protheros in a dictated letter that (for* Notes of a Son and Brother) *'the attitude of penmanship' was too painful, and that 'I am trying to finish a Book during the brief part of the day when I can command this helpful machinery' (Unpublished Houghton TS, bMS Am 1094.3 (104)). He moved into his Chelsea flat on New Year's Eve or Day, still suffering from shingles. On 2 January he sent Scribner's a portion of the final bit of* A Small Boy, *and the remainder on 15 January. The book was published by Scribner's on 29 March and by Macmillan on 1 April. On 23 January HJ told Harry how, financially and personally, 'it becomes vital for me to aim at returning to the production of the Novel, my departure from which, with its heart-breaking loss of time, was a catastrophe, a perversity and fatality, so little dreamed of by me or intended' (LHJ II, 291).*

On 16 March HJ acknowledged Pinker's cheque for £738 6s. 3d, the first half of Scribner's $8,000 advance on a novel (through Edith Wharton's scheming) minus Pinker's commission: 'I am unused to these fairy-tales of fortune & they almost scare me a little – this one making me for the moment sensibly nervous by all it constitutes a pledge & representation of. However the way to take it is as a great steadying & inspiring circumstance.' (Unpublished Yale MS, Za James 1, vol. 3.) He did discover – through his nephew Bill – her scheme to raise $5,000 in donations for his seventieth birthday on 15 April from American friends and admirers (to match the British subscription for a portrait by Sargent and a 'golden bowl', a silver-gilt Charles II porringer and dish). He cabled Bill: 'please express to individuals approached my horror money absolutely returned'; Wharton, whose divorce had just come through, told Lapsley 'the idea that he pictures me as a meddling philanthropist is too intolerable' (LEW, 291, 290).

Since 1912 Harry, who had abandoned his Boston law practice, had been manager

*of the Rockefeller Institute for Medical Research in New York. He was sensitive
about HJ's treatment of his father's letters, which he was himself to edit in 1920.*

Dictated.

2417 KENSINGTON.

21, CARLYLE MANSIONS, CHEYNE WALK. S.W.

April 24th. 1913.

Dearest Harry.

I rejoiced last night in your letter of the 13th., written from Quincey Street.
I had written myself in the p.m. so fully to Bill about the American Donation
matter – after having already sometime since gone into it very fully with your
Mother – that there is nothing more to say about *that*, and I refer you wholly
to them.[1] I also have put them in possession of all the facts relative to the very
charming Commemoration of my Birthday (you see what capitals I use!) Here,
and thereby provided I trust against any unpleasantness felt in the Boston and
New York air in regard to my taking an "invidious" line. If they had, in a
word, only offered me a modest piece of plate or suchlike (American silversmith
work being, at its best, so artistic and beautiful) all would have been well –
for I have sufficiently explained to the others that though I sit to Sargent here
I decline all retention or possession of the Picture. But enough!

I can't tell you how I rejoice in your delightful sustaining and inspiring
words about the Small Boy – for inspiring they are, in the sense that they will
help me so to go on well with its Sequel; which, in spite of everything, *is* going
on. The effect you speak of, the atmospheric and evocatory, the chemical
process rather than mechanical, is of course what I aim at and appeal to – so
that if I pull the thing off, so much the better. There is more to tell you of
how the volume insisted in coming, and in bulking so large, just as it is –
more, I say, than I can do in this fashion; though I should try it a little if we
were all sitting together again, as we did two years ago, in the Irving Street
library, the only right place for it. I should then explain a little how the Book
couldn't *but* become so egotistic, if it's fair so to call it – which it isn't! – if it
was to become anything. But this, and other like things, you will, and above
all your Mother and dearest Peg will, have made out for yourselves. The only
thing is that, after I have tried to put my whole expression, with a perpetual
remembering of the need of it, à la portée of the meanest intelligence, I seem

1. HJ's letter of 29 March to his nephew William about the donation scheme asks him to ensure
it is 'stamped out by any violent means (not, of course, of the newspaper) that may be all
necessary to really dispose of it' (HJL IV, 654).

to keep being told that of course I am well-nigh as "difficult" as ever to read, though "all right when you know" (that is understand) me. I groan at this, because I want to sell, and such remarks discourage sale. However, the thing seems, all the same, to flourish a good bit *less* mildly than my stuff in general, and such Notices as I have been aware of, both public and private, have been in the last degree pleasant – and some of them even perceptive! I shall before long be writing you on the question of what may be done, what you may help do, toward that idea of Illustrations for Book Two that we talked of when I was with you. The Volume will absolutely not be able to help growing larger, and containing more matter, a good deal more, than the Small Boy; and "pictures" *may* possibly too much swell it out.[2] The space I have wanted to make and shall have been so repaid, as to my whole effect, by making, for your Grandfather and a goodish many of *his* letters (with my own "egotisms" galore again!) – these things will contribute to the bulk. But I don't want to give up, in the least, the Illustration idea – we must cling to it unless it utterly beats us; and I should like you even to approach Willy Emmet – as soon as you've got your Secretary in train! – on the matter of your Dad's portrait of his Mother, which, supremely well photographed and photogravured, ought to be a high value. Wilfred von Glehn, Jane Emmet's husband, he and she being my close and most lovable neighbours here, told me but the other day that he considered it absolutely like a Manet of the best period.[3] However, these are details though they must be faced in time. I think I can already speak definitely about my use, or non-use, of some groups of the Letters. I shall use not one of the South American series, interesting and characteristic as they are; I can't fit them in, the space-question absolutely forbids; and they will stand over entire for the Collected Letters.[4] On the other hand I have used all that are usable of the early Newport– Cambridge series; it being vital, and the only way, to make these part of the time during which my own presence at, and participation in, them gives me a chance to breathe the right illuminating air all round them. By the same token I shall

2. In the event, *Notes of a Son and Brother* contained five illustrations apart from a frontispiece: sketches by WJ and reproduced pages of his letters. They also included a 'Portrait in oils of Miss Katherine Temple, 1861' (Minny's elder sister), which belonged to her son William Temple Emmet (1869–1918).
3. The Von Glehns lived at 73 Cheyne Walk. Wilfred was himself a painter. Édouard Manet (1832–83), who began like Velázquez and Goya painting darkly intense canvases, after 1870 moved to a brighter and lighter Impressionist technique and palette. In *Notes of a Son and Brother* WJ's 1861 portrait of Kitty Temple is described as 'a really mature, an almost masterly, piece of painting, having, as has been happily suggested to me, much the air of a characteristic Manet' (A, 293).
4. In *Notes of a Son and Brother* HJ refers to WJ's 1865 letters from the Harvard scientific expedition to Brazil led by Louis Agassiz (1807–73), 'for which, against my hope, these pages succeed in affording no space – they are to have ampler presentation' (A, 481).

like, I see, to incorporate such as I can of the '66–'68 European ones; I having been again so personally and closely concerned in the production of these. The air I can breathe round *them* again will, I think, be missed if they are published without it; but with the cessation of my nearness, as it were, that is with the opening of '69, that nearness begins to cease, and I leave everything thereafter for the Collection. Let so much serve, for the moment, as a sort of rough prefiguring statement. What seems to be indicated is that I can embody (for space-reasons) a good bit less of everything than I had dreamed. The Book mustn't be *too* fat and two vols. are out of the question. You see I write as if I were going on pretty well now – and so, thank goodness, I *am*. We are having a beautiful burst of very mild spring, and it does me all the good in the world – this being a perfect place to *get* good from it.

The Otis Place issue has given me immense pleasure – and I feel as if it would be fun for all of you, above all for your Mother and Peg.[5] Of course I have written the more closely interested parties. I congratulate you with all my heart on the prospect of the Secretary, and can only wish he may prove half the blessing to you that Miss B. is, as you see, to your Uncle. It will ease off immensely all my morbid scruples at hearing from you. Dear little Ruth Draper is here, and I am doing what I can for her (very, very tinily!) – and above all she gives me news of you more personal, as it were, than I have had from any New York source (outside of Mrs. Cadwal's writing me how she and Beatrix "intensely love" you!)[6] Little Ruth is a dear of dears, and her talent has really an extraordinary charm. She is here too briefly just now to show it off much, but has just telephoned me that she is stopping over a fortnight more because Lady Mountstephen, at whose house she has twice brilliantly performed, wants, practically engages, to arrange for her to do her little repertory (in fact it's rather big!) to the Queen.[7] But good-bye! Your fond old Uncle

Henry James

P.S. *Please* send this on to your Mother!

5. Billy James had married Alice Runnells in January 1912; they were living at 12 Otis Place, Boston. In 1913 he would become a teacher at the Boston Museum art school.
6. Ruth Draper (1884–1956) of New York, a friend of Henry Adams, was a monologuist of increasing reputation who was to have a long public career, but was still performing in private salons (including that of her brother Paul and his wife Muriel, where HJ heard Pablo Casals, Jacques Thibaud and Artur Rubinstein play). HJ wrote her a monologue (never performed) for an American woman ambitious to be presented to the king.
7. Lady Mountstephen is presumably the wife of the Scots-born George Stephen (1829–1921), first Baron Mount Stephen, successful as president of the Canadian Pacific Railway Company before settling in Britain in 1893. Ruth Draper performed successfully in Pall Mall to Princess Christian, Queen Victoria's third daughter, and to assembled royalty including George V and Queen Mary.

274. To Hugh Walpole
29 April 1913

Texas MS   Unpublished

On 28 April HJ acknowledged a cheque from Pinker for £592 15s. covering
Macmillan's advance for A Small Boy and Others, *Scribner's joint advance for*
that and Notes of a Son and Brother, *and royalties from Nelson for a cheap*
edition of The American.

Walpole called A Small Boy and Others *'quite glorious – so beautiful and so*
clear and so humorous', but evidently let drop in his letter of thanks (not extant)
some remark about his failure altogether to follow HJ's late style.

2417 KENSINGTON.
21, CARLYLE MANSIONS, CHEYNE WALK. S.W.

Dearest Hugh.

Your letter of April 20*th* gave & continues to give me, as it lies here before .
me & again & again engages my fondest attention, the greatest joy. But the
last ten days have been bad ones, the very worst, for writing. My prodigious
Birthday (prodigious by the measure of *my* sequestered vale of life) has taken
a vast deal of acknowledgment – under the vain effort of which push of the
pen I have languished, stumbled, almost quite collapsed. Which doesn't mean
however that so generous & gracious a demonstration hasn't deeply touched
& uplifted me – it has been really a most charming & reviving experience to
know. Be tenderly thanked, beloved boy, for your gentle & faithful share in
it. I think of your noble detachment from the scene about me here meanwhile
with infinite sympathy, envy, applause, & believe you are having, if the work
marches, days & weeks that you may count hereafter as among the happiest
of your life.[1] You will find – must already have found, your liberal sacrifice
on the Great Altar a great help to the knowledge of your own powers. May
that garden bloom & rustle & draw you on into more luxuriant bowers in
proportion as you trustfully explore it. I thank you ever so much for your
patience with the fatuous & presumptuous Small Boy; an extraordinarily
impudent attempt surely, that of regaling the world with the picture of my
rare consciousness from the age of 6 months to that of my earlier teens – &

1. At the end of February, to work on his next novel, *The Duchess of Wrexe*, Walpole had gone
to a cottage in the Cornish village of Polperro with his friend the theatrical designer Percy
Anderson (b. 1851), who had dressed *Guy Domville* and been involved with Morton Fullerton.

aggravated by the fact that when I began to tap the fount I found it come, the crystal stream – & *liked* the way of its coming. It's full at any rate of an ancient piety & a brave intention. You disconcert me a little – or call it much – by saying that some passages "defeat" you – that is if I know what you mean. I take you to mean that you found them difficult, obscure or *entortillés* – & that is the pang & the proof that I am truly an uncommunicating communicator – a beastly bad thing to be. Here at least I said to myself is a thing at every inch of its way on the [level of] the meanest intelligence! [And yet, as it] would seem, I don't get flat *enough* down on my belly – there's a cherished ideal of platitude that, to make "success", I shall never be able to achieve. Don't try for it *you*, dearest Hugh, for God's sake – if that's what your remark would imply; & when you come to town again *do* let me read you over the said baffling or bewildering morsels. I don't think I ought to so despair of driving them through your skull. But "thou hast great allies," as Wordsworth says to the captive Toussaint – since the acute Pinker told me a day or two ago that Arnold Bennett had said to him of the thing: "Not [easy to follow,] but how beautiful!"[2] [I am much] obliged for the beautiful but I lose myself in wonder at such a restriction on the part of an *expert* dabbler in the mystery, like A.B. It makes me indeed ask myself about the others; & indeed if you ask me in *what* "mystery" the aforesaid *is* a dabbler I shan't say in that of style. But don't think, dearest boy, that you have set me off – even though if you had called my complacent infant a prattler & a twaddler I should have found *that* quite in the line of the higher criticism & felt justly exposed. I think with a great elation of the possibility of seeing you here a month hence – if I understand you. I hope myself to hang on through June – that is if you'll sometimes put your legs under my poor mahogany.[3] Goodnight for now. My dear & delightful Von Glehns, neighbours & quasi-cousins, tell me they are starting for Cornwall & the hope of some small grab of you. See them if you (conscientiously) can, that they may tell me of you. I shall love you all the better for it. I lately had

2. HJ refers to the conclusion of Wordsworth's sonnet 'To Toussaint l'Ouverture', addressed to the former governor of Haiti, a slave's son, who had resisted the reimposition of slavery by Napoleon in 1802: 'There's not a breathing of the common wind / That will forget thee; thou hast great allies; / Thy friends are exultations, agonies, / And love, and man's unconquerable mind.' HJ had failed to meet the novelist and journalist Arnold Bennett (1867–1931) through Wells in October 1912 because of his shingles; but finally saw him in their common agent Pinker's office on 6 January 1913. Bennett's journal: 'Very slow talker. Beautiful French. Expressed stupefaction when I said I knew nothing about the middle-class, and said the next time he saw me he would have recovered from the stupefaction, and the discussion might proceed. Said there was too much to say about everything – and that was the thing most felt by one such as he, not entirely without – er – er – er – er – perceptions.'
3. Walpole dined with HJ on 3 June.

a Sunday p.m. hour or two with our lady of Ockham, who snuffled & yawned as sociably as ever. (Burn me at the stake *always*.) But she was very nice & believes entirely in Helen's marriage.[4] Let *us* therefore.

Your faithfully fondest old

H.J.

April 29*th* '13.

275. *To Louise Corrin Walsh*
23 *June 1913*

Houghton TC   Unpublished

On 18 May HJ began sitting to Sargent for the birthday portrait (the last session was 24 June). On 28 March he replied to Bruce Richmond (1871–1964), editor of The Times Literary Supplement, *that he would look at Émile Faguet's study of Balzac, but only started writing on 1 June, sending in his long essay on 15 June (it appeared on 19 June).*

In 1889 HJ, WJ and AJ had been upset that Aunt Kate Walsh, their mother's sister and a second mother to them, had left the bulk of her estate to her Walsh nieces and nephews of Stamford, Connecticut, including Louise Corrin Walsh (b. 1849) – daughter of Alexander Robertson Walsh.

21 Carlyle Mansions, Cheyne Walk. S.W.

June 23d, 1913.

My dear Louise,

First of all forgive my use of this cold-blooded machinery – I absolutely *have* in these days to depend on it; without it I should be able, through physical unfitness, to answer but one letter in twenty. And I want after all to tell you as distinctly and as legibly as possible that it gave me great pleasure the other day to hear from you. I rejoice that my fat book – really such an impudent attempt to interest my public, such as it is, in my little affairs between the ages of two and fifteen or sixteen – appealed to you and struck old chords of memory; as for that matter I hoped it would; so much matter of memory of the very old days have we in common. I wonder if you remember our Uncle John Walsh, whom I give an account of seeing in Fourteenth Street, and

4. I have not identified the Helen in whose marriage Lady Lovelace believes.

afterwards at your Father's house in Clinton Place during his last illness.[1] No, you must have been then too young – though he came back so visibly to *me*. But your recollections and impressions of poor dear Henry W. are most interesting and touching to me, and delightful your story of taking him to see Salvini and your adventure afterwards.[2] I'm so sorry you declined that part of it that concerned the ices, which would have made it so much prettier and more pathetic for retrospect. But I tried at least to do him and his queer quaint touching history and figure all possible justice – and think I did. The anecdote about his repressed puttings into the plate at church almost makes me cry, and I don't understand it on Cousin Helen's part, when she had such accumulations of his fortune to draw upon. It was her confounded narrow-minded conscience; she had such fear of being extravagant at his expense.

Very glad am I to hear of your having happily solved the problem of some solution of your solitude. It seems to me quite ideal, if your friend isn't too much on your back or your hands, or even your mind; and your wood-fire evenings and readings sound to me over here quite like one of Mary Wilkins's or Miss Jewett's New England tales.[3] Most of all do I thank you, however, for your news of the friend, your neighbour, Miss Havens, and of her having interesting letters of William's.[4] We are indeed gathering in, for the publication

1. In ch. x of *A Small Boy and Others* HJ first remembers his maternal uncle John Walsh, 'before the fire in the Fourteenth Street library', discussing the singing of the great soprano Jenny Lind (1820–87), the 'Swedish nightingale'; and then on his deathbed 'one dusky wintry Sunday afternoon, in Clinton Place . . . of the sinister twilight grimness of whose lot . . . I was to carry away a fast impression'. Clinton Place was the house of John's elder brother, Louise Walsh's father.

2. Henry Wyckoff (1815–90) was the rich, 'simple-minded' younger brother of 'Cousin Helen', Helen Rodgers Wyckoff Perkins (1807–87); they were HJ's cousins as the children of HJ's maternal grandmother's sister. Chs. x and xi of *A Small Boy and Others* ironically picture her 'strong simplicity', 'fine old New York ignorance and rigour', and conscientious managing of 'the odd, the eccentric, the attaching Henry'. For her, 'he was not to be trusted': he was 'suffered to indulge his passions on but ten cents a day'. Thus 'his imagination, in the long years, had been starved'; 'Henry's idea of a present was ten cents' worth of popcorn'.

3. Mary Eleanor Wilkins Freeman (1852–1930) was famous for grim tales of New England spinsters, notably in the collections *A Humble Romance* (1887) and *A New England Nun* (1891).

4. In May 1868 WJ, depressed and nervously out of order, told a friend he was invigorated at Frau Spangenberg's Dresden *pension* by the 'friendship of a young American lady here', Kate (Catherine E.) Havens of New York (1839–1939). It was not 'anything like flirtation. I soar in a region above that, I think.' (TCWJ I, 276.) She had bad nerves but was a talented pianist (and later taught music): 'Tonight while listening to Miss Havens's magic playing . . . my feelings came to a sort of crisis. The intuition of something here in a measure absolute gave me . . . an unspeakable disgust for the dead drifting of my own life for some time past.' (TCWJ II, 271.) No letters to Kate Havens were used in *The Letters of William James*, but she supplied a 'helpful memorandum' about Frau Spangenberg's. HJ's 'note' to her is not known to survive.

of his correspondence on a considerable scale, everything of interest, in that kind, that comes to our knowledge. I think the civil thing for me to do is to write and enclose herewith a note to Miss H., which I shall ask you kindly to deliver, leaving it open so that you may read it; I mean just to ask her to be so good as to send the letters on either to Alice at Cambridge or to Harry in New York (I will decide in a minute which;) for it will be of interest and importance to us to have at any rate seen them. If any of them are useable, as will probably be the case, they will be copied and carefully returned to the owner. It is Alice and Harry who are mainly concerning themselves with the collecting and editing of William's Letters simply as such. He was so admirable a letter-writer that *they* will constitute his real and best biography. I meanwhile, however, am doing a second Volume to the Small Boy, carrying on my too egotistical narrative some ten years more, or about up to my own twenty-fifth. This time, however, I shall be much less egotistical – and this second instalment is but an essential part of the book itself, the "Family Book", as first planned. I overflowed so much more than I intended about my babyhood and the few years after in the Small Boy that all that latter and more important part got crowded out. But you shall before very long have it as a volume by itself.

I am in no great state of reckless activity for overabounding vigour in this evening of my life; but I get on with care, though I haven't a superior trained nurse, like you, to sit with me "evenings". I now spend my winters, that is 6 or 7 months of the year, regularly in London: I found I could no longer stand, for long stretches of time, the solitude and confinement of the country. Of course your Stamford is a brilliant provincial city (if you will excuse "provincial") compared to my poor little Rye perched lonely, as one may say almost, upon a rock of ocean. Let me repeat how glad I have been, dear Louise, to hear from you, and believe me all faithfully yours,

Henry James

276. To Henry James III (nephew)
10 December 1913

Houghton MS   Unpublished

On 16 July HJ's nephew Harry and niece Peggy arrived for the summer. On 18 July HJ had a pectoral attack in Pinker's office, but after several days in bed went down to Rye on 22 July, resuming dictation of Notes of a Son and Brother *on 24 July. On 21 August, rereading* War and Peace, *he told Walpole, 'I now protest as much as I admire' (HJL IV, 681); on 31 August the widowed Howells and his daughter Mildred came down to Lamb House for the day; Edith Wharton swooped from France, 21–3 September.*

On 11 September HJ wrote to Theodora Bosanquet in Italy, about Notes, *that 'I am getting on very well with my revision – the effect of which is to show me that large, very large,* chunks *will have to come out' (Unpublished Houghton MS, bMS Eng 1213 (55)). On 13 October HJ told Pinker it was all but finished, and that, 'It is a better book than* The Small Boy *– that is it has in greater degree, I think, whatever merits & kinds of interest the S.B. had.' (Unpublished Yale MS, Za James 1, vol. 3.) He posted it to Macmillan on 6 November and on 19 November left Rye for Chelsea. On 8 December he sent another long article, on George Sand, to* The Times Literary Supplement; *but then transferred it to George Prothero's* Quarterly Review *(April 1914).*

In a long letter of 15–18 November HJ had replied in pained apology to his nephew Harry's pained response to the revisions made in the family letters of Notes of a Son and Brother, *which followed, as HJ explained, from 'that conception of an* atmosphere *which I invoked as, artistically speaking, my guiding star'. He promised, 'Never again shall I stray from my proper work', conceding that 'the sad thing is I think you're right in being offended' (HJL IV, 801, 803, 804).*

TELEPHONE 2417 KENSINGTON.
21 CARLYLE MANSIONS   CHEYNE WALK   S.W.
Dec: 10*th 1913*

Dearest Harry.

Katherine Loring has just sent me an old drawing of your Dad's which has been preserved these 45 years by miracle, & which I post off to you in all haste as it seems to me of absolute importance for my Book.[1] (I got your good cable with pleasure, but *this* is all I can pretend to speak of now.)[2] Katherine tells me that the drawing had the other day fallen out of an old book given her by your Aunt Alice & not opened for years, & that, recognising the probably great importance of it, she at once sends it to me. It is a pencil drawing by your Dad of *himself* – evidently done before a mirror, quite accidentally & casually & carelessly (as appears from the deplorable piece of cheap ruled paper on which it is done,) but so exceedingly good, characteristic & valuable that I feel it ought to go as Frontispiece to my Volume. It must have been done *about 1866* – it couldn't have been done later, & there are things about

1. The drawing became the frontispiece to *Notes of a Son and Brother*, captioned as 'Pencil-drawn portrait of William James by himself about 1866'.
2. Harry James's cable is not known to survive.

it that make it not much earlier. *I recognise* it perfectly – I don't mean simply as himself, but as a thing seen by me at the time & long forgotten: this sense of having seen it is absolute for me. It strikes me as one of the very best things in the handful of his relics that we have – your Mother & Bill & Aleck will, I feel, be intensely interested in it. I don't know of course what you have succeeded in arranging with Scribner about the reproduction of the other things – but I greatly hope it is going well – I mean that they have been successfully taken in hand. This one ought to reproduce very particularly well, I think – the only difficulty it can offer is perhaps in the unfortunately just visible ruled lines on the paper – but these are faint, & they must have ways of dissimulating such things. The drawing goes to you separately from this – in a registered packet marked outside with my initials. I won't say more now – but shall be very glad to hear anything whatever about the matter of the illustrations. By the time you get this 4/5'ths of the Macmillan's Proofsheets of the Book will be in Scribner's hands. I have all but seen it wholly through the Press here. Goodnight! Your affectionate old Uncle

Henry James

P.S. I find here carefully put away the original (original copies received from you) of all the Brazil letters – & I *think* of the German ones (I haven't had time to go through them yet.) I find it extremely good for me to be in Town again.

277. To James Brand Pinker
2 January 1914

Yale MS   Unpublished

From 16 to 18 December HJ spent each day in Tite Street, 'on exhibition' beside his portrait in Sargent's studio, thanking the subscribers (SLHJEG, 294). On 30 December HJ, who had agreements with Dent and Scribner's for Notes on Novelists, with Some Other Notes, *told Pinker he had 'already got the Contents of the Volume together and done all my work of revision on them' (Unpublished Yale TS, Za James 1, vol. 3). In the event he would also include 'The New Novel', a large and controversial two-part survey of recent fiction for* The Times Literary Supplement, *which he had proposed to Bruce Richmond on 19 December and for which he was already reading.*

Edward Montague Compton Mackenzie (1883–1972), son of Edward Compton (real name Mackenzie), the actor-manager who played HJ's American in 1891, had made his mark as a novelist with the bestseller Carnival *(1912). His* Sinister Street *(in two volumes, 1913–14) follows a hero warped by public school and*

Oxford, and having trouble reaching maturity. In 1914 he settled on Capri (partly for health reasons) and converted to Roman Catholicism. HJ's essay 'The New Novel' concludes by discussing Mackenzie and wondering if, 'moved by life, this interesting young novelist is even now uncontrollably on the way to style?' (LC I, 159).

2417 KENSINGTON

21, CARLYLE MANSIONS, CHEYNE WALK. S.W.

My dear Pinker.

I am obliged to you for your cheque for £25. 5. 8, representing Messrs. Scribners' remittance of semi-annual royalties on my New York Edition, less your Commission.

But alas how it shrinks & shrinks![1]

I have just been reading *Sinister Street*, by young Compton Mackenzie, of which you spoke to me some time since, & am so exceedingly struck by it as a *young* thing that I mean at once to read its 2 predecessors, or at least the immediate one. I should even like to get at him – (I've an old acquaintance with his parents,) didn't I seem to remember your telling me that he had gone off to live at Capri (?) or in some like retreat. In that case I must wait & perhaps will write to him.[2] He affects me at any rate as, putting one or two aside (or rather as putting Wells only, & Wells isn't as good for Wells [as] this little C.M. is for *him*,) as very much the greatest talent of the new generation. And the modernity of him! It's such a happy & unexpected change to be *interested*! If you write to him tell him I pat him very particularly on the back.[3]
Yours all faithfully

Henry James

Jan: 2: 1914.

1. The equivalent payment late in 1910 was $432.28, which with Pinker's commission deducted came to £80; in the summer of 1911 most of £104 4s. 5d. was a semi-annual payment on the New York Edition. On 20 December 1911 HJ got £52 8s. 8d., confiding to Pinker 'I am distressed & rather dismayed, I may add – can't *help* adding – at what the receipts from that source appear to be shrinking to' (Unpublished Yale MS, Za James 1, vol. 3). In the summer of 1912 it was £58 17s. 11d. On 8 February 1913 he explained his delay to acknowledge the latest payment by illness; also, 'I suppose I should have been more alert about the matter had the sum been less diminutive!' (Unpublished Yale TS, Za James 1, vol. 3.) The payment for the summer of 1913 was £36 18s. 5d.
2. HJ wrote to him on 21 January (see HJL IV, 696–8).
3. On 6 January HJ wrote again to Pinker: 'I am subtly, or at least awkwardly, conscious of some complications in my position – my position, I mean, of quasi-paternal delicacy of relation to several of the younger fry of "our profession"; that is of the "ructions", always, that might

278. To James Brand Pinker
5 February 1914

Yale MS   Unpublished

On 18 January HJ told AHJ that he was getting on with a novel for Scribner's (presumably The Ivory Tower*). HJ's two-part article on the fiction of 'The Younger Generation' (Conrad, Wells, Bennett, Walpole, Mackenzie, Lawrence and others) appeared in* The Times Literary Supplement *on 19 March and 2 April.*

TELEPHONE 2417 KENSINGTON.
21 CARLYLE MANSIONS   CHEYNE WALK   S.W.
February 5*th 1914*.

My dear Pinker.

I am obliged to you for the Macmillans' annual cheque – £25. 9. 6 – for royalties on my Edition de Luxe, minus your commission: for which amount please regard this as a receipt in full.

Yours ever
Henry James

J. B. Pinker esq.

P.S. I have just finished Conrad's very remarkable *Chance* – in which he affects me as having picked himself up extraordinarily from some comparative recent lapses.[1] It's a very great pleasure to recognise that power in him – after doubting it a little. The thing has great fineness & beauty & individuality (to J.C.;) but his perversity of method – his dealing with his material by relays of reporters 3 or 4 deep, like the chain of men passing buckets of water at a fire, strikes me as "rum" beyond all words.[2]

---

ensue on any impression or rumour propagated of my unfair, my too individual, patting of backs.' (Unpublished Yale TS, Za James 1, vol. 3.)

1. *Chance* was published on 8 January 1914, and through cunning publicity was a hit in the U.S. when published there on 26 March. Pinker was Conrad's long-suffering agent (they had quarrelled seriously in January 1910). What HJ terms his 'comparative recent lapses' (probably *Nostromo* (1904), *The Secret Agent* (1907) and *Under Western Eyes* (1911)) he was blunter about to Edith Wharton on 27 February as 'the last three or four impossibilities, wastes of desolation, that succeeded the two or three final good things of his earlier time' (HJEWL, 279).

2. In 'The New Novel' HJ reuses this image for Conrad's team of narrators, an image which recalls the circumstances of the 1861 Newport fire at which HJ sustained a back injury, 'a horrid even if an obscure hurt' (A, 415). The essay wonders at 'the Marlows and their determinant inventors and interlocutors, the Powells, the Franklins, the Fynes, the tell-tale little dogs, the successive members of a cue from one to the other of which the sense and the interest of the

279. To André Raffalovich
26 February 1914

Virginia MS   Unpublished

Throughout February and well into March, HJ paid regular visits to his London dentist, having at last all his teeth extracted.

Marc-André Raffalovich (1864–1934), a wealthy Russian educated in France, came to England in 1882 and was a protégé of Sidney Colvin. A poet and novelist, he wrote Cyril and Lionel, and Other Poems *(1884),* It Is Thyself *(1889), and a satire on the Wilde circle,* A Willing Exile *(1890). The poet John Gray (1866– 1934) left Oscar Wilde for him in 1892; they collaborated on a play. In 1896 Raffalovich wrote* Uranisme et Unisexualité: étude sur différentes manifestations de l'instinct sexuel *(1896), a study of homosexuality in the series Bibliothèque de Criminologie, incorporating his 1895 pamphlet against Wilde. He became a Dominican, Brother Sebastian – Gray became Father Gray – and they moved to Edinburgh, where Raffalovich built Gray St Peter's Church and they had a salon.*

In the autumn of 1913 Raffalovich sent HJ his 1904 edition of Last Letters of Aubrey Beardsley *(a former protégé), with an introduction by John Gray, inviting him to lunch at Claridge's. HJ asked Logan Pearsall Smith (1865–1946) on 17 November, 'Do you know whom I mean (and I may perhaps even say* What!*) by André Raffalovich? – with whom I had had some acquaintance, very limited, years ago, in London, but have never seen nor heard from since.' He added: 'I knew Beardsley a little – and found him personally pleasing and touching, though I detested his work – which made me sick – and does still.' (HJL IV, 693, 694.) Before Raffalovich's visit HJ wanted reports from Hugh Walpole, whose father was Anglican Bishop of Edinburgh: 'When you refer to their "immorality on stone floors," and with prayerbooks in their hands so long as the exigencies of the situation permit of the manual retention of the sacred volumes, I do so want the picture developed and the proceedings authenticated.' (HJL IV, 695.)*

21 CARLYLE MANSIONS   CHEYNE WALK   S.W.
February 26*th* 1914.

My dear Raffalovich.

I can only thank you again & always for your honeyed words. *The American Scene* is a better book than the *Bostonians* – if one may compare like with

---

subject have to be passed on together, in the manner of the buckets of water for the improvised extinction of a fire, before reaching our apprehension' (LC I, 151).

unlike. I seem to remember having done more or less what I tried to in the former & to recall a sense of comparatively thankless effort in the novel. But that was long ago, the book has become rather vague & obscure to me – & I don't quite catch on to your kind allusions, though I am touched by your good will. It was a rather rueful feeling about the B.'s that prevented my including it in the Edition, & I left it out partly because I hadn't the courage really to look at it again – & felt that revision would be formidable. I fear it seems more formidable now – when, with shrunken powers of application, I incline so much more to give my small stint of time to new work. That I am trying to do. I am glad poor dear old – though I fear it was rather more the superincumbent new – London supplied you with agreeable memories. May you now the more broodingly hibernate! I am sorry the occasion *didn't* seem to come to me to meet Cecil Wright again – I liked him so.[1] I had no proposal from the Sélincourts.[2] But I circulate in any case ever so little. Come & see me – & bring him – again & give him meanwhile my kind regards.

Yours very truly
Henry James

280. To Henry Adams
21 March 1914

Mass. Hist. Inst. MS   Published HJL IV, 705–6; SL2, 419–20; CHJHA, 88–9; LHJ II, 360–61

Notes of a Son and Brother *was published by Scribner's on 7 March (by Macmillan on 13 March). Henry Adams in Washington had been on the list of eighteen recipients of author's copies, so by 8 March could already reflect characteristically to Elizabeth Cameron, in the vein of* The Education of Henry Adams *(1918, privately printed in 1907): 'Why did we live? Was that all? Why was I not born*

1. On 16 January HJ wrote replying to Raffalovich's announcement that he was coming to London with a young friend he had been ' "cramming" ' with HJ's works; he had 'Raffalovich and friend' to luncheon on 10 February (Unpublished Scotland MS, Acc. 3868; N, 391). The friend may have been Cecil Wright (d. 1953), an art student first at Reading, 1910–14, then at the Edinburgh College of Art, who became a close friend and protégé of Raffalovich's in 1912. (See Brocard Sewell, *Footnote to the Nineties: A Memoir of John Gray and André Raffalovich* (1968).)
2. HJ's diary, 15 February: 'Basil de Selincourts lunch. 1.45.' (N, 391.) Basil De Selincourt was a writer on poetry (e.g. Whitman, Meredith and Blake), music and art. He was married to Anne Douglas Sedgwick (1873–1935), an American-born novelist.

in Central Africa and died young. Poor Henry James thinks it all real, I believe, and actually still lives in that dreamy, stuffy Newport and Cambridge, with papa James and Charles Norton — and me!' (LHA VI, 638.)

21 Carlyle Mansions Cheyne Walk S.W.

My dear Henry.

I have your melancholy outpouring of the 7th, & I know not how better to acknowledge it than by the full recognition of its unmitigated blackness. *Of course* we are lone survivors, of course the past that was our lives is at the bottom of an abyss — if the abyss *has* any bottom; of course too there's no use talking unless one particularly *wants* to. But the purpose, almost, of my printed divagations was to show you that one *can*, strange to say, still want to — or at least can behave as if one did. Behold me therefore so behaving — & apparently capable of continuing to do so. I still find my consciousness interesting — under *cultivation* of the interest. Cultivate it *with* me, dear Henry — that's what I hoped to make you do; to cultivate yours for all that it has in common with mine. *Why* mine yields an interest I don't know that I can tell you, but I don't challenge or quarrel with it — I encourage it with a ghastly grin. You see I still, in presence of life (or of what you deny to be such,) have reactions — as many as possible — & the book I sent you is a proof of them. It's, I suppose, because I am that queer monster the artist, an obstinate finality, an inexhaustible sensibility. Hence the reactions — appearances, memories, many things go on playing upon it with consequences that I note & "enjoy" (grim word!) noting. It all takes doing — & I *do*. I believe I shall do yet again — it is still an act of life. But you perform them still yourself — & I don't know what keeps me from calling your letter a charming one! There we are, & it's a blessing that you understand — I admit indeed alone — your all-faithful

Henry James

March 21. '14.

281. To Hugh Walpole
21 and 23 April 1914

Texas MS   Unpublished

On 29 March HJ told AHJ that in his reduced condition 'Complications and efforts

with people floor me, anginally, on the spot, *and my state is that of living every hour and at every minute on my guard' (HJL IV, 708).*

Walpole from Polperro expressed gratitude for HJ's restrictive praise in The Times Literary Supplement. *HJ's verdict: 'a juvenility reacting, in the presence of everything, "for all it is worth"' – but short of technique; 'The tract meanwhile affects us as more or less virgin snow' (LC I, 143). HJ complained to him on 8 April of 'inquiries from the Neglected Young as to* why *they were neglected' (HJL IV, 711). On 17 April Walpole wrote to Pinker: 'Quite between you and me I thought HJ's* Times *things all wrong. Anyone who prefers Edith Wharton to* Chance, *and* Sinister Street *to* Sons and Lovers*! Also no mention of E. M. Forster, who can put the rest of us in his pocket.' (HWB, 113.)*

105, PALL MALL, S.W.
April 21st *1914*.

Dearest Hugh.

It's a very sweet little letter, & this is a grateful little acknowledgment. You don't tell me very much – or rather *stay*: you do tell me that you have been as happy as ever before in your life – no, happier *than* ever before, this last week or two; & that surely is blest information, on which I congratulate you with all my heart. These are fairly golden days even here – & today a very amiable friend (Mrs. Sutro,) called for me after luncheon in her car, & motored me out across the vernal land to Box Hill, & up & over it, & down from it by the more long-drawn way, Walton Heath & Epsom Downs &c, to tea at Epsom town, & so home by 7; all of which, however, I reflect, must seem so cocknified to your bronzed & salted spirit that I blush to have seemed to swagger about it.[1] But it's this small beer, only, that I have to chronicle – though I did meet Arthur Benson 3 days ago at the Athenaeum (& have had a letter from him in consequence since;) talking with him for 30 minutes & the sight of him the first for a very long time. He has become in the interval extraordinarily big & red & rough as to surface, undergone a strange physical coarsening; but was most genial & welcoming & pleasant – ever so refined inwardly, even though I had the sense of our talking over a fence or through a window, as it were, so that he might fall back & away at any moment. His *clerical* tradition seems to me to account for him in all sorts of ways – he must be a blend of ancient pedagogues & parsons; but more of this another time –

1. Esther Stella Isaacs Sutro (d. 1934), herself a writer, was the wife of the fashionable dramatist and novelist Alfred Sutro (1863–1933), grandson of a German rabbi, who translated Maeterlinck's plays into English. They were close friends of HJ.

& of his letter taking back at once everything he had said in talk.[2] Also (if you can bear it,) a letter from Compton Mackenzie (today – & in consequence of my *Times* stuff;) barely legible – he *abbreviating* each word, reducing it to half, in the most inconsiderate fashion – & expatiative, & intelligible in thought; but with a spreading solemnity of self-commemoration that was notable enough.[3] He should live somehow with better people – if they will live with *him*; & get something considerable to happen to his sense of proportion & relation. Let us keep *ours*, dearest boy, very loose & flexible & convenient. And what else still? I am to be taken tomorrow to see Bernard Shaw's Tree-&-Mrs. Campbell-play; but X X X X X X X *April 23d.* "But," beloved little Hugh, I had yesterday – or was it day before yesterday? – to knock off in the act (I am liable to such sudden incapacitations,) & here I am belatedly picking myself up again. Let's see – where was I? Oh yes, kind Mrs. Sutro (again!) saw me through the B.S. thing last night – as she is to see her poor husband through a production of his own (& of Gerald du Maurier) tonight; & I was very grateful to the person (*for a* person) at my side whom I could suppressively gnash my teeth to at such flaunting (flaunt*ed*) ineptitude & infantility.[4] It's the loosest, emptiest, cheapest thing conceivable – helpless floundering farce, without point or form, without art or sense, with a small amusing effect in the early part of it soon drowned in dreariness, & of a general scenic *impudence* of nullity that must be seen to be believed. That is perhaps why the huge bête bovine public desire apparently in large numbers (as yet) to see it. The reflection it made me above all make, however, was on the still more incredible lack of any grain of intelligence or virtue in a state of "criticism" which appears to regard as its main office to promote the impunity of such misdeeds. So you see my whole impression is one of the blackest – & beside your simpering sea you too will smile at the power of a Haymarket, or a "rotten" play, the more or the less to trouble an urban mind. Well then, I blush for my urbanity! Let me also blush a little for not having more definitely said above that Compton Mackenzie's remarks (if you can stand him again,) were quite intelligent & interesting, & that I meant no *great* dig at the slight over-insistence with which

2. Benson's letter is not known to survive. However, on 24 April HJ wrote to Benson responding to his elaborately cryptic retractions apparently of things said about Percy Lubbock, who was on a motor tour in North Africa with Edith Wharton.

3. Walpole played up his jealousy of his contemporary's success – in the summer of 1913 he judged *Sinister Street: Volume One* 'too easily written', and declared 'Mackenzie, in spite of his cleverness, is no good'. HJ enjoyed this joke. Mackenzie's letter is not known to survive.

4. Shaw's play was *Pygmalion* at His Majesty's, with Mrs Patrick Campbell. Sutro's play was *The Clever Ones* at Wyndham's Theatre, with George Du Maurier's son Gerald (1873–1934) and Edmund Gwenn. On 13 May HJ went 'With Mrs. S. to Alfred's comedy' (N, 399).

he inspires himself. There is much play of mind in it – even though I remind myself a little of A.C.B. while so re-writing to explain away the previous! Good-bye now at any rate, before I trip up again. Yours all & always

H.J.

282. To Henrietta Temple Pell-Clarke
5 May 1914

Cornell MS   Published LPC, 533–7

Henrietta (1853–1934) was Minny Temple's youngest sibling, and thus interested in HJ's use of Minny's letters to her friend, the Harvard lawyer John Gray (who had sent them to WJ's widow AHJ). In the final chapter of Notes of a Son and Brother, *Minny's death in 1870 registers as 'the end of our youth' (A, 544). Henrietta appears in a letter of April 1869 where Minny refers to her as 'in that blissful state of babyhood peculiar to herself where everything seems delightful' (A, 523).*

Henrietta had married Leslie Pell-Clarke (1853–1904) in 1876. WJ, who had in 1869 called Henrietta 'a most uninteresting morsel', commented to HJ in 1887 that she 'has grown in ability and dignity every year of her life and kept her original geniality and good-nature intact' (CWJ I, 100; CWJ II, 364). In 1880 she gave Constance Fenimore Woolson her letter of introduction to HJ.

TELEPHONE 2417 KENSINGTON.
21, CARLYLE MANSIONS, CHEYNE WALK, S.W.
May 5th 1914.

Dearest Henrietta.

It is a very great pleasure to me indeed to have got your letter & to find myself really talking to you again – to say nothing of you talking to me. It links together again the chain of association across all the long years & gives the flush of life & reality to memories that struggle against the tendency of all the objects of the unspeakable past to become fictitious & spectral – at least to a poor old cousin whom the successive years – how these do go! – keep dragging away & away from them at such a rate! My pleasure is all the greater that you give me the impression of ease & peace & plenty in your own life & that I like so to hear of your interests, occupations & satisfactions – & above all of the prospect of your before very long swimming here into my Ken. I shall be delighted to see you when you do pull it off to come & take a holiday in this quarter of the world. Nothing could give me a better impression of your youth & confidence & energy than the happy fact of your planning with that confidence a year ahead – to which I wish all justification.[1] You will find me a good deal damaged by time, yet still bearing up, & really better than when I last had to write you, on your side of the sea, of my very poor power to rush about in the American manner.[2] Perhaps it's only that now I never move – save once in the autumn, late, to come up hither from Rye, & once again, early in July, to go back hence to that retreat – perhaps it's simply that that makes me feel a trifle less humiliatingly handicapped. I have *accepted* doing nothing & being more & more your great-great-uncle, & only moving, as the Vicar of Wakefield says, from the blue bed to the brown.[3] But what I want mainly to tell you is how touched I am by what you say of your interest in my ancient "Notes" & above all of your recognition of the devoted intention & the prompting tenderness & fidelity of that last chapter – so difficult as I found it to do, & yet now bearing the fruit of success as it appears to have done. My book was 3 quarters done when I received from J.G., through your cousin Alice at Cambridge, that packet of Minnie's letters of long ago, which, setting his affairs in order in these days of his own very impaired health & vitality, he asked Alice to read as preliminary to sending them to *me* (to do what I would with,) rather than bring himself to destroy them. She read them with intense interest & emotion & said at once "Do, *do* let me send them to Henry!" They came, & when I had read them (with *such* irresistible tears!) I recognised my chance to do what I had always longed in some way to do without seeing quite how – rescue & preserve in some way from oblivion, commemorate & a little *enshrine*, the image of our admirable & exquisite, our noble & unique little Minnie. It was not easy to do with all the right tact & taste – & there was danger that the long lapse of time would too much have bedimmed & weakened everything. But there at last was my material & my occasion, & I embraced them with all the art & all the piety of which I was capable. I was uncertain as to how Elly & you wd. be affected by the fact of the publicity – but it was out of my power to sound you in any way, & I felt

1. Henrietta Pell-Clarke's visit was prevented by the outbreak of the First World War in August 1914.

2. Apparently Henrietta Pell-Clarke burned all her letters from HJ but this one, including any from the period of HJ's unhappy visit to the U.S. in 1910–11.

3. At the opening of *The Vicar of Wakefield* (1766) by Oliver Goldsmith (1730–74), a novel to which HJ had written an introduction in 1900, the eponymous narrator, Mr Primrose, describes his domestic happiness with his wife: 'We had no revolutions to fear, nor fatigues to undergo; all our adventures were by the fire-side, and all our migrations from the blue bed to the brown.'

that the immense beauty would make the publicity right. So it appears universally to have done – that last chapter of the book has been extraordinarily acclaimed (with all the rest) in this country – where I can best judge of the impression, & dear Minnie's name is *really* now, in the most touching way, I think, silvered over & set apart.[4] I rejoice with all my heart that you feel nothing, so to speak, but the interest & the distinction of this. I haven't heard from Elly directly – though I have in a roundabout manner (that is heard *of* her & her impression;) but I gather that though her 1*st* impression, over my pages, was that of distress & wonder, she is now more than reconciled to what I have done.[5] Do *you* remember that far-away old 1*st* summer at North Conway & the Blue Blinds, with J.G. & O.W.H. & Aunt Charlotte & H.J., in short all of us, or were you too juvenile a little shrimp?[6] Since beginning this I have had an interruption – I have to stop things very often, for general *health* reasons, & wait to go on with them; & in the interval have had a dear little letter from Eleanor Lapsley, fine young mother of 6, on the subject of the emotion that record of Minnie had caused her.[7] But goodbye now, dearest Henrietta. Let me repeat that I delight in having had occasion, in your giving it me, to spend this hour with you. Yours all affectionately

Henry James.

4. HJ wrote to AHJ on 29 March that 'the early passage and the final chapter about dear Minny seem the great, the beautiful "success" of the whole. What I have been able to do for *her* after all the long years – judged by this test of expressed admiration – strikes me as a wondrous stroke of fate and beneficence of time: I seem really to have . . . made her emerge and live on, endowed her with a kind dim sweet immortality that places and keeps her.' (HJL IV, 707.)
5. On 29 March HJ told AHJ he had expected Ellen Emmet's initial distress 'in presence of my chapter', reported to AHJ by Elly's daughter Rosina (HJL IV, 707).
6. HJ recalls the August of 1865 that he and the Temple girls spent in the White Mountains in *Notes of a Son and Brother*, ch. XIII. He revisited North Conway from nearby Chocorua in the autumn of 1904, finding 'There was a latent poetry – old echoes, ever so faint, that *would* come back' (CTW:GBA, 379). S. P. Rosenbaum identifies those mentioned as John Gray, Oliver Wendell Holmes, and possibly Charlotte Temple Sweeney, a sister of Henrietta's father, who with another aunt, Mary Temple Tweedy, acted as guardian for the orphaned Temples after 1854. Rosenbaum reads the last (smudged) initials as an unidentified 'H.I.', but I take them to be 'H.J.'. The 'Blue Blinds' was possibly one of the numerous North Conway boarding-houses.
7. Eleanor Temple Emmet Lapsley (1880–1953) was Henrietta's niece, daughter of Katherine Temple Emmet, and married to John Willard Lapsley (1867–1921), a stockbroker relative of G. T. Lapsley.

283. To James Brand Pinker
8 May 1914

Yale MS   Unpublished

On 4 May a militant suffragette, Mrs Mary Wood, 'an elderly woman of distinctly peaceable appearance' as The Times *said, hacked Sargent's portrait of HJ at the Royal Academy – not irreparably – with a meat cleaver she had concealed about her person. A man who tried to defend her from the crowd before she was led away had his spectacles broken over his nose. 'I wish to show the public,' she said later, 'that they have no security for their property nor for their art treasures until women are given the political freedom.' HJ received a flood of sympathetic letters and was telephoned by all the newspapers. He commented on 6 May to the anti-suffragist Mrs Humphry Ward, 'Surely indeed the good ladies who claim as a virtue for their sex that they can look an artistic possession of that quality and rarity well in the face only to be moved bloodily to smash it, make a strange appeal to the confidence of the country in the kind of character they shall bring to the transaction of our affairs.' (LHJ II, 366.) Next day he told Pinker that a friend 'at once telephoned to me in jubilation – a literary friend! – to the effect that the row would immensely advertise my last book & make a sharper demand for it' (Unpublished Yale MS, Za James 1, vol. 3).*

Pinker had been to New York in March 1914, and presumably came back with word about Howells's professional standing.

TELEPHONE 2417 KENSINGTON
21 CARLYLE MANSIONS, CHEYNE WALK S.W.

My dear Pinker.

All thanks for your interesting note – for I do find it (that is the fact about W.D.H.) interesting. I had always been aware of his case, more or less – but always rather seen it as different from mine, through the difference of his production as to quantity. The fact named by you is but *one* of the facts about him – there are others that have been happier for him. One of them is that his relation to all the Harper periodicals, essentially to the "house", & especially the Magazine, has been long, constant & intimate – scarce a number appearing without a contribution of his – thanks to his abundant "journalistic" talent & the "kind of thing" he was willing to do! For years they paid him a definite annual fee – $10,000 for all his work – & may do so still; though probably not, as he now writes so much fiction *less* (than formerly.) And in the old days his fiction did sell – far more than anything of mine ever did, & he is rich today, thanks to small wants – in spite of a family – & great savings. Those old years are beyond Mr. Wells's ken – he knows of W.D.H. but this later time & the shrunken sale of his very occasional later tales, these less & less important. What it comes to is that he has been a very much bigger & easier & cheaper (in the labour or "quality" sense) & above all more perpetually serialised worker than H.J.; all of which has been to his great advantage & most of it to his honour. I don't in the least want to contradict Wells as to the *actual* state of his sales, combined with his reputation, but only to complete a little the story – which will also interest you![1] But good night & thanks again! Yours ever

H.J.

May 8*th* '14.

284. To Edward Emerson
4 August 1914

Princeton MS   Unpublished

On 3 June HJ told Gaillard Lapsley how touched he was by Eleanor Lapsley's appreciative letter about his volume of memoirs: 'I am trying my hand at another even now, & the most I can do is to assure her that it shall be very slow, very difficult, very delayed.' (Unpublished Houghton MS, bMS Am 1094.4 (70).) He dictated some chapters of this further volume, entitled The Middle Years, *during the autumn of 1914, then laid it aside for other work. On 1 July HJ had finished the proofs of* Notes on Novelists *for Dent, which Scribner's would set from in New York. He did not go down to Lamb House till the middle of July. War was looming, and on 31 July he wrote to Claude Phillips (of the Wallace Collection) about his 'terrible sense that the people of this country may well – by some awful brutal justice – be going to get something bad for the exhibition that has gone on so long of their huge materialized stupidity and vulgarity' (LHJ II, 377).*

Edward Waldo Emerson (1844–1930), son of the most influential American writer of the nineteenth century, trained as a doctor but was also a poet and an editor of his father's work. He wrote Emerson in Concord *(1888),* Henry Thoreau as Remembered by a Young Friend *(1917), and* The Early Years of the Saturday Club, 1855–1870 *(1918). His father and HJ Senior were friends, and he became friends with the James boys – linked to Wilky and Bob by going to Frank Sanborn's*

---

1. HJ had introduced Wells to Howells and his daughter when they were visiting England in 1904, and Howells gave a lunch for Wells in New York in April 1906.

experimentally coeducational school in Concord, and then to HJ and WJ by the physically impaired state (after a bout of typhoid fever) that prevented his joining up for the Civil War. He came down to stay with the Jameses in Newport in the spring of 1861, and in 1918 recorded the demonstrative quarrels of father and sons over dinner, which led HJ's mother to reassure the visitor: 'Don't be disturbed, Edward; they won't stab each other. This is usual when the boys come home.'

LAMB HOUSE RYE SUSSEX

My dear Edward.

I beg you very earnestly not to measure by the belatedness of this acknowledgment the pleasure, the delight I found in your beautiful & generous letter of too many weeks ago. There is no such straight & simple relation in these difficult days between my fond desires & impulses & the consequent action – when there *is* action, & when it retains any air of consequence. Too many things of the all but insurmountable order intervene – & mainly, not to say always, the steady leak in my energy represented by a very active physical ailment with which I have to reckon at every minute of the day, & which I am, I confess, at the same time, as I grow older & older, getting to live with on the most extraordinary terms. I have bad (very bad) & chronic angina pectoris, & nitro-glycerine is the chief of my diet; but wonderful to say I have come to find it not so very absolutely destructive if I can allow it to be sufficiently retarding.[1] It isn't so much that I can do nothing whatever as that I can sometimes do something – a few things – with the most elegant languor. Please note that quality in these poor lines that I write you nestling in the very lap of procrastination. But your letter, which I have before me, after reading it over, has only the more enjoyed its opportunity to sink in & in. I can't tell you how I value feeling that you are one of but three or four, at the most, who have known what most of my groping Notes so much as *mean*. You have been *able* to recognise what they supposed themselves, as they went on, to be talking about – & the mode of your recognition deeply touches me. In fact you remember things (of my own subject,) that I hadn't – like that fantastic little hat, acquired in Paris, that I must have worn to Concord & which lives again for me on your page.[2] How long our hats must have lasted us then! –

1. Nitroglycerine was a common treatment; on 9 June 1914 HJ heard of a man of seventy-eight 'who had lived with bad *angina pect.* for 25 years, and is now much better than formerly, having swallowed enough "dynamite" (mine) to blow up St. Paul's' (N, 402).
2. In *Notes of a Son and Brother*, ch. VII, HJ recalls only once visiting the Sanborn school, 'in the winter of '62–'63, I think'. The Jameses had returned from their most recent time in Europe (and Paris) in September 1860.

& how little I dared to re-visualise that one without this help of yours! Very moving indeed to me your memories of our intimate life of those days, of your first visit to Newport, which I perfectly recall, & of my dear & admirable parents in their habits as they lived – in those particular far-off years. I rejoice to hear from you that you are feeling yourself moved to call up some of the beloved old ghosts, & can wish you nothing better than to feel in doing so, even as I have been feeling, with what heart-breaking gratitude & confidence they come. They only want to & ask to – they hold out such answering hands, & there isn't a service they can render us that they don't seem to me to *look* their unspeakably touching delight at being able to perform. I wish you all happy fortune over the whole exquisite business. You tell me of bland Southern places that you have been to also – & when you speak of sunny nooks, or whatever, "angles", vistas, in the Virginia Blue Ridge I don't know what absurd nostalgic spasm passes over me in sympathy & as in privation – I never having been within even the furthest cry of the Blue Ridge, & being haunted doubtless but by some ancient American charm in its name. Well, I write you of these things with assurance enough, but we sit here in these days & more especially in these nights (for I am writing you very late – have had a longish nap & am not in bed yet,) under the blackness of the most appallingly huge & sudden state of general war. It has all come as by the leap of some awful monster out of his lair – he is *upon* us, he is upon *all* of us here, before we have had time to turn round. It fills me with anguish & dismay & makes me ask myself if *this* then is what I have grown old for, if this is what all the ostensibly or comparatively serene, all the supposedly *bettering* past, of our century, has meant & led up to. It gives away everything one has believed in & lived for – & I envy those of our generation who haven't lived on for it. It's as if the dreadful nations couldn't not suddenly pull up in a convulsion of horror & shame. One said that yesterday, alas – but it's clearly too late to say it today. The action of this country hangs in the balance as I write – but it's probable the scale will have dropped to something formidable, with possibilities fairly unthinkable, tomorrow.[3] It brings back to me the outbreak of the Wartime of our youth – but the whole thing here is nearer, closer upon us, huger, & all in a denser & finer world. I am sorry to say good night on the tragic note

3. *The Times* round-ups of the European situation bore alarming headlines. Monday, 3 August: 'Five Nations at War / Fighting on Three Frontiers / German Declaration to Russia / Invasion of France / German Troops in Luxembourg / British Naval Reserves Mobilized'. Tuesday, 4 August: 'The Menace of Germany / Campaign Through Belgium / Answer of Great Britain / Europe Armed / The Russian Frontier / Reported Naval Battle in the Baltic'. Wednesday, 5 August: 'War Declared / Note Rejected by Germany / British Ambassador to Leave Berlin / Rival Navies in the North Sea / British Army Mobilizing / Government Control of Railways'.

– which I mustn't prolong. But you will all be shaken with the misery of it too, & I am, with a sense of the renewal of your sympathy, yours, very dear Edward, all faithfully

Henry James

August 4*th* *1914.*

285. *To Charles Scribner's Sons*
26 *October 1914*

Princeton TS   Unpublished

On 2 September HJ wrote to Helena De Kay Gilder about the public situation: 'It leaves one small freedom of mind for general talk, it presses, all the while, with every throb of consciousness; and if during the first days I felt in the air the recall of our Civil War shocks and anxieties, and hurryings and doings, of 1861, etc., the pressure in question has already become a much nearer and bigger thing, and a more formidable and tragic one, than anything we of the North in those years had to face.' (LHJ II, 401.) He quickly became involved with charitable work for Belgian refugees, accommodating some in the chapel-studio by Lamb House; and came up to town late in September, some days after the end of the first battle of the Marne, in which the Germans retreated despite seeing the Eiffel Tower in the distance.

By 2 October HJ had received six copies of the Dent Notes on Novelists, *but told Pinker, 'I am unable really to* care *for anything but what happens to, and above all by, our Armies.' Dent's publication date, 13 October, was the second day of the first battle of Ypres (Scribner's published next day), and HJ confided to Pinker that the strain of the public situation, 'with its effect on my poor old physical condition', was not 'at all favourable for work' (Unpublished Yale TSS, Za James 1, vol. 3).*

. 21, CARLYLE MANSIONS, CHEYNE WALK. S.W.
October 26th. 1914.
Charles Scribner Esq.

Dear Mr. Scribner.

I am afraid I come late in the day to ask you to be so good as to send out a few copies of my Notes on Novelists which came into the world here, a direfully preoccupied world, alas, a little time back. It is our direful preoccupation that has mainly held my hand from giving you this very small number of addresses for Author's Copies of my book if you will kindly direct that they be dispatched. I inscribe them on another leaf – though with a fear, I confess, that you may have sent me out here, in your handsome way, a couple of copies of my allowance.[1] I say "fear", but I shall be very glad to get them, and really, I think, don't propose to distribute more than four in the U.S. – so that the half dozen will be exactly made up.

Mr. Pinker tells me that this autumn publication is languishing much less than he feared, that the world here shows in fact positive signs of wanting something other than the newspapers and the great oppressive topic to turn to. So much the better, and the appearance indeed rather strikes me; though if it be true on behalf of things prepared and appointed some time back, I fear the actual preparation of the publishable has the influences pretty badly against it in the poor authors' stricken minds. It's difficult to work in face of the War-monster – that is the trouble; he is so much bigger a reality than anything we can pit against him. If he ever comes to shrink again: – one can so but wonder *when*! – we shall doubtless leap astride of our own animals and set our lances in rest, performing in fact feats of gallantry beyond any in our record; but he looms too large for the moment for most of us, or for *me*, to do more than pretend just to keep in the saddle, sitting as tight as ever I can. See me please in this attitude, not unhorsed but a good deal held up; have patience with me as you have had it before, and I think I can promise you shall be justified. Those of us who shall outwear and outlast, who shall above all outlive, in the larger sense of the term, and outimagine, will be able to show for the adventure, I am convinced, a weight and quality that may be verily worth your having waited for. So, presumptuous as it may sound, those things are what I propose quite brilliantly to do – in testimony whereof I am yours, dear Mr. Scribner, very faithfully

Henry James

286. To Edmund Gosse
17 December 1914

Princeton MS   Published SLHJEG, 304–5; LHJ II, 430

In the summer of 1914 HJ had been working in Rye on his novel about contemporary American millionaires, but as Theodora Bosanquet noted, 'At the beginning of

1. The separate leaf with addresses was not located.

August the declaration of War brought dictation of The Ivory Tower *to an abrupt end. On* August 8 *he started dictating* The Middle Years' (*the never-finished third volume of autobiography*).

At the beginning of November he was thinking again about the abandoned Sense of the Past, *for 'now it seemed to him sufficiently fantastic and divorced from present day conditions to be worked up'. He sent Theodora Bosanquet to Rye on 3 November to fetch it, and next day started redictating.*

He explained on 9 November to Edith Wharton, who was in Paris organizing the American Hostels for Refugees, that, 'It's impossible to "locate anything in our time." Our time has been this time for the last 50 years, & if it was ignorantly & fatuously so the only light in which to show it is now the light of that tragic delusion. And that's too awful a subject. It all makes Walter Scott, him only, readable again.' On 1 December he told her, 'I have been lately attempting a go at one abandoned – at the end of some "30,000 words" – 15 years ago, & fished out of the depths of an old drawer at Lamb House . . . as perhaps offering a certain defiance of subject to the law by which most things now perish in the public blight.' (HJEWL, 316, 320.)

HJ was, as he told his nephew Harry on 30 October, 'utterly and passionately enlisted, up to my eyes and over my aged head, in the greatness of our cause' (LHJ II, 420); but despite this preoccupation made arrangements through Pinker with Martin Secker for the issue of a Uniform Edition of his longer short stories; on 14 November, 'I shall not *ask to see the proofs – I hate so reading over my old things! – if Mr. Secker will please engage to see that the Édition de Luxe is utterly and absolutely conformed to, to the very most lurking comma, and still more to the very most patent absence of one.' (Unpublished Yale TS, Za James 1, vol. 3.) (On 15 October to Gosse, good writing still mattered: 'nothing serious and felt and sincere, nothing "good", is anything but essentially in order to-day' (SLHJEG, 301–2).) From 20 November HJ was paying regular visits to wounded soldiers, first Belgian then increasingly British, in St Bartholomew's Hospital.*

21 CARLYLE MANSIONS, CHEYNE WALK. S.W.

My dear Gosse.

This is a scratch of postscript to my note this evening posted to you – prompted by the consciousness of not having therein made a word of reply to your question as to what I "think of things."[1] The recovered presence of that question makes me somehow positively *want* to say that (I think) I don't

1. Gosse's inquiry is not known to survive; HJ's other letter simply says he is engaged for Christmas by his neighbour Emily Sargent, sister of the painter.

"think" of them at all – though I try to; that I only feel, & feel, & toujours feel about them unspeakably, & about nothing else whatever – feeling so in Wordsworth's terms of exaltations, agonies & loves, & (our) unconquerable mind.[2] Yes, I kind of make out withal that through our insistences an increasing purpose runs, & that one's vision of its final effect (though only with the aid of *time*,) grows less & less dim, so that one seems to find at moments it's almost sharp![3] And meanwhile what a purely suicidal record for themselves the business of yesterday – the women & children (& babes in arms) slaughtered at Scarborough & Whitby, with their turning & fleeing as soon as ever they had killed enough for the moment.[4] Oh I do "think" enough to believe in retribution for *that*. So I've kind of answered you. Ever yours

Henry James

Dec: 17: 1914.

287. To Edward Marsh
6 June 1915

Berg MS   Published LHJ II, 472–4

HJ's war efforts only intensified; on 17 January 1915 he was at Walmer Castle in Kent staying with the prime minister, Herbert H. Asquith (1852–1928). He became honorary president of the American Volunteer Motor Ambulance Corps; and told Edith Wharton he was done 'a kind of unholy hideous good' by accounts of British victories and German deaths; he suffered 'the paralysis of my own power to do anything but increasingly & inordinately feel' *– but also wrote of 'the unspeakable adventure of being alive in these days' (HJEWL, 332, 337, 342).*

In April the first three of Secker's 'Uniform Tales of Henry James' were issued: The Turn of the Screw, The Lesson of the Master *and* The Aspern Papers. *On 10 April he told Walpole of his progress with* The Sense of the Past *– of the 'two or three hours each forenoon, when I have come back to the ability to push a work of fiction of sorts uphill at the rate of about an inch a day' (HJL IV, 751).*

2. HJ also cites this sonnet to Toussaint l'Ouverture in Letter 274, to Hugh Walpole.
3. The hero of Tennyson's poem 'Locksley Hall' clings to a basic faith despite his doubts: 'Yet I doubt not through the ages one increasing purpose runs, / And the thoughts of men are widened with the process of the suns.' (ll. 137–8.)
4. On the morning of 16 December, German cruisers fired on three undefended towns on the north-east coast of England, Scarborough, Whitby and Hartlepool, killing (by official figures) thirty-one people and injuring seventy-nine.

On 7 May, despite a week of poor health, HJ sent the Nation *his article on the founding of that magazine by his old friend Godkin.*

On 23 April Rupert Brooke, who had earlier been at the siege of Antwerp, died of blood poisoning on a French hospital ship in the Aegean. Sir Edward Howard Marsh (1872–1953), a scholar, high-ranking civil servant (associated with Winston Churchill) and patron of the arts, was Brooke's literary executor, and published in May 1914 and Other Poems, *a collection of thirty-two poems beginning with the* War Sonnets *and ending with 'Grantchester'.*

TELEPHONE 2417 KENSINGTON
21 CARLYLE MANSIONS CHEYNE WALK S.W.

Dearest Eddie!

I thank you ever so kindly for this advance copy of Rupert's volume which you were right (& blest!) in feeling that I should intensely prize. I have been spending unspeakable hours over it – heart-breaking ones, under the sense of the stupid extinction of so exquisite an instrument & so exquisite a being. Immense the generosity of his response to life & the beauty & variety of the forms in which it broke out, & of which these further things are such an enriching exhibition. His place is now very high & very safe – even though one walks round & round it with the aching soreness of having to take the monument for the man. It's so wretched talking really of any "place" but his place *with* us & in our eyes & affection most of all, the other being such as could wait, & grow with all confidence & power *while* waiting. He has something, at any rate, one feels in the volume, that puts him significantly apart even in his eminence – the fact that, member of the true high company as he is & poet of the strong poetic wings (for he seems to me extraordinarily strong,) he has *charm* in a way & of a kind that belong to none of the others, who have their beauty & abundance, their distinction & force & grace, whatever it may be, but haven't that particular thing as he has it & as he was going to keep on having it, since it was of his very nature – by which I mean that of his genius. The point is that I think he would still have had it even if he had grown bigger & bigger, & stronger & stronger (for this is what he *would* have done,) & thereby been almost alone in this idiosyncrasy. Even of Keats I don't find myself saying that he had charm – it's all lost in the degree of beauty, which somehow allows it no chance. But in Rupert (not that I match them!) there is the beauty, so great, & then the charm, different & playing beside it & savouring of the very quality of the man. What it comes to, I suppose, is that he touches me most when he is whimsical & personal, even at the poetic pitch, or in the poetic purity, as he perpetually is. And he penetrates me most when he is most hauntingly (or hauntedly,) English – he draws such a real magic from his conscious reference to it. He is extraordinarily so even in the War Sonnets – not that that isn't highly natural too; & the reading of these things over now, which one had first read while he was still there to be exquisitely at stake in them, so to speak, is a sort of refinement both of admiration & of anguish. The present gives them such sincerity – as if they had wanted it![1] I adore the ironic & familiar things, the most intimately English – The Chilterns & the Great Lover (toward the close of which I recognise the misprint you speak of, but fortunately so obvious a one – the more flagrant the better – that you needn't worry;) & of course Grantchester, which is booked for immortality. I revel in Grantchester – & how it would have made one love him if one hadn't known him.[2] As it is it wrings the heart! And yet after all what do they do, all of them together, but again express how life had been wonderful & crowded & fortunate & exquisite for him? – with his sensibilities all so exposed, really exposed, & yet never taking the least real harm. He seems to me to have had in his short life so much that one may almost call it everything. And he isn't tragic now – he has only stopped. It's we who are tragic – you & his mother especially, & whatever others, for we can't stop, & wish we could. The portrait has extreme beauty, but is somehow disconnected.[3] However, great beauty does disconnect! But goodnight – with the lively sense that I *must* see you again before I leave town – which won't be, though, before early in July.[4] I hope you are having less particular strain & stress, & am yours all faithfully

Henry James

June *6th 1915.*

1. The fifth and last War Sonnet, 'The Soldier', famously refers to Brooke's Englishness: 'If I should die, think only this of me: / That there's some corner of a foreign field / That is for ever England . . .'
2. 'The Chilterns' is a farewell to a lover, finishing: 'And I shall find some girl perhaps, / And a better one than you, / With eyes as wise, but kindlier, / And lips as soft, but true. / And I daresay she will do.' 'The Great Lover' lists, after a grandiose opening, the sensuous pleasures of the English human and natural world ('These I have loved: / White plates and cups, clean-gleaming . . .'). 'The Old Vicarage, Grantchester' whimsically praises the village (where Brooke lived after 1909) from a café in Berlin, and ends by asking, 'Oh! yet / Stands the Church clock at ten to three? / And is there honey still for tea?'
3. Sherill Schell's ethereally hazy photograph of Brooke in profile is the volume's frontispiece.
4. HJ did not get back to Lamb House till a ten-day visit in mid October.

288. To James Brand Pinker
29 June 1915

Yale TS (with MS insertions)   Partly published LHJ II, 482–3

On 23 June HJ wrote to Pinker that 'it wouldn't be at all disagreeable to make some money, in these strained conditions, and I will gladly do a small piece, about 3000 words, for the New York Tribune'. He had then two or three ideas, and without waiting 'I feel myself already choosing the rightest one' (Unpublished Yale TS, Za James 1, vol. 3).

> 2417 KENSINGTON.
> 21, CARLYLE MANSIONS, CHEYNE WALK. S.W.
> June 29th. 1915

My dear Pinker.

I am glad to hear from you of the conditions in which the New York Tribune representative thinks there will be no difficulty over the fee for the article. I have in point of fact during the last three or four days considerably written one – concerning which a question comes up which I hope you won't think too tiresome. Making up my mind that something as concrete and "human" as possible would be my best card to play, I have done something about the British soldier, his aspect, temper and tone, and the considerations he suggests, *as I have seen him since the beginning of the war in Hospital*; where I have in fact largely and constantly seen him.[1] The theme lends itself, by my sense, much; and I dare say I should have it rather to myself – though of course there is no telling! But what I have been feeling in the connection – having now done upwards of 3000 words – is that I should be very grateful for leave to make them 4000 (without of course extension of fee.) I have never been good for the mere snippet, and there is so much to say and to feel! Would you mind asking her, in reporting to her of what my subject is, whether this extra thousand would incommode them. If she really objects to it I think I shall be then disposed to ask you to make some *other* application of my little paper (on the 4000 basis;) in which case I should propose to the Tribune another idea,

---

1. This essay was 'The Long Wards' (eventually about 4,400 words), which was not used by the *Tribune*. It was first published in Edith Wharton's collection in aid of Belgian refugees, *The Book of the Homeless*, published on 22 January 1916. In August 1878 *Lippincott's Magazine* had published an essay by HJ (never reprinted) on 'The British Soldier', following a visit to the military camp at Aldershot, which echoes Ruskin's view 'that life loses a certain indispensable charm in a country destitute of an apparent standing army'.

keeping it down absolutely to the 3000. (I'm afraid I can't do less than that.) My motive would probably in that case be a quite different and less "concrete" thing; namely, the expression of my sense of the way the Briton in general feels about his insulation, and his being in it and of it, even through all this unprecedented stress. It would amount to a statement or picture of his sense of the way his sea-genius has always encircled and protected him, striking deep into his blood and his bones; so that any reconsideration of his position in a new light inevitably comes hard to him, and yet makes the process the effective development of which it is interesting to watch. I should call this thing something like "The New Vision"; or, better still, simply "Insulation:" though I don't say *exactly* that. At all events I should be able to make something interesting of it, and it would of course inevitably take the sympathetic turn. But I would *rather* keep to the thing I have been trying, if I may have the small extra space.[2]

And now here is another matter, purely personal, which I intended to write to you about to-day, and now clutch this convenient occasion for. You probably won't be surprised to learn that the force of events has brought to a head the disposition I have strongly felt, ever since the beginning of the War, to apply for naturalisation in this country.[3] I find myself wanting so exceedingly to do so that the question has simply settled itself for me, and I have taken the preliminary steps. I needn't tell you why and how much I have moved to this

2. This became 'Within the Rim' (just under 5,000 words), which re-creates HJ's scrutiny from Rye's ramparts of 'the bright mystery beyond the rim of the farthest opaline reach' – the invisible fighting in France and Belgium – during the incongruously beautiful August–September of 1914. HJ also speaks of his intensifying attachment to England, for 'reasons' which are 'the particulars of one's affection'. 'The blades of grass, the outlines of leaves, the drift of clouds, the streaks of mortar between old bricks, not to speak of the call of child-voices muffled in the comforting air, became ... with a hundred other like touches, casually felt, extraordinary admonitions and symbols, close links of a tangible chain.' (CTW:GBA, 331, 337–8.)

3. On 24 June HJ had written to his nephew Harry to tell him this, explaining that 'Hadn't it been for the War I should certainly have gone on as I was', and stating: 'I have spent here all the best years of my life – they practically have *been* my life: about a twelvemonth hence I shall have been domiciled uninterruptedly in England for forty years, and there is not the least possibility, at my age, and in my state of health, of my ever returning to the U.S. or taking up any relation with it as a country.' (HJL IV, 760.) And he told Gosse on 25 June that 'The disposition itself has haunted me as Wordsworth's sounding cataract haunted *him* – "like a passion" – ever since the beginning of the War.' (SLHJEG, 308.) On 3 July he told Frederic Harrison, 'As to the U.S.A., I am afraid I suffer almost more than I can endure from the terms of precautionary "friendship" on which my country is content to remain with the author of such systematic abominations.' (LHJ II, 484.) On 30 July he told Sargent he had been waiting for America to end its neutrality: 'It would really have been *so* easy for the U.S. to have "kept" (if they had cared to!) yours all faithfully, Henry James.' (HJL IV, 774.)

end – you will already have had your own observation of it. But the great point for the moment is that I am required to provide myself with four competent sponsors or guarantors of my respectability and good intentions, who will simply have to affix their signature (my solicitor or his representative waiting on them for the purpose) to their honest belief in these things – as well as to their judgment of my speaking and writing the English tongue with some approach to propriety. I have selected three of these friends, and the purpose of this is to ask if you will kindly act as the fourth. It will be giving me the greatest pleasure to be under that obligation to you. I will let you know even who your fellow sponsors are as soon as I hear from that one of the three to whom I applied but yesterday, and who is so immensely occupied a person that there may be a slight delay about his word.[4] I am saying nothing whatever generally about this, of course, till it is all settled and done. But if I can meanwhile feel I may look to you for your blessing on it I shall be very glad indeed.

Believe me yours ever
Henry James

289. To Herbert George Wells
6 July 1915

Bodleian MS   Published HJHGW, 261–3; HJL IV, 766–7

Wells had been wounded by his treatment, and his friend Arnold Bennett's, in HJ's 'The Younger Generation' in The Times Literary Supplement, *and added a chapter, 'Of Art, Of Literature, Of Mr. Henry James' to his long-accumulating, outspoken, parodic critique of the British literary world,* Boon, The Mind of the Race, The Wild Asses of the Devil, *and* The Last Trump: Being a First Selection from the Literary Remains of George Boon, Appropriate to the Times *(1915). Wells's character Boon talks about HJ: 'He has, I am convinced, one of the strongest, most abundant minds alive in the whole world, and he has the smallest penetration. Indeed, he has no penetration. He is the culmination of the Superficial type.' Further, 'In practice James's selection becomes just omission and nothing more.' In his fiction, 'These people cleared for artistic treatment never make lusty love, never go to angry war, never shout at an election or perspire at poker; never in any way* date . . . *And upon the petty residuum of human interest left to them*

4. HJ's other sponsors were Gosse, George Prothero and Asquith, the 'immensely occupied' prime minister himself.

they focus minds of a Jamesian calibre.' His climactic image mocks the unity of the Jamesian novel: 'The thing his novel is about is always there. It is like a church lit but without a congregation to distract you, with every light and line focused on the high altar. And on the altar, very reverently placed, intensely there, is a dead kitten, an egg-shell, a bit of string . . .' 'It is a magnificent but painful hippopotamus resolved at any cost, even at the cost of its dignity, upon picking up a pea . . .' Late in life Wells declared, 'Henry James asked for it'.

21 CARLYLE MANSIONS CHEYNE WALK S.W.
July *6th 1915*

My dear Wells.

I was given yesterday at a club your volume "Boon &c", from a loose leaf in which I learn that you kindly sent it me & which yet appears to have lurked there for a considerable time undelivered. I have just been reading, to acknowledge it intelligently, a considerable number of its pages – though not all; for, to be perfectly frank, I have been in that respect beaten for the first time – or rather for the first time but one – by a book of yours: I haven't found the current of it draw me on and on this time – as unfailingly & irresistibly before (which I have repeatedly let you know.)[1] However, I shall try again – I hate to lose any scrap of you that *may* make for light or pleasure; & meanwhile I have more or less mastered your appreciation of H.J., which I have found very curious & interesting, after a fashion – though it has naturally not filled me with a fond elation. It is difficult of course for a writer to put himself *fully* in the place of another writer who finds him extraordinarily futile & void, & who is moved to publish that to the world – & I think the case isn't easier when he happens to have enjoyed the other writer enormously, from far back; because there has then grown up the habit of taking some common meeting-ground between them for granted, & the falling away of this is like the collapse of a bridge which made communication possible. But I am by nature more in dread of any fool's paradise, or at least of any bad misguidedness, than in love with the idea of a security proved, & the fact that a mind as brilliant as yours *can* resolve me into such an unmitigated mistake, can't enjoy me in anything like the degree in which I like to think I may be enjoyed, makes me greatly want to fix myself, for as long as my nerves will stand it, with such a pair of eyes. I am aware of certain things I have, & not

1. On 9 November 1914 HJ had told Edith Wharton, about *The Wife of Sir Isaac Harman*, that 'I broke down utterly with Wells's last – found it of a looseness & cheapness scarce credible & sans everything that had made him one's joy before.' (HJEWL, 316.)

less conscious, I believe, of various others that I am simply reduced to wish I did or could have; so I try, for possible light, to enter into the feelings of a critic for whom the deficiencies so preponderate. The difficulty about that effort, however, is that one can't keep it up – one *has* to fall back on one's sense of one's good parts – one's own sense; and I at least shld. have to do that, I think, even if your picture were painted with a more searching brush. For I should otherwise seem to forget what it is that my poetic & my appeal to experience rest upon. They rest upon *my* measure of fulness – fulness of life & of the projection of it, which seems to you such an emptiness of both. I don't mean to say I don't wish I could do twenty things I can't – many of which you do so livingly; but I confess I ask myself what would become in that case of some of those to which I am most addicted & by which interest seems to me most beautifully producible. I hold that interest may be, *must* be, exquisitely made & created, and that if we don't make it, we who undertake to, nobody & nothing will make it for us; though nothing is more possible, nothing may even be more certain, than that my quest of it, my constant wish to run it to earth, may entail the sacrifice of certain things that are not on the straight line of it. However, there are too many things to say, & I don't think your chapter is really inquiring enough to entitle you to expect all of them. The fine thing about the fictional form to me is that it opens such widely different windows of attention; but that is just why I like the window so to frame the play & the process!

Faithfully yours
Henry James

290. To Herbert George Wells
10 July 1915

Bodleian TS   Published HJHGW, 265–8; HJL IV, 768–70; SL2, 429–31

Wells replied on 8 July: 'I have set before myself a gamin-esque ideal, I have a natural horror of dignity, finish and perfection, a horror a little enhanced by theory. You may take it that my sparring and punching at you is very much due to the feeling that you were "coming over" me, and that if I was not very careful I should find myself giving way altogether to respect. There is of course a real and very fundamental difference in our innate and developed attitudes towards life and literature. To you literature like painting is an end, to me literature like architecture is a means, it has a use. Your view was, I felt, altogether too dominant in the world of criticism, and I assailed it in tones of harsh antagonism. And writing that stuff about you was the first escape I had from the obsession of this war. Boon is just a waste-paper basket . . . I had rather be called a journalist than an artist, that is the essence of it, and there was no other antagonist possible than yourself.' HJ dictated a final letter to Wells.

21 CARLYLE MANSIONS CHEYNE WALK, S.W.
July 10th. 1915.

My dear Wells.

I am bound to tell you that I don't think your letter makes out any sort of case for the bad manners of "Boon", so far as your indulgence in them at the expense of your poor old H.J. is concerned – I say "your" simply because he has *been* yours, in the most liberal, continual, sacrificial, the most admiring and abounding critical way, ever since he began to know your writings: as to which you have had copious testimony. Your comparison of the book to a waste-basket strikes me as the reverse of felicitous, for what one throws into that receptacle is exactly what one *doesn't* commit to publicity and make the affirmation of one's estimate of one's contemporaries by. I should liken it much rather to the preservative portfolio or drawer in which what is withheld from the basket is savingly laid away. Nor do I feel it anywhere evident that my "view of life and literature," or what you impute to me as such, is carrying everything before it and becoming a public menace – so unaware do I seem, on the contrary, that my products constitute an example in any measurable degree followed or a cause in any degree successfully pleaded: I can't but think that if this were the case I should find it somewhat attested in their circulation – which, alas, I have reached a very advanced age in the entirely defeated hope of. But I *have* no view of life and literature, I maintain, other than that our form of the latter in especial is admirable exactly by its range and variety, its plasticity and liberality, its fairly living on the sincere and shifting experience of the individual practitioner. That is why I have always so admired your so free and strong application of it, the particular rich receptacle of intelligences and impressions emptied out with an energy of its own, that your genius constitutes; and *that* is in particular why, in my letter of two or three days since, I pronounced it curious and interesting that you should find the case I constitute myself only ridiculous and vacuous to the extent of your having to proclaim your sense of it. The curiosity and the interest, however, in this latter connection are of course for my mind those of the break of perception (perception of the vivacity of *my* variety) on the part of a talent so generally inquiring and apprehensive as yours. Of course for myself I live, live intensely and am fed by life, and my value, whatever it be, is in my own kind of expression of that. Therefore I am pulled up to wonder by the fact that for you my kind (my sort of sense of expression and sort of sense of life alike,) doesn't exist; and that wonder is, I admit, a disconcerting comment on my idea of the various appreciability of our addiction to the novel and of all the personal and intellectual history, sympathy and curiosity, behind the given example of it. It is when that history and curiosity have been determined in the way most different from my own that I myself want to get at them – precisely *for* the extension of life, which is the novel's best gift. But that is another matter. Meanwhile I absolutely dissent from the claim that there are any differences whatever in the amenability to art of forms of literature aesthetically determined, and hold your distinction between a form that is (like) painting and a form that is (like) architecture for wholly null and void. There is no sense in which architecture is aesthetically "for use" that doesn't leave any other art whatever exactly as much so; and so far from that of literature being irrelevant to the literary report upon life, and to its being made as interesting as possible, I regard it as relevant in a degree that leaves everything else behind. It is art that *makes* life, makes interest, makes importance, for our consideration and application of these things, and I know of no substitute whatever for the force and beauty of its process.[1] If I were Boon I should say that the pretence of such a substitute is helpless and hopeless humbug; but I wouldn't be Boon for the world, and am only yours faithfully

Henry James

291. To James Brand Pinker
27 July 1915

Yale TS   Unpublished

On 14 July Macmillan published The Book of France *in Aid of the French Parliamentary Committee's Fund for the Relief of the Invaded Departments, containing HJ's essay 'France' and his translation of 'Les Saints de la France' by Maurice Barrès (1862–1923). On 19 July HJ agreed to write to various writers and artists (including Kipling, Conrad, Sargent and Hardy – excluding Wells) on*

1. Replying to HJ on 13 July, Wells says, 'I don't clearly understand your concluding phrases – which shews no doubt how completely they define our difference. When you say "it is art that *makes* life, makes interest, makes importance," I can only read sense into it by assuming that you are using "art" for every conscious human activity. I use the word for a research and attainment that is technical and special . . .' (LHJ II, 488.)

behalf of Edith Wharton, asking for contributions to her Book of the Homeless *(1916). HJ's contribution was the essay not used by the* New York Tribune, *'The Long Wards', which ends with his hopefully wondering what, given the decency of the war-wounded, uncultivated though they were, a more nurturing society might not do for them – 'for I believe in Culture' (CTW:GBA, 350).*

HJ took the oath of allegiance at 4.30 p.m. on 26 July, and wrote to Gosse, 'Civis Britannicus sum!' (SLHJEG, 312). He had let Lamb House to an American diplomat, and the news that the Germans had torpedoed another American ship made him hopeful of American intervention on the Allied side. (The U.S. did not enter the war till April 1917.)

> 2417 KENSINGTON.
> 21, CARLYLE MANSIONS, CHEYNE WALK. S.W.
> July 27th. 1915.

My dear Pinker.

Here is the small passage, embodying my "reasons", extracted from my Application; I not only haven't, as I say, any objection at all to its being made public, but quite desire that this should be the case – for the sake of what I feel as the good example!

> Yours ever
> *Henry James*

Copy of Mr Henry James Reasons for Naturalisation.

[. . . . .] 'Because of his having lived and worked in England for the best part of forty years; because of his attachment to the country and his sympathy with it and its people; because of the long friendships and associations and interests he has formed here – these last including the acquisition of some property; all of which things have brought to a head his desire to throw his moral weight and personal allegiance, for whatever they may be worth, into the scale of the contending Nation's present and future fortune.'

292. To James Brand Pinker
28 July 1915

Yale TS   Unpublished

> 2417 KENSINGTON.
> 21, CARLYLE MANSIONS, CHEYNE WALK. S.W.
> July 28th. 1915

My dear Pinker.

Let me renew my thanks for your good office in respect to this morning's Times. The thing does exactly what I wanted of it – attests my fullest responsibility for my act, and has a sort of "exemplary" value which I shall rejoice in any degree to have established. So there we will let the business rest! It has been well done, and I am yours ever

Henry James

P.S. I talk of "rest" even while my telephone rings and rings again – rings out with the would-be approach of the interviewer or other worryer. However, I am cased in steel, and their want of wit in not seeing that the bit in The Times was designed very exactly to forestall them, to say everything that need be said about the matter, is – well, not worth talking about!

293. To Edmund Gosse
25 August 1915

Congress MS   Published SLHJEG, 313–15; HJL IV, 776–8; LHJ II, 496–9

On 30 July HJ was again taken ill. His diary: 'Date from that day the beginning, with intermissions, very brief, of all this late and present (Sept. 12th) crisis.' (N, 428.) On 10 August he told Rhoda Broughton of the many welcoming reactions to his naturalization; 'if there is a comfort in the absoluteness of my settlement (like old Martin Luther, "Here I stand, I can no other,") I enjoy it to the full' (Unpublished Cheshire MS, DDB/M/J/1/43).

TELEPHONE 2417 KENSINGTON.
21 CARLYLE MANSIONS CHEYNE WALK S.W.
August 25*th* 1915.

My dear Gosse.

I have had a bad sick week, mostly in bed – with putting pen to paper quite out of my power: otherwise I should sooner have thanked you for the so generous spirit of that letter, & told you, with emotion, how much it has touched me.[1] I am really more overcome than I can say by your having been able to indulge in such freedom of mind & grace of speculation, during these dark days, on behalf of my poor old rather truncated edition, in fact entirely frustrated one – which has the grotesque likeness for me of a sort of miniature Ozymandias of Egypt ("look on my *works* ye mighty & despair!") – round which the lone & level sands stretch further away than ever.[2] It *is* indeed consenting to be wooed aside a little into what was ere blest literature to so much as answer the question you are so handsomely impelled to make – but my very statement about the matter can only be, alas, a melancholy, a blighted confession. That Edition has been, from the point of view of profit either to the publishers or to myself, practically a complete failure; vulgarly speaking, it doesn't sell – that is my annual report of what it does – the whole 25 vols. – in this country amounts to about £25 from the Macmillans; & the ditto from the Scribners in the U.S. to very little more.[3] I am past all praying for anywhere; I remain at my age (which you know,) & after my long career, utterly, insurmountably, unsaleable. And the original preparation of that collective & selective series involved really the extremity of labour – all my "earlier" things – of which the Bostonians would have been, if included, one – were so intimately & interestingly revised. The Edition is from that point of view really a monument (like Ozymandias) which has never had the least intelligent critical

1. On 28 August HJ's diary would record: 'Unwell, dismally unwell and helpless, for many past days; almost, or quite, unprecedented and illuminated, or at least illuminating, stomachic and digestive crisis; with, suddenly, gout as climax.' (N, 430.) Gosse's letter is not known to survive.
2. The sonnet 'Ozymandias' of 1817 by Percy Bysshe Shelley (1792–1822) reports 'a traveller from an antique land', Egypt, telling of a vast, fragmented statue in the desert. Expressive details, like the face's 'sneer of cold command, / Tell that its sculptor well those passions read / Which yet survive, stamped on these lifeless things'. The pedestal bears a legend: ' "My name is Ozymandias, king of kings: / Look on my works, ye Mighty, and despair!" / Nothing beside remains. Round the decay / Of that colossal wreck, boundless and bare / The lone and level sands stretch far away.'
3. There were only twenty-four volumes in the New York Edition. On 6 February HJ had acknowledged Pinker's payment (with his 10 per cent deducted) of £36 9s. 10d., Macmillan's annual royalty.

justice done it – any sort of critical attention at all paid it – & the artistic problem involved in my scheme was a deep & exquisite one, & moreover was, as I hold, very effectively solved. Only it took such time – *and* such taste – in other words such aesthetic light. No more commercially thankless job of the literary order was (Prefaces & all – *they* of a thanklessness!) accordingly ever achieved. The *immediate* inclusion of the Bostonians was rather deprecated by my publishers (the Scribners, who were very generally & in a high degree appreciative: I make no complaint of them at all!) – & there were reasons for which I also wanted to wait: we always meant that that work shld. eventually come in. Revision of it loomed peculiarly formidable & time-consuming (for intrinsic reasons,) & as other things were more pressing & more promptly feasible I allowed it to stand over – with the best intentions, & also in company with a small number more of provisional omissions. But by the time it *had* stood over disappointment had set in; the undertaking had begun to announce itself as a virtual failure & we stopped short where we were – that is when a couple of dozen volumes were out. From that moment, some seven or eight years ago, nothing whatever has been added to the series – & there is little enough appearance now that there will ever. Your good impression of the B.'s greatly moves me – the thing was no success whatever on publication in the Century (when it came out,) & the late R. W. Gilder, of that periodical, wrote me at the time that they had never published anything that appeared so little to interest their readers. I felt about it myself then that it was probably rather a remarkable feat of objectivity – but I never was very thoroughly happy about it, & seem to recall that I found the subject & the material, after I had got launched in it, under some illusion, less interesting & repaying than I had assumed it to be. All the same I *should* have liked to review it for the Edition – it would have come out a much truer and more curious thing (it was meant to be curious from the first;) but there can be no question of that, or of the proportionate Preface to have been written with it, at present – or probably ever within my span of life. Apropos of which matters I at this moment hear from Heinemann that 4 or 5 of my books that he has have quite (entirely) ceased to sell & that he must break up the plates.[4] Of course he must; I have nothing to say against it; & the things in question are mostly all in the Edition. But such is "success"! I should have liked to write that Preface to the Bostonians – which will never be written now. But think of noting now that *that* is a thing that has perished!

4. Books of HJ's published by Heinemann were: *The American: A Comedy in Four Acts, Terminations, Embarrassments, The Other House, The Spoils of Poynton, What Maisie Knew, The Two Magics, The Awkward Age, A Little Tour in France, English Hours* and *Italian Hours*.

I am doing my best to feel better, & hope to go out this afternoon, the 1st one for several![5] I am exceedingly with you all over Philip's transfer to France.[6] We are with each other now as not yet before over everything & I am yours & your wife's more than ever

H.J.

294. To Longmans, Green & Co.
1 November 1915

University of Reading TC   Unpublished

On 22 September HJ told Edith Wharton of his still suffering from 'an interminable gastric crisis of the most vicious and poisonous order' (HJEWL, 354). He wrote on 4 October to Edward Marsh about his Preface to Rupert Brooke's posthumous Letters from America: *'I am doing the Preface with some steadiness, though you must still have a little more patience with me. I foresee it may run even to something like 10,000 words – & have already done 6,000; after which of course I shall as always have to do it all over: as it is ever the second doing, for me, that is the doing.' (HJL IV, 780.) It was to be his last completed piece of writing; the book appeared on 28 January 1916.*

HJ had received his Oxford honorary degree in 1912 at the same time as Robert Bridges (1844–1930), the Poet Laureate since 1913, who was compiling The Spirit of Man: An Anthology in English and French from the Philosophers and Poets, *made by the Poet Laureate in 1915 and dedicated by gracious permission to His Majesty the King (Longmans, Green & Co., 1916). HJ chose for it the ending of WJ's 'Is Life Worth Living?' of 1895, collected in* The Will to Believe and Other Essays in Popular Philosophy *(1897) – also published by Longmans, Green & Co. The passage as used by Bridges: 'I confess that I do not see why the very existence of an invisible world may not in part depend on the personal response which any one of us may make to the religious appeal. God himself, in short, may draw vital strength and increase of very being from our fidelity. For my own part, I do not know what the sweat and blood and tragedy of this life mean, if they mean anything short of this. If this life be not a real fight, in which something is eternally gained for the universe by success, it is no better than a game of private theatricals*

5. HJ's diary for the day says 'Nelson Ward, 4' (N, 430) – Ward being his solicitor (as well as Sargent's and the De Glehns'), who had handled his naturalization and whom he was seeing to add a codicil to his will.
6. Gosse's son Philip (1879–1959) was an army doctor whose medical unit, attached to the 23rd Division, was posted near the front (1915–17).

from which one may withdraw at will. But it feels like a real fight – as if there were something really wild in the universe which we, with all our idealities and faithfulnesses, are needed to redeem; and first of all to redeem our own hearts from atheisms and fears. For such a half-wild half-saved universe our nature is adapted. The deepest thing in our nature is this dumb region of the heart in which we dwell alone with our willingnesses and our unwillingnesses, our faiths and our fears. As through the cracks and crannies of caverns those waters exude from the earth's bosom which then form the fountain-heads of springs, so in these crepuscular depths of personality the sources of all our outer deeds and decisions take their rise. Here is our deepest organ of communication with the nature of things; and compared with these concrete movements of our soul all abstract statements and scientific arguments – the veto, for example, which the strict positivist pronounces upon our faith – sound to us like mere chatterings of the teeth . . .

'These then are my last words to you: Be not afraid of life. Believe that life is worth living, and your belief will help create the fact. The "scientific proof" that you are right may not be clear before the day of judgment (or some stage of being which that expression may serve to symbolize) is reached. But the faithful fighters of this hour, or the beings that then and there will represent them, may turn to the faint-hearted, who here decline to go on, with words like those with which Henry IV greeted the tardy Crillon after a great battle had been gained: "Hang yourself, brave Crillon! we fought at Arques, and you were not there!"' (The quotation is from Henri IV of France (1553–1610) in a 1597 letter to Crillon, as popularized by Voltaire.)

2417 KENSINGTON.
21 Carlyle Mansions, Cheyne Walk, S.W.
November 1st. 1915.
Messrs. Longmans Green and Co.
Paternoster Row, E.C.

Dear Sirs,

I have had a long illness, from which I am but now recovering, or I should sooner have written to ask your assent to the inclusion by Mr. Robert Bridges, the Poet Laureate, of a passage from my brother William James's "Will to Believe" in an Anthology of short pages from English literature bearing upon our public situation here now. He appealed to me some time ago to select for him such a page of my brother's as he was sure I should find, and I came upon just the right thing in "The Will to Believe." I sent it to him; it will figure admirably in his book, and its appearance there will give the greatest pleasure to my sister-in-law and her children. Please take for granted how much it will give me. The lines in question form about the final page of the essay "Is Life Worth Living?" in the volume I speak of. It will be a great satisfaction to me to be able to write to Mr. Bridges that I was happy in taking your assent for granted, and I am faithfully your

Henry James

295. To Rhoda Broughton
3 November 1915

Cheshire TS   Unpublished

HJ's indomitable, sharp-tongued old friend Rhoda Broughton, a novelist since 1867, lived at Richmond till 1900, then with a cousin at Headington Hill near Oxford, and was a regular playgoing companion, a friend also of Howard Sturgis and Anne Thackeray Ritchie.

2417 KENSINGTON.
21, CARLYLE MANSIONS, CHEYNE WALK. S.W.
November 3rd, 1915.

My dear Rhoda.

Yes indeed, I have been in pretty heavy trouble, such trouble as to have reduced me to this rude delay (to respond to your most kind letter) in the first place, and to this rude form in the second. I have really been quite miserably ill these three months, but only during the latter half of them have I emerged into a true intelligence of the source of my woe – which has been a bad heart-crisis. It needn't perhaps have been quite so bad had I not strayed by misfortune for a good while into the desert of false scents and wrong explanations; at any rate I am face to face with the right explanation now – which doesn't mean, however, as yet at least, any very desperate case; only one that has to be taken very strictly and firmly into account. I am in the light, of a sort, at any rate – rather than in the darkness in which I some time floundered; and gather that I'm doing well and going straight – though taking of course but short views.

I greatly appreciate meanwhile your fidelity and your explicit response to old perpetrations on the part of this fairly extinct literary volcano – your generous allusion to one of whose ancient masterpieces gives me, I assure you, the liveliest pleasure. I think of it, the masterpiece in question, as the work of quite another person than myself, at this date – that of a rich (so much rather than a poor) relation, say, who hasn't cast me off in my trouble, but suffers me still to claim a shy fourth cousinship.

But most of all does it regale me to know of your vision of a possible perch in town after Christmas, your really getting seated on which I shall keep praying for with all my heart. I am convinced that we shall truly set it up, we your friends here, between us all, and allow its knocker little rest – even though my actual hampered activity may reduce me to pushing the case on more by the fond spirit than by the bustling body. Bustling is at an end for me forever now – though indeed, after all, I have had very little hand in it for many a day. I cock my ear toward any echo of the triumphant chorus that awaits the confirmed prospect of your migration. Do indeed let Pullin keep her hand in for that blest matter of the tea-table cakes.[1] Never was such a hand – I trust she won't find me fulsome – whether for the fine art of purchase or for that of bold concoction. Yes, I have read Compton Mackenzie, with difficulty – but still read him. He is not, to my sense, keeping up the promise of his best earlier work, yet he has a queer cool mechanical cleverness, a kind of tiresome ease of substituted genius, which keeps him after a fashion possible to me.[2] Hugh Walpole's late volume I haven't so much as seen – any more than I have seen *him* yet, though just back from Russia, and then on his way to Edinburgh to greet his mother, did I a few days since hear from him by telephone that he was passing.[3] I hope for a sight of him a week or two hence. For a good while now of course I have seen almost nobody, only leading a life scraped bare – ! It will have to be kept pretty bare for the future – still, a certain social vegetation *will* doubtless sprout, and all roundabout you, as it were, the brave plashing and flashing pièce d'eau of the garden; the sound of whose clear cascades will be more welcome again than I can say to your affectionate old

Henry James

1. On 17 April, HJ had told Rhoda Broughton he missed her London establishment (she was taking a flat for part of each year), and especially 'dear Pulleyn in such liberal charge of the refreshment counter' (Unpublished Cheshire MS, DDB/M/J/1/42). In ill-health Rhoda Broughton often dictated her novels to her maid, correctly spelt Pullen.
2. Before going off to fight at Gallipoli, Compton Mackenzie had published his new book in 1914; HJ had told Walpole, Mackenzie's rival for his critical favour, on 21 November 1914, that, 'His huge II of *Sinister Street* is half a deadly failure and half an extraordinary exhibition of talent. The Oxford moiety . . . is of a strange platitude; but the London sequel, all about prostitutes (*exclusively*) offers a collection of these; studied *sur le vif*, which is far beyond anything done, ever, in English (naturally), and yet is not in the least an emulation of anything French – is really an original and striking performance.' (HJL IV, 730.)
3. Walpole, who had poor eyesight, had just come back, suffering with boils and insomnia, from Russia, where he had been first a war correspondent and then a Russian medical officer

296. To John William Mackail
26 November 1915

Princeton MS   Unpublished

On 13 November HJ wrote to Walpole of his latest illness: 'the past year has made me feel twenty years older, and, frankly, as if my knell had rung' (HJL IV, 781).

Mackail (1859–1945), a poet and mainly classical literary scholar, had been Professor of Poetry at Oxford, 1906–11, and was a Fellow (later President) of the British Academy. In 1888 he married Margaret, only daughter of Sir Edward Burne-Jones, and at the painter's funeral in 1898 HJ had found him 'beautiful and admirable' supporting the widow (HJL IV, 96). The newly naturalized HJ seemed a likely lecturer for the patriotic Shakespeare Tercentenary of 1916. Mackail himself published Shakespeare after Three Hundred Years.

TELEPHONE 2417 KENSINGTON.
21 CARLYLE MANSIONS CHEYNE WALK S.W.
Nov. 26*th* 1915.

My dear Mackail.

Your very kind invitation on behalf of the British Academy (whose own most flattering appeal hasn't yet reached me,) comes, alas, too late.[1] One blushes to give such graceless reasons in these days & conditions, but my poor old state of health which has for a long time past been one of great difficulty & during the last three or four months undergone great aggravation, puts it out of the question for me to undertake the glorious task you propose. I have been going through a bad heart-crisis, in addition to having suffered for several years previous from chronic angina pectoris. There are the intimate abject facts – my life is absolutely restricted by them – my activity practically reduced to naught. I can't count on myself at all; I should be able neither to prepare the Shakespeare lecture nor to utter it if prepared; & an engagement taken to perform such an act several months ahead is an idea simply appalling to me.

(decorated for valour). He had recently published a book of stories about children, *The Golden Scarecrow.*

1. The invitation from Israel Gollancz (1863–1930), Professor of English at King's College, London, and secretary of the British Academy, evidently arrived soon after this, for on 28 November HJ replied he was unable to promise any contribution: 'I am constrained to write you thus briefly and gracelessly, and can only very earnestly and sadly beg you to exonerate yours very truly / Henry James' (Unpublished Folger TS). Gollancz edited in 1916 *A Book of Homage to Shakespeare* and wrote *Notes on Shakespeare the Patriot.*

So horridly do I have to put the matter. Please believe how deeply touched I am by the light in which *you* put it. That does me the very greatest honour, & the devil of the thing is that I should immensely have *liked* to respond to your proposal, liked it beyond anything – & infallibly have said "Rather – !" The actual case would break my heart if that organ were not already smashed. It is a part of the whole general dreadfulness. I very gratefully acknowledge the honour done me by your colleagues. And I beg you to give my love, however irrelevantly, to Margaret. All faithfully yours

Henry James.

*

On the evening of 29 November HJ met Gosse for the last time. HJ's last recorded letter, on 1 December, to his niece Peggy, notes his months of serious insomnia; though dictated, it ends: 'the pen drops from my hand' (HJL IV, 784).

He suffered a stroke on the morning of 2 December, which paralysed his left side. Later in the day he supposedly told Fanny Prothero when she visited that in falling 'he heard in the room a voice which was distinctly, it seemed, not his own, saying: "So here it is at last, the distinguished thing!"' (Edith Wharton, A Backward Glance, 366–7.) He had a further stroke the following night and thereafter was cruelly confused about where he was. Delirious on 8 December, he had the Remington moved into his bedroom, and began dictating fragments of broken eloquence: 'I find the business of coming round about as important and glorious as any circumstance I have had occasion to record, by which I mean that I find them as damnable and as boring.' He seemed to be working on a novel, dictating two letters as 'Napoléone'. A last fragment specified that 'These final and faded remarks all have some interest and some character – but this should be extracted by a highly competent person only – some such, whom I don't presume to name, will furnish such last offices.' (HJL IV, 809, 812.)

But there were medical complications, and though HJ's condition stabilized, he was in a slow decline. His sister-in-law described his tired, tranquil state: 'He thinks he is voyaging and visiting foreign cities, and sometimes he asks for his glasses and paper and imagines that he writes. And sometimes his hand moves over the counterpane as if writing.' He died on Monday, 28 February 1916. At his own wish he was cremated, at Golder's Green on the following Friday.

When HJ became naturalized, Asquith, with support from Edward Marsh in his Private Office, had successfully moved to award him the Order of Merit in the 1916 New Year's Honours – despite opposition from Lord Morley, probably the hostile

reader for Macmillan's of French Poets and Novelists *in 1877, now a distinguished elder statesman and himself an O.M. Marsh later said: 'What Lord Morley's reasons precisely were I never knew; but I gathered that the novels did not appeal to him because they dealt too exclusively with the inconsequential dealings of the Idle Rich, and were therefore not what the Americans would call "worth while".'*

Gosse wrote the Times *obituary of 29 February 1916, calling HJ's life 'in a sense uneventful enough, except for the wide range of its points of social contact, yet in fact charged and brimmed as few lives are with ceaseless adventure of spirit and intelligence'. Gosse also recalled his conversation: 'When, at the right time and place, he would give the rein to his power of evoking and peopling a remembered scene, brushing in one vividly-marked figure after another with broad strokes of a vocabulary unmatched for splendour and grace, the finished picture was a work of art unforgettably enhanced by the careful deliberation of speech, the expressive gesture, the mobility of the finely-modelled face. At such times it was possible to realize a little how the passion for 'form,' in the critical and brooding mind of a consummate artist, could never rest, never be set aside, never be satisfied with anything short of the full imaginative possession and imaginative re-creation of all experience.'*

Textual Notes

To ensure a clear reading text, I have reserved some information about each letter to this separate section: library call-numbers; comments on the condition or provenance of the text; notes on the dating if necessary; comments on previous publications of the letter. Where the only source is a printed text or a copy, variants can usually not be given. Cancelled words are given in angle brackets (<>) and where illegible are marked by a row of x's roughly corresponding to the number of characters. Interlineations are marked in wedges (\/). The notations of particular textual variants are divided by vertical lines (|). Sometimes James rewrites a word to spell it correctly, or to make it more legible; sometimes he repeats words in haste or around line-end or page-break. All cancellations and insertions in typed letters are also typed unless described as '[MS]'. (I have not recorded brief corrections of mistypings.) Appendices like this can be unnecessarily arid: I have tried to quote enough to enable readers easily to find the passages concerned, and to give some sense of James thinking with his pen.

1. To Thomas Sergeant Perry 25 March 1864
Colby MS

walked \arm-in-arm/ with Shakespeare | novel I <mentio> spoke of |

2. To Charles Eliot Norton 11 November [1864]
Houghton MS or MC (bMS Am 1088 (3840))

The letter may have been copied in another hand than HJ's.

3. To Lilla Cabot (later Perry) [May 1865?]
Colby MS

Dating this letter is difficult. My dating is conjectural, but in May 1865 Lilla Cabot was seventeen and thus still a 'schoolgirl', the Jameses were living in Cambridge, and HJ had recently published a story under his name (' "an author" '). (In late April 1866 the James family left Cambridge for a summer in Swampscott, Massachusetts, so that year is less likely.)

you should have \had/ the trouble

4. To Charles Eliot Norton 31 July [1865]
Houghton MS (bMS Am 1088 (3843))

In this and some other early letters HJ puts a redundant apostrophe in 'your's', which I have let stand.

5. To Thomas Sergeant Perry Friday morn [1865]
Colby MS

6. To Charles Eliot Norton 28 February [1866]
Houghton MS (bMS Am 1088 (3847))

HJL reads 'popped up faint praise' where I read 'pumped up . . .'

7. To William Conant Church 21 May 1866
NYPL MS (William Conant Church Papers)

8. To William Dean Howells 10 May [1867]
Houghton MS (bMS Am 1784 (253) 1)

the real \levity/ <lightness> of your lightness

9. To Thomas Sergeant Perry 20 September [1867]
Colby MS

dira qui voudra<s> que | de ces \lettres/ folles | literature & \literary/ history | I feel <as if> \that/ my only chance for success as as a critic | enough of <this> "abstract speculation" | \A/ 1000 pardons | an ex\as/peration. | I \have/ used up | the grave, the <grave> \divine./ | I heard from \him/ yesterday.

10. To Francis Pharcellus Church 23 October [1867]
NYPL MS (William Conant Church Papers)

11. To Thomas Sergeant Perry 13 May [1868]
Colby MS

that <xxxx> any attempt | I alone <was> \am/ responsible, | which seem<ed>
overmuch | no reference to any\thing/ seen, | & \for/ my own part | to <xxx>
allow it | harbouring injurious \thoughts/ & | & by me forgotten & soon as uttered.

12. To George Abbott James 20 March [1869]
Houghton MS (bMS Am 1094.1 (56))

basement of \an/ ancient

13. To Henry James Senior 17 September [1869]
Houghton MS (bMS Am 1094 (1763))

I <think> \fancy/ a denser | *Cura MM. Em. Fenzi & Cie \Banquiers/ Florence* |
infernal \here/ just now | no \more/ Nations

14. To Grace Norton 11 November [1869]
Houghton MS (bMS Am 1094 (875))

Napoleon III <been> excavated | uncommonly magnificent<ly> & | as if I \have/
seen | all, \he/ will devote himself

15. To Charles Eliot Norton 25 March 1870
Houghton MS (bMS Am 1088 (3852))

continually <led to> \struck/ with | to go \back/ to Naples, | when \one of/ your
Florentine letters | that it <was[?]> \went:/ I hope | je <xxxx> \n'en/ reviens pas.

16. To Mary Walsh James (mother) 26 March [1870]
Houghton MS (bMS Am 1094 (1772))

vain to attempt \to/ utter | felt within \him/ (what I felt little enough!) | a world
to which she <is> \was/ essentially hostile. | what \a/ pure eloquent vision | she
\the/ very heroine of our common scene. | has <acted> \operated/ <on> \in/ my
mind as a gentle incentive to action & enterprise. | telling her – \so many stories by

which I had a fancy to make up her losses to her/ — as if | how strange it <was>
\is/ for me to be | You promise me \soon/ a letter

17. To James Thomas Fields 15 July [1870?]
Houghton TC (Lubbock: bMS Am 1237. 16)

18. To James Thomas Fields 25 July [1870]
Houghton TC (Lubbock: bMS Am 1237. 16)

19. To James Thomas Fields 15 November [1870]
Houghton TC (Lubbock: bMS Am 1237. 16)

I have corrected the TC's 'reccomend' and 'Millson'.

20. To Grace Norton 27 November 187[1]
Houghton MS (bMS Am 1094 (884))

distingué <of> German | I shall <always> \never/ know it | to see <as [?]> \what/
you may | wishing \him/ to write to the *Nation* | to see <xx> \what/ you may

21. To Charles Eliot Norton 4 February 1872
Houghton MS (bMS Am 1088 (3856))

not conducive \to/ that breakfast-table cheerfulness | in which, \or whom,/ you |
tastes \and/ <of> sympathies | assured \that/ in the interest of <my> "general
culture" | of \the/ two big foolish nations, | who <believe> \feel that/ the vexing
ghost | see. \With/ Longfellow | He is <delivering> \repeating/ before | seems to
me to <have [?]> \come/ less | \G/ive her my filial regards

22. To Charles Eliot Norton 19 November [1872]
Houghton MS (bMS Am 1088 (386))

23. To Charles Eliot Norton 31 March [1873]
Houghton MS (bMS Am 1088 (3863))

certainly <mine> \I who/ have | too \good/ a thing | my patriotism <as>
\being/ "serene." | judged by <common> \our usual/ standards,

24. To Henry James Senior and Mary Walsh James (parents) 14 August [1873]
Houghton MS (bMS Am 1094 (1813))

weather \– toward cold –/ had made my room | Homburg. <I too> \But/ A.M. will | had been <cool> \intensely/ hot | away \for miles,/ in their green interior stillness | in III parts to \the/ *Galaxy* | I did \think/ of making straight back <for> \to/ Italy; | believe. <I therefore> \But I/ give you

25. To William Dean Howells 3 May [1874]
Houghton MS (bMS Am 1784 (253) 7)

to <avoid> \write/ close, & avoid | be <your> \sure,/ to your

26. To William Dean Howells [19 or 26 March 1875]
Hayes MS (Ac 972)

27. To Francis Pharcellus Church 1 December [1875]
NYPL MS (William Conant Church Papers)

The text of the first page has been cut out.

consider that \it will interfere with/ such other

28. To Mary James (mother) 11 January [1876]
Houghton MS (bMS Am 1094 (1832))

it is a <boy> \girl/. I am | in my \mind's/ eye, I behold | The <xxxxx> \half/ dozen charming houses | sending it \to/ an English publisher

29. To William Dean Howells 3 February [1876]
Houghton MS (bMS Am 1784 (253) 9)

I think <your> \my/ extreme preference | insufferable *nonchalance*, <neglect [?]> \neglect/ & ill-manners | I would, \at any rate,/ rather | on many accounts \that/ the thing | very well – \on his novel – / he had | With \a/ friendly memory

30. To Grace Norton 31 March [1876]
Houghton MS (bMS Am 1094 (899))

read <your> \the/ review | to have \one's/ wounds bound up | because <your>
\of the/ balm | I should say \by analogy,/ a solvent | I don't remember – <that>
I chose it | happy that \that/ splendor

31. To Thomas Sergeant Perry [2 May 1876]
Colby MS

The letter is dated by the postmark.

<What> \Why/ the Flaubert circle

32. To Mrs Ellen Louise Chandler Moulton 20 October [1876]
Congress MS (Louise Chandler Moulton Papers)

Extremely good <xxx> \also/ are

33. To William Dean Howells 24 October [1876]
Houghton MS (bMS Am 1784 (253) 13)

was, \in the conception of the tale,/ in his losing her; I <the> \am/ pretty sure |
letting <letting> \the/ insolent foreigner | That he should <n't> only | I suppose
<it> \something/ will be. | thrive more \effectually/ than here

34. To Thomas Sergeant Perry 12 January [1877]
Houghton TC (bMS Am 1094.5 (21))

The 'word illegible' is in the typed copy, presumably made by or for Virginia Harlow
in TSPB – the only traceable text of this letter. The sense is not unclear.

35. To William Dean Howells 2 February [1877]
Houghton MS (bMS Am 1784 (253) 15)

to print <to> a *six-months' tale* | that only fills <a> \one/ volume | not that <the>
\any/ novel | a fatally <ill> \bad/ humor

36. To William James 29 March [1877]
Houghton MS (bMS Am 1094 (1975))

The texts in LHJ I and SL2 are minus the postscript. Where the boat-race is discussed, 'horri' is cancelled and replaced by 'bleak', which is in turn cancelled and replaced by 'supremely beautiful'.

the last \no. of the/ 19*th* Centy! | & \a/ monstrous cleverly-agreeably-talking M.P., | he hardly <opened> \opened/ his mouth. | (the <discoverer> \excavator/ of old Mycenae | the Bard, <who> \& heard/ most of his talk | not by \my/ own seeking, but | what he is talking \of,/ without a flaw. | I dont \particularly/ like him: | a <horri> <bleak> \supremely beautiful/ sight; | 2 or 3 days since <with> \at/ Mrs. Godfrey Lushington's

37. To William Dean Howells 30 March [1877]
Houghton MS (bMS Am 1784 (253) 16)

the interest of the <tale> \subject/ was, | fatally divide us<, &>\./ I have | I understand so well <well> \how/ M*me* | measure the <resemblance> \merit of a/ novel | "tragedies" <are> have | the brightest possible <for> sun-spot for | dyspepsia & <their> dissipates | as <the> \a/ picture of the conversion | it.) – \But I shall give you it, or its equivalent, by Nov. next./ It | show me <the> an inside-view of the school, | yesterday \in comp'y./ with Browning

38. To Alice James 8 April [1877]
Houghton MS (bMS Am 1904 (1582)) Unpublished

A later hand has dated the letter 1878, but internal evidence makes it certainly of 1877.

letter of <April> \March/ 24*th*, | dumb, & <which [?]> \who/ lived | a goodly margin <from> \for/ them, | will <probably> however compensate | from \my/ London observations, | complete \social/ stoppage; | that \on Good Friday/ I partook | he was <xxxxx> \shut/ up by the chattering | The <latter> \former/ never peeps out in society, & the <former> \latter/ hasn't | fresh-colored, <xxx> \blue-eyed/ simple-minded | of age, \in a Bath-chair,/ to | most romantic \of all/ people | another <afternoon> \day/ tried | lovelier spring \than me,/ & | optimistic acct. of \Hayes/ <the> & the | is he is charming in his conduct

39. To Elizabeth Boott 26 May [1877]
Houghton MS (bMS Am 1094 (527))

I have described in a footnote the emblem HJ draws in his text.

riding-habit, & <that> of your | very well for <the reader to expect it> \Newman to want it,/ & for | appreciated \it/. However | I salute you \both/ to the earth,

40. To his mother 15 March [1878]
Houghton MS (bMS Am 1094 (1863))

about the the Scribner cheque | I posted \instantly/ with | to the American "as <water> \wine/ unto water." | but \for/ this I must wait

41. To Frederick Macmillan [1 August 1878]
BL MS (ADD. 54931, fols. 28–9)

Rayburn Moore, following Michael Anesko, persuasively dates this undated letter as a reply to Macmillan's of 31 July 1878, agreeing to publish *The Europeans* (CHJHM, 16).

(both <from> \for/ himself & his publishers) | St. John's Wood, & & *bon voyage*

42. To William Ernest Henley [6 October 1878]
Morgan MS (MA 1617.9)

HJ was in Scotland on about 10–29 September. Taking the Turgenev piece here read 'many weeks since' as the one Henley was still to write on 28 August, and assuming that HJ's gift of *The Europeans* preceded Henley's writing his friendly review of the novel in the *Academy* of 12 October, and that 'Sunday' and '3 Bolton St.' are accurate, I have dated this to 6 October 1878.

proposed. \The other was full of well-said things./ He | I <hope> \wish/ George Eliot were a little more like him. | Attend \well/ to those French devils, | about \the/ Dramatic Art

43. To Elizabeth Boott 30 October [1878]
Houghton MS (bMS Am 1094 (543))

You are \a/ marvellous critic | its abrupt ending <rather than outward [?]> \came from outward/ pressure | you will \miss/ Miss B.; nor | Alice, thank heaven, is \ just/ lately

44. To Julian Hawthorne 15 January 1879
Bancroft TC (72/#236 z)

The TC reads 'As regards thus, however'

45. To William Ernest Henley 5 February [1879]
Morgan MS (MA 1617.3)

said to \have/ been tidied up

46. To Jane Dalzell Finlay (Mrs Frank Harrison) Hill 21 March [1879]
Princeton MS (Robert A. Taylor File Cabinet, Folder James, Henry, AM 86–121)

shall I confess it? < – > (you will | & <thinking over> \meditating on/ the matter | I remembered \that/ when I was fresh | irregular \manner,/ & use | to strike <quietly [?]> \quiet/ conservative people | seem to have \been so,/ with most people, | a resumé of \my view of/ English manners. | consummation \certainly/ does not suit | by which <it> the attitude of the duchess | the extension of his idea <into> \in/ which, | forthwith I <am> find myself responsible | I shall \live to/ make all sorts of representations | take a much <xxxxxxx> \cleverer/ person than myself | all sorts of <xxx> \unflattering/ \English/ pictures, | smile at <my> \the/ artless crudity | the American mind \alone,/ & its <xxxxx> \way/ of taking things.

47. To William James 15 June [1879]
Houghton MS (bMS Am 1094 (1986))

one from \your/ Alice) some | dispel the \impression of the/ rather dark account | was \in/ every way a most curious | & look<ing> at them | facts of London \life/ are tolerable | they exist to you \just/ <only> for the moment | sort. <From the Episode> Having in advance | represents <but> \but/ meanly so great a vogue | on the contrary, <but> \and/ I sometimes – or rather, often | at the "urgent request" \of/ *celui-ci* | promise to give <me [?]> \him/ a translation | The other \night/ John Fiske | are \staying/ <sulking [?]> at the Milnes Gaskells. | both very <brilliant> \pleasant/, & | a strong impression <&> I should

48. To William Dean Howells 17 June [1879]
Houghton MS (bMS Am 1784 (253) 20)

you of course \have/ known | I can't literally \afford/ <xxx> it. | a pecuniary
equivalent \almost/ grotesquely small. | 200 $ by the <sale> \whole American
career/ of D.M. | the pitiless \race/ of publishers. | I shall have made this year
\much/ more than | to issue your \own/ things here

49. To William Dean Howells [14 or 15 July 1879]
Houghton MS (bMS Am 1784 (253) 24)

letter of <July> \June/ 29*th*, | told in a <xxxx> \smaller/ number | pledge myself
<very> \so/ long in advance

50 To William James 16 December [1879]
Houghton MS (bMS Am 1094 (1990))

but I \also/ think that, read | town. \I gave up Italy, *rapport au* cold./ I

51. To John S. Barron 21 December [1879]
Virginia MS (6251 #583)

replied <by [?]> \to/ this | and <my> \I/ must repeat | the *North American Review*,
<for> \to/ which I must refuse myself

52. To John S. Barron 19 January 1880
Virginia MS (6251 #422)

no prospect \of/ being able to contribute

53. To William Dean Howells 31 January [1880]
Houghton MS (bMS Am 1784 (253) 26)

your <sage> graceful strictures seem to yourself | I think it <would> \is/ extremely
provincial | usages, habits, forms, <that> upon all these things matured & established,
that a novelist lives – they are the very stuff his work <has> \is/ made of; | such a

genius will get on \only/ by agreeing with your <xxx> \view/ of the case | he must feel as you <would> feel | whether such a genius \ – a man of the faculty of Balzac & Thackeray – / *could* agree with you! | made me feel <xxx> \acutely/ the want of the "paraphernalia." | for not feeling it; \i. e. the want./ You are entirely right

54. To William Dean Howells 18 April [1880]
Houghton MS (bMS Am 1784 (253) 26)

I throw myself on <my> \your/ mercy | that <it will> \the story/ shall be | pretexts for \one's/ haunting | a compatriot and a <Xtian> \Christian,/ & | England. <xxx> \Florence/ is delightful, | much \of/ the public | it won't matter \that my rude/ words

55. To Eliza Lynn Linton 6 October [1880]
Abernethy MS (M–2/145/11)

Steven Jobe, who located the original MS at Middlebury, Vermont, has established the correct date for this letter. (Edel had it as '[August 1880]'.)

56. To Charles Eliot Norton 13 November 1880
Houghton MS (bMS Am 1088 (3868))

LHJ starts at '. . . I wish you could take a good holiday', and stops (except for the final salutation), 'Lowell has to do *that* quite by himself . . .'

I have \now/ had, | it is the most valuable <sort [?]> knowledge | I don't \know/ when | from England <will> \must/ be for | you felt yourself in Florence \ – & lived again there – / & | the big scrambling <dinner> \banquet/ which | appreciated <here>, his talk enjoyed | Mrs. Lowell <will> \is/ not destined

57. To William Dean Howells 5 December [1880]
Houghton MS (bMS Am 1784 (253) 34)

abroad, \later in the winter./ Dizzy's | as to whom <she> \such/ telling | encounters \& acquaintances/ made | over here that \it/ offers itself | I mean for \dealing with/ a long period

58. To Thomas Bailey Aldrich 14 July [1881]
Houghton MS (bMS Am 1429 (2551))

makes your <October> \December./) Meanwhile, | I have \just/ come back from Venice,

59. To Alice Howe Gibbens James 6 August [1881]
Houghton MS (bMS AM 1094 (1610))

in spite of \one or two/ drawbacks,

60. To Thomas Bailey Aldrich 31 August [1881]
Houghton MS (bMS Am 1429 (2550))

the final pages of \my/ too, too solid serial,

61. To Houghton, Mifflin & Co. 23 November [1881]
Houghton MS (bMS Am 1925 (942) 20)

a new book, & a very <inferior> \superior/ one; | appears to be \in/ no hurry for it | the retail price of <the> my volumes | request then that it be raised then to <fifty> \twenty/. My \next/ half-yearly account

62. To Frederick Macmillan 27 December [1881]
BL MS (Add. 54931, fols. 88–9)

Cambridge, \Mass.,/ Dec. 27*th* | the <one> \copy/ to be addressed | nothing <in my [?]> particular in my letter | about 9 o'clock a.m., \daily,/ to considerably | we are having \moreover/ a winter

63. To Edwin Laurence Godkin 22 January [1882]
Houghton MS (bMS Am 1083 (389))

my opportunity nor \to/ my desires; | the outside, though <xxxxx> \pleasant/ enough,

64. To George Abbott James [2 February 1882]
Houghton MS (bMS Am 1094.1 (8))

65. To Edmund Clarence Stedman 20 April 1882
Berg MS

the Piazza: \the/ <)> best place | *Camere Mobigliate.* \There are dozens of such./
There | there are many \little/ apartments | house on \the corner of the/ Piazza
Sta. Maria Novella | to settle down for a \few/ weeks

66. To Edwin Laurence Godkin 5 June [1882]
Houghton MS (bMS Am 1083 (393))

The paper is embossed 'Reform Club'; there is a pencilled misdating, '1881'.

no inducement to <indulge> \resolve/ my <xxx> impressions

67. To Sir John Clark 13 November [1882]
Virginia MS (6251–N #161, Box 2)

I <wonder> \ask/ myself what | talking <with> \about/ you | makes it \also/
impossible

68. To Theodore Child 5 December [1882]
Virginia MS (6251 #154)

<Nov> \Dec/ 5*th* | What \the devil/ is coming over you Frenchmen? | interesting,
<but> \and/ which I await | not long ago <soley [?]> solely for

69. To James Ripley Osgood 8 April 1883
Congress MS (Benjamin H. Ticknor Papers, vol. 11)

discovered in her a <great> \remarkable/ natural talent | conceived <an exceeding>
\a passionate/ admiration | by the force \of/ a completely | she has <conceived>
\acquired a/ great influence. | the rich \young/ woman, | The struggle ends \(after
various vicissitudes,)/ with her | breaking <with> \forever with her/ friend, | that
the <thing> \story/ shall be | definitely <make> \make it/ of | length to be \that
of/ two instalments | in \these/ other things | as <she> \he/ has a good deal of

money | the <length> \relation/ of the *Atlantic* page | the "Lady Barberina" <&>
and, as well,/ the two short tales | having \in the interval/ let Proposal No I | so
that <you> \your magazine/ may have | short things \taken together/ – "Lady |
instalment. \For the *Siege of London* I got from the Cornhill $750./) A smaller <xxx>
\sum/ than this | the *volume*, <as well as> \in addition to/ the appearance | the
<books> \productions/ in question

70. To Thomas Sergeant Perry [June 1883?]
Colby MS

HJ was at this address between December 1882 and July 1883: more precisely, the
letter seems to refer to Perry's article, which is dated 'June'.

71. To Grace Norton 11 December [1883]
Houghton MS (bMS Am 1094 (954))

represent him <*him*> as "scolding"? | Surely, (<to> \for the impression they make
on/ the arrived European

72. To William Dean Howells 21 February 1884
Houghton MS (bMS Am 1784 (253) 50)

an allusion, in a late letter of T.B.A., \to/ <He> your having | I always (or generally)
have <) and> \and/ therefore, | to show you \also/ the sheets | Crawford's \last/
novel | trying to write <something> \anything/ decent | idiotic. \It must be totally
wasted./ I would rather | ferocity, <(> which | return to \the/ British scramble |
a tendency to <art [?]> \factitious/ glosses; | the <thing> \work/ is admirably |
owing him, <or rather> \& indeed/ his wife,

73. To Theodore Child 8 March [1884]
Virginia MS (6251 #144)

no \other/ human eye | disagreeable \to me/ in what that man writes | also, <for>
Dieu sait!, for | I should <drop> secretly poison him | like <xxxx> \refusing/ a riz
de veau

74. To Edmund Gosse 9 June [1884]
Leeds MS

thinking \<that\> \the thing/ is more solid | on p. 571, \exactly/ the allusion

75. To Alphonse Daudet 19 June [1884]
Houghton MS (bMS Am 1094.1 (1))

que \<je xxxx\> \je constate/ dans *Sapho* | moins éclairé \ – en comparaison de celle de la femme – / qu'il ne le faudrait | la conscience \<même\> de Jean Gaussin. | et ce \<qu\> \caractère,/ vous me faites | trouve bien la \<colo [?]\> \couleur/ et la forme. | un peu trop en blanc, \<c'est\> \ce n'est/ qu'avec vous même

76. To Edgar Fawcett 31 July [1884]
Princeton MS (Robert A. Taylor File Cabinet, Folder James, Henry)

77. To Benjamin Holt Ticknor 28 September [1884]
Yale MS (Za 18–23)

that article in the U.S. \<would\> \will have/ done me more good

78. To Grace Norton 14 November [1884]
Houghton MS (bMS Am 1094 (961))

& I \<have\> read it with | you speak of \in/ the *Nation*,

79. To Theodore Child 29 November [1884]
Virginia MS (6251 #153)

They don't seem to have made them \(the French)/ any tidier | I doubt think it a fault | escape \<xx\> \to this/ virtuous clime

80. To Robert Louis Stevenson 5 December [1884]
Yale MS (MS Vault Stevenson Files #4921)

contend with you here; \<for\> \besides,/ we agree, | & \<your\> \the/ current of your admirable style | the present \<xx\> Season

81. To Thomas Bailey Aldrich 3 January 1885
Houghton MS (bMS Am 1429 (2583))

George Eliot's \Life &/ Letters, which | to be treated \of/ in your pages,

82. To William James 14 February [1885]
Houghton MS (bMS Am 1094 (2021))

than they have \already/ said | drawn, & <was> \originated/ in my desire | in so
far <as they> \as they were/ otherwise represented | because <she> \so it/ would
be more touching, | go my way, \according to my own fancy,/ and make my image
as living as I saw <her> \it./ The | that my <absence> \paucity/ of data & not
\my/ repletion | but \only/ an imaginary figure | much nearer to <her,> \me,/
and | why you <can> \should/ call | the embodiment of pure \the purest/
philanthropy. | the money you \had/ *prélevé* (or borrowed) | to <print> \pay for/
Father's book | with a \very short/ note of Alice's, | evidently \now/ rather
stationary, | She <ha> \isn't/ in the least

83. To William James 15 February [1885]
Houghton MS (bMS Am 1094 (2022))

assigned this \as you know/ altogether | The later apparition \& death/ <in the
book> \of Miss B./ is the prettiest thing in the book, | it will be \an/ obloquy | if
the episode *does* <seem> \strike/ people as | in my mind, \or that they ever said
so;/ they | independence of any model <but> \that/ my own wits | about <F.'s>
\the/ review of your book.

84. To Theodore Child 16 February [1885]
Virginia MS (6251 #136)

the cruder civilization & less organised Priapism of some southern land present<s>
themselves | in the midst of \so/ much that is interesting, | And \for him/ to be
working | The only \engrossing/ topic | what is most alluded to \ – there are long
discussions as to whether she was "right" – / <is> is the scandalous | without
\having/ married him. | remember <that> how much

85. To John Hay 13 May [1885]
Brown MS

recognize something \human & Mississippian/. His

86. To Benjamin Holt Ticknor 26 June [1885]
Congress MS (Benjamin H. Ticknor Papers, vol. 11)

I must claim <that> this relief | rectify it \in some small degree,/ in

87. To Robert de Montesquiou 21 August [1885]
Bib. Nat. de France MS

HJL reads 'mesure trompeuse' as 'masque trompeur'.

attendent! <Chaque> Soyez certain, dans tous les cas, que chaque fois

88. To Benjamin Holt Ticknor 27 August [1885]
Virginia MS (96251 #438)

the amount of \the cost of/ them

89. To William James 9 October 1885
Houghton MS (bMS Am 1094 (2026))

than any reader can be \of the redundancy of the book/ in the way of | thing you
<anivader> \animadvert/ upon | reasons I <would> \won't/ take time | the
<Europeans; [?]> *Princess*/ *Casamassima*; | that it <is falling> \has fallen/ flat. |
with \extreme/ enthusiasm

90. To Thomas Bailey Aldrich 29 April [1886]
Houghton MS (bMS Am 1429 (2597))

the August & \this added/ September parts. | all deficiencies \of copy/ will be made
up. | I have been \feeling/ terribly squeezed,

91. To William James 13 June 1886
Houghton MS (bMS Am 1094 (2029))

to give you \at/ the same moment, | I \myself/ subscribe | make the picture
<alive> \substantial/ by thinking it out | thought the <book> \title/ simple &
handy, | very well \I shall write another: "The Other Bostonians."/. However, | to
float. < – Your> \If Aunt/ Kate | as soon as \you do/ this | to England. K. \L./
will stay | so that <he> \it/ might be done | but <here [?]> \seen/ on this spot |
of personal judgment, \before him,/ so complete.

92. To Robert Louis Stevenson 30 July [1886]
Yale MS (MS Vault Stevenson Files #4930)

I have <sent> \seen/ various reviews

93. To Julian Russell Sturgis 20 September [1886]
Houghton TC (Lubbock: bMS Am 1237.16)

94. To Thomas Bailey Aldrich 12 June 1887
Houghton MS (bMS Am 1429 (2605))

I send you you herewith | the more \submissively/ <xxxxxxxx> from \your/ having
it | The second half is <being [?]> \in/ London, | It <will> makes about a third

95. To Robert Louis Stevenson 2 August [1887]
Yale MS (MS Vault Stevenson Files #4938)

Misdated in HJL as 1886.

brutal should be \the/ thing that succeeds | like a buck, <to prevent his being> on
receiving the shot.

96. To Robert Louis Stevenson 5 December [1887]
Yale MS (MS Vault Stevenson Files #4941)

my productions are finished, <they [?]> \or/ at least thrust out | dwindle when
weaned – / removed | so it it is, & as it is, | an interesting subject, & \a/ good
deal | even your censure \pleases/ & your restrictions | the \Century's/ long delay |

any other prose <morsels> \specimens/ of my own genius | for \one who *knows* &
yet/ is famished:

97. To Edmund Gosse 24 December [1887]
Leeds MS (vol. II, 23)

a Xmas <cheer> \greeting/, & a friendly cheer, | & it <was> \is/ all accidental.

98. To William Dean Howells 2 January 1888
Houghton MS (bMS Am 1784 (253) 54)

to me \exactly/ as a new-year's gift. | all the <secrets> \reasons/ of things (of this
sort, to-day,) | Very likely too, \some day,/ all my buried prose | that \on occasions/
you mix things up | Edmund Gosse came to <xxxx xxx> \share my/ solitude & my
beefsteak, | imbroglio of a year \& a half/ ago | I find<ing> myself

99. To William James [20 February 1888]
Houghton MS fragment (bMS Am 1094 (2037))

told me <the other day> \some time ago/ that | with the <latter> \former/ & only
one other man<ner> (\2/ other women) | intellectual <type> \sort./ He is | &
badinage \&/, at the same time | who apparently \sincerely/ considers that Arthur
Balfour | & Scotland the *mind*; | as books. \I have good reasons for this./ I shall
publish | 2 or 3 \more/ short fictions | I am promised \remarkably/ good results |
to make \one's/ bargains & take charge \of/ one's productions | take all the
mercenary <& arranging> \& *selling*/ side off one's mind | compensation <from>
\for/ it.

100. To Thomas Bailey Aldrich 3 March 1888
Houghton MS (bMS Am 1429 (2608))

much other richness, <though> \and/ the scene will be in London,

101. To Mary (Mrs Humphry) Ward [March or April 1888]
Virginia MS (6251–a #366)

the mind \and the soul./ The things | conceptions \ – so fine as conceptions – / are
| But your \head/ carries it | shame \in/ which

102. To Daniel Connor Lathbury 9 June [1888]
Houghton TC (Lubbock: bMS Am 1237.16)

103. To Theodora Sedgwick 2 July [1888]
Houghton MS (bMS Am 1094 (1154))

the sodden \country./. But

104. To Grace Norton 30 September 1888
Houghton MS (bMS Am 1094 (977))

I seem \to myself/ to live with my pen | I am getting to know English life <as well> \better/ than American, of which today I see nothing – & to understand the English character \or at least the *mind*,/ as \well as/ if I had invented it: | very "clever" – \ – he is a charming host – / & the occasion | so ill with gout \&/ so gloomy | of the <lovable> \loveable/ & the annoying, | friendly to <him,> \me,/ & it | some people \here,/ (mainly | I have lately <xxxx> \seen/ a good deal, | scaled the <xxxxx> \long hill/ which | friend of mine & \has/ a charming | admirably on \early/ English literature | catarrhal \& curable;/ & is | tête à tête with a <wood man [?]> \man of straw./ What is the matter | to make the <xxx> \stupid/ world think me <xx> \more/ important than it supposed.

105. To Frederic William Henry Myers 20 October [1888]
Wren MS (Myers 2[134])

His \later/ "evolution" has been | that's <all> \the/ only criticism

106. To William James 29 October 1888
Houghton MS (bMS Am 1094 (2039))

health & happiness are <well> with you. | suddenly, \abt. Oct. 10*th*,/ that I wanted | being in \a/ foreign country, | stimulated, \healthily irritated./ She *is* homesick, | fragmentary, unre<sisting>\acting/ way in which she sees them. | if one <has lived> \is living in a/ country not ones own | as simply \different/ chapters | impossible \to an outsider/ to say whether I am, | attached to <it> \that exercise,/ combined | much more <stom [?]> \time/ for it <the> \as/ the months | I chose \the form of/ my saturation. | to spend only <my> \the/ interest of my capital. | seem to <be> \me/ wonderful the 1*st* time | with \profusion and/ evident <fr> sincerity. | keeping the \invalid/ child

107. To Henrietta Reubell 23 March [1889]
Houghton MS (bMS Am 1094 (1089))

a figure in a \missal or a/ mosaic, | her <splendid> \shining/ barbaric crown, which, \with/ a grand movement | People \in general/ will stare & be idiotic \& frightened,/ & not understand: | I have \tea'd/ <lunched> & dined at M*me* Waddingtons & felt promoted,

108. To Thomas Bailey Aldrich 2 November [1889]
Houghton MS (bMS Am 1429 (2617))

The greater \portion/ <part> of the of penultimate (February) part | that same \instalment/ <part> went | the greater part of the \ – as I calculate – / February number

109. To Florence (Mrs Hugh) Bell 5 February [1890]
Texas MS (Mrs Hugh Bell, recip., Folder 2)

But, <evidently> àpropos of her, | that <vul> banality would surely

110. To Florence (Mrs Hugh) Bell 7 February [1890]
Texas MS (Mrs Hugh Bell, recip., Folder 2)

yours \most/ attentively

111. To Frederick Macmillan 26 March 1890
BL MS (Add. 54931, fol. 220)

112. To Frederick Macmillan 28 March 1890
BL MS (Add. 54931, fols. 221–3)

HJL and SL2 print a 'P.S.' to this letter which correctly belongs to HJ's letter to Macmillan of 24 March.

113. To Alexander Pollock Watt 2 April 1890
Berg MS (70B6769)

I will <give> sign the agreement

114. To William James 16 May 1890
Houghton MS (bMS Am 1094 (2051))

LHJ omits: the first three sentences; the passage beginning 'I spent a day with Alice . . .'
as far as 'I hope you will have received . . .'; the passage about Howells (from
'Apropos . . .' to 'fish them up.')

a breathing-place, \well/ away from London, that, from day to day, <from> \for/
sometime past, | one thing (always "highly finished") after <xxxxx> \another/.
However | for a week \or two/ and then to Venice | when the book is \supposed/
to come out. | both \novels &/ money-making | a source of lucre to the <artist>
\author/ – I have | not perhaps, <xxxx> \envy,/ inasmuch | the whole question of
form, \style/ & composition | conceived by me <in> \with/ a religious & deliberate
view of gain | bringing <it> \in/ to me:) | a single word <of> \or/ touch of
*en*couragement | then \only/ an experiment | The only thing is \to/ do a \great/
lot. | so rarely \as/ for the last year.

115. To William Dean Howells 17 May [1890]
Houghton MS (bMS Am 1784 (253) 56)

The London address is a printed letterhead; the Milan address handwritten by HJ.

I should indeed be <an> sunk in baseness | an intensely <ful> professional eye |
better than \even/ the best of the rest, | I'll say \instead/ that to *read* | such a free,
full rich <thing> \flood./ In fact your reservoir <surprises> \deluges/ me, | shave
the truth – the general truth you aim at – <closer> \several/ degrees closer | *you*
see \a/ totally different | to be \that/ something you are | I <wonder at> \note/
certain things | because you <undertake to> communicate so completely *what* you
undertake to communicate. The novelist is a \particular/ *window*, | I could hang out
of <you> \it/ all day | I \should/ seem to be taking | the reader never touches the
<reader> \subject/ & the subject | to be <worse> \less/ good than | so many
things, \in future,/ will | Conrad D. is <also> \a/ *1st class* idea, | the place I see
\most/ & | rejection \at Washington/ of the | that we \in fact/ steal, | we do mean
it enough \not/ to care to | sorry the originality \of it/ should belong | another big
fight \before/ the civilization | the more to make up \to them/ for the unnatural
rigour

116. To Horace Scudder 30 August 1890
Houghton MS (bMS Am 1094.1 (1))

the usual <ly> Anglo-Saxon intelligence.

117. To Florence (Mrs Hugh) Bell 9 October [1890]
Texas MS (Mrs Hugh Bell, recip., Folder 2)

as early as \4. 15 or/ 4. 30, | from 3 to 4. \I am out of town Sunday p.m./ Yes, |
the simple \& essential/ fact | a play playable <into> \in/ 2 hours & forty minutes
| I didn't take it \(the idea)/ up *myself* | a passage \accidentally/ omitted | snatch
an hour or, \d'ici là,/ so | able \tomorrow/ to give

118. To Mrs Ariana (Wormeley) Curtis 18 December 1890
Huntington MS (HM 36064)

to whom I \have been/ reading it | the \provincial/ "1*ere*" draws \on,/ in the |
Sargent, <for> \to/ Egypt for the winter, | the big \new/ public library | interesting,
<but> \and/ Sargent as Ary Scheffer

119. To William Archer 31 December 1890
BL MS (Add. 45292, fols. 272–4)

whose principal merit \ – I admit it's a great one – / is that | I have gone in \above
all/ for *safe* lines

120. To George du Maurier 8 January [1891]
Houghton MS (bMS Am 1094 (645))

'1891' is pencilled in by the date.

a very big, <&> \a/ very attentive

121. To Elizabeth Robins 1 June [1891]
Boston Public Library MS (MS. Am. 1149)

such weight, \however slight,/ as I \may/ possess. | a success <cess> of the play, |

all of us. \Compton has a theatre, &/ *I* have | than to \work up to it &/ employ it | far more interesting \& practically far more inspiring & helpful,/ to work

122. To Edgar Fawcett 7 June 1891
Princeton MS (Robert A. Taylor File Cabinet, Folder James, Henry)

I haven't \yet,/ found leisure | her "vogue" in the U.S. \but/ an example | thanking \you/ meanwhile | lunch with \me/ one of

123. To Edmund Gosse [27 September 1891]
Leeds MS

124. To Dr William Wilberforce Baldwin 19 October 1891
Morgan MS (MA 3564)

bring out a play – \for the 1*st* time –/ to take the plunge | the "critics" have <had> a free field | inexperience, <have> \had/ given me | that \though/ my drama | The rest \of the acting/ is very good. | must look \to you/ in your retrospect. | the two Independents & <the> your letter

125. To Edwin Laurence Godkin 15 November 1891
Houghton MS (bMS Am 1083 (406))

so little, \however,/ that | this one was <forced> \pressed/ upon me | is at best \but/ a play | Robinson <that> (I mean | with me \with/ <xx> \a/ certain regularity. | wet windy \fiercely/ tempestuous autumn

126. To Florence (Mrs Hugh) Bell [23 February 1892]
Yale MS (Frederick R. Koch Collection)

The date is from the postmark on the envelope.

a candid & <xxx> primitive | to "catch on" to <most [?]> \four/ or five | speech \at the end/ was | Everything Oscar does is a \deliberate/ trap | The <Lang [?]> \Mitchell/–Lea affair was naturally, <last [?]> \yesterday/ afternoon, <in> \before/ a fatally female | compressibility into a <very> \quite/ practicable | a prologue, <but> \very/ well save that | a very \small &/ simple fantaisie

127. To Robert Louis Stevenson 19 March 1892
Yale MS (MS Vault Stevenson Files #4951)

HJRLS follows the omissions in LHJ: the sentence about 'Kipling's "future"'; 'In the way of published items . . . at the same time.'; the sentence starting 'I will send you both of these books . . .'; both say '[word illegible]' where I read '*ébauche* of an'.

superstition that you <are [?]> \enjoy/ some measure | the genius \or the *genus*, in himself,/ Rudyard, | we are <xxx> beginning soon | a painful mediocrity <of> \at/ the same time. | Hardy has <had> \scored/ a great success

128. To Robert Underwood Johnson 27 August 1892
Virginia MS (6251–as) [Formerly Morgan MS (Koch #966)]

ceased to care <xxx> to write about

129. To Edmund Gosse 30 August [1892]
Houghton TC (Lubbock: bMS Am 1237.16)

130. To Edward Compton 15 September [1892]
Texas MS (Mackenzie, C., Misc.)

the \same/ *names*, the same figures, | If I had kept \only/ the *general* idea | benefit \& advertisement/ of the association; | association <didn't> \did,/ on trial, so little, \in the way of "advertisement,"/ for us | only hampered <us> \me/ in the effort | a \wholly/ new (a *comedy*!!!) 4*th* act

131. To Mr and Mrs Edward Compton [20 November 1892]
Texas MS (Mackenzie, C., Misc.)

This letter (which Compton Mackenzie conjecturally dates as of 'October (?) 1892') seems, rather, immediately to precede one to Virginia Compton he prints as definitely of 21 November, in which HJ sends some 'little changes' for Claire's part, which 'make her say a nice thing or two *of* Newman, and *at* him, rather than straight *to* him' (MLT II, 301); 20 November *was* a Sunday in 1892.

Tomorrow <xxx> also shall go | what I have made her <to> *do* | in the \short/ scene with Newman | a far more complicated <thing> \one/ to make than by by the writing | together. \This too was the *shorter* way./ But | & \have/ therefore changed

132. To Julian Russell Sturgis [Early? 1893]
Houghton TC (Lubbock: bMS Am 1237.16)

133. To Robert Underwood Johnson 14 April [1893]
Horne MS

This letter (formerly seen by Philip Horne in 1989 as Morgan MS (Koch #96)) was purchased from Rick Gekoski of Bloomsbury for £400, 12 July 1996.

134. To Edmund Gosse [21 April 1893]
Leeds MS

if is his return be not

135. To Edward Compton 29 April [1893]
Texas MS (Mackenzie, C., Misc.)

I fully share <it> \them,/ for I had had | not so picturesque \or so romantic/ as to be strange; | diplomatically. \Above all I thought it *dramatic*!/ I accept | that I may \yet/ do something with it. | greatly *calculated*, \ – greatly counted – / the thing | effort) <to> *realize* | stooping, with a a vengeance, to conquer, | telling you <when> how the immediate future | I shall \still/ require ample time | living into the Domville story & <xxxx> \can't/ from one day to the other | aren't we, \after all,/ really mismated?

136. To Arthur Wing Pinero 28 May 1893
Pusey MS (Harvard Theatre Collection, MS Thr 65 (8))

137. To Mrs Elizabeth Lewis 1 June [1893]
Bodleian MS (Dep. c. 834, fols. 43–4, 45)

The year is written on the envelope.

138. To Henrietta Reubell [5 June 1893]
Houghton MS (bMS Am 1094 (1118))

The date is pencilled in.

No beauty – \no wigs,/ no clothes,

139. To Edward Compton 8 June [1893]
Texas MS (Mackenzie, C., Misc.)

better <so> \to/ do so | nor, I confess, do I <see xx> \understand/ what you see | to draw out. \They are things that make it very full./ I don't see | to be imported. \This I definitely said in my 1st letter./ Your objection | the end of the <third> \second/ act, | now that <I have> \you/ have seen | something with <the [?]> \it/ that will | For one <will> \can/ do nothing with a subject | my hatred, in general, of assemblages, \for assemblages' sake,/ of the characters at the end of the <play> \acts/ is extreme.

140. To Augustin Daly 3 December 1893
Pusey MS (Harvard Theatre Collection, uncatalogued)

141. To William James and Alice Howe James 25 May [1894]
Houghton MS (bMS Am 1094 (2089))

Alice's \magnificent/ diary. | in particular <by> \for/ the great hole | the \copious/ aid & comfort | a most devouring \an almost fatal/ job, | I had \just/ promised a splendid work of art, \in London,/ for the 2d number | the \covenanted/ 25,000 words | these feverish <words> lines | *impressedness* by \it,/ and, | disconcerted \ – I mean alarmed – / by \the/ sight | being \myself/ the source | able to <say> express anything | till \my/ <I> promise | God send you \have/ been

142. To Edmund Gosse 17 December 1894
BL MS (Ashley 929)

The envelope is postmarked 18 December, so probably the letter was written late at night.

dream, \<than\> \save/ of this ghastly extinction | quenching of an \indispensable/ light. | & yet \all/ the \<whole\> monstrosity

143. To Henrietta Reubell 31 December 1894
Houghton MS (bMS Am 1094 (1127))

LHJ omits 'Little Potter . . . clinging little chap.'

8 30 o'clk, \on that evening,/ in very fervent prayer. | alone \like the King of Bavaria at the opera./ There | the odious process of \practical/ dramatic production. | at \rare/ leisure-moments,

144. To Lady Elizabeth Lewis 1 January 1895
Bodleian MS (Dep. c. 834, fols. 54–5, 56)

Despite 'the distracted spirit that illegibly scrawls these lines', they are not very illegible by James's standards.

my presence \<was\> \proved quite/ horribly indispensable

145. To Henrietta Reubell 10 January 1895
Houghton MS (bMS Am 1094 (1128))

that yell\<xx\>\ing/ crew | thanks to \<th\> leathern | I am prepared, \as I say,/ for the worst, | treated \as I thought, at least,/ very ingeniously

146. To William Dean Howells 22 January 1895
Houghton MS (bMS Am 1784 (253) 64)

happy, \<I mean [?]\> \even/ if you | It lies open \<before\> \before me/ and I read | qualified \indeed/ by one | all will \yet/ be well"; | about this time to get \<in\> \into the/ motion of. | I'm the last \<person\> \hand/ that the magazines, | out of all relation \<to\> \with/ them. | not at all sorry. \I am indeed very serene./ I have always hated | same quality. \<xxxxx\> Forgive,

147. To Edmund Gosse [8 April 1895]
Leeds MS

qualified \<of\> \by/ such a sickening | this hideous \<xxxx\> human history

148. To Horace Elisha Scudder 8 June 1895
Houghton MS (bMS Am 1094.1 (15))

nothing I <see> \am/ likely

149. To Robert Underwood Johnson 24 June 1895
Virginia MS (6251–as)

In 1989 this letter was in the Koch deposit in the Pierpont Morgan Library in New York, but was subsequently sold.

Now \that/ she has been | the (today) all-invasive <stage> \theatre,/ with its cheapness of criticism, \its overestimated art,/ & | What I, \by the way,/ dropped | primarily the Author, <of the same,> the case | I <am> must concentrate,

150. To John Lane 13 August 1895
Texas MS (John Lane, recip.)

151. To Horace Elisha Scudder 4 October 1895
Houghton MS (bMS Am 1094.1 (17))

not able to day to send <today> \you/ the whole | (tomorrow's,) steamer <what> \as/ much as | the other day, <too> I find, | This little subject, \ – of an intense simplicity – / was tiny | tales which shall, \mainly,/ not already <of> \have/ appeared;

152. To Alphonse Daudet 10 November 1895
Houghton MS (bMS Am 1094.1 (7))

rivé à mon <pieux> \pieu./ Il m'a été, | accumulées, <xxx> \devant les/quelles j'ai dû | sans voir presque <xxx> \personne – / <xxx> dans une station d'hiver | à 7 frs. 50. \le volume./ On vient | un état d'<abbattement> \abattement/ complet, | qu'on a dû beaucoup relâcher \ – lui alléger – / la discipline | aucune <qualité> \faculté/ résistante | trouvé sur <la> ma table

153. To Horace Elisha Scudder 3 March 1896
Houghton MS (bMS Am 1094.1 (23))

as you have done before, \in the act/ of | that my optimism has originally deluded itself into <the> a belief in.

154. To Sidney Colvin [April–May 1896]
Yale MS (MS Vault Stevenson Files #4907)

the personal \ – i.e. the intellectual – / loneliness of the artist | as the hungry booksellers & newspapers insist more & more on its <do> being. | all the rest of you – \other & baser organs & members,/ more matches it

155. To St Loe Strachey 6 May [1896]
King's MS (John Maynard Keynes PP/87. 37)

H J has handwritten the Rye address, cancelling the printed De Vere Gardens letterhead.

one's reach, \or embrace,/ ampler; | the thing in the \May/ *Chapman.* | for *me* (!) ten \thousand/ would be all right. | something with pleasure \addressed to a public "not very intelligent" (inspiring thought!)/ – as soon as I have time: \si le coeur vous en dit./ I am | place I am <not> \now/ too wearily (& affectionately) *familiar.*

156. To Edmund Gosse [8 November 1896]
Leeds MS

Rayburn Moore persuasively bases this dating on the pencilled date of 9 November 1896 on the MS, and on the fact that 8 November was a Sunday in 1896.

some refined, <immaterial> \pathetic/ object | But \why/ do I speak of the chaste, | Du Maurier once said <to me> in a note,

157. To [Sir] Henry Craik 30 May 1897
Virginia TS (6251 #458)

This is the first dictated letter in the present selection. All cancellations and insertions in typed letters are also typed unless described as '[MS]'.

I won't pretend to say *all* [MS emphasis] the softening of the heart that I I should like

158. To William Blackwood 15 October 1897
Scotland MS (4660, fols. 140–45)

through various obstacles & complications – <xxxx> very little progress. | too
valuable, much, \for me/ <xx> to write Mr. Story's Life, | more than a one-volume
<book> book.

159. To Arthur Christopher Benson 11 March 1898
Bodleian MS (Dep. Benson 3/53)

that has been <in> \on/ my conscience | & partly \ – & much more – / because
there had *been* no details | into a <tale> \fantastic fiction/ which, | gruesomely
hideous <was [?]> \as/ my unbridled

160. To Mrs John Chandler Bancroft 21 March 1898
Yale TS (Frederick R. Koch Collection)

The sight of *your* [MS emphasis] hand | the situation; [MS semi-colon] and my climax,
arrived at, was marked *by*, [MS emphasis] and consisted *of*, [MS emphasis and comma]
the stroke of the hour | manageable <tea> \key/. Nothing particular, | deprecate
the marriage of two Bostonians! [MS exclamation mark] I always think | your sense
<of> \in/ [MS] manipulating him! | a longish stretch, [MS comma] so that |
sparsely-furnishing stage, [MS comma] and my

161. To Mary (Mrs Humphry) Ward 24 May 1898
Virginia MS (6251 #384)

give you some <time [?]> sign | that <yu [?]> you shld. take hold | the beauty of
the \personal/ drama that presents <it> \the case./ I am | if I \can/ read a novel
at all, | I <read> \remained/ under the completest charm | free, high \way/ you
walk

162. To Paul Bourget 19 August 1898
Unknown TS

The original letter is unlocated, so my source is LHJ, which gives no variants.

163. To Mary (Mrs Humphry) Ward [22 September 1898]
Virginia MS (6251 #386)

The date is on the envelope.

164. To James Brand Pinker 19 October 1898
Yale MS (Za James 1, vol. 1)

the months have <xxxxx> \gone/ round | my work has, save <for> \in/ rare cases, | kindly return to me <my> the unfortunate wanderers.

165. To James Brand Pinker 23 October 1898
Yale MS (Za James 4)

HJL is in error to say 'Dictated TS'.

my nerves, as it were, <has been> \is/ – with the vision | the whole <serial> \magazine/ question. | talk <to> with you.

166. To Herbert George Wells 9 December 1898
Bodleian MS (MS. Don. d. 122, fols. 4–7)

the difficulty \itself/ is the refuge | the childish <xxxx> psychology | subjective complications of <tone [?]> \her/ own – play of tone &c.; | little note of \neatness,/ firmness & courage

167. To Frederic William Henry Myers 19 December 1898
Wren MS (Myers 2[139])

the sort of \cerebral/ freshness required | what to say to you \on the subject on wh. you wrote,/ especially | the communication <of> \to/ the children of the most infernal imaginable evil | as we can humanly <expose> conceive children to be. | losing hold of <my> \some/ of my few chances | city lays a <charm> \spell/ upon me.

168. To William Leon Mead 27 March 1899
Virginia MS (6251 #467)

The Bourgets' address (on headed notepaper) is crossed through.

Complicated, \further,/ by extemporized | have never had anything to say <that> \to which/ some word

169. To Mary (Mrs Humphry) Ward [23 July 1899]
Unknown MS or TS

The logic for this dating is that a 'Sunday' between HJ's two adjacent letters to Mrs Ward (of 10 and 26 July) must be 16 or 23 July; and the 23rd seems more likely, since this feels like a rapid-fire exchange. LHJ records no variants.

170. To Mary (Mrs Humphry) Ward 26 July 1899
Virginia MS (6251 #388)

by the particular case; \ – involved in the writer's responsibility to it/ & each *then* \ – & then only – / "hard & fast" | (save <in> \when they use/ the autobiographic dodge,) | illustrations of <true [?]> \extreme/ & calculated selection, | I "go behind" right <in> \and/ left in | Therefore <acquit [?]> \acquit me,/ please, | Or rather, \ – more correctly, – / I was giving way | one could best work <my>\ones/self into the presence of it. | *for myself*, to write it, \rather – / – even | to a particular imagination \(her's)/ and that imagination, | the reader. \I, in fine, just rudely & egotistically thrust forward the beastly way *I* should have done it./ But | And yet I *must* \still/ add one or two things \more./ What I said | the artist must \(infinitely!)/ know <too [?]> \how/ he is doing it, | a perception of the interests of his subject that <holds> \grasps/ him as in a vise, | the way that \most/ presents it, | that comparatively give it <away [?]> \away./ And he must | that is <his [?]> \the/ hard-&-fastness | any other source than that; \can get it,/ from, e.g., | (which, \however enchanting,/ is a thing | the author himself, \without humiliating abdications,/ to my sense, | out of the <way> \process,/ which, having made out most what it \(the subject)/ is, | secretary of <legation> \embassy/. And | Eleanor <is> counts | standpoint \& centre/ of Tolstoi & Balzac | they \can/ get | *I* "present" \also – *anch'io!* – / enough

171. To Edward Prioleau Warren 13 August 1899
Huntington MS (HM 40272)

at a moment when I <am> \was/ a little de<pld [?]>\pleted/ & unexpecting. | my
little affairs \ – as bearing on a purchase – / a little differently | besides \endless
prints & photos. (*all* the latter valued for association &c,) &/ 5,000 books! | than
your <Crossways [?]> Cowley St. date

172. To William Dean Howells 25 September 1899
Houghton MS (1784 (253) 73)

contrive to <enhan [?]> \enhance/ the comparatively | *Awkward Age* that you <xx>
\so/ kindly | struck me as \having &/ being, | I'm afraid, <xx> awakened the
disgust, | anything of \anything *like*/ the length | Case," <the> your kind words |
doubtless,) <rather> a sickening effort. | of the \particular/ abyss, | shall find<ing
his> himself approaching

173. To James Brand Pinker 9 November 1899
Yale MS (Za James 1, vol. 1)

of time \ – which I gave;/ & I have | if <the> \my idea for/ Doubleday | One
<of> \or/ the other,

174. To Henrietta Reubell [12 November 1899]
Houghton MS (bMS Am 1094 (1140))

SL2 dates this as 12 November.

at any rate <explain> \mention/ that | actual) \London/ group & type & tone,
<who> \which/ seemed | more, <x> \rather/ than less, | I don't <keep [?]> keep
it | to the \Expositionist/ Kraals of the savages & <the> haunts of the cannibals.

175. To Katharine Prescott Wormeley 28 November 1899
Yale MS (Za Cortissoz)

animadversions. <Still> I'll tell you | rap on <the> \my/ knuckles | Balzac, \par
parenthèse,/ was,

176. To Sarah Orne Jewett 24 December 1899
Huntington MS (FI 5546)

that murmurs \me/ no relief & stretches me no perch \of excuse,/ my deep dark
guilt | reperusal,) <& un> \much less/ honoured | the Muse. \I find in/ The
Queen's Twin \all of/ everything | a <grave> \serious/ affection of the heart

177. To James Brand Pinker 17 January 1900
Yale MS (Za James 1, vol. 1)

diabolically, \tormentingly/ *difficult* | when I \can/ give large leisure | such chances
<of> \as/ this thing | for getting <in> \on/ with the thing | probably <too [?]>
as much | "The Sense of the <Truth> \Past"/ or

178. To Violet Hunt 1 April 1900
Virginia MS (6251 #285)

179. To James Brand Pinker 12 June 1900
Yale MS (Za James 4)

I shld. have \magnificently/ risen to it *then*, \ – was doing so;/ I believe, | the
\(intended-to-be)/ final type-copy | I am sending back \my copy/ for reproduction
with embodied new \inspired/ last touches. | few days. \You shall then have it all./
Believe me

180. To William Dean Howells 9 and 14 August 1900
Houghton TS and MS (bMS Am 1784 (253) 75)

Read P.S. (Aug. 14th) first! [MS] | a thing I <saw> \should see/ my way | some
<xxx> months ago, | and <permits> \carries with it,/ as I have "fixed" it, | another
quarter \, at still another angle, [MS]/ that | beginning then \ – a year ago – [MS]/
to *do* | economic. \(Because – now that I haven't to consider my typist – there was
nobody to "take" it! The *Atlantic* declined – saying it really only wanted "Miss
Johnson"!) [MS]/ It really | simkifies | all is for the <xxxxx> moment | something
that <ds> *is* in it, | make the world sit <upp> up; | lifting again, "Miss Johnson"
permettendolo, <lifting> its downtrodden head. | delighted to <hear> see

181. To Alice Howe James 1 October 1900
Houghton MS (bMS Am 1094 (1643))

interest on <the> \a/ mortgage, | for \publication in/ the autumn | writing now a <serial> \novel/ to begin | languishment \ – by my own dire detachment from *ways* – / the | Pinker is bringing \me/ up, | period of production \ – however brief – / that | was, \by the way,/ bought | Elly & <xxxxx> \Leslie/ (he being | impression,) <xx> yesterday | 2*d* lecture-copy \ (William,) / from | he <xxx> \put/ into an envelope \left with him,/ directed

182. To Edith Wharton 26 October 1900
Yale MS (YCAL 42 Series II 26: 812)

the \complete/ non-vision of Millicent | that <is [?]> \was/ really your difficulty. | I egg you on in, <the> \your/ study of the American life | your remarkable \ironic & satiric/ gifts;

183. To Mary (Mrs Humphry) Ward 22 November 1900
Virginia MS (6251 #390)

The square brackets round the sentence 'Irony (& various things!) . . .' are HJ's own.

when there *is* anything. <else> So | death in the \already so much unrolled/ Arnold family cycle! | potboilers – \of a sort/ which | anything \of a/ larger or more inspiring \order./ So I've done | I've done <xx> much longer things | re-writing, as I <do> read, such fiction | to have done \ – been able to do – / under the appeal | isn't a *real*, \a valid,/ antithesis. It was utterly built, \your subject,/ by your intention, | so that \if/ the book | the image of Lucy that you have tried to teach yourself to <have> \see has/ – no true, | brought her back \ – roughly speaking – / stranger. | reader in your millions \ – or critic in your hundreds – / will

184. To Mrs Mary (Humphry) Ward 15 March 1901
Virginia MS (6251 #391)

The Reform Club address is embossed.

crossing <xxxx> \them/ on the way, | books, or \must/ take | it appears to <xxxx> have been, | at the end – what in the world has put it into <the end> your head? | testify to <her> \Mrs. S. 's/ sense of a common fate | the *appearance* of a \sensible/ detachment | the same stroke <that> \by which/ Briss is | all an \ironic/ *exposure* of her \own/ false plausibility, | my deadly backward present <subject> \book,/ which *isn't* a <subject> \joke/ – unless

---

185. To Maud Broadwood (Mrs Waldo) Story 13 June 1901
Texas MS (Henry James Letters, Box 2)

I had <on> immediately after coming back | sitting down to <write> \put my Volume through/. Let it | turned up for me \directly/ after | more delay \about the book/ I was very much ashamed | hoped wd. be a <smaller [?]> \much/ shorter story | Blackwood (\some time/ last year) | the somewhat more or \somewhat/ less time <more> deliberately taken | may be <xx> moved | I wind up \with thanking you/ once more | extraordinary <success> \distress/ *not* to do so. | health is <largely> \wholly/ re-established.

---

186. To James Brand Pinker 31 June [1 July] 1901
Yale MS (Za James 4)

immediately <been> written | simply <that> \because/ from one | this business <were> \would/ have had *Finis* | with a strong & <xxxx xxxx> \insistent/ hand.

---

187. To William Dean Howells 10 August 1901
Houghton MS (bMS Am 1784 (253) 76)

everything \ – every hundred – / above 6 or 7 thousand words | àpropos of \the 1st named of/ these, | the idea of \the fiction/ <tale> in question | from Paris, \repeated to me/ <mentioned> five words you had said | the whole incident \ – suggestive/ – so far as | scene that you <mentioned> \wrote/ to me from, with so gleaming \a New England/ <an> evocation, | quartered for <a> \the/ time | hand over hand \at home/ to remain so.

---

188. To Sarah Orne Jewett 5 October 1901
Houghton MS (bMS Am 1743 (111))

I just now < – > (especially | even <with> \in/ cases of labour | that make \ours, that make/ the modern world | to *think* \with your modern apparatus/ a man, a woman | whose \own/ thinking | The childish <arts> \tricks/ that | by <xxx> \composing/ the whole thing | by rude & <convenient [?]> \provisional/ signs, | the palpable \present/ *intimate*

189. To James Brand Pinker 6 November 1901
Yale MS (Za James 1, vol. 1)

to do <some>\any/thing for the purpose | I understand now \(I wonder I ever blinked it,)/ the difficulty | that is of compassion \(&, a little, of gratitude,)/ to the afflicted Ortmans, | banquetted me \(& others)/ with fatal luxury | sufficient reality to print \& pay for/ other short things | to make up a <short> \full new/ vol. \of short stories – / – in addition

190. To Lucy (Mrs William Kingdon) Clifford [9 May 1902]
Houghton TC (bMS Am 1237.16)

This 'Friday' comes before 15 May, which fell on a Thursday in 1902; so is the 2nd or 9th. On 2 May HJ's letter to Clare Benedict comments on 'freezing' weather (HJL IV, 228), which fits 'this Arctic May'; but *The Times* records that while on the 2nd the minimum London temperature was a chilly 45° Fahrenheit, on the 9th it was a perishing 39° (there was snow in southern France). HJ was in London till about 27 April; 'I fled hither many days ago' I take as a further basis for preferring the 9th.

191. To Owen Wister 7 August 1902
Congress MS (Owen Wister Papers, Box 25)

having felt, as I read, <of> how | so <deeply> \clearly/ & finely felt by you, | questions, \elements/ of the art we practise & adorn, | studied \& dismissed/ to be, | something \equally American/ on this scale | I envy you the \personal/ knowledge of the W.W.,

192. To Edith Wharton 17 August 1902
Yale MS (YCAL 42 Series II 26: 812)

not to address <xxx> myself to you to that without | favour \your coming hitherward – / within | I feel \that/ just now | being <xxxxx> \crudely/ hinted | while you're <still> \in/ full command

193. To Lucy (Mrs William Kingdon) Clifford 8 September 1902
Houghton TC (Lubbock: bMS Am 1237.16)

The type-copyist has put 'sic' by 'So serve you write'; I therefore let it stand.

194. To Ford Madox Hueffer (Ford) 9 September 1902
Houghton MS (bMS Am 1094.6 (18))

I feel \ – have *been* feeling – / mainly as if I had deposited in the market-place an object \chiefly/ <mainly> cognisable, | in a certain way, \in order/ to come into being

195. To Mary (Mrs Humphry) Ward 23 September 1902
Virginia MS (6251 #392)

There are <xxxx> \three or/ four major ones | for Densher; \there's *no* consciousness – / none, I mean, | her Father, <who [?]> \in/ particular, | Mrs. Lowder \(& these are not the maximum faults, either!)/ has slipped away

196. To Viscount Field-Marshal Garnet Joseph Wolseley 15 October 1902
Hove MS (Wolseley Archive 72)

197. To Herbert George Wells 15 November 1902
Bodleian MS (MS Don. d. 122, fols. 33–5)

neglected <xx> \an/ interesting | *because* the <explanation> \acknowledgment/ involved | it *was* \the/ <a> statement, | ½ as long \& proportionately less developed./ *That* had | the thing \(the book)/ was then written, \the subject treated,/ on a more | no fiction of mine \can or/ *will* now be serialized; certainly I shall not \again/ draw up | do draw up <too> – that is | I always, \for easy reference,/ have it | unlikely. \It is too wantonly expensive a treat to them./ In the first place | *tone*, <are> \is/ too precious

198. To William Dean Howells 11 December 1902
Houghton MS (bMS Am 1784 (253) 80)

has <touched> \befallen me/ for years, | those <hear> \here/ (which I am told, | I mean had it \in/ any special way. | unsupported \unrewarded/ heroism; | having \accepted/ its bookish necessity | When, \if it meets my eye,/ I say | send me \either/ that *or* | benedictions on hour house

199. To Maud Broadwood (Mrs Waldo) Story 6 January 1903
Texas TS and MS (Henry James Letters, Box 2)

The printed letterhead '34, DE VERE GARDENS, W.' is crossed through; the 'P.S.' is handwritten. LHJ omits extensive passages: 'After that, Blackwood . . . what I mean'; 'The advantage . . . can stand off.'; 'I shall have used . . . it is plain sailing.'

200. To Frederick Macmillan 17 June 1903
BL MS (Add. 54931, fols. 260–61)

the book <of> \on/ London | able to read \ – a little – / even in America

201. To James Brand Pinker 1 November 1903
Yale MS (Za James 1, vol. 1)

202. To Brander Matthews 16 November 1903
Columbia MS (Brander Matthews Papers (X812M43/#S6))

The printed letterhead 'REFORM CLUB, PALL MALL. S.W.' is cancelled.

a little <xxxx>\care/ful proof-reading,

203. To Howard Overing Sturgis 18 November 1903
Houghton MS (bMS Am 1094 (1213))

a *positive* side, \ – all his own – / so that | for which I <want> \mean/ to thank – I mean

204. To Henry Adams 19 November 1903
Mass. Hist. Inst. MS (Henry Adams Papers)

to be precipate<d>ly obeyed | something \in the nature/ of a *book* might be made,

205. To Howard Overing Sturgis [28 November 1903]
Houghton MS (bMS Am 1094 (1215))

the \whole/ thing doesn't seem | happening?" <xx> \This/ is particularly sensible |

strangely, \ – in some way or *other* – / happening; | *adequate* \positive/ fact – of impression, | He couldn't afford \there/ (for interest,) to fail

206. *To Mary (Mrs Humphry) Ward 16 December 1903*
Virginia MS (6251 #394)

RRR's text differs in more than a dozen details.

"What <can> \can be/ expected for a novel | fearful, \though much patched over,/ fault

207. *To Millicent, Duchess of Sutherland 23 December 1903*
Yale MS (Frederick R. Koch Collection)

any hare, \however small,/ that might lurk by the way.

208. *To William Dean Howells 8 January 1904*
Houghton TS (bMS Am 1784 (253) 84)

LHJ omits ' – being contracted for . . . no brilliant terms.' and 'I am sorry . . . the truest loyalty!'

to do so \even/ across the wild winter sea.

209. *To Alice Stopford Green 10 January 1904*
Virginia TS (6251–a #254)

Very soon after I <had> \have/ got the wretched member

210. *To Violet Hunt 16 January 1904*
Virginia MS (6251–o #304)

In HJL this letter is misdated as 1902.

M*me* de Vionnet's visit to <Mrs.; it [?]> \Mrs./ P. – it gave her away | that indirectly revealing <value.> \virtue./ Maria G. is, dissimulatedly, \but/ a *ficelle*, | must know that –" <M*me* [?]> \She/ is not | Strether *is* the the subject,

211. To Mrs Eveleen Tennant (Frederic William Henry) Myers 8 April 1904
Wren MS (Myers 22 (74))

sure whether <now> \or no/ I am still possessed | great pleasure \in/ two or three happy chances

212. To James Brand Pinker 20 May 1904
Yale TS (Za James 1, vol. 1)

LHJ omits 'and Methuen's importunity does meanwhile, I confess, distress me.'

a straight <straight> step | last page, <now> [MS] comparatively close

213. To Joseph Pennell 23 June 1904
Congress MS (Pennell—Whistler Collection, Container 234)

in France, <I have [?]> \before/ it goes | a book \of Impressions,/ for the Harpers,

214. To Charles Scribner's Sons 17 September 1904
Princeton MS (Scribner's Archives 81: 2)

constructed & completed, <of my> \and it/ proved, | an artistic <xxxx> trap. | written you. \I appreciate this, but/ there are reasons, | "Book First: The <Princess> \Prince"/, &

215. To James Brand Pinker 22 October 1904
Yale MS (Za James 1, vol. 1)

movements <is> \are/ a devourer | to *see* all \of all this/ I can, | like a war-correspondent \writing on his knee or his hat,/ & I want | upon \the/ fulness of my observations. | the question being open \only/ as to | first in \corrected/ galley-proofs, | arranged \for/ the price | you <had> \have/ been having,

216. To Colonel George Harvey 25 January 1905
Congress MS (Henry James Papers)

to believe that \only/ good & valid, | & deliver \it/ in 2 or 3 places | having more \impressions & visions, more/ confidence & competence. | its intrinsic beauty <xx>

\shall/ strike you | hanging over \it/ <them> again, | to pay a \pair of/ promised & inevitable visits | till Monday \a. m./ next, | Biltmore, N.C. <for> \but/ 95 Irving St.

217. To James Brand Pinker 6 March 1905
Yale MS (Za James 1, vol. 1)

Will you – \thereafter – / I think | rather *starve* <xx> \at/ Lamb House | at St. Louis on the 7*th*, & then \ – 10*th* – 15*th* – / *4* times in all | known \this in/ <this> advance | I could <obtain> \have/ far more | my *2*/ Philadelphia evenings

218. To James Brand Pinker 6 June 1905
Yale TS and MS (Za James 1, vol. 1)

The brackets round '(This rather horrid heat ... muggy old London.)' are MS additions.

it <is> \should prove/ more difficult | you won't find <that> \the/ two or three days | the idea of which I \rather [MS]/ *don't* [emphasis MS] <rather> cherish. | his "phone" number is \234 Gramercy./ [number in MS balloon] Yours ever,

219. To Frederick Allen King 2 July 1905
Virginia TS (6251 #503)

220. To Robert Herrick 7 August 1905
Chicago MS (Robert Herrick Papers (1: 16))

You didn't even come \ – you told me – / to my fanatical Balzac lecture! | in respect to some \of the/ old stuff | will *in fact*/ bear but | felt close revision \ – wherever seeming called for – / to be | and \I fear/ it must go!) | of many \ – of all – / men's work | horrific. \You, also, will be ravished!/ Trust me | pardon my \untidy scrawl & my/ belated incoherence.

221. To Elinor Mead (Mrs William Dean) Howells 14 August 1905
Houghton MS (bMS Am 1784.5 (31) 3)

thinking of you \all, in your neighbourhood, / immensely, in Europe, | Portsmouth Drama, & I I should | so wondrous has <every> \everything/ become | his own particular \ruinous/ way | the sense of \the/ return to private life

222. To Edith Wharton 8 November 1905
Yale MS (YCAL 42 Series II 26: 814)

several things \ – interests – / that life | all your climax \is/ very finely handled. |
the thing <is;> – \his last book – is,/ I think, | in some degree \ – in a great degree
– / present | his so <insistent [?]> \inveterate, &/ so generous, gifts | Beatrix I
thought <not> \less/ well | with <so> \such/ softly-encircling arms | she \also/
greatly admires Mrs. Wharton. | tumbling herself \bodily/ into | will make <either>
\the other/ party out. | the commotion, <xx> \into/ which I foresee | I have \ – I
had – / heard of, | I know about <too> \your/ shock & your pang | to buy <a>
\some/ fine old Jacobean \(or other)/ house & estate. <& with whose> I roamed
\with them/ far over the land | Don't be morbid, *you*,/ in

223. To Herbert George Wells 19 November 1905
Bodleian MS (MS Don. d. 122, fols. 60–65)

HJHGW and HJL read HJ's praise of *Kipps*, 'so vivid & sharp & *done*', as 'so vivid
and sharp and *raw*'.

produced by <upwards of [?]> \almost/ a year's absence | by our \each/ contributing
Utopias | the \rare/ yearning individual | the \fantastic &/ romantic interference,
| George Eliot is so <misguidedly> \deviatingly/ full. You have <seen> \handled/
its vulgarity | till Jan. <1st> \31st/ – when | each vol. \but/ moderately thick | if
you, \at this late day,/ will have it.

224. To William James 23 November 1905
Houghton MS (bMS Am 1094 (2193))

I can't \tonight/ hideously further postpone \acknowledging/ your | to <Mrs>
\the/ Humphry Wards. | of imbecillity – of come back | he <is> (in addition to
being | the Kitty T. of <your> \our/ youth | 2 \moderately-long/ books (separate,
of course, not <xx> \2/ vols., | begins \in/ <this> December. | paying literature
is \a/ very great tension | artificial <cluth [?]> clutch! | her \simu[l]taneous/ social
début | that two-<& fo [?]>\&/ two-make-four system | express myself \on/ this
question | so that \all/ the intentions | about \me/ done or dreamed \of/ <off>
the things | having \margins of/ mornings in my room, through both <dinner [?]>
\break/fasting & lunching | your brother. \I had no *time* to read them there./
Philosophically, in in short, I am | garden – \setting it up better/ against | But <the>
hot-water pipes

225. To Auguste Monod 17 December 1905
Unknown MS or TS

I have emended HJLACBAM's reading 'a very appropriate rendering' to 'a very approximate rendering', on grounds of sense.

226. To Mary Cadwalader Jones 25 March 1906
Houghton MS (bMS Am 1094 (757))

227. To Charles Scribner's Sons 12 May 1906
Princeton MS (Scribner's Archive 81:3)

The printed letterhead of 'The Athenaeum, / Pall Mall. S.W.' is crossed through. HJ was briefly in London.

228. To Arthur Christopher Benson [31 May 1906]
Bodleian MS (Dep. Benson 3/53)

The letter can be dated from the postmark.

Pater <admirably> \assuredly/ is,) | the subject − \pressing it so intelligently hard, *le serrant de si près*, &/ playing all over it

229. To James Brand Pinker 27 June 1906
Yale MS (Za James 1, vol. 2)

containing \both/ the subordinate, | such \little/ papers | that \after/ I have sent Munro | as many <of> \in/ the 3000 words form | yes − \the question of issuing *here*/ the American vol. | I hope to <be> about July 10*th*.

230. To Frederick A. Duneka 28 August 1906
Yale TS (Za James 37)

undertook it \for your use,/ with

231. To Frederick A. Duneka 14 September 1906
Yale TS (Za James 37)

232. To Joseph Conrad 1 November 1906
Berg MS (216756B)

The manuscript is in very poor condition. Preceding published transcriptions of this letter have been unreliable.

the inexhaustible adventure. <of it> No one | & vous y avez, \en même temps que les droits les plus acquis,/ les plus rares bonheurs.

233. To Herbert George Wells 8 November 1906
Bodleian MS (MS Don. d. 122, fols. 71–2)

or a conjurer, \(juggler;)/ seems to show you | your vividness \& your force/ & your truth, | there are \still/ more things to say | of the same – <for> \of/ the vast uncomfortable subject. | find you – <xx> \amid/ what blooming

234. To Mrs Alice Dew-Smith 12 November 1906
Houghton TC (Lubbock: bMS Am 1237.16)

Following LHJ, I have amended the typed copy's 'I beg you to make and any early signal' to read 'make an early signal'.

235. To Alvin Langdon Coburn 11 December 1906
Virginia MS (6251 #190)

Do make \me/ a postal sign | outside, \ – *all round* – !/ *well*, | or even \ – & *better* at this season – / a good one | Make him your \"tipped"/ ally

236. To Charles Scribner's Sons 15 February 1907
Princeton MS (Scribner's Archives 81: 3)

my \long/ delay | the \aspect of the/ book | will <xxxx> \henceforth,/ let me

237. To Elizabeth Jordan 5 March 1907
NYPL MS (Elizabeth Garver Jordan Papers)

to Indianapolis itself, \another to the coeducative Berkeley Cal.,/ another to | would
be then be of *twice*

238. To Colonel George Harvey 6 September 1907
Congress MS (Henry James Papers)

239. To Mary Frances (Mrs Fanny) Prothero 18 October [1907]
Houghton MS (bMS Am 1094.3 (22))

the interests of of the Idol | "I hope you don't <xxxx xx> \mind me/ coming" | to
talk with you \about them"/ & then | She is <ind> \clearly/ indisposed – " | a
<shriek> \piercing wail,/ a heavy fall

240. To Elizabeth Robins 20 October 1907
Princeton MS (Robert A. Taylor File Cabinet, Folder James, Henry)

about \the secret &/ the silence; | & \through/ a limit | & \also of/ a value. |
complete (as \complete as/ it *can* become, | a particular \tense/ chord | a 100 000
sixpences \for the cause,/ very constantly

241. To Edmund Gosse 10 November 1907
Berg MS (216757B)

SLHJEG's text derives from Lubbock's typed copy, at my prompting in about 1986;
I subsequently came across the original in the Berg ('immensely' is correct, 'immediately'
in TC not).

these last days been \so/ leaving you | brilliantly maintained \ – carried through
with rare audacity./ <from beginning to end> You have | a couple of cases \ – places
– / in which | the subject treat<ment>\ed/ with so much more | on a side, I may
\further/ add, | I pray for something, \a week hence,/ *like*.

242. To James Brand Pinker 31 December 1907
Yale MS (Za James 4)

that <xxx> \we may/ take pleasure | reposing gloriously on on our tables!

243. To William Ernest Norris 30 January 1908
Yale MS (Za James 60)

I think, <before> \than ever in my life before./ I am | large \& most discreet/
omissions | & proof <collecting> \-reading,/ to say nothing | I *almost* vividly know
<about> \all your sad *essence*/ without your having | is that that you are probably
| & never acted \ – only in a manner printed – / but now dragged to the light |
mention <it> \them/ when

244. To Dr Charles E. Wheeler 25 March 1908
UCL MS (MS Add. 153)

that \benefit/ (& one or two others) <xxx> \&/ shall proceed

245. To Frederick Macmillan 5 April 1908
BL TS (Add. 54931, fols. 268–71)

have had to do so in the negatively. Mrs. Laurence Binyon | provincial, <but>
\though [MS]/ apparently | nothing can possibly <make more my> \conduce more
to/ my having

246. To William Dean Howells 17 August 1908
Houghton TS (bMS Am 1784 (253) 105)

City (as well \as,/ alas, more or less, Suburbs) | at the cost of all \imputable/
coherency | when I \receive/ the waft | I never had had such a sense | the too
personally and physically \arduous,/ and above all | one thing w which may

247. To James Brand Pinker 13 October 1908
Yale MS card (Za James 4)

only bought from \the/ Scribners

248. To James Brand Pinker 20 October 1908
Yale MS (Za James 1 or 4)

249. To James Brand Pinker 3 December 1908
Yale MS (Za James 1, vol. 2)

& I \have/ answered him | at the <st> \job/ – but | do two or three
\ – too irreducibly & irredeemably long, – / in order to pull off | the subject, \the
motive,/ has *had* | at least \ – & immediately/ another,

250. To James Brand Pinker 3 January 1909
Yale MS (Za James 1, vol. 2)

for Alden, \(Harper)/ as I wrote you | *will* be \a true/ 5000. | I can't but <accept>
\assent to/ for the money's sake | the \interrupting/ botherment is yet

251. To George Bernard Shaw 20 January 1909
Unknown TS

The late Leon Edel very generously reconstructed a few months before his death the
complicated manner in which he obtained texts of this and the following letter to
Shaw. Theodora Bosanquet told Professor Edel in 1929 of the existence of these letters;
but only at some point between 1937 and 1948 did his London friend Allan Wade
make contact with 'a German refugee named Lowenstein . . . who was sorting out
great masses of Shaw's received letters' (Leon Edel to Philip Horne, 1 July 1997).
Lowenstein found the letters and Wade transcribed them for Professor Edel, who first
reproduced them in *The Complete Plays* (1949). I have attempted to trace the originals,
without success, kindly helped by the Society of Authors, who are in charge of Shaw's
literary estate; and am grateful to Professor Edel for permission to use *The Complete
Plays* as my source.

252. To George Bernard Shaw 23 January 1909
Unknown TS

253. To Charles Scribner's Sons 8 March 1909
Princeton MS card (Scribner's Archives 81: 4)

254. To James Brand Pinker 1 April 1909
Yale MS (Za James 1, vol. 2)

255. To Violet Hunt 6 April 1909
Virginia MS card (6251 #327)

don't see how <xx> any man | your affair will be will be what the poor scratch shall avail you.

256. To William James 18 July [1909]
Houghton MS (bMS Am 1094 (2213))

your *all* coming \out/ to me | grow too fat & <eat> \move/ too little; | returning \to/ & leaning on dear Mother Nature | almost *as* dear – H.F. \himself/, who | that – \frequently/ a Welsh Rabbit!) | the effects (*local*/ *doctor-produced*) | then, \in town,/ in the 1*st* fit of gout, | two jobs \that/ are | it has been \ever since/ <long> convenient, | received <an> \my/ advance | during \all of/ which, | the next day \otherwise/ back through | with \a/ more thrilled interest | finding, in <the light of it> \comparison/ everything else

257. To James Brand Pinker 21 July 1909
Yale MS (Za James 1, vol. 2)

258. To William James 31 October 1909
Houghton MS (bMS Am 1094 (2215))

Franconia, \"autumn-tint" postcards/ &c, | I find <of> \it/ of thrilling interest, | you make out your case, (<as> \since/ it seems to me you so utterly do,) as \I/ under no romantic spell ever \palpitate/ now; | to <depict> \reflect/ a happy | & should \have,/ especially for | the climax \with/ diluvian | *definitely* \& *unmistakeably*,/ the finally proved *cul de sac* | from my of late \ – that is these last 3 months'/ very trying experience | I am <working> \worrying/ out my salvation | has had a rather a sad hole made in it | addressed to be by poor Ida Smalley | (Helen Fiske by name, \daughter of Vice-President of Metropolitan Insurance Company/) who, | when I got <him [?]> \her/ off | she was \ – & I trust *is* – / to sleep. | the \most/ extraordinary suggestiveness | your present volume \ – which I had read all individually before – / seems to me | feel \Pragmatic/ invulnerability | cross the <see> \wintry ocean/ to see | more successively \than/ < – > simultaneously, | will still, \together/ make | as regards <anylik [?]> \anything/ like content or character | in a \harmless &/ sad & imaginable way | a conscious\ness/ of comparative failure | (not \quite/ *in*expressible!) | which \just/ lately made | find a scrap <of> \of a/ moment to testify | the latter most <elevating> \interesting/ & uplifting!

259. To Elizabeth Jordan 14 November 1909
NYPL, RBMS MS (Elizabeth Garver Jordan Papers)

if it \ – my Life – / ever had any; | I work very expensively artistically speaking, \to myself – / to begin with.

260. To James Brand Pinker 6 January 1910
Yale TS and MS (Za James 1, vol. 2)

The text is TS up to 'the last outstanding thing to Putnam', and thereafter hurried MS; it seems possible that the letter as given here is not complete.

to *determine* [emphasis MS] it. | as \the/ other American magazines | secured by! \ – or *for* – ! – / – the author of *The Inner Shrine*. | hanged <If> if each | know as well as I \ – I only knowing through G. Barker – / that he | the best \possible/ for yours ever

261. To Hugh Walpole 13 May 1910
Texas MS (Hugh Walpole, recip., Folder 1)

utterly, <xx> \but/ necessarily | your "visible & tangible" <bility [?]> affection | change of air, \scene/ & circumstances | objects, \is so fiercely intense/ that | for me. \I adore it./ | the \grim &/ battered old *critical* critic | man & his wife – \ – since these *are* the key to the whole situation – / which have to be | to mean anything. \You don't tackle & face them – you *can't*./ Also | composition, \alternation,/ distribution structure, & other phases of presentation \than the dialogic – / – so that | you have \ – or, truly, only in a few places, as in Maradick's dive – / never got | you have never \made out,/ recognised,

262. To Theodora Bosanquet 1 August 1910
Houghton MS (bMS Am 1094 (635))

on <July> August 12*th* | my illness & \complete/ inability to superintend & be carry on rehearsal

263. To Sydney Waterlow 10 September 1910
Yale MS (Frederick R. Koch Collection)

HJ uses black-edged paper, marking WJ's death.

& \<sank> \struggled to/ his very threshold

264. To Gertrude Kingston 31 January 1911
King's College, Cambridge MS (Misc 6/ Bundle 4/ Item 84)

Also black-edged. HJ has handwritten 'New York' under the printed street address of the letterhead.

the little play \<will> \would/ more or less stand or fall | who "do" the \<newspaper> \theatres/ in their columns; | only intensely \<xxx> presumable

265. To Herbert George Wells 3 March 1911
Bodleian MS (MS Don. d. 122, fols. 80–83)

so alive & kicking \& sprawling! – / so vivid & rich and strong | disinterested. \R. Crusoe, e.g., isn't a novel at all./ There is, to my vision, no authentic, \& no really interesting & no *beautiful,*/ report of things | my \main "criticism"/ [above letter-head] on *The N.M.* | to England \in June,/ never again, | functional Love – \always/ suffers | by tracing \it/ through indirectness

266. To Lady Victoria Welby [August? 1911]
[Fragment only: original unknown]

My text comes from OD, which does not seem altogether reliable in some details.

267. To Henry James III (nephew) 26 November 1911
Houghton MS (bMS Am 1094 (1384))

putting in \the/ "week-end" | strenuously & \overwhelmingly/ munificent | illness \in her company/ here, | again, \even eventually,/ during | rather intense \<pressure> \remindingness, her urgency to me/ to come, | However, \<xx>\on/e has only | furniture of \<x> \our/ family annals. | so \to/ *keep* seeing it | very straight & \un/interruptedly & | by book-post \<some> \two/ of your Grandfather's volumes | renewal of co-operation \<of> \with/ Miss Bosanquet | & \that/ my so reasonable

268. To Henry Mackinnon Walbrook 5 January 1912
Houghton TC (Lubbock: bMS Am 1237.16)

269. To Herbert George Wells 25 March 1912
Bodleian MS (MS. Don. d. 122, fols. 88–93)

a mere \more *direct*/ effect of the energy of | as great as yours are \is/ able not to make

270. To Arthur Christopher Benson 9 May 1912
Bodleian MS (Dep Benson 3/53)

(the only <one> \approach/ possible

271. To Hugh Walpole 14 August 1912
Texas MS (Hugh Walpole, recip., Folder 2)

LHJ omits 'Dearest little Hugh . . . your fondest Methusaleh.'

I'm very glad \for you/ that | have plenty to <tell me> \thrill me/ & to confirm that passion withal. | return \to/ *these* platitudes, | you are \to be/ still | so *far* (<with> \given/ such an intellectual reach,) | the Ambassadors \have again engaged &/ still beguile you; | you probably \often/ sit | understand what \in that connection/ you miss | according to my method \only/ implied & indicated thing, | wondering sense, \a dimly envious sense,/ of all | Strether's discipline, \development,/ adventure & general history. All \of it/ that is

272. To Mrs Humphry Ward 24 October 1912
Virginia TS (6251 #411)

273. To Henry James III (nephew) 24 April 1913
Houghton TS (bMS Am 1094 (1398))

my \taking an/ "invidious" line. | had\,/ [MS] in a word\,/ [MS] only | contribute \to/ [MS] the bulk. | the '66–6\8/ [MS] <7> European | breathe round *them* [MS emphasis] again | practically engages, \to arrange for/ [MS] her | \P.S. *Please* send this on to your Mother!/ [MS]

274. To Hugh Walpole 29 April 1913
Texas MS (Hugh Walpole, recip., Folder 2)

The third sheet of the letter is torn, and I have suggested in square brackets words that fit the gaps and what I take to be the general sense.

it lies \here before me/ <before> & again | which \push of the pen/ I have languished, | that you \may count/ <count> hereafter | that some \passages/ <of my> "defeat" you | intelligence! [And yet, as it] \would seem,/ I don't get | But <though> \"thou/ hast great allies," | wonder at \such a restriction on the part of/ an *expert* dabbler

275. To Louise Corrin Walsh 23 June 1913
Houghton TC (Lubbock: bMS Am 1237.16)

276. To Henry James III (nephew) 10 December 1913
Houghton MS (bMS Am 1094 (1407))

the deplorable \piece of/ cheap ruled paper | but \so/ exceedingly good, | one of the \very/ best things | but I <confess [?]> \greatly/ hope | they have been \successfully/ taken in hand. | just visible \ruled/ lines | the \Macmillan's/ Proofsheets

277. To James Brand Pinker 2 January 1914
Yale MS (Za James 1, vol. 3)

I must <write> \wait/ & perhaps

278. To James Brand Pinker 5 February 1914
Yale MS (Za James 1, vol. 3)

the Macmillans' \annual/ cheque | he <strikes> \affects/ me | from \some/ comparative recent lapses. | strikes \me/ as "rum"

279. To André Raffalovich 26 February 1914
Virginia MS (6251 #545)

The name of the 'Sélincourts' has been scratched out at some later date.
a rather <feeling [?]> \rueful/ feeling

280. To Henry Adams 21 March 1914
Mass. Hist. Inst. MS (Henry Adams Papers)

I still, <have> in presence of life | It's, I suppose, \because/ I am that queer monster the artist,

281. To Hugh Walpole 21 and 23 April 1914
Texas MS (Hugh Walpole, recip., Folder 3)

& <xx> \the/ sight of him the first | ancient \pedagogues &/ parsons; | everything he had <had> \said/ in talk. | he *abbreviating* each word, \reducing it to half,/ in the most inconsiderate fashion | such flaunting \(flaun*ted*)/ ineptitude & infantility. | make, \however,/ was on the <even [?]> \still/ more incredible lack | smile at the <power [?]> \power/ of a Haymarket, \or a "rotten" play,/ the more or the less

282. To Henrietta Temple Pell-Clarke 5 May 1914
Cornell MS

planning with \that/ confidence | what you <tell me [?]> \say/ of your interest | rather than bring <her [?]> \himself/ to destroy them. | or were <xxxx> \you too juvenile/ a little shrimp?

283. To James Brand Pinker 8 May 1914
Yale MS (Za James 1, vol. 3)

The fact named <you> \by you/ is but *one* | small wants \ – in spite of a family – / & great savings, | he knows <but> \of/ W.D.H. but

284. To Edward Emerson 4 August 1914
Princeton MS (Robert A. Taylor File Cabinet, Folder James, Henry)

I have \come/ to find it not so <much> \very/ absolutely destructive | I can sometimes do \something – / a few things | I must have <xxx> \worn/ to Concord | speak of of sunny nooks, or whatever, \"angles", vistas,/ in the Virginia Blue Ridge | *bettering* past, \of our century,/ has meant | to something <dreadfu> \formidable/, with

285. To Charles Scribner's Sons 26 October 1914
Princeton TS (Scribner's Archives 81: 5)

the \half/ [MS] dozen will be exactly made up.

286. To Edmund Gosse 17 December 1914
Princeton MS (General MSS (bound) Series J, H)

feel about them <only> \unspeakably/, & | one seems to <xxxxxx> \find at moments it's almost sharp!/ And

287. To Edward Marsh 6 June 1915
Berg MS

one walks round <it> \&/ round it | a kind that <none> \belong/ to none of the others, | having it, <as> \since/ it was of his very nature | lost in the \degree of/ beauty, | he <has> \draws/ such a real magic | one had \first/ read | refinement \both/ of admiration & of anguish. | the Great Lover (<at> \toward/ the close | all so exposed, \really exposed,/ & yet

288. To James Brand Pinker 29 June 1915
Yale TS (with MS insertions) (Za James 1, vol. 3)

LHJ stops after the first paragraph, just before 'And now here . . .'

feels about his <island, and> \insulation, and his being/ in it and of it, | "The New Vision"; \or, better still, simply "Insulation:"/ though

289. To Herbert George Wells 6 July 1915
Bodleian MS (MS. Don. d. 122, fols. 106–7)

there \has then grown up/ the habit | various others that <I> \I am/ simply reduced to wish | nothing may even <xxx> \be/ more certain,

290. To Herbert George Wells 10 July 1915
Bodleian TS (TS Don. d. 122, fols. 108–10)

291. To James Brand Pinker 27 July 1915
Yale TS (Za James 1, vol. 3)

Enclosed with the letter is a purple typed copy of the 'Reasons for Naturalisation'.

embodying my <small> [MS] "reasons",

292. To James Brand Pinker 28 July 1915
Yale TS (Za James 1, vol. 3)

293. To Edmund Gosse 25 August 1915
Congress MS (Henry James Papers (Bound: vol. 3))

All previous editions follow LHJ's 'waved' where I read 'wooed'.

grace \of/ speculation, | Ozymandias of <Eyg [?]> \Egypt/ ("look on my *works* | what it does \ – the whole 25 vols. – / in this country | The Edition is \from/ that point | justice done it \ – any sort of critical attention at all paid it – / & the artistic problem | felt about it myself \then/ that | with you \all/ over Philip's transfer

294. To Longmans, Green & Co. 1 November 1915
University of Reading TC (Longman Archive: MS1393/122A/19)

295. To Rhoda Broughton 3 November 1915
Cheshire TS (DDB/M/J/1/45)

find me fulsome \ – / [MS] whether | seen *him* yet, \though/ just back from Russia,

296. To John William Mackail 26 November 1915
Princeton MS (Robert A. Taylor File Cabinet, Folder James, Henry)

an engagement \taken/ to perform | liked it <immensely [?]> \beyond anything – / & infallibly have said "Rather – "!

Glossary of Foreign Words and Phrases

(Alphabetically listed by first foreign word in each instance.)

à bientôt: till soon

à consulter: necessary to consult, of central importance

à demain: till tomorrow

à froid: coldly

à la bonne franquette: simply, without ceremony

à la guerre comme à la guerre: war is war, there's no choice

à la portée: within reach

à mon adresse: directed at me

à mon age: at my age

à peine: barely

a posteriori: from experience, after the event (Latin)

a priori: on principle (Latin)

à propos: with regard (to)

à qui le dites-vous?: to whom do you say it?

à quoi m'en tenir: what to expect, what to believe

ab ovo: from the start, from the egg (Latin)

absit omen: may it not be a bad omen (Latin)

accablé: overwhelmed

aetatis: of the age of (Latin)

agrément: pleasantness

Ah, je vous aime bien, allez!: Ah, go on, I love you well!

al solito: as usual (Italian)

Allons: Very well

allure: gait, bearing; presence

angoissé: in anguish

arida nutrix leonum: dry suckler of lions (Latin)

asservi: enslaved

attaché du cabinet: ministerial attaché

atteinte: hurt

attendri: touched

au besoin: in case of need

au complet: the complete set, in full

au grand sérieux: with high seriousness

au plus tôt: as soon as possible

Aussi: Also

avènement: advent

avertir: forewarn

Bäden: baths (German)

bafoué: flouted, scorned

Basta!: That's enough! (Italian)

Basta pure – basta!: Still, that's enough, that's enough! (Italian)

Bayadère: dancing-girl (also in English: striped pattern on fabric)

bel et bien: entirely

belles choses: beautiful things

bête: stupid

biais: shift, expedient

bien non: no indeed

Binnenleben: inner life (German)

bleu-ciel: sky-blue

bonheur: happiness

bouder: be sulky with

bouffées: whiffs, gusts

bousculé: buffeted

brin: scrap, fragment

624

C'est pour vous dire: This is to let you know

Ça ne m'est pas égal du tout – je vous prie de croire: It's not indifferent to me at all, please believe

ça ne vaut pas le diable: it's utterly worthless

ça se vend comme du pain: the thing sells like hot cakes (lit. bread)

ça y est: that's it, the thing is done

cachet: hallmark

Camere Mobigliate: Furnished Rooms

campanile: belltower (Italian)

Capo d'Anno: New Year's Day (Italian)

Carino amico: Dear friend

Ce que c'est de nous!: What poor mortals we are!

Ce que c'est d'être Allemand!: What it is to be German!

ce qu'il y a de mieux: the best thing

ce qu'on a (lately) fait de mieux: the best that's (lately) been done

cela s'est vu: it's been known

cela vous a porté bonheur: this was lucky for you

celui-ci: the latter

ces messieurs: those gentlemen

chargé d'affaires: ambassador's deputy

chatoyer: shimmer, glisten

chemisette: (woman's) blouse

choisi: select

ci-devant: fogeyish, out-of-date

ciselure: engraving, embossing

Civis Britannicus sum!: I am a British citizen! (Latin)

coeur d'oncle: uncle's heart

commandé: done by order

comme cela: in that way

compagnon de voyage: travelling companion

conférences: lectures

contorni: surroundings (Italian)

convaincu: full of conviction/by conviction

coram publico: in public (Latin)

coup: deed, exploit

cul de sac: dead end

dans le monde: in society

dans vos parages: in your region

d'autres choses encore!: other things as well!

de chic: with style

de confiance: on trust

dé de la conversation: die in gaming (also a thimble): (monopolize) the conversation

de passage: passing through

de province: provincial

de quoi: the wherewithal

de quoi vivre: something to live on

de retour: back

de rigueur: compulsory

déboires: unpleasant aftertastes

déjà assez difficile: already difficult enough

démodé: old-fashioned

dénouement: undoing, solution

déplacements: upheavals, movements

des loisirs inattendus: unexpected leisure

des rentes: a private income

désagrément: nuisance

désinvolture: freedom of manner, unselfconsciousness

destinataire: addressee

devotissimo: most devoted

d'ici là: between now and then

Dieu sait: God knows

disponible: available

distingué: refined, polished

donnée: given, premise

douche: shower

du bon: something good about it

du pied: full-length

du plomb dans l'aile: lead in its wing

D.V. (deo volente, dis volentibus): by the grace of God, if the gods are willing (Latin) *e tutti quanti*: and all such people

ébauche: rough sketch, skeleton

Ecco: There you are

écoeurement: disgusting business

écourté: curtailed, cut short

édition définitive: definitive edition

effondré: collapsed

effondrement: collapse

élève: pupil

elle est bien susceptible: she is very susceptible/touchy

Elle y serait plus en scène, après tout, que dans le Strug: She would be more on stage, after all, than in the Strug[gle]

elles étaient dans leurs malles: they were packing or unpacking their trunks

emménagements: movings-in

empoignée: gripped, attentive

en attendant: while waiting

en famille: in the family

en pleine crise: in mid-crisis

en première ligne: in the first place

en raffole: is crazy about it

en scène: on stage

en tête: in my head

encombrement: burden

enfantillage: piece of childishness

engrenage: gear-wheels

ennui: bother

entendez-vous?: do you understand?

entortillés: entangled, convoluted

entourage: setting, surroundings

Entre temps: Between times

Ergo: Therefore (Latin)

escamotage: sleight of hand

esprits d'élite: best minds

essoufflé: breathless

et encore!: if that!

et pour cause: and with good reason

était à trouver: was to be found

Excusez du peu!: Forgive the smallness of it!

exemplaire: copy

facile princeps: easily foremost (Latin)

façon de dire: style of expression

fait de chic: done with style

'faudra voir!: we'll have to see!

fausse anglaise: false Englishwoman

fiaschetto: small flask of wine (Italian)

ficelle: string (of a puppet)

fièrement campée: strikingly dramatic

finta: sham, artificial (Italian)

fond: background

font bien: look good

Fontaine de Jouvence: Fountain of Youth

frais & dispos: hale & hearty

frati: monks (Italian)

gargote: low-grade eating-house

genius loci: the spirit of place (Latin)

gentillissima sposa: most amiable wife (Italian)

giusto: exactly, that's right (Italian)

glas: death-knell

grand monde: high society, great world

grande nature: large character

grenier: attic, garret

grondement: rumbling, growling

gros: big, coarse

gros moyens: crude methods

grossissements: enlargements, swellings

guignon: jinx, bad luck

historiette: anecdote

il faut en prendre son parti: we must make up our minds to it

ils ne se connaissent plus: they are beside themselves

impayables: priceless

imprévu: unforeseen

in somma: in conclusion (Italian)

inédites: unpublished

inter alios: among others (Latin)

intimissimo: on the friendliest terms (Italian)

j'ai la main lourde: I'm heavy-handed

je me décide d'en finir: I make up my mind to have done with it

je m'y acharne d'autant plus: I slave away at it all the more

je n'en reviens pas: I can't get over it

je ne suis pas une bête: I'm not an idiot

j'en étais encore: I was still at the stage

j'en parle à mon aise: it's easy for me to say

j'en suis confus: I am covered with confusion by it

je t'embrasse . . . à la folie: I kiss you . . . to madness

je vous la souhaite bonne et douce: I wish it good and sweet for you

jeu d'esprit: witticism, display of ingenuity

jeune peintre quelconque: ordinary young painter

(jusquà [sic] nouvel ordre) Cura MM. Em. Fenzi & Cie Banquiers Florence: (until further instruction) Care of Messrs. Em. Fenzi & Company Bankers Florence

juste ciel: just heaven

Kur-orten: health spas (German)

Kursaal: spa assembly hall (German)

là bas: over there

la partie toute autre: the quite different matter

lâcher: let go of

le mien propre: truly my own

le serrant de si près: squeezing it so hard

lieu: grounds

literatim: word for word (Latin)

m'attachant à ses pas: hanging on his steps

mademoiselle & chère camarade: dear lady & friend

maîtresse de maison: hostess

mal àpropos: untoward

manière d'être: way of life, mode of being

marivaudage: elegant banter (in the manner of Marivaux)

mauvais tours: bad turns, nasty tricks

me prélassant dans mon fauteuil: taking my ease in my armchair

me voir venir: see where I'm coming from

mené à bonne fin: brought to a successful conclusion

merde à la vanille: vanilla-flavoured shit

merde au naturel: plain shit

méridional: Southern (from the South of France)

mes voeux très-sincères: my very sincere best wishes

mieux: better

mille amitiés: a thousand friendly wishes

mise en scène: setting, backdrop

moi chétif: miserable me

mon bon: my dear chap

mon cher ami: my dear friend

mon coeur d'oncle: my uncle's heart

mon vieux: old chap

mots: witticisms

moyens: means

naivement: naïvely

n'en éprouvant pas le besoin: never feeling the need of it

n'en parlons plus: let us say no more about it

ne saurais trop vous engager: will do my best to get you (to)

ne sort pas de là: never comes out of there

niaiserie: foolishness

non è vero?: isn't it true? (Italian)

non ragionam' [di lor]: let us not discuss [them] (Italian: Dante, *Inferno*, III)

nous verrons bien: we shall see

omnium gatherum: mixed assemblage (mock Latin)

on se débat: one struggles
Or: Now

panache: plume, feather in cap
pancartes: placards
par exemple, c'est trop fort: upon my
    word, it's too much
par le temps qui court: as time goes on
par parenthèse: by the way
par son naturel, ses dons & ses malheurs:
    by his disposition, his gifts & his
    misfortunes
partage: division
partagent: share
parti-pris: bias, premise
partout et toujours: always and everywhere
passagère: transitory
pavé de Paris: pavement of Paris
pax britannica: British peace (Latin)
peintre de moeurs et de caractères: painter
    of manners and dispositions
percer: break through
permettendolo: permitting (Italian)
persiflage & badinage: (ill-natured)
    banter & jesting
pièce d'eau: ornamental lake
pis aller: makeshift, last resort
plume en main: pen in hand
plume rebelle: rebellious pen
plus personne: nobody more
point d'appui: fulcrum
poncif: hackneyed effect
portier: janitor
Pourvu qu'elle en réchappe!: So long as
    she gets away again!
pourvu que ça dure: assuming it lasts
pranzo: dinner (Italian)
prélevé: set aside
primeurs: first pieces of news
    (*primeur d'une grosse nouvelle*:
    scoop)
Puisque souillon il y a: Once you're
    going to have a slut in it
qu'à cela ne tienne: never mind that

quand même: even so, come what may;
    notwithstanding
*Que diable allait-il faire dans cette
    galère?*: What the devil was he going
    to do there?
Que n'y suis-je-pas!: Why am I not
    there!
Quel genre!: What a line of goods!
quelque chose de bien méridional:
    something really Southern
qui ne tire pas à conséquence: which is of
    no importance
qui ont traîné: which have dragged about
qui que ce soit: anybody at all

raffinés: clever people
raffoler: rave, be infatuated about
raison d'être: reason for existing
rapport au: with respect to
râtés: misfired
réchauffées: warmed up again
recueillement: self-communion,
    contemplation
reflet: reflection
refroidissement: chill
Requiescat!: May he rest in peace!
    (Latin)
revanche: compensation
rien que d'y avoir passé: just from passing
    through it
riz [correctly *ris*] *de veau à la jardinière*:
    veal sweetbreads surrounded by
    glazed carrots, turnips, peas, French
    beans, etc.
*roman d'analyse, sans intrigue & sans
    ficelle, tant qu'il voudra*: the novel of
    analysis, without plot and without
    tricks, as much as he could wish
roman de moeurs: novel of manners

sac: bag
sagesse: wisdom, steadiness
sans découcher une seule nuit: without
    spending a single night away

sans le moindre talent: without the least talent

sans m'en vouloir: without bearing a grudge against me

sans vouloir me colleter: without wanting to come to grips

scabreuse: improper, indelicate

se prêter à merveille: to lend itself marvellously

séance: session

seconde: second night

segretissimo: most secret (Italian)

(selon moi): (according to me!)

sfogare: give vent (Italian)

si le coeur vous en dit: if your heart tells you so

si vous le voulez bien: if you are willing

soigné: carefully cultivated

souillon: slut

soutenu: sustained

Stia bene, caro amico, anche Lei: Keep well, dear friend, you too (Italian: 'Lei' is formal 'you')

suffrage: vote

Sur ces entrefaîtes: While this was going on; in the interval

sur le vif: from life

talent de dessinateur: talent at drawing

tant que vous voudrez: as much as you will want

tanti saluti: so many good wishes (Italian)

tarabiscotage: finickiness

tel quel, telle quelle: just as it is

Tiens! mon français qui me retrouve! Look! my French has found me again

touffu: involved (in style)

toujours: always, still

tout à vous: altogether yours

tout ce que vous savez: all you know about

train dont vont les choses: rate things are going

trattoria: eating-house (Italian)

treille: arbour

troisième: third-floor apartment

ultissimo: very last (Italian)

una bellezza: a beauty (Italian)

unberufen: touch wood! (German)

vade-mecum: companion, portable manual (Latin)

vale: farewell (Latin)

vécu: (the) lived

Venez donc, chère mademoiselle & amie: So come on, dear lady & friend

vidé: emptied

vie champêtre: pastoral life

vie intime: inward; homely

vieillards: old people

vieille noblesse: old aristocracy

vieux jeu: old-fashioned

villes du Midi: towns in the South of France

Voilà: There you are

Votre siège est fait: Your siege is laid

voulu: deliberate; forced

vous y avez, en même temps que les droits les plus acquis, les plus rares bonheurs: you enjoy there not only the most thoroughly earned rights but also the rarest felicities

voyez la différence!: look at the difference!

voyez plutôt: wait and see

vraie vérité: true truth

wüthend: furious (German)

Index

Norton, Elizabeth Gaskell (Lily), 125,
268
Norton, the Hon. George Chapple, 88n
Norton, Grace, 19, 21, 23n, 24, 27–32,
33, 34, 35, 39, 40, 41–5, 49, 51,
67–70, 124, 128, 149–51, 162n, 163–4,
167, 190, 378, 496n; *Studies in
Montaigne*, 27; review of *Roderick
Hudson*, 67–70; rejected *Nation* article
defending HJ, 163–4; *letters to:*
27–32, 41–5, 67–70, 149–51, 163–4,
205–9
Norton, Jane, 21, 23n, 24, 27, 32, 33, 34,
35, 48
Norton, Margaret, 125, 151, 421
Norton, Richard, 45
Norton, Sally, 44
Norton, Susan Ridley Sedgwick, 21,
23n, 24, 27, 35, 43, 45, 48n, 204
Notre Dame, Indiana, 446

Oberammergau, 229
Ockham Park, Surrey, 513
Olliffe, Dr, 70
O'Meara, Kathleen, 63n
Opera Comique, London, 238, 263
Oporto, 291n
Order of Merit, 566
Orr, Alexandra Sutherland Leighton,
128
Ortmans, Fernand, 361–2
Osbourne, Samuel Lloyd, 187, 192, 193,
248, 249–50; *The Wrecker*, 248
Osgood, James Ripley, xxii, 128, 131,
132n, 144–8, 151, 152, 154n, 161, 181,
277n; *letter to:* 144–8
Osgood, J. R. & Co., xxii, 59, 65n,
144–8, 162, 169, 171n, 177–8, 179–80
Osgood, James R., McIlvaine & Co.,
249n, 277n
O'Shea, Kitty, 233n
O'Shea, W. H., 233n
Ossian, 21n
Osterley Park, 139n, 183–6
Otway, Sir Arthur John, 79, 80n

Our Young Folks, 4n, 16n
Oxford, 24, 76n, 109, 156, 187, 241, 270,
293, 322, 462, 479, 482n, 513, 529,
560, 562, 563n, 564
Oxford and Cambridge Boat Race, 81

Pacific Coast (California), 446
Page, Walter Hines, 337
Pagello (Edith Wharton's car), 421, 422
Paget, Violet (pseud. 'Vernon Lee'), 189
Palazzo Barbaro, 189, 223n
Palazzo Capello (Venice), 444n
Palgrave, Francis Turner, 81; *The
Golden Treasury*, 81n
Pall Mall Gazette, 79n, 142, 156n, 166n,
256, 275n, 498n, 506
Palladio, Andrea, 25
Palm Beach, Florida, 409
Panhard (car), 447, 481
Pankhurst, Emmeline, 450
Pantheon, 29
Paris, 1, 13–14, 17, 18, 23, 24, 32, 35, 50,
51, 56, 61–74, 76, 87, 90, 92, 109, 114,
115, 119, 140–42, 143–4, 152, 153, 156,
165, 173–4, 180, 182, 207, 208n, 212,
215, 216, 217, 231n, 234, 238, 250, 257,
258, 259, 261, 263, 264, 272, 273n,
276, 286n, 304, 315, 330, 344, 347,
357–8, 370, 387, 439, 446, 447, 462,
487, 504, 507, 517, 541, 543, 545
Parisian, The, 96n, 142, 386
Parkes, George Richmond, 238
Parnell, Charles Stewart, 212, 233n
Pater, Walter Horatio, 110n, death
292–3, 433–4; *Gaston de Latour*, 293;
Marius the Epicurean, 293
Pater sisters, 293
Patti, Adelina, 410
Pavia, 24
Payne, James, 200
Payne, William Morton, 385n; *American
Literary Criticism*, 385n
Peabody, Elizabeth Palmer, xxii, 171,
172–3
Pearson's Magazine, 302

Sherman, General William T., 135n
Shropshire, 92
Siberia, 466
Sicily, xxi
Siddons, Sarah, 282
Siege of Paris, 414
Siena, 229, 250
Silsbee, Captain Edward, 189
Silver Lake, New Hampshire, 479
Simon, Sir John, 23n
Simpkin & Marshall, 361
Simplon, the, 318
Skinner, Dr Ernest, 480, 495
Skrupskelis, Ignas K., xvii
Smalley, George Washburn, 85, 87, 93,
  99, 173, 207n, 486n
Smalley, Ida, 486
Smalley, Phoebe Garnaut, 85, 87, 207
Smith College, Massachusetts, 411, 446
Smith, Elder & Co., 249n
Smith, George Barnett, 64n
Smith, Goldwin, 79
Smith, Logan Pearsall, 531
Smith, Miss, 86
Smith, W. H., 219
Smith, William Haynes ('The Babe'),
  386
Smiths, the (HJ's servants), 359
Smyth, Ethel, 492n
Society for Psychical Research, 181, 209,
  210n, 313, 488n
Society of Authors, 195n
Somers, Earl, 34
Sorbonne, 425
South, the (U.S.), 394, 408, 427, 542
South Berwick, Maine, 417n
South Seas, 191
Southampton, 402
Southport, 232, 236
Southworth, Alvan S., 64n
Spain, 13, 34
Spangenberg, Frau Johanna, 525n
Spectator, The, 99, 291
Spencer, Herbert, 48n, 79; *Principles of
  Psychology*, 79n

Spofford, Harriet Elizabeth Prescott, 5;
  Azarian, 5
Springfield Republican, 105
Stamford, Connecticut, 524, 526
Stanford University, 300n, 427n
Stedman, Edmund Clarence, 12, 15n, 71,
  137–8; *letter to:* 137–8
Stendhal (Marie Henri Beyle), 33; *La
  Charteuse de Parme*, 33
Stephen, Adrian, 443n
Stephen, Julia Prinseps Duckworth,
  270
Stephen, Leslie, 23n, 53n, 79n, 94, 102,
  119n, 270
Stevenson, Fanny Van de Grift
  Osbourne (Mrs Robert Louis), 180,
  187, 192, 193, 211, 249, 290, 313n
Stevenson, Margaret Isabella (mother of
  Robert Louis), 192, 193, 249
Stevenson, Robert Louis, 94, 95n, 157,
  166–7, 186–7, 190–94, 205, 211,
  247–50, 259, death 270–71, 290, 412,
  500; *Deacon Brodie*, 95; *Beau Austin*,
  95n; 'A Humble Remonstrance',
  166–7; *Kidnapped*, 186–7, 500; *The
  Strange Case of Dr Jekyll and Mr
  Hyde*, 186; *Memories and Portraits*,
  193; *The Master of Ballantrae*, 211;
  Across the Plains, 247; *The Wrecker*,
  248; *Vailima Letters*, 248n; *Weir of
  Hermiston*, 290; *letters to:* 166–7,
  186–7, 190–94, 247–50
Stewart, Mrs Duncan, 88
Stocks, Hertfordshire, 318
Stone, Herbert S., & Co., 277n, 299,
  303
Storey, Moorfield, 13–14
Story, Edith: *see* Peruzzi, Edith Story,
  Countess
Story, Julian, 448
Story, Maud Broadwood, 295–6, 352–5,
  379–82, 388–9, 392; *letters to:* 352–5,
  379–82
Story, Thomas Waldo, 295–6, 353, 355,
  382, 388–9, 392

Welby, Lady Victoria – *cont.*
501; *Witnesses to Ambiguity*, 502;
Significs and Language, 502–3; *letter
to:* 501–3
Weld, Mary, 353, 356, 365, 370, 448
Wells, Amy Catherine (née Robbins)
(Mrs H. G.), 425
Wells, George Philip, 425
Wells, Herbert George, xiv, xxiii, xxiv,
275n, 309, 311–13, 336, 374–6, 422–5,
429, 431–2, 440–42, 496n, 499–501,
509–11, 516–17, 523n, 529, 540,
551–5; *Boon*, xxiv; *Kipps*, xxiii, 422–4,
429, 432; *The Time Machine*, 311;
The Island of Dr Moreau, 311; *The
Invisible Man*, 311; *The War of the
Worlds*, 311; *When the Sleeper Wakes*,
312; *A Modern Utopia*, 422–4, 429;
The Future in America, 431–2,
440–42; *The New Machiavelli*,
499–501; *Marriage*, 516–17; *Boon*,
551–5; *The Wife of Sir Isaac
Harman*, 552n; *letters to:* 311–13,
374–6, 422–5, 440–42, 499–501,
509–11, 551–5
Wenlock Abbey, 109n
Westminster Abbey, 282
Weston, the Misses, 142
Wharton, Anthony P., 508n; *Irene
Wycherley*, 508
Wharton, Edith, xiv, xvii, 41n, 300n,
347–8, 350, 367–8, 386, 404, 407,
413, 418–22, 432, 434n, 446n, 447,
462, 467, 470, 479, 481–2, 496n, 501,
513, 516, 517, 518, 527, 530, 534, 535,
545, 546, 549n, 552, 556, 560, 565; *The
Age of Innocence*, 41n; *The Greater
Inclination*, 347–8; 'The Line of Least
Resistance', 347–8; *The Touchstone*,
347; *The Valley of Decision*, 367–8;
The House of Mirth, 418–19, 420, 516;
The Fruit of the Tree, 470n; *The Book
of the Homeless*, 549n, 556; *A
Backward Glance*, 565; *letters to:*
347–8, 367–8, 418–22

Wharton, Edward ('Teddy'), 367, 418,
422, 432, 434n, 446n, 447
Wheeler, Dr Charles E., 458–9, 471;
letter to: 458–9
Whistler, Beatrix Goodwin, 265n
Whistler, James Abbot McNeill, 152,
178, 215, 265
Whitby, 207, 217, 267, 546
White, Henry, 330n
White, Mrs Henry, 329, 330n
White Mountains, 8, 538n
White, Richard Grant, 101
White, Stanford, 235n
White, William, 23n
White, Dr William, 407
Whitman, Walt, 148, 149, 432, 532n;
Specimen Days, 148; *Leaves of Grass*,
432n
Whittier, John Greenleaf, 39, 72
Wild West, 366
Wilde, Oscar, xx, 135, 152, 215, 238,
245–6, 263, 264, 274n, 276n, 279–80,
283, 287, 288, 336, 513, 531; *Lady
Windermere's Fan*, 245–6; *A Woman
of No Importance*, 264; *An Ideal
Husband*, 274n; *The Importance of
Being Earnest*, 276
Wilkins, Mary: *see* Freeman, Mary
Eleanor Wilkins
Wilkinson, Dr Clement, 487; *James John
Garth Wilkinson*, 487
Wilkinson, James John Garth, 23n, 487
Wilson, Andrew, 64n
Winchelsea, 3n, 370, 371, 440
Winchester, 24
Windsor, 386, 387, 436n, 482n, 487
Winnetka, Illinois, 411
Wister, Owen, 63n, 192, 364–6; *The
Virginian*, 192, 365–6; *Lady
Baltimore*, 366n; *letter to:* 364–6
Wister, Mrs Owen, 162n, 366
Wister, Sarah Butler, 63n, 66, 78n, 249,
365, 366, 379, 382, 407
Wolseley, Garnet Joseph, first Viscount,
xix, 174n, 207, 279, 373–4; *The*

Index of Correspondents

The numbers after each name are the numbers of the letters, not page numbers